Living Together Separately

Living Together Separately

Cultural India in History and Politics

Edited by

Mushirul Hasan
and
Asim Roy

OXFORD

UNIVERSITY PRESS

OXFORD
UNIVERSITY PRESS

YMCA Library Building, Jai Singh Road, New Delhi 110 001

Oxford University Press is a department of the University of Oxford.
It furthers the University's objective of excellence in research, scholarship,
and education by publishing worldwide in

Oxford   New York
Auckland   Cape Town   Dar es Salaam   Hong Kong   Karachi
Kuala Lumpur   Madrid   Melbourne   Mexico City   Nairobi
New Delhi   Shanghai   Taipei   Toronto

With offices in
Argentina   Austria   Brazil   Chile   Czech Republic   France   Greece
Guatemala   Hungary   Italy   Japan   Poland   Portugal   Singapore
South Korea   Switzerland   Thailand   Turkey   Ukraine   Vietnam

Oxford is a registered trade mark of Oxford University Press
in the UK and in certain other countries.

Published in India
by Oxford University Press, New Delhi

ISBN-13: 978-0-19-566921-3
ISBN-10: 0-19-566921-5

Typeset in Perpetua 11.5/13
by Eleven Arts, Keshav Puram, Delhi 110 035
Printed in India by Sai Printopack Pvt. Ltd, New Delhi 110 020
Published by Manzar Khan, Oxford University Press
YMCA Library Building, Jai Singh Road, New Delhi 110 001

CONTENTS

PREFACE

L iving together but not separately was the raison d'être behind the founding of Delhi's Jamia Millia Islamia, a 'lusty child of the non-cooperation movement' (Jawaharlal Nehru). Hakim Ajmal Khan, its first Vice Chancellor, expected students to know each other's culture: 'The firm foundations of a united Indian nationhood depends on this mutual understanding.' Dr M.A. Ansari, who nursed the institution from its inception in October 1920, did not believe in a politically separate Muslim community, and often said that India's future must be a field of cooperation between those of different faiths. 'I consider the brotherhood of man as the only real tie', he wrote, 'and partitions based on race and colour are, to my mind, artificial and arbitrary, leading to divisions and factious fights.'

Many contested these formulations during Ajmal and Ansari's lifetime that coincided with the ebb and flow of nationalist currents, and many more did so in the 1940s when the Muslim League and its ideological allies, led by M.A. Jinnah, spearheaded the campaign for a Muslim nation. Even after India's Partition, the debates continued uninterruptedly at various levels. Along with many others, scholars at Jamia, especially Mohammad Mujeeb and Syed Abid Husain, intervened creatively in those debates with their books and articles. Today, they command respect and attention for their eclectic views and secular interpretations.

To pursue some of their favourite themes, Jamia's Academy of Third World Studies organized a conference on 18–21 December 2002. My colleagues and I were overwhelmed by the academic community's response. Overseas scholars bore their own travel expenses and participated; only a few could not accept our invitation. Most who came figure in the table of contents; the names of Shahid

Amin, Alok Bhalla, Sudhir Chandra, and Gyanendra Pandey are missing because they chose not to write.

We are immensely grateful to Mark Robinson, then Programme Officer at the Ford Foundation, for the generous grant that enabled us to organize the conference. Even before submitting a proposal, Mark agreed, at a dinner hosted by Gauhar Rizvi, Representative of the Ford Foundation in Delhi, to fund a seminar on composite culture.

We are immensely grateful to Jamia Millia Islamia's former Vice Chancellor, Syed Shahid Mahdi, for his support and understanding. To his credit, he gave me a free hand in organizing the conference. The University's Finance Officer and his staff in the Accounts Office facilitated various arrangements. Apart from hosting a fabulous Hyderabadi meal on behalf of Delhi's prestigious India International Centre, Promela Ghose tackled several administrative matters with her usual finesse. Pramod Kapur of Roli Books and his charming wife, Kiran, hosted an elaborate dinner for our participants. Manzar Khan, Managing Director of Oxford University Press, did likewise. Ramesh C. Jain of Manohar Publications laid out a fabulous lunch. This is what living together separately is all about.

Mohammad Shakir, who has gained worldwide fame for his organizational skills, carried the burden of organizing a huge conference diligently. This is what Barbara Metcalf, one of our distinguished participants, wrote to him: 'I am writing to thank you for the excellent arrangements you made for me and for all the participants in the conference .... The conference was a truly memorable occasion, and I offer my congratulations to you for the important role you played.' Francis Robinson, Farzana Shaikh, and Michael Fisher expressed similar sentiments.

It was a pleasure organizing the conference and being associated with a book that reflects so vividly my own long-standing engagements. I have dealt with the theme 'Living Together Separately' and its related aspects in my previous publications, and more recently in *From Pluralism to Separatism: Qasbas in Colonial Awadh* (2004), *Will Secular India Survive?* (2004), and *Reform and Renewal: Muslim Intelligentsia in Nineteenth Century Delhi* (forthcoming).

The theme 'Living Together Separately' has acquired unprecedented salience after the demolition of the Babri Masjid and the ensuing Hindu-Muslim violence. It will remain so despite the change of governments. The last six years or so have been disconcerting, especially for those nurtured in the Nehru era. Fortunately, though, there exists a much wider world that is inhabited by individuals and groups who value tolerance and live peacefully with their co-citizens. Fortunately, too, brave men and women continue to struggle against bigotry, obscurantism, casteist formations, and communal movements. We dedicate this book to them.

In recent years, I have edited a couple of books to promote a specific liberal and secular agenda. Whatever 'purists' might say, my reading of Jamia's institutional history has taught me that a historian *located* in India has to perform this role.

This inspired me to plan December's conference. However, the book in print is neither conceived nor tailored to serve that project. For this reason, as also for several other reasons, it does not have a message for our readers. If some were to discern one, it may run along the following lines:

In order to save mankind we have to learn to live together in concord in spite of traditional differences of religion, civilization, nationality, class and race. In order to live together in concord successfully, we have to know each other's past, since human life, like the rest of the phenomenal universe, can be observed by human minds only as it presents itself to them on the move through time .... For our now urgent common purpose of self-preservation, it will not be enough to explore our common underlying human nature. The psychologist's work needs to be supplemented by the archaeologist's, the historian's, the anthropologist's and the sociologist's. We must learn to recognize, and as far as possible, to understand, the different cultural configurations in which our common human nature has expressed itself in the different religions, civilizations, and nationalities into which human culture has come to be articulated in the course of its history .... We shall, however, have to do more than just understand each other's cultural heritages, and more even than appreciate them. We shall have to value them and love them as being parts of mankind's common treasure and therefore being ours too, as truly as the heirlooms that we ourselves shall be contributing to the common stock.

The British historian Arnold Toynbee penned these words of wisdom. I believe they deserve serious reflection.

Mushirul Hasan

INTRODUCTION

Asim Roy

I

The synthetic ethos of the Indian civilization is not only a pervasive notion but also a real historical experience shared by many Indians and non-Indians, which has been carried in varied forms and meanings across time and space in the region. To these millions of people, the genius of India expresses itself not only in a somewhat unique way of accepting and accommodating—rather than rejecting—diverse patterns of beliefs and thoughts, but also in the living of an infinite variety of people and cultures within a complex tapestry of life and culture. And this is what is variously characterized as India's 'unity in diversity', 'honeycomb', religious-cultural 'pluralism and tolerance', 'syncretistic' or 'composite'[1] culture—a type of characterization that has also induced many to extol it as a tolerant world view encapsulated in the old adage: 'Live and let live'. We have chosen, rather, to adopt another aphorism for it, namely 'Living together separately', with the hope of being able to read further and more realistic meanings into this time-honoured concept in the light of the various historical and contemporary challenges of both intellectual and political nature. In the eloquent words of one of the early and most powerful exponents of India's composite culture:

From immemorial times, India has been the meeting place of the conflicting races and civilizations. From immemorial times, she has tried to achieve a unity for the heterogeneous

---

[1]The term 'composite culture' in the Indian context is construed by some, in a restricted sense, to mean the coming together of the Hindu and Muslim cultures. We do not see any particular reason to delimit the scope and application of a pattern of cultural tradition extending in history long before and after the advent of Islam.

elements, which make up the totality of her life. Hers is perhaps the oldest civilization with an uninterrupted history. Most of her contemporaries have ceased to exist. She has not only survived but also maintained and developed a continuous culture. Different races have met and fought and fraternized on her soil. She has absorbed all of them into her blood .... She has lived through recurrent centuries of war and pestilence. She has triumphed over natural calamities and human misrule. Whence this vitality that overcomes destruction and death? Whence this wisdom that reconciles opposite truths? The story of India's culture unravels the secret of that vitality and that wisdom. It is a story of unity and synthesis, of reconciliation and development, of a perfect fusion of old traditions and new values.[2]

The distinctiveness of the assimilative and inclusive traits of the Indic culture came over a long period of time to acquire almost the salience of an unquestionable historical verity and a cultural given until relatively recent times. In the last couple of hundred years of colonial and post-colonial rule, the syncretistic tradition and perception have, at different stages, been engaged, challenged, and undermined by various historical forces and contesting ideologies. We can identify at least three major developments in South Asia's colonial contexts which countered the notion of syncretistic and composite culture. First, the British colonial perception and thinking on cultural tradition, especially emanating from Orientalist scholarship, largely anchored in high Hindu, Buddhist, and Islamic normative values and religious and other texts, helped to construct and perpetuate exclusive and competing, if not conflicting, models of religious-cultural traditions in the region. Having virtually ignored the intricate and complex processes of interaction of living religions and cultures in India, especially at a popular level, Orientalism contributed a great deal to the construction of barriers among plural cultural traditions in the land. The second serious challenge came, at a somewhat later stage, from the Islamicists or the Islamic 'essentialists' and the champions of Muslim 'separatism', who found their own ground considerably leavened by the earlier work of the Orientalists. The third is the most recent and potentially the most threatening and subversive challenge. This is embodied by the proponents of Hindu nationalism with its ahistorical, monolithic, cultural, and political credo of *Hindutva* during the colonial and, more aggressively and significantly, post-colonial periods. Relatively subdued in the late colonial and early post-colonial decades—the dormancy in the early stages of Independence being clearly attributed to its involvement in Gandhi's assassination—political Hinduism gained increasing momentum and stakes in India in the post-Nehruvian period.

II

A close examination of the historiography of composite culture reveals its strong linkage and responsiveness to its changing political contexts.[3] The clearest

---

[2]Humayun Kabir, *The Indian Heritage* (New Delhi: Asia Publishing House, 3rd edn, 1955), p. 33.
[3]See Javeed Alam, 'The composite culture and its historiography', in Asim Roy and Howard

evidence of this political relevance lies in the fact that the bulk of its literature belonged to the last six or seven decades, when nascent Indian nationalism, liberalism, and secularism had been seriously engaged and challenged, both intellectually and politically, by religious nationalists anchored in either political Islam or political Hinduism or other religious faiths. The colonial context of the imperialists' denigration and opposition to Indian nationalism, prior to the aforesaid internal challenges and direct interventions on a serious scale, offered the necessary political ambience for the persistence and growth of the composite culture as reflected in the shared experiences of millions of Indians. Many nationalist leaders, writers, and thinkers contributed to putting up the edifice of this culture.

The political and cultural momentum of the Muslim separatist movement reached its most critical stage in the 1940s. It is not surprising, therefore, that the year before India's Partition saw the publication, in 1946, of the two most powerful articulations and defences of the composite culture, namely Jawaharlal Nehru's *The Discovery of India*[4] and Humayun Kabir's *The Indian Heritage*.[5] After a brief lull in the wake of the stunning reality of Partition, the debate was revived in the early 1960s as a part of the struggle against the communal uses of history in both Pakistan and India. In the late 1950s and early 1960s, a number of major Pakistani scholars focused on Muslim ideology and history in the subcontinent, with special reference to Pakistan.[6] But undoubtedly, the two most politically sensitive publication series in Pakistan and India, dating from the late 1950s and contributing very largely to the rekindling of the debate on the composite culture, are the Pakistan Historical Society's multi-volume publications on the history of the freedom movement,[7] and the Bharatiya Vidya Bhavan's series on Indian history and culture.[8] I.H. Qureshi, in his 'Introduction' to the first volume of the Historical Society publications, stressed the exclusive nature of the Islamic and Hindu cultures and their separate destinies.[9] According to Aziz Ahmad: 'The divisive forces have proved much more dynamic than the cohesive ones .... Islam in India continued to retain throughout

Brasted (eds), *Islam in History and Politics: A South Asian Perspective*, South Asia, Special Issue, vol. XXII (1999), p. 29, n. 1.

[4]Jawaharlal Nehru, *The Discovery of India* (Calcutta: Signet Press, 1946).

[5]Kabir, *The Indian Heritage*.

[6]Javid Iqbal, *The Ideology of Pakistan and its Implementation* (Lahore, 1959); S. Muhammad Ikram, *History of Muslim Civilization in India and Pakistan, 712–1858* (Lahore, 1962); Ishtiaq Husain Qureshi, *The Muslim Community of the Indo-Pakistan Subcontinent 610–1947* ('S-Gravebhage: Mouton, 1962); Hafeez Malik, *Moslem Nationalism in India and Pakistan* (Washington D.C.: Public Affairs Press, 1963); Aziz Ahmad, *Studies in Islamic Culture in the Indian Environment* (London: Oxford University Press, 1964).

[7]Mahmud Husain et al. (eds), *A History of the Freedom Movement: Being the Story of Muslim Struggle for Freedom of Hind-Pakistan, 1707–1947*, 3 vols (Karachi: Pakistan Historical Society, 1957–70).

[8]R.C. Majumdar (gen. ed.), *History and Culture of the Indian People*, 11 vols (Bombay: Bharatiya Vidya Bhavan, 1951–81).

[9]I.H. Qureshi 'Introduction', in Husain et al., *History of the Freedom Movement*, vol. 1, pp. 1–57.

the centuries, despite secondary Indian environmental and ethnic influences, its original foreign character.'[10]

R.C. Majumdar, on the other hand, reciprocated the view that Hindus and Muslims were irreconcilable and it was unlikely that 'the twain shall ever meet'.[11] In the late 1950s, some Western historians too lent their support to this perception of exclusive Islam.[12]

The renewed interest in finding the common grounds in history was intended to counter the communal and political use of history as well as historical assessments of this nature. The year 1963 emerged as significant and fertile for the exposition of thoughts on composite culture. The most powerful of the earliest expressions of this renewed interest in the Hindu-Muslim composite culture was Tara Chand's well-known publication in 1963, although the work in its essence was known to have been accomplished over four decades earlier, in 1920.[13] The year 1963 also saw Abid Husain's first passionate contribution to this field, followed, in 1965, by his second.[14] Ziaul Hasan Faruqi's important study on the Deoband school belonged to the same year.[15] The year, however, reached its climax in the Indian National History Congress mounting a major symposium on the 'Contributions of Indian Historians to the Process of National Integration', and Nurul Hasan delivering his Presidential Address for the Medieval Period, speaking of 'the development of a composite culture tradition'.[16] The second half of the decade saw a number of major publications in quick succession seeking effectively to counter what was seen as 'communal' interpretations of Muslim history in India.[17]

The 1970s began to register marks of renewed communal tensions and conflicts, and initial concerns about secularism as well as the minority communities found expression at an academic level.[18] It is well known that the 1980s saw the

[10]Ahmad, *Studies in Islamic Culture*, pp. 73–4.

[11]Majumdar, *History and Culture of the Indian People*, vol. 4, p. 636.

[12]Percival Spear, *India, Pakistan and the West* (London: Oxford University Press, 1958), p. 88; Arthur L. Basham, *The Indian Sub-continent in Historical Perspective* (London: London University Press, 1958), p. 14.

[13]Tara Chand, *Influence of Islam on Indian Culture* (Allahabad: The Indian Press, 1963).

[14]Abid S. Husain, *The National Culture of India* (London: Asia Publishing House, 1961); his *The Destiny of Indian Muslims* (Bombay: Asia Publishing House, 1965).

[15]Ziaul Hasan Faruqi, *The Deoband School and the Demand for Pakistan* (Bombay: Asia Publishing House, 1963).

[16]See *Proceedings of the Indian History Congress* (Calcutta, 1963).

[17]S.A.A. Rizvi, *Muslim Revivalist Movements in Northern India in the Sixteenth and Seventeenth Centuries* (Agra: Agra University Press, 1965); Mohammed Mujeeb, *The Indian Muslims* (London: Allen & Unwin, 1967); A. Rashid, *Society and Culture in Medieval India, 1206–1556 AD* (Calcutta: Firma KL, 1969); Rafiq Zakaria, *Rise of Muslims in Indian Politics: An Analysis of Developments from 1885 to 1906* (Bombay: Somaiya Publications, 1971).

[18]Mushirul Haq, *Islam in Secular India* (Simla: Institute of Advanced Study, 1972); Attar Singh, *Secularism and the Sikh Faith* (Amritsar: Guru Nanak Dev University Press, 1973); Imtiaz Ahmad

beginning of a steady and steep rise of the Hindu militant communalist forces in the Indian body politic, with the gradual unfolding of their totalitarian cultural demands of Hindutva. The Indian cultural ethos was touched at its most tender point. The anxiety, fear, and commotion following in its wake was strikingly resonated in a huge corpus of scholarly reflections on this spectacular and somewhat incredible rise of the Hindu leviathan and its multi-level implications for the nation. It is of some considerable significance that the phenomenon drew as much response from national as from international scholars.[19]

The following decade of the 1990s—the last decade of the last century—was the decade of the national shame of the Hindu fanatics' orgiastic assault on

---

(ed.), *Family, Kinship and Marriage Among Muslims in India* (New Delhi: Manohar, 1976); Hasan Askari, *Inter-religion* (Aligarh: Printwell, 1977); Romila Thapar, 'The image of the barbarian in early India', in her *Ancient Indian Social History: Some Interpretations* (Delhi: Orient Longmans, 1978); Imtiaz Ahmad (ed.), *Caste and Social Stratification Among Muslims in India* (New Delhi: Manohar, 1978); Anand Coomarswamy, *Spiritual Authority and Temporal Power in the Indian Theory of Government* (New Delhi: Munshiram, 1978/ originally published in 1942); Nirad C. Chaudhuri, *Hinduism: A Religion to Live By* (New Delhi: Oxford University Press, 1979).

[19]Ashis Nandy, 'Counter-statement on humanistic temper', *Mainstream*, 10 Oct. (1981), pp. 16–18; his *The Intimate Enemy: Loss and Recovery of Self under Colonial Rule* (New Delhi: Oxford University Press, 1983); S.C. Dube et al. (eds), *Secularization in Multi-religious Societies* (New Delhi: Concept. 1983); Bipan Chandra, *Communalism in Modern India* (New Delhi: Vikas, 1984); Romila Thapar, 'Syndicated moksha', *Seminar*, 313 (Oct. 1985), pp. 14–22; J.C. Heesterman, *The Inner Conflict of Tradition: Essays in Indian Ritual, Kingship and Society* (Chicago: Chicago University Press, 1985); G.P. Deshpande, 'The plural tradition', *Seminar*, 313 (Oct. 1985), pp. 23–5; Ashis Nandy, 'An anti-secularist manifesto', *Seminar* 314 (Oct. 1985), pp. 1–12; M.S. Agwani, *Islamic Fundamentalism in India* (Chandigarh: 21st Century India Society, 1986); Lawrence A. Babb, *Redemptive Encounters: Three Modern Styles in the Hindu Tradition* (Berkeley: California University Press, 1986); Rasheeduddin Khan (ed.), *Composite Culture of India and National Integration* (Simla: Indian Institute of Advanced Study, 1987); Walter K. Anderson et al., *The Brotherhood in Saffron: The Rashtriya Swayam Sevak Sangh and Hindu Revivalism* (New Delhi: Vistar, 1987); T.N. Madan, 'Secularism in its place', *Journal of Asian Studies*, 46:4 (1987), pp. 747–59; Sarvepalli Gopal (ed.), *Nehru and Secularism* (Occasional Papers, No. 42, New Delhi: Nehru MM Library, 1987); Howard G. Coward (ed.), *Modern Indian Responses to Religious Pluralism* (Albany: New York State University Press, 1987); Brian Smith, 'Exorcising the transcendent: Strategies for redefining Hinduism and Religion', *History of Religion* (1987), pp. 342–55; Mark Juergensmeyer, 'The logic of religious violence: The case of the Punjab', *Contributions to Indian Sociology* (n.s.), 22 (1988), pp. 65–88; M.J. Akbar, *Nehru: The Making of India* (London: Viking, 1988); Joseph T. O'Connell et al. (eds), *Sikh History and Religion in the Twentieth Century* (Toronto: Toronto University Press, 1988); Ian Copland, 'Communalism in Princely India: The case of Hyderabad, 1930–1940', *Modern Asian Studies,* 22:4 (1988), pp. 783–814; Ashis Nandy, 'The politics of secularism and the recovery of religious tolerance', *Alternatives*, 13:2 (1988), 177–94; Romila Thapar, 'Imagined religious communities? Ancient history and the modern search for a Hindu identity', *Modern Asian Studies*, 23:2 (1989), pp. 209–31; Madeleine Biradeau, *Hinduism: The Anthropology of a Civilization*, tr. by Richard Nice (New Delhi: Oxford University Press, 1989); Khaliq Ahmad Nizami, *Akbar and Religion* (Delhi: Idarah-I Adabiyat, 1989); G.D. Sontheimar et al. (eds), *Hinduism Reconsidered* (New Delhi: Manohar, 1989).

the historic Babri Masjid in Ayodhya and its destruction, while the nation stood and watched. This shocking violence not merely to the mosque—consequential as it has been—but also to the fundamentals of India's Constitution, and more importantly, to the cherished image of her tolerant pluralistic religious-cultural tradition drew wide-ranging reflective responses from cross-sections of the global community. The prolific publications of this decade, articulating serious concerns about India's future as a nation, with particular attention to the seminal issues of her secularist ideology and religious-cultural pluralism vis-à-vis the growing ascendancy of fundamentalist ideology, have had an awesome quality. A broad sample of the relevant historical and social science publications alone of this decade would be a clear measure of this epiphenomenon in the perception of many—Indian and non-Indian.[20]

[20]Gyanendra Pandey, *The Construction of Communalism in Colonial North India* (New Delhi: Oxford University Press, 1990); Ainslie T. Embree, *Utopias in Conflict: Religion and Nationalism in Modern India* (Berkeley: California University Press, 1990); T.K. Oomen, *State and Society in India: Studies in Nation-Building* (New Delhi: Sage, 1990); Khaliq Ahmad Nizami, *Maulana Azad: A Commemoration Volume* (Delhi: Idarah-I Adabiyat, 1990); Sarvepalli Gopal (ed.), *Anatomy of a Confrontation: The Babri Masjid–Ram Janmabhumi Issue* (New Delhi: Viking, 1991); Gunther D. Sontheimar et al. (eds), *Hinduism Reconsidered* (New Delhi: Manohar, 1991); Martin E. Marty et al. (eds), *Fundamentalisms Observed* (Chicago: Chicago University Press, 1991); M.S. Gore (ed.), *Secularism in India* (Allahabad: Vidya Prakashan, 1991); Daniel Gold, 'Rational action and uncontrolled violence: Explaining Hindu communalism', *Religion*, 21 (1991), pp. 357–70; F.G. Bailey, 'Religion and religiosity: Ideas and their use', *Contributions to Indian Sociology* (n.s.), 25:2 (1991), pp. 211–32; Prasenjit Duara, 'The new politics of Hinduism', *Wilson Quarterly*, Summer 1991; Joanne Punzo Waghorne, 'Hinduism and the fate of India', *Wilson Quarterly*, Summer 1991; John Stratton Hawley, 'Naming Hinduism', *Wilson Quarterly*, Summer 1991; Wendy Doniger, 'Hinduism by any other name', *Wilson Quarterly*, Summer 1991; Mushirul Hasan (ed.), *Islam and Indian Nationalism: Reflections on Abul Kalam Azad* (New Delhi: Manohar, 1992); Prakash Chandra Upadhyaya, 'The politics of Indian secularism', *Modern Asian Studies*, 26:4 (1992), pp. 815–53; Irfan Habib, 'Observations on Akbar and his age: A symposium', *Social Scientist*, 20:9–10 (1992), pp. 68–72; M.M. Sankhder (ed.), *Secularism in India* (New Delhi: Deep & Deep, 1992); B.D. Graham, *Hindu Nationalism and Indian Policies. The Origins and Development of the Bhartiya Jana Sangh* (Cambridge: Cambridge University Press, 1993); Tapan Basu et al., *Khaki Shorts and Saffron Flags* (Hyderabad: Orient Longman, 1993); Satish Chandra, *Mughal Religious Policies, the Rajputs and the Deccan* (New Delhi: Vikas, 1993); T.N. Madan, 'Whither Secularism in India?', *Modern Asian Studies*, 27:3 (1993), pp. 667–97; Cynthia Keppley Mahmood, 'Rethinking Indian communalism: Culture and counter-culture', *Asian Survey*, 33:7 (July 1993), pp. 722–37; Peter van der Veer, *Religious Nationalism: Hindus and Muslims in India* (Berkeley: California University Press, 1994); Harjot S. Oberoi, *The Construction of Religious Boundaries: Culture, Identity and Diversity in the Sikh Tradition* (New Delhi: Oxford University Press, 1998); Martin E. Marty et al. (eds), *Accounting for Fundamentalisms* (Chicago: Chicago University Press, 1994); T.N. Madan, 'Secularism and the intellectuals', *Economic and Political Weekly*, 29 (1994), pp. 1095–6; André Beteillé, 'Secularism and the intellectuals', *Economic and Political Weekly*, 29 (1994), pp. 559–66; Partha Chatterjee, 'Secularism and toleration', *Economic and Political Weekly*, 29 (1994), pp. 1768–77; Gerald J. Larson, *India's Agony Over Religion* (Albany: New York State University Press, 1995); Robert Baird (ed.), *Religion in Modern India* (New Delhi: Manohar, 1995); Upendra Baxi et al. (eds), *Crisis and Change in Contemporary India* (New Delhi: Sage, 1995); Asim Roy, *Islam*

III

It has become long evident to students of the so-called New States of Asia and Africa—the countries newly liberated from the colonial yoke—that most of their endemic woes and confusions are attributable to the yawning lag between their polity and society. Not having the essential Western historical experience and the advantage of centuries of social and political development moving in tandem, the impact of colonial experience and colonial-nationalist polarities and contradictions on the New States tended to accelerate the pace of their political advance, leaving society, especially in the wake of colonial exploitation and underdevelopment, behind. In their slow and unsuccessful attempts to reduce the polarity of the two, the new leaders of those recently democratized countries often found themselves haplessly caught between politics and society pulling their countries in opposite directions, resulting in a political quagmire that ended up with the collapse of democratic constitution and government. India has been noted for being able so far to escape this predicament, and has accordingly earned the commendation from leading political scientist, Samuel Huntington, of being the 'Third World's most deviant case'.[21] The questions of how and why India has been able to avoid

---

in South Asia: A Regional Perspective (New Delhi: South Asian Publishers, 1996); Mushirul Hasan, Legacy of a Divided Nation: India's Muslims since Independence (New Delhi: Oxford University Press, 1997); Rajeev Bhargava (ed.), Secularism and Its Critics (New Delhi: Oxford University Press, 1998); Asim Roy et al. (eds), 'Islam in history and politics: South Asian perspectives', South Asia, 22, Special Issue (1999); Veena Das et al. (eds), Tradition, Pluralism and Identity: In Honour of T.N. Madan (New Delhi: Sage, 1999); Ashis Nandy, 'The twilight of certitudes: Secularism, Hindu nationalism and other masks of deculturation', in Veena Das et al., Tradition, Pluralism and Identity; Brenda Crossman et al., Secularism's Last Sigh? Hindutva and the (Mis)rule of Law (New Delhi: Oxford University Press, 1999); Neera Chandhoke, Beyond Secularism: The Rights of Religious Minorities (New Delhi: Oxford University Press, 1999); Sunil Khilnani, The Idea of India (New Delhi: Penguin, 1999/1997); Francis R. Robinson, Islam and Muslim History in South Asia (New Delhi: Oxford University Press, 2000); Stuart Corbridge et al., Reinventing India: Liberalization, Hindu Nationalism and Popular Democracy (New Delhi: Oxford University Press, 2000); T.N. Madan, Muslim Communities of South Asia: Culture, Society and Power, 3rd enlarged edn (New Delhi: Manohar, 2001); T.N. Madan, Religion in the Modern World (Bangalore: National Institute of Advanced Study, 2001); Gyanendra Pandey, Remembering Partition: Violence, Nationalism and History of India (Cambridge: Cambridge University Press, 2001); Mukul Kesavan, Secular Common Sense (New Delhi: Penguin, 2001); Mushirul Hasan, Islam in the Subcontinent: Muslims in a Plural Society (New Delhi: Manohar, 2002); Ashis Nandy, 'Unclaimed baggage: Closing the debate on secularism', The Little Magazine, 3:2 (2002), pp. 14–19; T.N. Madan, Modern Myths, Locked Minds: Secularism and Fundamentalism in India, 4th Impression, with a new Introduction (New Delhi: Oxford University Press, 2003/1997).

[21] Samuel P. Huntington, Political Order in Changing Societies (Connecticut, 1968). He also wrote: 'In terms of political institutionalization, India was far from backward. Indeed it ranked high not only in comparison with other modernizing countries in Asia, Africa and Latin America, but also in comparison with many more modern European countries' (ibid., p. 84). Cf. also: 'India's political order, parliamentary democracy, has a legitimacy paralleled in few nations of the Third World' [Richard L. Hardgrave, India under Pressure: Prospects for Political Stability (Boulder: West View, 1984), p. 3].

till now this rather common fate of the developing world are likely to throw up answers that may leave no room for comfort and complacency at Huntington's approbation.

Despite her considerable success in the political arena in the early years of Independence under the charismatic and vigilant leadership of the first Prime Minister, Jawaharlal Nehru, India did not quite bridge the aforesaid society–politics gulf.[22] Perhaps because of the same political success, Nehru's stature, as well as the traumatic and sobering effect on the nation of Gandhi's assassination at the very dawn of Independence, India had only managed to put the disquieting social forces on the back burner. Since the 1970s, the country started taking notice of these new players in the field, flexing their muscles in the 1980s, and taking command since the 1990s. With the steadily growing imprint of saffron hues on Indian politics, came the challenge of Hindutva—not only at political and ideological levels, but also at the level of physical violence and destruction. It provoked, overall, a sense of crisis in our perception and understanding of India's cultural pluralism, multiculturalism, and the hoary tradition of 'living together, even though separately'.

The chauvinistic claims made on behalf of a pan-Indian Hindu cultural monolith embodied in Hindutva assume much greater importance in light of the political power that was until recently vested in the Hindu-orientated political parties. Doubts have already been expressed in those extreme Hindu quarters concerning the historical legitimacy of the syncretistic process in the making of India's 'composite culture', with the corresponding claims made for a reconstructed exclusivist Hindutva. While the Bhartiya Janata Party (BJP) had been trying to create an impression that it was reluctant to push through its political and cultural agenda, in deference to the will of many of its political opponents, it had, in reality, been covertly engaged in promoting its ideological position. The most serious threat was posed in the educational-cultural sphere in polarizing society on communal lines.

In government schools in the BJP-ruled states and in over 20,000 Vidya Bharati schools and Shishu Mandirs all over the country, the prescribed syllabi present 'Indian' culture as 'Hindu' culture, totally denying its pluralistic character and the contribution of the minorities to the creation of the Indian identity in history. Everything Indian is shown to be of Hindu origin and the minorities are characterized as foreigners owing their first allegiance to political forces outside

[22]It may be recalled here that Prime Minister Nehru himself, the most powerful architect and builder of India's democratic and secular political culture, betrayed his mind on this issue, in the closing years of his government when he began to wake up to a sense of his mission unfulfilled. Questioned, in an interview with Andre Malraux, he affirmed that one of the two most difficult and intractable problems confronting his administration was 'creating a secular state in a religious society'. [Andre Malraux, *Antimemoirs* (London: Hamish Hamilton, 1968), p. 145; see also Madan, *Modern Myths*, pp. 245, 261.]

this country. Through a contrived process of distortion and concoction of facts, there is an effort to reconstruct history and tradition along communal and sectarian lines. Thanks to these books and the efforts of their 'dedicated' teachers, tens of thousands of children are growing up with prejudice and hatred towards the minorities, considering them alien, and in total ignorance of the rich and composite cultural heritage of India. The homogenized and predominantly Hindu imaging of Indian identity that these texts represent, is contrary to people's historical experience. A massive survey project by the Anthropological Survey of India published in the form of a series called the *People of India* proves a number of points which give the lie to the assertions of the Sangh Parivar. It shows that more than four thousand communities inhabit this country and their cultural profile is rooted and primarily shaped by their relationship with their environment, their occupational status, their language and so on, and that religion comes way down in the construction of their identities. This survey also shows that Hindus and Muslims share more than 95 per cent characteristics of various kinds in common and that it is shared lives that have given shape to the diverse cultural expressions. Among other things it also shows that nobody today can be characterized as an original inhabitant or a foreigner in South Asia.[23]

Where from here? India is indeed at a dangerous crossroads. There is no denying the fact that the challenge of Hindutva constitutes an unprecedented subversive threat to the Indian cultural tradition as evolved and known in history. Has, after all, the time for India to make her 'tryst with destiny' finally arrived? Is the fate of most of the developing world, as Huntington showed, closing in on her—a fate that the world judged, perhaps too soon, as not for her? The questions and issues are many and rather critical for India emerging into the new millennium. Where does it leave the plural and tolerant ethos of Indian culture—does it have a historical legitimacy or is it a convenient construct of India's nationalist demand? Imagined or real, does this tradition have the capacity to sustain India's cultural continuum through the new millennium? Again, how essential is it for the continuance of India's federal and democratic structure, and ultimately for her viability and survival? If so, are the historical traditions of pluralism and tolerance recoverable for that purpose?

It was in this critical milieu of endless questioning and intense soul searching in India and beyond, that the idea of our gathering took root, and we met together in Delhi a few months after the Gujarat pogrom. It is beyond the reach of a conference of this kind to be able to address all these questions and come up with all the answers, leave alone claim any finality about them. Despite the prescriptive unity and coherence of the overarching thematic umbrella of any academic conference, the actual depth and spread of its presentations always draw

[23]Nalini Taneja, *BJP's Assault on Education and Educational Institutions* (New Delhi, 1999), pp. 8–9.

its limits. It is for our readers and critics to measure the gap between our goals and achievements.

IV

The concept of composite culture in India has had a long history of being politicized all around—covering the whole spectrum of political ideologies and affiliations. Liberals, Marxists, socialists, and secularists have all found it expedient to use it politically to combat communalism and other forms of sectarian strife, just as the Muslim separatists and the champions of political Islam as well as their saffron-robed counterparts of political Hinduism have sought to undermine the notion of the composite cultural tradition and religious-cultural pluralism. In so doing, their objectives have been to 'harmonize' and 'totalize' the votaries of their respective faiths, primarily in the interest of galvanizing their political influence and dominance. As logical corollaries of a political agenda and efforts of this nature, various questions and issues have come to the fore, which are not merely the core concerns of India's historical evolution, but remain rather critical for her emerging into the new millennium.

Of the two most dominant issues to emerge from the vortex of the Hindutva discourse, one is that of the legitimacy of the pluralistic religious-cultural processes in India's historical development and their continuing relevance and recoverability. Unquestionably, the monolithic cultural stance appropriated by Hindutva is based on the total rejection of India's time-honoured plural and tolerant religious tradition. In recent years, some doubts have been raised about the assumptions underlying Hinduism, with particular reference to the question of its antiquity and tolerance. The other issue, virtually overwhelming the discourse on Hindutva, is the explosive one of secularism. The concept of religious-cultural pluralism, based on the principle of recognition and respect for all religious systems, clearly intersects the notion of secularism as embodied in the Indian Constitution. A substantive part of the Hindutva agenda constitutes a fierce attack on the so-called 'unjust, discriminatory, and impotent' ideology of secularism, believed to be fully loaded against the 'Hindu majority' and pandering to the non-Hindu 'minorities', especially the Muslims. The aspiring fathers of the Hindu state have been assiduously striving to popularize the spurious notion of 'pseudo-secularism' and deploy it to sap the foundation of the multicultural secular state. Undoubtedly, the most critical question facing India today is the future of secularism. And, in as much as the secularist ideology has been carefully ensconced within a perception of tolerant pluralistic tradition, the challenge to secularism is no less a challenge to India's pluralistic culture.

With the spectre of religious fundamentalism and terrorism stalking people in various countries today, there is a pervasive sense of a crisis in secularism. A fairly common perception is based on an understanding that secularist ideology, evolving in the West, and being innate to Western political culture, is peripheral and unsuitable for non-Western peoples. Despite an element of truth in this position, it is difficult to be persuaded entirely by such an orthogenetic and *sui generis* view of social and cultural change in history. Non-Western countries, failing the model of secular government, quite successfully adapted themselves to many other facets of development in the West. More importantly, the issue of secularism has also troubled the West. The intersection of secularism and religion has remained a subject of intense and acrimonious debate not only in the non-Western world, but also in the West from secularism's very inception. Born of a critical combination of some major historical developments, such as the emergence of the nation state system, Protestant Reformation, and Enlightenment, the notion of the 'separation of church and state' has often been contested and compromised. Even more so challenged, contradicted, and disfavoured, in some quarters, has been the most radical 'anti-religious' view of secularism and secularization pledged to the undermining of religion and unreason, and promoting rational and scientific values and outlook on life. These idealistic radical goals were to be achieved not simply by driving religion to the domain of the private, but also by relegating it to the realm of backwardness. One would scarcely find a Western secular country today daring to subscribe to this radical secular ideology. Even the principle of 'neutrality' for government in religious matters is carefully eschewed as 'offensive' and 'impolitic'. The British Constitution is based on the recognition of a single religion. The enlightened secular democratic Western countries begin their daily parliamentary deliberations by invoking the Grace of God. The Government of the United States, which proclaimed the principle of the separation of church and state by the First Amendment of 1791, has continually wavered—in its religious dealings, especially through its judicial interventions—between the principle of 'neutrality' and that of 'non-preferentialism'. In one of the latest developments in this area, it took the US Supreme Court all this time to remove a marble plaque, inscribing the 'Ten Commandments', from the precinct of the highest court in the State of Alabama amidst rather disturbing reactions from many Christian protesters.[24] Again, it has been a very familiar sight, particularly in recent years, for every speech of the President of the United States of America, or other high official dignitaries, especially trying to rouse the patriotic fervour of the people, to end invariably with the prayer 'God Bless America!'

None of all this should come as a surprise, given the fact that religion has not waned, as hoped for by the Positivists, Marxists, and Secularists. Rather, there has been a significant revival of religiosity both in the West and East since the twentieth century. More significantly, there are good reasons to believe that the

[24]Widely reported in the media on 28 August 2003.

rise of religious fundamentalism—violent or non-violent—all over the world is a reactive response, inter alia, to what are often perceived as the constraints and narrowness of the secular ideology.

V

So, if secularism in its primary Western context had moved away from the ideal of total separation between religion and governance, it was far less likely for the secular ideology and practice in India to capture or even aspire to reflect its classical Enlightenment spirit. The obvious dilemma and challenge here for the makers of the Indian Constitution are there for all to see in their treatment of the subject of secularism in the Constitution. It is clear that they preferred not to make heavy weather of the highly loaded and problematic term of 'secularism', the term occurring in the Constitution only once and the term 'secular' only a couple of times. The term 'democracy' is originally used in the Constitution, while 'secularism' and 'socialism' have been incorporated into the Preamble by the 42nd Amendment in January1977. Secularism, however, is unquestionably implicit and ingrained in the ideal of democracy itself, as the latter is totally opposed to, and inconsistent with, any notion or practice of discrimination of any kind, including religious. Without specific use of the term 'secularism', religious freedom and the corresponding rights of the individual and minority religious communities have been secured in the Constitution broadly under the provisions ranging from Articles 20 to 30 of the 'Fundamental Rights' (Part III).

The need for a definition and direction in some form has, nonetheless, been felt and canvassed. Sarvepalli Radhakrishnan, the renowned philosopher President of the Indian Republic, considered it 'strange' that the Indian government should be a 'secular' one, while the people's culture was 'rooted in spiritual values'. 'Secularism', he urged, needed a 'new, appropriate definition' in India, laying 'stress on the universality of spiritual values, which may be attained in a variety of ways'.[25] Despite his opposition to the concept of a divorce between religion and politics, Gandhi was not uncomfortable with the idea of secularism committed to the principles of non-interference with the people's religious lives and impartiality. The essence of such ideas found expression in the working definition of Indian secularism. Within the broad framework of religious pluralism, it came effectively to construe the principle of 'equal respect for all religions' (*sarva dharma samabhava*)—a position rather akin to the American constitutional concept of proactive 'non-preferentialism', rather than passive 'neutrality' of government in religious matters.

Has the system put in place in India worked? The answer to this question, in

---

[25]S. Radhakrishnan, 'Foreword', in Hussain, *The National Culture of India*, pp. vii–viii.

the first second and even the third decade of Independence, would have elicited dissimilar answers. From the 1980s, and surely from the 1990s, there would be scarcely anyone foolhardy enough to deny that secularism is in deep crisis in India. Today, there is a very serious question facing students of the history, politics, and society of post-colonial India: Why were we not able to read and forewarn about the crisis that was going to challenge the very foundations of the nation and to what extent was it due to complacency and/or a conspiracy of silence?[26]

Starting from the very beginning of the debates in the Constituent Assembly, it is possible to find a trail of doubts, sporadically expressed, on the feasibility and efficacy of the secularist ideology in the Indian context from various quarters, including the most obvious Hindu nationalist. Within the Congress Party itself, there were critics of the ideology like Dr Rajendra Prasad, the first President of the Indian Republic.[27] And yet it is interesting that the country seemed to have evolved a rather complacent and broad consensus about secularism being, to use a paradox, the 'sacred cow of New India', and seemed also to have developed a practical 'conspiracy of silence' about speaking out against this shibboleth of 'political correctness' that could and would easily have been castigated as fundamentalism or religious reaction. This wall of silence about the growing problems of secularism was rudely shattered by Ashis Nandy's powerful and successive volleys on secularist ideology in the 1980s, especially his 'anti-secularist manifesto' that largely set off a protracted and continuing debate.[28] The most informed and penetrating critique of secularism in the Indian context emanated, however, from T.N. Madan, whose writings and contributions in this area are simply majestic in breadth, depth, and style.[29] From a shared position, though not fully, both Nandy and Madan raised

[26]As early as 1963, Donald Eugene Smith saw 'the forces of Hindu communalism' as a potential threat to the future of secularism in India, and predicted 'much that could go wrong'. See his *India as a Secular State* (Bombay: Oxford University Press, 1963), pp. 493–501. Such premonitions were, however, few and far between.

[27]*Constituent Assembly Debates* (Delhi: Govt of India, November 1949), vols 10–12, pp. 705 and 993–4.

[28]Ashis Nandy, 'Counter-statement on humanistic temper', *Mainstream*, 10 Oct. (1981), pp. 16–18; his, *The Intimate Enemy: Loss and Recovery of Self under Colonial Rule* (New Delhi: Oxford University Press, 1983); 'An anti-secularist manifesto', *Seminar*, 314 (October 1985), pp. 1–12; his 'The politics of secularism and the recovery of religious tolerance', *Alternatives*, 13:2 (1988), pp. 177–94; his, 'The twilight of certitudes: Secularism, Hindu nationalism and other masks of deculturation', in Veena Das et al. (eds), *Tradition, Pluralism and Identity: In Honour of T.N. Madan* (New Delhi: Sage, 1999); also his, 'Unclaimed baggage: Closing the debate on secularism', *The Little Magazine*, 3:2 (2002), pp. 14–19.

[29]T.N. Madan, 'Secularism in its place', *Journal of Asian Studies*, 46:4 (1987), 747–59; his 'Whither secularism in India?', *Modern Asian Studies*, 27:3 (1993), pp. 667–97; his 'Secularism and the intellectuals', *Economic and Political Weekly*, 19 (1994), pp. 1095–6; *Modern Myths, Locked Minds. Secularism and Fundamentalism in India* (New Delhi: Oxford University Press, 1997); his *Muslim*

vital questions about some of the basic assumptions underlying the policy and practice of secularism in India. The floodgates were thrown open, and with Hindutva now firmly saddled on political power and threatening the multi-religious plural state, in the 1990s and after, the volume of literature interrogating and critiquing the problematic of a god that clearly failed to deliver became abundant.[30]

Our major concern here is not to take stock of the whole history and predicament of secularism in India. Rather, we have a much greater and more specific interest, in consonance with the aims and objectives of our Conference, in plotting the trajectory that establishes a clear linkage between the new concept of 'secularism' and the older tradition of 'religious-cultural pluralism' in the new Indian discourse. We have sought, in this Conference, to revisit, explore, and understand the forms and meanings of India's tradition of pluralistic living, currently threatened by Hindutva, which has been presented as our Conference theme with a slightly different slant—'Living Together Separately'. It is of particular importance for us that the gradual realization of the lacunae and lapses of the secular processes has given rise to a set of rich and fruitful literature, with its focus turned on the need, as well as the strength and capacity, of India's multi-religious, and multicultural plural tradition to represent and sustain the secular values and institutions. Both Nandy and Madan, as initiators of this new discourse on the intersection of secularism and the plural and tolerant tradition in India, remain at the forefront of it. Its major preoccupations have been to project the critical importance and relevance of India's religious-cultural pluralism, its philosophical underpinning of 'tolerance', and the question of the 'recoverability' of the tradition of tolerance and pluralism.

Responding in 1981 to a much publicized public statement from a number of leading Indian intellectuals expressing deep concern about 'the accelerating pace of retreat from reason' and the 'decay of rationality' in the country,[31] Nandy fired his first salvo, airing his now-too-familiar invectives against uncritical exaltation of 'hegemonic' science and modernity.[32] From this position he develops a radical critique of ideological secularism: it has pernicious effects in the form of religious devaluation; religious bigots and not people of faith breed religious intolerance, and it is the secularists who undermine religion; religious tolerance cannot sprout from religious devaluation but from inter-religious understanding and respect; hence the essence of the anti-secular message is to repair the damage done to social cohesion by the ideology of 'godless secularism', with the recovery

---

Communities of South Asia: Culture, Society and Power, 3rd enlarged edn (New Delhi: Manohar, 2001); his *Religion in the Modern World* (Bangalore: National Institute of Advanced Studies, 2001); and *Modern Myths, Locked Minds: Secularism and Fundamentalism in India*, 4th Impression, with a new Introduction (New Delhi: Oxford University Press, 2003).

[30]For fuller lists of the relevant publications since the 1980s, see ns 19 and 20.

[31]Amit Bhaduri et al., 'A statement on scientific temper', *Mainstream*, 25 July (1981).

[32]Nandy, 'Counter-statement on humanistic temper', pp. 16–18.

of religious tolerance dwelling in the Indian tradition of religious pluralism. Secularism, he insists, 'must respect and build upon the faiths and visions that have refused to adapt to the modern worldview'.[33]

Madan is in clear agreement with Nandy on the 'hegemonic' and 'homogenizing' potentials of ideological secularism, and its consequences for religious devaluation and delimitation. In his words: 'The construction of an Indian ideology of religious pluralism and tolerance ... had been rendered problematic by the processes of secularization which tend to, if they do not actively seek to, delimit and devalue the role of religion in society.'[34] He is also 'in sympathy with the main thrust of ... [Nandy's] arguments' on religious tolerance, as he shares with him the belief that 'religion itself can be a resource in the fight against religious bigotry'.[35] They differ, however, in regard to their respective understanding of India's religious tradition. Madan is not comfortable with Nandy's 'idealization' of tradition. But what is of much greater significance for the reconstruction of plural and tolerant religious tradition in history is admittedly Madan's disinclination to accept 'all the claims Nandy makes on behalf of abstract religion as against historical religions'.

The other important point of difference between the two relates to the issue of the recovery of religious tolerance. While Madan is supportive of the idea and efforts towards recovery, he is inclined to 'stress' that the process is 'not going to be easy', as Nandy 'does not recognize the enormous philosophical doubts and practical difficulties' besetting the task.[36] But the critical point of distinction between these two early challenges to ideological secularism is in that they proceed from two very different positions. Nandy's categorical rejection of secularism is a part of his general hostility to hegemonic, authoritarian, and science-driven world views of modernity. Madan's, on the other hand, is a 'scepticism' about an 'unreformed secularism' and its 'easy passage to India', as well as its 'universalizability', rather than total rejection of it out of hand. Underlying his scepticism are his two major concerns, namely the secular ideology's 'rootedness' in the 'dialectic of Protestant Christianity and the Enlightenment', on the one hand, and its 'incompatibility with India's major religious traditions', on the other,[37] as 'none of India's major religious traditions, with the exception of Christianity', he says, 'entertains the notion of privatized religion and the separation of the sacred and secular domains of everyday life. In "the prevailing circumstances", secularism was not, therefore, likely to make much progress'.[38] The 'prevailing circumstances' clearly

---

[33]Nandy, 'An anti-secularist manifesto', p. 2 ff; also 'The politics of secularism and the recovery of religious tolerance', *Alternative*, pp. 177–94, passim.

[34]Madan, *Modern Myths*, p. 276.

[35]Ibid., p. 275.

[36]Ibid., p. 276.

[37]Ibid., pp. 275–6.

[38]Ibid., p. xiv.

make reference to the 'problematic' that 'the modern processes of secularization … proceed in India without the support of an ideology … such as one legitimized by religion. What exists empirically, but not also ideologically, exists but weakly'.[39]

Madan's particular intervention in the area of secularism in India drew all kinds of responses for all kinds of reasons—some positive[40] and some critical.[41] Some of the criticism was clearly based on a misunderstanding of his position, which could not have been for lack of clarity in his style, but perhaps because of his occasional indulgence in a highly nuanced thought process that demands very close reading. The general tenor of the doubts expressed in this critical literature largely concerned the precise locus of his critique on secularism. More often than not he is cast in the same mould as Ashis Nandy. This is unfair and wrong. While Nandy is an acknowledged 'anti-secularist', Madan is not. We have probed in the preceding discussion the major facets of difference between the two, Madan's 'scepticism' about the 'prevailing circumstances' of secularism being interpreted and implemented in India, and also the specific sources of his 'concerns'. In one of his most recent reflections on the question—his new 'Introduction' to the Fourth Impression (2003) of his magnum opus—Madan comes closest to saying what may be misconstrued, if not 'closely read', as a rejection of secularism: 'Throughout *Modern Myths, Locked Minds*, from the first epigraph to the last paragraph, runs the conviction that *participatory pluralism* [emphasis ours], rather than a hegemonic and homogenizing secularism, is what will serve India's interests best.'[42] The key phrase here is 'participatory pluralism' which, with its corollaries of 'tolerance' and 'inter-religious understanding', is what Madan consistently canvassed to reinforce a hapless secularism with a much needed relevant Indian ideology that has been missing since its birth in the Indian Constitution. This is no call to bury secularism, only a plea to resurrect the dead pretending to be alive. There is an even more definitive statement from him: 'The conclusion is not that the secular state should be jettisoned … but that special efforts are needed to give it clear definition, work out its relation to civil society, and reinforce it ideologically.'[43]

[39]Ibid., p. 261.

[40]See, among others, Peter van der Veer, *Religious Nationalism: Hindus and Muslims in India* (Berkeley: California University Press, 1994); Larson, *India's Agony over Religion*. It should be noted here that Madan's case has found wider and better appreciation in recent years. Even some of his critics have come round to incorporate his viewpoints in building up and refining their own critiques of secularism.

[41]F.G. Bailey, 'Religion and religiosity: Ideas and their use', *Contributions to Indian Sociology* (n.s.), 25:2 (1991), pp. 211–32; Upendra Baxi, 'Secularism: Real or pseudo', in M.M. Sankhder (ed.), *Secularism in India* (New Delhi: Deep & Deep, 1992); Andre Beteille, 'Secularism and the intellectuals', *Economic and Political Weekly*, 29:10 (1994), pp. 559–66; Javeed Alam, 'Tradition in India under interpretive stress: Interrogating its claims', *Thesis Eleven*, Massachusetts Institute of Technology, No. 39 (1994), pp. 19–38; Stuart Corbridge et al., *Inventing India: Liberalization, Hindu Nationalism and Popular Democracy* (New Delhi: Oxford University Press, 2000).

[42]Madan, *Modern Myths*, p. xxi.

[43]Ibid., p. 261.

VI

Regardless of what they stand for, represent, and contribute, in relation to the discourse on the failing secularism in India, both Nandy and Madan have at least ended the long and cultivated silence on a subject enjoying the highest rating on the score of 'political correctness', and set off a trend of serious and open engagement with the 'burning' issues facing the 'secular' nation. Unquestionably, the horrors of recent years perpetrated on the minorities by the 'majoritarian' upholders of 'true', rather than 'pseudo', secularism, have also dragged many secularist intellectuals out from their slumber and complacency. It is not surprising in the least to find that issues concerning the protection of the minority communities have come to dominate—and quite rightly so—the thinking of most recent writers. Also, in seeking and securing such safety and protection, the promotion and deployment of the resource of religious tolerance have been assigned a major complementary role. For Rajeev Bhargava,[44] the severity and persistence of such communal conflicts have effectively reduced the meaning of secularism to 'a strong defence of minority rights', which is to be reinforced by the religious resource of tolerance. He advocates a practical notion of 'political secularism', which makes 'the right' come before 'the good', and 'provides a way of living together', but not the optimal goal of living together 'well'. The latter goal is perhaps left to the long-term ideological objectives of what Bhargava calls 'ethical secularism'.

Another major contribution belongs to Partha Chatterjee,[45] who is equally concerned with the 'challenge of Hindu majoritarianism' and calls into question the capacity of the current rhetorical secularism 'to meet' this threat. Like others, searching for a more practical and effective way of dealing with this serious threat, he suggests some pragmatic solutions within the framework of 'a strategic politics of toleration'. Dipankar Gupta's[46] intervention is a realistic and bold exposure of the feebleness, debility, and infirmity of time-worn secular rhetoric, on the one hand, and the traditional notion of tolerance, on the other. His answer to the urgent need of the dangerous hour—brilliantly phrased 'secular intolerance'—would directly reach out to the hearts and minds of all who feel enraged and helpless at the endless and organized destruction of jobs, properties, and lives of children, women, and men belonging to the minority communities in a 'democratic' and 'secular' India. Gupta's is the most basic and sensible call—for the government to discharge its first responsibility to 'govern' under the first principle of the Constitution to uphold the Constitution and law and protect its citizens.

It is our belief as well that no amount of debates and deliberations on the nuanced definition, nature, and form of secularism can obscure these basic

[44]Rajeev Bhargava, 'What is secularism for?', in Rajeev Bhargava (ed.), *Secularism and Its Critics* (New Delhi: Oxford University Press, 1998).

[45]Partha Chatterjee, 'Secularism and toleration', *Economic and Political Weekly*, 29:28 (1994), pp. 1768–77.

[46]His contributions in various newspaper articles, cited in Madan, *Modern Myths*, pp. xix–xx.

responsibilities of governance. It is perhaps logical to raise questions about the reliability of government when a government looked the other way as the Babri Masjid was being pulled down, or when a government connived at the horrific massacre of thousands of Muslims in Gujarat. True, but this can still not distract us from the main issue. There is no 'life' without law and no law without government. All our multitudinous and multifarious academic discourses on secularism remain totally irrelevant—only empty sound—unless we find an effective constitutional-legal way of protecting the minorities not only against a murderous 'majority', but also against a delinquent government and state. It is generally well understood that the ultimate protection of the right and dignity of individual citizens and groups, as well as the recovery of tolerance cannot be achieved without the eventual development of 'civic ties' and 'civil religion' in society. This is a slow and difficult process, and until such developments, disparate social forces cannot but be kept within bounds by appropriate legal-administrative and political measures. It appears that there was no lack of clear perception, at the dawn of Independence, on the gravity of this critically important question, as Nehru put at once his conviction and uncanny premonition with his usual poignancy:

We have got to deal with this minority in a civilized manner. We must give them security and the rights of citizens in a democratic State. *If we fail to do so, we shall have a fastering* [sic] *sore, which will eventually poison the whole body politic and probably destroy it* [emphasis ours].[47]

VII

Finally, we are left with the issue on the flip side of Indian secularism, that is religious pluralism founded on its twin props of non-discrimination or non-preferentialism (*dharma nirapekshata*) as state policy and equal respect for all religions (*sarva dharma samabhava*), inter-religious understanding, and tolerance as social philosophy. At the very outset of this Introduction we broached the issue of the pervasive notion of India's plural, tolerant, and composite cultural tradition, on behalf of which strong claims have often been made, like the following one: 'There is some basic element in India's genius, something in its "genetic code" as it were, which has always moved towards an underlying unity despite apparent diversity.'[48] The notion of plurality and heterogeneity of the Indian society is commonplace. India's diversity is so easily noticed, but the claim of underlying 'unity' is not so obvious and has attracted adverse opinion from time to time, since the colonial period, as already discussed. But the mere fact of India's continued existence

---

[47]Jawaharlal Nehru, *Letters*, 15 October 1947, vol. 1, p. 2, also vol. 2, p. 84; cited, Mushirul Hasan, *Legacy of a Divided Nation: India's Muslims since Independence* (New Delhi: Oxford University Press, 1997), p. 151.

[48]M. Mohiuddin, 'The elements of composite culture', in Rasheeduddin Khan (ed.), *Composite Culture of India and National Integration* (Simla: Indian Institute of Advanced Study, 1987), p. 84.

through millennia bears witness to her capacity to hold together an enormous variety of people and culture divided by every conceivable criteria known to divide one human being or group from another. Any answer to the immeasurably complex question about Indian 'unity' has indeed to grapple with a simple but profound historical truth that the people in this region have lived together for over 5000 years of prehistory and history, despite all internal differences, and strict caste and religious taboos vis-à-vis other castes and religions. How does one approach this question? This has, over a long period of time, been a major preoccupation of Indology, social sciences, and other disciplines across the world. Like other major questions of this nature facing cognitive knowledge of modern times, the answers have been sought within a 'structural' and 'cultural' frame. There is no room or reason for us to get involved here in a prolific discourse of this magnitude. We cannot, however, overlook it in so far as the wider discourse on continuity and stability of the Indian civilization and their structural and cultural basis are significantly relevant to the issues of religious pluralism and tolerance and its recoverability.

We should like to state our view at the very outset that the essence of the concept of India's so-called 'unity in diversity' is best construed at its most basic level in a 'functional' sense, and one cannot ignore that India has remained 'functional' over nearly five millennia. Stability and continuity are to be identified as the effective forms of this functional unity. Questions can be raised, and have indeed been raised, about many religious and ideological concepts and institutions of Hinduism, long accepted as incontrovertible factors in the unity of the Hindu and Indian world, as will be discussed. No doubts, however, could or have been raised, about the historical truth of India's social stability and continuity through millennia, which are there for all to see. What made India stable, continuous, and, so, functionally united? India's social diversity and pluralism had always been her strength. A vast mosaic of cross-cutting divisions of class, caste, tribe, religion, sect, language, and region, each social compartment was more or less insulated from the other and compartmentalized. In this sense, society functioned on the principle of fission. The principle of fusion was, on the other hand, equally operative in that there were competing and interacting groups and interests, which held the balance of order and stability. As Indian society had not been organized on the basis of a single mega-circuit system, but as a multiple-circuit system, a breakdown in one circuit kept the others going. For the same reason, change and challenge were structurally quarantined and their impact cushioned. The problems of one sector did not generally spill over to the others. Successful protest and dissent did not bring about a structural change in the system; it only ended up creating new groups within the system. The caste structure integrated into the village system of traditional India together provided the basic site at ground level for the system to work. It is fairly well known to the informed that there were no 'structural' changes in the caste system, only 'positional' changes within it. The system did not conduce to much displacement or replacement in this social arrangement, especially of conflicting matters, only juxtaposition and coexistence—often neither rationalized nor reconciled, but accepted. Above all, there was 'tolerance' of change born of diversities, and of 'living together, even though separately'.[49]

Unlike the structural foundation, the cultural, religious, and ideological bases of the togetherness of living, or at least coexistence, have not been as free of major controversies, especially in recent years. Both Hindu and Muslim communalism, based on the notion of their respective religious exclusiveness, have obviously presented the bigger and more rounded political challenge, as noted before. Of late, the issue of 'tolerance' as a component of India's pluralistic tradition has been caught up in the debate on secularism, or rather 'anti-secularism'. We have already discussed at length that one of the main planks of the critique of secularism is a call to return to and recover the tradition of Indian religious pluralism and its underpinning of tolerance and mutual recognition and respect for other religions. The rationale underlying this position, as discussed earlier, is not only that the principle of separation of religion and politics is not grounded in the social-religious realities of India and is, consequently, unable to provide a sound basis for the promotion of mutual understanding among its diverse religious communities. The position is also predicated on the belief that inter-community understanding and harmony are achieved better and quicker by drawing upon the indigenous resources of the nation in the form of its people and tradition. The authors of this critique of secularism undoubtedly include professed anti-secularists, like Ashis Nandy, but an uncritical association of this critique with *anti*-secularism per se is as wrong as is calling every secularist *anti*-religious. Javeed Alam, one such critic of the 'anti-secularists', has chosen, on

[49]The above reflections and analyses are based on some major social science studies in the structural and cultural foundations of the Indian civilization. Most useful among these are: Bernard S. Cohn, *India: The Social Anthropology of a Civilization* (New Delhi: Oxford University Press, 2000); Milton Singer, *When a Great Tradition Modernizes: An Anthropological Approach to Indian Civilization* (New York: Praeger, 1972); his 'The cultural pattern of Indian civilization', *The Far Eastern Quarterly*, 15 (1955–6); his 'The social organization of Indian civilization', *Diogenes*, xlv (Spring 1964); Milton Singer et al. (eds), *Traditional India: Structure and Change* (Philadelphia: The American Folklore Society, 1959); Milton Singer et al. (eds), *Structure and Change in Indian Society* (Chicago: Aldine Publishing Co., 1968); Nirmal K. Bose, *Culture and Society in India* (London: Asia Publishing House, 1967); D.G. Mandelbaum, *Society in India*, 2 vols (Berkeley: California University Press, 1970); McKim Marriott, *Village India: Studies in the Little Community* (Chicago University Press, 1955); his 'Changing channels of cultural transmission in Indian civilization', *Journal of Social Research*, 4:1–2 (1961); M.N. Srinivas, *Social Change in Modern India* (Berkeley: California University Press, 1966); also his *India: Social Structure* (Delhi: Hindusthan Publishing Corporation, 1980); V. Raghavan, 'Variety and integration in the pattern of Indian culture', *The Far Eastern Quarterly*, 15:4 (Aug. 1956), pp. 497–507.

his own admission, to build his whole case on 'Madan's anti-secularism',[50] which is clearly a misreading of Madan's position, as already discussed.

The case of the critics of secularism has been countered nationally and internationally in recent years. Questions have been raised as to 'whether and how far *tradition* has been or can continue to remain a *resource* for people in India'.[51] There are, however, rather significant differences of approach and perception to be found in regard to the understanding of tradition and tolerance. Javeed Alam clearly recognizes the historical legitimacy, continuity, and importance of the tolerant tradition in the pre-modern/colonial period, as he affirms:

It is true that, historically, Hinduism had displayed an amazing capacity to tolerate diverse forms of competing world outlooks and philosophies. While the record is not totally unblemished, it had generally not persecuted the adherents of other religious orders or taken a hostile stand vis-a-vis other religions.[52]

He is, however, quick to point out the limits of this tolerance, Hinduism being 'highly tolerant towards those who were outside its folds', and 'extremely intolerant to those within its fold'. As a non-proselytizing religion, it could afford to overlook other religions outside its pale, and, while not having a scripture or a fixed dogma to defend, Hinduism developed and enjoined a 'rigid pattern of living'.[53] The tragic fate overtaking India's tradition of tolerant pluralism in modern times may be viewed as an unhappy outcome of a gradual extension of Hinduism's 'intra-community' intolerance to engulf its tolerant 'inter-community' outlook and relations. Within the larger context of the historical process of negotiation, reinterpretation, and reworking of tradition in India, Alam focuses on its development in the last century that saw it 'divided between its lived versions and the articulated forms', that is the bifurcation 'between tradition that fills the public sphere of politics or intellectual contentions and the private face of traditions available in their varied unreflective forms to the people—unreflective given the non-literate conditions ... in Indian society'.[54] He is pessimistic about the recoverability of tolerance in the current political context of tradition 'hijacked by the communal forces to build a politics of confrontation'. It 'seems unlikely', he concludes, 'that it can provide an alternative basis for a politics based on social harmony'.[55]

[50]Alam, 'Tradition in India under interpretive stress', p. 20. He writes: 'In this article I will *mainly* use Madan and that for one simple reason, his is a neatly argued out position cast in a rational mould.' P. 36, n. 2.

[51]Ibid., p. 19. Emphases in the original.

[52]Ibid., p. 28.

[53]Ibid., pp. 28–9.

[54]Ibid., p. 23.

[55]Ibid., p. 35.

The concepts of 'tradition' and 'tolerance' are not only at the heart of the discourse critiquing the anti-secularist thesis, these have also emerged as significant in the current debates on the vexed question of the historical roots of 'communalism'.[56] Posing the question of 'just how primordial or ancient communal affiliations in India really are', the seekers of deeper cultural roots of communalism in history have come to challenge the prevailing 'notion that the current communal divisiveness is solely a product of modern politics, a temporary anomaly in the long sweep of a basically harmonious Indian history', which is also branded as a 'political myth of communal conflict today' that 'it is a modern phenomenon out of sync with the rest of Indian history'. This particular view seeks to raise doubts about the long-established, but 'demonstrably false notion that pre-modern Indian civilization was one characterized by tolerant pluralism'.[57] To Cynthia Mahmood, who argues against the widely accepted view of the 'recency' of Hinduism as a rather structured religious system, 'India is clearly a plural society', except that it does not accord equality to its diverse communities. Rather, 'the dominance and continuity of the Hindu tradition remains the defining feature of the culture'. The 'long-term reality of Indian civilization' is that 'it is a civilization with a single (not necessarily coherent) tradition at its core, around which almost all other dialogue necessarily revolves'. Given its continuity and civilizational structure, it takes the form of an extended dialogue between a network of overlapping core groups and other largely peripheral groups in the society interlocked into a relationship of dominance and subordination, or bound in 'the dynamics of dominance and resistance'. This is indicative of Hinduism's 'persistent attempts at intellectual hegemony', evidenced by the non-Hindu religious literature of the Buddhists and Jains. Mahmood ventures to say: 'The decline of Buddhism in India … is not really very hard to understand once the ideological lens of "India the land of tolerance" is removed.'[58] Elsewhere she asserts: 'The great fact of Indian history that is suppressed in nearly the whole of the Indian educational system and even in its world of scholarship is the religious persecution that plagued nearly all the heterodox defectors from Brahmanism.'[59] Strong words and very tall claims indeed, especially within the compass of a short fifteen-page essay. It is a well-known adage of scholarship on India that for every statement there is a counter-statement waiting to confront it. Some of Mahmood's main concerns raised in the paper spanning a history of over four millennia are highly contentious, to say the least. The determination of the relative importance of

---

[56]See Ainslie Embree, *Utopias in Conflict: Religion and Nationalism in Modern India* (Berkeley: California University Press, 1990); Cynthia Keppley Mahmood, 'Rethinking Indian communalism: Culture and counter-culture', *Asian Survey*, 33:7 (July 1993), pp. 722–37; Achin Vanaik, *The Furies of Indian Communalism* (London: Verso, 1997).

[57]Mahmood, 'Rethinking Indian communalism', pp. 722, 724, 726, 730, 734 and 737.

[58]Ibid., p. 736.

[59]Ibid., p. 732.

the cultural and political contexts of communalism or ethnicity, as well as that of their pre-colonial, colonial, and post-colonial settings is perhaps the most explosive issue of South Asian historiography, and the volume of literature on this subject is simply overwhelming. Even all well-researched hypotheses are likely to look shallow without taking the counter-arguments on board, and without exercising caution in treading this delicate ground. Likewise, the issue of 'intolerance' in the context of Indian civilization is one to be treated with more than usual circumspection. Historical records of civilizations or societies are as much about tensions, rivalries, intolerance, hatred, and conflicts as about stability, cooperation, tolerance, love, and peace. What makes Indian civilization stand out is, therefore, not the absence of such common traits of history in it, but its staggering capacity to survive, with its size, and proverbial and matchless diversities, to reach the dizzy height of history of being known to have, along with China, 'the oldest continuous' civilization in the world.[60] To play around a little with Cynthia Mahmood's own words, it is 'really very hard to understand' and explain this historical feat 'once the ideological lens of "India the land of tolerance" is removed'. Indian civilization has undoubtedly had its own share of religious and social intolerance and conflicts,[61] but we cannot take and use these as an exclusive source of dynamism in the evolvement of Indian civilization, with special reference to the vital questions of its phenomenal continuity and stability. It is inconceivable that a historical development of this nature and magnitude could be explained within an analytical frame of 'intolerance', 'persecution', and 'exclusion'. Within the rather limited scope of this Introduction, we have focused in the preceding pages on some basic structural explanations underlying this historical phenomenon that reveals the dialectical principles of 'exclusion' and 'inclusion'—'fission' and 'fusion'—holding up and sustaining this civilization through millennia.[62] Nonetheless, Mahmood and other writers of her ilk deserve serious attention for making uninformed readers of Indian civilization aware of the facile and uncritical assumption of a pervasive and idyllic tradition of equalitarian pluralism in Indian religious and cultural development. Scholars have already probed the hierarchical orientation of Indian tradition, with its pluralism and tolerance, largely modelled and rested on the caste system, which is pluralistic in principle, though clearly inegalitarian and exploitative in practice. In reference to the early proto-Indian social formation of 'a variety of communities, determined by location, occupation and caste', it has been pointed out that those communities, living 'in

[60]Arthur L. Basham, *The Wonder That Was India: A Survey of the Culture of the Indian Sub-continent* (New York: Grove Press, Evergreen edn, 1959), p. 4.

[61]Romila Thapar, *Interpreting Early India* (New Delhi: Oxford University Press, 1992), pp. 73–5; M.N. Srinivas, *On Living in a Revolution and Other Essays* (New Delhi: Oxford University Press, 1992); p. 123; Wilfred Cantwell Smith, *Islam in Modern History* (Princeton University Press, 1957), p. 81.

[62]See p. 20 here and Mohiuddin, 'The elements of composite culture'.

a state of close though highly structured interaction' would have found pluralism 'an obvious basis for developing a general view of everyday life'.[63] The organizing principle of the caste system has, in fact, been extended to cover the intra-religious and inter-religious relations on the basis of a hierarchized pluralism.[64]

In today's India, however, tolerant pluralism is totally meaningless and impotent unless it is thoroughly rooted out of its traditional hierarchical mores, and is relocated on the basis of equalitarian and egalitarian principles. Such relocation cannot be achieved in a religious and political environment charged with fundamentalist credos and vitiated by a confrontationist polarity between 'majorityism' and 'minorityism'. Equalitarian pluralism demands a lot more than a mere plea for mutual respect and understanding among clearly differentiated religions and religious communities. Also, it is not achievable under the umbrella of the widest and most liberal of the definitions of Hinduism, leave alone Hindutva. Each of these religions must be prepared to transcend itself to embrace an overarching higher spiritual ideal binding all separate religious groups into a togetherness of living—a kind of spiritual message that we heard from the Rig Vedic seers, 'Truth is one, the sages call it by many names' (*ekam sad, viprah bahuda vadanti*), some saints of the medieval bhakti cults, and later Mahatma Gandhi, Radhakrishnan, and Maulana Azad, all rising above the denominational religious barriers of Hinduism, Islam, and all other religions.

This is precisely the point where the notions of social harmony and egalitarian and equalitarian pluralism as a social-religious philosophy—'equal respects to all religions' (*sarva dharma samabhava*)—may be seen to come so easily and logically to intersect with the spirit of secularism as understood and accepted in the Indian Constitution, namely the principles of 'non-discrimination' and 'religious neutrality' (*dharma nirapekshata*). It is not necessary for India to look for an alternative ideology to secularism, being driven to this course by the spectre of an 'anti-religious' message associated with secularism in its pure ideological form as separation between sacerdotalism and regnum, God's and Caesar's, heaven and earth, spiritual and temporal, and religion and politics. Regardless of the arguable question of the long-term justification and desirability of this ideology commensurate with a transformed and new face of India in the distant future, the clear intention of the makers of the Indian Constitution appears quite clearly against its adoption in the prevailing state of Indian society and politics. There is no reason, therefore, to look for anything beyond what is already there, except that there is a real and urgent need that the rules of the game are to be defined, once

[63]Thapar, *Interpreting Early India*, p. 75; also Madan, *Modern Myths*, p. 195. M.N. Srinivas holds that tolerance is 'provided by, strangely enough, caste. It is true that at the level of individual castes, exclusivism is the rule, but if one looks at the system as a whole, an acceptance of life-styles lies at its heart'. Srinivas, *On Living in a Revolution*, p. 123.

[64]Srinivas, *On Living in a Revolution*; Madan, *Modern Myths*, pp. 176–201.

and for all, with the clarity, certitude, and authority of the uncompromising political-legal system. Rules are perhaps not unknown to the breakers of the same, all that we need is to convey a new and stern message that rules are there for compliance and not to be broken, and if broken, the transgressors—either members of government or civil society—*must* face the full weight of the law. Until the values of a civil society take root, laws and rules are not expected to be honoured only because these are in the Book, which are to be enforced strictly and impartially. With the iron-clad guarantee of the secular state remaining strictly non-preferential in its legitimate dealings with people and communities, and the complementary civil process committed to promoting inter-religious and inter-community understanding, India can begin to re-learn how to live together, even if separately, but as equals, and also 'well', as Rajeev Bhargava would have it.[65]

[65]See Bhargava, 'What is secularism for?'.

PERSPECTIVES

THINKING OVER 'POPULAR ISLAM' IN
SOUTH ASIA: SEARCH FOR A PARADIGM

Asim Roy

The dawn of the new millennium saw a major sociological publication (not entirely original, rather an enlarged third reincarnation of it), focusing on the South Asian Muslim communities, under the competent editorship of T.N. Madan,[1] in which the editor speaks of a relative weakness of sociological studies compared to the volume and quality of historical studies on the region. Madan expresses his regret that

While historians have for long regarded South Asia as an area of immense if not unique interest from the Muslim point of view, and many approaches and schools of historiography flourish, high quality sociological studies of these Muslim communities are rather rare. Some improvement in this regard has been, however, noticeable, in recent years.[2]

At least some historians of South Asian Islam would have some understanding of the serious problems encountered by their sociology counterparts in building up their strength in this area, because of two major reasons. One is, in Madan's expressive words, 'the constrictive identification of Hindu society with India', treating communities other than the Hindus as minorities of relatively less scholarly interest. Besides, the avant garde of Indian sociology made very little effort to address this problem no less because of the biases of their theoretical positions, than because of the dearth of ethnographic studies of Muslim societies.[3] Within

[1] T.N. Madan (ed.), *Muslim Communities of South Asia: Culture, Society and Power*, third enlarged edn (New Delhi: Manohar in association with the Book Review Literary Trust, 2001).

[2] Ibid., p. 15.

[3] Ibid.

this relatively limited output, however, sociology and social anthropology of Islam in South Asia deserve the highest commendation for having raised serious issues with many historical certitudes and assumptions made by historians in this particular field. Historians, having their own reasons to feel uneasy with some of these generally received historical assumptions, cannot afford to be as dismissive to these disciplines as often seems to be the inclination of some historians and Islamicists.

The whole issue of the relationship between historical and sociological understandings of the Islamic process in the context of South Asia has come to the fore again with the publication of a historical work in the same field almost concurrently with that of Madan. This refers to Francis Robinson's latest major publication in 2000.[4] One of Robinson's chapters in this new publication, 'Islam and Muslim Society of South Asia', originally appeared in 1983, as students of South Asian Islam may recall, in Contributions to Indian Sociology, edited by no other than T.N. Madan. In this particular essay, Robinson's critique of the thesis of a distinguished sociologist, Imtiaz Ahmad, on South Asian Muslim societies sparked off a lively debate in the pages of Contributions in the 1980s, in which Gail Minault, a historian, and Veena Das, a sociologist, rallied in support of Ahmad. Among other major issues, the Ahmad–Robinson contentions almost came down to asserting the 'superiority' of one discipline over another. Robinson wrote:

In the Introduction to volume three[5] [of his four-volume study of Islam in South Asia] Ahmad set out his credo. He asserted the superiority of the sociological vision over that of the Islamicist. 'The sociological and social anthropological understanding of religion', we are told, 'is at once more comprehensive and more concrete.'[6]

Further, Robinson senses in Ahmad 'a dismissiveness towards the achievements of other disciplines, as well as a jarring confidence in the superiority of the sociological vision'.[7] Paralleling Ahmad's claim for the sociological understanding being more 'comprehensive', the historian warns the sociologist: 'Perhaps, the sociological understanding of religion, and religious change, is not as "comprehensive" as he [the sociologist] would like to think,' and then goes on to affirm the historian's 'extended view'.[8]

Such contestations for territoriality in disciplinary terms raise enormous problems for the ever-growing academic trends in multidisciplinary studies. Even within the old, generically defined parameters of disciplines, there have always been and will always be sociologically minded historians as there are historically

---

[4]Francis Robinson, Islam and Muslim History in South Asia (New Delhi: Oxford University Press, 2000).

[5]Imtiaz Ahmad (ed.), Ritual and Religion among Muslims in India (New Delhi: Manohar, 1981)

[6]Robinson, Islam and Muslim History, 'Introduction', p. 4.

[7]Ibid., pp. 44–5.

[8]Ibid., p. 62.

minded sociologists. Historians can turn, and have so often turned, to other disciplines either to reinforce or re-examine their historically derived understanding of problems. It is not reasonable to think that sociological perception is necessarily limited, while historical perception is necessarily and meaningfully 'extended'. We need each other and every other relevant discipline to enhance our knowledge and understanding of often complex historical matters. This is not to deny the historian the liberty and the total justification of critiquing specific issues of sociological findings from the vantage point of their historical perspective and understanding, as Robinson has demonstrated clearly the significant divergence between the apparent and the real meanings of people's practices during 'attendance at saint's shrines'.[9] Academic discretion of this nature is not necessarily antithetical, rather it is often integral to multidisciplinary studies. One most recent and excellent example of a multidisciplinary study of Muslim communities, with special reference to South Asia, is *Islam, Communities and the Nation: Muslim Identities in South Asia and Beyond,* edited by Mushirul Hasan.[10] In the editor's own words, the volume is 'intended to bring together scholars from different countries, from widely different political standpoints and disciplines, which include history, political science and sociology'.[11] It is, therefore, of quintessential importance for all concerned that sociology and social anthropology of Islam in South Asia have raised some serious questions—albeit within the frameworks of their own disciplines—about our historical understanding and assumptions regarding the Islamic process in the same region. Given the sociologist's approbation of the relative good grounds made by historians of South Asian Islam, it seems ironical that historians themselves find their house still significantly divided on their conceptual understanding of some key questions concerning the Islamizing process, and about the true meanings and significance of being and becoming Muslim in this region, both in historical and contemporary perspective. Let us, then, try to problematize the debate and the issues involved.

I. THE PHENOMENA

The students and sundry observers of Islam in South Asia and even beyond have long been familiar with the inner divergences of the Muslim communities crystallized into two broad clusters and strands of Muslim beliefs and practices, most commonly perceived to represent the distinction between the universal attributes of the religion derived from its scriptural and textual sources (*kitab*), and its particular formulations cast in the mould of its local geo-cultural and

---

[9]Ibid., p. 48.

[10]Mushirul Hasan (ed.), *Islam, Communities and the Nation: Muslim Identities in South Asia and beyond* (New Delhi: Manohar, 1998).

[11]Ibid., pp. 11–12.

customary beliefs and practices (*adat*). The former is viewed as the formal, transcendental, normative, universal, and macro segment of the twin complex of Islam, while the latter is seen to represent its proximate, pragmatic, practising, and living domain. In both literature and life, a multiplicity of descriptive labels are found to be widely used in the contrastive forms of 'high versus low', 'elite versus folk', 'learned versus popular', or 'syncretistic versus purist'. There is, of course, a much wider perception of this significant historical phenomenon going beyond the Islamic world.[12]

In one of his contributions on South Asian Islam, Ali Asani spoke of two distinct Muslim traditions. One he labelled the 'rustic tradition', which 'on the basis of its appeal and popularity among the rural, illiterate masses' was characterized 'variously as the folk, low or little tradition'. In reference to the other, he makes an extremely meaningful observation in regard to the issue of interrelationship between these two strands—an issue we intend to explore rather fully later:

Contrasting, or perhaps some would say, complementing this rustic tradition[13] is the more sophisticated, intellectual facet of Islamic civilization that developed in urban areas under the cultural influence of the immigrant Muslim elite of Persian or Central Asian origin.[14]

Sundry historical sources from the medieval times bear testimony to the inner divergences of Indian Islam, especially through the occasional outbursts of 'purist' sentiments and reactions of both religious and non-religious elite. As early as the fourteenth century, Ibn Battuta, the well-known Moorish traveller visiting India, was known to have been struck by some distinctive features of Indian Islam, much in the same way as Babur, founder of the Mughal dynasty and a keen and perceptive observer, noted its 'Hindustani' peculiarities in the early sixteenth

---

[12]See James G. Frazer, *The Golden Bough*, and Pt 6: *The Scapegoat*, 3rd edn (London, 1925), pp. 89–90. Cf. also: 'It has been found in countries where there are two distinct classes, the one intellectual and learned, the other illiterate and ignorant that the common religion which they profess has two sides, the one higher and the other lower, the one more or less esoteric and the other popular.' [Louis S.S. O'Malley, *Popular Hinduism* (UK: Cambridge University Press, 1935)]; and also:

There have always been two distinct strata of society in India, the one higher and the other lower; the first small in numbers, but in possession of highly developed religions, social ideas and institutions; the second comprising the great mass of the people who occupy a humbler rung on the cultural ladder. The first provides the intellectual and aristocratic and the second the folk element in India's culture. These two in their interactions have supplied two strands of the pattern.

[Tarachand, *Influence of Islam on Indian Culture,* 2nd edn (Allahabad: The Indian Press Publications, 1963), 'Introduction', ix.]

[13]Emphasis in this quotation is mine. Henceforth all emphases in quotations are mine unless otherwise indicated.

[14]Ali S. Asani, 'Sufi poetry in the folk tradition of Indo-Pakistan', *Religion and Literature*, 20:1 (Spring 1988), p. 81. The opposite connotations of the terms 'contrasting' and 'complementary' remain at the heart of the controversy between the Islamicists and their opponents among historians and social scientists, as we shall examine in the following pages.

century. Mandelslo, a widely travelled visitor in India, proposed to 'treat of the manner of life of the Mahumetans [sic] of the Indies, which is much different from that of the Turks and Persians'.[15] In the fourteenth century again, an influential Sufi divine, Makhdum-i Jahaniyan Jahangasht, is said to have forbidden Muslims to use Indian equivalents for the name of Allah.[16]

Since the late eighteenth century, and particularly in the nineteenth century, besides the sporadic references in Muslim revivalist writings, rather direct and much fuller accounts of Muslim beliefs and practices revealed the varieties and depth of the 'scriptural' and 'living' Islam in South Asia. One such pioneering account of foreign authorship concerning Muslim social-religious practices in India is that of Garcin de Tassy, who occupied the Foundation Chair in Urdu at the Ecole des Langues Orientales Vivantes between 1828 and until his death in 1878. As a sequel to his earlier publication, in 1826, on the Qur'anic doctrines and duties, he chose to study 'the festivals peculiar to Musulman India, as well as the solemnities practised in Persia, and even throughout the Musulman world, which are distinguished in India by peculiar ceremonies.' The 'first thing' that struck him 'in the external worship of the Mahomedans of India' was the 'alteration which it has undergone in order to adapt itself to the native indigenous physiognomy.' He considered the classical Islamic festivals 'not numerous enough for countries accustomed to the multiplicity of Hindu festivals'.[17] With occasional lapses, understandable in a pioneering effort of its nature, de Tassy, in support of his argument, 'depended almost entirely on whatever the Indian Muslims themselves had written on their festivals', as he cited as many as ten Muslim sources, four of which were very largely used.[18] Two other accounts of similar nature were published about the same time, one a voluminous work by Ja'far Sharif,[19] and the other by Mrs Mir Hasan 'Ali.[20] While Sharif's study covered Muslim life primarily in the Deccan, Mrs 'Ali, an Englishwoman, who married a wealthy, well-educated

---

[15]J.A. Mandelslo, *The Voyages and Travels of J. Albert de Mandelslo ... into the East Indies*, Eng. trans. by John Davies (London, 2nd edn, 1669), p. 62.

[16]Annemarie Schimmel, 'Reflections on popular Muslim poetry', *Contributions to Asian Studies*, 17 (1982); also Asani, 'Sufi poetry in the folk tradition', p. 82.

[17]M. Garcin De Tassy, *Memoire sur les particularites de la religion musulmane dans l'Inde* (Paris: De L'Imprimerie Royale, 1831), p. 9; Eng. extract in *The Asiatic Journal*, 6 (1831) (n.s.), pp. 352–3; see also its new recent edn, *Muslim Festivals in India and Other Essays*, trans. and ed. by M. Waseem (New Delhi: Oxford University Press, 1997), pp. 31–2.

[18]Of the ten works mentioned, eight were published from the Fort William College of Calcutta (now Kolkata) under the guidance of John Gilchrist (d.1841), Professor of Hindustani in the College, founded in 1800. All originally hailing from Delhi, the extensively used four writers were Mir Shair Ali Afsos (d.1808), Mirza Kazim 'Ali Jawan (d.1816), Haidar Baksh Haidari (d.1828), and Amanatullah Shaida (d.1846). See Waseem, *Muslim Festivals in India,* pp. 3, 5, 13–16.

[19]Ja'far Sharif, *Qanun-i Islam*, English trans. by G. Herklot and ed. by William Crooke (Oxford, 1921).

[20](Mrs) Meer Hussein Ali, *Observations on the Musulmauns of India*, ed. by William Crooke (Oxford, 1917).

aristocrat Shi'a in Lucknow, wrote largely on the basis of her personal knowledge and experience of Muslims, particularly of her own sex, in and around this region and Hyderabad. The Report of the Indian Census of 1901 observed that 'the Musulman religion is an *exotic* one in India and consequently does not contain a great number of *pure Moslems*'.[21] In one of the earliest major works of historical research, in the last century, embracing 'life and conditions of people in Hindustan', during the period largely of the Delhi Sultanate, K.M. Ashraf wrote, in 1935, with particular reference to the Muslim festivals observed in India, that 'the atmosphere' of the 'Muslim gatherings' was 'too sombre and austere to call them social festivals', and added:

Indian tradition and environment were bound to react in course of time on this rigidity of Muslim ritual. As a result, although the form of the orthodox religious congregations remained, their nature and purpose underwent a great deal of modification in the environment of Hindustan. Other new festivals were super-imposed on the Muslim Calendar which were predominantly social and indigenous.[22]

Bengal has long been known for the masses of its Muslim votaries practising a rather 'lax' and 'spurious' form of the religion, and for a consequent derogatory attitude of the high-born 'immigrant' Muslims towards their indigenous Bengali Muslim counterparts. This dichotomous perception of Islam in the land goes back long in history. The consciousness of the distinction between these two strands of Muslims was clearly articulated in a potent remark of Ihtimam Khan, the Mughal admiral in Bengal during the viceroyalty of Islam Khan (1608–13). Displeased with an instance of unbecoming conduct on the part of the viceroy, the former remarked to his son, Mirza Nathan, 'Islam Khan is behaving with us as he would behave with the natives.'[23] In the late eighteenth century, Ghulam Husain Tabatabai observed the 'deviance' of Muslim Bengal.[24] A late-nineteenth-century British medical practitioner in Muslim-dominant Eastern Bengal, Dr James Wise, noted 'the corrupt Hinduized rites' of Muslims in Bengal.[25] The most graphic depiction and the most venomous condemnation of such 'debased' Islam in Bengal came from the large volume of polemical and didactic writings of the Islamic

[21] *The Report*, Census of India, 1901, vol. 18, pt 1, p. 152. Also Asani, 'Sufi poetry in the folk tradition', p. 82; and his, 'The Khojahs of Indo-Pakistan: The quest for an Islamic identity', *Journal Institute of Muslim Minority Affairs*, 8:1 (January 1987), p. 31.

[22] K.M. Ashraf, *Life and Conditions of the People of Hindustan* (AD *1200–1550*) (Calcutta: Asiatic Society of Bengal, 1935), p. 300.

[23] Mirza Nathan, *Baharistan-i Ghaybi*, Eng. trans. by M.I. Borah (Gauhati: Dept of Historical and Antiquarian Studies, 1936), vol. 1, p. 51.

[24] *Siyar ul-Muta'akherin*, cited, Qazi Abdul Wadud, *Hindu-Musalmaner Birodh* [in Bengali] (Santiniketan: Visva-Bharati, 1936), p. 16.

[25] James Wise, *Notes on the Races, Castes, and Trades of Eastern Bengal* (London: Harrison & Sons, 1883), p. 6.

fundamentalists, revivalists, and reformists in the nineteenth century and later.[26] At the beginning of the last century Syed Ameer Ali, a distinguished member of the modern Muslim social and intellectual elite, contrasted 'the Mahomedan settlers from the West who had brought with them to India traditions of civilisation and enlightenment' with the Eastern Bengali Muslims who were 'chiefly converts from Hinduism' and 'still observe[d] many Hindu customs and institutions'.[27] Derogatory remarks on the piety of Bengali Muslims are often attributed to contemporary West Pakistani politicians and officials. Malik Feroze Khan Noon, the Punjabi Governor of East Bengal in 1952, regarded his wards as 'half-Muslims'. President Ayub Khan was also known to hold similar views.[28] Anthony Mascarenhas, a noted journalist covering the Bangladesh Liberation War, pointed out that 'the absurd denigration of the piety of the Muslims in the east wing by those in the west' was among the 'major points of discontent' between the Bengalis and West Pakistanis. He also reminisced about a Punjabi military officer, placed in an East Pakistan district during the Bangladesh crisis, who grabbed a handful of the 'the rich, black earth' of the place and exclaimed, 'My God, what couldn't we do with such wonderful land,' and then added: 'But I suppose we would have become like them.'[29]

II. CONVENTIONAL APPROACH AND DIAGNOSIS

The perception of the variance and divergence in Indian Islamic development is, therefore, rather evident and common. But the understanding, explanation, and conceptualization of the phenomenon at the level even of academics, including historians and Islamicists, clearly lack translucence. Faced with the challenge of resolving this historical problem of great magnitude, crying for serious intellectual engagement, the dominant approach of historians is marked by indifference and naivete. The most common approach for them has been to measure up all 'popular' expressions of the religion against the norms, practices, and prescriptions of 'scriptural' Islam, and trash everything that fails to measure up into the dark and bottomless pit of 'folk' Islam. The sheer convenience of resorting to this ill-defined and amorphous intellectual dumping ground of 'folk Islam' lies at the roots of an endemic failure on the part of historians and Islamicists to offer a critical and convincing analytical frame to probe this phenomenon. Analysis is

---

[26]Asim Roy, *The Islamic Syncretistic Tradition of Bengal* (Princeton: Princeton University Press, 1983); also its Indian edition, (New Delhi: Sterling Publishers, 1987) (henceforth Roy, *Syncretistic Islam*), Preface, ix–x, xiii–xxi.

[27]*The Moslem Chronicle* (Calcutta), 28 January 1905, p. 193.

[28]Cited in Anthony Mascarenhas, *The Rape of Bangladesh* (Delhi: Vikas Publications, 1971), p. 18; M. Ayub Khan, *Friends Not Masters* (London: Oxford University Press, 1967), p. 187.

[29]Mascarenhas, *The Rape of Bangladesh*, pp. 11, 14.

substituted in such academic efforts by a few uncritical assumptions and assertions in the form of either 'incomplete' or 'semi' 'conversion' or a largely conjectured and unhistorical logic of 'degeneration'. Arguments of this nature are often buttressed with a whole range of subsidiary and ancillary explanations, like animism, aberration, corruption, accretion, and anomalies. It may seem extraordinarily intriguing that whereas for all other kinds of historical debates on South Asian Islam, the respective positions of historians are almost invariably found to correspond to their known ideological and intellectual orientations, such as that of the Islamicist, essentialist, purist, empiricist, instrumentalist, separatist, nationalist, secularist, and Marxist, there is an astonishing degree of the unity of purpose, attitude, and approach among historians, cutting across their ideological and even ethnic boundaries, as they are challenged by the problematic of conceptualization of popular expressions of Islam. Let us make a brief survey of the field.

For Mohammad Mujeeb, the practitioners of popular Islam were 'partly converted';[30] for Peter Hardy 'census Muslims',[31] and for Francis Robinson 'half-Islamized peoples'.[32] 'At the *popular level*,' according to Aziz Ahmad, 'Indian Islam represents a mosaic of *demotic, superstitious and syncretistic beliefs*.' Further, he affirmed, '*animism* in Islam, as in other religions throughout the world, is to some extent rooted in popular beliefs, while in India it may have been influenced to some uncertain extent by Hinduism.'[33] All this, for him, meant nothing more than 'add[ing] color to the bizarre pageantry of India'.[34]

The case of Imtiaz Ahmad is particularly significant in this context, underlining the magnitude and complexity of the problem. He has been one of the strongest protagonists of the varieties and diversities in South Asian Islam as well as an opponent of the monolithic perception of orthodoxy and orthopraxy in Islam. He identified three separate and somewhat 'autonomous' strands or 'levels' in South Asian Islam. Referring to the third, representing 'pragmatic' concerns of believers such as 'supernatural theories of disease causation, propitiation of Muslim saints, and, occasionally at least, deities of the Hindu pantheon and other *crude* phenomena as spirit possession, evil eye, etc,' Ahmad declared: 'One

---

[30]Mohammad Mujeeb, *The Indian Muslims* (London: Allen & Unwin, 1967), p. 22.

[31]Peter Hardy, *Muslims of British India* (Cambridge University Press, 1972), p. 27. He avers: 'The real challenge to *purity of belief and practice* in Islam in medieval India was to be found ... in the convert's countryside—in the ignorance of new Muslims of the requirements of Islam and in the insidious infiltrations of "creeping Hinduism" into the daily life of the convert.'

[32]Francis Robinson (ed.), *Atlas of the Islamic World Since 1500* (Oxford University Press, 1982), p. 119.

[33]Aziz Ahmad, *An Intellectual History of Islam in India* (Edinburgh: Edinburgh University Press, 1969), pp. 44, 46.

[34]Aziz Ahmad, *Studies in Islamic Culture in the Indian Environment* (London: Oxford University Press, 1964), pp. 163–4.

would be *perfectly justified in excluding them* almost completely from considerations under Islam, except that those who observe them are *nominally Muslims* and are so regarded by others.'[35]

Sumit Sarkar, with his pronounced leftist leanings, offered no different perspective:

It has to be admitted that the premodern synthesis had serious limitations. Social barriers and taboos remained sufficiently formidable for both communities to retain always a sense of separate identity even at the village level. *Syncretist tendencies* all too often *took the form of irrational devotionalism* and *superstitions shared in common*; religious reform movements in the nineteenth century—both Hindu and Muslim—were bound to regard such cults and rites as a *debasement* of the pristine purity of their respective faiths.[36]

Bengali Muslim historians such as Momtazur Rahman Tarafdar and Rafiuddin Ahmed followed the beaten track on 'folk Islam'.[37] Azizur Rahman Mallick's was perhaps the baldest articulation of the Islamicists' case. In reference to Bengal, 'where *corrupt and irreligious practices* gained considerable ground', he spoke of the 'ignorance' of the 'half-converted Muslims' and identified 'incomplete conversion' as 'a channel through which un-Islamic practices passed' into Islam. '*Incomplete conversion* in the rural districts of Bengal', Mallick wrote, 'left these people only *nominal followers* of the Faith.' He raised the issue of the Mughal decline and the 'loss of political power', which, in his opinion, 'undoubtedly contributed to the *degeneration* of Islam'. Mallick, in an intriguing statement, betrayed his inclination not even to count 'the half-converts from Hinduism' among 'Muslims': 'Thus long years of association with non-Muslims who far outnumbered them,[38] cut off from the original home of Islam, and *living with half-converts from Hinduism, the Muslims had greatly deviated* from the original faith and had become "Indianised".'[39]

It appears, therefore, that there have been two broad lines of reasoning to account for the deviance and divergence of popular Islam. The theory of 'incomplete conversion' or 'semi-conversion' is, in essence, a variant of that of 'folk Islam', both seeking to underscore the cultural limits of the masses of indigenous converts. The theory of 'degeneration', on the other hand, offers a much different kind of

[35]Imtiaz Ahmad, 'Unity and variety in South Asian Islam: A summary', in Dietmar Rothermund (ed.), *Islam in Southern Asia: A Survey of Current Research* (Wiesbaden: Franz Steinar Verlag, 1975), pp. 6–8.

[36]Sumit Sarkar, *The Swadeshi Movement in Bengal 1903–1908* (New Delhi, 1973), p. 409.

[37]Momtazur R. Tarafdar, *Husain Shahi Bengal, 1494–1538* (Dhaka: Asiatic Society of Pakistan, 1965), pp. 163–4; Rafiuddin Ahmed, *The Bengal Muslims 1871–1906: A Quest for Identity* (New Delhi: Oxford University Press, 1981), pp. 54–5.

[38]In a study of Muslims in Bengal, Mallick seems to overlook here that while Muslims formed a minority in the Indian subcontinent, they were a majority of the Bengal population.

[39]Azizur Rahman Mallick, *British Policy and the Muslims in Bengal 1757–1856* (Dhaka: Asiatic Society Press, 1961), pp. 3, 7–9.

argument. None of these explanations could, however, be sustained either by logic or history.

To begin with, the arguments of incomplete conversion and degeneration contradict each other. Degeneration could not have logically followed from a situation which was already regarded inadequate and 'incomplete'. Besides, descriptive labels such as 'half-converts', 'census Muslims', or 'nominal Muslims' raise serious questions about the place for value judgments in academics. To call a Muslim something less than a Muslim is a value judgment and not a description or analysis of the meaning of being a Muslim from the point of view of one who calls himself a Muslim and claims the religion as his own. Such a presumptuous and judgmental stand on the nature and depth of piety of individual believers seems more akin to a religious posture than an academic analysis. Finally, the most serious objection to the theory of Islam's degeneration in Bengal is that it is patently unhistorical. There is no historical evidence to suggest that Islam as practised by the masses of its votaries in Bengal, in the declining years of the Mughals, was anything different from what it had been there in the past, or that the so-called 'corrupt', 'degenerate' and 'Hinduized' Islam, confronted by the Islamic revivalists and reformists since the nineteenth century, was a sharp fall from an imagined golden or classical age of Islam in Bengal lying in the past.[40] On the contrary, the earliest extant Muslim Bengali literary sources, dating largely from the sixteenth century, provide the clearest possible evidence of the early existence in Bengal of masses of believers who, having been linguistically cut off from the Arabic and Persian sources of Islamic tradition, and denied of such tradition in their vernacular Bengali, continued to remain steeped in the locally popular non-Muslim tradition readily available in the vernacular Bengali.[41] The authors of this early Muslim Bengali literature were themselves instrumental in recasting Islamic tradition in syncretistic moulds. We shall return to this theme later.

III. CONVENTIONAL CONCEPTUALIZATION AND PROGNOSIS

It is regrettably true that historians, who are obsessively preoccupied with the search for a master narrative of the triumphal march and victory of 'essential' Islam in history, either totally ignore popular Islam, or make only passing references to it. Even when this perceived 'non-issue' found more than a mere mention from them, its historicity still remained totally marginalized. A fairly common position, as seen in the preceding discussion, was to treat such deviance as aberration, anomaly, and accretion, devoid of any historical import and not worthy of serious consideration. There was some predisposition even to treat such popular

[40]Roy, *Syncretistic Islam*, p. 6.
[41]Ibid., p. 7.

developments as 'festers' that could be 'cured'. Aziz Ahmad's prescriptive 'proper perspective' on how the folk beliefs should be viewed was simply that these 'should not be over-emphasized or over-rated.' He assured us:

They are specific to microscopic Muslim communities and are generally *the exception rather than the rule*. They were challenged by the fundamentalist, orthodox and modernist movements alike in the nineteenth and twentieth centuries. They have *completely ceased to exist in the Westernized upper class and nearly so in the orthodox lower middle classes*. In the predominantly Muslim regions, which now constitute West Pakistan, their hold was not very strong even in the lower classes, and *fundamentalism is now rooting them out*.[42]

Mushirul Haq laid the blame on 'social scientists', who had 'generally been underrating the position of religion in the life of people', and also found those 'wrong' who would 'explain away the reality of religion' in 'sociological terms' and 'invariably' took 'the outwardly socio-religious practices of a people as their religion'.[43] Haq thus effectively spoke for the exclusion of 'socio-religious practices' from the purview of religion. We only need to juxtapose here sociologist Imtiaz Ahmed's affirmation, as noted in the previous section, that one would be '*perfectly justified in excluding*' the 'pragmatic' concerns of popular Islam '*almost completely from considerations under Islam*, except that those who observe them are *nominally Muslims* and are so regarded by others'.[44]

Alongside the supreme indifference and utter naivete inherent in the academic approach discussed above, there is a relatively more serious academic effort to bridge the cleavage between the two sectors of the Islamic religious complex with the help of the analytical concepts of 'great' and 'little' traditions, which are again conflated respectively with the corresponding concepts of 'orthodoxy and orthopraxy' as against 'heterodoxy and heteropraxy'. A workshop on Islam in Southern Asia, held in Heidelberg (December 1974), was a major attempt at conceptualization along these lines.[45] With an obvious element of contradiction in his use of the term 'the *general trend* of opinion' earlier and '*some* participants' later, Imtiaz Ahmad, in his 'summary' statement for the workshop, reported on a predisposition at the workshop towards conceptualization of Islamic diversities 'in terms of a dichotomy of orthodoxy and heterodoxy in religious affairs'. The point he wished to make is unmistakable:

[42]Ahmad, *Intellectual History*, p. 51.

[43]Mushirul Haq, 'A note for the ICSSR workshop on religion, politics and society', held on 25 Oct., 1979, cited in Ahmad, *Ritual and Religion Among Muslims*, p. 8.

[44]Ahmad, 'Unity and variety in South Asian Islam', pp. 6–8. See n. 16 here.

[45]It may be noted here that I came to realize, as early as the late 1960s, the relevance and appropriateness of Robert Redfield's concepts of great and little traditions for my purpose, and was *perhaps* the first to apply this model to a serious study in the area of South Asian Islam. For more detailed discussions, see Section V in this chapter.

Using the concept of the Little and Great Traditions as defined by cultural anthropology, some participants contended that the theological and philosophical principles enshrined in the Islamic scriptures and other sources of [the] religion constituted the orthodox religious tradition and the local or regional beliefs and practices represented a heterodox tradition .... The process of Islamization, understood as an increasing tendency amongst Muslims towards new identity formation based on *an increase in conformity to orthodox Islamic principles in social and cultural life and a conscious rejection of syncretic elements* that previously persisted as remnants of their pre-conversion orientations and beliefs, was said to link the orthodox and heterodox religious complexes, resulting in *a gradual shrinkage of the sphere of the heterodox complex of the little tradition*.[46]

Ziaul Hasan Faruqi is another to adopt the great–little tradition model. He showed awareness of the important contributions made by 'recent sociological and anthropological researches' on the 'regional communities to show that they are mutually distinct and different in many respects'. In regard, however, to the vital question of interrelationship between the great and little traditions, and the corresponding one between orthodoxy and heterodoxy, Faruqi's position, as well as the view reported by Imtiaz Ahmad at the Heidelberg Conference of 1974, as quoted in the previous paragraph (especially the portion with my emphasis), diverged very little from the lines of the conventional scholarship.

Faruqi maintained:

Muslim communities belonging to the Little tradition, with all their distinct cultural traits, have *always aspired to relate their social and cultural values to those of the Islamic Great Tradition*, thus asserting their identity, through a two-way process of Islamization, as an integral component identity of a larger and over-all religion-wide Muslim community.[47]

The clear and consistent assumption about Islamization, underpinning the conventional perception and conceptualization of this internal divide in Islam is unmistakable. It is presented as a simple, unbroken, and unidirectional process in history of transition and transformation from popular to learned, lower to higher, custom to scripture, heterodoxy-heteropraxy to orthodoxy-orthopraxy, little to great tradition, and syncretistic to purist Islam. Long ensconced in the terrain of South Asian Islamic studies, without any serious academic challenge and hence almost by default, this assumption forms the core area of difference between the conventional Islamicist and alternative revisionist perspectives on Islamization. The conventional position has, over a period of time in recent decades, come to be very seriously questioned by many new studies and new findings—

[46]Ahmad, 'Unity and variety in South Asian Islam', p. 6; also Yogindra Singh, *Modernization of Indian Tradition* (Delhi: Thompson Press [India] Ltd, 1973), p. 76, which provided some ideas and language for Ahmad.

[47]Ziaul Hasan Faruqi, 'Orthodoxy and heterodoxy in Indian Islam', *Islam and the Modern Age*, 32 (1979), p. 34.

both in the social sciences and history. Let us explore the material thrown up by them separately in the three following sections.

IV. NEW PERSPECTIVE: SOCIAL SCIENCE

The revisionist perspective, projected in the social science research on practices of South Asian Muslims, canvasses a pattern of interrelationship between the great and little traditions as well as between the so-called orthodoxy-orthopraxy and heterodoxy-heteropraxy in Islam that is, on one hand, quite complex and variable, rather than simple, flat, linear, and uniform. On the other, their interrelationship is seen not necessarily as dichotomous and adversarial—often, in reality, appearing interactive and complementary. The empirical findings are full of implications for a fuller appreciation of the process of Islamization in the South Asian setting. The weight of the evidence is to clearly reject Islamization as a simple, unidirectional, and unvarying process of the so-called heterodoxy or little tradition inevitably succumbing under the impact of the orthodox or orthoprax great tradition of Islam. The process, in this perspective, seems considerably more interactive and even discontinuous than generally understood in the Islamicist's terms. The boundary of 'orthodoxy', howsoever well defined in Islamic scriptural works or by the religious professionals, does not appear often to coincide with the one that is locally determined. Quite often, elements of the little tradition, 'rather than being rejected or eliminated', are actually accepted through Islamization, either in their original or somewhat modified form, and 'incorporated into the corpus of the orthodox religious complex'. Imtiaz Ahmad found that 'beliefs and values not derived from the Islamic literature' and not necessarily 'always [in] accord ... with orthodox Islam', are 'regarded by Muslims who hold them as truly Islamic'. He came to the conclusion that 'popular Islam in South Asia is not merely the heterodox side of the Great Tradition of Islam. Looked at from the viewpoint of those who subscribe to its corpus of beliefs and values, it is as much orthodox as the Islamic beliefs derived from the religious texts'.[48]

Ahmad's observation was very largely grounded on the empirical studies of a number of other sociologists and social anthropologists, covering Islamic beliefs and practices in various parts of South Asia—Mattison Mines on Tamil Muslims, Ismail Lambat on the Sunni Bohras of Surat, Partap Aggarwal on the Meos of Rajasthan and Haryana, Lina Fruzzetti on the *rites de passage* and rituals among Muslims of Bishnupur in West Bengal, and, finally, Jean Ellickson on Bangladesh with its large Muslim-majority population. The realities of living and practising Islam emerging from these studies constitute a significant challenge indeed to some long-standing assumptions concerning Islamization on the ground level.

Ismail Lambat's investigations into the conditions of the Sunni Surati Vohras

---

[48]Ahmad, 'Unity and variety in South Asian Islam', pp. 6–7.

(Bohras) revealed an intensification, in recent years, of a 'struggle between custom and religion', but 'the customary rites and ceremonies', he added, 'continue to hold a very strong hold on the group and have not been replaced by alternate [*sic*] religious practices'.[49]

Partap Aggarwal's findings on the Meos in Rajasthan and Haryana showed that they continued to oppose, in the face of sustained pressures of Islamization on the community, preferential cousin marriage, as prescribed in the *shari'a*.[50]

Mattison Mines noted about Tamil Muslims that they 'marry among themselves and only rarely marry Muslims from other groups'. According to Mines, this was 'largely a result of Tamilians' marriage preference for kinsmen' and thus 'what is considered orthodox by Pallavaram's Muslims is influenced by local beliefs'. In villages, he found, 'Tamil Muslims do not differentiate themselves so much from the rural social structure. There they accept and practice customs, which are anathema to them in their urban-based orthodoxy .... Village behaviour provides a striking contrast to urban behaviour.'[51]

Mines' study, with this significant exposition of the divergent response of the Tamilian Muslims to Islamization in rural and urban settings, poses a serious challenge to the prevalent notion of Islamization as a continuous and uniform process. The greater propensity for Islamization in the urban, rather than rural setting was noted in other South Asian regions as well.[52] Mines, however, provided cogent explanations of this differential response to Islamization. He stressed on the difference in 'the structural basis' of these two settings as well as that of their twin identity. Hierarchy defined by interaction, and closed corporate status determined by birth were two major features of village social structure. 'Descent, interaction and displays of wealth' established 'religious identity and status in the village', and 'an identity based on orthodoxy' contributed 'little to the Muslims' identity and status in the village'. Urban structure, in contrast, was 'relatively open', and identity in open urban context could not be 'based on corporateness, because fellow villagers are dispersed'. Religious identity is 'all that remains and orthodoxy helps to establish and maintain this identity', and so they found it 'necessary to create a new group sense through Islamization'.[53]

[49]Ismail A. Lambat, 'Marriage among the Sunni Surati Vohras of south Gujarat', in Imtiaz Ahmad (ed.), *Family, Kinship and Marriage Among Muslims in India* (Delhi: Manohar, 1976), p. 80.

[50]Partap C. Aggarwal, 'Changing religious practices: Their relationship to secular power in a Rajasthan village', *Economic and Political Weekly*, 4:12 (1969), pp. 547–51.

[51]Mattison Mines, 'Islamization and Muslim ethnicity in South India', in Rothermund, *Islam in Southern Asia*, pp. 55, 69, 72, 76–7.

[52]Singh, *Modernization of Indian Tradition*; Faruqi, 'Orthodoxy and heterodoxy', pp. 9–36; Partap C. Aggarwal, 'A Muslim sub-caste of north India: Problems of cultural integration', *Economic and Political Weekly*, 1, pp. 159–67; Satish C. Misra, *Muslim Communities in Gujarat* (Bombay: Asia Publishing House, 1964).

[53]Mines, 'Islamization and Muslim ethnicity', pp. 84–5.

Likewise, studies of Lina Fruzzetti and Jean Ellickson on the Bengali-speaking Muslims clearly revealed the coexistence and interpenetration of the twin religious complex of orthodoxy and heterodoxy. Fruzzetti's perceptive study of the *rites de passage* and rituals among Muslims of Bishnupur in West Bengal led her to the conclusion:

Bengali Muslims adhere simultaneously to the fundamental orthodox principles of Islam and to a Bengali culture. They state that one can be a 'Muslim' and a 'Bengali' without creating any contradiction or conflict between the two spheres, though both the boundaries are sharply defined by their ideology and practice .... The universalistic aspect of Islam is not the only concern of the Muslims; in everyday practical life, the Muslims share in a 'Bengali culture', which is common to both Hindus and Muslim Bengalis.[54]

Besides 'the prescribed Islamic rules', concerning life-cycle rites, Fruzzetti noted that 'a number of local rules, loosely defined as *desher adat* (customs of the land) accompany the rituals'. Both the Islamic and local cultures were 'maintained and followed by the Muslims'. [55] They seem to have 'forged a unique culture' based on a combination of 'Islamic precepts' with 'the experience of everyday life ... and the elements that come from a non-Islamic culture'. They saw 'no contradiction between strictly Islamic and non-Islamic practices', and 'whatever does not fit into the one fits into the other. Whatever is not in the Koran is *niom* [*niyam*] (Bengali), complementing though never contradicting, the spirit of Muslim *dharam* [religion]'.[56]

While Fruzzetti's evidence came from the Hindu-majority area of West Bengal, Ellickson's field study embraced the Muslim-majority area of Bangladesh, and the findings of both reinforced each other. Ellickson reported a substantive conflict between Islamic personal laws and the customary practices of the rural Muslims, who perceived no serious violation of Islamic injunctions in their customary acceptance of inheritance by a grandson. The same perception was corroborated by their customary attitudes to divorce. Here again, Ellickson noted no perceived sense of conflict between the family laws of the shari'a and the dominant social values obtained locally, disfavouring divorce by wife. In the words of the locals: 'According to *our religion,* a woman cannot divorce her husband.'[57] The underlying rationale, which Ellickson offered for this position, is a clear vindication of the revisionist model of a shifting boundary between orthodoxy and heterodoxy. In her opinion: 'The argument was couched in terms of what a good Muslim

[54]Lina M. Fruzzetti, 'Muslim rituals: The household rites vs the public festivals in rural India', in Ahmad, *Rituals and Religion Among Muslims*, pp. 92–3.

[55]Ibid., p. 91.

[56]Ibid., p. 111.

[57]Jean Ellickson, 'Islamic institutions: Perception and practice in a village in Bangladesh', *Conributions to Indian Sociology*, 6 (n.s., 1972), p. 62.

should do ... and all that is required is general local consensus as to what "good Muslims" do.'[58]

Social science research findings of this nature have unquestionably challenged the Islamicist's perception and understanding of the process of Islamization in South Asia. It is unfortunate that the significance of these findings has not received much historical appreciation or recognition. Rather, questions have been raised, in some quarters among historians, about the specific social science affiliation of this recent literature, with its limited empirical disciplinary focus, and hence about its appropriateness in matters of historical concern. I have already broached this issue at the very beginning of this chapter, and quite emphatically expressed my discomfort with this largely unnecessary and totally unhelpful disciplinary wrangling between the social sciences and history in regard to the study of South Asian Islam, crystallized in the Ahmad–Robinson debate.[59] It may be noted here that, apart from Mushirul Haq (1979), mentioned above, we have on record at least two other Jamia Millia-based scholars, A.R. Momin (1977) and Mohammad Talib (1979), who preceded Robinson in critiquing the sociological understanding of Islam, and upholding the Islamicist's position in the South Asian context.[60]

Robinson has, undoubtedly, been the most powerful advocate of this position, having asked considerably more substantive questions for the opponents of the Islamicists to answer. For an adequate understanding of the differences between these two contrary viewpoints, it is necessary to take his arguments on board. Robinson's opposition centres on the sociologist's perception of Islam that tends to place, for him, exaggerated and misconceived emphasis on 'the gulf which exists between Islamic law and Muslim practice in India', as well as reject the Islamicist's explanations of the 'contradictions between law and local practice'. The Islamicist's basic explanation is focused on the historical development of Islamic society in terms of long, slow, and gradual processes of Islamization eventually bringing about a heterodox-heteroprax to orthodox-orthoprax religious orientation. Sociologists refuse to accept this explanation, as 'syncretic and folk beliefs are still widely found in Indian Islamic practice'. This takes us to the hard core of these opposing viewpoints, as Robinson boldly underlines the difference: 'Ahmad rejected this understanding of a dynamic relationship between ideas and society through time in favour of a concept of coexistence. For him the high Islamic

[58]Ibid., p. 58.

[59]See Section I here for Ahmad–Robinson debate. See also note 43 for Mushirul Haq's relevant remark.

[60]A.R Momin, 'The Indo-Islamic tradition', *Sociological Bulletin*, 26 (1977), pp. 242–58; Mohammad Talib, 'The social context of the contemporary Muslim studies in the sub-continent', Seminar on Recent Trends in Muslim Studies, held at Jamia Millia Islamia, New Delhi, 28 March 1979.

and custom-centred traditions peacefully "coexist as complementary and integral parts of a common religious system".[61]

That Imtiaz Ahmad 'can discover no dynamic situation in which a high Islamic tradition is steadily eating into local custom-centred traditions' and, on the contrary, 'finds the orthodox and orthoprax living harmoniously side by side with the heterodox and heteroprax', and that he 'would rather talk of coexistence' seemed, to Robinson, a total violation of his understanding of, and fundamental belief in, the making of Islamic history and actual historical processes of Islamization. Central to his understanding and vision of Islam in history are his shibboleths: 'Islam offers a pattern of perfection for men to follow,' in Islamic history 'there has been a movement towards, or occasionally away from, the pattern of perfection', and 'what there cannot be, as Ahmad *asserts*, is a state of equilibrium.'[62] In a review of this particular book of Robinson, soon after its publication, Simon Digby wrote:

In a manner which may be related to his own elitist academic environment, Robinson's sympathies are engaged with 'the emergence of Protestant or scriptural Islam'[63] .... Robinson's arguments may be seen as a valiant struggle on behalf of a South Asian Muslim elite with whom he has identified himself, mainly Sunni, replete with an exclusive tradition of scholastic learning, ultimately concerned with the promotion of 'fundamentalist' religious belief and ritual observance .... The cumulative impression of Robinson's arguments is of the *exclusiveness* and *inalterability* of his own and their vision.[64]

If Digby's final statement contains even a modicum of truth, the prospect of any total resolution of this academic contention would seem very bleak indeed. Yet, a few broad observations are called for. If, in the nature of this controversy, an agreement looks difficult to reach, we need to appreciate the depth of the essential polarity between these two perspectives. The contradiction and conflict between the ideal and actual, or the norm and practice, are as old as the inception of ideology and morality. Total and exclusive adherence to any side of this equation cannot but yield wrong results. Scanning history in search of answers, in one way or another, may not bring this dispute to an end either, as history, such as that in the enormously rich and protean field of South Asian Islam, is replete with proofs of all kinds which are quite amenable to suit particular conclusions, as is abundantly evident in the contentious literature on this debate. A good example of the conflicting nature of evidence impeding a convincing conclusion may help elucidate the point.

[61]Robinson, *Islam and Muslim History*, pp. 4, 44–6.
[62]Ibid., pp. 46, 50 and 62.
[63]Robinson's own words, see ibid., p. 7.
[64]Simon Digby, 'Anglo-American scholarship on South Asian Islam', *The Book Review*, 25:3 (March 2001), p. 29.

Robinson has made a similar, though more documented, claim than Aziz Ahmad that the process of Islamization was ascendant, and popular Islam and syncretistic values had been undergoing steady erosion in many parts of the Muslim world, especially South Asia, including Bengal, since the Islamic reform and revivalist movements in the early nineteenth century.[65] About 150 years later, after the creation of Pakistan, a field-study in popular Muslim beliefs and practices, was undertaken in a district of East Pakistan (now Bangladesh). It was conducted under the supervision of A.K. Najmul Karim, later to become Professor and Head of the Sociology Department in the Dacca (now Dhaka) University, and the district of Noakhali was chosen for its reputation of being 'the most orthodox district of Bengal', where 'the influence of reforming priests has been most persistent'.[66] Robinson and Aziz Ahmad, along with the entire school of Islamicists, would be most unlikely to derive much satisfaction and hope out of the following revelation in the survey:

There are some rites observed by the Muslims ... which have no doubt been originated from the Islamic sources. But even in such cases, sometimes Hindu beliefs and rituals are mixed up with the Islamic rites. On the other hand, a purely Hindu ritual at times would bear an Islamic facade.[67]

What do we make of our evidence—historical or sociological? Are we, then, left with the principle of individual truth inculcated in the parable of the four blind men's touching experiences of the elephant?

Francis Robinson's approach to the history of Islam, largely shared in common with that of the Islamicists, raises some questions. Students of Islamic history are given a splendid choice of tracing in history a significant religious vision of a total community life emanating from Arabia in the seventh century. How do we begin to read this history? Do we start off with a blueprint of this ideal conduct of life, look for the Muslim 'diasporas' across the globe, stop and admire where we find them, and turn our back on those who would not measure up, waiting for their redemption through a 'long and gradual' process of Islamization? Robinson betrayed a curious sense of history and historical 'inevitability', almost in the sense of a 'scriptural determinism', as he wrote: 'We should not be deceived by the fact that in many societies non-Islamic practices had acquired the force of law in Muslim minds. This is often a matter of imperfect knowledge or *temporary expedient, although temporary in this sense may well be several hundred years.*'[68]

[65] Robinson, *Islam and Muslim History*, pp. 58–62.

[66] A.K.N. Karim, 'Some aspects of popular beliefs among Muslims of Bengal', *Eastern Anthropologist* (Lucknow), 9:1 (Sept.–Nov. 1955), p. 29.

[67] Ibid., p. 36.

[68] Robinson, *Islam and Muslim History*, p. 50.

Clifford Geertz's model of a slow process of Islamization has been lauded in Robinson's study, found several mention, including Imtiaz Ahmed in one, because 'he cannot find Clifford Geertz's pattern in Islamization in India'.[69] It is rather interesting to note, in this particular context, that Geertz, in his brilliant comparative study of Islam in Morocco and Indonesia, raised serious doubts about an approach to the study of a religion that began with its 'definition' and accepted or rejected everything to the extent that it measured up to this standard. He urged, instead, a more meaningful approach to 'find' it in the life and world of its believers.[70]

In his analysis of shortcomings of the social science approach, which he considered 'limited in understanding, place and time', Robinson emphasized the importance of the 'written word' and 'study with the help of texts' beyond mere behaviour, that is 'how Muslims actually behave, and how this behaviour is at variance with preferred Islamic practice'.[71] Though it may not be entirely correct and fair to make an assumption about social science investigations being totally divorced from written material, or at least from a perspective based on such material, one of Robinson's major concerns here would have been to turn the focus on the importance of historical perception and understanding informing the outcome of such empirical research. In the following two sections, I have made some efforts to bridge this gap by seeking to reinforce such empirical data with material of historical import, not merely limited to our chosen region of South Asia but beyond it into South East Asia.

V. NEW PERSPECTIVE AND PARADIGM: HISTORICAL: SOUTH ASIA

It has surely been an unedifying spectacle for sociologists and historians of South Asian Islam to have locked horns with each other in a contest for disciplinary 'superiority', while both are given a common ground to explore the complexity, variety, and creative dynamism of the process of Islamization in this region. The sociological and social anthropological explorations in South Asian Islam virtually began since the publication of the special volume of *Contributions to Indian Sociology* (no. 6) in 1972, devoted exclusively to the 'Muslim communities of South Asia'. My postgraduate historical research in Islam in the region of undivided Bengal, beginning at the School of Oriental and African Studies, London University, in the late 1960s, reached its completion at the Department of Oriental Civilizations, Australian National University, Canberra in 1970. My doctoral thesis entitled

[69]Ibid., p. 46.
[70]Clifford Geertz, *Islam Observed: Religious Development in Morocco and Indonesia* (New Haven & London: Yale University Press, 1968), p. 4.
[71]Robinson, *Islam and Muslim History*, pp. 47–8.

'Islam in the environment of medieval Bengal, with special reference to the Bengali sources' used the great–little tradition model as well as raised serious issues concerning their interrelationship from a historical perspective. This academic effort may claim, as mentioned earlier, the distinction of perhaps being the first to apply this sociological model to a study of South Asian Islam.[72] This is no covert attempt here, on my part, to reopen the history-sociology contest by creating a new front in terms of claiming chronological 'precedence' over and above the one of 'superiority'. For me, the issue ends here and now, for the simple reason that I drew my inspiration largely from Robert Redfield's studies.[73] My sole purpose here is to draw clear attention to the fact that the research findings of at least some historians, as much as those of sociologists and social anthropologists of South Asian Islam have made them distinctly aware of the inadequacy of the conventional perception of a simple, exclusive, and monolithic great tradition as also that of a necessary contradiction and conflict between syncretistic developments and Islamization.

One of my primary concerns in my doctoral and subsequent studies of Muslim Bengal has been the interrelationship between the great and little traditions of Islam in this region. It has been my contention that Islam, in this region, has not been a 'primary' but a 'secondary' culture, that is exogenous and not indigenous to the region. Also, here in this region, Islam has not been a 'single' or the only 'great tradition' since it entered a land which was not culturally virgin, and confronted the long-established indigenous great tradition. Islamic conversion forced a break in the pre-conversion cultural continuity between the great and little traditions of the converts. To remedy the situation, a medieval group of Bengal Muslim literati, conceptualized as 'cultural mediators' in my study, constructed a rather rich alternative model of great tradition for the Bengal Muslim masses in the Bengali language and on a syncretistic model. In the process they restored the broken continuity between the great and little traditions of the converts.

'Syncretism' is often seen by 'purists' as spurious—a perception that seemed to inform the beliefs and attitudes in a large section of higher classes of Muslims in South Asia, including Bengal, berating such developments as a jumble of 'folk' or 'popular' Islam. Writing in 1951, Qazi Abdul Wadud, a supreme rationalist among Bengali Muslim writers and thinkers in this century, noted that the pre-nineteenth-

[72]See n. 45 here. See also, my 'Islam in the environment of medieval Bengal, with special reference to the Bengali sources', unpublished Ph.D. thesis, Australian National University, Canberra, 1970. 'The social factors in the making of Bengali Islam', *South Asia*, annual no. 3 (1973). My claim in this respect is based on a general survey of the literature in this particular field. I should be pleased to have my claim confirmed or otherwise

[73]Robert Redfield, *Peasant Society and Culture: An Anthropological Approach to Civilization* (Chicago: University of Chicago Press, 1936); his, *The Folk-Culture of Yucatan* (Chicago: University of Chicago Press, 1941); also his *Little Community: Viewpoints for the Study of a Human Whole* (Chicago: University of Chicago Press, 1955). See also note 41 here.

century revivalist culture represented 'an accord between Hindu and Muslim thoughts', and the truth of this cultural coalescence was 'generally distressing to educated Muslims today' because 'they regard it as an admission of denial of their own identity'.[74] The issue is, however, considerably deeper and more significant than what appears on the surface of Wadud's highly perceptive observation. What Wadud saw as true about 'educated Muslims today' in Bengal, stretches back long in the history of the region and even beyond. I have adduced earlier considerable evidence of derogatory attitudes toward 'popular' and 'syncretistic' expressions of Islam in Bengal and elsewhere in South Asia.[75]

Rafiuddin Ahmed's is a revealing case in example. He differentiates, like others, between an 'Islamic orthodoxy' and 'folk beliefs and practices',[76] but brings, like many of his Islamicist peers, a rather patronizing and supercilious attitude to bear on the whole question, writing: 'Until late in the nineteenth century the masses had hardly *any idea about the virtues of their own religion*; they had no way of knowing them'.[77]

He used the word 'sacrilegious' for syncretistic beliefs and ideas, and daubed as 'un-Islamic' the creative attempt by a leading Bengali Muslim mediator-writer to present Prophet Muhammad alongside the Hindu divinities.[78] Apart from the fact of overlooking the mediatory concerns and roles of those authors of the syncretistic tradition, Ahmed revealed his unfamiliarity with similar attempts made by many reputed north Indian Sufis, who justified their actions on the ground of the Quranic revelation that Allah did send prophets to all peoples. My own studies in the Islamic syncretistic tradition precisely sought to bring out the religious concerns and purposes underlying the literary efforts of the Muslim cultural mediators. A detailed textual examination of Saiyad Sultan's *Nabi-bamsha* (The Lineage of the Prophet) clearly revealed to me his ingenious and creative adaptation and reformulation of Hindu mythology with the ultimate objective of proclaiming the finality of the Islamic prophetic mission. Based on the Quranic knowledge of the divine message being bestowed on other messengers before Prophet Muhammad, he used the Hindu tradition of successive 'avatars', especially the Krishna myth, to underscore the failure of those earlier missions, and thus set the stage for the final mission of Muhammad. It is more than ironical that Rafiuddin Ahmed questions the faith of this leading Muslim pir-poet on the ground that, in his *Nabi-bamsha*, the name of Prophet Muhammad appears with 'the Hindu *avatars*

[74]Q.A. Wadud, '*Banglar Musalmaner Katha* [On the Musalmans of Bengal]' [in Bengali] in his *Shashvata Banga* [The Eternal Bengal] (Calcutta, 1951), p. 98; also Roy, *Syncretistic Islam*, 'Preface', pp. xviii–xxi. (All translations from the original Bengali, quoted in this study are mine, unless otherwise indicated.)

[75]See pp. 112–14 in this chapter.

[76]R. Ahmed, *Bengal Muslims*, pp. 54–5.

[77]R. Ahmed, 'Contradictions in Bengali Islam', p. 126.

[78]Ibid., p. 125.

in a list of prophets'. Ahmed concluded: 'Surely this was not quite Islamic.'[79] There is no reason to doubt that other Islamicists, with their preconceived and stereotypical understanding of the 'popular' and the syncretistic processes in Islam, would nod their heads in approval of Ahmed's interpretation.

The construction by the Bengal Muslim mediator-literati of the 'Islamic syncretistic tradition' also raises the vital question of interrelationship between syncretism and Islamization, which constitutes another significant component of my studies. I have already noted that the syncretistic developments in Islam remain generally disfavoured from the purist's point of view. Perceived as mere 'relics', 'remnants', or 'survivals' from the pre-conversion cultural substratum of the locality or region, they are usually seen as antithetical to the process of Islamization. The syncretistic developments and tradition presented in my studies are not a medley or pot-pourri of irrational, animistic, and superstitious folk beliefs and practices, 'pre-dating the advent of Islam' in the land. The adaptive process inhering in the Islamic syncretistic tradition has emerged in my studies as 'conscious' efforts of the Bengali Muslim cultural mediators. This conclusion flies in the face of an entrenched simplistic view of the cultural substratum and its relics. It is significant that sociologist Imtiaz Ahmad, referred to 'the process of Islamization, understood as a tendency involving a conscious rejection of syncretic elements that persist as *remnants of pre-conversion* orientations and ethos'.[80]

Richard Eaton expressed his reservations about 'Roy's mediators' being engaged 'quite self-consciously and deliberately' in 'concocting their syncretic brew for the masses', and added: 'Possibly much of Roy's literature reflected not so much the product of a conscious selection ... as the survival of a purely Bengali substratum of values and ideas.'[81]

There was of course much, coming from their long historical past, that the Bengalis, like any other people, held in common. Anyone, with the slightest degree of familiarity with the cultural world of medieval Bengal, should know about the pervasive nature of beliefs, superstitions, and practices shared in common among the people. It *has not been my purpose* to concern myself with this general area of common beliefs and practices obtained in medieval Bengal. The purpose of my

---

[79]Ibid., p. 126. It is rather baffling that Ahmed, in his first major excursion into the world of pre-colonial Muslim Bengal in this particular contribution, has either chosen to ignore or failed to explore the substantive research pre-existing in this field of study, including mine, as evidenced by his markedly deficient bibliography in this particular area.

[80]Ahmad, *Ritual and Religion Among Muslims*, p. 10.

[81]Richard M. Eaton, 'Review' of Roy, *Syncretistic Islam*, in *Journal of Asian Studies*, 44:2 (February 1985), p. 443. It is interesting that Eaton, in his later publication on Islam in Bengal, conceptualizes the process of Islamization in terms of 'inclusion', 'identification', and 'displacement'—clearly suggesting a conscious process of selection and rejection. Richard M. Eaton, *The Rise of Islam and the Bengal Frontier, 1204–1760* (Berkeley: University of California Press, 1993), pp. 270–90.

study has not been to deny such developments nor to explore them. My specific concerns have been to 'find', as Clifford Geertz would like to put it,[82] and explain the presence of such indigenous matters in the literary efforts of the mediators which clearly evince their anxiety to win the latter's allegiance to a reconstructed Islamic tradition in the vernacular Bengali, couched in familiar and popular syncretistic forms and symbolisms. The focus of my attention has been an unmistakable and 'deliberate' construction and creation of an 'Islamic' tradition for Bengali Muslims, running parallel with the non-Muslim traditions in Bengal. This is again the rationale for my exclusion from the purview of my study 'non-Islamic' syncretistic cults, despite substantive Muslim participation in them, like the Baul. The problem set for my investigations has been as limited and specific as perhaps the objectives of 'my mediators'. The syncretistic tradition of my concern and interest has been a thoughtful and purposeful construct by the hearts and minds of a section of both religious and non-religious members of the Bengal Muslim literati, and the nature and outcome of their efforts and achievements are there for us to see in the vast corpus of the literature that they left behind.

It is in this specific context that we begin to see and appreciate the linkage between the syncretistic tradition and the process of Islamization in Bengal. It was precisely because of the converts continuing to be steeped in the non-Islamic cultural heritage of Bengal that the Muslim literati were compelled to construct a tradition which Bengal Muslims could call and claim as their own. Saiyid Sultan bemoaned the fact that Bengali Muslims 'in every home', denied of any comparable Islamic alternative in the Bengali vernacular, resorted to the Hindu epics, the Mahabharata and the Ramayana.[83] This prompted him to compose his magnum opus, *Nabi-bamsha*, to wean Muslims away from the Hindu epics, puranas, and *mangal-kavyas*. His subtle and purposive tampering with and construction of new myths about Krishna to vindicate the mission of Muhammad provides clear and incontrovertible evidence of the mediators' 'self-conscious and deliberate' role in constructing a popular and meaningful tradition for Bengali Muslims.[84] Viewed in its proper historical context, the syncretistic reformulation of Islam in Bengal rather emerges as a necessary stage in the progress of Islamization in the country. This tradition continued, for centuries, to dominate the religious-cultural perceptions of the Bengali Muslim masses as well as of other Bengali Muslims, who shared the mediators' world views and values. The syncretistic tradition met its first frontal challenge from the Islamic revivalist and purificatory movements in the nineteenth century, which condemned the syncretistic tradition and values and urged suppression of non-Islamic accretions. Despite decades of Islamization in religious,

---

[82]See n. 66 on p. 46.
[83]Roy, *Syncretistic Tradition*, p. 69.
[84]Ibid., pp. 96–8.

cultural, and political terms, however, the syncretistic values and practices of Bengal Muslims did not seem to have been overwhelmed by it, even in the 'most orthodox' East Bengal district after Partition, as shown in the preceding discussion.[85] The syncretistic tradition thus performed, until the revivalist challenge, a significant historical function in the dissemination of Islam in Bengal, and was not, therefore, an antithesis of Islamization but a necessary stage in its historical development in Bengal. Syncreticism remained as integral to the process of Islamization in the land as did the later revivalist, reformist, and fundamentalist contributions.[86]

The 'conscious' promotion of an 'Islamic purpose' in the Muslim vernacular literature in South Asia finds equal recognition in Susan Bayly's studies of the Tamil-speaking south Indian Muslims. Despite the pervasive syncretic religious and cultural ethos of the Tamil maritime people, she rightly reminded us that they were 'converts rather than Hindus'. Even worshippers at 'the most eclectic of the Muslim and Christian shrines', she informed us, 'preserved some sense of a distinct religious identity, however strongly this was overlaid with elements of a joint and undifferentiated religious culture'. She mentioned their 'legends', which 'employ Hindu terminology and language to describe Muslim and Christian victories over explicitly Hindu enemies'. This was, she affirmed, 'as much a confrontation with alien religious traditions as an expression of shared values and shared ideology'.[87] The adaptive process could, and did indeed, become quite purposefully 'conscious' rather than remain a mere survival of the cultural 'substratum'.

Bayly also raised some seminal issues concerning the 'actual meaning' of the terms 'purist' and 'syncretic' as well as their 'usefulness' as analytical 'categories'. She queried 'the relationship between "purist" and "syncretic" religious behaviour within individual Muslim communities', with particular reference to 'the idea of a confrontation between distinct sets of "purist" maritime Muslims and "syncretic" peasant or rural Muslims—the sort of people who are so often dismissed as "half-Islamized" or even degenerate, "backsliding" or simply "bad Muslims".'[88] Her findings and observations are emphatic endorsement of the revisionist critique. She totally rejected the 'notion of distinct and opposing realms of Muslim worship, of "high" and "low" or "scriptural" and "non-standard" Islam'.[89] With a view to setting southern Indian Islam in the wider contexts of the indigenous social and religious systems, Bayly sought 'to trace some of the ways in which the Islam practised by Tamil

[85]See n. 66 on p. 46.

[86]Roy, *Syncretistic Tradition*, pp. 250–2.

[87]Susan Bayly, 'Islam in southern India: "Purist" or "syncretic"?', in Chris A. Bayly and D.H.A. Kolff (eds), *Two Colonial Empires* (Dordrecht: Martinus Nijhoff, 1986), pp. 64–5.

[88]Ibid., pp. 36–7.

[89]Susan Bayly, 'The limits of Islamic expansion in south India'. Paper presented at a Conference on Regional Varieties of Islam in Pre-Modern India, held in Heidelberg in July 1989, p. 6.

Muslims was shaped and moulded by an equally complex local religious system'.[90] On the basis of her findings, she warned us:

It is no longer satisfactory to conceive of the Tamil country—and indeed many other parts of South and Southeast Asia—in terms of separate and distinct religious cultures confronting one another across rigid communal boundaries. Surely the traditions and practices enacted at these Labbai centres indicate that there has long been a close and subtle relationship between religious traditions which are often thought of as distinct and mutually exclusive. Certainly the population of this region cannot be divided into the old bald categories of purist/maritime traders ('santri') and 'syncretic' hinterland peasants ('abangan').[91]

Further,

It must not be thought that this Tamil Muslim trading elite had evolved by the eighteenth century into a population of 'Islamized' Muslims who had divorced themselves from the values, culture and religious motifs of the wider society .... It is clear that the maraikayyar [maraikkayar/the Tamil maritime traders] retained very complex links to a world of elite and exclusive Muslim piety, but they also pursued much wider ranging religious connections.[92]

There is no dearth of other historical evidence of such linkages between elite and folk levels of South Asian Islam. In no inconsiderable way, social and socio-religious practices and values such as 'caste',[93] 'child marriage',[94] and 'forced

[90]Bayly, 'Islam in southern India', pp. 36–7.

[91]Ibid., p. 57. Cf. also, 'Surely what begins to emerge then is a picture of a single religious culture of great complexity and variability but with fundamental elements of belief and practice held in common among a very large part of the population.' (Ibid., p. 59.)

[92]Bayly, 'The limits of Islamic expansion in south India', p. 3.

[93]The tenacious persistence of castes, caste analogues, and caste values cutting across the class barriers in the Muslim community, in direct violation of clear Islamic norms, has been common knowledge in the past, especially in the region of Bengal. Buchanan-Hamilton, in the early nineteenth century, observed 'a practical ascendancy' of the idea of caste over Muslims in Bengal and Bihar. [M. Martin, The History, Antiquities, Topography, and Statistics of Eastern India, compiled from Buchanan mss. (1807–14) (London, 1838), vol. 3, p. 150; Roy, Syncretistic Islam, pp. 36–7.] In 1896, Maulavi Muhammad Khan, a Muslim observer of Bengal, noted: 'Certainly Islam does not recognize caste distinctions yet paradoxical though it may seem, people among Muhammadans do ask "so and so what caste is he?" ... There are some classes that hold in great regard the custom of early marriage. Forced widowhood although prohibited by religion is rather the rule than the exception.' [Maulawi Muhammad M. Khan, 'Social divisions in the Muhammadan community', in the Calcutta Monthly, 6:1 (July, 1896), p. 3; Talke, 'Islam in Bengal', The Muslim World, 4 (1914), p. 12; Roy, Syncretistic Islam, pp. 35–8. p. 3.]

[94]Nawab Siraj ud-Daula and his brother Akram ud-Daula were married quite early. Their descendants consistently followed this practice. Siraj's daughter left four daughters before she died at the age of 20. The daughters themselves married quite early. [See B.N. Banerjee, Begams of Bengal (Calcutta: M.C. Sarkar, 1942), p. 36.] According to the Census Report of Bengal (1901),

widowhood'[95] straddled the barrier between the *ashraf* and *atraf* or elite and folk Muslim societal divisions. But the most obvious and effective linkages between the twin social-religious strands in the South Asian Muslim world are found in the common resort to the cults of saints (*pirs*) and shrines (*dargahs*) and in the extensive range of shared magical and supernatural beliefs and superstitions. Aziz Ahmad, a champion of the 'purist' Islam, conceded: 'At the popular level Sufism itself became distorted, and even orthodox orders developed irreligious (*bi-shar'*) offshoots, and most of them absorbed at that level *malami* (blameworthy) features.'[96]

In the same context he provides a detailed account of the 'heterodox variants' of the orthodox Sufi orders in South Asia, and adds:

A number of practices, which from the fundamentalist viewpoint appear heterodox, were common even among the orthodox Sufis .... Amulets, (*ta'widh*) containing verses of the Qur'an or other pious formulae, were prepared and distributed in the Sufi hospices. Shah Wali-Allah and Shah 'Abd-al-'Aziz deal with them in their writings with pious credulity. Amulets are still very much in use in India, as indeed in other parts of the Muslim world ... as a charm against misfortune or disease. By the end of the eighteenth century there was an extensive variety of these amulets suitable for almost every conceivable calamity and misfortune .... Even the great Sufis of the thirteenth and fourteenth centuries believed in magic and witchcraft as a cause of illness .... Tombs of orthodox Sufis were, and are, held in veneration by mystics, the elite and the common people.[97]

Referring to the belief among Muslims in 'the evil eye' and its 'antidote' in the 'concealment or multiplication of names', Aziz Ahmad informs us that 'Mughal emperors were sometimes given as many as three names'.[98] Further: 'In medieval and pre-modern India, belief in astrology and magic was quite common among Muslims. Astrologers thrived even under the pious and puritan Awrangzib. In the early nineteenth century, Tipu Sultan, otherwise an orthodox Muslim, had recourse to esoteric practices prescribed by Hindu astrologers.'[99]

Susan Bayly explicated the 'mixed and overlapping religious traditions' of

---

twelve girls in 1000 among Muslims were married under 5 years of age, and 108 in 1000 between the ages of 5 and 10. Amongst males the corresponding figures are four boys and nineteen boys. [See E.A. Gait, *Report on Bengal, Census of India, 1901*, vol. VI, pt 1 (Calcutta: Bengal Secretariat Press, 1902), p. 261.]

[95] According to the Census Report of Bengal (1901), Muslim widows were 'comparatively fewer than amongst Hindus', but they 'still number more than a sixth of the total female population'. [Gait, *Report on Bengal*, p. 262.] The Urdu translator of the *Khulasat ul-Ta'rikh* lamented that 'Hindu notions of widowhood have infected the Muslims, especially in the villages, and have led to their women remaining widows contrary to Islamic injunctions'. [*Journal of the Royal Asiatic Society* (1894), p. 748.]

[96] Ahmad, *Intellectual History*, p. 44.

[97] Ibid., pp. 45–6.

[98] Ibid., p. 48.

[99] Ibid., p. 50.

the shrine cults, even of the 'purist' Muslim trading towns on the Coromandel coast.[100] She notes:

Devotees from almost every class and community ... flocked to ... [these] towns to venerate their dargahs, to obtain blessings, amulets and spiritual counsel from their pirzadas, and to take part in the shrines' ecstatic ... festivals .... Their donors and worshippers clearly did not make any rigid distinctions between acceptable and unacceptable or Islamic and un-Islamic forms of worship: what mattered most was that their dargahs were universally revered as repositories of miraculous and transforming divine power, or barakat ... these expanding networks of devotion and cult worship are not to be seen as elements of a parochial, debased or unlettered 'folk Islam'.[101]

The strong beliefs in the saint and shrine cults, divination, astrology, charm, and witchcraft among the pre-Mughal as well as Mughal rulers and elite in Bengal are clearly evidenced by the interesting account of Mirza Nathan, a Mughal naval official under Governor Islam Khan (1608–13), and also by other sources. On his authority we know that his father Ihtimam Khan, also a Mughal official, when ordered by Jahangir (1605–27) to proceed to Bengal, made his preparations 'at an auspicious astrological hour', and that he kept under his employ a physician who was also 'very expert in the science of astrology'.[102] As the imperial fleet under his command entered the river Karatoya, wrote Mirza Nathan:

On account of great tumult raised by the sailors, the sound of the victorious trumpets and the artillery, the fish of the river, jumping out of the water, began to fall on the boats. This was taken to be a good omen for the conquest of Bhati, and suppression of the rebels.[103]

Buzurg Ummed Khan, son of Shaista Khan, Governor of Bengal (1664–78) under Aurangzeb (1658–1707), started his march against the Firingis (Portuguese pirates) and the Maghs of Burma/Arakan 'at a moment auspicious for making a beginning'.[104] About Mir Qasim, the last post-Plassey Nawab of Bengal (1764–5), it was said that he: 'understood a little astrology and believed in its maxims and predictions; he procured the child's horoscope to be accurately drawn by able astrologers'.[105]

The belief in necromancy and charm permeated all sections of society. Mirza Nathan also spoke about his experiences in Ghantaghat, which was 'notorious

---

[100]Bayly, 'Islam in southern India', p. 44.

[101]Bayly, 'The limits of Islamic expansion in south India', p. 5.

[102]Mirza Nathan, *Baharistan-i Ghaybi*, Eng. trans. by M.I. Borah (Gauhati: Government of Assam, 1936), vol. 1, pp. 6, 167.

[103]Ibid., p. 53.

[104]Shihab ud-Din Talish, *Fathiya-i 'Ibriya*, English trans. by J.N. Sarkar, in his *Studies in Aurangzeb's Reign* (Calcutta: Calcutta University Press, 1933), p. 198.

[105]Ghulam Husain Tabatabai, *Siyar ul-Muta'akhirin*, Eng. trans. by Haji Mustafa (Calcutta, 1926), vol. 2, p. 387.

for magic and sorcery'. The people there could make anyone 'produce the voice of a fowl from inside his stomach', and could also turn mango leaves into fish by 'breathing words of magic and sorcery' on them, which, if eaten, resulted in death. Muhammad Zambian was reportedly 'bewitched by some person so that for two or three days he used to produce sounds of beasts, like dogs, cats and other animals of that class, and thus he died'.[106] Mir Shams, 'an expert in the science of necromancy', used 'magic spells' to kill Shaikh Kamal, as a result of which 'lumps of blood began to come out of his stomach and throat', and 'after a week he expired'.[107] The people of Koch Bihar attracted the attention of Shihab ud-Din Talish as 'enchanters', who 'read formula upon water and give it to the wounded to drink, who then recover'.[108] He also spoke of his and the general belief that the Bengal Governor Mir Jumla's (1660–3) fatal sickness, following upon his conquest of Koch Bihar and Assam, was 'the result of witchcraft practised by the Rajah of Assam'.[109] Nawab Shuja' ud-Din (1727–39) built a 'magnificent garden' at Dehpara on the banks of the Bhagirathi in west Bengal. When he came to know that 'fairies used to come down there for picnics and walks, and to bathe in its tanks', 'dreading mischief' from them, he 'filled up the tanks with earth and discontinued his picnics in that garden'.[110]

Muslim governing elite often took part in the indigenous festivals. According to Ghulam Husain Salim, the Hindu spring festival of Holi, observed in the months of February–March, held a special appeal for the Muslim upper class.[111] Prince 'Azim us-Shan (1697–1712), son of Aurangzeb, on his arrival at Dacca (Dhaka) as the Governor of Bengal, took part in this festival so readily and thoroughly that the emperor wrote him a sarcastic letter, saying: 'A saffron-coloured helmet on thy head, a red garment on thy shoulder, thy venerable age verging on forty-six years; hurrah on thy beard and moustache!'[112]

Karam 'Ali witnessed Nawab Aliwardi Khan's (1740–56) nephews, Sahamat Jang and Saulat Jang, enjoying the Holi festival for seven days in the garden of Motijhil palace. About 'two hundred reservoirs were filled with coloured-water' for the occasion, and 'heaps of abir (coloured powder) and saffron' were used.[113]

[106]Ibid., pp. 273–4.

[107]Mirza Nathan, *Baharistan-i Ghaybi*, vol. 2, p. 671.

[108]Ibid., p. 191; also cited in Henry Blochmann, 'Koch Bihar and Assam', *Journal of the Asiatic Society of Bengal*, pt 1:1 (1872), p. 67.

[109]Mirza Nathan, *Baharistan-i Ghaybi*.

[110]Ghulam Husain Salim, *Riyaz us-Salatin*, Eng. trans. by Maulavi Abdus Salam (Calcutta, 1902), p. 291.

[111]Ibid., p. 246.

[112]Ibid.

[113]Karam 'Ali, *Muzaffar Nama*, cited in K.K. Datta, *Studies in the History of the Bengal Subah (1740–70)*, (Calcutta, 1936), vol. 1, pp. 94–5.

VI. NEW PERSPECTIVE AND PARADIGM: HISTORICAL: SOUTH EAST ASIA

Historians and social scientists of South Asian Islam, challenging the Islamicist's perception of a monolithic Islam and a uniform pattern of Islamization, based on the assumption of a total cleavage between the 'high' and 'low', have every reason to derive strength of support from similar findings of their counterparts in South East Asia. In this region as well, the dominant views of the polarity between a 'high, orthodox and purist' *santri* Islam and its 'low, heterodox and syncretic' *abangan* version, as well as that of 'the typical mode of Islamization' and its transformative effects seen as unidirectional,[114] have been countered in some recent studies. John Legge did not consider it 'a very precise model'. In his opinion, the abangan tradition of the village community was 'a compound of Islamic as well as earlier traditions, and that the Indonesian peasant finds no great difficulty in combining in varying mixtures his obligations as a Muslim with his acceptance of older beliefs and customs'.[115]

Deliar Noer took a similar position: 'This division into the *putihan* [or santri] and *abangan* in Java at the turn of the century was not of a hostile character. It merely distinguished one's particular type of devotion to Islam. They all called themselves Muslims, wong selam.'[116]

Views suggesting a more subtle process of interplay and interpenetration between Islam and adat (custom-centred practices), in the context of Indonesia, have been proffered by others like Ricklefs, Christine Dobbin, and Peter Carey.[117] In Ricklefs's study, the new perception finds a strong articulation: 'It [Islam] was tolerant. It gave greater richness to Javanese religion without requiring the complete abandonment of older ideas. Thus Java came to be a Muslim society, but one in which Islam was only part of the vast cultural heritage.'[118]

The interactive linkages between the two broad strands of Islam and varying degrees of accommodation, compromise, and even coexistence have indeed been there if one is looking for them and caring to read serious meaning into them. The

[114]Clifford Geertz, *The Religion of Java* (Glencoe, Illinois: 1960). passim; also his 'Modernization in a Muslim society: The Indonesian case,' in Robert N. Bellah (ed.), *Religion and Progress in Modern Asia* (New York: The Free Press, 1965), pp. 96–7.

[115]John D. Legge, *Indonesia* (Sydney: Prentice-Hall of Australia, 2nd edn, 1977), pp. 59–61.

[116]Deliar Noer, *The Modernist Muslim Movement in Indonesia 1900–1942* (Kuala Lumpur: Oxford University Press, 1973), p. 19. Noer uses the term putihan for santri.

[117]M.C. Ricklefs, *Jogjakarta Under Sultan Mankubumi 1749–1792: A History of the Division of Java* (London, 1974); also his 'Islamization in Java', in Levtzion (ed.), *Conversion in Islam*, pp. 100–128; Christine Dobbin, *Islamic Revivalism in a Changing Peasant Economy: Central Sumatra, 1784–1847* (London, 1983); Peter Carey, *Babad Dipanagara: An Account of the Outbreak of the Java War (1825–30)* (Kuala Lumpur, 1981).

[118]Ricklefs, 'Islamization in Java', pp. 126–7.

landscape of Islamic beliefs and practices, beyond the rigid and narrow confines of the 'Islamicist's Islam', set out here in a comparative and historical perspective, covering both South and South East Asia, presents itself as a rather familiar terrain already visited, explored, and documented by the social scientists.

VII. CONCLUSION

'Popular' Islam, like popular culture, conjures up myriad images in people's perception subject to their social and cultural-ideational orientations. I have introduced this phenomenon here as a gateway to explore some vexed and unresolved matters that continue to cloud and confuse a clear perception and understanding of the total domain of Islamization in South Asia and its adequate interpretation.

Students of the historiography of Islam are well aware of the two dominant perspectives on Islamic developments in history. Reflecting the tensions between the 'transcendental' and the 'pragmatic' or between the 'universal' and the 'particular' in Islam and Muslim societies, these perspectives are situated in varying degrees of proximity to the opposite ends of a spectrum. On one side of this, stand the Islamicist, who would interpret Muslim developments in history in light of the perceived uniqueness and centrality of Islam. He/she is keen on seeking out the Muslim diasporas in history, and the corresponding implementation of the blueprint for a scripturally ordained 'pattern of Islamic perfection'. A natural consequence of this perception has been to promote an unhistorical process of essentializing and homogenizing an infinitely diverse and complex world of human developments. It is interesting, particularly in the context of the opening discussion in this chapter on claims and counter-claims of history and social science disciplines, that a noted social anthropologist and a historian of the ilk respectively of Ernest Gellner and Hamilton Gibb both made substantive contributions to the formulation of the Islamicist's position. On the other side of the spectrum also there are historians and social scientists, who cannot overlook the local geographical, social, and cultural contexts of Islamic developments in a particular country or region. They share a common attitude and approach of looking at the diversities in the Muslim world and the totality of Muslim life, not ignoring the masses of believers across the internal social and cultural divides in the community.

I have, in the analysis here, raised issues with the monolithic, normative, essentializing, and homogenizing perception and understanding of the process of Islamization with particular reference to South Asia. A central concern of this chapter has been to focus on the weakness and inadequacy of the Islamicist's position in relation to the whole complex of Muslim religious beliefs and practices at variance with his/her scripturalist view of Islam, for which I have chosen a generic or omnibus label of 'popular Islam'. The chapter clearly reveals a singular apathy, unconcern, and failure on the part of Islamicists in regard to probing the popular and syncretistic Islam in this region, with a view to providing a conceptual basis for the accommodation and explanation of what is, in reality, a very complex, subtle, and nuanced phenomenon. What emerge clear and important from a wide variety of historical and empirical sources are the presence and persistence of such popular expressions of the religion in both space and time. The material lifted out of scattered historical sources, spanning a very large part of Dar al-Islam, comprising South and South East Asia, with its clear majority of the Ummat al-Islam, is, by its very nature, exhaustive. These are mere samplings—enough to raise doubts about the assumptions underlying the perception of a totally dichotomized world of Muslim believers between a purist strand of the high Islam of the elite—'learned and pious'—and that of the aberrant, corrupt, popular, and syncretic products of 'imperfect knowledge', the latter being destined to be overcome by the juggernaut of the unrelenting process of Islamization, even if it takes 'several hundred years'. The empiricist scholars of South Asian Islam may well be expected to take heart from some of these historical findings. Additionally, the social-religious polarities as well as convergence between the 'higher' and the 'lower', evident in the South Asian history of Islam have also been unmistakably traced outside, in the region of South East Asia, further strengthening this perception.

While seeking to deepen and promote the understanding of the historical significance of the phenomenon of 'popular' Islam, my central purpose has, however, never been to deny or undermine the significance of the scriptural, textual, and high Islam. I have spoken here a great deal about the Islamicists' dedicated efforts in vindication of the centrality of high Islam in Muslim developments, with its corollary process of devaluation and rejection of popular Islam. This analytical frame is not wrong so much as inadequate and unsatisfactory. The issue is clear: it is a patently simplistic academic exercise to resort to the convenience of denying everything in Islamic developments that one is unable to accommodate easily within the framework of a textual and ideal monolithic orthodoxy. Islam, as practised by teeming millions of believers in South Asia, clearly emerges in this study as possessing much greater elasticity, flexibility, tolerance, accommodative spirit, richness, and diversity than what is encapsulated in the Islamicist's rather one-dimensional, scriptural, and limited view of Islamic orthodoxy. It seems ironical that the Islamic scripturalists seek to save Islam from what they regard as its weakness, namely its 'popular' and syncretistic expressions, by turning away from where the real strengths of historical and living Islam have been, namely its creative dynamism and the spirit of accommodation and adjustment. The sociological perception of Islam has a close resonance to the revisionist historical understanding of the so-called popular Islam, as articulated in the following excerpt:

While Muslim fundamentalists may assert and maintain that there is one, and only one, version of what is orthodox from the Islamic point of view and whatever does not conform to it is to be dismissed as heterodox, the people's own beliefs and behaviour admit of much greater variety in what they regard as truly 'Islamic'. Clearly it seems to me that the Islamicists' vision has tended to obscure the inherent and underlying pluralism within Indian Islam as a practised religion.[119]

The sociology of religion has long been differentiating between the 'transcendental' and 'pragmatic' within a single religious complex, often cutting across the inner social and cultural barriers. In reference to this internal divide within a religion, David Mandelbaum maintained: 'Whatever terms are chosen, the important fact is that both are used as part of the whole setting of religion in India, each is employed for generally differing (though frequently overlapping purposes) within the frame of religion and each is popularly considered to be complementary to the other.'[120]

In his important study of the popular 'Sufi poetry' in the Sindhi language, Ali Asani underscored the 'seminal role' of the so-called 'folk, low or little tradition', in 'propagating Islamic ideas within this population'. He affirmed: 'Most studies of Indian Islam, while focussing on the elitist facet, have treated the folk tradition marginally—a treatment that is rather surprising considering the tradition's impact on a substantial proportion of the Muslim population, not to mention it's [sic] seminal role in propagating Islamic ideas within this population.'[121]

Similar understanding of the role of the popular Muslim tradition found expression in the writings of Farhan Nizami. In his study of Islam in the Indian subcontinent, he has noted the complementarity between syncretism and Islamization. 'Syncretism', he observed, 'was not always the reassertion of popular religion but very often the Islamisation of local religious forms.'[122]

In its empirical development, no system of ideology, belief, and practice could be divorced from its spatial context. For an alien and intrusive religion in a particular geographical-cultural context, the social and cultural mores of the convert would more often than not instil special and particular meaning and symbolism into its beliefs and practices. This refinement was designed to bring his new world closer to his Weltanschauung, and leave the rest of his pre-conversion cultural baggage to coexist, generally harmoniously, with his new possessions, as long as such perceptions remained unchanged. A student of this phenomenon— a historian or not—is more meaningfully challenged to unravel this complex interface between the old inheritance and the new acquisition.

Finally, we may have a special reason today for underlining the genius of Islamic

---

[119]Ahmad, *Ritual and Religion Among Muslims*, p. 18.

[120]David G. Mandelbaum, 'Process and structure in South Asian religion', in Edward B. Harper (ed.), *Religion in South Asia* (Seattle: Washington University Press, 1964), p. 10.

[121]Asani, 'Sufi poetry in the folk tradition', p. 81.

[122]F.A. Nizami, 'Islam in the Indian subcontinent', in Sutherland Stewart (ed.), *The World's Religions* (Boston, Mass: GK Hall, 1988), p. 381.

tolerance, adaptability, and creative dynamism in bringing an incredibly diverse world together into a whole of unity in diversity, as clearly evident in its progress in the history of South Asia as well as the far larger world beyond. The in-house discord between the Islamicists and their opponents over issues such as the nature and interpretations of the relationship between scriptural and living Islam or that of Islamization as both historical and empirical experiences and processes is problematic enough within an academic parlour. It is, however, incalculably damaging for the entire Muslim world today, steeped in fundamentalism and militancy welded together by a perceived sense of denial, deprivation, betrayal, and injustice. Threatened and haunted, on the other hand, by the spectre of the fundamentalist and militant–inspired unitary perception of Islam, the culturally rich and diverse Muslim communities in the world today have been desperately seeking reaffirmation of their freedom to define themselves as Muslims in the way they have understood and accepted Islam. The claim for a single monolithic, universal perspective on Islam is not only unhistorical and untenable, but also fraught with grave danger in this global environment. The need and the challenge to establish a consensual understanding of the unity and dynamism of Islam within the variety, plurality, and creativity of the Muslim world has never been greater and so critical.

REFERENCES TO TRADITION IN SOUTH ASIA

Peter van der Veer

I. INTRODUCTION

According to Annie Besant, India was the spiritual leader of the world and even Nehru believed what she said.[1] One could therefore say that Robert Oppenheimer followed established tradition when he quoted the Bhagavad Gita at the first testing of the atomic bomb. Perhaps that was a warning for the believers in India's spiritualism, since today politicians in India and Pakistan have seriously raised the possibility of the use of nuclear weapons in their current stand-off on Kashmir. The current conflict between Pakistan and India is one in a succession of violent conflicts since Partition that are always related in some way or another to communal conflict between Hindus and Muslims in India. Since 1980, communal violence in India has been on the rise.[2] Much of this violence originates in the campaign to replace the sixteenth-century Babar mosque in Ayodhya with a temple for the Hindu god Ram. In 1992 activists of the Vishwa Hindu Parishad (VHP) and Bharatiya Janata Party (BJP), organizations allied to the Rashtriya Swayamsevak Sangh (RSS), destroyed the mosque. Widespread violence followed, especially in Mumbai and cities in Gujarat. In the years following that destruction, these activists have continued to demand that a temple should be built. Most recently, in the early morning of 27 February 2002, *karsewaks* (volunteers offering their service in building the temple) on their way back from Ayodhya provoked Muslims in Godhra in Gujarat into an attack on the train.

---

[1]Peter van der Veer, *Imperial Encounters* (Princeton: Princeton University Press, 2001).
[2]Peter ven der Veer, *Religious Nationalism* (Berkeley: University of California Press, 1994).

According to some reports, some of the Muslim attackers had contacts with the Pakistani secret service. Although the details are disputed, it is clear that some fifty-eight people, mostly women and children, died in the clash. In the following months more than a thousand Muslims in nearby Ahmedabad were killed and more than 100,000 people (mostly Muslims) were made refugees in makeshift camps. The evidence we have shows clearly that the killings have followed a pattern of ethnic cleansing that has completely transformed the nature of this city with its Muslim name, in which some 3,000,000 Hindus lived interspersed with Muslims numbering around 600,000. The kind of violence as well as the nature of responses by the authorities shows a pattern that is chillingly similar to that of 1992. Such a replay of past events seems to make even critical reporting by the media and by human rights organizations part of an already existing script.

All this is well known to those who follow current events in India, but how to interpret the violence between Hindus and Muslims today? Violence is a total social fact with many sides to it: social, economic, political, religious. Violence is also an intrinsic part of human relations and can thus be found everywhere. Causal explanations are often not easy to give. For every instance of large-scale violence in which two communities (ethnic, religious, racial) are involved, one has to come up with a detailed analysis in which all these elements are taken into account. In such a way, one finds out what triggered the violence off, who the participants were, what the economic circumstances of competition and conflict were, what happened in the political arena, and what the police did. In some cases, like in Ahmedabad, one finds an institutionalized riot system in which specialists in such things turn small-scale violence into large-scale mob violence.[3] Such specialists build on experiences in earlier riots and can be organized by political parties (such as the Shiv Sena in Mumbai) or trade unions or criminal gangs. Communication plays a significant role in the spread of violence and it is especially the media that narrate the story of violence. As has been shown also in the case of Gujarat, English-language newspapers tend to be more even-handed in the reporting and are branded as pseudo-secular (and pampering the Muslim minority) by their opponents, while Gujarati-language newspapers are on the side of the Hindu majority for a number of reasons including circulation numbers. There is clearly a split public and neither side trusts the other.[4]

The difficulty, as always, is also one of representation.[5] A riot happened and a struggle emerges about how to represent it, in terms of numbers of casualties, in terms of who started it, in terms of the role of the police. That struggle makes use of certain master narratives and tropes, such as 'communalism or the engrained

---

[3]Paul Brass, *Riots and Pogroms* (London: Macmillan, 1996).

[4]Arvind Rajagopal, *Politics After Television* (Cambridge: Cambridge University Press, 2000).

[5]Peter van der Veer, 'The victim's tale', in Weber and De Vries (eds), *Violence, Identity and Self-determination* (Stanford: Stanford University Press, 1995).

antagonism of Hindus and Muslims' or 'the machinations of dirty politics behind the scene' or 'the foreign hand'. Hindu–Muslim violence since the 1980s can be explained in a variety of ways, but at some level, at least, it is connected to the rise of Hindu nationalism and the success of the VHP and BJP in the social and political arenas. These organizations have an ideology claiming that the Hindu majority has the right to balance wrongs from the past and that the Hindu religious traditions should be the core of national identity. Minorities in this view have to submit to the majority perspective. In this master narrative, the secular state is seen as pseudo-secular since it pampers the minorities. Hindus should be proud of their traditions and not be marginalized in their own country.

In this chapter I want to examine some references to religious traditions in the antagonistic relations between Hindus and Muslims.[6] The past is sometimes invoked in connection with utopian views on the 'just state'. The past is also sometimes invoked in relation to traditions of conversion (religious expansion) and conflict as well as to traditions of harmony and tolerance. But first it would be useful to discuss what is meant by the concept of 'tradition'.

II. TRADITION, INVENTION, MODERNITY

References to tradition are mystifying. As a textual scholar one can adopt a superior position (like Max Muller did) from which one adjudicates what is invented and what is authentic, but such ex cathedra judgments are often unacceptable for the players in the field and also quite unacceptable from a scholarly point of view since authenticity is such an intractable concept. The predicament of anthropologists is no less than that of the textual scholar. Nowadays, they often forget about the text and focus on practice, the cultural performance of a tradition (for example a ritual) in a particular context. Cultural meaning is produced in symbolic action and it has both subjective (intentional) and objective components. In the view of many anthropologists, ritual enactments of tradition are demarcated from the practices of everyday life. Again, it is the anthropologist who puts himself in the position to adjudicate this demarcation and what to make of it. Authentic may be the native's point of view (in Geertz's terms) but authoritative is the anthropologist's superior interpretation of that view. References to cultural praxis and to everyday life are thus not a solution to the problem of the interpretation of tradition. This is even clearer when the anthropologist's understanding of a community's culture gives him also the key to understand violence as resulting from some deeper cultural logic. It is then the interpretation of a particular cosmology that makes violence culturally interpretable. For example, in Bruce Kapferer's work on Sri

---

[6]Daud Ali, *Invoking the Past* (New Delhi: Oxford University Press, 1999); Peter van der Veer, 'Religion in South Asia', *Annual Reviews in Anthropology* (2002).

Lanka there is a hierarchical cosmology in Sinhalese society that sees demonic possession and violence as a sign of an inverted hierarchy and exorcism and counter-violence as a means to return from chaos to order. Similarly, Tamil violence against the Sinhalese is interpreted as demonic.[7] This kind of argument, in which violence is an enactment of culture, is often counterbalanced by an argument that shows tolerance and syncretism to be culturally embedded. The anthropological notion of 'culture' is akin to the textual scholar's notion of 'tradition' and these notions can be drafted for all kinds of purposes.

Talal Asad[8] has given a definition of tradition that is relevant for both historians and ethnographers: 'A tradition consists essentially of discourses that seek to instruct practitioners regarding the correct form and purpose of a given practice that, precisely because it is established, has a history'. These discourses relate conceptually to a past (when the practice was instituted, and from which the knowledge of its point and proper performance has been transmitted) and a future (how the point of that practice can best be secured in the short or long term, or why it should be modified or abandoned), through a present (how it is linked to other practices, institutions, and social conditions). Central to this then is a community's debate about boundaries and transgressions, about orthodoxy and orthopraxis. Traditions often project themselves as timeless, transcending history and politics, and part of their discursive power lies in that claim, so that historicizing them is often felt by practitioners as 'debunking' and showing a lack of respect. This is even worse in situations in which Western modernity is perceived as the enemy of tradition. Those who use modern scholarly methods and observations are then declared to be part of the enemy as Nasr Abu Zaid, the Egyptian scholar of the Qur'an, experienced. Again, the outsider's point of view is also problematic given the fact that Orientalist scholarship is so much part of authorizing discourses.

Traditions are crucially concerned with correct practice and opinion and therefore it is in the field of boundaries and transgressions, of syncretism and conversion that some of the hottest issues lie. These issues are not only hotly debated, but often also lead to violent conflict. That conflict is perhaps even more intra-communal than inter-communal. The hottest debates are between competing groups and they tend to be close together. A good example is the Khalistani movement of Sant Bhindranwale who had come to power because of his claim to defend orthodoxy against heterodox Sikhs and who played a role in the murder of the Nirankari, Gurbachan Singh, in 1980. Besides that there is, obviously, also

[7]Bruce Kapferer, *A Celebration of Demons: Exorcism and Aesthetics of Healing in Sri Lanka* (Bloomington: Indiana University Press, 1983).

[8]Talal Asad, *The Idea of an Anthropology of Islam* (Washington: Georgetown University Press, 1986).

considerable inter-communal violence. Such is true for both the colonial and pre-colonial periods. Criticism of Sufi saint-worship predates Shah Waliullah of Delhi and Muhammad bin Abd-al Wahhab of Arabia who themselves are both eighteenth-century thinkers who predate colonialism proper. We know also of a lot of conflict between Shaivas and Vaishnavas, partly doctrinal, partly about control over resources. Of course, there has been pre-colonial inter-communal violence also, as Chris Bayly has argued, but the interesting thing is how the arena, the participants, and the political context all change in the colonial period and thus give old issues of syncretism, conversion, and conflict a new salience. To some extent, it is attractive to posit a traditional opposition between the defenders of orthodoxy, the Brahmin or Sayyid jurists, and the bringers of poetic syncretism and transgression, the leaders of the Bhakti and Sufi movements. The recurring problem, however, with posing this kind of structural opposition is that it fails to do justice to the historical salience of recurrent traditional arguments in changing contexts. Traditions do have continuity, but their transmittance is historically and contextually specific.

I do think that the colonial state and practices of modern governmentality have had a huge impact on the conditions of transmittance of tradition, on the questions asked and the answers given by practitioners. This is immediately clear in the field of education where modern education and new fields of knowledge compete with traditional education. It is not only that other languages and other forms of knowledge push existing ones aside, but also that modern and traditional forms of knowledge penetrate each other. This was obviously not a level playing field, since knowledge of languages such as Persian, Urdu, Hindi, and English, all gave access to some opportunities for jobs and money. This is a complex field of interaction that can only be touched upon in passing, but for our purpose it is important to note that Christian missionaries were very active in the field of education and that this very fact forced Hindus, Muslims, and others to respond. This response was very much in terms and organizational forms adopted from the missionaries. To give one example: the Arya Samaj wants a rational religion with one god and one central text. It organizes schools with a mixture of traditional and modern subjects. Dayanand is a great debater and a public sphere of debate on religious and social issues emerges. The importance of modern forms of knowledge, especially the authority of science, is immediately clear from these debates. This produces a creative mixture of argumentative styles, sources of authority, and so on. The Arya Samaj is at the same time at the forefront of a movement to create a national state on the basis of 'tradition'.

III. TRADITIONS OF THE JUST STATE

BJP politicians increasingly make use of references to Hindu traditions. They do not have to be very learned in these references, since they can just choose what they need for a particular purpose. This is, more in general, the feeling one gets when political leaders use traditional references for putting their political programmes in a moral framework. Famous are the references to the biblical tradition made by American Presidents in their inaugural or State of the Union addresses. In Robert Bellah's much cited view, they constitute a civil religion, a religion of the modern nation state.[9] Many of the references made by political leaders in India seem to be of the same category. However, while in the case of the USA, such references are more or less interpreted as metaphors with an emotional appeal to what constitutes the Moral Majority, there is a tendency to take them much more literally in the case of Islam and of Hinduism. This is especially true for Islamic and Hindu references to a 'just' state where it is sometimes suggested that those who make these references really want to go back to ancient political practices.

The state can be seen as a nexus of institutional arrangements in which power and violence are crucial. According to Max Weber, the state has a monopoly on legitimate force in society. Similarly, Norbert Elias's story of Western civilization connects the civilizing process with the growing monopolization of violence by the state.[10] It is odd that Elias wrote his book during the formation of the Nazi totalitarian state and ignores Weber's dark misgivings about the dangers of state bureaucracies. There is enough reason to be less optimistic about the modern state than Elias. Especially those colonized people who object to a 'foreign', colonial (and 'Christian') state sometimes couch their criticism in terms of a religious past. This is in principle not so different from, say, the neo-Gothic fantasies that characterized nineteenth-century nationalism in Europe, but the reference to the past by the colonized is primarily in opposition to a colonial state that itself has a nationalist project 'at home' but not in the colony. While the romantic impulse is strong in all nationalisms, it refers in colonial nationalism to a past that is seen as essentially opposite to the present form of the state, and thus a source of resistance. This continues after independence when the post-colonial state is seen as the instrument of a deracinated, Westernized elite.

This is the background to references to the Islamic state (*dawla*) or to Ram's Rule (*Ramrajya*). The first thing that has to be observed here is that references to earlier political forms show a deliberate misunderstanding of the radically different nature of the modern, developmental state. Those who call for the foundation of an Islamic state often use the Arabic term dawla that refers to 'dynasty' and indeed the pre-modern societies are governed by *sultans*, *nawabs*, *rajas*, and the like. The modern state, on the contrary, is an instrument of the will of the people and penetrates deep into people's lives with a number of developmental projects, such

[9]Robert Bellah, 'Civil religion in America', in *Beyond Belief* (New York: Harper & Row, 1970), pp. 160–89.

[10]Nobert Elias, *The Civilizing Process* (Oxford: Basil Blackwell, 1994).

as education and healthcare. It is, even when it is a weak state in Gunnar Myrdal's sense, still a beast of completely different nature than the pre-modern state.

The second observation that has to be made here is that the references to a religiously based 'just state' are relatively recent in modern Indian history and are actually quite marginal in Indian political thought and practice. The call for going back to the time of the Prophet or the time of Ram and establishing a so-called theocratic state is a very recent demand that has to be understood within the framework of modern political ideas of true Islamic democracy and so on. Contrary to what is often thought, there is no clear definition of the Islamic state in Pakistan.[11] What about the tradition of *dar-al-islam* (the Abode of Islam) to which Muslims should migrate (*hijrat*) if they are in a minority position, or that of the *jihad* (holy war) against the *dar-al-harb* (an Abode of Unbelief or War)? None of this makes much sense in India where Muslims were always a minority and there were no Islamic states, but merely Muslim dynasties with Islamic legitimation. It also ignores the fact of current large-scale migration to the dar-al-harb, or the West, rather than away from it. Similarly the reference to the rule of Rama, the virtuous king (*dharmaraja*) and the 'Lord of Propriety' (*maryada purushottam*), has very little specific content, even less than in the Islamic context where the establishment of the Law (*shariat*) can at least be part of a political programme. Certainly in Hindu kingdoms, the Ramayana may have given some guidance to the behaviour of rulers, but there is little in it that specifies the nature of the caste order and the rules of poltics. One should understand references to such traditions in the modern period primarily as a utopian rejection of current political formations rather than a theological interpretation of the tradition. This is not to say that there are no theological interpretations of the tradition that have political implications. They certainly exist and are important, because they show that the tradition is alive. The violent political projects of activists like Osama Bin Laden, however, do not engage the tradition in such a fundamental manner. It is, in fact, striking how little theological training leaders of the major religious nationalist movements have had. They tend to be journalists, engineers, graduates of the humanities, educated in modern subjects rather than in the tradition.

The same is true for leaders of Hindu and Muslim movements who want a just rule. Gandhi was certainly not a theologian and when he came up with the notion of Ramrajya he used a cultural repertoire in which he had been socialized from his early youth, but not a political theology. In the case of Gandhi and many other great populist leaders, one sees the function of a traditional religious repertoire as bridging the gap between elite politics and mass politics. However, it is also clear that this kind of reference to tradition for purposes of mass mobilization needs to allow for a wide range of interpretations, as Shahid Amin has beautifully

[11]Muhammad Qasim Zaman, *The Ulama in Contemporary Islam* (Princeton: Princeton University Press, 2002).

demonstrated in his piece on Gandhi as Mahatma.[12] Similarly, Gananath Obeyesekere and Richard Gombrich have mapped what they consider to be the major departures from Buddhist Tradition in Sri Lanka and the invention of new traditions, such as the Sarvodaya movement that purports to give a Buddhist model of development.[13] Here we get to the heart of the matter: Hobsbawm and Ranger's invention of tradition or what recent scholarship has called 'the manufacturing of religion' or 'the invention of religion'. I would suggest that while the universal category of religion is a European invention that affects the development of religious traditions (of a Hindu, Buddhist, Christian, Muslim nature), these traditions exist and have a history of change, polemics, and so on that cannot be reduced to the encounter with European thought. I do think that modern references to Ramrajya and dar-al-islam are inventions of tradition, but at the same time there are a number of living traditions in which there are discourses and practices relating to state and violence. However, we are not speaking about separate universes (one of tradition, one of invented tradition) here, but about interaction, conflict, polemics. Some people are willing to use a lot of violence to establish their idea of traditional justice in the form of an Islamic state or of a Hindu state and others who think they are living in harmony with tradition are completely mystified by what the first are doing.

IV. CONVERSION

Conversion from one tradition to the other is probably the most contentious issue in India today.[14] This perception clearly has to do with the rise of communal politics of numbers after the first colonial Census of 1872. Political mobilization and strengthening of Hindus and Muslims as antagonistic religious and political communities made the issue of conversion, of moving from one community to the other into a crucial one. It also created an anachronistic history of Islam in India as one of violence, of invasions, of destruction of Hindu shrines, of mass conversions by the sword. Conversion to Islam is often read by Hindus today as the result of coercion—either by violence or by economic and political means—while 'being a Hindu' is seen as a fact of nature, a natural identity. Muslims, obviously, regard conversion to Islam in the highly positive light of a moral and religious change for the better. Hindu leaders often see conversion to Christianity again as a sign of coercion, but with an emphasis on mental coercion of the disenfranchised poor by way of education and spreading literacy. While Islam

[12]Shahid Amin, 'Gandhi as Mahatma', in Ranajit Guha and Gayatri Spivak (eds), *Selected Subaltern Studies* (New York: Oxford University Press, 1983), pp. 288–351.

[13]Gananath Obeyeskere and Richard Gombrich, *Buddhism Transformed* (Princeton: Princeton University Press, 1988).

[14]Gauri Vishwanathan, *Outside the Fold* (Princeton: Princeton University Press, 1998).

spreads through oil money, Christianity spreads through literacy programmes paid for by Western philanthropy. When Amartya Sen received the Noble Prize for Economics, Ashok Singhal, president of the VHP, argued that Sen's plea for spreading literacy was part of a plan to spread global Christianity and wipe out Hinduism.[15] In recent years there have been a number of attacks on Christian missionaries by the VHP in the context of their own expansion in tribal areas.

The upsurge of Hindu nationalism and the successes of the VHP/BJP in fact began with the highly publicized conversions to Islam of untouchable communities in and around Meenakshipuram in south India in 1981. The press interpreted these conversions as 'induced by oil money' and 'a threat to Indian unity'. Indira Gandhi and her Congress government warned against the Muslim conspiracy, in line with a long-standing secular apprehension about conversion, expressed in recurring debates about the constitutional right to proselytize. A fear of 'the foreign hand', of global developments such as migration to the Gulf, and of a severe weakening of national unity when untouchables and tribals leave the Hindu fold all come together in a fierce rejection of Muslim and Christian religious activities. Interesting is the slippage from 'Hindu' to 'national' in the secular Congress response to Meenakshipuram and this aspect has, obviously, been brought to the forefront by the VHP. This plays on a notion that was prevalent in pre-modern Europe, 'cuius regio eius religio', that relates political loyalty to religious allegiance. In the modern European nation state, this has been disentangled in a long history of creating national identities, but this process cannot be taken as a model for India where precisely in modern history communal identities have been politicized in opposition to the (colonial) state.

I find it quite important to point out that the 'naturalness' or 'givenness' of Hinduism is a myth. Saints, traders, and soldiers were agents of Muslim and Christian expansion, but as much of Hindu expansion. Often Sufis were all in one. Sufi shrines were spiritual and material centres, just as *baraqa* was poltical, economic, as well as spiritual power. Like their counterparts, Brahmin priests and ascetics were the vanguard of agrarian and civilization expansion and played a significant role in the settlement and very slow conversion of nomadic and tribal peoples to Hindu traditions. Hindu *sadhus* have always been soldiers as well as traders, and fighting ascetics during the larger part of their history. Militancy, not pacifism, is the core of their traditions, whatever nineteenth-century views on Hindu spiritualism may have posited. The current activities of the VHP among tribal people (interestingly calling them *vanavasis* instead of *adivasis* in line with their theory of the original Aryan inhabitants of India) are, therefore, to be regarded as part of a *longue duree* expansion of Hindu traditions. It is one of the

---

[15]Gauri Vishwanathan, 'Literacy in the eye of the conversion storm', in Derek Peterson and Darren Walhof (eds), *The Invention of Religion* (New Brunswick: Rutgers University Press, 2002).

saddest aspects of the recent conflagration in Gujarat that Muslims have been widely attacked by tribals, showing the success of the VHP strategy.

Hindu revivalist movements and certainly the contemporary BJP argue that Hindus have been too tolerant, that they have been taken advantage of for too long and that in independent India they have to take what is their own. This is the rhetoric behind the *Ramjanmabhumi muktiyajna* that led in 1992 to the destruction of Babar's mosque in Ayodhya. It is, in fact, also something all Indian schoolchildren get in their history lessons, even long before the 'textbook controversies' of the late 1990s. Mahmud of Ghazni is the well-known villain of that story while similar raids by Shaiva rulers on Vaishnava temples or vice versa are hardly mentioned. It is at the same time clear that this story of 'foreign invasions' into pristine India is so well entrenched by now that it is almost unassailable. It is hard to see what the role of modern history writing is in the face of popular history. One wants to talk truth to power, but when it is a discursive framework that one is challenging, courage is not enough. The flat denial of violence and destruction by Muslim conquerors is in any case too ideological to be either true or powerful. It is the nature of violence and the conceptualization of it in history that is important.

The story of conversion is decisively reshaped under the conditions of modernity.[16] In north India, the Arya Samaj, despite all the hybridity of its Hindu ideology, desires to strengthen the ranks of the Hindu community. A series of successful but very aggressive campaigns, such as the very violent cow protection movements and the equally important reconversion or *shuddhi* (purification) movements, are initiated. The latter movements to reconvert Muslims, Sikhs, tribals, and low castes created an immensely contentious atmosphere in north India and were in some important respects forerunners of the ethnic cleansing (*safaya*) that took place during Partition. Shuddhi built upon accepted elements of Hindu tradition, such as *prayascitta* (expiation) rituals, but these had never been used in collective action for reconversion of the lapsed (*patita*) before. Conversion and violence were very close together and experienced as the same: an attack on the boundaries of the community. *Tabligh* (internal mission) was the answer given by Muslims to the shuddhi activities of the Arya Samaj. To prevent the Arya Samaj from making inroads in the Muslim Meo community in Mewat near Jaipur, small groups (*jamat*) of dedicated Muslims (mostly Deobandis from Nizamuddin in Delhi) tried from 1925 onwards to educate the Meos in proper, orthodox Islam.[17] The Meos, like so many other groups, had a wide range of traditions in common with their Hindu neighbours and these traditions were read by both the Arya Samaj and the Tablighi Jam'at as a sign that they were not really converted to Islam. The Meos are Muslim, but the boundaries between them and their environment had

---

[16]Peter van der Veer (ed.), *Conversion to Modernities* (New York: Routledge, 1996).
[17]Shail Mayaram, *Resisting Regimes* (New Delhi: Oxford University Press, 1997).

to be redrawn in the arena of communal politics in the 1920s and 1930s. The practices of groups such as the Meos can be called syncretistic and this brings us to the other side of the coin of religious expansion: syncretism.

V. SYNCRETISM

Syncretism is historically a term that refers to attempts in the seventeenth century to promote tolerance among Protestant sects within the context of religious war and violent conflict in Europe. The term is, therefore, less a descriptive than prescriptive one. It shows an acceptance of a multiplicity of truth claims and of fundamental differences within a polity. This use of the term is also found in writings on Indian traditions. Ashis Nandy, for instance, has a strong belief in the syncretic traditions of ordinary Indians and blames the modern, secularizing state for the communalism that rips the social fabric apart. In Nandy's view, it is in particular the modernizing, Westernizing middle class that has lost touch with India's syncretism and thus with tolerance. Nandy refers to Gandhi as the apostle of this culture of tolerance:

Gandhi used to say that he was a sanatani, an orthodox Hindu. It was as a sanatani Hindu that he claimed to be simultaneously a Muslim, a Sikh, and a Christian and he granted the same plural identity to those belonging to other faiths. Traditional Hinduism, or rather Sanatan dharma, was the source of his religious tolerance.[18]

Nandy does articulate here something that one finds in Gandhi and perhaps in Hindu traditions more generally. I interpret this tradition of tolerance as a tradition of inclusivism, a form of hierarchical relativism. There are many paths leading to God and there are many gods, but that does not do away with the fact that there is a hierarchy of these paths. People follow paths that belong to their 'being'; there is a co-substantiality between the believer and his *dharma*. That includes Muslims and Christians, but in an inferior position. When Nandy therefore argues that 'it is religion-as-faith which prompted Indians to declare themselves as Mohammedan Hindus in Gujarat in the census of 1911'[19] he forgets that the VHP does not demand that Muslims give up their religion but that they recognize themselves as Hindus first. Islam becomes then a *sampradaya* within Hinduism and it should be clear that Muslims do not want to be syncretized in such a manner. Nandy's argument ignores completely the internal debate among Muslims about orthodoxy.

The most important example given of Hindu–Muslim syncretism in India is always the Sufi shrine.[20] Observers report that both Hindus and Muslims frequent

---

[18]Ashis Nandy, 'The politics of secularism and the recovery of religious tolerance', in Veena Das (ed.), *Mirrors of Violence* (New Delhi: Oxford University Press, 1990), p. 91.

[19]Ibid., p. 70.

[20]Prina Werbner and Helene Basu (eds), *Embodying Charisma* (London: Routledge, 1999).

this kind of shrine and that members of both communities worship the saint for all kinds of purposes. Such observations lead to the notion that popular (or 'folk') Islam is as tolerant as Hinduism and that it is only modern fanatics who want to destroy this and replace it with intolerant purism. Unfortunately, one has to reject such easy views. First of all, there is a long tradition of Islamic criticism of Sufi saint-worship as *bida* or innovation or as *shirk* or polytheism even by some Sufis themselves. The issue is as usual the definition of orthodoxy. This debate about the orthodoxy of some Sufi practices is an internal Islamic one to which Hindus mostly have no clue. Moreover, historically Sufi saint-worship has been in decline since late nineteenth century, not only in India but in the entire Muslim world. Mass education and direct lay access to sacred scripture and debate about it as well as the waning of the economic and political power of shrines seem to be factors in that decline. Hindus often have their own motivations and stories that led them to seek the blessing of a Muslim saint. In some cases this is precisely because the saint as a Muslim is seen as having power over a world of demons and dangerous ghosts. From a sociological point of view, it is important to observe not only that Hindus and Muslims participate in the same Sufi rituals, but also why and how. At least in my own ethnographic experience, traditions on which participation was based were often understood and recited in very different ways. Moreover, the shrine often is part of a larger complex of Islamic institutions of prayer and education such as mosques and *madrasa*s, in which Hindus do not participate, as long as they are not converted. It is perhaps better to see the Sufi shrine as an arena of contestation and conversion than as a site of inter-faith dialogue.

This is also clear from recent work by Shahid Amin on the shrine of Ghazi Miyan or Salar Masud, a famous Sufi shrine in Bahraich. Over the last century or so, this is an arena of contestation in which the Arya Samaj attacks some popular versions of the founding myth of this shrine. But it is not only modern nationalism and reformism that have brought contestation and violence. These are elements at the heart of the shrine itself. Like many other Sufi shrines, this is a shrine for a warrior-saint (*ghazi*) who was martyred at the spot. The founding myth of the shrine deals directly with violence and conversion. It is the constant reworking of this myth in history that gives us a perspective on the changing relations between Hindus and Muslims, but also on Hindu and Muslim understandings of violence itself. In the Ghazi Miyan story, one element is very striking: the killing of the virginal saint at the time of his wedding. It is this story of mystical power that emerges from an act of violence against it that is such a powerful metaphor we live by. One finds it in the story of Jesus Christ, of African earth cults, of Mahatma Gandhi. It is such root metaphors that trigger off collective memory and bring Hindus and Muslims together with interpretations embedded in their own traditions. The story of violence is thus multifaceted and religiously potent.

VI. BY WAY OF CONCLUSION

Reference to traditions is made in debates about correct beliefs and practices, about orthodoxy and orthopraxis. Such debates may not only be verbal. Liberal government allows for debates in the public sphere and for the expression of the will of the people in elections, but, according to its own theory, it has to monopolize violence by suppressing violence between individuals and groups in society. The theory presupposes, therefore, a distinction between the free expression of opinion and the use of violence, between speech act and other acts. However, words can hurt and the role of insults, slander, rumours, and propaganda is quite important in the dynamics of civil violence. When slogans like '*Babar ki santan: Jao Pakistan ya Kabristan*' are uttered freely in the streets and in writing, there is reference to tradition and to certain understandings of history. Physical violence is an extension of verbal engagement.

Debates about tradition define the boundaries of a community. They define the 'other' of the community and this is done within different contexts. In some contexts Shi'a–Sunni or Sanatana–Arya antagonisms are relevant, in other contexts they are replaced by Hindu–Muslim or Hindu–Christian antagonisms. In some cities in India, one finds elaborate riot systems with collective memories of previous violence, with rituals of provocation that feed on religious traditions of purity and impurity. One would think that one would also find systems of pacification with rituals of tolerance that feed on traditions of syncretism and non-violence. A sad story about the Ahmedabad riots of the recent past was that Gandhi's Sabarmati ashram in the city closed its gates for refugees at the moment of the riots. In such circumstances, one expects the state to be proactive in controlling communal violence, but this expectation is based on another tradition, the liberal tradition of the state as arbiter between interests. In the case of Gujarat and in other cases, such as the destruction of the Babar mosque, it is sufficiently clear that the institutions of the state are involved in civil society to the extent that political leaders are the main instigators and organizers of communal violence. Democratization in India implies a growing participation of larger sections of the population both in the political process and in communal violence.[21] To expect that the liberal tradition will give answers that religious traditions will not provide seems to be a fallacy of the secular mind.

[21]Thomas Blom Hansen, *Wages of Violence* (Princeton: Princeton University Press, 2002).

COLONIAL LANGUAGE CLASSIFICATION, POST-COLONIAL LANGUAGE MOVEMENTS, AND THE GRASSROOT MULTILINGUALISM ETHOS IN INDIA

Annie Montaut

T he Constitution of India viewed linguistic diversity as a reflection of the 'composite nature' of Indian culture and of its pluralism: the composite nature of Hindi was celebrated by the liberals among the founding fathers, as well as the multilingual situation;[1] and the preference of an official language over a national language was meant to discard all emotional identification between language and the nation. However, the eulogist praise of diversity was at the same time blurred off in the vague slogan, 'Unity in diversity'. Nehru himself went to the extreme of practically dismissing the concrete reality of linguistic plurality as a mere fantasy grown out of the restless brain of philologists, since one could easily reduce this proliferating diversity to a few main languages all very close structurally, except some 'petty', illiterate, hill-tribe languages which should not be taken into account, being 'undeveloped' and 'uncultivated', therefore 'insignificant'.

Besides, whatever the recognition of difference, it did not mean equality, and the discrimination between major and minor languages was not only a matter of number regarding the speaking communities—numerous people noticed and still notice that the claim for Sindhi or Sanskrit as major language, disregarding the four million plus Santali speakers, had nothing to do with the mass of speakers.[2]

---

[1] See the most celebrated (when not loathed) Articles of the Constitution (347–51) regarding the definition of Hindi, the would-be official language of India, invited to get enriched by other major languages and dialects.

[2] The proposition for including Santali (by the Constituent Jaypal Singh) in the Eighth Schedule listing major languages was rejected without even being discussed. The ambivalence of the criteria required for the status of major language is extensively analysed and criticized in several chapters of

Positive discrimination as a principle encapsulated in various provisions of the Constitution, with its varying implementation at practical level, exhibits the paradox of democratic equity (equal citizens with equal rights) coping with the need to protect minorities and to preserve plurality. Integration may lead to the levelling of contained differences, minority rights to the fragmentation of the state into communities—a paradox that Khilani places at the root of the Nehruvian view of the nation as an abstract idea, above its substantial contents, whether in terms of regional or linguistic communities.[3] This well-known dialectics of national integration versus diversity, right from the beginnings of independent India, reached a particularly acute polarization regarding the language question.

I. EVENTS: A BLOODY HISTORY

It may seem amazing that the language problem (finally a script-cum-numeral problem) came to be the major conflict among constituents between 1948 and 1950 and that only language debates compelled Nehru to call—twice—for a vote although he was determined to avoid a vote in order to preserve the consensual basis for democracy.[4] But if we see language not merely as a tool for communication, nor even as a way of enacting one's social role(s), but as a means of asserting one's cultural or religious identity and an icon for a group identity, one can understand how it can become an intensely burning issue. Still, for these tensions to become a bloody issue, a process of politicization is needed, and this is precisely what was already going on before Independence when Gandhi had to give up his dream of Hindustani (in both scripts) as a would-be national language,[5] Hindustani being religiously unmarked and quite loose regarding regional and cultural identity. The question of the national language, in fact, condensed the problems raised by the exploitation of language for expressing the political claims of a community, and later language claims and riots can only be explained by the political link, more or less artificially created, between language and political or administrative needs.

One of the most convincing examples of the politicization of the language 'problem' and of the tension between national integration/security and maintenance of linguistic diversity is the question of the so-called 'linguistic states'. It is still an ongoing process (with the recognition of Konkani in 1994 as a state

---

R.S. Gupta, A. Abbi, and K.S. Agarwal, *Language and the State: Perspectives on the Eighth Schedule* (New Delhi: Creative Books, 1995).

[3]Sunil Khilani, *The Idea of India* (New Delhi: Penguin, 1998).

[4]Granville Austin, *The Constitution of India: Cornerstone of a Nation* (New Delhi: Oxford University Press, 1966), pp. 300–5.

[5]And to resign from the leadership of the Hindi Sammelan, an assembly more and more dominated by the 'Hindiwallahs' as those in favour of a Sanskritized Hinduized Hindi were then called. For the question of Hindi/Urdu conflict, see following discussion.

language within its territory and the still unsuccessful claim for Maithili), and the military, administrative, and political factors involved[6] go back to the first years of the twentieth century when the 'linguistic principle' was first mentioned by the British to legitimate the transfer of some Oriya-speaking communities during the first partition of Bengal (1905), then for a further bifurcation of the province into Assam, Orissa, and Bengal. What stopped the British administration from generalizing the principle and led them to oppose the Andhra Mahasabha claim for a Telugu-speaking province was the well-known dictum that nobody rules in the colonial tongue (Montague-Chelmsford report).[7] The Congress itself was initially in favour of linguistic states and the Nehru Committee in 1928 and the election manifesto (1945–6) supported the principle but identified several unsolvable difficulties (Maharashtra/Karnataka in Bombay, Maharashtra/Mahavidarbha in Berar, Andhra/Tamil Nadu in Madras). When the Dar Commission appointed for solving such problems submitted its report in 1948, it advised against linguistic states: 'The formation of provinces on exclusively or even mainly linguistic considerations is not in the larger interest of the nation. Oneness of language may be one of the factors to be taken into consideration along with others but it should not be the decisive or even the main factor', since it would 'create new minorities'. Similarly the JVP Committee (Jawaharlal, Vallabbhai, Pattabhi)[8] during the Jaipur session in 1948 concluded that language is 'not only a binding force but also a separative force', thus endangering national unity and security. As a result, the various states to be created in 1950 (distributed into four groups) were all linguistically heterogeneous, especially Tamil Nadu (Madras) which included considerable masses of Telugu speakers. This infuriated the Congress leader Sanjiva Reddy and acted as an incentive for the Vishal Andhra Movement in protest.

It is the Telugu-Andhra problem which started real violent conflict on language issues. In July 1952, a motion for a Telugu-speaking state by a communist leader, supported by several Congress members against Nehru, was finally rejected because of party solidarities.[9] After the meeting of an all-party Andhra Convention, Potti Sriramulu, the leader of Vishal Andhra Movement, started a fast unto death for the Telugu state and died on the fifty-sixth day, leading to violent riots in which several people were killed. The government gave up and decided in December 1952 to create the new state which actually came into existence in October 1953, a result of violent language protests which triggered off the official will to reorganize states on a linguistic basis. The State Reorganization Commission

---

[6]It was easier to administer small units.

[7]The Andhra Mahasabha, later to launch the Vishal Andhra Movement, was active since 1913. Parat Prakash, *Language and the Nationality Politics in India* (Bombay: Orient Longman, 1973), p. 30.

[8]From the first names of Nehru, Patel, and Sitaramayya.

[9]Ending in 261 votes against it and only 77 for it, the Congress Party ultimately uniting against the proposal.

appointed in 1953 to that effect, although reluctant to organize the creation of states on a purely linguistic basis, suggested sixteen states and three centrally administered areas, which finally amounted to the fourteen 'linguistic states' created in 1956 along with six union territories.[10] Soon after, the most feared danger of 'balkanization' induced by the creation of new minorities again came to the fore with violent language riots in Bombay (*Midnight's Children* gives a vivid description of them) for division into a Gujarati-speaking state separated from the Marathi-speaking state (the Maharashtra/Gujarat bifurcation occurred in 1960). Violent episodes also marked the north-west area with the Sikh Akali Dal agitation for a Punjabi state separated from the Hindi-speaking areas. Sant Fateh Singh on a fast unto death for the Punjabi state, stopped his fast on the order of his spiritual leader Tara Singh, but after the failure of negotiation between the Akali Dal and the government, Master Tara Singh himself started a forty-eight days fast in July 1961. However, negotiations again failed, and Sant Fateh Singh once more in 1965 started a fast and threatened the government with self-immolation in the manner of South Vietnam Buddhists. Only then, after the Pakistan war, was the new state granted (separated from Haryana).

Meanwhile, the Tibeto-Burman-speaking Nagaland, already separated from the Indo-Aryan speaking Assam (in 1962) witnessed the violent agitation of hill tribes from Garo, Khasia, North Cacchar, Jaintia for a hill state of their own in 1966. After the All Party Hill Leaders Conference decided on a complete strike in Shillong (25 May 1968), new states and territories were created in 1971 on the recommendation of the Ashok Mehta Commission (Meghalaya, Mizoram, Manipur, Tripura). Although only Manipuri to this day has acquired the status of a major language listed in the Eighth Schedule (1994), Khasi (Meghalaya), Mizo, and Tripuri have to some extent achieved their language claims. If in the case of Punjab and Punjabi, the intimate link between language and religion was more than instrumental in the success of the language movement,[11] in the case of the Nagaland bifurcations the relevance of religion is less obvious (as it is in the bifurcation of Maharashtra/Gujarat or Tamil Nadu/Andhra). But what is common to all these movements is the politicization of the language issue, still highly emphasized by the language activists themselves. For instance, a Konkani militant (who learnt Portuguese in elementary school and 'was a Portuguese', then Gujarati in Diu and 'was a Gujarati', then in college 'was a Marathi', discovering that Konkani is a language, incidentally his language, only after the Konkani conference in 1939) clearly states that he had to become a politician in order to fight for his language. He remarks that politicians accepted Ahirani poetry and popular dramas

---

[10]Himachal was added to the union territories, Vidarbha was withdrawn, Karnataka was created instead of Mysore and Hyderabad.

[11]Paul Brass, *Language, Religion and Politics in North India* (Cambridge: Cambridge University Press, 1974).

in Malwani, 'dialects' of Marathi which did not threaten the territorial entity of Maharashtra but opposed Konkani literature since the recognition of its distinctiveness would have gone against the Marathi-Konkani fusion and supported the political distinction of Goa from Maharashtra.[12]

The proliferation of new 'linguistic states' is the obvious proof that the language principle for reorganizing states was indeed like opening the floodgates to a never-ending process of secession if not balkanization, with a continuous creation of new minorities enduring increasingly worse conditions. With one language made the official basis of the state and getting the status of the 'major' language, all the other languages spoken in the state locally become minor languages— with the exception of Hindi and English, the official languages of the Union. The new minorities created by the formation of linguistic states become like outsiders within the state, towards whom the linguistic majority has a 'discriminatory attitude, blatant or patent', according to K.M. Munshi,[13] who describes the miserable condition of minorities in the linguistic states at the end of the 1960s in Macaulay's words: 'In such a case, the rule of the majority, exercised more often under the title of a democracy, is a true tyranny. It is the worst—which is the corruption of the best …. The lot of a member of a national minority is indeed a hard one'. Siddiqi (1998) gives various examples to show the miserable status of Urdu in its very cultural homeland and birthplace, Uttar Pradesh.[14] Although Urdu-speaking minorities are officially entitled to get official documents in Urdu, official positions advertised in Urdu, ration card applications in Urdu, practically it is almost never the case, and the civil suppliers officer never accepts demands for ration cards written in Urdu. The Moradabad schools have unsuccessfully tried for ten years to obtain recognition for Urdu medium since more than ten of forty parents are willing to educate their children in Urdu, but registration of the students is always postponed and more than 200 demands are waiting in government courts.[15]

The situation is, of course, even worse for those minor languages which are not listed in the Eighth Schedule, particularly the 'tribal' languages, and Ho, Kurukh/

[12]Ravinder Kelekar, 'Planning for the survival of Konkani', in B.D. Jayaram and K.S. Rajyashree (eds), Goals and Strategies of Development of Indian Languages (Mysore: CIIL, 1998), p. 117.

[13]K.M. Munshi, Indian Constitutional Documents (New Delhi, 1967), vol. 1.

[14]A.A. Siddiqi, 'Evaluation of implementation of developmental programme regarding Urdu', in Jayaram and Rajyashree, Goals and Strategies, 55–68.

[15]Siddiqi contrasts the 2853 and 2103 Urdu-medium schools respectively in Karnataka and Maharashtra with the bare 422 in UP and 251 in MP where there are more important Urdu minorities, but where the political tension with Hindi is far more acute than with Kannada or Marathi (see following discussion). For the case of Sindhi, see C. Daswani, 'Language attrition: The case of Indian Sindhi', in Z. Veneeta and Richard L. Leed (eds), For Gordon H. Fairbanks (Honolulu: University of Hawai Press, 1985); C. Daswani, 'Minority languages in multilingual India: The case of Sindhi', in E.C. Dimcock, B. Kachru, and B. Krishnamurthi (eds), Dimensions of Sociolinguistics in South Asia (New Delhi: Oxford & IBH, 1992).

Oraon, and Mundari, although recognized for primary education in Bihar, are not implemented,[16] nor is it in Orissa, a state with more than a hundred mother tongues, or Rajasthan and Madhya Pradesh, also with many tribal languages. If such languages are really 'endangered' languages, and India's tribal languages now represent less than 2 per cent of the speaking mass (from more than 13 per cent in 1961 and 3.5 per cent in 1981), this decline is partly linked to the side effects of language planning.[17]

The official recognition of a major language with its explicit (financial support in the media, education, and printing) and implicit privileges necessarily entails frustration and often violent protestation from minor languages speakers. The three-language formula, for instance, supposedly aimed at providing linguistic skills in the relevant language of a given region, can end in acute conflict, as was the case in the 1980s in Karnataka after the Gokak Committee was asked to evaluate the relevance of the hierarchy of the taught languages (1979): mother language studied first initially included Sanskrit as a choice with Kannada and Urdu and the final report of the committee in 1985 relegated Sanskrit as a possible choice for third language only along with Persian and Arabic, making Kannada compulsory as a first language. This decision was greeted by strong agitation from the Brahmins, angered by the new downgraded status given to Sanskrit, and the Muslims, angered by the compulsion of taking Kannada instead of Urdu as the first language. Interestingly, the Muslim population (11 per cent) which entered the 'jihad' (the movement indeed was termed a jihad[18]), included the non-Urdu speakers (1 per cent) whose mother tongue was Kannada. Interestingly also, this same population which were now revolting against the compulsory study of Kannada had asked for a Kannada education in 1971 and 1981 through the Urdu delegates in the assembly (Praja Pratinidhi Sabha). That means that language loyalties shifted during the period, becoming more associated with religious loyalties (even without any linguistic basis at all), which confirms the growing instrumentalization and politicization of languages since Independence, and especially since the 1980s.

It thus appears that language planning in independent India, although constantly elaborating new formulae and devices[19] cannot manage to peacefully

[16]They were, at least to a small extent, used in the 1950s and 1960s.

[17]There are, of course, exceptions, among which the vitality of Tulu (Dravidian speech), Bhili (Indo-Aryan), and Santali (Austro-Asiatic), the first one certainly explained by the local language politics and support of the CIIL in Mysore, an institute which has prepared a considerable amount of teaching material in Tulu. Another exception is Nagaland, where sixteen 'tribal' languages are currently used as teaching medium in primary schools, during three years, English medium being used after.

[18]B. Mallikarjun, 'A language movement in Karnataka: Gokak movement', in A.K. Biswas (ed.), Profiles in Indian Languages (Kanpur: Indian Languages Society, 1985), pp. 264–79.

[19]The history of the three-language formula itself is symptomatic of these unsatisfactory efforts, since it was launched by the Central Advisory Board of Education in 1957, criticized and

and efficiently ensure the maintenance of linguistic diversity. If language now seems to act more as a separative force than as a cohesive one, as feared by opponents of linguistic state reorganization, the reason is not linguistic diversity itself, but rather the consciousness of language as a monolithic entity and as a direct expression of community identity. Such a consciousness, widely absent in pre-modern India, gradually developed with the British efforts to map and survey the languages of the colony, providing a radically new representation of the relation of the speaker to his speech (one language, one name, one identity).

II. REPRESENTATIONS: THE WEIGHT OF PHILOLOGISTS IN THIS BIRTH OF LANGUAGE CLAIMS

The integrating political view of languages expressed in the Constitution of India, in fact was not neutral: it both countered and continued the philological tradition which dominated the nineteenth and early twentieth centuries linguistic studies in Europe and India.[20]

It continued the Indo-Aryan comparative studies by echoing the historical approach (language families) of language studies current at the time and by emphasizing the common origin of the great variety of modern Indo-Aryan languages, implicitly validating the genetic approach. This genetic view of language evolution and growth was started by the German school of Neo-grammarians in the early nineteenth century (Pott, Bopp, Lassen, etc.) who first gave scientific arguments to establish the first linguistic family described, Indo-European (at the time rather called as Indo-Germanic). The discovery of a common source beyond the present variety of mutually unintelligible languages happened to be the first modern attempt in the history of language science to explore linguistic evolution with rational 'laws' of change, rational according to the then Western standards. The birth of language 'science' in Europe with the Neo-grammarian and comparatist school, itself the first step in what was to become linguistics, is part of the more general history of sciences at the time; as such, it belongs to an epistemological trend viewing the natural sciences (with Cuvier in palaeontology and botanics, Darwin and his theory of determinism in natural species, Adler in heredity) and their methods as a model for studying any living entity, including language, a

---

reformulated by the Kothari Commission in 1966, tentatively implemented with complex adjustments to local situations by the NCERT (National Commission for Education, Research and Teaching) and is still ignored by many schools.

[20]That the integrating and integrative official language later on turned out to be a support for fundamentalism and itself an integrist rather than integrative language is another matter (see on that shift, my 'Le Hindi en 1947: la question de la langue nationale, ses origines, ses consequences', in *Sahib*, 5, pp. 131–51; and my 'Vaid's poetics of the void: How to resist communal and global terror', *Hindi*, 6 (2002), pp. 81–114.

subclass of human science. Linguistic variety and change were accounted for by the laws of evolution, such as Wackernagel's, Brugmann's, Bartholomae's, and Caland's, in the same way as the classification of natural species resulted in the grouping of various families, and its diversification, too, was accounted for by the laws of evolution (like adaptation).

The German school of scholars who argued for an Indo-Germanic family was, as is well known, triggered off by William Jones's discovery in 1786.[21] In his Third Discourse on the Hindus for the Asiatic Society, Jones unveiled the 'marvellous structure' of Sanskrit grammar along with its 'antiquity' superseding Latin and Greek, two ancient languages exhibiting striking grammatical affinities with Sanskrit.[22] So Sanskrit was immediately recognized as the most ancient hence pure and perfect ancestor of European civilization, the Ursprache for all European languages derived from the unattested Indo-European which was to be reconstructed in the following years. Sanskrit was welcomed as the cradle of European civilization, dethroning Hebrew in the position of absolute origin.[23] The 'marvellous structure' mainly consisted in the flexional structure of the language (casual morphology and highly synthetic verb forms), a marvel further emphasized by philosophers as the very sign of intellectual perfection and fitness for expressing abstract ideas. As early as 1808 in his *Essay on the Language and the Wisdom of Hindus*, Friedrich Schlegel made the flexion a matrix figure in his argument for Indo-Germanic linguistic and cultural perfection.[24] It exhibits, he said, both 'natural simplicity' and a 'power of germination' since it is endowed with an inner strength allowing the word to transform from the inside and behave as a living germ. Such languages were presented as an evidence of the cultural capacity of the Indo-Germanic race, the only one 'naturally gifted for the expression of high spirituality'. They contrasted with agglutinative (aggregative) languages 'naturally rude and imperfect' with their sterile and burdening endless aggregate of suffixes or prefixes, 'particles', sounding like rocks, unpleasant to the ear and hard for the mind to connect.[25] Isolating languages (like Chinese) were even lower in the

---

[21]A discovery which had however already been made by a French missionary, Révérend Père Coeurdoux, who had a few years earlier sent to the Academy of Inscriptions in Paris a memoire regarding the parallel flexional structure of Sanskrit, Greek, and Latin, and their common lexical stock, but the memoire failed to attract the attention of its few readers in the board of the Academy, was kept unnoticed, and was not given any circulation.

[22]William Jones, 'On the Hindu: The third discourse', *Asiatic Researches*, 1 (1788 [1786]).

[23]A more welcome candidate than ancient Egyptian (deciphered just before by Champollion) since it was related to European classical languages.

[24]Friedrich Schlegel, *Essai sur la langue et la sagesse des Hindous* (Paris: Parent Desbarres, 1837 [1808]).

[25]Like Turkish or Dravidian languages, typical examples of agglutinative languages; yet Schlegel's favourite example is Arabic and Hebrew, rather considered today as flexional languages. The poor knowledge about language typology at that time may partly account for this strange classification, but Schlegel's agenda and his bias against Semitic culture were probably more responsible.

hierarchy, closer to the animal cry, with no syntax and no intelligence, a small step above the imitation of natural noise.

Such a formulation was, of course, in tune with the times,[26] when the agenda of philosophers and intellectuals was mainly concerned with shaking off the overwhelming and embarrassing antiquity of Hebrew and the Bible (over Latin and Greek) as the origin of European culture and trying to legitimize a less religious and 'foreign' patronage.[27] Even Jules Michelet, the well-known historian of the French Revolution and rebellious historian, did not resist the sweeping movement to establish the Aryan origins of the family against the Semitic. The *Bible of Humanity* (1864), a book he considered his masterpiece since it summed up the history of mankind from its origin to 'the end of history', is divided into two contrasting parts: the bibles of light (Ramayana, Shah Nameh, Eneida, Iliad, and Odyssey) and the bibles of darkness (the Jewish Bible, the Koran). He, too, lavishly uses the philologists' authority as a new, revolutionary scientific power, which he compares with the recent discovery of electricity, for contrasting the marvellous power of light, sight, female chastity, and purity (the virgin and the mother), male bravery and reason in the three great Aryan cultures, to the sterility, duplicity, darkness, lascivity, weakness, and immorality of the Semite bibles.[28]

The Neo-grammarian school entered the scene at the same time as Michelet, a little later than Schlegel, but philologists usually avoid such extreme formulations[29]—on the contrary, Bopp's monumental *Comparative Grammar of*

---

[26]See Daniel Droixhe, *Genèse du Comparatisme Indo Européen, special issue of Histoire Epistémologie Langage* (1984). Half a century after Schlegel's bestseller had swept European intelligentsia circles, for it soon became a prerequisite of the cultural baggage for every intellectual, we find similar formulations in Pictet, a student of Saussure, who viewed Indo-Europeans as a race designed by Providence to reign all over the world ('race désignée par la providence pour régner sur le monde') and in Lassen (1847), a student of Schlegel. Adolphe Pictet, *Les Origines Indo-Européennes ou les Aryan's primitifs. Essai de paléontologie linguistique* (1859–63); Christian Lassen, *Indische Alterthumskunde* (1847).

[27]Connected in Germany with the nascent nationalism (Creuzer group of mythology scholars, first national grammar of the German language by Fichte).

[28]The opposition (Aryans have the 'enormous privilege, the unique kinghood to see where other races do not see anything, to penetrate worlds of ideas and signs ... by the sheer strength of a lucid vision, a marvellous optic', p. 51) is moulded in the familiar poetic patterns of Michelet (the arid Judea gives him a headache, and 'when I see the caravans of camels in the Arabian desert, I have no other reaction than feeling dreadfully thirsty, dessicated to the bones', whereas the gorgeous greenery of Indian valleys refreshes him like a generous 'river of milk' [sic]. As for the influence of the 'tune of the times' on Michelet, it is obvious he was a reader of Herder's *Philosophical Ideas on the History of Mankind*, translated in French in 1834 by his friend and supporter in College de France Edgar Quinet (Paris: Berger-Levrault). In this book Herder locates the origin of humanity not in Palestine but in Asia, a reason why the work enjoyed huge popularity in Germany and Europe during the nineteenth century. See my 'De La Bible des lumières à la Bible des ténèbres chez J. Michelet', in *L'Europe: Reflets littéraires*, C. Astier et Cl. de grève (eds), (Paris: Klincksieck, 1993), pp. 45–55.

[29]Although Max-Mueller, who is usually sober in his philological work, does not hesitate, however, to refer to the new findings of craniology (measurements of skulls) for hierarchizing human races.

Indo-Germanic Languages (1833) proves the suffixal origin of the flexion, which should have cut short the Schlegelian theory about flexion and flexionality. Yet the burden of this new philology, a 'science' always used for legitimating purposes by historians and philosophers, weighs right from the beginning on nineteenth-century cultural thought, hence irretrievably caught up in the problem of securing a noble and antique cradle for the family of Aryan brothers, opposed to the lower language cultures and races. The most extreme repercussion of Jones's philological discovery occurred, of course, in the twentieth century with Hitler's (or rather his ideological propagandist Rosemberg's) version of the Aryan myth, but, as clearly analysed by Poliakov in the chapter 'The tyranny of linguists', philology was a prerequisite for the theorization of the Semite/Aryan duality in German racial mythology.[30]

Modern (nineteenth century) philology is then ultimately linked to this recurring quest for origins and the construction of the community-group as threatened by the other—it is the emasculated Hellenistic culture and its decadent language and cults that caused the ruin of the Greco-Roman civilization in Michelet's view. According to a now well-accepted analysis, the construction itself of group identity, which is coupled with the quest for origins, requires the construction of an opposite other, necessarily represented as aggressive and dangerous for the survival of the community. As ironically put by Sibony, 'un groupe, ça lie = un groupe s'allie' [a group is a linking factor (ça lie) means that a group gets allied (s'allie)].[31] Organic community is necessarily equal to military alliance.

The descriptive tradition which developed in India after Pischel in 1900—Beames, students of Bloch (himself a pure product of the French philological tradition in the early twentieth century), and Chatterji—is of course totally devoid of such assumptions.[32] Works even quite late in the century like U.N. Tiwari, R.B. Saxena, and S.K. Chatterji, typically entitled 'Evolution of x language' (or its equivalent in Hindi) rather tend to reappraise vernacular modern languages (long seen as a degenerate product of a formerly perfect language), but the discipline itself consolidates the building of language families in documenting the evolution of many Indo-Aryan speeches as historical sprouts of Sanskrit via Prakrits and Apabhramshas in a quasi-organic way. The quest for origins (and its anxiety in European nineteenth-century ideology) is not given foremost status.

And Pott, a major pioneer of the Neo-grammarian school came to associate with the well-known French theoretician of racial superiority, Gobineau (*Die Ungleichheit menschlichen Rassen haupsächlig von Sprachwissenschaftlichen Standpunkte, unter besonderen Berücksichtigung von des Grafen von Gobineau*, 1856).

[30]Léon Poliakov, *Le Mythe Aryen* (Paris: Calman–Levy, 1971).

[31]Daniel Sibony, *Le Lien et la peur* (Paris: Christian Bourgois, 1980).

[32]Although we find in Beames such arguments for the redundant plural agreement of Punjabi adjective and participle (*jatiyan hain*) as the following: this 'useless repetition' (not found in Hindi/Urdu) is a necessity only for the 'uncultivated' and 'rude' mind of Punjabis, unable to grasp things at their first mention.

Besides, Sanskrit had always played the role of absolute origin in the local linguistic tradition and there was nothing new in relating spoken languages to their grand ancestor. The novelty was the 'scientific' method, rationally arguing and providing evidence of the development of the family tree. This family had to be distinguished from others. Although the distinction does not involve racial standards and a hierarchic view, it creates the perception of otherness and categorizes groups as radically distinct with clear-cut boundaries, whereas previously the distinction rather juxtaposed the noble pure Sanskrit and all its 'degenerated' by-products, more or less subsumed into the vast amalgam of Prakrits or Apabhramshas (sometimes including Dravidian languages).[33]

But already since Grierson's times, in a parallel way, similar and reactive, the Dravidian family emerged as a group created by linguistic research collapsed with the quest for origins.[34] In *The Tamilians Eighteen Years Before*, Pillai[35] juxtaposes Dravidian descent with the Indo-Aryan family to the former's advantage, on the very same grounds that Western scholars discarded Semitic ancestry in European culture: more ancient and culturally superior, Tamils not only were a consistent linguistic and cultural family, not to be confused with the Indo-Aryan (their antiquity and originality[36] is proved by the 'letter' *l*, borrowed from the high plateaus of Tibet), but they were the best candidate for qualifying as ancient Indian culture, having already attained a highly sophisticated and urban culture when the primitive Aryan tribes made their appearance.[37] In Pillai, as in scholars of the time, linguistic evidence for this antiquity in the competition with Sanskrit for origin is more lexical than grammatical: among contested etymologies, a number of names of spices, metals, animals, vegetables, quoted by Roman travellers around the first century (Chtesias, Ptolemea, Plinius, and moreover the anonymous author of the *Perypleus of the Erythrean Sea*) usually attributed to Sanskrit, are proved to

[33]For example, in earlier Prakrit grammarians. Markandeya (sixteenth century) clearly excluded the Dravidi (as well as the Odri) from the list of Prakrits.

[34]The huge *Linguistic Survey of India* of Grierson (11 vols, Delhi: Motilal Banarasidass 1967 [1905]) was published in the first years of the century. The case for the other two major families is far less clear and documented than those for Indo-Aryan and Dravidian (the Munda family emerged as such not much later, but due to lack of reliable description and ancient written material, a comparative grammar had to wait until 1875, and there are no competitive claims for origins, although it would not lack historical arguments).

[35]Kanakabhai Pillai, *The Tamilians Eighteen Years Before* (1904).

[36]Jones's arguments for choosing Sanskrit over Latin and Greek as the origin language were exactly the same.

[37]See today the recurrence of this competition in the struggle (linguistically evidenced) for the legacy of the Harappan culture. The ancient Tamils in Pillai, made highly noble and ancient by their Himalayan ancestry, have to be distinguished from the low substrata speaking other languages than the cultivated ones: Minawar and Villavar are recorded as black savages (ultimately related to the Rajasthani Mina and Bhil tribes), a picture retained in Barnett's *Cambridge History* (vol. 1, p. 595). Here again a group joins ranks in making alliance against the outsider.

belong to the Dravidian stock—for example, the names for camphor, ginger, peacock, pepper, rice, and cinnamon.[38] This clear stand against the Indo-Aryan group obeys the same dynamics out of the same premises (quest for origins, competition for antiquity, purity and higher cultural achievements). Such a contrastive construction means that the implicit superiority of Sanskrit conveyed in the designing of the Indo-Aryan family and drawing of its borders is perceived by the other as a kind of rejection to the subaltern world of inferior languages. Even in sound scholarly linguistic research like Caldwell's masterpiece,[39] much more sober in its ideological implications than Pillai, the posited consistency of the group as both distinct (original) and ancient (true cradle of Indian civilization) sounds a clearly vindictive note against Sanskrit and Indo-Aryan, although there is no racial mythology involved. The philologist agenda in India is clearly different from that in Europe, but in both cases there is room for the competition with the other, framed by the methodological pattern: genetic linguistics aiming to form families and sub-families creates outsiders to the family. This initial linguistic consciousness on the part of descriptors, informed by Western science (patterned after natural sciences), was significantly contemporary with the requirement of census to identify one's language, hence perceive it as distinct from the neighbouring languages and as one homogeneous entity which could be named.

The Dravidian family of languages was, a century later, integrated by the Constituents, not as a family of its own (a distinct group eventually conflicting with the other group or groups) but as a number of major languages at the same level as Indo-Aryan languages. Interestingly, neither the Austric family, although identi-fied as such by Smith in the first years of the century, nor the Tibeto-Burman family got any recognition, in spite of Jaypal Singh's motion in the Constituent Assembly for including such tribal languages as Santali (today with twice the number of speakers than Sindhi), Ho, Kurukh, a motion rejected with hardly any discussion. We may ponder on what were Nehru's intentions in scaling down the linguistic diversity to a few major languages supposedly very similar. The refusal to let family groups prevail with their genetic delimitation was certainly consistent with his 'idea of India'[40] as an abstract global idea rather than a con-crete aggregate of well-defined linguistic, regional, and cultural entities,[41] as

[38]Argumentation vehemently opposed by Swaminatha Aiyyar who denounces the ideological bias of such origin fantasies. *Dravidian Theories* (Delhi: Motilal Banarasasidass, 1987 [1975, 1922]). Collection of Lectures by Aiyyar previously published in supplements to *The Tamilian's Friend*, 1922–3, Journal of the Tamil Education Society, Madras.

[39]Caldwell, *Comparative Grammar of Dravidian or South Indian Family of Languages* (1856).

[40]As developed in Khilani's *The Idea of India*.

[41]One of the main bases of Nehru's 'secularism' was his insistence on the impossibility of finding a unity (cultural, religious, historical) other than artificial in the history of India; and that an abstract idea was the only way to shape the new state as one without letting regional particularisms, prevail. However, the refusal of Nehru's followers to let linguistic claims shape the administrative

well as with his extraordinary denigration of linguistic diversity in India. However, the contradictory notion of quotas (for positive discrimination) for certain groups resulted in the well-known situation where regional, cultural, gender, linguistic identities more and more came to substitute group claims and lobbying to a political creed in democracy. Besides, the listing of a few 'major' languages, later on widely criticized,[42] inevitably opened up a dynamics of competition for entering the magical schedule and benefiting from its advantages (education, publishing, media, etc.).

At the same time, the definition of the official language[43] and the linguistic provisions in the Constitution seemed to go against the very notion of grouping languages by 'blood links' with organic roots, and yet the very wish of identifying separate languages and making this identification the condition of recognition or non-recognition was deeply indebted to the previous hundred or so years of historical linguistics. It is the tradition of historical linguistics in India that made possible language classification and linguistic cartography, where boundaries were mainly drawn according to the genetic (vertical) criteria of linguistic affiliation. To describe a language was essentially to assert its genetic affinity in order to put it in the appropriate category (refer to the discourse on Khandeshi or Bhili changing classification). The huge survey of Grierson at the beginning of the century (and the numerous monographs which followed on till the mid-twentieth century), without which the language census would not have been possible, are contemporaneous—the first census dates from 1837. Both enterprises resulted in the requirement for each individual to name his language as a clearly distinct entity (necessarily different from another or other entities) and to choose one language as his mother tongue, although every census officer has met with people not knowing which their 'real' language is (a situation still current). In Ganjam district in Orissa, for example, an oft-cited case in Indian sociolinguistics, speakers are unable to say whether they speak Oriya or Telugu, although the Indo-Aryan and Dravidian families are supposed to radically differ from each other. As Paul Brass states, 'The language censuses in north India are political, not philological, documents,'[44] but it should be borne in mind that philological documents too are far from language reality in usage and consciousness.

Linguistic consciousness then seemed to have stemmed from the classificatory passion of the colonial agenda, at least a certain type of linguistic consciousness with clear-cut boundaries juxtaposing same and other, grounded on rigid structural

---

map of India when they opposed a linguistic state reorganization, for fear of 'balkanization', was not to prevail in the end as is well known (see preceding pages).

[42]Gupta et al., *Language and the State.*

[43]Deliberately not national language. See my 'Le hindi en 1947: La question de la langue nationale, ses origines, ses conséquences', *Sahib* 5 (1997), pp. 133–51.

[44]Brass, *Language, Religion and Politics*, p. 190.

systems, which was not (and still is not) present in the grass roots multilingual ethos. Later, encouraged by identity claims of many different orders, the initial perception of language as a boundary has coincided with the first descriptive attempts shaped by historical linguistics, with all its European, more or less implicit, ideology. The British requirement to classify, name, and map greatly contrasted with the local perception which used different, more intuitive, fuzzy ways of locating as described in Kipling's *Kim*, for instance. The superimposition of 'scientific' and rational methods of categorizing provided the grounds for a distinctive language consciousness later on to develop into language claims and conflicts. In a similar way, David Scott, studying the emergence of Sinhalese religious consciousness, points out after Carter and Malalgola that words referring to concepts of 'religion' and 'Buddhism' are of fairly recent origin.[45] This is not to say that people did not think about Buddha or dhamma or *sangha* prior to British colonization, but that such a concept in the modern meaning of a 'natural, abstract, systematic entity', a 'demarcated system of doctrines-scriptures-beliefs' was not available prior to the encounter with missionaries, and became a reified ideological entity readily available for polemical and adversarial use through the religious debates and controversies between Christians and Buddhists during the mid-nineteenth century. Languages as demarcated systems and fixed entities, similarly, do not seem to be part of the native representation, and still are not in many parts of traditional India untouched by modern education.

I will show in the next section (III) that a given language, even the same feature in a given language, can be accounted for in two ways: inner (vertical) evolution and areal (horizontal) contact, which blurs boundaries drawn by genetic grouping. Moreover, the study of lower colloquial varieties (generally neglected by historical grammar) and their interactional use pattern by sociolinguists shows that the axiom one person/one language/one linguistic system has little relevance in a grass roots multilingual environment (Section IV).

III. VERTICAL OR HORIZONTAL LINKS: BLOOD OR NEIGHBOURHOOD? THE INTERNAL EVIDENCE OF LANGUAGES

Even if we wish to contain the description within the limits of genetic affiliation only, it may happen that evolution produces quite original developments within the family, sometimes to the point that it loses all resemblance with its ancestor. Such is the case with the so-called ergative structure in western Indo-Aryan speeches like Hindi/Urdu or Punjabi: the agent (subject?) is marked (+*ne*) and the predicate, without personal endings, agrees with the patient (object?), a major typological feature found in Caucasian or Australian languages too. This structure has long

---

[45]David Scott, 'Toleration and historical traditions of difference', in *Subaltern Studies* (New Delhi: Oxford University Press, 2000), vol. 11, pp. 288–9.

been described in terms of traditional (Sanskrit) grammar as a passive (*karmani*) or middle (*bhavi*) voice, with the result of making Hindi like Sanskrit in this respect. The description of nominal morphology within the flexional frame of the eight Sanskrit cases is still in vogue in traditional grammars used in schools and suggested by the Kendriya Hindi Sansthan[46] for the teaching of Hindi in government exams. Relating Hindi and other modern Indo-Aryan vernaculars to the prestigious ancestor at the expense of the language's own specificity has been the usual drawback of early grammars. Continuing this tradition now amounts to emphasizing a lost flexional structure and obliterating affinities with the non-flexional languages spoken in the area.

The ergative structure indeed comes from the evolution of the purely Indo-Aryan system, as shown by philologists like Bloch[47] or Chatterji[48] on textual sources: the use of the passive past participle, agreeing like an adjective with what is now perceived as the object:

Sanskrit	*mama / maya*	*tat*	*krtam*	
origin of	I-gen/-instr (of/by me)	this-ns	done-ns	'I did this'
Hindi	*maine yah*	*kiya*		
	I-erg this-ms	done-ms	'I did this'	

(*ne* being a recent reinforcement of the oblique, absent in Braj: and in many dialects we still find the oblique without *ne*, in Jaisalmeri for instance.) This pattern was generalized in classical Sanskrit for the expression of a past/perfect transitive event, the result being treated as the pivot of the statement, the agent as a peripheric figure. But in the modern language it is no longer a passive pattern, nor is it active or middle, it represents a distinct pattern well known in other natural languages, which makes Hindi typologically closer to Georgian or Dyirbal on this respect, although the inner logic of the system itself accounts for the apparent aberration of western Indo-Aryan ergative languages within the Indo-European family.

But the same Sanskrit syntactic pattern is also at the origin of the eastern Indo-Aryan languages which do not have ergative structure but a 'normal' predicate with personal endings and a 'normal' direct subject, like Bengali:

ami boita porlam
I book read-past-1   'I read the book'

[46]Aryendra Sharma's reference grammar (1958) in Hindi mentions the eight cases and three voices. Modern, 'linguistic' grammars like Kachru's (1980) on the contrary align the ergative structure (and other categories) on the English language, considering the morphology as an archaic, irrelevant relic of the past, a surface feature for the 'normal' deep structure subject verb object. In both descriptions, a foreign categorical frame serves as the underlying model for description.

[47]Jules Bloch, 1935, *Indo-Aryan from the Vedas to Modern Times* and his *Formation de la langue marathe* (Paris: Campion, 1919).

[48]S.K. Chatterji, *The Origin and Development of the Bengali Language* (Delhi: Motilal Banarsidas, 1926).

Asoka's well known first sentence of the first edict uses an instrumental agent and nominative

iyam dhammalipi-fs nom *devanampriena Priyadassena* ranna-ms-instr *lekhapita-fs* nom
This law scripture by the god-loved friendly-looking king written-causative
'the friendly looking king loved by the gods wrote this law scripture'

This pattern gave both the ergative western IA and the non-ergative eastern IA. If we look into older stages of languages, we also find traces of ergativity (*mai bhujila* by-me understood, in old Bengali, *kahini sunili*, story listened, '[they] heard the story', before the erosion of gender agreement during the fourteenth–fifteenth centuries), forms later reshaped into an active pattern with personal endings like 'I read the book' above.

In a symmetric way the formation of future was also adjectival and also with an oblique agent. It too happened to lose its ergativity, retaining only the –b- from the obligative passive participle (*tavya*) in eastern speeches.[49]

Then there is clearly a process of differentiation stemming from the very inner logic of systems (and sometimes amounting to major typological differences), but one cannot explain why the eastern (Magadhean) and western (Saurasenic) speeches differ so strikingly, each having followed a logic of its own, similarly yet differently evolving logical paths from the original pattern in keeping with its logic.[50]

What the best scholars of the early twentieth century[51] could already see, in complete deviance from historical linguistics, is that areal contact has played a major role in the whole area, geographically close languages deeply influencing

----

[49]The structure involves a passive obligative participle and agent in the oblique case if present:
    tribhir yatavyam 'the three will go' (literally by the three should be gone)
Asoka's formulation in the same context as above has:
    iha na samajo kattavyo (Sauraseni) *na samaje kattavye* (Magadhean)
    here no meeting is to be made = one shall not do meeting,
This passive obligative adjective in *-tavya* gave the specific –b- future in Neo Magadhean speeches like Bengali and Eastern Hindi, further turned into an active with personal endings (same story as for the ergative) whereas the Western languages have periphrastic futures. More rarely, the old sigmatic future (Sindhi, old Jaisalmeri). The above two structures in classical Sanskrit also happen to be the basis for late Latin perfect and future, of passive formation, later also reshaped into the active pattern but by different means (the have verb):
    mihi id factum = *maya tat krtam, mihi id faciendum*= *maya tat kartavyam*,
    later on > *ego id factum habeo*, giving the *avoir* perfect and future in Roman languages: *j'ai fait* in the perfect, *je fer-ai* in the future.
[50]My *Hindi Grammar* (München: Lincom Europa, 2004), pp. 185–199.
[51]Bloch, J. *Formation de la langue marathe* and S.K. Chatterji, *The Origin and Development of the Bengali Language*. The latter was a disciple of Bloch, himself a Dravidologist (*La Structure grammaticale des langues dravidiennes*, 1946). As opposed to Meillet (the French father of comparative historical linguistics), Bloch was ready to accept areal influence because of his double formation (Dravidian and Indo-Aryan studies).

each other. The evolutions discussed were probably helped by contact, since the eastern Indo-Aryan languages also started differentiating from western Indo-Aryan by a number of correlated features like the loss of gender and agreement other than person agreement, which is closer to the Dravidian than the Sanskrit pattern. Whatever the reason for convergence with Dravidian languages, a reliable scholar like S.K. Chatterji could relate the Bengali verbal system to the Dravidian one, which has only the verb–subject agreement and no verb–object agreement.[52] Such features create what linguists call isoglosses (defined by the extension of a special feature or a cluster of features) within the major structural family. Micro isoglosses are observable in the eastern Indo-Aryan speeches: Magahi and Maithili[53] present a very complex pattern of agreement with more than one argument, including subject, object, indirect arguments, and this pattern has been shown to present strong similarities with the Munda pattern, which indexes all major arguments on the predicate.[54]

This shows that convergence and diffusion have been as important as differentiation. The discovery of the impact of such contacts prompted first Kuiper then Andronov and Emeneau[55] to posit an Indian linguistic area, in many features homogeneous and consistent in spite of the many specificities still distinguishing the various languages spoken in the area. The first finding was to trace back to Sanskrit some early borrowings from Dravidian at phonological, lexical, and syntactic levels (retroflexion,[56] a fair amount of words like *phalam / paLam* ripe, fruit, the five grammatical meanings of the Dravidian -*um* particle diffused in the five uses of Skr *api* > Hin *bhi*, Mar *i*,[57] the conjunctive participle which came to be one of the pan-Indian features, etc.). And borrowing from the so-called Austric or Austro-Asiatic languages (*punya, purush* are of Munda origin according to Kuiper) have been studied up to Witzler's study on Vedic language and its

---

[52]Chatterji, *The Origin and Development of the Bengali Language*, pp. 807, 967.

[53]Ramawatar Yadav, *A Reference Grammar of Maithili* (Delhi: Munshiram Manoharlal, 1997).

[54]See in Magahi the verb agreement with both subject (1st person) and object (3rd person) : *ham okraa dekh-l-i-ai* (I he-object see-past-1–3) 'I saw him'. Similarly in Mundari, verb see (lel) agrees with both subject and object : *lel-jjad-in-a-e* (see-present-perfect-1s-predicative mark-3s) 'he has seen me'.

[55]F.B.J. Kuiper, *Proto-Munda Words in Sanskrit* (1948); his *Aryans in the Rig Veda* (Amsterdam/ Atlanta: Rodopi, 1991); and his 'A hunt for possible objections', *Indo-Iranian Journal*, 38 (1995), pp. 238–61; M.S. Andronov, 'On the typological similarity of New-Indo-Aryan and Dravidian', *Indian Linguistics* 25 (1964), pp. 119–26. Murray B. Emeneau, *Essays on Language and the Linguistic Area* (Stanford: Stanford University Press, 1980).

[56]Although controversial, cerebralization can be spontaneous, Deshpande (1979), yet its phonological role, clear opposition with dentals, has certainly been favoured by the contact with Dravidian.

[57]Emeneau (*Essays on Language*) shows that the five meanings of *api* (concessive, generalizing/ indefinite, coordinative, augmentative) are, in fact a calque from the Dravidian suffix -*um*.

foreign borrowings (conference in College de France in 2001). Such affinities are, of course, far more developed in modern languages and it is now widely acknowledged that all the four original families (Indo-Aryan, Dravidian, Austric, Tibeto-Burman) of languages in contact on the subcontinent today share more specific features among themselves than any one does with an external member of the family: for instance Bengali and Irish, both Indo-European, are typologically more distant than Bengali and Telugu, although both Bengali and Telugu stem from distinct genetic families. To mention only a few of the pan-Indian features: retroflexion (the dental d contrasts with the retroflex D), serial verbs (*aa jao, kha lena, nikal jana*, come go, eat take, leave go, with aspectual and attitudinal meanings), dative 'subjects' (*mujhe pyas lagi hai, mujhe malum hai*, to-me thirst is, to-me know, for 'I am thirsty, I know'), subject-object-verb word order, lack of 'have' verb, verbo-nominal predicates (*intazar karna, yad hona*, waiting do, memory be, for 'to wait, to remember'), marking of the human or specific object (*usko bulao, isko rakh do*, to-him call, to-it place give, for 'call him, put it down'), reduplication and echo formation (*garam-garam, chai-wai*, hot-hot, tea). Some of these features can be traced from diffusion: retroflexion and word order are said to have been diffused to Indo-Aryan from Dravidian, marked object from Dravidian, later favoured by Persian influence; some seem to be innovations, new features unknown in each of the languages in contact: verb seriality, maybe oblique subjects, the wide use of reduplication, pairing lexical synonyms *maa-baap* (mother-father, 'parents', *lena-dena* take-give, 'exchange'), and other forms of iconicity frequent in Creole languages.

Such a concept of linguistic area means that contact has been even more prevalent than genetic affiliation: the links of blood, so to speak, were superseded by links of neighbourhood. But this is a fact that was always hard to swallow for the traditional comparatist, as suggested by the famous quarrel between Meillet the Indo-Europeanist, and Schuchart, the first Creolist, a German scholar specializing in eastern Asian languages, at the beginning of the twentieth century.

At a micro level similar processes have been observed, defining micro linguistic areas, the most commented being Marathi, since the founding work of Jules Bloch in the 1920s, to the extent that is has been described[58] as a Creolization of Indo-Aryan by Dravidian (acting as the substratum): for instance Marathi has three genders (a typically Old-Indo-Aryan feature) but an inclusive versus exclusive distinction for 'we' (*apan* includes the speaker whereas *amhi* does not, like the Dravidian pair *nam/nangal* for 'we'), it uses the *ki* 'that' for reported speech and thought, but also the typically Dravidian device of the 'quotative' (a 'say' verb grammaticized into the meaning of 'that', *mhanun*, like Tamil *enru*, [literally 'having

---

[58]Franklin C. Southworth, 'Detecting prior Creotization: An analysis of the historical origins of Marathi', in D. Hymes (ed.), *Pidgnization and Creotization of Languages* (Cambridge: Cambridge University Press, 1971); Franklin C. Southworth and M.L. Apte, *Contact and Convergence in South Asian Languages.* (Special volume of the *International Journal of Dravidian Linguistics*, 3 (1974).

said'] which is also used for conditional *mhanje* in Marathi and *enraal* in Tamil), it has the local reflexive *swatah* (co-referring with a term in the clause in a typically Indo-Aryan manner) but also the long distance reflexive *apliya* (co-referring with a term outside the clause) like the Dravidian *tan/tanu*.

The study of Dakkhini Hindi/Urdu, a southern non-standard variety of Hindi/Urdu spoken in Dravidian environment (Mysore, Madras, Hyderabad), leads to similar findings: it has a quotative (*bolke* literally 'having said') used for reporting speech or thought instead of *ki* 'that', it exhibits partial loss of grammatical gender and de-aspiration, erosion of agreement, all features probably due to the Dravidian influence. The following example of Dakkhini Urdu (DU) exhibits two Dravidian features (use of quotative and of a specific word for 'tomorrow' distinct from 'yesterday' as does Dravidian whereas standard Hindi/Urdu (SH/U) has the same lexical unit for both, *kal*, and uses a 'that' conjunction, *ki*):

DU   *un/o saban   atu   kako   bolya*
        he to-morrow come-1s disant dit-ms
        he said he will come tomorrow
SH/U   *usne kahaa   ki main kal   aaungaa*
        he-erg say-ms that I tomorrow come-fut-ms (same meaning)
Tamil   *avan   naalai varukkireen   en̠ru   connaan*
Telugu *vaaDu reepu   vastaan   ani   ceppyaadu*
        he tomorrow come-pres-1s quot say-past-1s[59] (same meaning)

If not Creolized languages in the restricted meaning, Indian languages are all more or less hybrid languages—de Selva claimed that Prakrits were the result of a Creolization of Sanskrit.[60] Hybridization has been highly productive in the entire area, including more radical forms like the pidgins used as lingua franca like *bazari* Hindi[61] or new languages like Nagamese (an Assamese IA structure with a Tibeto-Burman Naga lexicon).[62]

[59]From Mohiddin Khader, *Dakkhini Urdu* (Annamalai, 1980); Hans R. Dua, *Language Use, Attitude and Identity among Linguistic Minorities: A Case Study of Dakkhini Urdu Speakers in Mysore* (Mysore, 1986). Quotative is also used in Dakkhini for expressive hypothesis, with a special form of verb 'say' (*ka-*) to which the correlative *to* is suffixed ('that, then' *to*). This correlative, which initiates the main clause in standard Hindi/Urdu after a hypothetic clause, is then in the same position as the Dravidian quotative (the special *en̠raal* form for hypothesis). A clear case of re-analysis is also observable in the Dakkhini relative construction (a Dravidian structure with an Indo-Aryan morphologic expression).

> DU   *tu aatuu kato mai bii aatuun* you come pres say-then I too come-pres
> Telugu *niivu vastaananTe neenu kuuda vastaanu*   you come-pres-quot.cond I too come-pres
> Tamil *nii varukkireen en̠raal naanum varukkireen*   same gloss
>   'if you come I too will come'

[60]A.M. de Selva, and W.M. Sugathpala, *Linguistic Diversity* (Annamalai, 1975).

[61]K.S. Rajyashree, 'Sadari of Orissa', in K.P. Acharya, Rekha Sharma, Sam Mohan Lal, and K.S. Rajyashree, *Pidgins and Creoles as Languages of Wider Communication*, CIIL Series in Sociolinguistics 4 (Mysore, 1987).

[62]M.V. Shreedhar, *Standardized Grammar of Naga Pidgin* (Mysore: CIIL, 1985).

All these micro and macro processes of convergence can only be explained by a prolonged contact involving societal bilingualism, and the present 'grass roots multilingualism' is still a reflexion of the ancient pluri-lingual situation, responsible for the dynamics of linguistic change. They rely on specific social interactions.

IV. A SPECIFIC PATTERN OF INTERACTION: LANGUAGES LIVE TOGETHER SEPARATELY

One of the most frequent observations in Indian sociolinguistics and language-shift studies is the extraordinary resilience of language maintenance in diasporic situations all over India.[63] This very high degree of language maintenance in communities living in a different linguistic environment has even been seen as the linguistic specificity of India, as opposed to the usual language-shift observable in other countries resulting in the 'melting pot' phenomenon (typical evolution of language migrant communities in the USA and Europe). One of the oft-quoted examples is that of the Saurastri-speaking (a variety of Gujarati) community in Tamil Nadu, which is still speaking its original mother tongue after centuries. Similarly, Tamil speaking migrants to the Kannada-speaking Bangalore still maintain their language, to varying degrees according to the various communities, depending on the language-use patterns and cultural habits.[64]

The sociolinguists' findings on the present situation[65] can certainly apply to the ancient one although it is not historically documented or very scantily so. The fact that languages are strikingly well maintained in multilingual settings cannot be separate from the language-use patterns widely dominant in traditional India, where there is no such thing as one language for each and every communication.

Years ago Pandit noted that one of the reasons for this remarkable main-tenance is the pattern of language use.[66] The classic example is of the Gujarati merchant one century ago, who uses Kacchi (a dialect of Gujarati) in the local market, Marathi for wider transactions in the region, standard Gujarati for read-ings, Hindustani when he travels (railway station), Urdu in the mosque, with some Persian and Arabic, but also *sant bhasha* in devotional songs, his variety of Gujarati for family interaction, English when dealing with officials. Many examples of the kind can easily be provided in the Punjabi context. Such a situation provides the multilingual speaker with a setting where each language has a definite role with little overlap. What is very important is that there is no competition between the various segments of the verbal repertoire, each one in its appropriate sphere being the main language, the choice of language being determined by the type of exchange, each language being equally part of the social exchange and required

[63]P.B. Pandit, *Language in a Plural Society* (Delhi, 1977), p. 9.

[64]S. Mohan Lal, *Convergence and Language Shift in a Linguistic Minority: A Sociolinguistic Study of Tamils in Bangalore City* (Mysore, 1986).

[65]Pandit, *Language in a Plural Society*; Dimcock et al., *Dimensions of Sociolinguistics*.

[66]Pandit, *Language in a Plural Society*.

by the socio-economic life of the community. As stated by R.N. Srivastava, each language is part of the whole and none is apart, which provides for the real integration of plurality.[67] A speaker is not defined as a one-language user but as a shifting user of a multi-layered repertoire, each segment being connected with a specific role of the individual within a highly segmented society. Interactional patterns echo that segmentation with fluid adjustments. For instance, studies on Bengali and Punjabi maintenance[68] convincingly show that the degree of maintenance is proportionate to the selective use of the language under consideration in shifting social roles.[69] One of the consequences on the linguistic system is a large degree of linguistic tolerance, no normative judgment, and a great flexibility in uses gained by the constant adjustment of speaker and addressee, aiming more at communicational performance than correctness. Everyday interaction and its typical adjustments, of course, involve the colloquial (lower) variety of languages and not the highly standardized high varieties.

Incidentally, we may wonder if the very notion of linguistic system as a bound stabilized monolithic entity still retains its meaning in such settings—think of the speakers of border villages, like Ganjam in Orissa, bordering Andhra, who cannot tell if their mother tongue is Telugu or Oriya and return either one to the Census officer. Gumperz has shown for the Kuvrup speakers (Ku) in southern Madhya Pradesh that a word by word equivalent is achieved in the local varieties of Marathi (M), Kannada (K), and Hindi (H), with a heavy lexical borrowing.[70] For instance, see the lower local varieties of Kannada and Marathi (Ku), far closer and simpler (no 'about' post-position, genitive formation for the possessive in K) than their standard equivalent (S):

KKu   *id nam de garibstiti heLi.d.ew nawr*
MKu   *he am ca garibstiti sangit.l.a ami*
       this we of poverty have spoken we
       'we spoke of our poverty'

[67]R.N. Srivastava, *Studies in Language and Linguistics, vol. 3, Bi/multilingualism* (Delhi: Kalinga, 1994).

[68]Aditi Mukherjee, *Language Maintenance and Language Shift: Punjabis and Bengalis in Delhi* (Delhi: Bahri, 1996); Rangila Ranjit Singh, *Maintenance of Panjabi Language in Delhi, A Sociological Study* (Mysore: CIIL, 1986).

[69]See also M.V. Shreedhar, introduction of *Standardized Grammar of Naga Pidgin* for language-use patterns in Nagaland, and in general the publications of the CIIL on language-use patterns (Himachal Pradesh, Punjab). Such interactions and correlation of language switch (code switching) and role change is sometimes surprising. G.M. Trivedi (*Sociolinguistics Study in an Andhra Village* [Calcutta, 1983], for instance shows the role of the use of Urdu by Telugu Brahmins between themselves in an Andhra village for asserting their social prestige in exhibiting some knowledge of the once culturally dominant language, whereas the same individual never considers modern local Urdu as being connected with the high variety of Urdu).

[70]John J. Gumperz, *Language in Social Groups*, essays selected and introduced by Anwar S. Dil (Stanford: Stanford University Press, 1971).

KS   *navu namma baDatanada bagge heLidevu*
       we we-obl poverty-obl about speak-past-1p
MS   *am amci garibstiti badal sangitlaa*
       we we-gen-fs pauvreté-fs about speak-past-ms

In the next example, local Kannada uses interrogative for tag questions (a typical Indo-Aryan device), omits specific accusative marker with non-human (Indo-Aryan omits it more freely than Dravidian), and, conversely, Urdu and Marathi local variants have subject agreement like Dravidian languages, whereas their standard counterparts have either subject–object agreement (Marathi in the first two persons) or only object agreement (Urdu):

UKu   *kya baba ghoRi di.ya kya?*
MKu   *kya baba ghoRi dil-as kya?*
KKu   *yan appa kuddri kwatti yan*
       how father horse give-past interr
       'eh, you have sold the horse, no?'

H/US   *kyaa, bhaii, ghoRii bec d-ii kyaa ?*
       interr. brother, horse-fs sell give-past-fs inter
MS   *kay baba ghoRi vik-un Takl-i-s ka ?*
       interr brother, horse-fs sell-part throw-past-fs-2s « tag »[71]
KS   *eno appa heNNu kudurey-annu mar-id-ir-a ?*
       how (adress), father, horse-acc sell-past-2p-Q

The standard varieties in Punjabi (SP), Hindi (SH), and Urdu (SU) for the statement 'how much does it cost?', show numerous differences at every level:[72]

1 SH   *iskaa kyaa bhaav hai?*
2 SU   *iskii kyaa qiimat hai?*
3 SP   *edaa kii pàaw ai?*
       of-it interr price is

(2) in Urdu has a distinctly Urdu lexical item, *qiimat*, feminine (< Arabic, pronounced with the distinctively Urdu back velar q) for price, whereas (1) in Hindi uses the *tadbhav* term *bhaav*, masculine. High Punjabi in (3) uses a word with the same origin, but with the initial voiced consonant devoiced and followed by a low tone vowel,[73] a feature ignored by neighbouring languages: *pàaw* corresponds to Hindi *bhaav* (like *kàr* to *ghar* 'house'). The Hindi nominal relator

---

[71] For such 'tag' questions expressing surprise or asking for confirmation, Marathi would rather use a verbal element (derived from 'seem' verb, *vaTle*).

[72] Gumperz examples enlarged (in Gumperz the only comparison for lower variety is the standard Punjabi, *edii kii pàuu haigii*, of which several segments are not accepted by all standard speakers).

[73] According to the tonal system of Punjabi.

(genitive) k + gender-number, 'of', has the Punjabi correspondent d + gender-number, so that it is easy to transfer from one language to the other by simple rules, which is not the case for the pronominal form (no oblique-direct distinction in Punjabi) nor for the toned lexical item. These are the two elements that Delhi colloquial Punjabi (P') calques from spoken Hindi (CoH), lexically close to colloquial Urdu (CoU) :

P'	*isdii kii kimat aigii ?*
CoH/CoU	*iskii kyaa kiimat hai / ai ?*

P' maintains the relator d- of Punjabi, the interrogative k- common to all three languages, and selects the common word used in spoken varieties of Hindustani, itself devoid of its typically Urdu phonetic specificity (q, unknown in Indo-Aryan, becomes k). A common denominator obtains at the lexical, morphological, and phonetic levels, facilitated by conversational convergence (phonetics diverges between Hindi and Urdu in the high registers). Delhi Punjabiphones are known to replace numerous grammatical Punjabi words by their Hindi equivalents (Hin *itna* for Punj *enna* 'so much', of similar origin, *saath* for *naal* 'with', from different origin), and to borrow usual vocabulary (Hindi *dukaan* for Punjabi *haTTi*, 'shop'). Conversely, in Punjabi Hindi speakers, the typically Punjabi devoicing-de-aspiration cum low tone is a dominant feature, and the compensating vowel lengthening with cluster simplification is not realized (P *gajjar, satt*, H *gaajar, saat*).[74]

Linguistic identity as well as a distinct linguistic system (a notion challenged by Creolists too like Le Page[75]) have little relevance in such multilayered settings where multiple belongings according to the various social roles echo the variety of the linguistic repertoire.

What is at stake in this 'grassroot' multilingualism—certainly a good image of ancient past—is the dialectic of 'functional heterogeneity' as labelled by Khubchandani[76] within this specific communicational ethos: each language is dominant in its domain of use, favoured by the fact that languages are more like a continuum with no clear boundaries (for instance north India is a 'fluid zone' from Punjab to Bengal), with a good deal of inter-intelligibility between two adjacent languages, favoured by the constant adjustment required by the traditional pattern of life. The HUP fluid zone claimed to be characteristic of the Hindi-Urdu-Punjabi continuum by Khubchandani is definitely a major north Indian feature, and it is echoed by the north-south continuum (see Ganjam speakers), as well as by the

---

[74]A feature which could be accounted for as conservatism, since it reflects the middle-Indian phase when distinct consonants were assimilated (germination) but not yet simplified into a single consonant with lengthening of the vowel.

[75]R. Le Page, 'You never can tell where a word comes from: Language contact in a diffuse setting', in Hakon yaar Ernst (ed.) *For Gordon Fairbanks* (1992).

[76]Lakchman M. Khubchandani, *Revisualizing Boundaries: A Plurilingual Ethos* (Delhi: Sage, 1997).

diglossic continuum (between low and high varieties). According to Srivastava, 'There is a continuous chain from the most illiterate variety of local village dialect to the highly specialized role of the (formally learned) official language, with a reciprocal intelligibility between the hierarchically ordered adjacent areas.'[77]

All this started to change with the institutionalization of clear-cut linguistic identities, standardization, and normative behaviour. A new dynamics of competition tends to substitute the traditional functional heterogeneity, domains of use largely overlap, and dominant languages appear as a threat for dominated languages (competition for hegemony, regional, national, or even local). The considerable attrition of tribal languages, some of them already extinguished, is sad evidence of these trends.[78] The roots of such a shift can be traced back to the contradictory provisions of the Constitution. Articles on the protection of minority rights ensure that minority languages be granted certain rights in a democratic way (to be classified as such, therefore defined as clear-cut entities, calling for exclusive identification). On the other hand, the very listing of the so-called scheduled languages in the Eighth Schedule was the starting point of a competitive dynamics aiming at including other languages for proper recognition, which means that a language not included is endangered.[79] A few years earlier, an important book on the Eighth Schedule has shown the perverse effects of linguistic recognition for dominated languages,[80] to that extent that D.N. Pattanayak, a fervent opponent of the Eighth Schedule, simply proposed its abolition since it encourages both a competitive anti-democratic dynamics and also results in exclusive and aggressive linguistic loyalties totally irrelevant in the traditional grass roots, multilingual setting.

Clear-cut identities, and moreover the necessary standardization and modernization of scheduled (or otherwise recognized) languages, have brought out artificial neology, burdened with unnatural *tatsam* and their phonological patterns opposed to the new Indo-Aryan phonemics, normative attitudes, and more and more distinctive features so that the grassroot fluidity and continuum seem to be endangered. 'Modernization' as it has been implemented so far goes against the 'composite' nature of the would-be national language in the Constitution (Art. 351 seq), which advocates large borrowings from the regional languages and dialects. Srivastava's continuum between dialectal and official varieties (which may be a continuum between regional or socially lower varieties and the standard) is getting more and more broken. Education in the formal variety (in its most rigid and cut-off form) may then alienate regional speakers, especially of Hindi which

---

[77]Srivastava, *Bi/multilingualism*, p. 58.

[78]K.S. Singh and S. Manoharan, *Languages and Script (People of India, vol. 9)* (Delhi, 1993).

[79]No tribal language is included in the Schedule until now, and only one non-Indo-Aryan non-Dravidian one is. The need for inclusion of major tribal languages (Santali, with more than 5 million speakers, Ho, Kurrukh) was dismissed by Nehru and others when proposed by Jaypal Singh in the Constitution Debates.

[80]Gupta et al., *Language and the State.*

encompasses a high number of diverse dialects (331), in such a way that they become semi-literate or inarticulate,[81] because of non-intelligibility between mother variety and official standard. Non-intelligibility of standard Hindi in the Hindi belt has often been stigmatized as a major cause of social injustice (for instance, administrative documents, police complaints have to be filed in something like a foreign language to villagers), in a present situation which paradoxically comes very close to the ancient diglossic situation (Persian as the court language) which MacDonnell tried to solve when imposing Hindi as a court language.

Today, linguistic loyalties and identity claims of 'endangered' languages build their arguments on the implicit rejection of such a 'fluid continuum', helped in this rejection by schooling strategies and official 'modernization' and standardization. The struggle for recognition in the Eighth Schedule may secure advantages[82] but endangers the grassroot type of language evolution and interaction, since it construes distinct rigid entities, eventually conflicting entities, where there was previously something like a fluid continuum.

One of the most extreme cases is the separation of Hindi and Urdu, two enemies born out of the splitting of colloquial Hindustani, the popular (lower variety) language paradoxically claimed by Gandhi as the should-be national language. Its integrative ability (linguistic vector of both Hindus and Muslims in Gandhi's view) paradoxically turned into the maximal separatist device when high varieties (Persianized versus Sanskritized) are concerned, to such an extent that the Hindustani speaker, Nehru, confessed that he did not understand a word in either the Hindi or Urdu version of the Constitution. This linguistic war, documented by Rai,[83] started in the nineteenth century (*Hindi Urdu ki Larai*, 1886, is not its first episode), and it is interesting to see a liberal writer and critic like Raja Shiv Prasad (compared to Lakshman Singh, Raja Shiv Prasad was not only tolerant but wishing for a hybrid Hindi) come to exactly the same radical conclusion as Michelet: Urdu is viewed as a Semitic element alienating Aryans from their Aryan speech.[84] Other writers of the time view Urdu as a seductive and degenerate harlot whereas Hindi is viewed as the chaste virtuous elder wife or the pure virgin, both threatened by the destructive seduction of the harlot. P.D. Tandon, more than half a century later (8 April 1946), still claimed: 'Those who oppose Hindi as a

---

[81]K.M. Tiwari, 'Linguistic Deprivation among the socially disadvantaged in Bihar', *International Journal of Dravidian Linguistics* (1985), pp. 8–81. Alok Rai, *Hindi Nationalism* (New Delhi, 2001).

[82]This is not even certain, given the market situation (Peggy Mohan in Gupta et al., *Language and the State*): vitality of a language (maintenance) cannot be compelled by mandatory bilinguism in schools and official areas (Sumi Krishna forthrightly states that administrative vernacularization is largely an empty decorum). A newly 'recognized' language like Konkani may feel threatened by English now even more than by Marathi previously (Kelekar, 'Planning for the Survival of Konkani').

[83]Rai, *Hindi Nationalism*.

[84]Shiv Prasad's Memoir in 1868.

national language and Nagari as a national script are still following a policy of anti-national appeasement.' And in the 1960s, the same discourse—'a foreign script and alien culture'—was still enacting the classical scenario 'un groupe ça lie = s'allie'. But in Michelet's case, the binary opposition aimed at discarding non-Indo-European languages and cultures within a genetic pattern, whereas in the case of the Hindiwallahs, since nobody could deny the Indo-Aryanness of Urdu, genetically as well as structurally, the tension focused on the script question: only the script was a possible linguistic pretext to divide brothers, a script which indeed compelled Nehru to rely twice on vote, although he claimed that democracy could only be secured by consensual resolutions (see Section I here). The divisive device worked and brothers became more and more estranged: I do not think many non-Muslim citizens today declare Urdu as their mother tongue. They were more than ten million in the early 1960s.

This takes us back to the questions raised in Section I: how to reconcile official protection of plurality (the rights of linguistic minorities in Articles 29 and 30) and avoid the perverse dialectic of hegemony and competition; how to recognize separate identities in order to prevent the small being absorbed by the bigger and levelled in a melting-pot model and without endangering the weakest by showing their difference; how to reconcile linguistic identity and loyalty as one and single and respect of diversity and pluralism.

There are counter-examples, like the Sadari-speaking Munda tribes, who dissociate ethnic and cultural identity from linguistic identity, since they shifted to a dialect of Bihari from their native Mundari.[85] But usually it works the opposite way, and the powerful language symbol, the history of which I have briefly tried to outline, indirectly indebted to the colonial agenda and then to the nationalist agenda, is utilized to shape clear-cut identity claims against other clear-cut identities, leading to linguistic communalism.

V. CONCLUSION: HOW CAN A PLURAL CULTURE BE WORKABLE NOW?

Going back to the functional heterogeneity and the grass roots multilingual ethos of traditional India cannot be more than a utopian dream in the drastically changed socio-economic environment. But one of the few things intellectuals can do,

[85]K.S. Rajyashree, 'The Sadari of MP, Bihar and WB', in Acharya et al., Pidgins and Creoles Tribals still constitute a fair percentage of Madhya Pradesh and Bihar population. There are 400,000 Sadari speakers, and for most of them Sadari, originally a link language, has become the mother tongue. Descriptions of Sadari, as well as other 'pidgins', show quite a number of features (at least paths for change) similar to the evolution of Dakkhini (a meridional variant of Hindi/Urdu spoken in a Dravidian setting) at the phonetic and syntactic levels, which themselves evoke the 'regular Prakritization' of 'major' languages. Linguistic change is as much social as historical, in India intimately linked to multilingualism.

since they are teachers and language practitioners, is to show the importance at school level of emphasizing not the link with the prestigious ancestor (Sanskrit or ancient Tamil) by substituting to real analysis the largely irrelevant categories of classical grammar, but of emphasizing rather the common structure which make the transition easier from regional minor varieties to the standardized one, as well as from one 'family' to the other. This will provide a means for activating the continuum instead of breaking it by projecting distinctive and rigid normative systems. Flexibility and tolerance of the standard should be emphasized, and not only primary teaching in the mother tongue, but scalar access to the regional language should be favoured by exploiting all the available affinities of both languages instead of separating them. Hierarchies in valuating languages should be avoided so as not to induce derogatory feelings towards non-standard varieties, and convey the notion that linguistic qualification should not be confused with social or political status of a language.[86] Efficiency rather than conformity to the expected normative linguistic behaviour should be favoured, as it is in successful 'full literacy campaigns' which are always also integrative programmes (connected with other training in medical, childcare care, women rights, juridical, environmental skills).

On the other hand, language planners dealing with neology and official language should elaborate more adjustable and popular strategies and give up morphological Sanskritization or syntactical Anglicization which increases the gap between the colloquial and technical varieties. The present modernization of Indian languages ends up in diglossic situations largely responsible for the linguistic deprivation of those who have access only to the lower 'restricted code' in Bernstein's terms. This is what Cobbarubias coined the ethics of language planning, now encapsulated in the general 'ecology' of language.[87]

We should use every occasion to trigger off awareness about the meaning and consequences of language manipulations. But what about culture, so often associated with language and sometimes assimilated with it in language movements? Can the linguistic experience of diversity and hybridity induce a specific cognitive and cultural mode of relation, although without any direct iconic correlation involved? That is what Edouard Glissant claims with his poetics of interrelatedness.[88] A Creole himself from the French Caribbean Martinique, he claimed that the best stand to face 'postmodernity' was from the viewpoint of 'Creolized' cultures, absolutely devoid as they are of a proper ancient culture which belongs to them, which they can own. Why should it be the best stand? Because the radical emptiness of the past prevents a looking back towards a mythical origin and they have to make with mongrelization as a starting point, leaving aside any fantasy of original

---

[86]R.N. Srivastava, *Studies in Language and Linguistics*, vol. 1 *Literacy* (Delhi: Kalinga, 1993).

[87]Juan Cobarrubias, 'Ethnical issues in status planning', in Juan Cobarrubias and Joshua Fishman (eds), *Progress in Language Planning* (Mouton, 1983), pp. 41–82.

[88]Edouard Glissant, *Poétique de la relation* (Paris, 1990); his *Traité du Tout-Monek* (Paris, 1997).

purity; because the past is blank, leads to no root, an absence which necessarily develops a rhizomatures present.[89] This traumatic experience of being erased from one's own history Glissant calls the 'chaos monde' or 'chaos-world'. Out of chaos with only the language of the other to nurture, newness emerges, new combinations and new forms that can only be created by unexpected confrontations, undesired encounters: le 'tout-monde' 'world-as-whole' in Glissant's words, which amounts to the very post-colonial poetics.

However, there is a radical difference between 'true' Creolization[90]—although such a notion has become controversial—and the South Asian situation, even if the word has been often used to describe the Prakritization of Sanskrit.[91] The difference is that in the latter case there has been no eradication of the past, no radical break, no forced mass isolation from the mother tongue. On the contrary, linguistic evolution has been continuous, along with the maintenance of the prestigious ancestor as a language used for literate communication (Sanskrit; to a lesser degree ancient Tamil and the reference to the *Tolkapiyam* as an absolute origin and purity standard for *cen tamil*). Roots are then highly accessible, with the danger of selecting one to make it the absolute origin. Still, the long prevailing grass roots multilingualism in India has something to do with the situation described by Glissant:[92] the constant interactions between flexible and adjustable systems, the many hybrid features, the 'functional heterogeneity' described by Khubchandani fit the notion of plural identities and plural belongings, they can resist the opposite notion of a single unitary pure identity and single belonging. Linguistically speaking, the necessity in the Creole situation for renouncing the mythical purity of origins and singleness of identity is only an available possibility in the Indian context, more available than in monolingual countries.[93]

But can the ethics of a hybrid culture, even deeply marked by the contact with Muslim culture in the syncretic Mughal realizations, be equated with the

[89]A concept borrowed from Deleuze, which was for a time a war engine against 'onto-theo-logocentrism': the rhizome, a botanic term, refers to the spreading out and dissemination of roots, none of them being the main.

[90]Traditionally defined as the appropriation of a pidgin as mother tongue, more or less stabilized and enriched, the so-called substratum (usually African) no longer activated by linguistic exchanges, forgotten. And linked to a specific historical and economic situation (the plantations). Theories of the substratum/adstratum versus spontaneous genesis of a language born without past, that is, by the sheer enactment of the innate 'language faculty', the most natural in that way (iconicity prevailing over syntax and grammatical devices).

[91]By, for example, de Selva (*Linguistic Diversity, Diglossia and Literarcy*) and Shrivastva (*Literacy; Bi/multilingualism*).

[92]In his works like *Traité du Tont-Monde*, or *Poétique de la relation*.

[93]We may deplore that such a possibility has not yet been taken seriously in the modernization of major languages, which instead of opening to the new combinations offered by integrating other languages and dialects into a composite creation has more and more cleansed languages of impure elements.

process of linguistic Creolization as Glissant claims? That might be true for 'true' Creole culture, which was robbed at the same time of its language and its culture and religion. Even if Creolized Indian languages like Marathi have not been born out of a cultural disaster, we may say that Indian culture suffered some form of disaster, colonization as a mild form of wiping off. The contemporary Hindi writer Nirmal Verma makes it very clear in an illuminating essay about 'Indian fiction and colonial reality' (mainly devoted to Prem Chand):

He lived in an abnormal situation, where he had to come in contact with the most brutal aspects of western civilization and most moribund version of Indian society—colonialism being the corrupting factor common to both. The alien intervention was not merely confined to political and economic sphere, it was something far more subtle and insidious, it was an intervention on a colossal civilizational scale, uprooting the entire peasantry not merely from land but from all that which connected it from past. As Simone Weil once observed, 'for several centuries now, men of white race have everywhere destroyed the past, stupidly, blindly, both at home and abroad. Of all the human-soul's needs, none is more vital than this one of past. The destruction of past is perhaps the greatest of all crimes'. It is a crime, because it alienates a man from all that gives a meaning to his life on earth. By uprooting him from the past, it distorts man's relation to his own self. It is precisely this damaged 'self' of a common Indian, neither purely traditional, nor completely colonized, a lacerated soul, which became the most sustained, poignant theme of Prem Chand's novels and short-stories.[94]

Given these affinities between an authentically pluri-lingual colonized culture as is India, and Glissant's thought about the challenging power of pluralism and uprootedness, India too should be better equipped than monocultural monolingual cultures to meet the challenges of this century. If we admit, with Touraine, that the major threats against humanity now lie in the uniformization of thought and de-socialization, with its two opposite poles of communalism and mass culture (globalized individualism, instrumentalization of people), then societies able to deal with pluralism are the best resisting forces to liberal neo-capitalist globalization.

According to the French sociologist in a book significantly entitled *Can We Live Together?*,[95] both threats are an extreme result of liberal capitalism, both only superficially antinomic. In a previous book about the *Critique of Modernity*,[96] Touraine showed that modernity—a process which started with the industrial revolution—brought together the concept of individualism, the rights of the individual within a democratic state or nation, and the faith in ideology as the right tool for shaping such a system, both a product of rationality. Even if trade unionism (with more pragmatic programmes) has become, after the World War

[94]Nirmal Verma, *Word and Memory* (Bikaner: Vagdevi, 1986), p. 35.

[95]Alain Touraine, *Comment Vivre Ensemble: Egaux et Différents* (Paris: Fayard, 1997).

[96]Alain Touraine, *Critique de la Modernité* (Paris: Fayard, 1992).

II, more efficient than political parties in the fight for democracy, it was the last movement still belonging to an area where power was dominated by ideology. But with the erosion of faith in ideology and even in trade unions, more or less contemporaneous with the breakdown of Eastern European nations, there was a void at the centre of power. This ideological vacuum then got filled with an essentially different source of power, because it is in a way abstracted from reality: power now relies on the new technologies of information, market strategies being more and more dependent on the circulation of information. The domination of uniformized mass culture which now threatens the West is part of the same logic, and even if it seems to advocate plurality and diversity it brings people to a culture of oneness and unity of thought and eradicates from deep down the real differences. The logic of rationality (modernity) produced the reign of ideology, the logic of this logic produces the reign of information and its technologies (postmodernity). Touraine's book on 'living together' studies the process of de-socialization which, in Europe, accompanied this change of power centre. Since people were no longer united in an ideological struggle with a particular goal and identified enemy, they, more and more, took to an individualist stand, cultivating the 'values' of the self (the culture of leisure, of 'souci de soi' [self-care], pleasure, healthcare, hobbies, as the only thing under control), more and more disconnected from the public space. No identity is left except private. Values have become strictly a matter of personal interest. At the same time, the desire for collective existence and shared values, also resulting from the feeling of being marginalized from the public space and losing one's identity, can end up in the new fascination for sects or religious communities. Although this appears as the opposite of the process of privatization, it proceeds from the same logic of de-socialization: the group allows the individual to fuse with others who are indeed the same, creates an organic, strongly emotional link based on simple shared values, generally under a non-controversial leader, ruling out all interactive dialogue since this is a universe of sameness: it provides an easy way of re-socializing but a very dangerous one at the same time (back to square one: a group links in standing against, 'un groupe ça lie = s'allie'). Faced with these two antagonistic threats of sheer individualism with no interaction with the public space and sheer fusion of the individual within a dream community of sameness, ruling out the other, what future is left?

The alternative advocated by Touraine, against both the mass culture of a globalized world and communalism, equally de-socializing, is a different construct of self, which he calls a subject. A subject is neither an individual, nor a collective item produced by the fusion of the individual in an indistinct organic group of the fusion kind. It is also distinct from the classical connotations of subjectivity resulting from modern psychology. The very word 'subject' has a complicated history, in France at least. One of its worst *avatars* was during the 1960s and 1970s when it got conflated with the individual—as a result of Freudian, then Lacanian, analysis that such a thing as a subject did not exist as an entity, split as it was between the biological world of drives (impersonal 'pulsions') and the social world of symbolic rules and norms (impersonal too). A great deal of the 1960s new critique vigour was directed towards calling for the 'death of the subject' as well as of 'meaning'—meaning intended as the embodiment of 'theocentrism' and 'logocentrism'.

Touraine reverses this trend when calling back the subject as the only way of resisting both the individualism of mass culture and the fusion of collective identification, both perceived as de-subjectivizing devices, ultimately leading to dehumanization. Becoming a subject is a prerequisite for maintaining humanism, since to be a 'subject' means to be a person who is able to accept others as subjects (and not as radical others with a distinct identity, nor identically same, sharing the same clear-cut identity), same and different at the same time. Same in that sense that every 'subject' knows he is not one but essentially plural, with plural belongings, and also that he can only act and think through interaction and inter-subjectivity. As far from the de-socialized individual as from the individual fused in the communal group, the 'subject' is the social actor of a plural society. In Indian terms, we could say that the path from individual to subject is the path from *vyakti* to *manushya*.[97] Such a process of 'subjectivation' cannot be achieved by the mere promotion of awareness, it needs participative action. Touraine reached these conclusions after close observation of the so-called associative movements in France, which today are, according to him, the only active and efficient resistance against the major threats of our times, because they can restore the disintegrated social tissue (degraded by modernity). The main difference of such participative movements compared with previous (modern) patterns of action is that they are not ideology bound—they do not share a distant ideological programme. Rather, what unites the people who participate in such networks is a short- or medium-term project, essentially local and concrete, and shared values at ethical level. The fact that there is no institutionalization, no centralization, allows practical flexibility. Many such small, hardly visible projects are disseminated in various spheres of social life, and they are fast extending to areas where official action has proved inefficient: solidarities for homeless and paperless people, associations working with prostitutes or AIDS patients, district associations to fight expropriations or insecurity, peasant associations opposing the European agricultural policies along with similar associations in other countries, ATTAC movement, etc. These unconnected projects can be conceived as glocalization, the new term coined as an alternative to the market globalization: the motto 'think global act local', global in Amartya Sen's sense, with a strong rootedness in locality, produces the new 'glocal' alternative.

Such a stand can be observed in literature, at language as well as content

[97]See the chapters 'India and Europe: Some reflections on the self and the other', and 'The self as a stranger', in Nirmal Verma, *India and Europe* (Shimla: IIAS, 2000).

level: Krishna Baldev Vaid's use of Persian or Arabic or Sanskrit in Hindi along with the peace programme of his *divanas* in his great novel on Partition, *Guzra Hua Zamana*, Nagarjun's depiction of human solidarity within a world where nature, spiritual relationship with cosmos, divine and social are equally part of the agency of the subject. *Varuna ke Bete*, literally 'The Sons of Varuna', the Vedic god of waters, one of his famous novels, says something other than 'The Fishermen'. *Baba Batesarnath*, 'The sacred lord of the banyans', another of his novels, is the story of the conquest of freedom and justice as told by a tree, a sacred tree, and enacted by a young villager and his friends, who act exactly as dictated by the tree. Literature, indeed, and its proper teaching in schools, can act as a precious link in adjusting to our differences, because the words it uses have their own agency in blurring the boundaries between languages. The young fools (*pagal, divana*) of *Guzra Hua Zamana*, including the narrator, an ironic *nastik mahatma* (agnostic Mahatma), who freely interact in the three communities of Vaid's Punjabi *qasba* are 'the true soldiers of Peace' but in Hindi it says something far more concrete because of the Arabic words mixed with Hindi: *aman aur ittahad ke sacche sipahi*.[98] Similarly, the Sikh who married a Muslim woman, is said to 'have settled for the whole village the fundamentals of a new religion which teaches that all of them are men, not only Hindus, Sikhs or Muslims'; the narrator uses a markedly Urdu word for 'only' (*mahaz*) in this sentence which refuses distinctive and restrictive identity, an identity restricted by the prominence of one single identity in multiple identities:[99] *un donon ne darasal is qasbe men ek nae mazahb ki buniyad dal di hai, jo yah sikhata hai ki ham sab insaan hain, ki ham mahaz hindu ya sikh ya musalman nahin*.[100]

---

[98]Krishna Baldev Vaid, *Guzra Hua Zamana* (Bikaner: Vagdevi, 1997 [1981]), p. 426.
[99]Montaut, 'Vaid's poetics of the void'.
[100]Vaid, *Guzra Hua Zamana*, p. 436.

REINVENTING DEMOCRATIC CITIZENSHIP IN A PLURAL SOCIETY

Gurpreet Mahajan

I. FROM PLURALISM TO MULTICULTURAL EQUALITY

Cultural pluralism may be a visible feature of most societies today but it is by no means a distinctive attribute of the contemporary world. The ancient empires of Persia, Egypt, and Rome were also culturally diverse. India too included within its fold people of many different religions and languages. Closer to our time, the Ottoman and Habsburg empires of the nineteenth century were known to be internally heterogeneous. 'At the turn of the century', Mark Mazower notes, 'the Habsburg city of Czernowitz was home to Hungarians, Ukranians, Romanians, Poles, Jews and Germans. Further south, the dock workers of Ottoman Selanik (Salonika) routinely spoke six to seven languages; the city included some 70,000 Jews as well as Greeks, Armenians, Turks, Albanians and Bulgarians.'[1] Thus, the co-presence of several cultures, religions, and, ethnicities within the same political unit is not a new phenomenon. But in liberal democracies today, cultural pluralism and diversity raise significantly new and different concerns.

Perhaps the most striking difference is the concern for equality and non-discrimination. Democracy brings in the issue of equal treatment of people who have different social and cultural identities. The questions that emerge, therefore, is liberal democracy related to the status and rights of individuals belonging to different communities. Are they treated as equal in the political and public arenas?

[1]Mark Mazower, *Dark Continent: Europe's Twentieth Century* (New York: Vintage Books, 1998), p. 44.

Do they enjoy the same opportunities as members of the dominant majority community? Do the laws and policies of the state give due recognition to the diversity of cultures that exist in the polity?

Living together, in other words, translates into living together as equals. The mere presence and survival of different cultures is therefore never enough. In contemporary liberal democracies, diversity must coexist with equality. The question therefore is whether different communities, or individuals as members of different communities, are treated as equal. The idea that all individuals, irrespective of their ascribed identities, be treated as equal is central to modern democracy. More specifically, democracies must affirm a commitment to the principle of non-discrimination: this means that identities with which we are born, such as caste, race, religion, or gender, must not be the basis of disadvantage or discrimination in the public domain. Historically, it is the struggles that revealed, highlighted, and then tried to eliminate existing sources of identity-based discrimination in the political and social spheres that contributed to the process of democratization. At first, it was the distribution of political privileges and rights on the basis of noble birth that was challenged. Subsequently, it was the exclusion of individuals from the political and public arenas, on the grounds of their religion, gender, race, and caste, that came under scrutiny. Today, the challenge before the developed and the developing worlds is to ensure that cultural identities are not a source of discrimination and disadvantage in the democratic polity.

The concern for equal treatment in this sense marks a departure from previous frameworks of plurality and accommodation of difference. In most pre-modern societies when communities lived together and entered into the public arena, they did so within an acknowledged structure of hierarchy. Public recognition of difference, institutionalization of legal pluralism, thus existed along with the accepted dominance, or special status, of one community—usually the one to which the ruler belonged. Under the Millet system of the Ottoman empire, Orthodox Greeks, Jews, and Orthodox Armenians received official recognition as semi-autonomous entities. So long as they paid their taxes and lived peacefully, the state did not interfere in the lives of these communities. However, this autonomy existed within a structure where Islam was the official religion of the empire. Thus, while recognized religious communities enjoyed a degree of freedom vis-à-vis their own members, they were subject to the same restrictions, on matters of dress, proselytizing, intermarriage, etc. vis-à-vis the Muslims, who were the ruling community.[2]

Further, this system of legal and cultural pluralism operated within a community-centred framework. While the rest of the population was 'communicated through the public criers', it was the communal heads of the Millet who

[2]Michael Walzer, On Toleration (New Haven: Yale University Press, 1997), pp. 17–18.

were 'summoned to receive news on behalf of their constituencies'.[3] A plural structure functioned, thus, with elite control of population.

In medieval India, similarly, syncretism grew and tolerance flourished when the subject population, or its leadership, avowed their loyalty to the ruler of the kingdom. To take just one example: in much of the seventeenth century, officers of the Mughal court initiated the renewal of the Jagannath cult, but by establishing quite clearly their supremacy as rulers. 'By sitting on a canopied chariot while accompanying the cult's annual festival, Shah Jahan's officials ritually demonstrated that the Mughal emperor, operating through his appointed officers (mansabdars), who was the temple's—and hence the God's—ultimate Lord and protector.'[4]

Thus pluralism thrived and different communities lived together but within a framework where the symbolic and political dominance of the ruler's community was unchallenged. Diverse cultural communities may have received public recognition and privileges to establish their religious institutions and continue with their own ways of life, but within a well-defined boundary where each knew whether the *shivalaya* could be higher than the minaret of a mosque, or the spire of the Evangelic church taller than that of the Methodist church.

This does not, however, imply that social and intellectual interactions between communities were actively discouraged or even penalized. There were indeed periods when intercommunity interactions were supported, but such policies were most often prompted by the personal and political interests of the rulers. Akbar, for instance, consciously tried to build linkages with the Hindu Rajput community. In part, at least, this was intended to check the influence of the Afghan rulers who controlled the southern region of India.[5] Phillip B. Wagoner argues that changing balance of power 'affected the attitude of south Indian elites toward Muslims'.[6] When Hindu polities were faced with the superior power of the 'Turkic Muslims', anti-Muslim rhetoric dominates the inscriptions of the period. However, in the fifteenth and sixteenth centuries, when a balance is reached between the Delhi Sultanate, that controls the north-western portion of the peninsula, and the Vijayanagara empire that prevails in the southern part of the peninsula, there is 'no demonization of the Muslim. Rather than an anti-Muslim polemic, the

---

[3]Daniel Lerner, *The Passing of Traditional Society: Modernizing the Middle East* (Glencoe, Illinois: Free Press, 1958), p. 14.

[4]Richard Eaton, 'Temple desecration in Modern India: When, where and why were Hindu temples desecrated in pre-modern history? And how were they connected with this rise of Indo-Muslim states?', *Frontline* (5 Jan. 2001), p. 71.

[5]Mohammad Yunus, *Islam: A Threat to Other Civilizations* (New Delhi: UBSPD, 2003), p. 207.

[6]Quoted in Cynthia Talbot, 'Inscribing the other, inscribing the self: Hindu–Muslim identities in pre-colonial India', in Richard M. Eaton (ed.), *India's Islamic Traditions 711–1750* (New Delhi: Oxford University Press, 2003), p. 95.

[7]Talbot, 'Inscribing the other', p. 95.

inscriptional sources display a tolerance of Muslim warriors and political power'.[7] Indeed, 'Muslims are depicted as respected political rivals, just like the other major Hindu powers of the peninsular'.[8]

Such incidents of intercommunity interactions and co-presence were also evident in Europe. All through the nineteenth century, people of different ethnicities were present in courts, and at times they even held high positions there. However, once again, this was possible because the empires claimed 'legitimacy on the basis of dynastic rule'.[9] 'Ethnic Germans could,' therefore, 'rise to high position in Tsarist administration' and 'diplomats representing the Ottoman empire in international congress could be Greeks.'[10] Examples of this kind can easily be multiplied. The point really is that pluralism, tolerance, and symbiotic relationships between communities have existed in the past, but most of the time they operated against the backdrop of a structure of hierarchy and dominance that was widely acknowledged and accepted. Dominance was not always coercive in nature but it was certainly apparent, most of all in the symbolic domain of the public arena. What is aspired for today, within contemporary liberal democracies, is a framework of governance where different communities are legally and constitutionally recognized as equals in all spheres of social, political, and public life.

Democracy, in other words, questions tacit and even implicit forms of dominance. To live together as equals, therefore, implies living in a context where there are no fixed markers of dominance, no acknowledged or pre-given hierarchy, and no special privilege for a select few. Negotiations and interactions were relatively easier in societies when hierarchies were well defined and more readily accepted or acknowledged as the basis of action. Peace was also relatively longer lasting under those circumstances. By comparison, democracy, with its concern for equal treatment, disrupts existing equations of power and this often creates potentially volatile situations that can go either way.

Living together with difference thus takes on a whole new meaning in the context of contemporary liberal democracies. It poses radically different challenges and rules out certain ways of reconciling and dealing with social and cultural differences. In the Millet system of the Ottoman empire, for instance, elite control over community members went hand-in-hand with public recognition of certain religious groups. In liberal democracies today, such forms of accommodation appear less than satisfactory. The democratic commitment to non-discrimination entails not merely equality between communities but also equality within the community. Structures of legal pluralism, irrespective of their content, may have been sufficient for accommodating the demands of minority populations in the

[8]Talbot, 'Inscribing the other', p. 95.
[9]Mazower, Dark Continent, p. 41.
[10]Ibid., pp. 41–2.

past. However, in contemporary democracies, the political community has an additional obligation to ensure that recognized community codes and institutions do not exclude or systematically marginalize sections of the community. It is this twin concern for inter-group as well as intra-group equality that has set a new agenda in which previous modes of accommodation and living together remain inadequate and, at times, even unacceptable.

II. PURSUING EQUALITY THROUGH GROUP RIGHTS

The question of equal treatment for individuals belonging to different communities has been an ongoing concern of democratic theory over the last three centuries. However, when the issue of religious, racial, or even gender discrimination was first discussed, it was segregation and exclusion from the public arena that was seen as the main ground of discrimination. Accordingly, to minimize and eliminate this form of discrimination, democracies tried to include hitherto excluded populations by giving them equal rights of citizenship. In other words, to offset the disadvantage that stemmed from exclusion, citizenship rights were de-linked from considerations of religion, race, and gender. It was assumed that if all individuals were to receive the same rights as citizens, then equality would prevail.

Thus, till the first half of the twentieth century at least, the dominant voices within democratic theory advocated that community identities be erased, consciously set aside, and considered irrelevant in the political and public arenas. This is not because collective community identities were irrelevant or superfluous but because distribution of rights and obligations on the basis of community identities had for long been a source of discrimination. Theorists of the liberal persuasion, following John Stuart Mill, were of course critical of the community as an institution. They associated it with the tyranny of the majority and maintained that, within it, the orthodoxy of custom stifled a person's creativity and individualism.[11] Hence, there were always voices within democratic theory that opposed recognition of community as a structure of political governance, and argued that priority be given to the individual. Combined with the possibility that linking rights to community identities is likely to be a basis of disadvantaging and discriminating against some, theorists of democracy overwhelmingly pleaded for an identity-blind criterion for distributing rights.

This ideal of justice and fairness has, however, been challenged in recent times. Debates around cultural diversity and equality have highlighted another source of discrimination in society. If previous analysis focused on exclusion and segregation as ways of disadvantaging some cultural groups and communities, these debates revealed that forced inclusion and assimilation are equally potent

---

[11]John Stuart Mill, *On Liberty, Representative Government, the Subjection of Women* (London: Oxford University Press, 1971 [1859], pp. 10–11.

modes of discrimination within the nation state. And, much more importantly, simply extending the same identical rights to all cannot eliminate these forms of discrimination. Countering discrimination that ensues from assimilation requires rights that allow communities, and individuals belonging to minority groups, the opportunity to continue with their distinct way of life. In short, it requires public recognition, and not effacement of community differences and identities.

Contemporary liberal democracies have then to contend with the fact that a colour/difference–blind criterion is far from adequate for minimizing the different modes of cultural discrimination that exist in the nation state. Granting equal civil liberties and rights to participation in the political process are important but they are not enough for realizing the goal of non-discrimination. This is because equal political rights bring in people of different religions, races, and gender but as members of a homogeneous political community. Consequently, as long as the culture of the public arena remains homogeneous and reflects the culture of the dominant community or the majority, members of minority populations will remain disadvantaged. At least they will not be equal members of the polity. To be treated as equal, minority-community members must enjoy all those opportunities that majority population takes for granted and their members must not face greater hardships in pursuing the same ambitions and goals. Group rights enter into the picture here. They are intended, on the one hand, to counter the effect of existing laws that advantage majority population and, on the other, to make the public arena more diverse and hospitable to the expression of difference.

Group rights may take many different forms. They may be given to the community as a collectivity or to those individuals who are members of a recognized minority community. The subject of group rights may thus differ and so may the nature of the given right. At the most basic level, group rights may take the form of exemptions, that is, exemptions from social, religious, or cultural practices that are currently endorsed by the state. For instance, Sikhs may seek, and receive, exemptions from laws that prescribe helmet wearing for motorcycle riders. All such exemptions take cognizance of the specific practices of minority communities, and aim to give the members of these communities an opportunity to live in accordance with those collectively shared norms or practices. Exemptions, of the kind just mentioned, are rights that some individuals receive on account of being members of a given minority community. These are not rights that are given to the community to enforce or to interpret as it deems best.

Exemptions are, in a manner of speaking, the mildest expression of group rights for they place no positive obligations upon the state. By comparison, group rights that take the form of extending assistance and recognition to community practices, institutions, and codes involve the state more substantially. Assistance from the state, both financial and institutional, is usually desired to enable members of minorities to do things that the majority can take for granted, or do unaided: for instance, establish separate educational institutions and museums, promote or protect the cultural and intellectual heritage of the community. Recognition rights have several different dimensions that bring in fairly distinct considerations. Since language is a crucial node of personal identity, and in democracies a medium of participation and communication, almost all communities seek language rights. They desire recognition for their language: to offset disadvantages in the market they want the language to be included as the medium of instruction as well as public examinations and selections. More substantially, communities want the right to address the state and have access to public communication in their language.

Linguistic communities, as in the case of India and Quebec, also wish to perpetuate themselves. In addition to ensuring that their users are not disadvantaged in the public arena, they want the culture and world view embodied in their language to survive and flourish. Consequently, they present themselves as viable units of governance that may receive special representation in various legislative bodies or be treated as separate federal entities. In both cases, political rights, including those of self-governance, are seen as being necessary for protecting the language community and ensuring its survival within the polity.

At another level, group rights may provide recognition for the distinct cultural practices, institutions, and codes of the community. In India official acceptance of community personal laws is a case in point. Quite often, and particularly in the form of acceptance of community family law, the right is given to the community. While individuals may, if the state permits, opt out, the right is actually given to the community. It is the community which, through its institutional mechanisms, determines the content of these codes and the way they will be interpreted and applied to specific cases.

All group rights—be it exemptions, separate representation, self-governance, assistance/inclusion in the symbols of the state, or recognition—introduce cultural diversity into the public sphere and meet claims of respect and recognition that come from minority populations. However, there is one basic difference between rights that are given to individuals, as members of a community and rights that are given to communities per se. The former brings in community identities but it usually gives options to individual members of a community: the option to wear a helmet or an Indian dress at workplace if they so choose. The latter, by and large, promote and protect a given way of life. They can, in other words, restrict options for community members. What is also equally important is that they empower traditional community leadership and institutional structures.

In the contemporary world, most votaries of such community rights strongly argue for democratization of community institutions. In the words of Partha Chatterjee, a community may say that it has its own reasons for doing what it does. However, it cannot say that it has no reasons at all.[12] In a democracy it is essential

---

[12]Partha Chatterjee, 'Secularism and tolerance', *Economic and Political Weekly* (9 July 1994), p. 1775.

that these reasons be discussed and made known to others; and vice versa the reasons that others offer for amending or abandoning a practice be heard and taken into account while determining collectively valued goods. No community can therefore be exempt from collective deliberation through democratic participation and decision-making processes. It cannot, in the name of difference, deny the necessity and justification of deliberative consensus within a democracy.[13]

It is, of course, paradoxical that a framework that seeks respect for different ways of life nevertheless remains intolerant of different institutional mechanisms. It accepts that exclusion is a form of discrimination and that community practices may disadvantage some internal groups. Hence it supports and even mandates democratic modes of participation and decision making. However, this is not the main issue. The more serious issue is whether the mere fact of inclusion is enough to offset existing inequalities. Can individuals and groups that have been victims of systematic oppression and subordination participate as equals in the deliberative process? Much more importantly, is participation a sufficient and adequate indicator of democracy? Should we be concerned about all individuals being treated as equal or can this be left open to negotiation? Does the state have an obligation to its citizens to see that they be treated as equal or should it let the outcome be determined by deliberation within the community? Within the democratic nation state, rights receive priority because participation can, and often does, yield results that express the interests of the dominant majority. Should the same considerations not apply within the community? How can the rights of vulnerable minorities be protected within the framework of group rights? These are issues of democratic citizenship that arise within the framework of group rights, and we need to consider how they may be addressed without sacrificing the twin concerns of inter-group as well as intra-group equality. However, before discussing these questions further, it is necessary to recall the context in which the concern for minorities has arisen in recent times.

III. ETHNIC CONFLICT AND MINORITIES

The growing concern for equal treatment and recognition for members of diverse cultures living within the nation state is essentially a sign of the deepening of democratic consciousness. There are, however, a number of contingent conditions that have placed this issue on the anvil of liberal democracies today. Almost all societies are internally plural and diverse. Globalization has certainly contributed to this phenomenon but even if this catalyst was not present, the issue of democratic citizenship in a diverse society was bound to arise. Current estimates reveal that there are 'some 5,000 to 8,000 ethno-cultural groups in the world and

[13]See Jeff Spinner-Halev, 'Feminism, multiculturalism, oppression and the state', *Ethics*, 112 (Oct. 2001), pp. 84–113.

only around 200 states'. Hence 'arithmetic dictates that most states (at the moment over 90%) are inevitably going to be shared by more than one ethnic group, and often by dozens'.[14] Effectively, this means that nation states have to learn to live with diversity; they have to innovate and think of ways in which different communities may coexist as equals. Failure to do so will result in escalation of ethnic conflicts as more and more communities seek equal political rights and recognition for their cultural membership. Classical liberal theories of justice attended primarily to issues of political participation but ignored the question of recognition and cultural membership. Consequently there is a real need to devise institutional mechanisms which give expression to these demands for equal political and cultural membership.

Further, the strategies that nation states had previously chosen for managing diversity and ethnic conflict have proved to be inadequate and even unacceptable for democracies. Most often nation states dealt with diversity through policies of assimilation, elimination, and/or, to borrow a term used by McGarry and O'Leary, hegemonic control.[15] In the twentieth century forced mass population transfers have been by far the most extensively applied strategy for constructing a homogeneous nation state and compelling absorption into the latter. The Greco-Turkish exchange of populations in the early decades of that century was perhaps the most striking example of, what E.H. Carr called, repatriations but it was by no means the only one. Mass expulsions, for one reason or another, were a common phenomenon in much of twentieth-century Europe. Between 1945 and 1947 itself, approximately 12,300,000 Germans were expelled from Central Europe alone. If we look at the historical atlas of East Central Europe we find that between 1930 and 1991, the number of Jews in Poland fell from 2.7 million (approximately 8.5 per cent of the population) to 15,000; in Czechoslovakia during the same period, the number decreased from 354,000 (2.4 per cent of the population) to 12,000; and in Hungary from 500,000 (4.8 per cent of the population) to 100,000 (1.3 per cent of the population). Several other ethnic groups also met with the same fate. In Romania, in 1930 Ukranians were a community of about 582,000 but by 1977 their numbers were down to just 54,000. Around the same time, in Yugoslavia they were approximately 28,000 in number but by 1981 there were merely 13,000 Ukranians left in that country.[16]

Thus mass transfers were a common phenomenon but they have few defenders among liberal democrats today. Indeed few would question the conclusion that these were unacceptably coercive and undemocratic ways of managing and coping

[14]Will Kymlicka and Wayne Norman (eds), *Citizenship in Diverse Societies* (Oxford: Oxford University Press, 2000), p. 13.

[15]J. McGarry and B. O'Leary, *The Politics of Ethnic Conflict Regulation* (London: Routledge, 1993), pp. 23–5.

[16]P.R. Magocsi, *Historical Atlas of East Central Europe*, cited in Mazower, *Dark Continent*, p. 414.

with diversity. Is assimilation into the constructed national culture less coercive and more in line with democratic aspirations? It would not appear so if we were to look at the experiences of the indigenous populations of North America. In any case, the growing assertions for recognition and power sharing have compelled most liberal democracies to accept the presence of 'unmeltable ethnicities'. This has prompted theorists to rethink the assumptions of classical liberalism and the conception of citizenship and justice that came with it.

This task gained further urgency in the decades following the 1970s. The decline in the economic conditions in America provided the context in which immigrant populations became the target of right-wing mobilizations and jingoism. The immigrant communities and minorities responded to this attack by raising the demand for recognition and accommodation of cultural-community identity through special rights. In this polarized situation, community rights for minorities gained considerable support but they also came to be associated with separatism. In the words of Arthur Schlesinger Jr, the cult of ethnicity and multiculturalism is 'breaking the bonds of cohesion' that 'hold the (American) republic together'[17] and 'exaggerating differences'.[18] Yet others, on the right, associated the framework of group rights with a new form of apartheid that is likely to destroy the basic principles of a liberal democratic polity. The response from the votaries of special rights for minorities was equally strident. Justifying 'Africanity' as the ultimate reality, Mofi Kete Asante claimed that 'the idea of mainstream American is nothing more than an additional myth meant to maintain Eurocentric hegemony'.[19]

These conflicting pictures of what special rights for minorities entail lies at the heart of the present debate on democratic citizenship. Should cultural membership be regarded as a relevant consideration? Can diversity coexist with equality and the democratic commitment to non-discrimination? These are questions that confront modern liberal democracies. In India, the recurring experience of communal violence that results in the destruction of life and property of a targeted community, and in Europe, the explosion of ethnic conflict after the collapse of the Soviet Union, have only served to underline the inadequacies of liberal remedies and ways of accommodating/managing diversity. It is these circumstances that have collectively triggered off the present debate on multicultural accommodation.

As I mentioned earlier, multicultural accommodation entails something more than peaceful coexistence of different cultures and communities. In violence and strife-ridden situations, peaceful existence is no doubt important, but for peace

[17]Arthur M. Schlesinger, Jr, *The Disuniting of America* (New York: W.W. Norton, 1991), p. 112.
[18]Ibid., p. 13.
[19]Quoted in Neil J. Smelser and Jeffrey C. Alexander (eds), *Diversity and its Discontents: Cultural Conflict and Common Ground in Contemporary American Society* (Princeton: Princeton University Press, 1999), p. 7.

to last in a democracy what is perhaps even more important is that diverse populations learn to live as equals. Can the framework of special rights for minorities provide the basis of accommodating diversity with the concern for equal treatment for all? This is the question that must also be considered while discussing ways of living together with differences.

IV. THE NORMATIVE AND THE EMPIRICAL

The concept of group-differentiated rights or special rights for minorities addresses the normative concerns of democratic theory. It deals with the principles that should form the basis of liberal political institutions. However, while discussing the limitations of existing liberal principles of justice and presenting an alternative to them, it draws upon historical experience. The experiences of particular minorities in specific democracies provide reasons for moving away from notions of identical rights for all and for supporting special rights for minorities. While anchoring the idea of group rights in notions of a situated self, the value of cultural-community membership, and diversity, its advocates invariably point to instances where absence of such rights leads to grave injustice and disadvantage for minority populations. The normative is here informed, and to some extent even constituted, by the particular that is both historical and empirical.

An appeal to the historical and the empirical is not uncommon in studies dealing with ethnic conflict and minorities. Images of 'us' and 'them' that sustain the politics of 'friends and foes' draw upon history and so do analysts who challenge such representations of the past. If the former select and de-contextualize the past, the latter provide the much-needed corrective. They focus on encounters between cultures and civilizations that enriched the given society and sustained interactions between members of different communities. In so far as living together as equals requires deconstruction of the cultural narrative of the nation state that is based on exclusions and negative representations of otherness, these historical narratives are of critical importance. Their absence allows representations of difference as hostile otherness, that is foreign and threatening, to circulate unchallenged.

However, an appeal to historical truth is rarely enough for settling present-day political disputes. Even though history is often placed at the service of the present, to assume that discovering what actually happened would resolve conflicts decisively is to misunderstand the nature of political rhetoric and competitive politics. Democracy unfurls the aspiration to be treated as an equal but it also creates room for the construction of identities. In situations of acute scarcity and competition for limited resources, the manipulation and refashioning of identities has a logic that defies historical reasoning. Under the circumstances, it is essential to invoke and affirm values around which some kind of historical consensus has been achieved. The notion of non-discrimination on the grounds of ascribed social identity serves just this task. It offers a principle by which different claims that come from the majority and the minorities can be assessed and weighted.

What needs also to be reiterated here is that living together with difference poses new questions and challenges in a democracy. In situations of communal violence and ethnic cleansing, the question of peaceful coexistence of diverse communities tends to become the primary concern. However, in a liberal democracy, the mere fact of living together and tolerating difference can never be enough. It cannot satisfactorily fulfil the condition of non-discrimination. To realize the latter, different cultural communities living within the same polity need to be treated and accommodated as equal. Equal membership is a critical factor both for establishing lasting peace and for promoting the value that is central to modern democracies.

The terms of discourse have thus changed and for this reason historical examples and references to the past serve a limited purpose. But this is not peculiar to historical accounts and narratives. Empirical studies that try to measure the degree of 'trust' between communities also face an analogous difficulty. In the case of the latter, the difficulties are compounded by the fact that recent studies of Robert Putnam indicate a negative relation between diversity and social capital. While economic equality is positively linked to social capital, societies that are diverse show lower levels of social capital both across communities as well as within the community.[20] Even though Putnam is quick to add that this does not imply that homogeneity is more desirable, it does pose a question mark against the purported value of diversity as a social good. For Putnam the negative relation between social capital and diversity suggests that we need new forms of social capital in plural societies—bridging rather than bonding capital. The underlying assumptions, however, remain the same. It is assumed that networks of interaction between communities will act as 'buffers' in situations of ethnic conflict.

Empirical reality does not always sustain this supposition. Interactions between communities, particularly in situations of acute scarcity and contested sovereignties, do not necessarily build trust. They also generate hostility and resentment. Reports on the recent riots in Gujarat, for instance, reveal that in many cases, the victims knew the perpetrators of violence.[21] People engaged in brutal acts of violence were not always individuals from outside; at times they were persons with whom the victims and their families had some degree of social interaction. To assume, therefore, that stereotypical images will dissolve and sustained interactions will

---

[20]Robert Putnam, 'Community equality and diversity in contemporary society', Keynote lecture at the 53rd Annual Conference of the Political Studies Association of the UK, University of Leicester, 14–17 Apr. 2003.

[21]Fact Finding by a Women's Panel, Sponsored by Citizens' Initiative, *How has the Gujarat Massacre Affected Minority Women? The Survivors Speak* (Ahmedabad, 16 Apr. 2002); Sahmat Fact Finding Team, *Ethnic Cleansing in Gujarat: A Preliminary Report* (10–11 Mar. 2002).

yield a more tolerant society, with a high degree of trust, is something that needs to be interrogated.

Perhaps the most serious problem with this form of reasoning is that it reduces the concern for equal citizenship to promoting certain civic and social virtues. The presence of social capital or trust is not just a supplementary condition that nurtures democracy, rather it is seen as a condition that is necessary for sustaining democratic citizenship. It is this priority given to social capital that raises a variety of anxieties, both about the relationship between social capital and diversity and the nature of organizations which can be high on social capital. Since this is not a subject that this chapter seeks to discuss, suffice here to say that in a democracy equal treatment, or non-discrimination, must be a systemic value that informs all political institutions and interactions.

A number of conditions can be said to help in the flourishing of democracy. William Galston identifies a set of general, social, economic, and political virtues in this regard, and they cover attributes such as the capacity to be loyal and law-abiding, independent and open-minded and the capacity to delay self-gratification and respect for the rights of fellow citizens.[22] However, none of these, like social capital, can be regarded as being distinctive to democracy and democratic citizenship. It is the idea of non-discrimination and, linked with that, of equal treatment that defines and distinguishes contemporary democracies. Consequently, non-discrimination or equal treatment cannot merely be a contingent effect of some attitudes and conditions, it must be the operative principle of democratic life. It is for this reason that theorists of democracy locate equality in a structure of rights, and it is for this same reason that we need to analyse whether granting the same identical rights to all citizens is enough in a democracy? Whether equal treatment in a democracy requires special consideration for vulnerable minorities? And whether a system of group rights can promote democratic citizenship?

V. GROUP-DIFFERENTIATED RIGHTS AND THE QUESTION OF EQUALITY

In the second half of the twentieth century, feminist scholarship introduced a new element into democratic theory. Against the difference–blind approach of the liberals, it argued that women and men differ; their experiences and needs differ. On issues such as family, childcare, income, and discrimination, men and women have divergent interests and perspectives and these needed to be represented separately.[23] Two arguments were made in this regard: 1) to be treated as equal,

---

[22]William Galston, *Liberal Purposes: Goods, Virtues and Duties in the Liberal State* (Cambridge: Cambridge University Press, 1991), pp. 221–4.

[23]Martha Minow, *Making All the Difference: Inclusion, Exclusion and American Law* (Ithaca: Cornell University Press, 1990).

women require special consideration, and even special rights; and 2) including women separately will enrich social and public life. It will bring in new perspectives and ways of thinking into the deliberative process.

Reasons that had here been offered to bring in the difference which women represent, have today been applied to include vulnerable minorities within the state. The idea that cultural-community identity is a relevant consideration that needs to be factored in while determining who are alike and who must therefore be treated in an identical manner, has found systematic expression in the notion of group-differentiated rights. A strident defence of this point of view came in Iris Marion Young's book, *Justice and the Politics of Difference*. She argued that in a society where some groups are privileged while others are oppressed, insisting that everyone should efface their particular identities and affiliations works to the advantage of the dominant group. It allows privileged groups to define the standards according to which all will be measured;[24] and it makes the point of view and experience of the privileged group appear 'neutral and universal'.[25] This perpetuates a kind of cultural imperialism. Special rights for minorities or group-differentiated rights are needed to dislodge this prevailing structure of dominance and to make space for oppressed communities to participate as equals in the affairs of the polity.

Two clarifications are in order here. One, not all rights are to be linked to group/community membership. In a democratic state, almost all would agree that rights of political participation and civil liberties must be extended to all citizens irrespective of the community to which they belong. Hence group-differentiation is not intended to be a means of excluding some communities from political membership. Special rights may supplement these rights, for instance special representation or even self-governance rights may be given to identified communities. But these cannot be the basis of denying other communities their rights to participate in the deliberative process as citizens of the polity. Two, the concept of group-differentiated rights does not undermine or decry the value of political-community membership. Membership of the state remains a crucial, if not primary, source of identity; however, it once again supplements this form of identity with that of cultural community. The latter is perceived to be an important part of personal identity and it is further assumed that these two identities can intersect and even complement each other. There is no reason therefore to assume that affirming, or bringing in, the cultural community would undermine or weaken the commitment to the nation state. On the contrary, as Joseph Carens points out, due recognition to one's cultural community might well be an essential condition for developing a sense of belonging to the nation state.[26] Special rights are intended

---

[24]Iris Marion Young, *Justice and the Politics of Difference* (Princeton: Princeton University Press, 1990), p. 165.

[25]Ibid.

[26]Joseph Carens, *Culture, Citizenship and Community: A Contextual Exploration of Justice as Evenhandedness* (Oxford: Oxford University Press, 2000), pp. 166–73.

therefore to ensure fair treatment to all; more specifically to ensure that members of different communities have an equal opportunity to live in accordance with their distinct ways of life within the framework of democratic citizenship.

The idea that individuals associate with and owe allegiance to groups and communities other than the state is not entirely new. In medieval Europe it was widely acknowledged that men, as part of the universal Christian order, had an obligation to the wider 'society of believers'. Since the state was not the creator of moral law, it followed that it could not claim all of man's allegiance. In a slightly altered form, early Puritanical thought visualized society as comprising different free and voluntary associations; in fact, the church itself was seen as a voluntary congregation of equals. As these associations and organizations did not owe their origin to the state, and men owed their loyalty to them directly, it was assumed that the state could not prevail in conflicts between the government and these associations. The space that early modern thought created for groups and associations was significantly diminished later by theories of state sovereignty and the liberal notion of individualism. However, this strain of thinking continues to be expressed in theories of group rights. In India, for instance, Ashis Nandy and Partha Chatterjee advocate some degree of autonomy for communities and their value systems with a view to curbing the increasing power and intrusiveness of the state and for encouraging plural sovereignties.

Advocacy of group rights for purposes of curtailing state totalitarianism is, in normative terms, substantially different from frameworks where group rights are intended to promote equality of treatment for members of diverse communities. Even though both legitimize structures of legal pluralism and value community membership positively, the moral reasoning is different. It is necessary to make this distinction, for group rights may be justified on many different grounds. They can be an instrument for curbing state power or promoting diversity; or acknowledging community membership as a valuable social good or enhancing equality between groups. In the context of a culturally diverse society, committed to the ideal of non-discrimination, it is the latter alone that can be unequivocally defended. Group rights that are necessary to minimize disadvantage and to promote equal treatment and equal opportunities for members of diverse communities can, and indeed they must, be accommodated within the structure of basic rights.

VI. DEMOCRATIC CITIZENSHIP, NON-DISCRIMINATION, AND GROUP RIGHTS

Even when group rights are associated with the concern for non-discrimination and supported only for promoting that end, they raise serious anxieties and concerns. Most liberals fear that they would lead to hardening of group identities and loyalties, and this is likely to fragment the state or threaten its territorial integrity. Others claim that special rights are a new form of group-based discrimination. It gives special status and with it special privileges to a few. When, for instance, only one community or its members alone have the right to carry swords, then they enjoy a special status. In a liberal democracy, either a right or a privilege of this kind should be extended to all or to none.[27] Concerns of this kind, arguing that group rights for minorities imply partiality towards them, are expressed in almost all societies and in India this has been the constant refrain of the critics. One needs, therefore, to address this issue and examine whether liberal democracies should make room for special rights for minorities in the interest of promoting equal treatment for all. And, more importantly, what kind of understanding of democratic citizenship may be appropriate in a diverse society.

All nation states invoke some notion of sharing and collective being. Shared historical experiences, memories of the past, common language and culture are some of the elements that can be instrumental in imagining the state as a homogeneous political community. It is feared therefore that collective/group rights, that seek to replace this constructed homogeneity with heterogeneity of cultures and practices, would fragment the political community. It would destroy the universality that the state must represent as the highest sovereign authority. In the contemporary world, where we are witnessing a resurgence of identity politics, the fear that particular identities will displace or 'crowd out'[28] common citizenship identity is indeed a real one. However, the question that needs to be asked is, 'Is the politics of identities engendered by group rights?' Also, is the relation between the universal and the particular necessarily one of antagonism?

If the Indian experience is any indication, it would appear that identity politics thrives in situations where there is acute scarcity of resources and opportunities. In the absence of any substantial agenda of redistribution, groups and communities consolidate and organize themselves by appealing to ascribed social identities. Besides, community identities harden and become more inflexible and closed when there is significant inequality of opportunity and treatment. If group rights enhance equality, if they enable marginalized minorities to be included and counted as equal members of the polity, they can assist in minimizing the sense of alienation that is present among minorities in the nation state. Indeed they may even help to build a sense of belonging to the wider polity.

In other words, there is no reason to assume that particularistic identities are antithetical to the existence or consolidation of a collective identity. The linguistic reorganization of states in India has shown that it is perfectly possible to be a Maharashtrian or a Punjabi or an Assamese and yet be an Indian. These identities can coexist and even reinforce each other. On the issue of group rights giving

---

[27]See Brian Barry, *Culture and Equality: An Egalitarian Critique of Multiculturalism* (Cambridge, Massachusetts: Harvard University Press, 2001).

[28]Kymlicka and Norman, *Citizenship in Diverse Societies*, p. 35.

special/preferential treatment to some, it is necessary to make some distinctions. First, in situations where group rights provide equal opportunity to minorities to live in accordance with their distinct ways of life, special rights require little justification. If, for instance, Catholics can wear the cross without it being prohibited on the grounds of being a religious symbol, it appears only fair that Muslims be permitted to wear the headscarf if they so choose. After all, religious symbols of one community alone cannot, or must not, be disallowed. Here permission for the minority-community members only provides them with the opportunities that are enjoyed by the majority-community members. Group rights here take the form of exemptions or recognition but they do not smack of partiality.

Problems arise only when group rights sanction practices that curtail/violate the rights of other citizens or seek to protect a culture. Rights that single out minority institutions and practice for support and endorsement are not being included in this category for, here again, considerations of equal opportunity and integrity, rather than special treatment, prevail. When Sikhs alone have the right to carry *kirpans*, or American Indians get the right to use the peyote on ceremonial occasions, even when it is prohibited for all others, and Quakers are exempted from service in war-time, it may appear that minorities are receiving special privileges. However, in each of these cases, special treatment is predicated on the assumption of 'moral integrity' of the citizens. Individuals' 'sincerity in their professed beliefs' is accepted,[29] and it is accepted for it does not in any way limit the rights of others. Hence these too can be accommodated within the framework of democratic citizenship.

In contrast to these cases, when collective group rights seek to protect a culture, to ensure that it survives and flourishes, or when these rights curb the right to equal treatment or the right to life, their accommodation within the framework of democracy becomes deeply problematic. When cultures are conceived as ends in themselves that are irreplaceable and therefore worthy of protection, rights that are sanctioned often limit options for internal members. If, for instance, the survival of French or Sanskrit is regarded to be intrinsically valuable and therefore worthy of protection, then the choice of reading and learning that language cannot be left to the members. It is restrictions of this kind that such collective rights place upon members of the community that raise concern. If individual users were to make that choice themselves and all that was required is for the state to ensure that they have the possibility of exercising that choice, there would be little difficulty in accepting them. At least they would fit more easily within a liberal democracy. However, it is questionable whether a culture or a language has any intrinsic worth in a way that individuals are valuable and

---

[29]See Vinit Haksar, *Rights, Communities and Disobedience: Liberalism and Gandhi* (New Delhi: Oxford University Press, 2001), p. 88.

irreplaceable. Likewise, practices such as sati, child sacrifice, community personal laws, that violate the basic right to equal treatment and the right to life, cannot be accommodated within a democracy.

Three conclusions follow from this. One, not all forms of collective or group rights can, or need, be accepted in a democracy. Rights that are intended to promote equal treatment for minorities by giving them opportunities that the majority takes for granted, or rights that follow from deeply held religious beliefs or cultural norms, can be accommodated. In fact, efforts have to be made to make space for them so long as they do not violate the rights of others or the ideal of non-discrimination. Two, pursuit of the ideal of non-discrimination requires restructuring of the relation between the universal and the particular. In a culturally diverse democracy, the universal that is embodied in the law and practices of the state should be animated and constituted by the particular. Only when the diversity that comprises the totality is reflected in the universal can different communities have a sense of identity and equality within the polity. Third, the ideal of non-discrimination places obligations on the state. It calls upon the state to acknowledge and accommodate diverse cultural communities as equal partners and at the same time it is required to see that cultural and community norms do not become the basis of subordinating vulnerable individuals and groups. The responsibility for promoting equal treatment lies with the state; at least the state cannot abandon it in the name of promoting and protecting diversity. The pursuit of diversity has therefore to be linked to the principle of non-discrimination. Deliberations upon the nature of democratic citizenship have also to be placed within these parameters. The notion of non-discrimination alone can provide a framework for deliberating upon the claims of diverse groups and communities as well as for constructing a collective identity that can be the basis of imagining a political community.

PROCESSES

A 'HOLI RIOT' OF 1714: VERSIONS FROM AHMEDABAD AND DELHI*

Najaf Haider

This chapter examines a set of evidence on an event in Ahmedabad in AD 1714. The evidence appears to be the earliest description of a conflict involving Muslims, Jains, and Hindus in Ahmedabad or, for that matter, the whole of India. It offers us an insight into the causes, organization, form, and control of group violence in the capital city of a highly commercialized region. A complete and fresh translation of the descriptions of the incident found in two Persian chronicles is presented here, followed by a schematic reading of both versions. I hope that by adding to our empirical knowledge, and by raising questions and inviting criticisms, some contribution may be made to the study of the tensions and challenges of living together separately in pre-colonial India.

I. THE TEXTS AND THEIR AUTHORS

The incident has two versions, one contained in a local history of Gujarat, the *Mirat-i Ahmadi*, and the other in a general history of the Mughal empire, the *Muntakhab ul Lubab*.[1] The local version is longer, more detailed, and the lesser known of the two.

*I am grateful to Professor Irfan Habib for making valuable suggestions while going through the translations of the sources. All errors, whether in translation or the text are, however, mine.
[1] There is a third version of the Ahmedabad incident in a short entry in the Diary (AD 1718–27) of a retired Mughal official. See I'timad Ali Khan, *Miratu-l Haqaiq*, MS. Bodleian, Fraser 124, ff. 170b-171a. I shall refer to this later in the discussion.

The *Mirat-i Ahmadi* is a history of the Mughal province (*subah*) of Gujarat completed on 10 September 1761 (10 *Safar* 1175 AH). It begins, after an introduction and a physical and fiscal description of the subah, with an account of the 'Rajput Rajas' of Gujarat and ends with the second battle of Panipat in AD 1761. The author, Ali Muhammad Khan, tells us that he reconstructed his history from official chronicles and, for the period AD 1668 to 1708, for which no such work was available to him, from the oral testimony (*isgha*) of older people (*kuhn salan*). The account after AD 1708, the year of his arrival in Gujarat as a young boy of 8 years, is based on the author's personal observations (*faham*).

This brief statement shows that the local narrative was written independently of the other one which deals with the period for which Ali Muhammad Khan had to rely on oral history. It also places the author close to the event. At the time of the incident he was 14 years old and although he may not have been present at the scene of action, he may have heard about it from people circulating the news locally. He may even have read about it some years later when, as the *diwan* (finance officer) of Gujarat, he gained access to the archives of the state, which he made liberal use of both in the narrative as well as the gazetteer parts of his work.

The other version appears in the *Muntakhab ul Lubab*, a history of the Mughal empire from the date of its establishment (AD 1526) to the fourteenth year of Muhammad Shah's reign (AD 1723). It was written by Khafi Khan, who worked in Gujarat as a news writer (*waqa'i' navis*) but moved out to the Deccan as the diwan of the Viceroy, Chin Qulich Khan Nizam ul Mulk, a year before the incident. When his patron was transferred and replaced by one of the Saiyid brothers, Khafi Khan lost his job. A bit of lobbying secured him a relatively lower position but he lost that too when he failed to remit the sum of money urgently required by his new employer. Deprived of his livelihood, he came back to Delhi, sometime after AD 1718 and began to write the book. To the extent that he worked with state papers, personal observations, and memory, Khafi Khan may have found his residence at Delhi useful in recapturing an event that began in the province but reached its climax in the metropolis.

II

The Version from Ahmedabad

A description of the Holi disturbance (*hangama i holi*) between Hindus (*hunud*) and Muslims (*ahl-i islam*)

One of the events (*sawanahat*) of this year [1126 AH] was the occurrence of a disturbance between Hindus and Muslims over the playing of Holi (*holibazi*). A brief account of it is that at that time, Madan Gopal *sarraf* had an agent (*gumashta*) named Hari Ram. He [Madan Gopal] came to this province as the treasurer of Khan Firoz Jung and built a very grand house in the city. On account of his wealth, and as treasurer of the Governor, he became the leader of the sarrafs. After the death of Firoz Jung, having established a sarraf's shop in Ahmedabad, which was very profitable, he left for the imperial capital [Delhi].

At the door of his [Madan Gopal's] house, Hari Ram was indulging himself in enthusiastically playing Holi with a group of sarrafs and companions (*hum mushriban*), pouring colour, smearing *gulal* in a bacchanalian manner (*badmasti*) as is their custom. Perchance, a Muslim happened to pass through that street and fell in with them. Taking hold of him, they showered colour, gulal and dust, and abuses on him (*ahanat pardakhtand*). He, considering the situation, got away by some means and, in that very condition, took some people and went to intimate to his holiness (*haqaiq u marif*) Muhammad Ali, the *wa'iz* (sermon reader) who was at the head of those who occupied the pulpit for delivering [Friday] sermons, [and] who, by the aid of his speech, used to satiate the thirsty dwellers of the desert of disappointment (*tishnakaman i wadi i hiraman*) and guide those lost in the wilderness of vices to the path of salvation (*nijat*).

The high and low of the Muslim community, being his devotees and his followers, went to him and, reporting the whole incident and story, appealed for justice (*tazallum*). The regard for the honour of Islam and the cause of the true faith seized him and compelled him to go to the Jami Masjid. He sent a message to Mulla Abdul Aziz, the head (*rais*) of the Sunni Bohra community, about his own arrival and the incident. He too went to the mosque with the people of his sect.

Most of the Muslims, whether soldiers or artisans, residents of the city or inhabitants of the suburbs, arrived in groups and bands from every nook and corner shouting 'faith, faith!' (*din, din*). A general concourse and assemblage of Muslims took place and, determined to kill and plunder Hindus, marched in a crowd to the house of Qazi Khairullah Khan to urge that since it was a matter of enforcement of (Muslim) law (*muqaddama-i shara*) and the cause of Islam, he should come out and join them.

His Worship (the *Qazi*), sensing the situation, closed the doors of his house, and fearing to be a part of the crowd, procrastinated, and so the ignorant among the public, losing hope of getting the door opened, hurled abuses and insults. The unruly fellows among them set fire to His Worship's house. Soon thereafter, they resorted to riot and lawlessness, and insolently took to murder and plunder. They ransacked and put to fire many shops of the cloth market and of the sarrafs, which were full of money (*naqd*).

The conflict lighted such flames of fire
That everything got burnt in their heat

They now turned to the house of Madan Gopal, from where the trouble had started, and the residential quarters of the Hindus, of which the greatest is the Jauhari-wara [jewellers' quarter]. The house of Kapur Chand Bhansali, who was then the leader of the Hindu community (*sar-guroh-i firqa-i hunud*), whom they call *nagarseth*, was also [located] at that place. This was either on account of religious prejudice (*taassub-i din*) or of the professional rivalry (*humchashmi*) between him [Kapur Chand] and Mulla Abdul Aziz, the *seth* of the Bohra community, there being since old times an innate and natural animosity between the two. [The other side] trying to repel them for their own protection, took to fighting by throwing stones and bricks from their roofs.

Kapur Chand Bhansali always had access to the courts of the Governor and the diwan of the province. A group of soldiers native to Gujarat (*mutawattinan-i gujarat*), who were devoted to him, gathered around him out of a desire to please him, and he set them as watch over his house and the gate of the Jauhri-wara. The out-of-job soldiers considered this disturbance to be an opportunity to earn their livelihood (*wasila i rozgar*), and upon a settling of their daily pay (*rozana*), they posted themselves at the outlets of the localities of the sarrafs and merchants and became ready to fight for the cause of unbelief, giving up all pretence of defending the faith out of worldly considerations. They sold their faith (din) for the world (*duniya*). Their musket balls reinforced[2] their [the Hindus'] volleys of stones and bricks. Many people from both sides were killed and wounded. The fight continued for two days and nights.

At that time, Daud Khan had gone to Sabar district to collect tribute from the zamindars and deal with the refractory; he had camped at Bagh i Shahi. He dispatched soldiers to intervene between the [two] sides and separate them, and to disallow anyone to raise his head [in defiance] and cause bloodshed. Meanwhile several notables (*ayan*), men with foresight and wisdom in the city, offered with temperate tongue salutary words of advice, with arguments based on reason and tradition (*dalail-i aqali wa naqali*), to hold the two parties back. The fire of sedition (*atish-i fitna*) was put down and Daud Khan marched [towards Ahmedabad] for purposes of administration ....

When reports of the Holi disturbance and the barricading [of roads] were conveyed by dispatches of the news writers to the imperial court, and the group of Hindu sarrafs and merchants of Gujarat (*jama-i hinduan sarrafan wa tijarat peshagan*), who had their branch-shops in the imperial camp having suspended their business and dealings, collectively approached the Court about the ransacking and burning of their shops, the killings, and the looting of their cash and goods, alleging in this the instigation of Muhammad Ali Waiz and Mulla Abdul Aziz, an order was issued that harsh mace bearers should depart and bring the above-mentioned persons as well as Kapur Chand Bhansali and Hari Ram, in chains and fetters, to the imperial court of Justice. Mulla Abdul Aziz came to know about this before the arrival of the mace bearers from the letters of the Bohras, present at the court, and tipped off Muhammad Ali Waiz. Both of them thought it expedient to proceed to the court on their own and so departed [from Ahmedabad]. Kapur Chand Bhansali and Hari Ram, learning of the circumstances, [also] made their way [to the Court]. The mace-bearers turned back midway. The [two] parties, making their journey, reached the capital one after the other.

That foremost preacher, Muhammd Ali, [having arrived] ascended the pulpit of the Jami Masjid [of Delhi] and started delivering sermons. As the Glorious God had given him the power of speech and purity of diction (*taqat-i lisan wa uzubat-i biyan*), he was very impressive in his sermons and gained immense fame instantly. Group after group of people, high and low, gathered at the foot of the pulpit to listen to his sermons and became his disciples and followers, until his merits were brought to the Emperor's attention by Fazail Khan. An order was issued granting him audience (*mulazamat*). He [Fazail Khan] brought His Holiness (*u ishan*) and Mulla Abdul Aziz, himself in no small measure an embodiment of virtue and excellence, before the Emperor. The truth of the entire matter was now revealed directly to the Emperor. His Majesty, being greatly affected, observed that the Hindus[3] by

[2]For *ma'adin* in the text, read *mu'awin*.
[3]For *hunuz* in the text, read *hunud*.

their falsification (*khilaf numai*) caused this unique person to take to wandering. An imperial order was issued that Kapur Chand and others be seized to be fettered and imprisoned. An order was also sent to the Governor and diwan of the subah of Gujarat that they should confiscate his house, and this was accordingly done at Ahmedabad. When His Majesty listened to [Muhammad Ali's] sermons he became more and more attached to that spiritually elevated voice [lit. voice interpreting divine revelations] and showered upon him abundant words of praise. This became very well known and the majority of people became inclined towards him. After some time, Kapur Chand saw that there was no means of redemption except for him to make appeals and solicitations to Muhammad Ali and Mulla Abdul Aziz. He sent a message [to them] that [since] we have come from the same native place and region (*yak watan wa dayar*), let us overcome our quarrel, and turning our mutual hostility into friendship, we should so act that we leave for our native place in safety and harmony (*ba salamat ba ittifaq*). Thus when Mulla Abdul Aziz obtained leave to depart from the Court of Imperial Dignity and Government of the World, he also secured leave for departure for him [Kapur Chand] and embarked upon his journey. The people [of Delhi], pleading with Muhammad Ali with much humility made him stay on till he died [lit. found a place in the vicinity of Divine Mercy].[4]

The Version from Delhi

A Description of the Events of the Third Regnal Year of Farrukh Siyar, the Martyr

Now I turn my pen to the description of an event which took place in Ahmedabad in the third regnal year of Farrukh Siyar [AD 1715]; [viz.] the flame of riot and enmity (*fasad u inad*) which flared up between the communities of Hindus and Muslims, and the end of it saw a conflict between Khwaja Muhammad Jafar Darwesh and Shaikh Abdullah Waiz at the imperial capital.

To give a summary of it, in the first regnal year Daud Khan Panni became Governor of Ahmedabad-Gujarat. In the second year [AD 1714], on the night when the *holi* of Hindus is set alight, one of the Hindus, opposite whose house lived some Muslims, with a common street (*kucha-i mushtarak*) between the courtyards of the two houses, wished to set alight the holi in front of his own house. The Muslims objected to it. The Hindu, having support and protection from Daud Khan, who often came to the aid of the Hindus, asserted that he was entitled to do what he wished in his own house. Despite much argument and importunities of all kinds, he set the holi afire.

The next day, a Muslim, who lived opposite the house, desired to give a feast [on the eve] of the death anniversary of the Prophet, the purest of all beings. Arguing in the same manner as the Hindu that this was his house, he brought and slaughtered a cow (*gau*) there. The Hindus of the entire locality assembled and a crowd came to attack the Muslims. The Muslims, not being strong enough to resist, hid themselves in their houses. The Hindus carried their boldness to such extreme that they were said to have dragged away the 14- or 15-year-old son of a cow butcher (*gau qassab*), and so it is said, one of the Bohras who had fallen into their hands, and slaughtered him. Observing this atrocity committed by

---

[4]Ali Muhammad Khan, *Mirat-i Ahmadi*, 2 vols and *Supplement*. Ed. Syed Nawab Ali (Baroda, 1927–30), vol. 1, pp. 405–7, 410–12.

the Hindus, Muslims collected from all sides, raised the cry of a general onslaught and prepared to do battle with the Hindus.

A few thousand Afghan soldiers, from amongst the servants of Daud [Khan], for the sake of the honour and prestige of Islam, without the pleasure of their master, and the Afghans from the suburbs of Ahmedabad, and the Bohras of the city assembled to form a riotous crowd and arrived at the door of the house of the Qazi. The Qazi, seeing the disturbance and the crowd, and keeping in view the partiality of the Governor, shut the doors of his house in the face of the tumultuous gathering. According to a popular account, as a result of this act of the Qazi, which was due to the favour and partisanship Daud Khan showed to Hindus, the Muslims burnt the doors of the Qazi's house and set fire to shops on the street of the square and other houses of the Hindus. In the riot, many shops of the cloth merchants (*bazzazan*) and other traders were destroyed. Subsequently, they set out to burn the house of Kapur Chand, the ill-famed jeweller (*nam badnam jauhari*), who was the source of all the trouble, and a companion of Daud Khan, and an intensely bigoted Hindu. Kapur Chand was alerted and, fortifying the gates of his locality with a group of matchlock men (*barqandazn*), took to fighting and a number of Hindus and Muslims were killed.

The riot reached such a pitch that for three [to] four days [all] business in the market and of the professional class was closed and suspended. Later, many people from both sides decided to make representations to the imperial court. Daud Khan drew up a signed statement (*mahzar*) to which he put his own as well as the seals of the Qazi and other officials, gave it to Kapur Chand who left [with it] for Shahjahanabad. From the side of the Muslims, Shaikh Abdul Aziz, Shaikh Abdul Wahid, and Shaikh Muhammad Ali Waiz, adorned with the virtues of honesty and probity, with a group of the Bohras and Muslims of other denominations, proceeded to the court. Since Raja Ratan Chand, the diwan of Qutub ul Mulk [Abdullah Khan] thought it necessary to take the side of his co-religionists (*hum qaum*), he got Shaikh Abdul Wahid, Shaikh Muhammad Ali Waiz, and other Muslims arrested and imprisoned on the basis of the document which the Hindus were holding in their hands. Khwaja Muhammad Jafar, who was renowned among hermits and recluses, got the information of the above-mentioned matter [lit. truth] and of the incarceration of the Muslims. He sought the release of this group through the mediation of Khan i Dauran [Khwaja Asim Khan].[5]

III

The Flashpoint

There is usually an incident that precipitates a riot. It is close in time and place to the outbreak of violence and is causally related to subsequent events. The precipitant for the Ahmedabad riot was the celebration of Holi, a festival of

---

[5]Khafi Khan, *Muntakhab ul Lubab*, 2 vols. Ed. Maulvi Kabiruddin Ahmad (Bibliotheca Indica: Calcutta, 1874), vol. 2, pp. 755–7. The author of *Siyar ul Mutakherin*, Ghulam Hussain Tabatabi, has reproduced this version with minor modifications. See the Nawal Kishore edn (n.d.), vol. 2, pp. 398–9.

colour, games, and merrymaking. The versions concur on this but they differ in describing the precise act which triggered the conflict.

The Delhi version, indicating the inevitability of contact between communities living in close proximity, adds a serious note to the precipitant by bringing in cow slaughter and the killing of a Muslim youth, apparently the son of the same butcher who slaughtered the cow, in what was seen as an act of revenge.[6] There is no mention of the two slaughters in the Ahmedabad version and it is difficult to imagine that, if anything of this nature actually happened, the author could have missed it altogether. However, in the account of the subsequent year, he mentions another dispute which took place in Ahmedabad involving a cow, a *havaldar* (junior military official), and the Bohras on the eve of the Sacrificial Feast or *Id al azha*.[7] Except for the feast, the cow, and a mob of Bohras, there is nothing common between the above incident and the one reported in the Delhi version, and it is difficult to ascertain whether the former was the source for the latter. The idiom used by the author of the Delhi version (*ba qaul*) suggests that he found the two incidents—the Holi celebrations and the slaughter—already fused in the version circulating in his city from the time when the Muslims appeared to be badly placed in an ongoing court case.

The Mobilization

Mobilization for a riot is done for the purpose of expressing rage, conquering fear, and legitimizing violence, things which individuals find difficult to accomplish on their own. In the Delhi version, mobilization became easier once the atrocious nature of the precipitant was revealed. The people, who witnessed the slaughter, as well as those who lent willing ears to stories of the atrocity, were outraged and felt, at the same time, an impending threat of aggression.

Due to the soft nature of the precipitant, the author of the Ahmedabad version pays more attention to the act of mobilization. At primary level, the person, the 'victim' of Holi celebrations, circulated, with physical evidence, the story of his humiliation among those who were known to him to get their support. To broaden participation, however, the agency of those commanding informal or formal authority over people was required. Thus the leader of the sermon readers of local

---

[6]See Tabatabi, *Siyar ul Mutakherin*, p. 398 ('*iwaz i gau ba kushtand*).

[7]A havaldar, 'inspired by his religious beliefs and emboldened by the Governorship of Maharaja Ajit Singh', seized a sacrificial cow from Kalupur, a predominantly Bohra locality in Ahmedabad. The Qazi reported the matter to the Governor. When no response came from the administration, 'the Muslims from the city and the suburbs gathered to form a riotous mob'. They were pacified only after an assurance was given by the Governor that 'the Muslims have freedom of action in accordance with [the tenets of] their religion and regulations of the state (*muwafiq i din wa a'in*)', and that this freedom can not be taken away from them by anyone. Soon after, the Qazi carried a cow [the cow!] to the mosque and sacrificed it after the Id prayer. Ali Muhammad Khan, *Mirat-i Ahmadi*, vol. 2, pp. 5–6.

mosques was approached for the second, and higher, level of mobilization that took place at the central mosque of the city. The wa'iz lost no time in getting to the Jami Masjid knowing well that to wait till Friday would strip the matter of urgency and immediacy. He also used his religious and moral authority to persuade the leader of the Sunni Bohra sect, who lived in a different locality, to join him with the members of his *jama'at*.

Religion provided an important source of strength. It was used both to express rage and induce a sense of legitimacy and invulnerability. Slogans of 'din din' were raised to announce the threat posed to the honour of the true faith (*din-i mubin*) and to signal that the crowd was acting in unison. To extract greater legitimacy, the office of the Qazi was invoked and the demand on him to accompany the mob was made to put the seal of authority on the course of violence.

The role of religion is emphasized in both versions, but more strongly in the one produced at Delhi. It was articulated by words of praise for those who came out to defend the honour of Islam, regardless of risks and dangers (such as the Afghan soldiers of the Governor), and of condemnation for those who were either seen as enemy (such as Kapur Chand) or siding with the enemy (such as the Muslim matchlock men and the Governor). Interestingly enough, the Qazi's refusal to give in to the demands of the Muslim mob was seen not as an act of prejudice but prudence by the author of the Ahmedabad version. The author employs the rowdiness of the crowd as a trope to direct the audience's allegiance and sympathy towards the jurist and his burnt house.

The Riot

Violence began with the burning of the house of the Qazi for his refusal to yield to the pressure of the mob. This was the declaration of intent which also made it quite clear what the mob meant by 'defence of honour and protection of faith'. The targets were selected with precision. They were not difficult to locate and lay within striking distance from the place of congregation of the rioters, the Jami Masjid. Just across the mosque, and leading up to Tin Darwaza and Manek Chowk, the commercial hub of the city, was the principal market street of Ahmedabad arrayed with shops of all kinds but more particularly of the cloth merchants, money changers, and bankers (sarrafs).[8] The rioters hit the high street first, looted cash and goods from one set of shops, and set another on fire.[9] The discriminate acts of plunder and arson indicated not only the urge to gain from violence but also complete hostility. Apparently they met with no resistance as no casualty is reported at this stage.

[8]Makrand Mehta, 'Social base of Jain entrepreneurs in the 17th century: Shantidas Zaveri of Ahmedabad', in his, *Indian Merchants and Entrepreneurs in Historical Perspective* (Delhi, 1991), pp. 92–4.

[9]I'timad Ali Khan, *Miratu-l Haqaiq*, f. 170b.

The mob moved from the market towards the second target, the reputed Jauhari-wara (Zaverivad) which housed the residential quarters of the commercial elites of Ahmedabad such as Kapur Chand and Madan Gopal. It was here that they met with resistance by Kapur Chand whose house was specifically selected for attack. Kapur Chand fortified the gates of Jauhari-wara by posting matchlock men and supervising the lines of defence. By now the residents of Jauhari-wara were also ready to counter-attack. Bricks and stones flew from both sides but the use of muskets, expensive but effective, gave the defenders a definite edge over the attackers. The fight continued for two days and nights or probably more. In the absence of precise figures available to them, the authors favoured approximation and indicated that 'many' people from both sides were killed or wounded. Violence was stopped after the intervention of the state administration and civilian population. The Governor, then camping on the northern borders of the city, sent soldiers to handle the situation without using excessive force, and influential citizens of Ahmedabad came out with custom-made messages meant exclusively for such occasions.

Both versions are remarkably similar in describing the course of the rioting, the nature of the violence, target selection, and resistance. The termination of violence, however, receives treatment only in the Ahmedabad version with an emphasis on the role of the local administration and citizenry. In that sense, the riot episode in the *Mirat-i Ahmadi* appears to be more complete. The *Muntakhab* passes up all this although there is a reference to the impact of violence on business which the *Mirat-i Ahmadi* omits. None of the two versions justifies the act of violence explicitly, although Ali Muhammad Khan uses expressions such as oppression, plunder, and murder to suggest condemnation and reveals his indignation and sorrow in a couplet.

The Participants

The participants in the Ahmedabad episode can be classified into three groups: organizers, supporters, and neutralizers. Among the organizers of the riot and the resistance, the two principal actors, Abdul Aziz and Kapur Chand, were merchants—one a cap merchant (*topiwala* or *kulah farosh*), the other a jeweller (*jauhari*)—and leaders of the Sunni Bohra and 'Hindu' communities respectively.[10]

In both versions, the term Hindu, and its plural (hunud, *hinduan*), is used several times. On two occasions in the Ahmedabad version (once in the title of the episode), it is coupled with, and used in opposition to, the term Muslim and it's plural (*ahl-i islam*, *muslamin*). On both occasions, it is used in the sense of a group of people, particularly when Kapur Chand is identified as the 'leader of

---

[10]For Abdul Aziz's professional status, see I'timad Ali Khan, *Miratu-l Haqaiq*, ff. 170b, 453b. Kapur Chand is described as a jeweller in ibid., f. 170b and Khafi Khan, *Muntakhab ul Lubab*, vol. 2, p. 756.

the Hindu community'. In a separate section (*Khatima* or *Supplement*) of his work, the author of the Ahmedabad version offers a definition of the term 'Hindu' under the title 'A Description of the Inhabitants of the City'.

The description begins with a passing reference to the primary group identity of the population of Ahmedabad as 'Gujarati': those who lived in Ahmedabad from the time the city was founded by Sultan Ahmad Shah of Gujarat (AD 1411), and their descendants, as well as those who came and settled from neighbouring localities.[11] The Gujarati population was divided into two main groups, Hindus and Muslims, of which the former are described as follows:

The Hindu community consists of various castes (*aqwam*) and professions (*asnaf*), viz. Brahman, Sevra, Khatri, Rajput, Bania or Baqqal, Kait, Kunbi or farmer, Koli, and artisans, such as gold-smith, iron-smith, fuller, oil-presser, carpenter, weaver, tailor, dyer, tanner and sweeper, and other similar people on whom the term Hindu is applied. Some are original inhabitants and some have come from other places and settled in this kingdom. In every caste, with the passage of time, various [sub] castes are born, in branches and divisions, either due to some unworthy action or due to the appearance of a breach in the purity of the father and the mother .... Since an account of all the divisions will lengthen and complicate the discourse, the following treatment is limited to the castes of Brahman, Sevra, [and] Maisri and Sravak Baqqals who are in greater multitude.[12]

It can be seen from the above passage that Ali Muhammad Khan is using Hindu as a term of reference for people of all religions, castes, sub-castes, and professions who can be classified as a group different from the Muslims.[13] He reckons the Jain clergy (Shevra) and the laity (Shravak) as Hindus even though he is aware of the difference in the religious persuasions of, as well as the antagonism between, the Jains and the Vaishnavites (Maishris).[14]

---

[11]Ali Muhammad Khan, *Mirat-i Ahmadi, Supplement*, p. 129.

[12]Ibid., p. 132.

[13]The author follows a tradition in Persian scholarship of medieval India where all Indians other than Muslims are described as Hindus. Kaikhusrau Asfandyar, the author of a celebrated Indian work on world religions (c. AD 1653), places the belief systems of various schools, sects, and religions of India (including Jainism) under the rubric Hindus. *Dabistan-i Mazahib*. Ed. Rahim Rezazadeh Malik (Tehran, Solar 1362), vol. 1, pp. 121–212. For other examples, see Heinrich von Stietencorn, 'Hinduism: On the proper use of a descriptive term', in Gunther D. Sontheimer and Herman Kulke (eds), *Hinduism Reconsidered* (Delhi, 1989), p. 12; Carl Ernst, *Eternal Garden: Mysticism, History and Politics at a South Asian Sufi Center* (Albany, 1992), pp. 22–4.

[14]Ali Muhammad Khan, *Mirat-i Ahmadi, Supplement*, pp. 135–7, 139–40. 'The Sevra, also called Jati, are a group of mendicants who live in solitude ... and practice strict asceticism. They reckon Parasnath as their God and beg their subsistence, water and bread, from the houses of their followers, the Sravak *baqqals* .... The Maisris, who are the followers of the Brahmans, abhor the Sevras and consider it despicable (*mazmul*) to associate or even converse with them .... Both [the Maishris and the Shravaks] have their places of worship (*ma'bad*) in this kingdom but the one does not have faith in the other'. A statement is made in Asfandyar, *Dabistan-i Mazahib* (vol. 1, pp. 185–6) that the Jains 'rejected the religious principles of the Hindus (*munkir-i shari'at i-hinduan bashand*)' and also made fun of them.

A possible reason for the consolidation of two separate religious communities into a single group could be that both the Maishris and the Shravaks were traders by profession and therefore constituted the sub-group of the Vaishya caste known as Bania. Ali Muhammad Khan treats the group as one when he gives a common list for the eighty-four sub-castes of Maishris and Shravaks and calls them all 'Banik or Bania or *baqqal* in Arabic'.[15] The close connection between the two was reinforced by the freedom to move, with the exception of the Brahmans, from one religious group to another.[16] In Ahmedabad, a strong indication of the cohesive nature of the Bania community, as well as the dominance of one group over the exchange economy of the city, was the appointment of Jains, such as Kapur Chand and his putative successor, Khushhal Chand, as nagarseths.[17]

If the title nagarseth conveyed the leadership of the entire 'Hindu' population of Ahmedabad, then the organizational structure would have imparted some internal coherence to it as well. However, there is a possibility that the nagarseth was the head of the business community of Ahmedabad and not simply of the 'Hindus'. If it was not an aberration, members of the Sunni Bohra community held the post of the nagarseth of Ahmedabad in the 1730s, and the appointment order of Khushhal Chand to the post does not give any indication that his responsibilities were limited to managing the affairs of the 'Hindus'.[18] However, the virtual monopoly of the leading Jain merchants of the city over the post of the nagarseth and the fact that they were, at the same time, leaders of their own respective guilds (*mahajans*), gave the title and the leadership a predominantly 'Hindu' character which Ali Muhammad Khan took for granted.[19]

While a common profession, common sub-castes, and freedom of conversion

[15]*Mirat-i Ahmadi, Supplement*, pp. 138–9. Cf. Irfan Habib, 'Merchant communities in pre-colonial India', in James D. Tracy (ed.), *The Rise of Merchant Empires, Long-Distance Trade in the Early Modern World 1350–1750* (Cambridge, 1990), p. 380.

[16]Ali Muhammad Khan, *Mirat-i Ahmadi, Supplement*, pp. 137, 163; Banarasidas, *Ardhakathanaka*. Ed. and trans. Mukund Lath (Jaipur, 1981), Hindi text, p. 224 (verses 8–9).

[17]Khushhal Chand, who was the grandson (The *Mirat-i Ahmadi* mistakenly calls him the son) of the famous Jain merchant and jeweller, Santidas, is similarly described as the leader of the Hindus (*firqa-i hunud*) and the nagarseth. Ali Muhammad Khan, *Mirat-i Ahmadi*, vol. 2, p. 158. Also see Dwijendra Tripathi and M.J. Mehta, 'The nagarseth of Ahmedabad: The history of an urban institution in a Gujarat city', in Satish Chandra (ed.), *Essays in Medieval Indian Economic History* (Delhi, 1987), pp. 267, 268.

[18]Ali Muhammad Khan, *Mirat-i Ahmadi*, vol. 2, pp. 139, 158, 172.

[19]Gangadas, who remained the nagarseth from 1726 to 1731, was a Jain and the leader of the silk merchants (*sar-guroh i abresham faroshan*). Similarly, nagarseths Ahmad and Abu Bakr, were the leaders (seth) of the Sunni Bohra group of merchants. Ibid., pp. 92, 139, 172. Although this is not stated in any of the sources available to me, Kapur Chand and Khushhal Chand must have been the leaders of their own guild of jewellers. For the mahajans of Ahmedabad, see Shirin Mehta, 'The Mahajans and the business communities of Ahmedabad', in Dwijendra Tripathi (ed.), *Business Communities of India* (Delhi, 1984), pp. 173–83.

facilitated the conceptualization of Banias as a community and an important component of the Hindu population, specialization of functions and the pursuit of commercial interests also turned them into distinct and separate sub-groups, each with its own identity, rules, and leadership. The Banias specialized in various branches of commerce, such as commodity trade, brokerage, money changing, and banking (sarrafi) and insurance (bima). Madan Gopal, who had no part in the story, except for keeping an agent on his payroll who played Holi with passion, is identified as an influential member of the community of sarrafs. These distinctions are maintained in the account of the Gujarati Banias doing business at the imperial court in Delhi. They are first described as 'Hindus' and then as 'sarrafs' and 'merchants'. It is interesting to note that whenever Ali Muhammad Khan speaks of these groups in isolation, he never uses for them the word Hindu (such as in the incident described in the following paragraph). The term is used only when they are seen as a group in relation to the Muslim community, as in the Holi riot.

Ali Muhammad Khan is deeply aware of the underlying tension between two groups of the mercantile community of Ahmedabad, the Bania merchants, and the Bania bankers (sarrafs), which came out in the open and led to an armed conflict in the midst of the Holi episode. The tension was inherent in their business relations and their pursuit of profit. The Banias needed cash for investment in the right seasons of the year and also needed to keep transaction costs to the minimum while circulating their liquid capital. The sarrafs provided both the services by lending money, discounting negotiable bills of exchange (hundis) to maintain cash flow, and by using entries in their ledger to accept deposits on interest and settle obligations through book transfers (giro banking).[20] In ordinary circumstances, the system worked to the advantage of both parties. At the turn of the century, however, Ahmedabad suffered from a serious cash crunch and the sarrafs tried to handle it by introducing a system of floating credit in which cash payments against commercial papers and deposits were discouraged by raising the rate of anth (conversion of credit into cash) to a very high level. In medieval market economies, credit was reckoned as a supplementary artifice of money, and not its substitute, since all transactions were structurally tied to settlement in specie. Thus the demand for cash and a rise in transaction costs pitched the merchants against the sarrafs and brought the entire exchange market to a standstill. Negotiations between the two parties, led by Kapur Chand and the representative of the sarrafs, Hari Ram, acting on behalf of Madan Gopal, failed. The two groups organized their defences and prepared for a battle (jang). The war of attrition continued for two days and was stopped from turning violent only by the 'wise men' of the city.[21]

---

[20]Najaf Haider, 'The monetary basis of credit and banking instruments in the Mughal empire', in Amiya Bagchi (ed.), *Money and Credit in Indian History* (Delhi, 2002), pp. 58–79.

[21]Ali Muhammad Khan, *Mirat-i Ahmadi*, vol. 1, pp. 410–11.

This minor episode of a potential riot is perhaps indicative of the strains and stresses afflicting the mercantile economy of Gujarat at the turn of the eighteenth century. A downturn in the hinterland, rising transaction costs due to fear, uncertainty, and lack of safety for goods and money in transit, and Maratha expeditionary raids which began in AD 1703 and reached their high point in the second quarter of the eighteenth century, boded ill for the vigorous conduct of business.[22] Stiff competition for the shrunken markets and concern for a greater stake in the city affairs may have lowered the threshold of tolerance that existed between communities with complementary interests.

The principal organizer of violence, Abdul Aziz, was the leader of a sub-group of Ahmedabad's mercantile population, the Sunni Bohras, who were junior partners of the Banias in the trading network of Gujarat. They descended from that section of the mercantile population of Gujarat (probably of the Vohra caste) which converted to Ismailism in the eleventh century and later split to form the Sunni sect in the fifteenth century.[23] Rest of the Vohras remained Jains and Hindus. The merchant prince of Surat in the seventeenth century, Virji Vora, was a Jain and his counterpart (umdat ut tujjar) in the eighteenth century, Mulla Abdul Ghafur, was a Sunni Bohra. The Sunni Bohras were in a majority and were wealthier and more powerful than the Ismailis.[24] They had their shops, offices, and correspondents in Ahmedabad, and Surat as well as the imperial camp at Delhi. In all these places, they had Banias as their competitors. How much the crisis of the early eighteenth century was responsible for turning the seth of the Sunni Bohras and Kapur Jauhari, his Bania counterpart, into organizers of violence can only be speculated. The Ahmedabad version indeed imputes motives of professional rivalry, which probably also included claims over the coveted post of the nagarseth, when it clubs the two principal actors together in the run-up to the riot.[25]

[22]Georges Roques, *La maniere de negotier dans Les Indes Orientalles dedice a mes Chers amis Et Confreres Les Engages de la Royalle Compagnye de France*, Bibliotheque Nationale, MS Fonds Francais 14614, ff. 239–40; Ashin Das Gupta, 'Trade and politics in eighteenth century', in D.S. Richards (ed.), *Islam and the Trade of Asia* (Oxford, 1970), p. 189; Ali Muhammad Khan, *Mirat-i Ahmadi*, vol. 1, pp. 356, 359–69, 377–9. With each pay out to the Marathas (such as the one exacted by Balaji Vishwanath in 1706), Ahmedabad got poorer, lost business, and moved investments towards strengthening the defences of the town.

[23]Farhad Daftary, *The Ismailis: Their History and Doctrines* (Cambridge, 1992), pp. 292–302.

[24]Ali Muhammad Khan, *Mirat-i Ahmadi*, vol. 2, p. 139; *Supplement*, p. 131; I'timad Ali Khan, *Miratu-l Haqaiq*, f. 349a.

[25]For the bitter rivalry and enmity ('adawat') between Seth Khushhal Chand and Seth Ahmad, see Ali Muhammad Khan, *Mirat-i Ahmadi*, vol. 2, pp. 170–2. When Ahmad died, Khushhal Chand was pleased (Khushhal Chand ... khushhal-i chand namuda) and ordered the body of his Bohra adversary to be exhumed and vandalized by the Kolis specially hired for this purpose. For the relationship between Khushhal Chand and Abdul Aziz, also marred by mutual rivalry, see I'timad Ali Khan, *Miratu-l Haqaiq*, f. 453b.

The supporters of Islam, mostly artisans and unnamed citizens—'high and low', 'believers and faithful', 'rowdy and ignorant'—are identified purely on the ground of their attachment to the cause of religion. Among them, the Afghans receive attention in the Delhi version as soldiers of Daud Khan. They came from the suburbs of Ahmedabad, across the river Sabarmati, where there was a large and 'ancient' settlement of the Afghan community.[26] Although praised for defiance of authority, it is doubtful whether they were in regular employment of the provincial administration or in the personal service of the Afghan Governor. They were unavailable for the Governor's campaign and the man, although not a very good administrator, was known for exercising strict control over his troops (*lashkariyan*) during expeditions.[27] Chances are that the group was once in the personal contingent of some warrior noble and that at the time of the riot, was probably out of employment.[28] Chris Bayly has offered a sociological explanation for the general involvement of the Afghans in conflicts: their 'undisciplined' and 'mercenary' character and their isolation 'in an urban environment', providing the 'impetus for communal violence in the early stages of state building'.[29] However, more findings on the exact nature of their professional status, command structure, and religious persuasions are needed before their motives can become fully explicable.[30]

No such doubts could be entertained about the motives of the Gujarati musketeers who were Muslims but threw in their lot with the Banias and practically saved the Jauhari-wara from being overrun by the attackers. They were mercenaries and currently out of job. Ali Muhammad Khan rues the fact that they became embroiled for purely mundane reasons, either immediate gains or future employment. They were paid by Kapur Chand (their wages were fixed in advance) and they also knew that he was close to the administration and that appealing to his good offices was worth the fight against the defenders of the 'true faith'.[31]

[26]Ali Muhammad Khan, *Mirat-i Ahmadi, Supplement*, p. 17; vol. 1, pp. 356, 392–3.

[27]Ibid., vol. 1, p. 412.

[28]Muhammad Beg Khan, 'a noble and a warrior', who served the Gujarat administration in various capacities, had in his service, at the time of his death in Ahmedabad in AD 1712, six to seven thousand Afghans, foot soldiers and cavalrymen, for a 'very long time'. Ibid., vol. 1, pp. 392–3, 397.

[29]C.A. Bayly, 'The Pre-history of "Communalism"? Religious Conflict in India, 1700–1860', *Modern Asian Studies*, 19, 2 (1985), pp. 194–5.

[30]In the Delhi riot of 1729, the Afghan soldiers of Raushan ud daulah Zafar Khan fought spiritedly in order to defend their employer against the attacks of the Muslim show sellers. Saiyid Athar Abbas Rizvi, *Shah Wali-Allah and His Times* (Canberra, 1980), p. 201.

[31]Khushhal Chand, similarly organized the defences of Jauhari-wara with the help of Arab soldiers against a possible attack on his locality and his own establishments from the forces of the deputy governor, Anup Singh Bhandari, a man responsible for the murder of the previous nagarseth, and a fellow Marwari, Kapur Chand Bhansali. Ali Muhammad Khan, *Mirat-i Ahmadi*, vol. 2, p. 170.

The neutralizers were aligned on two axes. The Governor of the subah, Daud Khan, and the Qazi, Khairullah Khan, were part of the higher bureaucracy of Farrukhsiyar's provincial set-up and their interest lay in maintaining peace in the province.[32] Their job was to uphold the law of the land (a'in) and, at the same time, to watch for anything which appeared violative of the shari'ah.

In the Delhi version, the Governor is portrayed as a person no less vicious than his associate, the 'bigoted infidel', Kapur Chand. His reputation as an 'intimate friend of the Hindus' was good enough a reason to establish his complicity in the murder of the butcher's son, the Qazi's refusal to act and, above all, in the court case against the Muslims. After all, he sent a report to the court blaming only one party for the violence that landed most Muslim petitioners in jail.

The 'intimacy' between the Governor and nagarseth Kapur Chand was perhaps natural owing to the latter's position as an intermediary between the powerful business community of Ahmedabad and the administration as long as the Mughal institutional structure remained intact. The Qazi too was an important link between the Muslim civilian population and the administration and his choice to under-react betokened religious and official disapproval of the campaign and any potential act of violence. The two officials were convinced that the campaign had no legal basis and that the Muslims were indeed at fault.

The other group comprised the 'wise men' of the city, unnamed and unidentified except by their virtues and wisdom, apparently from both communities. The culpability of the heads of the corporate bodies opened up the space for them to negotiate and arbitrate. That the riot was put down by the collective efforts of the military and civilian population does not find a place in the Delhi version.

Reading both accounts together, and rereading the Delhi version, one feels as if Khafi Khan was trying to make a case against the Governor. Daud Khan had a reputation for holding unorthodox opinions, keeping an idol in his house, and 'favouring' the Hindus.[33] One can also guess, after reading his history, where Khafi Khan's sympathies would lie in a dispute such as this. But there could be another reason for a hostile portrayal of the Afghan noble. Daud's patron, Hussain Ali Khan, replaced Khafi's patron in the Deccan and ended the author's career as a diwan, the highest office of his life. Also at the head of a powerful faction at the Court, Hussain Ali Khan wanted to stay in Delhi and appoint his protégé, Daud, as his deputy. Khafi Khan's tormented soul may have placed the Deccani Afghan somewhere in the Court politics precipitating these appointments.

[32] Ali Muhammad Khan, *Mirat-i Ahmadi*, vol. 1, p. 401.
[33] Satish Chandra, *Parties and Politics at the Mughal Court 1707–1740* (4th edn, New Delhi, 2002), p. 149.

The Climax

Just as the two versions differ in their description of the flashpoint, they also differ in their treatment of the climax. The Ahmedabad version spins the narrative entirely around the personality of the preacher, Muhammad Ali, for whom the author, Ali Muhammad, shows enormous respect. When representations were made at the court, the response of the state was to bring all the accused, Abdul Aziz topiwala, Muhammad Ali waiz, Hari Ram gumashta, and Kapur Chand jauhari, to trial. A trial could have gone against all four or, worse still, against the first two. But the preacher descended from the pulpit of the Delhi Jama Masjid, like some dues ex machina, and delivered the Muslims from the peril. The author clears the ground for it by valorizing the eloquence of the preacher. A trial was indeed superfluous and, in what appears as a turnaround, the verdict was pronounced against the 'guilty'.

Ali Muhammad Khan cares to mention Kapur Chand's conciliatory gestures which provided the pretext for intercession. References to a common homeland (*yak watan wa dayar*) formed the basis for reconciliation and for 'closing the social distance'. Kapur Chand's claim to the citizenship of Gujarat, and of Ahmedabad, was acceptable to Abdul Aziz who appealed to secure the release of his adversary on the eve of his departure.[34] One might perhaps question how a man convicted by the highest court of law in the empire was acquitted purely on the pleading of a co-accused, but the author of the Ahmedabad version seems convinced of the genuineness and efficacy of the rapprochement. Muhammad Ali, meanwhile, showed no disposition to return and by now had enough reasons to stay in the capital where he was well looked after till his death. Before that, however, he indulged in a fierce polemical exchange on behalf of a liberal Sufi, Khwaja Muhammad Jafar Darwesh, against an orthodox theologian from Multan, Shaikh Abdullah, which kicked up a sectarian row in Delhi.[35]

A trial did indeed take place if the Delhi version is to be believed, and the 'Muslim party' lost the case. Although the court may have had at its disposal the report of the waqa'i' navis, petitions of the Gujarat merchants and bankers at Delhi, and statements from the accused, the clinching evidence was provided by the Governor's report (*dastawiz*) which, rather unusually, Kapur Chand was made to deliver. Khafi Khan is not interested in the merits of the case and attributes the outcome of the trial to the predilective affinity of Raja Ratan Chand, a Bania and a close associate of the Saiyid brothers (being the diwan of one of them, the *wazir* Qutub ul Mulk Abdullah Khan), for Kapur Chand. However, it seems more probable

---

[34]Kapur Chand Bhansali originally came from Marwar, had a house in Jodhpur, and maintained contacts with his homeland. In 1707, he sent from Ahmedabad the news of the death of the emperor, Aurangzeb, by a courier (*qasid*). *Ajit Vilas*. Ed. Shivdattdan Barhat (Jodhpur, 1984), p. 113.

[35]Khafi Khan, *Muntakhab ul Lubab*, vol. 2, pp. 757–60; Tabatabi, *Siyar ul Mutakherin*, vol. 2, pp. 399–400.

that factionalism in Farrukh Siyar's court provided the real ground for the release of the Muslims when Khan i Dauran Khawja Asim, one of the two leading favourites of the king in his struggle against the Saiyids (the other was Mir Jumla), interceded on their behalf. The basis for the reversal of the verdict remains unknown.[36]

IV. RIOT, HOLI RIOT, COMMUNAL RIOT?

The dictionary definition of riot is 'a disturbance of the peace by a crowd' or 'an occurrence of public disorder'. In this sense, the Ahmedabad 'disturbance' qualifies to be called a riot and the terms used for it in our sources—*hangama*, *fasad*, *fitna*—convey the same impression. A crowd (*hujum*, *majma*), the size of which is unknown but which was certainly big, indulged in murder, arson, looting, and street fighting, provoked retaliatory measures, and the conflicting parties were disciplined by the agency responsible for maintaining law and order.

The Ahmedabad version formally calls it a 'Holi disturbance', and the Delhi version, using stronger expressions, also considers the festival ritual to be the reason behind the slaughter of the animal, and a man, and, ipso facto, the riot. However, the fact that members of one community were not only unwilling to participate but were hostile to the celebrations suggests an underlying tension which made the need for violence seem exigent when an appropriate precipitant occurred. It seems that if there was no Holi riot, there may well have been an Id riot.[37]

In modern accounts dealing not specifically with Ahmedabad, the event is referred to as a communal riot or a Hindu–Muslim riot although, as Bayly has argued, they may not always mean the same thing.[38] In the aftermath of the recent Gujarat carnage, the Ahmedabad riot of 1714 was recalled to buttress the position that communal conflicts in the city have a long pedigree and that all incidents of violence involving Hindus and Muslims, past or present, fit into a pattern which is indicative of the precarious nature of their coexistence.[39] In a sense, then, all

---

[36]Money was the basis for the dismissal of the case, says the author of the third version when he accuses Kapur Chand of bribing the nobles of the imperial court (*ba umara' zar dada*). 'The Muslims got killed, their blood was spilled in vain and Kapur Jauhari was treated in Shahjahanabad with dignity and honour until he left for Gujarat .... This case was the most unusual.' I'timad Ali Khan, *Miratu-l Haqaiq*, ff. 170b-171a.

[37]Reflecting on the sorry state of affairs in his province in AD 1732 which affected Hindus and Muslims alike, the author of the Ahmedabad version also considered the ban on cow slaughter and 'humiliation of Muslims' during Holi as veritable signs of a decline in the fortune of Islam. Ali Muhammad Khan, *Mirat i Ahmadi*, vol. 2, pp. 139–40.

[38]M.S. Commissariat, *A History of Gujarat* (Bombay, 1957), vol. 2, pp. 388–9; Rizvi, *Shah Wali-Allah and His Times*, p. 197; Bayly, 'Pre-history of "Communalism"?', pp. 178–9, 194.

[39]In a televised programme ('The Big Fight', 7 December 2002), a minister in the Indian government and a member of parliament from Ahmedabad, while answering questions on whether

such acts of violence could be seen as a natural outcome of a situation in which two communities viewed each other as separate and mutually antagonistic groups living in a lawless environment where disputes could not eventually be settled peacefully. The matter is further complicated by the suggestion that a sharp and self-conscious Hindu (and Muslim) identity was created in pre-colonial India out of rivalry and violent conflicts between Hindus and Muslims.[40]

The Ahmedabad riot of 1714 is the only incident of its kind in the recorded history of the city from AD 1411 to 1761. It was confined to a particular locality during the course of the rioting and invited participation from groups drawn from three religious communities. Commercial rivalry appears to have lain at the heart of the conflict and signs of it were manifest also in subordinate cases of dispute cutting across religious lines. The presence of other Muslim groups in the mob indicates that the Bania community, the butt of their attack, was viewed with an obscure sense of mistrust or fear. Cow slaughter and Holi celebrations were two contentious issues which heightened hidden pressures and provided the pretext for open provocations. Even in the midst of volatile situations, communities were not divided completely on religious lines and individuals or groups are found to have taken narrower views of their membership while expressing support for or opposition to a particular act or policy. Finally, except for the lapse on the part of the local administration to maintain order at the outset of the violence, the Mughal state apparatus appears to have been effective in containing and adjudicating the dispute in the province and the metropolis.

---

the recent Gujarat riots were an unusual phenomenon, proclaimed that riots have taken place in his constituency 'ever since 1713 [sic.]'.

[40]David N. Lorenzen, 'Who invented Hinduism?', *Comparative Studies in Society and History*, 1999, pp. 630–59.

LIVING TOGETHER: AJMER AS A PARADIGM FOR THE (SOUTH) ASIAN CITY

Shail Mayaram

I. INTRODUCTION: CHARTING DISCIPLINARY WATERS

The major challenge in researching a project on inter-ethnic relations in Ajmer was to delineate its methodological and conceptual dimensions. While there is an established mode of dealing with conflict, say, when one is doing a study of sectarian violence, there are, to my knowledge, no accounts of communities living together. What confronted one was the striking absence of

Acknowledgements: The Sasakawa Peace Foundation's Program on Culture and Identity: Ethnic Coexistence in Asia funded the research for this chapter. I am indebted to Ghanshyam Gurjar and Somoti Lal for their assistance with fieldwork done in Ajmer and its vicinity between 1995 and 1998. Professor Ashis Nandy, Daya Krishna, Mukund Lath, Imtiaz Ahmad, Darini Rajasingham, Rajendra Joshi, N.K. Singh, and Daniel Gold have had discussions and drafts inflicted on them. I must acknowledge the tremendous response and encouragement I received from audiences at the University of Texas at Austin, the Ecole Pratique des Hautes Etudes, Sorbonne, Paris, and the Social Science Association, Mumbai.

The exchanges with Komal Kothari and Sattar Khan, Dominique Sila Khan, S. Liyaqat Hussain Moini, and P.K. Mathur have enhanced my understanding of popular religion. In Ajmer I could not have done without the warm hospitality of Veenu and Devendra Gupta and Colonel Paul. At Beawar Shekhar and Laxman Singh proved a mine of information and contacts. Other persons who contributed their life's experiences at Ajmer, Beawar, and Jaipur were Bhalchand Vyas, Vinita, Shagufta Khan, Salim Sherwani, the Marfatias, Zafar Mohammad, Shankar, Father Wali, Suraj Chaturvedi, Dhulichand Patwari of Pushkar and members of different communities. The institutional support of the Institute of Development Studies and the Committee for Cultural Choices and Global Futures, New Delhi, has been indispensable to this work. For assistance with printouts and library searches, as always I am grateful to Rajan and Khan saab. Rajan and Mohan Das have provided invaluable secretarial support. Arvind Mayaram and Francine E. Krishna have, as usual, been my backbone. This chapter is part of a larger project titled, Communities in Interaction: Discourses of any methodological guidelines, conceptual frameworks, or available literature to handle the universe of ethnic interaction and coexistence. It is important that we reflect on this *absence*. On the contrary, most institutions and the academy are grounded in an epistemology and ontology that celebrate binarism, the bifurcation of the cultural self from the ethnic other.[1]

The dominant episteme of the West defines the lens through which the 'Orient' or the cultures and societies of the non-West are viewed. The juxtaposition of the cultural self with an ethnic other(s) is based on the generic treatment of the self/other in Western philosophy.[2] The ruling notion of Western thought views the integral person as a monad and the other as an entity bounded, separate from, and external to the self. This reverberates within disciplinary territories.

The emergent field of cultural studies purportedly emphasizes the constructedness of identities and diasporic hybridities and challenges essentialism and primordialism. But it is as implicated in sustaining the self–other dualism. This is done as it highlights genealogies of otherness, as in the critique of Orientalism and its variants, in the deconstruction of colonialism and its various discourses of knowledge and power.[3] Balslev points out that the self–other division subsists despite the fact of simultaneously present multiple perceptions of the self and the other.[4] It pervades a good deal of contemporary discussion that focuses on difference and its constituents and on alterity.[5]

Conflict, Conversion, and Coexistence in Cosmopolitan Contexts. Crosscultural Perspectives from Certain Asian Cities, supported by Ford Foundation, December 2002–5.

[1]For a detailed treatment of this theme, see Shail Mayaram, *Resisting Regimes: Myth, Memory and the Shaping of a Muslim Identity* (New Delhi: Oxford University Press, 1997); and my 'Rethinking Meo identity: Cultural faultline, syncretism, hybridity or liminality?', Special issue on Muslim Identity in South Asia and beyond, fifty years after Indian Independence, *Comparative Studies of South Asia, Africa and the Middle East*, guest edited by Mushirul Hasan, 17 (1997), pp. 35–45.

[2]Schools of Buddhist, Hindu, and Islamic philosophy as also discourses of 'popular' religion such as spirit possession suggest very divergent formulations regarding the self and the other.

[3]Said, Inden, Halbfass and others have shown how the Orient is both exoticized and demonized as the domain of unreason, magicality/spirituality, and the primitive in contrast to the rational, enlightened, secular West. Edward Said, *Orientalism* (Harmondswroth, Middlesex: Penguin, 1985); Ronald Inden, *Imagining India* (Oxford: Basil Blackwell, 1990); Wilhelm Halbfass, *India and Europe: An Essay in Philosophical Understanding* (Delhi: Motilal Banarsidass, 1990 [1988]). As Said puts it, much of nineteenth-century thought is characterized by what is fitting for us and what is fitting for them, the former designated as inside, belonging, in a word *above*, the latter, as outside, excluded, aberrant, inferior, in a word *below*. These ideas permeated all disciplines and even the works of Marx. Edward Said, 'Secular criticism', in Hazard Adams and Leory Searle (eds), *Critical Theory since 1965* (Tallahassee: Florida State University Press, 1986), p. 612. For a cogent critique of Said's thesis, see R.K. Kaul, *Studies in William Jones: An Interpreter of Oriental Literature* (Simla: Institute of Advanced Study, 1995).

[4]Anindita Niyogi Balslav, *Cultural Otherness: Correspondence with Richard Rorty* (Shimla: Indian Institute of Advanced Study, 1991). One of the problems with Richard Rorty's pragmatism is that it sees the asymmetry between East and West as inevitable.

[5]For a discussion of alterity, see Emmanuel Levinas, 'The trace of the other', in Mark C.

Historiographies are no less indicted in othering for, after all, history and centres of power have been closely related. Koselleck has argued that the historical-political semantics of historical writing since ancient times defines the other negatively as spatially and culturally alien. Greek and Christian, histories used asymmetric counter-concepts such as Hellene and Barbarian, Christian, and Heathen.[6] Arab conquest accounts and Persian statist chronicles likewise juxtaposed the warrior self of Islam with conquered peoples.[7] Ranajit Guha draws our attention to how world history discarded not only the pasts of the so-called historyless people but 'also the modes adopted by their languages to integrate these parts in the prose of their respective worlds'. He uses the term historicality borrowing from Rabindranath Tagore to refer to the 'space beyond World-history'. This suggests the several continents and their populations that cover the greater part of humanity with its cultures, literatures, religions, philosophies, etc. 'The noise of World-history and its statist concerns has made historiography insensitive to the signs and whispers of everyday life.' It is in the everyday, as Guha asserts, that individuals encounter one another in the process of mutual recognition.[8] The problem is also that the archive even when constituted by the decolonized of 'prehistory' yields primarily a history of conflict. The universe of ethnic interaction is rarely deemed worth recording.

Anthropology has been centrally implicated in setting up the opposition between the self and the other. The very notion of culture is postulated on its sameness, sharedness among members, from which follow its incommensurable differences with other cultures and the identification of boundary.[9] Bourdieu might well prefer the notion of habitus but this constructs 'archaic' enclaves (such as Algeria, which the becomes a foil of modern France), as Tsing points out.[10] Anthropological monographs on communities tend to be based on ideas of cultural continuity, identity, and a shared temporality. Different conceptions of time are often seen, as Fabian maintains, at the heart of the 'denial of coevalness' of lesser cultures.[11]

Taylor (ed.), *Deconstruction in Context* (Chicago: University of Chicago Press, 1986); also his *Totality and Infinity: An Essay in Exteriority*, trans. Alphonso Lingis (Pittsburgh: Duquesne UN Press, 1969); and Robert Young, *White Mythologies: Writing History and the West* (London and New York: Routledge, 1990).

[6]Reinhard Koselleck, *Futures Past: On the Semantics of Historical Time*. Translated by Keith Tribe (Cambridge: Massachusetts, 1985).

[7]See Andre Wink's *Al-Hind: The Making of the Indo-Islamic World I: Early Medieval India and the Expansion of Islam 7th–11th Centuries* (New Delhi: Oxford University Press, 1990).

[8]Ranajit Guha, *History at the Limit of World History* (New York: Columbia University Press, 2000).

[9]Lila Abu-Lughod, *Writing Women's Worlds: Bedouin Stories* (Berkeley: University of California Press, 1993).

[10]Pierre Bourdieu, *The Logic of Practice*. Translated by Richard Nice (Stanford: Stanford University Press, 1990); Anna Lowenhaupt Tsing, *In the Realm of the Diamond Queen: Marginality in an Out-of-the-Way Place* (Princeton, N.J.: Princeton University Press, 1993).

[11]Johannes Fabian, *Time and the Other: How Anthropology Makes its Object* (New York and London: Columbia University Press, 1983).

The debate on positionality has been a significant source of the critique of anthropology. It has made the anthropologist self-conscious about the absence of the (native) Other and of our own voices in our texts. To this Handleman adds the need to radically inlay the voices of other ethnographers in our texts.[12] What is ignored, however, in this exercise in self-reflexivity, is how the ethnographer's 'ethnic' baggage and biography influence the interpretation of 'ethnicities'. The need for hermeneutic, dialogic, and polyphonic approaches has been highlighted but not the need to look for inter-ethnic dialogue.

Self/other (S/O) framing has also deeply impacted the fields of political science, multiculturalism, ethnic studies, and the understanding of inter-ethnic relations therein. Elsewhere I have critiqued Taylor's celebrated work that tends to re-primordialize ethnic, 'multicultural' identities. It congeals ethnic identities into majorities and minorities—a move that is fraught with grave dangers of reproducing categorial identities.[13]

In the South Asian context, the S/O divide pervades the representation of the Hindu–Muslim or the Sinhala–Tamil relationship. As van der Veer points out, a major element of Orientalist discourse on India is the essentialization of difference between Hindus and Muslims. Indigenous discourses were transformed under the influence of Orientalism to support the imagination of the religious community as a 'nation'.[14] This became what Gyan Pandey calls the master narrative and, one may add, the master cleavage. A good deal of colonial and contemporary writing seeks to explain community conflict in these terms.[15] Media reports of ethnic conflict the world over and in the region foreground oppositional images of violence.[16]

[12]Don Handelman, 'The absence of other: The presence of texts', in Smadar Lavie, Kirin Narayan, and Renato Rosaldo (eds), *Creativity/Anthropology* (Ithaca: Cornell University Press, 1993), pp. 133–52.

[13]Shail Mayaram, 'Recognizing whom? Multiculturalism, Muslim minority identity and the Mers', in Rajeev Bhargava, Amiya Bagchi, and R. Sudershan (eds), *Multiculturalism, Liberalism and Democracy* (New Delhi: Oxford University Press, 1999), pp. 380–99.

[14]Peter van der Veer, 'The foreign hand: Orientalist discourse in sociology and communalism', in C. Breckenridge and P. van der Veer (eds), *Orientalism and the Postcolonial Predicament* (University of Pennsylvania Press, 1993).

[15]For a recent use of the self–other framework, see Amrita Basu and Atul Kohli (eds), *Community Conflict and the State in India* (New Delhi: Oxford University Press, 1998). Vasudha Dalmia and Heinrich von Stietencron argue that 'Hinduism' developed in opposition to a Muslim Other so that the self was set off and defined against a negative projected other. 'Introduction', in V. Dalmia and H. von Stietencron (eds), *Representing Hinduism: The Construction of Religious Traditions and National Identity* (New Delhi: Sage, 1995), pp. 17–32.

[16]Recent examples are J. Stanley Tambiah, *Leveling Crowds: Ethnonationalist Conflicts and Collective Violence in South Asia* (Berkeley: University of California Press, 1996); and Paul Brass (ed.), *Theft of an Idol* (New Jersey: Princeton University Press, 1996). Olsen suggests articles published between 1988 and 1993 in the popular Indian journal *Economic and Political Weekly* project 'Homogenous groups of Hindus and Muslims'. They are portrayed as incited to riotous frenzy on the basis of

Whether one follows the primordialist or constructivist approaches to ethnicity, since identities are conceived as immutable, violence seems to follow as a matter of course. I myself have been a participant in the burgeoning genre of ethnic studies, a strong demand for which comes from the publishing market and university courses on ethnic conflict and identity politics.[17]

Combined with the technologies of governance of the modern state and the productiveness of the academy, what we have is a reinforcement of the binary construction of the social universe. In South Asia we need to ask ourselves the question why in the bureaucracy, media, and the academy, there is a virtual celebration of violence. The state foregrounds each event—for instance, the elopement of a Muslim boy and Hindu girl (the ethnicities are substitutable in different cultural contexts) is read not as desire but as potential communal strife by the police and bureaucracy. The 'riot' similarly provides the frame for under-standing any 'event' concerning the Hindu–Muslim relationship in instant write-ups/intelligence reports by journalists/state and police bureaucracies. Academic studies more often than not are grounded in assumptions of incommensurable cultures and communities. Needless to say, this renders politically insignificant the fact of living together, the *longue duree* over which conflict was managed and intercommunity relations regulated and worked out.

The challenge was not only to explore social phenomena and group interaction, but also to be methodologically and conceptually innovative in order to write an ethnography of cultural encounter. This chapter is, therefore, in the nature of a prolegomena to future work that will investigate this universe both in Ajmer and in the larger Asian context. Cities, of course, inhabit a spectrum in terms of competition-conflict-coexistence. Ajmer, Lucknow, Bhopal, and other Indian cities inhabit one end of the spectrum. The discussion in the following sections is grounded in the historical specificity and experience of Ajmer, in western India.

II. SIX PROPOSITIONS REGARDING ETHNIC COEXISTENCE

Living together derives from:
   1. The existence of a shared mythic space between communities.
   2. Everyday life being a zone of inter-ethnic intersubjectivity that is strongly combative of fundamentalisms.

---

primordial or ideologically determined religious identity. These crowds are constructed as irrational in contrast to rational and secular forces. Keri Olsen, 'Reading the masses', draft paper.

[17]Ashis Nandy, Shikha Trivedi, Shail Mayaram, and Achyut Yagnik. *Creating a Nationality: The Ramjanmabhumi Movement and the Fear of Self* (New Delhi: Oxford University Press, ms of Committee for Cultural Choices and Global Futures and United Nations Research Institute for Social Development, 1995).

3. The management of difference through institutions and existential mechanisms of dispute resolution.

4. Medical pluralism or the existence of multiple traditions of healing. This fosters new healer–client relations and those that develop between the clientele at different healing centres.

5. The existence of intermediate identities that blur categorial identities and boundaries.

6. The possibilities of network identities that derive from the activities of the life-world.

The above six propositions are of general applicability to a larger urban–rural (South) Asian context. They indicate a paradigm, an alternative imagery of inter-ethnic relations.

III. AJMER: HISTORICAL CONTEXT AND COMPETING POLITICAL AND RELIGIOUS AUTHORITY

Situated in central Rajasthan amid the Aravalli hills, Ajmer may be described as a shatter zone: it developed over a millennium into a multi-religious centre. Over time it became a major nucleus for Hindu and Muslim pilgrimage and for the activity of numerous tribes, castes, and sects that have been classified as Hindu, Muslim, Jain, Christian, Sikh, Parsi, and others (Appendix Map).

Ajmer-Merwara, as it was called in the colonial period, is then a terrain that is highly meaningful for a plurality of religious sects. Pushkar, which has the only Brahma temple in the country, has been one of the 'centres' of the Hindu sacred world. The pilgrimage is simultaneous with one of the largest animal fairs. The Sufi saint Khwaja Mu'in ud-din Chishti's *dargah* has been since Akbar's rule the subcontinent's most important Muslim shrine drawing Muslim and Hindu masses from all over the world for pilgrimage. The United Presbyterian Mission at Beawar was the first Christian Mission to be established in Rajputana. Like the Roman Catholic Church of India (RCI), headquartered here, it controlled operations in western and central India. Ajmer presently has the only Parsi (Zoroastrian) temple in Rajasthan; three Sikh gurudwaras; and Pushkar has an all-India centre of the Saivite-Sakta Nath ascetics. Nathism, incidentally, is now being recognized as one of the important, relatively autonomous strands within 'Hinduism'.[18]

Pushkar is a sacred-profane complex for numerous castes such as the pastoral Gujars and Raikas and Dalit groups. The Ramdev shrine at Pushkar houses the caste association of the largest caste of Dalits in western India called the Meghwals that is called the Meghwal Mahasabha. Ajmer also has Jain and Buddhist (and

---

[18]Personal conversation, Roxanne Gupta, Jaipur, November 1998. For an early account of Nath yogis, see George Weston Briggs, *Gorakhnāth and the Kānphaṭa Yogīs* (Delhi: Motilal Banarsidass, 1973, reprint).

before Independence, Jewish) populations. At the level of popular practice, observers have noted the plurality of folk god and goddess cults and ancestor shrines, the Ramdev cult of the Dalit and erstwhile untouchable castes as also Hindu and Islamic tantrik practice.

What is remarkable and calls for explanation is the absence of any major history of violence in Ajmer. This despite its sectarian plurality over a millennium. No 'communal riot' has taken place although since Independence Muslims and Sindhis have been living in mixed/adjacent residential areas. To this is often attributed an economic rationale, of Sindhi–Muslim interdependence, their livelihood being centred on the market of the Dargah Bazar that has a massive turnover from the four hundred thousand or so pilgrims who visit every year. This does not, however, account for most of Ajmer's past as the Sindhi diaspora has been relatively recent, result of the Partition of the subcontinent. But what slowly became clear to us over the course of our fieldwork is that 'living together' was also rendered possible because of the spiritual life of the various communities involved in the religious life of the city. Added to this was the operation of factors such as music and poetry that, as one Ajmer resident told me, 'is *rūhānī* relating to the higher life of the spirit'. The story of coexistence, at any rate, is much more complex than the mere market factor!

McNeill refers to the 'permanent poly-ethnicity' of the great cities of Asia and Europe and Ashis Nandy to forms of 'alternative cosmopolitanism'.[19] The growth of Ajmer as a multi-religious centre over the millennium was facilitated by constant changes in political control as no power held it for very long; and also because of the fair balance that was achieved at the religious institutional level. Ajmer saw swiftly changing political authority and rulers who brought with them constant changes in its religious complexion and political economy. The initial transformation of Ajmer from a pastoral centre occurred when it became the capital of the Rajput clan of Chauhans in the eighth century AD.[20] The Chauhan rulers were responsible for the early wave of Rajput state formation. Ajmer witnessed a highly urbane culture in contrast to the later Rajput states. Ajmer's conquest by the Turko-Afghan Sultanate of Delhi in 1192 was followed by the Sufi saint, Khwaja Mu'in ud-din Chishti's (d. 1235) arrival in Ajmer. It was by then already a religious centre for both Hindus and Jains. It also had a major presence of Nath yogis, Gujars, and of forest communities such as the Bhils and Mers. The Shias and Ismailis came later. Liaquat Hussain Moini maintains that the dargah

[19]Cited in Susanne Hoeber Rudolph, 'Introduction: Religion, states and transnational civil society', in S.H. Rudolph and James Piscatori (eds), *Transnational Religion and Fading States*, (Boulder, Colorado: Westview Press, 1997), pp. 1–24.

[20]Ahmad Yadgar, *Tārīkh-i Shāhī* or *Tārīkh-i Salātīn-i Afāghinā* (Persian, AMU collection) (Calcutta, 1939), pp. 20–1; see also Kali Ram Kayasth of Ajmer, *Masab ul-Ansab Tārīkh-i Rājasthān* (Arabic and Persian Records Institute, Tonk, 1209/1794).

was a centre for pilgrimage even before Akbar. Alauddin Khilji, Muhammad Tughlaq, and Bahlol Lodi were known to have visited the tomb. As kings liked to make offerings, the making of the road was expedited.

Ajmer was successively annexed by the Sisodia Rajput rulers of Mewar and by the Tughlaq dynasty of Sultans during the early fourteenth century, and was reconquered by Sultan Mahmud Khilji in 1455. The Khiljis of Malwa and Mandu in central India were closely connected with the shrine in the last half of the fifteenth century. The Muslim ruler of Gujarat, the ruler of Marwar, and Sher Shah, the Afghan ruler of Delhi, then took it over in succession. The city became headquarters of a province of the Mughal empire until Scindia brought it under Maratha suzerainty in 1756. It was taken over by the British in 1818 and Ajmer-Merwara became a small enclave under British rule amid the princely states of Marwar, Mewar, and Jaipur.[21]

For the past century and more, Ajmer has been witness to a fierce competition of sects and proselytizing movements. Its establishment as an important colonial centre accompanied by the development of road and rail links facilitated missionary activity and the movement of priests. The oldest mission in Rajputna began work in Beawar as the United Presbyterian Church Mission in 1860. Following its amalgamation with the Free Church of Scotland, it was renamed the Scotch United Free Church Mission. The Presbyterians were followed by the Methodist Church (Madar) in 1874 and the RCI in 1880. The latter undertook the most sustained educational and evangelical activity in the region. The 108 million people inhabiting north India had been brought under the three dioceses of Agra, Allahabad, and Lahore. These were further split into three Prefectures—Bettiah (from Allahabad), Kashmir (from Lahore), and Rajputana (from Agra). On 17 March 1892, the Mission was designated an Apostolic Prefecture.[22]

Ajmer also became a major centre for work by the Arya Samaj in the Rajputana States in the late nineteenth century. Its founder, Swami Dayanand, is said to have returned to have his last rites performed at Ajmer. The Arya Samaj Pratinidhi Sabha was active with headquarters at Ajmer and Mathura from where śuddhi (literally purification and a euphemism for conversion) was organized. It brought out from Ajmer the *Arya Martand*, Rajputana's first newspaper, which celebrated its centenary in 1993. This poised the Arya Samaj against the Christians and Muslims. Famine sites and drought relief became occasions to contest the work of Christian

---

[21]For details, see Har Bilas Sarda, *Ajmer: Historical and Descriptive* (Ajmer, 1911); Rajendra Joshi, 'A century of British rule in Ajmer-Merwara (1818–1918)' (unpublished thesis, University of Rajasthan, 1966); *Ajmer-Merwara Text*, Rajputana DG, vol. 1-A, compiled by C.C. Watson (Ajmer: Scottish Mission, 1904).

[22]For an account of Christian missions based on the records of the French Capuchins and other original sources, see Father R.H. Lesser's *The Rajputana Mission: Pioneers and Shepherds* (Ajmer: St. Anselm's Press, 1989).

missionaries.[23] More recently, the Vishva Hindu Parishad (VHP) claims to have made the largest number of (re)conversions anywhere in India in Ajmer's Beawar subdivision.[24]

IV. SOURCES OF ETHNIC COEXISTENCE IN AJMER

The Shared Mythico-Religious Space

The Sufi shrine of Ajmer dominates the making of this shared space. Through the medieval-modern period, Ajmer was a site of religious competition and conversion. Nonetheless, human agency plays a major role in consciously developing traditions of tolerance. The Chishtiyya *silsilah* came to Ajmer, then the capital city of Rai Pithaura, in the first decade of the thirteenth century. According to Rizvi, none of Chishthi's disciples were interested in low-caste Hindus and there was hardly any genuine commitment to the betterment of Hindus, particularly untouchables.[25] But the question, to my mind, is not of what Khwaja Mu'in al-Din Chishti did or did not do but of how he is remembered and what the traditions of the dargah are.

Although initially associated with conversion, the shrine was later far more of a symbiotic statement that emphasized the healing and miraculous powers of the *Khwaja*. It brought persons associated with different sects together in a shared participation in acts of worship; also in economic activity (chiefly of the Dargah Bazar) that grew out of pilgrimage—particularly during the annual Urs, the festival held at the tomb that commemorates the saint's marriage with God after his death.

The Chishtiyya is widely regarded as the most tolerant of the Sufi *tariqās* or brotherhoods.[26] Hindu yogi ascetics are said to have frequented the shrine during Mu'in ud-Din Chishti's lifetime and he is said to have referred to a local Hindu as a saintly man of God. There has obviously been a conscious attempt to develop

---

[23]See on this the large number of Famine Reports particularly of 1891–2 and 1901–2. The famine of 1868–9 decimated approximately a fourth of the human and a third of the cattle population. Famine prevailed again in 1872, 1891–2, 1898–1900, 1901–2, and continues to be repeated at an average interval of approximately four years.

[24]According to VHP sources, 103,025 persons from 900 villages and 19,460 families had been (re)converted by the end of the 1980s. For an analysis, see my 'Canonizing Hinduism: The politics of VHP conversion', draft.

[25]S.A.A. Rizvi, 'Islamic proselytisation: Seventh to sixteenth centuries', in G.A. Oddie (ed.), *Religion in South Asia: Religious Conversion and Revival Movements in South Asia in Medieval and Modern Times* (Delhi: Manohar, 1991), p. 29.

[26]P.M. Currie points out that although hagiographers have stressed his envangelical role, the attitude of the early Chishtis towards non-believers was one of tolerance. *The Shrine and Cult of Mu'in al-din Chishti of Ajmer* (New Delhi: Oxford University Press, 1992), pp. 52–4, 93; see also on philosophy of the Chishtiyya silsilah, R.S. Bhatnagar's *Dimensions of Classical Sufi Thought* (Delhi: Motilal Banarsidass, 1984).

the dargah as an incorporative space. Considerable Hindu and Buddhist ceremonial was incorporated into the making of shrine ritual such as the bowing before the *shaikh*, the *samā* (sessions of mystical music that bring on an ecstatic trance), and the shaving of the head of mystic initiates.[27]

The acculturation of Sufism is indicated by shrine traditions of *chirāgh-batti* or lighting of the lamp, celebration of the spring festival of Basant when visitors carry the auspicious *basantī* yellow handkerchief whereas children are dressed in a yellow *angochā* shirt with a sprinkling of red colour. The ritual food that is 'looted' and distributed among pilgrims is vegetarian and comprises not meat but sweet rice so that it can be eaten by anyone. The *sajjādā nāshīn* or the custodian of the shrine wears the ochre saffron robes of a Hindu renouncer. As the gates are closed, the *qawwal* recites in Persian that is mixed with the local dialect. The *banrā*, a regional genre of wedding songs, launches the *qawwali* at the Urs, the death anniversary of the saint that is also his marriage with God. Quite clearly the shrine assisted the peaceful penetration of Islam, that was itself transformed in this process.

Not surprisingly, the shrine received the patronage of both the Mughals and Hindu princes. Several Rajput rulers such as Sawai Jai Singh of Jaipur endowed the tomb-shrine with land grants and other forms of support. Ironically, the anti-Mughal Scindias were, according to Bishop Heber, 'magnificent benefactors'. The Urs or commemoration of the death anniversary of the saint is held from the 1st to 6th Rajab as the precise date of the death of Mu'in ud-din Chishti is not known. This is the only time when the number of Muslim pilgrims is larger, the rest of the year Hindus comprise an estimated 60 per cent of visitors to the dargah. Even the priest of the Brahma temple at Pushkar (who has been involved with Hindu nationalist organizations such as the VHP) admits that the dargah does not distinguish between Hindus and Muslims and is open to everyone.[28] Yusuf, one of the major *khadims* (literally servant of the shrine) who has conducted the ritual offering of the Nehru-Gandhi family, maintains that the eclecticism of the shrine is because of its non-Arab character. The Khwaja came from Persia bringing with him a good deal of Persian culture.[29] Even as the over one thousand khadims proudly relate to the traditions of the dargah, they are under criticism from the more orthodox (but globalized) Tablighi Jama'at which derives its ideology from the Deoband school of Islam.

It is difficult to convey the mystical-ecstatic atmosphere of the shrine and the widespread belief in the saint's ability to perform *karāmāt* or miracles. During the 1996 Urs we interviewed pilgrims who had come from all over South Asia. Non-Muslim and Muslim poor congregate on the occasion, many of them carrying

---

[27]For details, see Currie, *The Shrine and Cult of Mu'in al-din Chishti*, pp. 52–4, 93.

[28]Bansi Dhar Vashistha, personal interview, 1996.

[29]Khadim Yusuf Maharaj, personal interview, 18 Jan. 1997.

dried bread for the entire duration of their pilgrimage. All are moved by the faith that 'Gharīb Nawāz' or the benefactor of the poor and downtrodden will alleviate their suffering. 'I was destined to come,' one man told me, 'even the train turned up late so I could catch it.' There is a mad rush for the Jannati Darwaza before it closes as passage through this door guarantees access to *jannat* or heaven.

There is a conscious awareness among Muslim pilgrims that shrine ritual and the tradition of worship of the saints is not wholly sanctioned by Islamic orthodoxy. Surprisingly, even Deobandis and persons involved with the Tabligh Jama'at have been drawn to the shrine. M. Madani, longstanding President of the Jamiat-ul Ulama-i-Hind, bought and carried a basket of flowers on his head as offering at the shrine. When he kissed the *chādar* (sacred sheet covering of the tomb), a follower quizzed him, 'But you say this is *bid'at* [innovative belief and ritual]'. He replied, 'This is my *tarīqat*, the rest is a matter of books.' Tarīqat suggests the process of ritual, intellectual and spiritual initiation beyond the *sharī'at*, to the truths of esoteric Islam, the *haqīqat*.[30] A pilgrim told me, 'They say *sajdāh* [bowing in adoration] is only for Allah, but this sajdāh is liked even by God.'

There is a realization that the shrine transgresses the normative model of Islam as women are not supposed to be present within the premises. But as one *ziarin* or pilgrim informed me, 'Women have as much *aqīdat* [faith] as men. And then, in this ambience of ecstasy everything is permissible [*is madhoshī ke alām main sab kuch jāiz hai*].'

Among non-Muslim families, one finds an association with the shrine maintained for generations. For example, Gauri Shankar Ojha's family, associated with the Kapasan dargah, has been coming to the shrine for seven generations. My own first visit to the shrine took place shortly after my marriage. I was travelling then with a Rajput family from Jaipur to Jodhpur. Thakur Onkar Singh insisted we stop and visit the dargah. His only son is attributed to the blessings of the Khwaja. About nine months later when I delivered my first-born, Onkar Singhji insisted it was all due to Khwaja *sa'ab*'s benediction and that I must now offer a chādar (sheet).

The custodians of the shrine continue to take great pride in the eclectic traditions of the dargah: persons of other religions can read their religious texts; the shrine has on the whole avoided indulging in proselytization and commission is on a purely voluntary basis.

The shared mythic space of the city and its hinterland goes way beyond the dargah. Western Indian religious traditions indicate that agricultural castes of whatever religious denomination and tribal groups such as Bhils share Saivite and Sakta traditions of worship. Siva is locally called Mahadev and the devis or

---

[30]See Azim Nanji, '*Sharī'at* and *haqīqat*: Continuity and synthesis in the Nizari Isma'ili Muslim tradition', in Katherine P. Ewing (ed.), *Sharī'at and Ambiguity in Islam* (New Delhi: Oxford University Press, 1988), pp. 63–76.

goddesses, variously called Śitālāmātā (the deity against smallpox), Chāvandā, etc., are venerated by both Hindu and Muslim Rajputs and lower castes. They are frequently narrativized as carnivorous consumers of blood sacrifice.

There is much evidence of a cultic life that is relatively autonomous. One of the popular cults in Ajmer and in western India in general, is that of Ramdev or Ramsha Pir, as he is popularly called. Ramdev is one of the famous *panch* or five *pirs* of Rajasthan, the other four of whom are Goga, Pabu, Harbu, and Meha. This famous saint and folk deity of Marwar is generally worshipped in the form of footprints, and more recently, in the form of an image. This creative, dynamic movement has represented a challenge to the social order of Brahmanism and caste. Cults such as of Ramdev and Ai Mata span religious boundaries as worshippers are drawn primarily from the low Dalit, Sudra, and Muslim castes. Hence his original characterization as (*dhedhon kā dev*) or the deity of the 'untouchables' although more recently the cult has demonstrated a Sanskritization/Rajputization and popularity with high castes as well. The worship of Ramdev that once drew around 20–25,000 persons, now attracts 2–2.5 million. The priests at Ramdev shrines can belong to the low Kamad caste but can also belong to one of the 'untouchable' castes, that is, be a Balai or Raigar leather worker.

The ritual and symbolic aspects of the Ramdev and Ai Mata cults, as well as those of Jambha and of Jasnath, respectively popular among the large peasant communities of the Bisnoi and Jats, are also transgressive with respect to religious boundaries.[31] Followers belonging to these cults were buried, indicating the Islamic sources of this movement. Ramdev is sometimes worshipped as 'Allahji' and a shrine in Beawar is locally known as the Allahji *thān*. It is believed that it is legitimate for Muslims to recite the *fatihah* or the first chapter of the Qur'an, a part of Islamic mortuary ritual, at the Ramdev shrine. Not surprisingly that the Meghwal, one of the largest Dalit castes of western India, were regarded as 'half Hindu and half Muslim'.[32]

---

[31]Jambhaji was a pir of the fifteenth century whose main shrine is at Mukam near Deshnok, Bikaner. The *samādhi* or grave is covered by a saffron sacred sheet, underneath which is a green one. Worshippers must wash their hands and feet, a requirement of Islamic ritual. Ai Mata who is worshipped as a goddess has a dargah that is also called a temple at Bilora, near Jodhpur. The sect is headed by a Pir-Murshid or Diwan. The cult is popular among Sirvis, a peasant caste akin to the Jats.

[32]For a review of the traces of Ismailism, see Dominique-Sila Khan, 'The Kamad of Rajasthan—Priests of a forgotten tradition', *Journal of the Royal Asiatic Society*, 6:1 (1996), pp. 29–56. She argues that Ai Mata, Jasnath, Jambha, and Ramdev were Ismaili missionaries. Ramdev's grandfather had been converted by Pir Shamsuddin. The Ismailis were a secret, underground sect of Shia Islam who suffered persecution. Mahmud Ghazni's first attack was against Da'ud, the Ismaili ruler of Multan. He slaughtered a large number of Ismailis and destroyed their mosque before he came to India. Ismailism spread over a large part of western India. There is a close relation between Sufism and Ismailism as many adopted the garb of Sufis and like them emphasized the inner, non-ritualistic aspects of worship. Ali incidentally figures very centrally in Sufi qawwalis. Instead of building mosques, the Ismailis focused on symbols such as footprints and ideas such as

Carstairs' fieldwork in the region highlighted secret cults known by generic title such as *lāja dharma*, variously called *kāchli panth, kundāpanth, bīj mārg*, or *jot mārg*. Their rites begin with singing of bhajans and later non-members are asked to leave. High and low castes sit together and eat from a single dish that might include prohibited cow's meat. They culminate in sexual union (that might even be incestuous with one's mother or sister) as a form of worship. Participants partake of male and female semen as *prasād* (sacred food offering). Strangers are tested by being asked the name of the guru. Active members to this come from the lowest Sudra castes but might also include the higher, 'twice-born' castes such as Rajputs and Banias. Carstairs describes this as a 'stubborn and active cult, which has survived many attempts at suppression by scandalised Rajput rulers; and it flourishes in secret still, although proscribed by civil law'. Such *mandlīs* or gatherings are often held in precincts of the Ramdev temple.[33]

Accustomed as we are to cleaving myth on sectarian lines in terms of the Sunni Islamic, the Christian, the Hindu, we ignore the shared myths between communities. This is a space I have explored extensively in my work on the Meos.[34] Bardic genres indicate forms, themes, metaphors, and narrative tropes shared between castes and communities. These include forms like the *gīt* and *dohā*, the *vārttā* and the *bāt* (inspirational historical stories), and genealogies that are not merely chains of descent but include conquest accounts. Hiltebeitel highlights the existence of an underground pan-Indian oral and folk Mahabharata tradition that exists parallel to but independent of Sanskrit traditions. This is centred on the myth of Draupadi as goddess, a cult found among Muslims and Dalit groups among others.[35]

A good deal of shared belief and practice is foregrounded in the performing art traditions of Ajmer and Rajasthan, in general. This is an arena that requires independent investigation.

The *kuldevīs* or clan goddesses and *istadevs* are shared by family lineages across religious boundaries, Hindu, Muslim, and Jain.[36] Harlan cites Komal

---

reincarnation, and their literature had strong affinities to the *nirgun* Bhakti canon. I am grateful to Dominique for a discussion of these and related points.

[33]G. Morris Carstairs, *The Twice Born* (London: Hogarth Press, 1961), pp. 102–4.

[34]See my *Resisting Regimes*, esp. chs 2 and 8; also my *Against History, Against State: Counter Perspectives from the Margins* (New Delhi: Oxford University Press, forthcoming); and my 'Selections from the Mewati Oral Tradition', transcribed in Devnagari and Roman and translated into English (unpublished ms).

[35]Alf Hiltebeitel, *India's Oral and Classical Epics: Draupadi Among the Rajputs, Muslims and Dalits* (Chicago: University of Chicago Press, 1999). For the Mahabharata as a story of the Hindu–Muslim civilizational encounter, see my 'Framing epic and kingdom: The Mahabharata of the Meo Muslims', paper presented at Workshop on Framing: Narrative, Metaphysics, Perception, Israel Academy of Sciences, Jerusalem, 23–27 May 1999; and my 'Of cow killing and identity politics: The goddess and the guru in the Mahabharata of a Muslim community', draft.

[36]Lawrence Alan Babb, personal conversation, Nov. 1998.

Kothari on the *jāgran* associated with birth and marriage celebrations as well as with ceremonies for death, house building, and land purchase and well digging. Women of Hindu and Muslim castes sing songs devoted to kuldevīs and *satis, pitrs* and, *pitrānīs* (male and female ancestors) and *jhūnjhārs* (prematurely dead ancestors).[37] Women's genres such as the *jhikri* dedicated to the five pirs, sung among most communities immediately after the birth of a child, also memorialize this mythic space. The singing of this genre brings on a possession trance, as a deceased ancestor is embodied in a living being.

Several ethnographers refer to the common cosmologies in rural Ajmer comprising beliefs shared by both Muslim and Hindu castes. This magical world is populated by the *churel* or ghost of a young woman who has died in childbirth; *bhūt-preta* or prematurely dead spirits who have not been transformed into ancestors through funerary ritual and who inhabit a threshold existence in and out of the world; *balās*, wandering spirits embodied through possession; and deified ancestral spirits worshipped as household deities called *pātar* (pitr) or jhūnjhār.[38] The spirits of the recently dead, also called *devatā* or *pūrbaj*, often take possession of a descendant, causing the body to shudder and gasp. Painted *jhūnjhārjīs* can be found in the fields of Muslim castes such as the Merat and Hindu castes. In this world view, death and life are not distinctly demarcated, as the ancestral dead are responsible for the fertility of both the fields and the family.[39]

Warrior, peasant, pastoral, artisanal, and specialist groups that comprise both Hindu and Muslim branches and others have common deities and shared traditions.[40] These include castes such as tailors, washer-persons, barbers, potters, genealogists, leather tanners, liquor brewers, and cloth printers.

[37]See Komal Kothari, 'Epics of Rajasthan', in Stuart H. Blackburn, Peter J. Claus, Joyce B. Flueckiger and Susan S. Wadley (eds), *Oral Epics in India* (Berkeley: University of California Press, 1989); Lindsey Harlan, *Religion and Rajput Women: The Ethic of Protection in Contemporary Narratives* (Berkeley: University of California Press, 1992), p. 47.

[38]The understanding of good and evil within popular religion is connoted by an elaborate classification terminology for demons, spirits, and ancestors including balā, *piśaca* (flesh eating demonic beings), bhūt, preta, *vetāla, rakśasa* (demons), *jinn, shaitān* (demonic *jinn), farishtā* (angel), *dakan* (witch), and *joginī*. See Ann Grodzins Gold, *Fruitful Journeys: The Ways of Rajasthani Pilgrims* (New Delhi: Oxford University Press, 1989 [1988]), pp. 64–6; Lindsey Harlan, *The Goddesses' Henchmen: Reflection on Gender in Indian Hero Worship* (New York: Oxford University Press, forthcoming); and G. Morris Carstairs, *Death of a Witch: A Village in North India 1950–1981* (London: Hutchinson, 1983), pp. 13–16, 42. C.J. Dixon describes people as extremely superstitious and fearful of witches. *Sketch of Mairwara* (London: Smith, Elder and Co. 65, Cornhill, 1850).

[39]For further details, see my 'Spirit possession, spirit mediumship and exorcism in a rural shrine: Medical pluralism and inter-community relations', in Imtiaz Ahmad (ed.), *Women and Islam* (Delhi: Manohar, forthcoming).

[40]Munshi Hardyal Singh, *Report Mardumashumari Raj Marwar* (Hindi), 3 vols (Jodhpur: Vidyapeeth, 1895) reprinted as *The Castes of Marwar*, English trans., Introduction by Komal Kothari (Jodhpur: Books Treasure, 1990). For instance, the Muslim sections of Bhati and Chauhan Rajputs were respectively known as Sindhi Sipahis and Kayamkhanis after their conversion.

The shared mythic space will be further apparent from the discussion on medical pluralism but we need to consider a larger question: why is the realm of the popular so subversive whether it is with respect to popular Islam or Hinduism? Is it because the space it inhabits is that of cultural encounter?

Everyday Life

The idea of everyday life draws upon Goffmanian usage. James writes,

The world of everyday life, the common-sense world, has a paramount position among the various provinces of reality, since only within it does communication with our fellow-men become possible. But the common-sense world is from the outset a sociocultural world, and the many questions connected with the intersubjectivity of the symbolic relations originate within it, are determined by it, and find their solution within it.[41]

Ethnic inter-subjectivity can be witnessed on numerous axes in Ajmer. The Sindhi–Muslim interface derives from the activity centred on the shrine. Sindhi traders dominate the Dargah Bazar and benefit considerably from the annual Urs turnover of something like Rs 80–100 million. Their post-Independence economic prosperity is, hence, dependent on the continuous flow of pilgrims.

The market plays a major role in the quick settlement of disputes but the Sindhi–Muslim relationship is more complex than that. There is among Sindhis a profound belief in the dargah. Despite their affiliation with right-wing parties, several shopkeepers begin their day by first placing the keys to their shop at the feet of the tomb.

Inter-subjectivity derives from the spatial organization of the city. Sindhi homes and business are concentrated in the Dargah and Nalla Bazar areas adjacent to Anderkot, the Muslim area. Similarly, the Dalit neighbourhoods (of the Bhangi or sweeper and Mochi or leather-worker castes) adjoin the Muslim areas. Sometimes Sindhi and Muslim houses meet roof-to-roof. Muslims remark on the marked absence of ideas of purity–pollution among Sindhis as a result of which there is considerable social contact between Sindhis and Muslims in the residential neighbourhoods. Muslims make their purchases and take credit from Sindhis. As the writer Nagaraj puts it, it is the 'unheroic quality of everyday life' that sustains pluralism.[42]

Kinship terminology used in urban neighbourhoods indicates everyday relations forged between individuals that are carried over from rural contexts. Helen Lambert points out how kin terms are used to refer to village co-residents

[41]Cited in Erving Goffman, *Frame Analysis: An Essay on the Organization of Experience* (Harmondsworth: Penguin, 1974), p. 4.

[42]D.R. Nagaraj, 'Beyond the essentialist and constructivist paradigms', unpublished paper presented to Fondazione Giovanni Agnelli's Conference on Politics, Culture and Socio-Economic Dynamics in Contemporary India, Turin, 3–5 Feb. 1997.

such as *dharam kī bahin* or *dharam ki mā* for sisters and mothers. These locality-based social identities and forms of relatedness run counter to conventional anthropological views of kinship as restricted to persons related either consanguineous or affinal.[43] 'Fictive kinship', is the anthropologists' very limited term for relationships that denote complex ties of affect. As we left the residence of a doctor who belongs to the major Ellis-David Christian clan of Ajmer, a Hindu girl arrived with her children to ask after the health of *nani* (mother's mother) Dr Constance David. Laxman Singh, the Rajput lawyer of Beawar, has a 'sister' called Badami who is a (Muslim) Merat woman. When her young son died leaving a grandchild, Laxman Singh assumed responsibility for his rearing.

Ritual and religious life brings people together for moments of celebration and particularly in mourning connected with cultural ideas that both joy and sorrow can be and ought to be shared. In city and village I noticed how women from different castes would come together for the *rātījagā* or night wake held on the two specific occasions connected with death and life. Devātā or deity songs are sung through the night to the drumbeat of the Dholi drummer. During one such occasion, the participants included women of various Hindu castes and a Merat (Muslim) woman with her two giggling daughters and daughter-in-law. While the rātījagā songs were sung they lit a lamp (*diyā*) and offered food to the pitr or ancestor. The night-long ritual saw some women busy with worship, while others applied henna to each other's hands and shared a bit of gossip. Needless to say, this rite derives from non-Brahmanical traditions and commemorates women's autonomous ritual space where the upper caste male priest or Brahmin can be dispensed with.

Men from different castes collect on the occasion of a death rite called *mausar*. This is believed to ensure transcendence for the ancestral spirit. Often seen as a feast after death, it is also a rite of succession. It confers recognition on the lineage heir by different castes symbolized by the application on his forehead of the *tikā* or vermilion mark and the tying of the turban (*pāg*). The rite reproduces patrilineal political structures that receive a consensual legitimation from members of other patrilineages.

The Communitarian Management of Difference

The question of Hindu–Muslim conflict has often been addressed by counterposing it with ideas of 'communal harmony', which to my mind, are quite illusory. The question with respect to a multicultural centre such as Ajmer is how people live with and manage difference? What are the institutional mechanisms that help resolve conflict and contain it within manageable levels?

[43]Helen Lambert, 'Locality, affection and bodily constitution in Rajasthani kinship', unpublished paper presented to Third International Seminar on Rajasthan, Jaipur, 14–18 Dec. 1994.

Sectarian competition in Ajmer was institutionalized through dialogue and other mechanisms. Dayanand, founder of the Arya Samaj, spent considerable time in Rajputana. His exchange with Christians and Jains was mediated by the long-standing Indian tradition of *śastrarth* or intellectual debate. In the fifteen days that he spent in Beawar he had continuous dialogue with Reverend Scholbread and undertook śastrarth with Jains at Masuda.

There is extensive evidence of the verbalization of conflict between Christian missionaries and the Arya Samajists so that it does not degenerate into physical violence. One such story describes the encounter of a priest and pandit. To the former's suggestion that the wooden cross and stone *Siva linga* be both placed in water to see which floated (and was therefore superior), the latter retorted, let us now place them in fire to see which one burns! Despite the fact that the Arya Samaj press was bringing out considerable polemical anti-Muslim literature, leaders of the Arya Samaj such as Pandit Jialal personally regulated religious processions so that there would be no violence.

During the last three decades, several major cities of India and Rajasthan have witnessed the play of communal politics and violence. Ajmer is a noticeable exception. Curfew was declared in the city for a brief period in 1991 over a minor incident involved with the administrative agenda of cleaning up the Dargah Bazar. Muslim cart-owners expressed their resentment by pelting the police-administration with stones (a Muslim Station House Officer or SHO was also targeted). The conflict that was essentially between some Muslims and the administration witnessed a minor attempt at communalization when the grain market was set fire to reportedly by some Hindus in an attempt to put the blame on Muslims.[44]

Administrative sources maintain that curfew was declared in view of the 'communal tension' and as a preventive measure following the declaration of curfew in Delhi, Jodhpur, Jaipur, and other cities. Both Sindhi and Muslim leaders, however, maintain that there was no cause for declaring curfew as there was no Hindu–Muslim conflict and jointly protested that a 'communal riot' was non-existent. One might underline that there are available, in any given situation, different and competing readings of a 'communal riot'. In this case, the contrast between the statist reading of tension and the communitarian perspectives is evident.

Further, this renders the 'communal riot' a patterned structure of meaning that the administration can impose onto a given situation. It often might have to do with what is taking place in the larger world rather than the locally available situation so that difference, which is under control and being contained and managed, is instead read as symptomatic of communal tension.

What is the role of institutions and individuals in contexts of Hindu–Muslim animosity? In most disputes, known leaders on both sides are summoned. On

[44]D.B. Gupta, former Collector, personal interview, March 1997.

the Sindhi side, leaders like the Congress legislator Mr Motwani and the respective Presidents of the Nalla and the Dargah Bazars are summoned and on the Muslim, members of the Dargah Committee and respected khadim families such as the Qayoom and Gurdezi are brought in to arbitrate.

There have been other localized quarrels such as one involving a Muslim family from Bombay staying in a Hindu guest house. The children's throwing of fruit peels led to tension but the Dargah Committee played a role in containing the situation and not allowing it to erupt. In another dispute between a Muslim shopowner and Sindhi tenant over the extension of a shop, both sides were brought together and eventually agreed that permission from the administration would be sought first for the extension.

Interestingly, the actual lines of division in Ajmer are not Hindu/Muslim but suggest much intra-Hindu and intra-Muslim conflict. Sindhi upward mobility has been fiercely resented by (Hindu) Marwari traders as the former lowered margins of profit to corner a major share of the market. Several Hindu communities in Ajmer hold Sindhis in marked distrust.

Within the city's Muslim politics, there is a triangular division involving the Dargah *Diwan*, the khadims, and the *Nazim*. The Dargah Diwan who is also the sajjādā nashīn (the lineal descendant of the Khwaja) is enormously critical of the khadims for having commercialized the shrine: the 400,000 odd pilgrims' offerings amounting to millions, he claims, are all appropriated by the khadims. They have distorted both Sufism and Islam, he alleges! The Diwan's ritual role includes presiding over the night-long qawwali sessions of mystical music along with the khadims and performing the rite of *ghusl* that re-enacts the washing of the Ka'aba.[45]

The struggle is clearly over the income of the shrine that most pilgrims hand over to the khadims whom they consider the ritual intermediaries between the pilgrims and the saint. The third party to dargah politics comprises the government nominee to the Dargah Committee called the Nazim. He is equally critical of the money-making orientation of the khadims, and denounces the powerlessness of the Dargah Committee and would like to see it remodelled along the lines of a (Hindu) temple trust.[46]

With regard to the dargah area, as mentioned earlier, the market factor is

[45]During the 1996 Urs, the Diwan complained to the Government of India alleging that he had been fired at by the khadims and survived only because of his bullet-proof jacket. Eventually he refused to produce the evidence demonstrating this but not before the hotline was buzzing in many directions regarding a conflagration at the shrine. According to the Diwan, the Privy Council and Supreme Court have pronounced that the Diwan, as the lineal descendant of the Mu'in ud-din Chishti, will perform the rites. This is, however, challenged by the khadims whom he refers to derisively as the offspring of a tribal convert, Teka Bhil. 'But who looks like a Bhil?' retorts a khadim. 'In any case, the last lineal descendant of Khwaja sa'ab went over to Pakistan'!

[46]This section is based on interviews with Nazim K.D. Khan, the Dargah Diwan, and khadims from the Moini and Gurdezi families, 17–23 Jan. 1997.

advanced as explanation for the low degree of tension. The following case of Pushkar, however, suggests that it is not material gain alone that moves the resolution of difference.

For residents, the city's tradition of 'communal harmony' is constantly invoked as a narrative trope. This possibly impacts their own response to situations. A local leader of the right-wing Bhartiya Janata Party (BJP) whom we met bewailed the Hindu inhabitants of the city who failed to take up the protest that he initiated with respect to the Riaya Haveli. This case involved the sale of a mansion by a Rajput to a Muslim family. As the lower portion of the mansion houses a temple, some persons attempted to organize violence against the Muslim Pathan family to whom it had been sold. This was strongly resisted by a large number of local persons including by a BJP member of the municipality who insisted that the dispute be peaceably resolved.

Ironically, the institutional framework of dispute resolution is wholly communitarian. The state, on the whole, ignores or refuses to recognize and take advantage of this site. Intelligence personnel, in particular, see communitarian institutions as the embodiment of backwardness and primitivism.

Medical Pluralism

Medical pluralism deals with the cultural resources of communities. Spread all over Ajmer, as in the subcontinent more generally, are a multiplicity of specialist-healers of *nazar* (evil eye), poison such as from snakebite, of minor ailments like boils or thorns, and of major problems such as rheumatism, kidney stones, paralysis and polio. Most of them derive their powers from folk deities. What makes these distinct from other pan-Indian gods and goddesses are their capacities of both vengeance and benefaction, for when they are pleased they assist the human project of living.[47] Carstairs highlights the religious life of lower-caste villagers, centred on the open-air shrines of lesser gods whose priests, called *bhopas*, are healers of witchcraft and sickness.[48] The bhopa or healers belong to the low castes and may be a Sudra and even Dalit or Muslim.

In three major shrines of rural Ajmer where I did fieldwork, the spirit mediums were low-caste women.[49] At Husain Tekri, in the vicinity of Beawar town, the

[47]Komal Kothari points out that although Krishna is a cowherd deity, he cannot help ailing cows. This requires intervention of the performer of the Hir Ranjha narrative to make them well. Opening address, Workshop on Sati, University of Rajasthan, Dec. 1996. Also see Komal Kothari, 'The shrine: An expression of social needs', in *Gods of the Byways* (Oxford: Museum of Modern Art, 1982). Aditya Malik describes the cult of the snake god Teja and the Bagarāvat in western and central India. 'Avatara, avenger, and king: Narrative themes in the Rajasthani oral epic of Devnarayan', in Heidrun Bruckner, Lothar Lutze, and Aditya Malik (eds), *Flags of Fame: Studies in South Asian Folk Culture* (Delhi: Manohar, 1993), pp. 239–67.

[48]Carstairs, *The Twice Born*, p. 26.

[49]For an ethnography of the practice of two women healers, see my 'Spirit possession:

Hindu Rawat woman, Sushila, goes into a trance every *jumme rāt* (Friday eve) possessed by the spirit of Pir Baba or Imam Husain (the martyred *shahid* of the Karbala massacre). In two other shrines, a Hindu and (until recently) a Muslim woman were the spirit mediums for the collective mother goddess, Baya Sa'ab Mata, comprising seven sisters. In all three shrines, the healers go into a trance at a designated time and space.[50] The shrines have a large clientele in the region drawn from different communities and castes.

Sushila Rawat is known for her exorcizing skills specially with regard to women. Several visits by the afflicted to the shrine usually culminate in a 'remand' or successful exorcism when the spirit is nailed to the tree or buried in a bottle in the ground. The rite concludes with the ritual circumambulation seven times around the Ramdev shrine and tomb of Abbas Alamdar (both the Prophet and Ali's half-brother and, hence, Hussain's uncle).

Sushila draws upon Islamic mythology of the five pirs including Muhammad, Ali, Fatima, Hasan, and Hussain who are said to have come from Medina. The localization of the spirits of Ali and Hussain has been noted all over the subcontinent. Clients at Sushila's shrine are told to tie the *pānjtan kī dorī* or five threads of help from five pirs on the three windows with seven knots each. The iconography of the shrine relates the Ali myth to that of Ramdev, who is said to have been 'tested' and proven by the five pirs who acknowledged him as 'the pir of pirs'. The main shrine includes small silver replicas of both the *pañjā* (hand) and the *pagaliyā* (footprints) that symbolize the five pirs and Ramdev respectively.

The relations across lines of ethnic division that the shrine has established are symptomatic of the consequences of 'traditional' 'indigenous' therapeutic activities. Sushila uses considerable Islamist terminology and so do her clients. As the exorcism of a childless, Dalit Hindu Raigar woman called Sampati takes place, the demon spirit swears on both Aka Hussain and Ramdev that she will not trouble Sampati again. Her husband, Madholal, is possessed by a Muslim jinn who is a positive benign and actually helpful presence as he even fights the spirit who has bewitched his wife! Madholal's case is indicative of the range of popular belief, diagnostics, and cosmologies shared among inhabitants of rural society irrespective of religious affiliation.

This is only one of the many shrines that relate to the world of suffering and desire. Although there is considerable cultic variation in shamanistic practice so that the specific deity and details of ritual vary (with Ramdev, Pabu, Teja, Goga,

---

Reframing discourses of the self and other', *Purushartha*, 21 (1999), special issue on La possession en Asie du Sud: parole, corps, territoire (Paris) (eds), Gilles Tarabout and Jackie Assayag, pp. 101–31.

   [50]See Rex L. Jones on designated possession, 'Spirit possession and society in Nepal', in J.T. Hitchcock and R.L. Jones (eds), *Spirit Possession in the Nepal Himalayas* (Warminster: Aris and Phillips, 1976), pp. 1–11.

and Bhairu shrines), there is, nonetheless, a shared grammar that is quite striking. The shrines usually called thāns are referred to as *chaukīs* when the custodian-priest goes into a trance. The *sevak* or Bhopa/Bhopi demonstrates his/her calling by embodying the deity/saint. In most spirit exorcism shrines, the *peshī* or presence of the embodied divine establishes contact with the jinn or bhūt. Its identity revealed, a *bujh* or dialogue takes place with it. The forms of spirit possession at a 'Muslim' and 'Hindu' shrine are strikingly similar, blurring the distinction between popular Hinduism and popular Islam. There is obviously considerable mutual borrowing among the shrines.

Taussig has presented an effective anti-structural analysis to shamanism demonstrating how possession rites worked as resistance to colonialism; Kapferer identifies ritual as resistance to the order of caste.[51] I have argued elsewhere that it disrupts the totalistic ethnic categories. Kapferer describes a ceremony that took place to heal the wounds caused by conflict between Sinhala and Tamil ethnic groups when three Tamil and Sinhala women danced entranced at the Pattini shrine.[52] This does not mean that shamanism is a space that is immune to communal conflict. Indeed Kapferer's work has brought out how the participants of exorcism rites become participants in ethnic strife.

Nonetheless, shamanistic ritual globally tends to comprise a more inclusionary space suggested by the eclectic borrowing in its vocabulary, ritual, and symbolism. It is important to underline that shamanism relates to a bi(if not multi)-religious universe.[53] The conceptual and symbolic universe of medical pluralism reveals a dynamic field of cultural encounter.

Suffering and its alleviation forge relationships that are across community. The shrine is a sacred space that fosters new social networks. We witnessed this in Ajmer city with respect to several hakims who practise the Islamic Yunani (Greek) system of medicine; a Dalit (Meghwal) wrestler who mends bones; and a Christian priest widely loved and acclaimed for his therapeutic capabilities. Medical pluralism, as I have argued elsewhere, has operated in the Indian subcontinent as one of the strongest sources of inter-ethnic bonding. It also provides villagers with low-cost and effective psychiatric resort. It is, however, dismissed by the Western medical system and its practitioners as symptomatic of superstition!

---

[51]Michael Taussig, *Shamanism, Colonialism and the Wild Man: A Study in Terror and Healing* (Chicago: University of Chicago Press, 1987).

[52]Bruce Kapferer, *A Celebration of Demons: Exorcism and the Aesthetics of Healing in Sri Lanka* (Chicago and London: University of Chicago Press, 1991 [1983]), p. xv.

[53]Donn V. Hart shows how in the Philippines, there is an amalgamation of indigenous Filipino and Spanish and Greek medical concepts and folk Catholicism, 'Culture in curing in Filipino peasant society', *Contributions to Asian Studies*, 5 (1975), pp. 15–25. Gananath Obeyesekere demonstrates how it conjoins Buddhism and Hinduism in Sri Lanka. 'Psycho-cultural exegesis of a case of spirit possession in Sri Lanka', *Contributions to Asian Studies*, 8 (1975), pp. 41–89.

The Existence of Intermediate Identities

The significance of bi-religious, interstitial communities has been elaborated in my work on the Meo Muslims and on the Mers (presently called the Rawat/Chita/Merat/Kathat community) of Ajmer.[54] Both groups have inhabited a complex space in between Hinduism and Islam. The Chita-Merat-Kathat have been practising both religions since the seventeenth century, hence the colonial ethnographer's description of their religion being 'undefined'.

The Merat are called the 'Muslim' branch and the Rawat the 'Hindu'. The Merat follow three Islamic norms of circumcision, burying the dead, and eating *halāl* meat, and in all other respects are indistinguishable from the Rawat. Conversely, Dixon commented that although the Rawat call themselves Hindu 'their observances of that religion are extremely loose' and that most Hindus would not 'acknowledge them as associates' because of the 'extraordinary melange, dignified by the name of religion' that the Mairs represented.[55] The crossing and blurring of boundaries is indicated by intermarriage between the Rawat and Merat (until the intervention of Hindu and Muslim reformist groups) and by the fact that the Chita continue to have Hindu, Muslim (and a fractional Christian) sections.[56] Similarly, the Merat include both Hindus and Muslims and others who say they are neither. Not surprisingly, after we had done a considerable stretch of fieldwork in rural Ajmer, an assistant told me, 'I really can't understand the difference between Hinduism and Islam.'

Several Muslim organizations such as the Rajasthan Dini Talim Society, Jaipur, the Majlis Tamir-i Millat, Hyderabad, Tablighi Jama'at, Jama'at-i Islami, Jamiat ulama-i Hind, and the militant Students Islamic Movement of India have been working in the area to rectify the liminal identity of the Rawat-Merat. The VHP continues the Arya Samajist intervention of 'Hinduizing' them. The identity of the Merat is being contested just as Meo identity was earlier in this century.

But it is interesting to note the aspects of resistance as even after their so-called 'conversion', persons continue with their customary religious practices. Households still maintain their jhūnjār ancestral shrines. There are three old Śiva *dhunīs* at Śivapuraghata, Jhak, and Shamgarh. The one at Jhak has a Merat

---

[54]Mayaram, 'Rethinking Meo identity'; and my 'Recognizing whom? Multiculturalism, Muslim minority identity and the Mers'.

[55]Dixon, *Sketch of Mairwara*, pp. 7, 28.

[56]In 1891, the 1568 Chitas comprised 370 Hindus and 1198 Muslims; the Mer population had 30,467 Hindus and 32 Musalmans; the 21,887 Merat included 9022 Hindus and 12,865 Muslims; and the 30,919 strong Rawat population included 30,844 Hindus and 75 Muslims. The inclusion of both Hindu and Muslim sections is also the case with castes related to the performing arts such as Mirasis, Dhadhis, Dholis, the Garmanga, and Bhaud; artisanal castes like the Lohar (blacksmiths), Nilgar (dyers), Teli (oil-pressers), Kumhar (potters); and 'menial' castes such as the Mehtar (scavengers). B. Egerton, *Census of India, 1891*, Report on the Census of the Districts of Ajmere-Merwara (Calcutta: Superintendent Government Printing, 1893), p. 28.

sevak (priest-servant) who has become a Nāth yogi ascetic. Elsewhere Merat Muslims are also Bhopa custodians at other shrines. The expenses of local shrines are borne by both the Rawat and Merat who have to pay a contribution of Rs 3 per household and special endowments on ritual occasions. Many Muslim Chitas continue to use the name Singh.

With the exception of certain villages such as Rup Nagar, the Merat continue to participate in festivals such as Śivratri and Diwali and the worship of Ramdev. The Tablighi Jama'at group from Bombay I spoke to commented on the highly 'backward' Kathat Muslims. Despite the large number of Muslim reformers working in the area, a local Maulvi complained how difficult it was to get the children to come to the *madrasa*, 'They learn for two days, then disappear for the next four so that all that was learnt is forgotten!'

Hyphenated identities designate bridge communities, literally and metaphorically. They can provide a potential zone of resistance to 'fundamentalist' and reformist ideologies. One of the factors responsible for the close Sindhi–Muslim interface in Ajmer is the liminal identity of the Sindhis that lies at the intersection of Hinduism, Islam, and Sikhism. Most Sindhis are Nanak Panthis or followers of Sufis like Lal Shahbaz Qalandhar and Shah Latif. They follow the Muslim calendar and resemble Muslims in their language and dress. Not surprisingly, there is a large Sindhi presence in the Middle East.

The Existence of Network Identities[57]

The foregoing description should not lend the impression that 'tradition' is pluralist and modernity is exclusivist or that this is an anti-modernist argument. Indeed, what begs investigation is how modernity offers an architecture with new sites for the interaction between ethnic groups. Scholars such as Tambiah have argued that democracy enhances ethnic conflict.[58] It does and does not. Electoral politics produces cleavages but also new network identities manifest in political parties and lobbies. Local governance has been launched with the landmark 73rd and 74th Amendments to the Constitution which seek to extend the process of democratization and caste and gender-based affirmative action. The participation by women and backward and low castes and tribals as members and chairpersons of panchayats is throwing up new alliances. Sushila Raigar, a Dalit *sarpanch* in Sawai Madhopur fought the dominance of the local Muslim caste. She was abused and assaulted on several occasions and made history when she filed the *first* Dalit case in the district. Her closest confidante during this very disturbed period of her life was, however, the local (Muslim) 'Master' Zafar Mohammad.

[57]This section draws on Harrison White's notion of network identities. Distinct from categorial identities, these involve networks of concrete social relations that develop as human beings come into contact. *Identity and Control* (Princeton: Princeton University Press, 1992).

[58]Tambiah, *Leveling Crowds*, and his Daniel Thorner Memorial lecture, Paris, May 1998.

'Civil society' provides numerous instances of network identities, albeit the ethnicization of this sphere proceeds apace. The Mazdoor Kisan Shakti Sangathan, a radical organization of peasantry and landless labour in rural Beawar has both Merat and Rawat member-activists. It has been spearheading a nationally significant movement on the right to information that demands transparency in governance and empowers the poor. State programmes introduced in partnership with the women's movement such as the Women's Development Programme (WDP) have created rural women 'change agents' called *sathins* and women's collectives all over the state that work with women across ethnic lines. A people's hearing organized by women activists in May 1999 highlighted the problems of both Hindu and Muslim women representatives in the panchayat system.

Modernity has brought a new political economy of spirituality. It has meant the development of a large sector of activities associated with both the Pushkar and Ajmer shrines.

Late-twentieth-century Ajmer has become a major centre for drugs and arms smuggling. Instead of the mono-ethnic impression that we have of crime, I would argue that modern criminal activity tends to be multi-ethnic involving individuals in new networks that cut across community. Take, for instance, the pornography scandal of 1992 that caused a good deal of tension. Approximately 100 girls from well-to-do Jain and Sindhi families are said to have been involved with a gang supplying girls to farmhouses for high-level officials and politicians from Jaipur. Many of them were filmed on pornographic videos made for widespread circulation. Some eight khadims' sons were named in the initial report filed with the police. There is obviously a lot of money coming into the dargah with some khadims having monthly incomes up to Rs 500,000 that has transformed both lifestyle and values, particularly for the younger generation.

What the pornography scandal suggested was the existence of networks of friendship and alliance between young persons from khadim families and non-Muslims. Angela McRobbie points out the importance of different, youthful subjectivities.[59] In Ajmer, the activities were initiated by a Sindhi, owner of Bharosa Lab, a major photo-video business. He employs a dozen or so photographer employees who make video films. Some of them took photographs of three-four girls at a wedding who happily posed for them. The gang traced the colleges of the girls and they were lured into relationships by a combination of desire and blackmail and supplied to clients at poultry farms, most of them owned by khadim families.[60] Some of the girls died in suspicious circumstances,

---

[59] Angela McRobbie, 'Different, youthful subjectivities', in *The Post-colonial Question: Common Skies, Divided Horizons* (London: Routledge, 1996), pp. 30–46.

[60] State-level politicians and officials such as Vishnu Modi, Navin Sharma, and others were named by newspapers.

some have committed suicide, and others have refused to give evidence because of constraints of familial honour! The case is being heard *in camera* in the District Sessions Court.[61]

The non-cognition of sources of ethnic coexistence by the state and non-state institutions, particularly the agencies of coercive power, leads to irreparable damage. Police intelligence accounts of forty-six cases of alleged 'icon breaking' in rural Ajmer assumed the culpability of the Merat Muslims. This fed into press reports and everyday conversation, arousing ethnic tensions and bitterness. Our investigation found that contrary to the assumed Muslim identity of the culprits, the 'icons' vandalized were the ancestral deities of the Merat. Indeed, they were the custodians of several shrines and temples. Was it more than coincidence that most cases of icon breaking occurred in the villages where Hindu nationalist organizations had a strong base?[62]

Cities intimate the complex interaction of cosmologies and are subject to processes to change and the constant drawing and redrawing of boundaries. Interventions of classical textual frameworks seek to regulate the patterning of everyday cultural encounter. Colonial and contemporary politics and reformist agendas have over a century come to regulate the realm of categorical identities.

Despite the extensive evidence of sectarian contention during this period, there has also been something strange and inexplicable going on at the interface of the cultural encounter. This is a phenomenon that the historical record hardly cognizes and sociological theory is hard put to explain. Western philosophy and disciplinary traditions, in any case, prioritize binarism given their emphasis on monadic selfhood, incommensurable identities, and boundaries around cultural isolates. But human agency subverts boundaries at the most unexpected sites: say the realm of desire as in the passion of a Sindhi girl for a Muslim painter; Colonel Dixon's marriage with Bibi, a Merat Muslim woman; Gibson's willing of his property to his gardener;[63] in the friendship and close professional relationship that grew between Hakim Nizamuddin and the Vaidya Ramchandra

[61]More recently a blackmail case was registered by a Sindhi girl involved with some boys of the merchant caste, in which police were also attempting to extort money. The First Information Report (FIR) was lodged at the Kotwali police station under section 376 on 31 Dec. 1996.

[62]See Shail Mayaram, 'Canonizing Hinduism: The politics of Visva Hindu Parishad conversion' draft; and my 'Who broke the idols? Reflections on recent conversion to Hinduism', *Seminar* (August 1996).

[63]Gibson, OBE, was Principal of the famous elite Mayo College originally meant for the Indian princes; Colonel Dixon was Political Superintendent of Mairwara (1842–57) and later Chief Commissioner of Ajmer-Merwara (1853–7). On the significance of such marriages, see Ashis Nandy's 'Contending stories in the culture of Indian politics: Traditions and the future of democracy', paper presented to Fondazione Giovanni Angelli's Conference on Politics, Culture and Socio-Economic Dynamics in Contemporary India, Turin, 3–5 Feb. 1997.

Vyas as the latter tried to convert mercury into gold in his quest for alchemy and was isolated by other practitioners of Ayurveda; in the collaborative ventures of civil society and crime.

The incommensurability of communities and identities, therefore, requires to be sustained by high energy levels of ideological intervention, to override the universes of coexistence and encounter that are constantly eroding and subverting boundary-making enterprises.

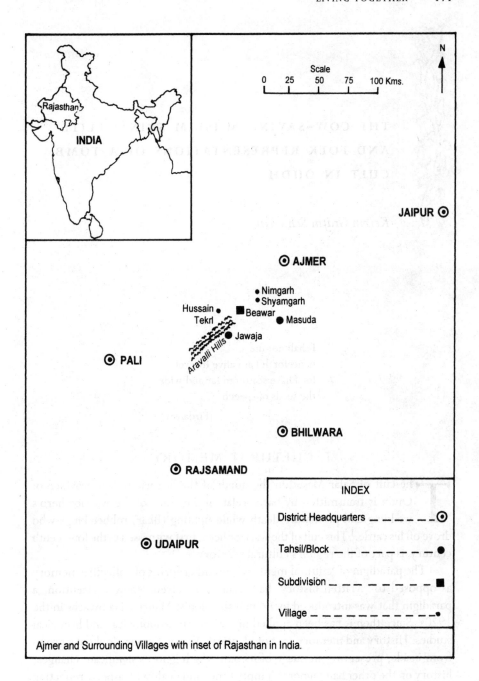

Ajmer and Surrounding Villages with inset of Rajasthan in India.

THE COW–SAVING MUSLIM SAINT: ELITE AND FOLK REPRESENTATIONS OF A TOMB CULT IN OUDH

Kerrin Gräfin Schwerin

> I shall not die
> henceforth I am alive forever
> for I have scattered far and wide
> the seeds of speech
>
> [Firdausi]

I. CULTURAL MEMORY

The cult of Salar Masud in the north of the historic Indian province of Oudh is transmitted by bards relating the story of the warrior hero's wedding and premature death while fighting (Bhar) robber kings who drove off his cattle.[1] This cult of the warrior hero, first witnessed in the fourteenth century, is part of the region's cultural memory.

The paradigm of 'cultural memory' and other forms of collective memory as opposed to 'written history' has recently received renewed attention, a paradigm that was introduced by French sociologist Maurice Halbwachs in the 1920s. Since then it has been applied in various anthropological and historical studies. History and memory are not identical. While memory looks at a group from inside, presenting an image of its past which ignores significant changes, history on the other hand ignores 'empty time' and deals with aspects reflecting

---

[1]Kerrin Gräfin von Schwerin, 'Besuche am Grab eines Maertyrers: Salar Masud und die Muslims in Audh' (Visits at the Grave of a Martyr: Salar Masud and the Muslims of Oudh), in Dirk Loenne (ed.), *Tohfa-e-dil. Festschrift Helmut Nespital* (Reinback, 2001), pp. 821–44.

processes and change. History begins only where memory ends. Memory originates in a group constituting its identity, while history belongs to everybody and nobody. Memory is closely related to the concrete, to space, to a gesture, a picture, and object. History deals with continuity in time, with development and relationships. 'Memory is absolute, history relative.' Or: 'Memory is life, borne by living societies', whereas 'history ... is the reconstruction, always problematic and incomplete, of what is no longer'.[2] Memory is an active process, reformulating the past for purposes of the here and now. Cultural memory is handed down from generation to generation not biologically, but by stored knowledge, in the form of myth, songs, dances, sacred texts, images, whole landscapes. Cultural memory 'belongs' to a group of people. This knowledge which is part of the group's identity is circulated in rituals which are regularly repeated. It is kept alive by repetition.[3] Ritual is the mnemotechnic tool to keep cultural memory alive. A sacred text, an epic of heroic deeds persists due to its sacral energy:

The sacral is outside of time, it is 'for ever' .... The sacred defies time, since it is itself a means or a weapon for the overcoming of it. By its very nature it refuses history .... Once a memory has survived intact for a significant period, sometimes for as much as a thousand years, its continuity is established once and for all.[4]

Cultural memory is transmitted by specialists. This is true for illiterate as well as literate societies. The specialists are poets, bards, artists, priests, learned men, teachers, etc. Their memory consists of 'ritual knowledge'. In India these are usually Brahmins with their special training of memory. In Islam it is the *maulvi* or any learned person. Folk literature has its own specialists: in Gujarat they are called *bhagats* specializing in folk poetry and *bhakti* (devotional) songs, in Rajasthan they are called *bhopo*, story-tellers who travel from village to village performing their art with the help of a *par*, an intricate picture of the story's sequences. There are numerous groups on India's roads earning their living by circulating songs and tales of heroism and asceticism.[5] In medieval times some of these singers of the road belonging to pastoral or martial castes were attached to Rajput or Muslim noble houses and served as informers or spies. Muslim secular and religious elites encouraged the performance of songs in vernacular languages.

The ballads or songs of praise of Salar Masud are usually shorter and less complex than the Rajput epics. They are transmitted by members of the Dafali/

[2]Pierre Nora, 'Between history and memory', *Representations*, 26 (1989), p. 8.

[3]Jan Assmann, *Das kulturelle Gedachtnis. Schrift, Erinnerung and politische Identität in frühen Hochkulturen* (Cultural memory script, memory and political identity in early cultures) (Munchen, 1997), p. 102.

[4]Alphonse Dupront, p. 127.

[5]Catherine Servan–Schreiber, 'Tellers of tales, sellers of tales: Bhojpuri peddlers in northern India', in Claude Markovits et al. (eds), *Society and Circulation: Mobile People and Itinerant Cultures in South Asia 1750–1950* (Delhi, 2003), p. 275.

Abdal caste. The Dafalis belong to a low caste, their primary occupation is playing the *daf* or tambourine, but they are also working as contractors, masons, tailors, barbers, etc. They remember having migrated from the west into Uttar Pradesh and Bihar and claim a connection with the Hashmi tribe of Arabia. They proclaim to follow the Islamic tenets, but also propitiate Hindu deities and saints like Baba Balak Nath, Lakhdata, and Guga. 'At marriage, the turmeric and oil ceremony [*batna* and *mehandi*] are observed before the main ritual of the *nikah* [marriage contract]',[6] a ceremony that has entered the narrative of Salar Masud's wedding. Dafalis also call themselves Sheikh Derwesh. In Himachal Pradesh they used to be singers of Rajputs, leading funeral processions playing a stringed instrument (*sarangi*) and singing mourning songs. They lead large processions of pilgrims attending the *mela* of Salar Masud, the festival of flags in the months of May–June (Jeth) at Bahraich and other places. They also function as kind of priests for low castes and perform at weddings: 'They (the wedding parties) sit up all night with music and singing songs recording the exploits of Saint Ghazi Salar Masa'ud. Some hang up a curtain on which are painted scenes of his battles and martyrdom.'[7] According to Hoey, the ballad praising Salar Masud was called *jangnama* (song of praise),[8] a term I will adopt to distinguish the ballads from oral epics.

Nowadays Dafali sardars must register at the Dargah Sharif (the shrine) in Bahraich if they want to perform at the mela. The Dafalis of eastern Uttar Pradesh are organized and hold annual meetings. They perform their songs by beating a daf, a kind of tambourine. The text of their song may contain the name of its author or performer. In the course of his performance, the bard may add to the story and elaborate or drop episodes. But the narrative usually follows a consequent pattern. There are regional differences in language, content, and length—some emphasize the martial aspect, others the ascetic character of the hero. The three songs compared in this chapter are examples of oral folk songs performed by Dafalis.

Qawwali music, group songs in praise of the saint, is another way of conveying the story of the martyr. *Qawwals*, specialists in devotional poetic music at Sufi shrines, perform regularly in Salar Masud's dargah. It is not clear since when they have been so doing. It is highly emotional, powerful rhythmic music, a solo recitative followed by the group picking up the refrain. 'The singer's aim is always to move, to arouse, to draw the listener towards his Sheikh, the Beloved.'[8] *Sama'* is commonly practised.

Salar Masud is not a Sufi saint, but a popular hero-martyr. Neither did he belong to a Sufi *tariqa* (order) nor was he an individual spiritual teacher of students

[6]K.S. Singh (ed.), *India's Communities*, 3 vols (Delhi, 1998), vol. 1.

[7]Jafar Sharif, *Islam in India or the Qanun-e-Islam*, ed. by M.D. Herklots (London, 1972), p. 67.

[8]Regula Burckhardt Qureshi, 'Sufi Music in India and Pakistan', *Sound, Contents, and Meaning of Qawwali* (Cambridge, 1986), p. 4.

(*murids*).[9] Tradition calls him a military leader (*salar*), a pious soldier. The qawwalis presented at his tomb today, however, are entirely modelled on those performed at Sufi centres such as Nizamuddin Auliya in New Delhi. The recorded qawwals on sale at the dargah relate the story of a pious Salar Masud coming to India to spread Islam (*tabligh*). The language of the text is a Persianized Urdu. The tradition of qawwals goes as far back as the poet Amir Khusrau (thirteenth century). It is a hereditary profession; the musicians are closely related among themselves (*baradri*) and to the saint and his tradition. This dependency gives them something like a monopoly to perform at 'their' dargah. The group is made up of at least three or four musicians (vocal, harmonium, tabla, or drum). The central event is the saint's '*urs*, his final union with god with large groups for an audience. Qawwals are usually present at Friday prayers. The qawwali also functions purely for instruction, entertainment, and pleasure.

Qawwali songs are based on oral transmission, handed down from generation to generation. Language and music differ widely from folk tradition. While oral epics are usually performed in local languages like Bhojpuri or Purbhi in Oudh and adjacent Bihar, the qawwals use a poetic language inspired by Persian devotional poetry.

Why does a cult such as that of Salar Masud Ghazi in Bahraich survive hundreds of years without having lost any of its vitality, in spite of attacks of 'rational' or 'scientific' arguments, in spite of political interference and historical reinterpretation? While 'history' challenges the historic existence of the object of the religious cult, the longevity of the cult itself is a proof of its sacred power. Salar Masud may not have existed as a historic person, but he lives in the cultural memory of a large region of north India. The annual re-enactment of his death sacralizes the present. The cult of Salar Masud serves, as so many other folk cults, a therapeutic purpose. It means to cure, to end human suffering, and to provide new energy for life. And like so many other religious cults, it has to do with death. Salar Masud died a martyr's death, a premature death at the age of 19, on the day of his wedding.

After looking at arguments raised about the historicity of Salar Masud and his deeds, I will discuss or rather speculate on structural parallels between Indian oral folk epics and the songs of praise (jangnama) of Salar Masud's life and death. And finally an attempt will be made to estimate the relevance of folk cults for the study of history.

II. POLITICS OF HISTORY

There are numerous versions of the life and death of Salar Masud Ghazi. These are usually songs of praise (jangnama) sung by bards at the festivals (mela), on

[9]Kerrin Gräfin von Schwerin, 'Der Islam in Indien', in Dietmar Rothermund (ed.), *Indien Ein Handbuch* (Muenchen, 1995), p. 169.

the way to or at his dargah (shrine consisting of Salar Masud's and Zohra's tomb, a mosque, and numerous other graves) in the city of Bahraich, commemorating the death of the martyr-hero ('urs). It is not uncommon that bards use place names and dates to authenticate their story.[10] What makes one of the texts of Salar Masud's life so controversial for historians is the fact that it is not a jangnama, but a narrative clad in the garb of a chronicle. This is the only known pre-colonial written version of the martial epic of the martyred hero Salar Masud: Abdur Rahman Chishti is the author of the '*Mirat-i-Masudi*'. Extracts of its 214 pages were published by Elliot and Dowson[11] and translated by one B.B. Chapman in the nineteenth century. William Hoey considered the *Mirat-i-Masudi* 'a debased translation or rather amplified paraphrase in Urdu of the Persian work *Saulat-i-Masudi*.' Hoey possessed a copy of the Persian version which he had translated. Apparently he never published it as planned.[12]

Abdur Rahman Chishti states that his chronicle of the life of Salar Masud is based on 'an old book' by Mulla Muhammad Ghaznavi, in the service of Sultan Mahmud Subuktigin and Salar Masud's father Salar Sahu. 'Sundry incidents, and miraculous statements, which have been found in trustworthy books, have been selected, and after being verified by oral communications with the author's spiritual visitors, have been inserted in the book.' Abdur Rahman Chishti, a contemporary of the Mughal emperor Jahangir (early seventeenth century) made it quite clear that he wanted to establish the saint as a historic person living and fighting the Hindus and dying a martyr for the sake of Islam in the region of Oudh/north India in the early eleventh century.

The 'chronicle' narrates the birth of Salar Masud (AD 1015), son of Salar Sahu and his wife Satr Ma'alla, a sister of Mahmud of Ghazni, his career as a soldier, and his final conflict with an alliance of *rajas* in the north Indian region known as Oudh. He and his loyal comrades are involved in numerous battles and are finally annihilated by the said group of rajas (1033). The region is strewn with graves of the martyred soldiers of the army of Salar Masud who is referred to as 'the Lord of the Universe'.[13] Details of battles, conversations, dates, and reference to witnesses intend to establish the character of a chronicle. By relating the hero to Mahmud of Ghazni, Abdur Rahman Chishti means to emphasize the prestigious pedigree of the saint and ancient origin of the cult in earliest Indo-Muslim history. Thereby he follows a pattern of legitimation common in folk cults.[14] The note added by the editor identifies place names with actual cities in Oudh.

[10]Mira Reym Binford, 'Mixing in the colors of Ram of Ranuja', in Bardwel L. Smith (ed.), *Hinduism: New Essays in the History of Religion* (Leiden, 1976), p. 120.

[11]H.M. Elliot and J. Dowson, *The History of India as Told by Its Own Historians* (Allahabad, 1869), (EHI), vol. 2, pp. 513ff.

[12]William Hoey, 'Sahet mahet', in *JASB*, extra no. (1892), p. 17.

[13]*EHI*, vol. 2, p. 547.

[14]Dupront, p. 131.

The selective publication of medieval Muslim chronicles of the *EHI*, including the *Mirat-i-Masudi*, with its emphasis on battle and brutal conquest, for some time now has been held responsible for having constructed an image of a militant, fanatical Islam. By contrast, Hindus in colonial historiography were represented as passive, peace-loving, and tolerant victims of aggression. Lawrence calls it 'an elitist battle' that, after the Mutiny of 1857, came to be fought by Hindus and British as a common, if not coordinated, front against the Muslims.[15] The preoccupation of the 'British imperial school' with India's military history had a lasting impact on the minds of the British as well as the Indian people. The thesis that Salar Masud had not only reached Bahraich, but also Ayodhya and Varanasi[16] has become a political issue in present-day India. Although the editor of the *Mirat-i-Masudi* renounced it as an unhistoric 'romance', settlement reports and gazetteers in their narrative of the early history of Muslims in Oudh and Uttar Pradesh in general relied on the *Mirat-i-Masudi* and on local folk tradition echoing this version of Salar Masud's life and death. Alexander Cunningham's archaeological studies on the remnants of Bhar architecture in northern Oudh tended to confirm the validity of these texts. The fact that there was no trustworthy contemporary source documenting a Muslim military excursion into northern and eastern Oudh in the eleventh century was not explicitly discussed.

Speculations on the expedition of Salar Masud into Oudh are related to the general question of conversion. The alleged intention of the Muslim martyr to spread Islam by whatever means, the sword or ascetic spirituality, is a case in point. What was the function of local Sufi saints in the process of mass conversion? While there is abundant evidence of the spiritual effect of Sufi *Sheikhs* on an inner circle of 'elite members of society', the non-elite followers of Sufi Sheikhs have left hardly any records. This is particularly true for the thirteenth to fifteenth centuries. 'The earliest saints are the most important,' says Lawrence,[17] and lasting the longest.[18] This would include Salar Masud, although not strictly a Sufi. But the question how Sufis were 'Indianized', how their cults became part of a local religious culture, their role in any process of mass conversion is still open, likewise how Sufi saints and in particular martyrs like Salar Masud maintained their distinct, non-Indian identity over hundreds of years in a predominantly Hindu environment.[19]

The Gazetteer of Bahraich district related 'the facts' as follows:

He [Salar Masud] was the son of Salar Sahu and the nephew of Mahmud of Ghazni. It was here [Bahraich] that he met his death in 424 Hijri at the hands of the Hindus, under

[15]Bruce B. Lawrence, 'Early Indo-Muslim saints and conversion', in J. Friedmann (ed.), *Islam in Asia* (Boulder, 1984), vol. 1, p. 121.

[16]*EHI*, vol. 2, p. 549, *Bahraich, A Gazetteer, UP, Agra and Oudh* (Lucknow, 1921), p. 119.

[17]Lawrence, 'Early Indo-Muslim saints', p. 129.

[18]Dupront, p. 131.

[19]Lawrence, 'Early Indo-Muslim saints', p. 142.

the Raja Soheldeo. His shrine ... is said to occupy the site of a former temple of the sun and to have been erected by Zohra Bibi, the blind daughter of Saiyid Jamal-du-Din of Rudauli in Bara Banki, after she had regained her eyesight by a pilgrimage to the burial-place of the martyr. She built herself also a tomb here, and died and was buried at the age of eighteen. Her mother and other relatives made a pilgrimage to her grave yearly, performing a ceremony like that of a marriage, saying that they were marrying the virgin Zohra Bibi to the unmarried martyr Masud.[20]

Even a post-Independence gazetteer remained ambivalent: 'Much credence cannot be given to Salar Masud's expedition but a number of Muslim families of eastern Uttar Pradesh particularly those of Oudh, claim descent from the nobles who accompanied him.'[21]

While taking the dates and events of this 'chronicle' for a fact, nineteenth-century British authors considered the 'Indian national memory' 'defective' and the history of the Indians 'a cloud of fables'.[22] Folk traditions collected by officials were pronounced in a derogatory manner as 'debased' or 'vulgar'.[23]

Politics of History, that is the use of 'history' for political ends is not an exclusively modern phenomenon. Whether in Europe or Asia, ficticious genealogies, falsified records, and invented chronicles have always served a particular purpose. Political elites may monopolize the interpretation of 'history' and impose and define cultural symbols, values, and norms, thus constituting a cultural hegemony. While British colonials had an interest in making Indian history look degenerate and chaotic, Indians—Hindus as well as Muslims—tended to glorify their past to make it look more prestigious. Gommans shows how the Afghans of Rohilkhand disliking their reputation as 'barbarous' pastoralists invented a more suitable past 'coupled with glorious traditions of Ghaznavid and Ghorid dynasties and their holy wars against the infidels of India'.[24] In the seventeenth and eighteenth centuries they produced a whole set of Indo-Afghan literature to create and strengthen ethnic cohesion. Migrant Rajputs took pains to establish a genealogy linking them to the great Rajput houses of Gujarat and Rajasthan.

The legendary battles fought by Salar Masud in Oudh related in the *Mirat-i-Masudi* fitted into the general picture of Muslim invasions, plunder, and 'conversion by the sword' in the construction of exclusivist identities of Hindus and Muslims. There are, however, good reasons to question this thesis. In the face

---

[20]*Bahraich, A Gazetteer* (1921), p. 149.

[21]*Bara Banki, Gazetteer* (1964), p. 124.

[22]Thomas R. Trautmann and Carla M. Sinopoli, 'In the beginning was the word: Excavating the relations between history and archaeology in South Asia', *Journal of Economic and Social History of the Orient* 45:4 (2002), p. 496.

[23]Richard C. Temple, *The Legends of the Punjab* (Patiala, 1963 [1884], vol. 2, p. 299.

[24]Jos J.L. Gommans, *The Rise of the Indo-Afghan Empire c. 1710–1780* (Leiden, 1995), p. 167.

of these stereotypes Shahid Amin demands a deconstruction of the traditional military history of Muslim invasions.[25]

Studies on medieval history by Muhammad Habib, Irfan Habib, Peter Hardy, Athar Ali et al., and more recent regional works on the north Indian military labour market, on supply of horses and elephants, on demography, and military technology and fiscalism[26] put military history on a sounder footing. Our military hero Salar Masud and the battles he fought usually do not much concern this type of history writing. Historians generally have difficulties with oral tradition: 'What do we do with a legend?' Legends and myths are not considered reliable sources of factional history which actually they are not. Oral epics and ballads are rather part of literature and literature part of cultural history or of anthropology. But still it is legitimate to ask about their origin in historic time and meaning, and speculate about the circumstances of their creation.

The first explicit report of the cult of Salar Masud Ghazi is that of the Moroccan traveller Ibn Batuta. In the year AD 1341 he accompanied Sultan Muhammad Tughlaq to Bahraich where he intended 'to visit the tomb of the pious shaikh, the warrior Salar 'Ud who made the conquest of most of these territories. There are wonderful stories told of him and celebrated expeditions.' Gibb in a footnote established the identity of Salar 'Ud as 'the name of Salar Mas'ud al-Ghazi who died in 557 H. (1162) in the war with the Hindus. Another account is that he was born in 1013 and was killed at Bahraiyij in 1033'.[27] Whatever the name of the Ghazi and whatever the meaning of the wonderful stories, it attracted large crowds. Its Islamic character was certainly established. While some Muslim rulers like Firoz Shah Tughlaq (1374) visited the tomb as pilgrims, granted rent-free land, and had the dargah and other buildings constructed, other rulers objected indignantly to the 'un-Islamic' practices of its cult. The Mughal emperor Aurangzeb even issued a decree to close down the pilgrim centre. This may have been one of the reason for the cult's multiplication in the entire north Indian region, possibly in the form of the *Panch Pirs*.

Oral literature has no 'date of publication'. Five hundred years after Ibn Batuta's visit, the French Orientalist Garcin de Tassy related conflicting views on Salar Masud's background. 'Some people say that he was Syed, or a descendant of Muhammad, through Husain, and at the same time a close relation of Sultan Mahmud of Ghazni; while others say that he was a Pathan (that is, an Afghan).'[28]

---

[25]Shahid Amin, 'Making the nation habitable', paper presented at the conference 'Living together separately', New Delhi (19–22 Dec. 2002), p. 5.

[26]Dirk A.H. Kolff, *Naukar, Rajput and Sepoy. The Ethnohistory of the Military Labour Market in Hindustan. 1450–1850* (Cambridge, 1990); Jos J.L. Gommans and Dirk H.A. Kolff (eds), *Warfare and Weaponry in South Asia, 1000–1800* (Oxford, 2001).

[27]H.A.R. Gibb, *The Travels of Ibn Batuta* (Cambridge, 1971), vol. 3, p. 726.

[28]M. Garcin de Tassy, *Muslim Festivals in India and Other Essays*, ed. by M. Waseem (Delhi, 1997), p. 81.

Crooke relates a version of the Bhangis which places Salar Masud and his parents as contemporaries of Prithviraj (late twelfth century).[29]

We know nothing of how and when elements of the stories were included or changed. What, for instance, is to be made of the fact that 'the worthy Muhammad Ghori' who in 1175 led an expedition against the Ismaili 'heretics' in Multan, was Salar Masud's standard bearer? Or of the use of cannons and muskets? Or of Salar Masud fighting in the army of Guga or Zahir Pir, whose horse bears the same name as that of Salar Masud's—Lilli? Temple opines: 'Bala Ghazi, alias Salar Masud, the well known hero ... appears as Guga's partisan and nephew (sister's son) though beyond doubt he was really the nephew of Mahmud of Ghazni. He must probably be a contemporary of Guga'.[30]

If ever Salar Masud was a historic person, he could possibly have lived in the late twelfth century, participating in Mohammad Ghor's campaigns against Multan and Delhi, a date related by Ibn Batuta. But there are no contemporary sources confirming this assumption.

III. FOLK EPICS

Salar Masud's legend is only one of innumerable stories of Indian saints, heroes, and gods. Some of them share some central characteristics. While the *Mirat-i-Masudi* follows the style and pattern of Muslim chronicles, the songs of praise (jangnama) collected by British officials (Greeven, Temple, Hoey) in the late nineteenth century are modelled on oral folk epics of the Afghan-Rajput tradition such as Pabuji or Ramdev, Guga or Desing in terms of 'ideology' and structure. Studies on Indian oral folk epics tend to link them to the great classical epics Mahabharata and Ramayana because of 'structural parallelisms'[31] while emphasizing that folk epics have a different value system motivated by 'belief systems and group identity'.[32] Hiltebeitel considers these folk epics as 'reemplotments' of the great classical epics by elaborating on selective themes. 'As the heroes and heroines of the classical epics veer into their new lives, things are turned inside out; winners lose, losers win'.[33] 'Little kings' are depicted as local incarnations of the great heroes of the Mahabharata and Ramayana. But while the latter are set in mythic time, the folk versions are clearly located in the Middle Ages (twelfth to fifteenth

---

[29]William Crooke, *Popular Religion and Folklore of Northern India*, 2 vols (Delhi, 1968), vol. 2, p. 289.

[30]Temple, *The Legends of the Punjab*, vol. 1, p. 121.

[31]Schomer

[32]Komal Kothari, 'Performers, gods, and heroes in the oral epics of Rajasthan', in Stuart Blackburn et al. (eds), *Oral Epics in India* (Berkeley, 1989), pp. 115–17.

[33]Alf Hiltebeitel, *Rethinking India's Oral and Classical Epics: Draupadi among Rajputs, Muslims and Dalits* (Chicago, 1999), p. 17.

centuries). This thesis, applied to our texts means that 'the little kings' resist superior powers—and win.

The answer to the question of which side the Muslim Salar Masud is on in this plot of resistance is ambivalent. Remembered as a Muslim military commander invading India from the west, he may be looked at as an early outpost of an imperial power spreading Islam with the sword (*Mirat-i-Masudi*). Where he resembles those who defend the cows of their subjects against an encroaching power, his actions correspond to the plot of resistance. It is the caste structure of his clientèle that makes the difference, a clientèle that shares the memory of 'the cow saving Muslim warrior-saint'. These are, like in the cult of Pabuji, untouchable and low peasant castes, some of them claiming Rajput status like the Meos and Ahirs.

The British official Sleeman, travelling through Oudh in the middle of the nineteenth century, talks of 'gangs of ruffians', Rajput as well as Muslim, 'landholder of whatever degree who is opposed to his government, from whatever cause, considers himself in a state of war'.[34] Is he talking of 'ruffians' like our hero-saint and his comrades?

IV. RAJPUTS

The first Muslim armies appeared in the region around the middle of the thirteenth century. The early Muslim governors of Oudh fought the local Bhar opposition. The district was then largely covered by forest, agriculture being confined to the river valleys of Gagra and Sarju. Muhammad Tughlaq on his visit to Bahraich in 1341 conferred the first grants of land to Sayyids. Firoz Shah Tughlaq on his visit in 1374 was accompanied by one Bariar Shah, son of a Janwar (Rajput) chief of Gujarat. He was appointed *sultan* of the unruly region. By the middle of the fifteenth century, various Rajput clans, particularly the Raikwards had moved in from west India and settled in northern Oudh. At this time, the (Muslim) Sharqi dynasty had established itself in Jaunpur, south-east of Bahraich, with the help of an army consisting of Afghans, Mughals, Tajiks 'and significantly of Rajputs'.[35]

The Gazetteer of Bahraich suggest that the Bhar ruling elite preceding the advent of the new masters were absorbed into Rajput status. Even after the advent of Muslims in Oudh, Bahraich seems to have remained very much on the periphery of Muslim power at least up to the time of Akbar (late sixteenth century). Rajputs then owned most of the land, the leading families each ruling its part of the district with the help of an army recruited from the lower peasant castes. This was, incidentally, the time when Abdur Rahman Chishti wrote his 'chronicle' of Salar Masud's battle against the Bhar/Rajput rajas. The Janwar Raja of Ikauna, the

---

[34]W. Sleeman, *Sleeman in Oudh*, ed. by Peter O. Reeves (Cambridge, 1971), p. 100.
[35]Kolff, *Naukar, Rajput and Sepoy*, p. 160.

seventh generation of Bariar Shah, obtained a farman in 1628 from Shah Jahan which confirmed his power over eight parganas including Bahraich. These Bahraich Janwars still considered Gujarat their home.[36] Afghans who 'have been almost masters of the town of Bahraich' were allies of Ikauna against Gonda, from where they 'carried off his [Datt Singh's] kettledrums, which were for years paraded in the streets of Bahraich on the occasion of Moharram'.[37]

Muslim sultans east of Delhi generally relied on intimate alliances with Rajput warlords with their Hindustani peasant infantry, recruited in the east (*purab*). Rajput chiefs served as brokers. 'Their [the sultan's] overriding interest in recruitment alliances and consensus with Rajput chiefs were expressed, ideologically, in the syncretist, conciliatory idiom that dominated their courts.'[38] Rajput warriors converted to Islam without necessarily giving up their way of life. These pre-Mughal Rajputs were not the Rajputs of the seventeenth century Great Tradition but, rather, 'an open status group of warrior-ascetics in search of patronage and marriage'.[39] Via a process of Rajputization, peasant castes (like Bhar and Ahir) of eastern Hindustan (*purbiya*) were integrated into the open status group of warrior ascetics, adopting Rajput values. The warrior hero's death in the battlefield represents the values of kingship. If he does not sacrifice himself he loses his honour. After Salar Masud is slain his spirit appears to Rai Sahar Deo, the Kshatriya who has just killed him, in a dream saying: 'Thou hast slain me— dost think to escape? This is not manly.' So Sahar Deo returns to the battlefield to be killed.[40]

Rajput culture was represented in folk literature, ballads, and songs reflecting the warrior-ascetic's absence from home, bloody battles and heroic death, as well as marriage as a means of building alliances and a symbol of home. Women served as pawns and were as good as contracts between allies in war.

V. HINDU–MUSLIM RELATIONSHIP

We may assume that the majority of visitors to the grave of Salar Masud at the time of Ibn Batuta were, just as nowadays, predominantly Hindus as well as converted Muslims of peasant castes. The massive participation of Hindus in pilgrimage to the site has proved quite a puzzle.[41] The previous sanctity of the place called Surajkhund may be a possible answer.[42] Muslims were and still are in a minority

[36]*Baharaich: A Gazetteer* (1921), p. 129.

[37]Ibid., p. 133.

[38]Kolff, *Naukar, Rajput and Sepoy*, p. 161.

[39]Ibid., p. 84.

[40]*EHI*, vol. 2, p. 547.

[41]Sleeman, *Sleeman in Oudh*; Shahid Amin, 'On retelling the Muslim conquest of north India', in Partha Chatterjee and Anjan Ghosh (eds), *History and the Present* (Delhi, 2002).

[42]Kerrin Gräfin von Schwerin, 'Saint worship in Indian Islam: The legend of the martyr Salar Masud Ghazi', in Imtiaz Ahmad (ed.), *Ritual and Religion Among Muslims in India* (Delhi, 1981).

in Oudh. According to Barani, there was—to his dismay—no official discrimination of Hindus under Muhammad Tughlaq (1325–51), on the contrary. Even in the capital 'and in the cities of the Musalmans the customs of infidelity are openly practised, [and] idols are publicly worshipped'.[43] The fact that Hindus and Muslims attended the festivals at the shrine of Salar Masud together does not necessarily mean that they came for the same reasons or performed identical rituals. According to the dargah administration, the two festivals—'urs and mela—drew each a different crowd, 'urs being mainly attended by Muslims, the mela by Hindus. At the same time, a large part of these 'Hindus' are synonymous with 'Dafalis', borderline Muslims. Muslims distinguish between the Hindus' worship of a saint on the one hand and the Muslims' prayer at the saint's dargah asking for his blessing on the other.[44] But rigid boundaries may be of more recent origin. We know little of how the low peasant caste pilgrims at the shrine in pre-colonial times defined their religious differences.

After making clear that Muslims fight against Hindus and Hindus against Muslims, the songs of praise (jangnama) do not strictly distinguish between the two religions. Hindu and Muslim names and traditions stand side by side. Allusions to classical Hindu epics, Hindu heroes like Bhima, and Hindu/Muslim marriage customs are common in the texts. There are obvious parallels with martial epics such as Pabuji and Ramdev which originated in the west of India between the twelfth and fifteenth centuries. Kolff believes that these folk epics are part of a pre-Mughal, older lower-status medieval Rajput tradition, based on a close Afghan–Rajput power relationship. Originally composed by Charan poets, they were then orally transmitted by low-caste bards with former Rajput status.[45] Their cults were most important for low castes and Dalits, their bards and village priests.[46]

VI. THE MARTYR

Oral Hindu epics and songs praising a Muslim warrior protecting cows show obvious parallels in content and structure with the jangnamas. Rituals celebrating Pabuji or Salar Masud, the prince of martyrs, centre on 'heroic death'. 'A premature, violent death often forms the basis of an epic tradition. A hero who achieves his aim or object for which he performed heroic deeds who continues to live in the story is not deified ... but the dead man's spirit must manifest itself in some form or another'.[47] Schomer, on the other hand, does not believe that the heroes are deified. 'They are clearly folk heroes rather than courtly Rajput heroes of the

---

[43]Stephen Conermann, *Die Beschreibung Indiens in der 'Rihla' des Ibn Batuta* (The description of India in Ibn Batuta's 'Rihla') (Berlin, 1993), p. 160.

[44]Christopher A. Bayly, *Origins of Nationality in South Asia* (Delhi, 1998), p. 47.

[45]J.D. Smith, *The Epic of Pabuji: A Study, Transcription and Translation* (Cambridge, 1991), p. 19.

[46]Binford, 'Mixing in the colors of Ram', p. 121.

[47]Kothari, 'Performers, gods, and heroes', p. 108.

elite.'[48] Muslims are usually called martyrs (ghazi) instead of heroes, particularly if killed defending their faith.

The armies of these warrior heroes belonging to low castes are usually portrayed in Rajput epics as egalitarian due to Muslim influence. The spirit of a dead hero is called bhomiya in Rajasthan. Bhomiyas are warriors who lose their lives in pursuit of cattle robbers. Cattle theft was a common occurrence as reflected in local oral village traditions. The standard story follows a common pattern with more or less complex sequences added. Cows grazing near a village are being driven off by robbers. The defenceless cowherds are killed. An armed Rajput follows the robbers and retrieves the lost herd. After the removal of many obstacles, a battle ensues. The hero dies in the battle. To make his fate even more tragic, the warrior is young and dies on the very day of his wedding.

Pabuji is supposed to have lived in the fourteenth century. He is widely venerated as a deity by herdsmen, but also by Jats and Rajputs, and is served by Scheduled Caste Nayak priests.[49] Pabuji, the Hindu warrior, fights the cow-killing Muslim ruler Mirza Khan, retrieves stolen cattle, and protects women, thus doing his Rajput duty. Smith believes that 'Pabuji and his associates serve as projection-screens for the frustrated aspirations of a certain class of Hindus. This too, is probably a major function of epic heroes everywhere'.[50]

The folk version of Salar Masud's fate in the jangnamas shares the structure of the epic of the Rathor Rajput Pabuji. The jangnamas usually concentrate on the central plot—the wedding, theft, battle, and heroic death. Versions unknown to us may have narrated his earlier exploits on the way to Bahraich in a more ample style. In some versions Salar Masud is killed,[51] in others he survives victorious.[52] In some instances his fate is compared with that of Husain in the battle of Kerbala.[53] Pabuji's death is also not explicitly mentioned. He is taken to heaven. The Rajput Guga, who is sometimes associated with Salar Masud, disappears into the earth after having adopted Islam. Pabuji is venerated in a small temple in the village Kolu. The graves (mazars) of Guga, Pabuji, and Salar Masud are venerated by regional Hindu and Muslim peasants and low castes. In the case of Ramdev, his grave is inscribed with a Qur'anic verse. He is considered an avatar of Vishnu/Krishna.

All three jangnamas represent the ideal of the horse-riding warrior hero or sacral king of the Rajput tradition. The horse is of central importance in folk

[48]Schomer, p. 150.

[49]Smith, The Epic of Pabuji, p. 4.

[50]Ibid., p. 5.

[51]Mirat-i-Masudi (as cited in EHI, vol. 2, pp. 513ff); R. Greeven, The Heroes Five (Allahabad, 1892)

[52]Temple, The Legends of the Punjab; Hoey, 'Sahet mahet'.

[53]Marc Gaborieau, 'Legende et cult musulman. Ghazi Miyan an Népal occidentale et en Inde du nord', Object et Mondes, 15:2 (1975), pp. 289–318.

epics. There is a rule that within his own territory, the king rides an elephant (like Suhel Deo, Salar Masud's opponent),[54] but once he sets out to conquer (like Salar Masud), he rides a horse. Conquest is the Rajput's, the Kshatriya's business. Since a Rajput is not supposed to accept any presents, he has to take what he needs, if necessary by conquest. It is also part of his *dharma* to defend 'the *brahman*, the cow, the women and children' against robbers and enemies.[55] Warrior hero and horse are one entity: The horse itself stands for the vir, the deified hero king. In the epic of Pabuji providing him with a horse is imbued with great importance. Finally Deval, the Charan lady presents him with one of her horses: Kesar Kalami. It is his mother returned to him. Salar Masud's horse or 'charger' is named Lilli, meaning 'in the name of God'; it is less ceremoniously introduced. In one of the versions current in Bahraich, the horse is said to have protected the wounded hero. Horses are sometimes personified. They die with their riders. Salar Masud's faithful horse Lilli lies buried right next to his tomb in Bahraich.[56]

VII. CELIBACY

Pabuji and Masud share not only the fate of becoming martyrs in the process of rescuing cows (that is, doing their Kshatriya duty), they also lose their lives the moment they are to be married. There is an obvious tension between the warrior as ascetic and as bridegroom.

The character of the warrior hero is ambivalent: on the one hand he is engaged to be married, on the other he is an ascetic. The ascetic represents moral perfection. Oral folk epics (like Alha or Pabuji) often refer to warrior-ascetic-minstrel traditions.[57] A current version of Salar Masud stresses his ascetic withdrawal from the life in the battlefield. The tree under which he is said to have meditated is marked by a commemorative building about a mile from the main dargah. Only the ascetic warrior, not the married man, has sufficient power to fulfil his duty in battle. Therefore the wedding ceremony is not completed. In the epic of Desing, the bridegroom, on his way to battle, exclaims, 'For a sepoy who holds a sword, what does he need a woman?'.[58]

All the details of Pabuji's and Salar Masud's prenuptial ceremonials are elaborately narrated: the coming of the Brahmin for the horoscope, the invitation and entertainment of guests, fireworks, games and songs, the oil- and mehndi-ceremonies, the wedding pavilion, the tying of the nuptial thread—but not the

---

[54]Hoey, 'Sahet mahet', p. 33.

[55]Helene Basu, 'Die Götter und die Charan: Das Gedächtnis des königtuns, Verwandtschaft and Askese in Kacch' (The gods and the Charan: The memory of kingship, kinship and ascesis in Kacch), unpublished ms (2000).

[56]Crooke, *Popular Religion and Folklore*, vol. 2, p. 204.

[57]Hiltebeitel, *Rethinking India's and Classical Epics*, p. 356.

[58]Ibid., p. 378.

final wedding ritual. Before it can be completed, before the warrior can enter the state of a householder, the theft of cattle by a hostile Hindu raja is reported to the wedding party. Salar Masud, the Muslim warrior takes leave from a grieving mother, 'who once gave her milk to her son' and from a disappointed bride. (Pabuji was suckled by a tigress.) Kolff explains the 'great value set on asceticism' as a consequence of the 'difficulties of the separation of the individual from his "primorial" ties',[59] that is, the young boy leaving home and his parents to become a soldier.

> Pabuji's bride Phulvanti clings to his stirrups.
> 'Oh daughter of the Sodhos,' he cries,
> 'let go of the stirrups of my foot;
> Pabuji cannot delay when cows have been driven of!'[60]

Salar Masud, in identical situation, asserts:

> When the call for the rescue of the cow is raised
> how shall I refuse to answer it?
> how shall I care for my life?[61]

Is this the cry of a Rajput, disguised as a Muslim, or a converted Rajput holding on to his tradition?

Like Pabuji, Salar Masud is killed in battle without having consummated his marriage. Zohra laments:

> A barren stock was I, and a barren stock I remain.[62]

And just like in the epic of Pabuji, the tragic fate of the bridegroom Masud is revealed by omens and dreams.

> I saw a dream [says Salar Masud's mother]:
> Shepherds came and taunted me, saying:
> On the wedding day shall the chief become a martyr.[63]

And Pabuji's reference to Fate

> It was written in heaven
> that we (should have only) a short (time in)
> our father's home[64]

---

[59]Kolff, *Naukar, Rajput and Sepoy*, p. 199.
[60]Smith, *The Epic of Pabuji*, p. 423.
[61]Greeven, *The Heroes Five*, p. 135.
[62]Ibid., p. 137.
[63]Ibid., p. 129.
[64]Smith, *The Epic of Pabuji*, p. 129.

is echoed in Salar Masud's ballad:

What caprice of God was this?[65]

These almost identical verses are no accident.

Hoey translated a curious omen from the *Saulat-i-Masudi*: Shortly after Salar Masud's parents died, the grieving son saw them in a dream 'encamped on a river bank, and he seemed to go to join them, and his mother held out a chaplet and said she had his wedding feast laid. This was the presage of the coming end'.[66]

The equation of wedding feast and death here can only mean the union with god: 'urs *karna* may have both meanings: to celebrate a wedding as well as the union of a deceased saint with god.

By comparing various Indo-European epics of the twelfth/thirteenth century, de Vries identifies a number of features common to them: The hero who dies will be young, making his death all the more tragic; his death is announced by omens, signs, or dreams. His mother is usually a virgin (a barren woman), his father a god (or godlike). His young life is threatened, his character extraordinary, courageous, virtuous, learned, etc. His death is to be understood in terms of 'rites de passage':[67] at the end of puberty the boy enters a liminal stage of chaos (the battle). The child 'dies' before being initiated into adulthood. It is a life crisis of the lonely young man in danger. It also means the evolution of the male individual, his reproductive ability. The time has come for the young lad to look for a wife.[68]

VIII. THE CONTEMPORARY CULT

While the epic and songs maintain the tension between the ascetic and the bridegroom, a symbolic performance of the wedding has become part of the contemporary cult at the tomb of Salar Masud.

The *jangnamas* talk of two types of weddings: the unconsummated wedding before the battle, and the wedding (=death) that unites the hero with god. The martial epics usually end with the death or victory of the hero. There are no weddings after the battle, no happy return home, no family life. This is the soldier's fate. However, in Bahraich there is another wedding: Salar Masud's wedding with Zohra Bibi that never was to be, is celebrated each year in a grand manner in the dargah with half a million pilgrims as wedding guests, among them many newly-wed couples who come for the blessings of the saint. It is performed at the mela in the month of Jeth (May/June). Dafalis lead processions of pilgrims

---

[65]Temple, *The Legends of the Punjab*, vol. 1, p. 113.

[66]Hoey, 'Sahet mahet'.

[67]Arnold van Gennep, *The Rites of Passage* (London, 1977 [1908]).

[68]Jan de Vries, *Heldenlied und Heldensage* (Muenchen, 1961), p. 291.

coming from various directions to Bahraich. The procession from Rudauli/ Bara Banki brings the wedding gifts which are deposited on the bride's grave, wedding gifts symbolically representing dowry, that is, household goods. These gifts make up a considerable amount of the income of the shrine.

Zohra Bibi in this legend is a Sayyid's blind daughter from Rudauli. When she is told about the miraculous powers of the martyr, she travels to his tomb, and after regaining her eyesight (*zohra*) she dies and is buried beside the saint. Her family keeps coming every year to celebrate her wedding with the young hero in heaven.[69]

Some time later this ceremony turned into a festival. The wedding is called mehndi, referring to the custom of colouring the hands of the bride and bridgegroom with henna, as related in the jangnama of Salar Masud. Following the wedding, hundreds of flags symbolizing battle are carried into the dargah where they are made to touch the golden pinnacle on top of Salar Masud's mazar to be reloaded with his spiritual power.

The performance of wedding and flag procession in Bahraich is modelled on the Muharram celebration as it used to be performed in Lucknow and other parts of India, celebrating the wedding of Qasim, the nephew of Husain, the grandson of the Prophet Muhammad, with his daughter Sakinah on the eve of the battle of Kerbala.[70] Qasim's wedding is not historical since he was too young at the time to be married. According to Hollister, this custom originated in Gujarat and Shi'ite Hyderabad.[71] The Shi'ite Nawabs of Oudh celebrated Muharram, including Qasim's wedding, with great pomp. [72] But it is possible that the performance of the wedding itself is of older date.

In the middle of the thirteenth century, Ithna Ishariya Shi'as established *sultanates* in the Deccan with strong ties to the Shi'ite sacred sites of Kerbala and Najaf. By employing Rajput and Afghan soldiers in their armies, the Shi'ite custom may have disseminated into the north. But only when the Shi'ite dynasty of the Nawabs of Oudh adopted Muharram as a show of official Shi'ite identity did Muharram become a popular festival. Numerous Sunnis and rural magnates like the Raja of Mahmudabad converted to Shi'ism. Even Sunni and Hindu rajas performed Muharram like the Raja of Nanpara who 'kept Shi'i ulama ... at his provincial seat to read elegies for the Imam Husain'.[73] The seventh day of Muharram 'commemorated the battlefield wedding of Qasim, Imam Husain's doomed nephew, to the Imam's daughter. In Awadh, mourners remembered the

[69]de Tassy, *Muslim Festivals in India*, p. 85.

[70]Gaborieau, 'Legend et cult musulman'; Schwerin, 'Besuche an grab eines maertyrers'.

[71]J.N. Hollister, *The Shia of India* (London, 1953), p. 175.

[72]William Knighton, *The Private Life of an Eastern King* (London, 1855), p. 288.

[73]J.R.I. Cole, *Roots of North Indian Shi'ism in Iran and Iraq: Religion and State in Awadh 1772– 1859* (Berkeley, 1988), p. 104.

wedding through the staging of premarital processions and formalities'.[74] Husain's nephew and Mahmud's nephew became one: their fate was identical even if invented in both cases.

IX. OTHER IDENTITIES

The Nizari Shi'ites appeared to have influenced the development of oral martial epics in west India as well as in the Deccan, contributing to the multi-language of Indian religious traditions.

Salar Masud (Ghazi Miyan) is venerated by the Lal Begis, Jolahas, Doms, Mirasis, and Nats, castes with borderline identities. Lal Beg, the saint and founder of the Lal Begis is sometimes identified with Ghazi Miyan.[75] Khan considers the Lal Begis among the 'lost branches of the Ismailis'.[76] She attributes the overlapping of Hindu and Muslim elements in medieval saint cults to the possible influence of an 'embedded' Nizari (Shi'a) tradition. The Nizaris were brutally persecuted by Sunni rulers; taqiyya (concealment) was therefore widely practised. Shams Pir was one of their prominent missionaries. He is said to have 'installed a sacred footprint engraved on a stone, as a symbol of the new faith in which idol worship was prohibited, although followers were permitted to retain most of their customs, their dresses and even their Hindu names'.[77]

The footprint of the Prophet, Qadam Rasul, is a widespread element of the veneration of pirs and warrior heroes. In the context of Muharram, it is 'encased in a coffin-shaped box' and carried along with other standards ('alams) symbolizing Ali's horse (Nal Sahib), the Panch Pirs, and Twelve Imams, and an ornate Bibi (Fatima) ka alam in the Muharram procession.[78] A large tomb constructed by the Nawabs of Oudh in the eighteenth century, housing the Qadam Rasul allegedly brought by Salar Masud, stands between the dargah of Salar Masud and the city of Bahraich.[79] Adjacent to the shrine of Salar Sahu, Salar Masud's father, at Satrikh, another Qadam Rasul carved in marble is set in the wall of a separate building. The original footprint is that of Vishnu or Buddha.

Fatima, the mother of Husain and Hasan is identified with the 'great goddess' (sakti).[80] Klemm's study on the origin and development of the legends of Fatima

---

[74]Ibid., p. 112.

[75]Schwerin, 'Saint worship in Indian Islam', p. 155.

[76]Dominique-Sila Khan, 'Ramdeo pir and the Kamadiya Panth', in N.K. Singhji and Rajendra Joshi (eds), Folk, Faith and Feudalism: Rajasthan Studies (Jaipur, 1995), p. 271.

[77]Ibid., p. 311.

[78]Hollister, The Shia of India, p. 169.

[79]A photograph of the building in Herklot's edition of Jafar Sharif's Islam in India is erroneously labelled 'Shrine of Sayyid Salar'.

[80]Khan, 'Ramdeo pir', p. 50.

serves as an example of how and why legends of symbolic saints originate. It took about four hundred years after Fatima's death for her legend to take shape. While contemporary sources know little about the genealogically important mother of Husain and Hasan, the development of Shi'ism, along with its legitimizing literature and cults, led to the invention of a symbolic figure based on mythical elements and historic memory as part of the passion play of Muharram. She eventually became the ideal model for Shi'a women and mothers and Queen of paradise. The genre of so-called Maqatil literature (eighth–tenth centuries) collected reports of violent (martyrs') deaths especially concerning the fate of the Alide family and its supporters.[81] Some time later Fatima's myth entered the *ginans* (songs) of Ismaili Muslims in India. Shams pir of Gujarat sings:

> The virgin of the universe will drink it (the cup of light)
> and wed Syama, Lord of the universe. (Ali/ Krishna)
> She is called Bibi Fatima—
> known as the virgin of the universe.[82]

In a ballad recorded by Gaborieau in Nepal, the hero at Bahraich is Hasan and Husain (one person), whose mother Fatima wants to marry him to Johara, the daughter of a *sayyid*.[83] At Salar Masud's wedding his mother performs the ceremony called 'partakers of the dish of the Lady Fatima', which dish is then presented to virtuous women.[84] The genealogies of Salar Masud draw a direct line of descent to Hasan and Husain and thus to Fatima. Thereby the warrior attains the high status of a classical Sufi saint (sayyid).

In the course of Hindu–Muslim contact via Ismaili teaching, 'a kind of bilingualism' developed, 'a religious language mutually recognized by Hindus and Satpanth Ismailis alike'.[85] The jangnamas made use of this bilingualism. The Prophet's name stood next to Devi Bhawani and Raja Basak (Vasuki, the serpent). The Brahmin priests and sayyids jointly attended the wedding.

X. GUGA PIR

Guga was a Rajput prince and hero believed to have the power to control snakes. This theme is part of Pabuji's narrative, while Salar Masud is sometimes identical with or at least related to Guga. Guga received his powers from Lord Shiva. His ballads, relating his birth, marriage, and conflict with his cousin, are sung by

---

[81]Verena Klemm, 'Die frühe islamische Erzählung von Fatima bint Muhammad: vom habar zur Legende' (The early Islamic stories of Fatima bint Muhammad: From habar to legend), *Der Islam*, 79, pp. 47ff.

[82]Hiltebeitel, *Rethinking India's Oral and Classical Epics*, p. 354.

[83]Gaborieau, 'Legende et cult musulman', p. 294.

[84]Temple, *The Legends of the Punjab*, vol. 1, p. 110; Jafar Sharif, *Islam in India*, p. 69.

[85]Hiltebeitel, *Rethinking India's Oral and Classical Epics*, p. 255.

Bhagats and Gorakhnath *yogis*. Guga pir 'is now one of the chief Muhammadan saints of the lower classes of all sorts. In life he appears to have been a Hindu and a leader of the Chauhan Rajputs against Mahmud of Ghazni about AD 1000, in Bikaner'.[86] Guga's horse is prominent in the cult. Its name is Lilli, alternately Nilata or Javadia. Guga is besieged by Prithviraj Chauhan (*c*. 1175) of Delhi. Before Guga disappears into the earth, that is, dies, he converts to Islam. Guga and Salar Masud are both born to formerly barren mothers who conceive only after visiting saints. Is Guga alias Salar Masud the prototype of the converted low status Rajput?[87] But Guga is also the hero fighting Feroz Shah of Delhi (1351–88) three hundred years later, supported by Salar Masud. He is called Zahir pir. References to the snake-god are made in Salar Masud's jangnama; the spear rests 'like sleeping snake in earth'.[88]

XI. THE PANCH PIRS

One of the many graves inside the fort (*qila*) of Dargah Sharif in Bahraich is dedicated to the Panch Pirs. The cult of the Panch Pirs in some parts of north India includes not only Guga and Ghazi Miyan (Salar Masud), but also Ramdev and Pabuji. Pabuji again, on his way to Pushkar, travels with Lakhmana, Harbu, Meyo Magaliyo, and Gogo, all five making up the Panch Pirs.[89] Crooke associates the Panch Pirs with the five Pandava brothers of the Mahabharata.[90] The Muslim version follows the Shi'i-Ismaili tradition of the five saints: Muhammad-Ali-Fatima-Husain-Hasan,[91] symbolized by the open hand, carried as an 'alam in Muharram processions. The Khalafiyya, a subsect of the Zaidiya, developed a pentadist doctrine of devotion including five primary angels, five chosen creatures on earth, five fingers, five pillars of Islam, and five prayers.[92] The 'Five' 'often is a single personality,' according to Briggs,[93] with the first person dying in a village (the founder) becoming Panch Pir. Salar Masud and his soldiers are often considered the founders of lineages.

XII. CONCLUSION

Traditional historiography has often been indifferent to anthropological studies of oral literature and, in particular, to folk representations of Islam. 'Tracing the

---

[86]Temple, *The Legends of the Punjab*, vol. 1, p. 121.

[87]Hiltebeitel, *Rethinking India's Oral and Classical Epics*, p. 336.

[88]Hoey, 'Sahet mahet', p. 36.

[89]Smith, *The Epic of Pabuji*, p. 293.

[90]Crooke, *Popular Religion and Folklore*, vol. 1, p. 206.

[91]Cole, *Roots of North Indian Shiism*, p. 103.

[92]Farhad Daftary (ed.), *Medieval Ismaili History and Thought* (Cambridge, 1996), p. 174.

[93]G. W. Briggs, *The Doms and Their Near Relations* (Mysore, 1953), p. 489.

threads of Hindu influence' (on Indian Islam) has even been stigmatized as 'a popular academic sport'.[94] Studies using non-elite records have, however, recognized the value of oral folk literatures. According to Kolff, 'These songs add an entirely new dimension to the extremely limited number of historical sources available and, taken together as a genre, they are convincing evidence that the new Rajput Great Tradition of the seventeenth century is an unreliable guide to pre-Mughal north India'.[95] Dupront even pleads, in addition to an anthropology of the sacred, for a study of 'sacred history' involving the listing and mapping of popular cults, of sacred space and its history, pilgrimages, legends and practices, and of features and models common to them. As an instance he quotes the discovery of a sacred object, a well or a tree by 'the simplest of lay people, by a shepherd or a little peasant girl watching over her flock'. Outside the official authority, this laity 'is able to bestow upon itself ... the sacral object which it needs'. He also observes the tendency to predate the origin of a rather recent cult into mythical time.

This is a history of the depth which is transparent to the present. Through the picture which it reveals we are able to investigate the great shifts in religion, i.e. the transformation in the sacral vision and the participation of the previously silent masses, who have had a voice of their own restored to them even in this rudimentary account.[96]

The traditions of the martyr Salar Masud are the creation of those previously silent masses. Chronicle and jangnama represent different types of cultural memory. The songs of praise (jangnamas) with their 'cow-saving Muslim warrior' belong to an oral folk tradition modelled on oral folk epics of a lower Rajput–Afghan culture, which originated in pre-Mughal India of the thirteenth to fifteenth centuries. They are current in a milieu of low and untouchable peasant castes exposed to this very Afghan–Rajput value system. A cultural memory of the cow-saving Muslim warrior is part of their identity whose religious multilingualism is equally understood by Hindus and Muslims.

The *Mirat-i-Masudi* of Abdur Rahman Chishti, a child of Mughal India, pursues another strategy: he intends to establish a virile 'Islamizing' Muslim presence in the region of Oudh, a Muslim presence threatened by a rural Rajput dominance.

A section of the affected Muslims in Awadh seemed to be dreaming of acquiring power vis-a-vis the local Rajput magnates through inexplicable divine sources, by arousing the memory of the past heroes .... One can speculate that Chishti (the author) thus sought to reinforce the legitimacy of Muslim political power in the region.[97]

[94]Francis Robinson, *The Ulama of Farangi Mahall and Islamic Culture in South Asia* (New Delhi, 2001), p. 183.

[95]Kolff, *Naukar, Rajput and Sepoy*, p. 84.

[96]Dupront, p. 131.

[97]Hiltebeitel, *Rethinking India's Oral and Classical Epics*, p. 333.

The concerns of Chishti were shared by later generations who continued to present his chronicle as factual history.

The martyr's spiritual power was enhanced by his manifold representation in the religious culture of the region, integrating a landscape of graves into a meaningful system of cultural memory. A cultural multilingualism was and is tolerated at the dargah as an essential element of its attraction; it is even encouraged. Dafalis and qawwals perform side by side in the dargah. But by holding on to the 'elite' version of the chronicle, the 'Sword of Islam' version,[98] his Muslim devotees as well as the dargah administration perpetuate the memory of a once ruling Muslim minority and culture. In the present climate of Hindutva-inspired politics of history, this may turn out to be a backfiring 'strategy of survival'.

---

[98] Amin, 'On retelling the Muslim conquest of north India', p. 42.

A GENRE OF COMPOSITE CREATIVITY:
MARSIYA AND ITS PERFORMANCE IN AWADH

Madhu Trivedi

Here I aim at exploring how *marsiya,* an Islamic/Iranian literary tradition, developed in Awadh as a genre of composite creativity. It did not remain merely a medium for invoking sorrow. As a literary genre, it represented a synthesis of multiple Indian cultural traditions and provided glimpses of the *ganga–jamuni tehzib* of north India with Lucknow as its centre. As a musical genre too, it assimilated the traits of both classical canonized forms as well as folk musical varieties then current in Awadh, and developed from *khwanandagi,* chanting, into a most sophisticated musical style. Under the patronage of the Shiite rulers of Awadh (1765–1856), the marsiya rose to unprecedented heights.

The term marsiya (elegy) is a derivative of the Arabic *risa,* which means an oration in mourning. Marsiya, generally speaking, is a poem recited to express sorrow on the death of a person; it is also a poem to commemorate a particular pathetic event. This type of compositions was not rare in Persian literature. The marsiyas of the famous poets Firdausi and Shaikh Sa'di, who wrote to commemorate the events of the death of Sohrab and the destruction of Baghdad respectively, are well known. In India, Amir Khusrau Dehalvi, the doyen of Persian poetry, composed two marsiyas in *tarkib-band* after the death of Prince Muhammad, the son of Sultan Balban (AD 1267–87), that can be found in the anthology entitled as *Ghurratul-Kamal.* According to Badauni, 'folk used to sing those *tarkib-band*s and used to chant them as threnodies over their dead from house to house.'[1] Gradually,

---

[1] Abdul Qadir Badauni, *Muntakhab ut Tawarikh*, trans. by George S.A. Ranking (Delhi, 1973 reprint), vol. I, pp. 196–7. Badauni has quoted one of these on pp. 197–216.

marsiya came to narrate the event of the martyrdom of Imam Husain, the grandson of Prophet Muhammad and his kinsmen at Karbala (in Iraq), during Muharram, the first month of the Islamic calendar. This event, which has great sentimental value for the Shi'ite sect of Muslims, provided a tragic panorama of deep human interest, so much so that a literature wholly dedicated to it came into existence. The *Rauzatus-Shohda*,[2] containing elegies on the incidents of Karbala by Husain Waiz Kashafi, a contemporary of Sultan Mirza Baiqara (1469–1506), and the *Dwazdeh Band* of Muhatshim Kashani, a poet of the court of Shah Tahmasp (1524–76) set the mode for marsiya compositions in Persian.[3]

The history of the evolution of marsiya in India is unique. From solitary verses and songs of wails and laments, it came to acquire the characteristics of epic and heralded a new era in Urdu poetry.[4] It thrived on religious ritualism and in this process came to integrate ceremonies and rituals of Indian origin as well. It portrayed the ethics typical of the Indian way of life and presented a cultural canvas of northern India. The significance of marsiya is, thus, much more than just religious. One important feature, that distinguishes marsiya from epic poetry, is that it does not present the story of Karbala as a whole. Instead, it deals with single episodes in each poem. This was in keeping with the requirements of mourning assemblies, organized to commemorate the events on a particular day during Muharram. This feature, however, provided enormous freedom to a marsiya writer who elaborated his theme by portraying his own surroundings. As an audience-oriented literary tradition, marsiya changed in accordance with the social environment and patronage patterns, leading to experimentations and variations incorporating traits of folk and urban theatre and *qissa-khwani*.

Marsiya writing in Awadh was popularized by the local poets of Fyzabad—Afsurdah and Gada—and luminaries from Delhi who included Sikandar and Sauda.[5] An indigenous style of marsiya writing developed in the north with

---

[2]The *Rauzatus-Shohda* held overwhelming sway over the Shia community in India.

[3]Reza Jadeh Shafiq, *Tarikh-i Adabiyat-i Iran* (Persian) (1958), pp. 369–70. In India, however, marsiya took its own roots and set up its own traditions, at times independently of Persian tradition, and it first developed in the Deccan as a folk form of poetry. The poetic metres are in quite a few cases distinctly indigenous and the metric pattern corresponds to the *chhand-vistar* metric pattern of Braj *bhasha*. Moreover, the language of these marsiyas is characteristic of the spoken idiom and contains elements of popular speech. It is only in the seventeenth century that marsiyas began to imbibe Persian influence in respect of language and choice of metres. For details, see Madhu Trivedi, 'Invoking sorrow: *Marsiya-khwani* and *Marsiyago'i* in north India', in Satish Saberwal and Supriya Verma (eds), *Tradition in Motion: Essays for Shereen Ratnagar* (forthcoming).

[4]The early Daccni marsiyas are akin to *git* (a song) form in its rhythmic structure with a *tek*, a segment that is repeated after every stanza in the song.

[5]Shah Kamal Kara Manikpuri, *Majma ul-Intikhab* (1219 AH/1804, Persian), ed. by Nisar Ahmad in *Teen Tazkire* (Delhi, n.d.), p. 52; Shaikh Ghulam Hamadani Mushafi, *Tazkira-i Hindigoyan* (1209 AH/1794), Persian ms., Reza library, Rampur, f. 80; Karimuddin Khan Panipati, *Tabaqatus- Sho'ra -i Hind* (1848), Urdu ms., Reza library, Rampur, f. 315.

Delhi as its centre, which grew due more to its popularity and cultural vitality and not royal patronage, and it drew from Indian literary and folk forms.[6] Even the marsiyas of the late seventeenth and early eighteenth centuries, which followed Persian style and tradition and were written for a select group mostly in *qasida* form, have more the appearance of *desi kavya* (folk poetry). Their lines are in segment and echo the *chal* (movement), which shows that these were rendered in the *dhrupad* style. In the later period in marsiyas, which were written for a wider audience, there is inclusion of the *savaiyya, doha*, and *chhand* of Braj bhasha. *Murabba dohra-band*[7] metre was Sauda's favourite, and his intimacy with Braj bhasha lent further colour to the *murabba dohra-band* style. Folk poetry metres also remained in currency.[8] Sikandar and Sauda extensively used the *mutadarik* metre and their compositions were rendered in dhrupad form. In view of the growing popularity of marsiyas with a larger audience, Sikandar composed marsiyas in Marwari, Punjabi, and Purbi dialects also.[9] Sauda also composed some marsiyas in Awadhi and Punjabi.[10]

It is important to note at this juncture that Sikandar and Sauda represented two traditions in the realm of marsiya writing. Miyan Sikandar represents a phase in the development of marsiya wherein the dominant trend was to produce marsiyas in a popular manner. He was a professional storyteller (*qissa-khwan*) and in *marsiya-khwani* he used traits of the recitational form of drama and included song, narration, and intonation, which he borrowed from qissa-khwani and folk forms like *pandavi* and alha. He was also highly accomplished in classical and folk music. Miyan Sikandar's style had great appeal among the masses.[11]

Sauda was one of the leading Urdu ghazal writers of Delhi who brought the folk form of marsiya on a par with other forms of literary expression, and it

[6]A number of marsiyas of Qasim Dehalvi, Murad, Saleh, Qurban 'Ali, Sa'dat Yakrang, Hatim, and Asim, in all 113 compositions of twenty-one poets are found in a manuscript, *Marasi-i Rekhta*, transcribed about AD 1738. Qasim Dehalvi is said to have initiated marsiya writing in north India. Sifarish Husain Rizvi, *Urdu Marsiya* (Urdu) (Delhi, 1965), p. 190. For details, see Trivedi, 'Invoking Sorrow'.

[7]A four-line verse followed by a doha in Braj bhasha.

[8]Rizvi, *Urdu Marsiya*, p. 191; Abul Lais Siddiqi, *Lucknow ka Dabistan—Shairi* (Urdu) (Lahore, 1951), pp. 668–9.

[9]His well-known Purbi marsiya as well as another in Marwari are both in a folk metre which has been identified in India as *bahar-i mutadarik*, precisely similar to the *chhand-vistar* (metric span) of *alha* of Jagnik Kavi. Their opening lines are:

> *ban karbal mein banu bitiya naina nir bahavat hai.* [Purbi]
> *kaain kahi ab mhaako shahan ghani katak charh chhai chhin.* [Marwari]

[10]His Punjabi marsiya opens with the line '*kuk di jainub pitt ke sar nu, sade jind khapadan*' and his Awadhi marsiya as follows: '*chav bhare aye banre kasim, aa banri teri yaad mein rove*'. Both compositions are in bahar-i mutadarik. Rizvi. *Urdu Masriya*, p. 195.

[11]Abdullah Khan Zaigham, *Waqyat-i Karbala ra dar jigar kharash alfaz bayan me dada u marsiya nez khub me gufta* (Persian) (Hyderabad, 1886), p. 60.

appealed to both the elite and the populace. Up to the middle of the eighteenth century, there was no clear distinction between literary and musical compositions and, as one finds in a Persian travelogue *Muraqqa'-i Dehli*, all were meant for musical rendering.[12] Due to the efforts of Sauda, however, marsiya's literary worth began to be recognized. He set new standards of marsiya writing and lent a literary colour to his marsiya compositions.[13] He was of the opinion that a single piece of imagination could be depicted in a thousand colours even in this branch of poetry and claimed that he had evolved an intricate style of marsiya writing.[14] Sauda made several innovations in the form of the marsiya. He enhanced the element of tragedy by emphasizing bravery and chivalry as a concomitant of the narration of the actual warfare (*jung*). He composed marsiyas in the memory of individual heroes and warriors and described combats, which also necessitated characterization. This descriptive trend led to the addition of historicity. He also introduced scenic description (*manzarnigari*) in his marsiyas. Some elements of Sauda's style became fixed features of marsiya writing: for example the *tamhid* (introduction), which came to be known as chehra in Lucknow, was imbibed from qasida; with certain variations, his style of concluding his marsiyas on bain also became an essential feature of marsiya writing and was maintained in Lucknow. Sauda was also the first to write marsiyas in *musaddas* (hexametre) metre.[15] These innovations led to an increase in the length of marsiya.[16] As such, the marsiya in Delhi now prepared itself for the heights it was to reach in the kingdom of Awadh where experimentation was carried much further. A distinct style developed in marsiya poetry in terms of language and idiom, content, literary, and musical form at Lucknow, which became the capital of the kingdom of Awadh from the time of Asaafud Daulah. These later marsiyas are invariably written in musaddas metre, which was found most suitable for lengthy marsiyas.[17]

[12]Dargah Quli Khan, *Muraqqa'-i Dehli* (1739) (Persian), ed. by Nurul Hasan Ansari (Delhi, 1982), pp. 75–80.

[13]Rizvi, *Urdu Masriya*, p. 191

[14]Madhu Trivedi, 'Cultural history of the kingdom of Awadh', Ph.D. Thesis, Aligarh University (1977), pp. 9–10.

[15]Rizvi, *Urdu Masriya*, p. 191; Siddiqi, *Lucknow ka Dabistan*, pp. 668–9.

[16]Even though the traditional concept of invoking sorrow remained intact in the compositions of Sauda (*khud rove aur dusron ko rulave*), his style was apparently not liked by people. Their main criticism was that his compositions lacked the essence of pathos (*marsiyat*) and were mere poetry. (Muhammad Husain Azad, *Ab-i Hayat* (Urdu) [Lucknow, 1982], p. 157. There were, however, some supporters too, like Mir Insha and Ahad Ali Yakta, who opined that these 'blind persons' do not understand that the marsiya too is characterized as poetry. Trivedi, *Cultural History of the Kingdom of Awadh*, p. 10. This suggests that there was a controversy in this period regarding the literary status of marsiya. However, it soon began to develop in accordance with the standards set by Sauda.

[17]Previously marsiyas in north India, were generally written in qasida form and consisted of twelve or twenty-four bands indicating the number of twelve Imams or twenty-four *masumin* (children) respectively. *Masnavi* form was rarely used in the north.

Traditionalists like Afsurdah, Gada, and Nazim Lucknawi, who popularized the art of marsiya-khwani, stressed the element of pathos, and paved the way for the refinement of the marsiya as a musical genre. The art became standardized with its own rules and came to be known as *soz-khwani* during the nineteenth century. It included the full-fledged rendering of marsiya, *salam* (verses rendered as compliments or bidding farewell) and *ruba'i* (a verse of four hemistiches), and served as a prelude to the mourning assembly.

The pioneers in this sphere were Khwaza Hasan Maududi and Mir Ali *soz-khwan dhrupadiya*.[18] The soz-khwani till now is rendered largely in the style evolved by Mir Ali. It is a sad and sombre style of music wherein an effort is made to conceal the musicality (*ragdar*i) of the melody: *layakari* (execution of rhythmic variations and patterns) is not as such maintained. The musical phrases employed in soz-khwani adhere to a unique cadence. The *bandishes* (rhythmical compositions) do not conform to any rhythmic pattern although the *bol banao* (improvization of rhythmic passages) and *tan taraf* (melodic turns for creating a cacophony of wails) move in *khayal* and *thumri* styles.

The soz compositions have two segments: *sthayi* (the first line or verse of the song) and *antara* (the verse that follows sthayi, employing higher notes of the musical scale). In larger compositions there is a *laghu antara* (smaller antara), also called *dehur,* and sometimes a *tan antara* called *teep*. This term is derived from the Sanskrit word *tipi,* which means rendition in notes of high register. Soz compositions are set in those ragas that evoke pathos and are sung from morning to midnight. Although, in soz-khwani, the khayal style prevailed, it also incorporated the characteristics of dhrupad, *tappa*, and thumri. Its high-pitched vigorous tonal pronunciations were derived from dhrupad; the *zawaid* or glosses of *tan-paltas* (intricate rhythmic turns) from khayal; *zamzama* and *tahrir* (swift zigzag melodic turns employed in Persian music) from tappa. The techniques of bol-banao (improvisation of rhythmic passages) and *ras-bhav* (evoking a sentiment) are taken from thumri. Thus soz assimilated the characteristics of all musical styles, then current in Awadh, especially tappa and thumri.[19] It is interesting to note that Syed Mir Ali was a renowned *tappa-baz* and a pupil of the legendary Miyan Shori.[20]

[18]Muhammad Karam Imam Khan Unnami, *Ma'dan ul Musiqi* (1856, Urdu) (Lucknow, 1925), p. 37; Azmat Ali, *Muraqqa-i Khusrawi,* Urdu ms, Tagore Library, Lucknow University, Lucknow (1869), f. 226a; Abdul Halim Sharar, *Ghuzishta Lucknow: Mashriqi Tamaddun ka akhiri namuna* (Urdu), ed. by Rashid Hasan Khan (Lucknow, 1965, rpt, Delhi, 1971), p. 304.

[19]Madhu Trivedi, 'Hindustani music and dance: An examination of some texts in the Indo-Persian tradition', in Muzaffar Ali, Francoise 'Nalini' Delvoye, and Marc Gaborieau (eds), *The Making of Indo-Persian Culture: Indian and French Studies* (New Delhi, 2000), pp. 281–306; and also, Madhu Trivedi, 'Tradition and transition: The performing arts in medieval north India', *The Medieval History Journal,* 2:1 (1999), pp. 73–110.

[20]Imam Khan Unnami, *Madar ul Musiqi,* pp. 23, 30; tappa was an intricate musical genre evolved by Ghulam Nabi Shori. It was a unique blend of indigenous classical and folk traditions with techniques used in Persian *muqam* (i.e. raga).

Soz-khwani was rendered in Persian tradition by a group, which consisted of a minimum of three performers. The main performer was called *sar* and he was flanked by two supportive singers known *bazu* and *sarbazu*. Sometimes there were two additional singers also, *aas* and *baas*. The aas provided drone, as instruments do not accompany soz-khwani, while baas created tonal varieties by sounding the accordant note involved in the particular raga performed by the *soz-khwans*. In present times the famous dhrupad singers, the Dagar brothers, as well as *shahnai* player Bismillah Khan perform soz-khwani, and they represent two distinct performance traditions, the dhrupad style and khayal style respectively.[21]

Soz-khwani became so popular that it did not remain confined to professional singers only, and began to be learnt (with all its rules and techniques) by many, even women.[22] It was learnt and performed as a mark of reverence by them. There were professional women soz-khwans too. Amongst these, the *domni* used to perform exclusively in *zanana majlise*s only. Some of the courtesans of Lucknow, such as Haideri Begam, Muhammadi Begam, and Nanhi Begam, were outstanding performers in the art of soz-khwani. King Wajid Ali Shah also trained a group of performing women who were known as *marsiya-waliyan*.[23] One may notice here a break from tradition. In Deccan and Delhi sources do not mention women *marsiya-khwan*s.

Due to the efforts of those who cared for literary excellence, the marsiya as a newly graded item of poetry heralded a new era in Urdu literature. It was the time when Shia rituals connected with Muharram (in the Indian context) were taking shape and a sort of social exclusiveness and sect consciousness were gaining ground among the Shias. Separate Shia congregational prayers were already established practice.[24] *Mujtahid*s (ecclesiastical leaders) had assumed religious power, and the period of mourning was extended from ten to forty days, up to the 20th of Safar, the second month of the Islamic calendar.[25] Mourning assemblies (*majlis-i aza*) and *ta'ziya*[26] processions became frequent. Significantly, these processions were elaborate and provided an arena to performing artistes for a display of their skills without discrimination of caste, creed, or social status. King

[21]Information by courtesy of Mr Shahab Sarmadee, a famous musicologist.

[22]Sharar, *Ghuzishta Lucknow*, pp. 305–6.

[23]Najmul Ghani Khan, *Tarikh -i Awadh* (Urdu) (1919), vol. 5, p. 54.

[24]Muhammad Faiz Baksh, *Tarikh-i Farah bakhsh*, Persian ms, Abdul Salam Collection, Maulana Azad Library, Aligarh Muslim University, Aligarh (1815–16), f. 252-a. The Shia *namaz-i zamat* was conducted by Syed Dildar Ali Ghufran Ma'ab during the reign of Nawab Asafud Daulah on 13th Rajab 1200 AH. Sarfarazud Daulah Hasan Reza Khan made arrangements for it. Syed Dildar Ali Ghufran Ma'ab (d. 1820) was the first Shia mujtahid at Lucknow.

[25]Ahad Ali, *Waqai Dilpazir* (Persian), English trans. by Taqi Ahmad as *Tarikh -i Badshah Begam* (Allahabad, 1938 [1837]), p. 13.

[26]*Ta'ziya*s (tableau). In Iran *ta'ziya*s were used to dramatize the events of the siege and carnage at Karbala. In India, however, these have a different connotation with the replica of the tomb of Imam Husain being taken out in procession on the tenth day of Muharram.

Wajid Ali Shah himself used to play *dhol-tasha* (a band of a large and spherical drum) at the time of the *mehndi* procession. The *imambaras* became centres of these activities.

Many new rituals were accepted in the mourning ceremonies. Marsiya audience now extended from the capital town to tiny villages. In this process, many Indian customs became associated with *azadari* (mourning), which was performed with great pomp and show, to the extent that Muharram became the living symbol of the Shia culture. It attained the colourfulness of the Dussehra festival. Some of the practices such as mehndi, *jhula*, or even the elaborate processions and *ghasht* and illumination were of Indian origin. All the events of the seventh Muhurram (the day of the martyrdom of Imam Qasim) were actually depicted, reminiscent of the picturesque Iranian processions as well as the grandeur of Ramlila. This compositeness was largely due to the fact that many Hindus also adopted azadari. Amongst Hindus, the Saxena and Shrivastava Kayasths and the Khatris, were *hamkasa* with Muslims, that is they had cultural affinity with Muslims and shared their cultural practices. Local chieftains and influential zamindars also adopted azadari. Marsiya audience, therefore, was larger than ever before and marsiyas were now written as pieces of art and literature and not merely to evoke the emotions of pity and sorrow. A highly respected class of marsiya writers emerged—quite different from the professional class of marsiya-khwans.

Marsiya took shape in accordance with these developments in language, musical form, and Shia ritual, and came to reflect all aspects of the culture of Awadh. It became thematic and predominantly descriptive and increased in length. Marsiyas, invariably written in musaddas form, were recited from the *mimbers* (pulpit) in the mourning assemblies, which imparted to the marsiya-composers a hallowed significance. The recital of these compositions was in the manner of poetry (*tahatu'l lafz*), but they retained some of the traits of the rendition of oral epics, especially the intonation and, to a certain extent, the histrionics. Tradition has it that Anis used to rehearse in front of a mirror for hours together in order to obtain the desired effect in intonation and gesticulation. What is more significant here is the fact that these mourning assemblies of Lucknow had the essence of the *mushaira* (literary gatherings), where poetic talents were judged. It meant that pathos was no longer the keynote in marsiya composition and literary overtones became dominant.

With this, the quality of marsiya writing underwent remarkable change. Not only was its form standardized as a literary genre with variegated technique, it also widened the scope of Urdu poetry, which was till this point confined to erotic themes only. Besides, it did not remain confined to the Muslim community and Hindu poets also contributed greatly to marsiya poetry: for instance Chhunnu Lal Dilgir, who wrote about 500 marsiyas that were extremely popular. According to Munshi Nawal Kishor, the soz-khwani and khwanandagi of Syed Mir Ali, Sultan

Ali and many other renowned soz-khwans was mostly based upon the marsiyas and salams of Dilgir.[27]

There were structural changes also in the technique of marsiya writing. Previously marsiyas comprised, apart from tamhid (introduction), which was initiated by Sauda, vaqyat (events), rivayat (incidents and anecdotes), jung (war), and bain. Now the components of marsiya were the chehra (introduction), rukhsat (bidding of farewell to the hero by his kith and kin), amad (the arrival of the hero in the battlefield), sarapa (the description of the hero from top to toe), rajaz (verses read in the battlefield to arouse martial spirit), majra (events), rudad (an account of circumstances), makalimah (dialogues), ghore aur talwar ki ta'rif (description of the horse and sword of the hero), jung (war), shahadat (martyrdom), and bain (mourning). The makalimah was probably inspired by the samvads of Ramlila and other theatrical representations of folk origin as well as the sawal u jawab of urban theatre which was coming to the fore about this period.

Many leading ghazal writers of Lucknow adopted the marsiya as the sole medium of poetry. The names of Mir Zamir (1191–1855) and Mir Khaliq (1774–1814) appear foremost among those who greatly enriched the art of marsiya composition in Lucknow. Zamir brought about changes in the technique of marsiya and evolved, together with Khaliq, a new pattern. They standardized the form of marsiya.[28]

After Sauda, Zamir, a pupil of noted ghazal writer Musahfi, seems to have been the only successful poet to make a conscious effort to raise the marsiya to a status of adab-ul-marsiya and evolve a new style in its rendition.[29] On the aesthetic side he diluted the predominant strain of pathos and sorrow with that of enthusiasm in his marsiyas, and he was the first to impart to marsiya the elements of epics. Zamir claims in one of his marsiyas to have invented a new style (tarz-i navi):

aage to ye andaz sune the na kisi ke ab sab ye muqallid huye is tarz-i navi ke.[30]

In this Zamir is correct to a great extent as his style was followed later on. He added chehra as a permanent feature of marsiyas and introduced many new themes such as sarapa[31] (description) of the hero, which was a common practice in many Indian poetical forms and oral traditions, for instance the raso, alha, and man.[32]

---

[27]Munshi Nawal Kishor, Ibarat-I Khatima-i Kulliat-i Marsiya-i Dilgir (Lucknow, 1897), p. 496.

[28]Rizvi, Urdu Marsiya, pp. 285–7; Siddiqi, Lucknow ka Dabistan, p. 676.

[29]See his marsiya opening with the line: 'Yaron, taqrir se main kar-i qalam karta hun.'

[30] See his marsiya that opens with the line: 'kis nur ki mehfil mein meri jalwagari hai'.

[31] Zamir observes as one of his innovations:

   tarz ye marsiya ki thaharai ke sarapa ho aur saf- arai.

[32]Raso—an early medieval oral tradition of poetry recited by bards (charans) to arouse heroic sentiments. Prithviraj Raso by Chandra Kavi, documented for the first time under Akbar's patronage, was the oldest and the most popular work in the raso tradition. A whole lot of raso

But he does not confine himself to a description of the physical strength of the hero, he describes virtually every limb of his hero from top to toe and here he is, apparently, inspired by the *nakh-shikh varnan* of Sufi and *riti* poets. The only difference is that instead of a heroine, he describes the nakh-shikh of his hero who is ready for combat.

Zamir also added vividness and colour to *jung* (battle) by introducing *ghore aur talwar ki tarif* (the description of the horse and arms), an element that he probably borrowed from the charan (bard) tradition. Previously description of jung was either avoided or treated in brief. But Zamir regarded it a necessary part of the marsiya and specialized in the description of battle (*razmiya mazamin*) and provided authentic details about war techniques, arrangement of forces in different formations, and weapons and many other articles of war equipage. Besides, he described the arts of combat and self-defence practised in the Awadh region such as *bank* (combat with knives); *binaut* (combat with staves); *fikiyat* or *fhankainti* (combat with long wooden sticks); *nezabazi* (combat with short spear); and *patabazi* or *pata hilana* (combat with wooden swords). In fact, these were actually displayed during the mourning processions and to this day form part of the ritual. Depiction of landscape (manzarnigari) was another item added to marsiya by Zamir. Here Zamir has made use of similes, metaphors, and exaggerated analogies and a profuse Persian diction. His style is otherwise simple and lucid. His marsiyas are very lengthy and number more than 200.

Khaliq specialized in describing assemblies (*bazmiya mazamin*), leave-taking, martyrdom, and bain. He wielded these elements deftly and presented them in a novel manner. For instance, he introduced the element of dialogue at the time of rukhsat. It is no longer simply bidding of farewell by the hero to his kith and kin; he goes to battle with certain assurances and expectations of them. One of the important features of the marsiyas of Khaliq is his portrayal of socio-religious customs, especially those which describe the martyrdom of Imam Qasim. Most of his marsiyas deal with this theme. Khaliq is noted for the simplicity and the sweetness of his language. He imparted a lyrical quality to marsiyas and composed about 200 of them.

Dilgir (1781–1846), a pupil of noted ghazal writer Nasikh, was attracted to marsiya writing on account of the range of literary expression it offered and the respectability a marsiya writer enjoyed at that time. He does not conform to the style of Zamir and claims to have introduced a new style (*naya andaz*) of marsiya writing.[33] For instance, he does not open his marsiyas with chehra but

---

literature was produced in Rajasthan in Braj bhasha, Dingal, Pingal, and Bbangri, the dialects of the region. Alah—oral epic of the raso tradition woven around the themes of battles of the legendary heroes Alah and Udal of the twelfth century. Man—a musical composition in Prakrit and Bhakha. Its theme was self-exaltation.

[33] *ye be sanad ahwal nahin maine likha hai, Dilgir haqiqat mein ye andaz naya hai.*

rather with some moral theme and he builds up the atmosphere for some dramatic event on the fateful day of martyrdom, with details of preparations and evocation of chivalry. Also, he does not portray the adversaries of his hero as non-entities and Imam Husain and his followers as superhuman beings. The sermonizing element is prominent in his marsiyas as are narration and quotations from the *Hadis* (sayings of the Prophet) and other sources. Thus he lays emphasis on the authenticity of details, except in the context of bain.[34]

He deals elaborately with rites and rituals, particularly those shared by Hindus and Muslims, in his marsiyas, which present the martyrdom of Imam Qasim. To describe the family of the Prophet he refers unconsciously to highest nobility of his days, and the overall picture that emerged in his marsiyas is that of a Hindu joint family. The concepts of *kutumb* and *biradari* are quite pronounced in his marsiyas. Ethical values are highlighted in his marsiyas. His choice of poetical metres indicates his knowledge of popular musical airs. He was a prolific writer and his marsiyas became immensely popular during his lifetime.[35]

The early marsiyas of Fasih (b. 1780) centre on the theme of pathos and affliction and he is faithful to the style developed in Delhi. Later he shifted to lengthy marsiyas, which do not, however, necessarily include all the components of the Lucknow style, as chehra and such other formal elements do not form part of his marsiyas. Like Dilgir, Fasih too gives prominence to narration (*waqyanigari*). But he has versified only the traditional narrative *(rivayat)* and that too in a ritualistic manner. He seems interested in the description of battles *(rajaz, jung)*. The tone of ethical values (*akhlaqi mazamin*) is prominent in the marsiyas of Fasih too.[36] The use of lengthy metres is a peculiar characteristic of Fasih's marsiyas, as if he were still writing not for recital from the pulpit but for the mourning processions. This is reminiscent of the marsiyas of the Deccan and Delhi. There is a certain archaic touch to his language. He uses words and phrases no longer in common usage such as *talwar-karna, daryav, aave, and lave* and also phrases in Awadhi such as *sammukh* and *paithana*, which were considered *matruk* in the poetic language of the time. He composed more than 100 marsiyas.

The various components of marsiya assumed new proportions in response to new aesthetic urges in the poetry of Mir Anis (1802–74) and Mirza Dabir (1803–75). They popularized and perfected the trends set by Zamir and Khaliq and their contemporaries, and imparted to this branch of poetry such high poetic standards that it was considered by some as the finest of poetic forms.[37] They did

---

[34]*Dilgir ne hadis se hai marsiya kaha han bain mein to dakhl- i tabi'at hai ja ba ja*
   ravi ka nam aaya na us mein kitab ka khali sanad se par nahin ye nazm-i mutaligha
   aagah rah ru hai har ek is tariq ka
   is ja pe ittifaq hua har fariq ka

[35]Siddiqi, *Lucknow ka Dabistan*, p. 680.

[36]Ibid., p. 686.

[37]Azad, *Ab-i Hayat*, p. 101; Taqi: 8; Sharar, *Ghuzishta Lucknow*, p. 84.

not introduce new elements but widened the scope of every ingredient of marsiya. Their marsiyas represented the Awadh of their time, the dictates of the society they lived in, and its socio-cultural norms. The heroes of both these poets reflect the values of aristocratic Awadh society. Social etiquette, the behaviour of youngsters towards their elders, the rites and rituals that ruled the life of aristocratic women, and the chivalry of the heroes have a definitely dated quality. The characters in the tragedy talk and behave like the gentry (shurfa) of Awadh. The more poignant the situation, the more subtle the sentiment and greater the whiff of the atmosphere and surroundings in which the marsiyas of Anis and Dabir were composed. Their marsiyas show a deep insight into human nature and have all the grandeur of qasida.

Anis, who hailed from a family of littérateurs,[38] is noted for his fluent and idiomatic diction, simplicity of style and expression, and flight of imagination. Dabir displayed lofty ideas, great erudition, and grandeur of language.[39] The Lucknow style of poetry is more pronounced in his marsiyas. Both of them enriched the language of marsiyas and endowed upon it vigour. Anis proclaimed that he used the rozmarrahi, the spoken dialect of the gentry of Lucknow.[40] But Dabir went a step further and he chose his diction in accordance with the scholarly tradition of his period. In this way he echoed Nasikh, one of the prominent ghazal writers of Lucknow who favoured a language peppered with high-flown Arabic and Persian words.[41] Every marsiya of Dabir follows a different pattern:

> shukr-i khuda ke sirqe ki had se bai'd hun
> har marsiya mein mujid-i tarz-i jadid hun.[42]

Dabir's marsiyas are different in yet another way. He does not portray a single event or project a single hero. Instead, he provides the details of events in a way that everyone in the family seems to be busy as if on a stage and the central figure in every marsiya is Imam Husain. Anis treats his theme in a different manner. His description revolves around a particular hero, the martyr of a particular day of Karbala. Dabir does not observe this pattern; the entry of the martyr of the day is quite late in his description.

---

[38]His grandfather Mir Hasan was a famous Urdu poet from Delhi, whose masnavi, Sahar ul Bayan, earned fame far and wide; he also authored a tazkira (an account) of contemporary poets in Persian. His father Mir Khaliq was one of those Urdu poets who along with Zamir standardized the form of marsiya writing.

[39]Azad, 539–40, 540–1; Sharar, Ghuzishta Lucknow, p. 84.

[40]rozmarra ho shurfa ka salasat ho vahi lab u lahja vahi sara ho mutanat ho vahi

[41]The highly Persianized language of Dabir can be seen in the following:
aqs –i chaman-i rukh se ayan qudrat-i haq hai rang gulshan –i jannat ke muraqqa' ka varq hai (Akbar Hyderi (ed.), Intikhab-i Marasi Mirza Dabir (Lucknow: Uttar Pradesh Urdu Academy, 1980) p. 495/1.
Dabir also uses Arabic phrases in his marsiyas quite liberally and quotes from the Quran. Ibid., 16: p. 520/28; 15: p. 499/20.

[42]Ibid., 6: p. 240/20.

The early marsiyas composed in the Deccan and Delhi merely expressed the emotions of a sect of mourners having immense faith in Imam Husain. Beyond this other sentiments were almost excluded. Anis and Dabir widened the scope to portray other sentiments also, especially Anis in whose poetry it is not very difficult to recognize the nine *ras* of Braj poetry. The theme of marsiya was undoubtedly the tragedy of Husain. But this tragedy was a complete picture in action in the hands of Anis and Dabir. It provided aesthetic pleasure from sublime pathos. It excited passions which were healthy. Anis has even used *shringar ras* at some places. The wife of Abbas, while performing bain over the dead body of her husband, suddenly reminisces about her beloved:

> *Allah tha yeh aaj ki shab tak, hamara pyar uth uth ke dekhte the mere munh ko bar bar*
> *main kahati thi ke so raho, ik aan mein nisar kahte the ro ke, ab yahi suhbat hai yaad gar*
> *furqat mein vasl ki sahar u sham fhir kahan*
> *sona to hashr tak hai ye aaram phir kahan.*[43]

It may be noted here that Anis represented a long-standing tradition of learning nurtured in medieval north India, wherein knowledge of Indian literary traditions was deemed as essential as that of Arabic and Persian. He had great expertise in Braj poetry.

Both Anis and Dabir emphasized greatly the literary aspect of marsiya. Anis echoed Sauda when he proclaimed:

> *Guldasta-ma'ani ko naye dhang se bandhun*
> *Ek phul ka mazmun ho to sau dhang se bandhun*

One of his marsiyas opens with these lines:

> *yar ab ab chaman-i nazm ko gulzar iram kar*
> *Aye abr-i karam khushq ziraat pe karam kar*[44]

At times Anis does concede that mourning and lamentation have religious significance and marsiyas should evoke grief:

> *jalsa nahin mazlum ki yeh bazm-i 'aza hai*
> *yan rone ki lazzat hai rulane ka maza hai*[45]
> ....
> *Mardum ke liye vajib 'aini hai ye zari*
> *Rona hi wasila hai shifa'at ka hamari*[46]

[43]Saleha Abid Husain (ed.), *Anis ke Marsiye* (Delhi: Taraqqi-i Urdu Board, 1977), 13:p. 375/151.

[44]Ibid., p. 61/1.

[45]Ibid., p. 409/48.

[46]For marsiya opening with the lines, *yaar ab chaman- nazm ko gulzar iram kar*, see ibid., pp. 61–91.

However, this objective does not dominate his poetry and his marsiyas denote literary excellence.

As we have noted, mourning assemblies at Lucknow also had the essence of literary gatherings wherein poets were appreciated for their poetic achievements. Dabir consciously used marsiya as a medium for the display of his literary skill:

> ab rayat-i zaban sar-i mimbar 'alam karun ... phir ma'ani- i buland ka lashkar ba ham karun
> majlis pe aashkar viqar-i 'alam karun ... rayat mein silk-i nazm ke parcham ko zam karun[47]

Dabir is one of the foremost exponents of rubais, salams, and marsiyas in a variety of styles. One of his marsiyas, *'mehr-i 'alam sarvar-i akram hua tala'*, is entirely *ghair-manqut*, that is, in it only those words are used which do not have diacritical marks.[48] Once in a gathering, wherein Dabir presented a marsiya in this style, one of the leading ghazal writers, Atish, applauded, saying that in diction he found it of the same stature as Faizi's *tafsir*:[49]

> 'aqs- i 'alam u 'alam –i ma'mur ka 'alam
> gah mah ka, gah, mehr ka gah taur ka 'alam.[50]

The *mazmun-bandi* (delineation of a theme in all its vividness) of Dabir is, unquestionably, excellent. He has explored a variety of themes and delineated them in detail:

> mimber pe kya main peshkash-i Murtaza' karun
> han nazar nazm ke gauhar-i bebaha karun.[51]

---

[47]Ibid., p. 1: 38/6; one of his marsiya opens with the line: *'aye dabadaba-i nazm, do 'alam ko hila de;* see, Hydari, *Intikhab-i Marasi Mirza Dabir*, pp. 86–125. Even verses expressive of extreme devotion to Husain have literary overtones. For instance in the marsiya, *'angushtari -i 'arsh ka yarab nagin dikha'*, he says:

    han josh-i taba' tarz na hasha bigarne paaye misra na apni rast qadami par akarne paaye
    khud nazm bol uthe ke naya intazam hai afsana yeh nahin jihad -i Imam hai.

Ibid., 11: p. 99/63.

[48]Ibid., p. 31. A style wherein words without diacritical marks are used is known as *san'at-i mahmal.*

[49]Ibid., p. 33. In the marsiya, *'mehr -i 'alam sarvar –i akram hua tala'*, there are 72 bands (verses) having only ghair-manqut words.

[50]Ibid., 19: p. 592/2.

[51]Ibid., p. 11:391/21. Although he mentions at one place that *'apne sukhan ki aap shina sakht 'aib hai'* (ibid., 7: p. 300/149), at several places he boasts of his literary skill:

    ho dhum jahan mein ke ye ta'id-i khuda hai ye bandish-i mazmun na dekha hai suna hai (ibid., 2: p. 86/3)

    mazmun naye karta hun ijad hamesha (ibid., 2: p. 87/4).

    main bulbul-i khush lahja-i bosatan-i chman hun (ibid., 2: p. 87/5).

    main aaj baam-i khutba-i insha –i nazm hun husn –i bayan se martaba afza –i nazm hun (ibid., 6: p. 240/20).

    kis tarz ki raunaq ho is andaz ke aage jadu kahin chal sakta hai 'aijaz ke aage (ibid., 2: p. 87/6).

In the marsiya opening with the line '*jab mah ne nawafil-i shab ko ada kiya*' he claims:

> *is nazm se khazal hain cheh Sa'di cheh Anwari*
> *har misra-i buland hai shamshir-i Hyderi*[52]

One may find in the marsiyas of Anis and Dabir the delineation of familial love and such other bonds, which tie one individual to another. A person's relationship with others—as father, brother, sister, son or as a faithful servant—is of foremost consideration to him/her. Dabir and Anis also try to portray the temperament and qualities of their characters, the way they conduct themselves, and their moral values and virtues. Their loyalty, obedience, allegiance, reverence, devotion and faithfulness, and sometimes even contrariety and dissension are delineated in great detail.

As for their characters—they are universal in time. The best aspects of Indian women are chivalrously depicted. For example, Anis's portrayal of the character of Zainub, the sister of Imam Husain, highlights all the positive aspects of a woman in an Indian household. She virtually keeps the family going, supervises each and every thing, sensitively handles the emotions of others, and has tremendous control over her own emotions even in great distress. The other female character, whom Anis has portrayed in great detail, is Sakina, the youngest daughter of Imam Husain, who is innocently unaware of the hardships of the family. Through her Anis captures childhood in all its innocent curiosity, and beauty but also its tantrums and unending demands. Banu, the wife of Husain, on the contrary, is shown as a very quiet person, extremely respectful of her sister-in-law and with immense faith in family traditions.

In the marsiyas of Dabir also Zainub occupies an important place. She bids farewell to every warrior and we find her busy making arrangements in the family for all sorts of things.[53] However, she appears slightly subdued contrasted with the aura of her brother. Instead, Dabir has projected the character of Banu. She is the granddaughter of Noshervan, the ruler of Iran.[54] In the marsiya, which opens with the line '*ran ki zamin namuna-i 'arsh-i jalil hai*' and deals with the martyrdom of Akbar, even the enemy Umar mentions this fact with reverence.

The marsiya opening with the line '*parchum kisi 'alam ka shu'a'i aftab ki*' is woven around the theme of '*alam* (banner) of Imam Husain and at least hundred bands are written on it by way of *mazmun bandi*, a characteristic of the Lucknow school of Urdu poetry (ibid., 1: p. 37–57).

[52] Ibid., 3: p. 164/184; he concludes this marsiya with this verse.

[53] *Zainub ne kaha hai meri qismat ka yahi kam dene lagi matam ke syah jore wo na kam*
Fiza se kaha sog ka karti hun saranjam thand hua, hai hai 'alam-i lashkar-i Islam.
(Hyderi, *Intikhab-i Marasi Mirza Dabir*: 8: p. 327/129).

[54] Ibid., 6: p. 253/84.

In another marsiya also, Dabir has projected Banu's emotions at the rukhsat of Akbar in a poetic manner:

> Akbar ki har ik baat pe tharrati hai Banu maathe pe shikan dekh ke bal khati hai Banu
> kuchh sochne lagte hain to ghabrati hai Banu murte hain jo run ko to mui jati hai banu
> ik haath kaleje pe dhare, ik jabin par
> ankhon ko jhukaye huye baithi hai zamin par

She is emotionally charged, but not crying or performing bain in the manner of Zainub, instead, pouring her heart into words, she says:

> pala tha esi din ke liye to ke juda ho aankhon ki na 'ainuk ho na piri ke 'asa ho
> ham dhundhe dulhan aur tumhe shauq-i qaza ho irshad samajh kar karo nahaq na khafa ho
> han karti hun, vari, na nahin karti hun, vari
> nazuk hai mizaj aapka, main darti hun vari[55]

Sakina, too, is not portrayed like an innocent girl. Her dialogues at the time of bidding farewell to her father are quite mature.[56] She performs bain at the death of Abbas and says to his wife:

> maine tumhe bewa kiya, randsala pinhaya hai hai meri ik pyas ne sab ghar ko rulaya.[57]

Anis depicts Imam Husain as an ordinary human being. He takes every care of his relatives ('khayal-i khatir-i ahbab chahiye har dam') and mourns and betrays emotions over his dead like an ordinary person.[58] By contrast, Dabir depicts the Imam with a halo of divinity.

The family of Imam Husain in both Anis and Dabir is shown as an aristocratic Indian family in the socio-cultural set-up of Awadh. In describing the dress of Imam Husain and his warriors, Anis virtually describes the contemporary sartorial fashion of Lucknow. Imam Husain wears shamla[59] and patka.[60] Even in the desert, the establishment of the Imam has all the luxury typical of the rulers of Awadh. There are no images of hardships associated with travellers when the Imam arrives in the plains of Karbala; instead there is all the glamour of the procession of a ruler:

> hoshiyar ghafilon ke sawari qarib hai[61]

---

[55]Ibid., 13: p. 446/19; 13: p. 446/23.

[56]Ibid., 4: p. 181–3/79–89, 'adam ka dadras ...'.

[57]Ibid., 8: p. 328/137.

[58]Imam Husain performs bain over the dead body of Hazarat Abbas. (Husain, Anis ke Marsiye, 5: p. 170/ 235; 8: p. 237/115.) Some people expressed reservations about this kind of depiction of the Imam.

[59]Ibid., 7, p. 207/73. Shamla was the headgear in fashion in Awadh among the shurfa from the time of Nawab Sa'adat 'Ali Khan. Madhu Sharma, 'Costume and costume craft in the kingdom of Awadh', Proceedings of Indian History Congress, Jabalpur Session (1971).

[60]Husain, Anis ke Marsiye, 12: p. 322/412; patka is a waistband and part of the ensemble of the Indian upper classes.

[61]Ibid., 13: p. 350/1.

The camp of Imam is visualized by Anis as a *darbar*.[62] The pleasing sounds of *naubat* and *shahna* fill the morning.[63] *Parda* for the ladies of the Imam's household, *haramsara* as he calls it, is carefully observed.[64] Anis generally uses the expression *deorhi*, which was prevalent amongst Rajputs and was also in use in the household of the rulers of Awadh.[65] The Imam's family is referred as a *kunba*, a colloquial expression for *kutumb*, and a *gharana*.[66] The members of the family of Imam Husain converse with him with folded hands (*hath jor ke*), an Indian way of showing respect to elders or superiors.[67] There are several examples: '*dast-i adab ko jor ke*';[68] '*hathon ko jorti hai ye bhaina asir-i gham*';[69] '*qadmon pe gire hathon ko jore jo vo zi jah*';[70] '*bachchon ne ki jo jor ke haathon ko yeh taqrir*;'[71] '*rakha pisar ne pavon pe sar haath jor ke*'.[72] At his deathbed Hazrat Abbas desires: '*rakh do mera sar qiblq-i 'Alam ke pavon par*.'[73]

When Hazrat Abbas leaves for the battlefield and bids farewell to the family, Zainub blesses his wife:

> sar ko laga ke chhati se Zainub ne ye kaha tu apani mang kokh se thandi rahe sada.[74]

This is a typically Indian blessing, conferring longevity of husband and the happiness of children. Similarly, the expression *mang ujarna* signifies widowhood. The youngest son of Hazrat Abbas alludes to the demise of his father in this manner:

> amma ki mang ujar gayi, sadme guzar gaye.[75]

At the time of leaving for Kufa, Akbar, the son of Imam Husain comes to meet his sister Sughra, who reminds him to remember her on auspicious occasions and keep the gift (*neg*) for her:

> haqdar hun main neg ki mera bhi rahe dhyan.[76]

---

[62]Ibid., '*darbar mein haazir the rafiqan-i dilavar*', 10: p. 269/11.

[63]Ibid., 10: p. 275/42.

[64]See Dabir's lines:
parda uthaya laundiyon ne bargah ka (Hyderi, *Intikhab-i Marasi Mirza Dabir*, 10: p. 360/10).
aayi jo dar pe kheme ke paya Husain ko de kar qasam mahal mein bulaya Husain ko (ibid., 11: p. 398/56)

[65]Husain, *Anis ke Marsiye*, 5: p. 153/133.

[66]Ibid., '*kunbe se munh chhipa ke jangal mein ja rahen*', 16: p. 426/20; Dabir also uses the expression kunba, kutumb, and gharana. '*Hashim ke ghar ko dekhiye ipne gharane ko*' (Hyderi, *Intikhab-i Marasi Mirza Dabir*, 4: p. 189/121).

[67]Husain, *Anis ke Marsiye*, 2: p. 94/16; 4:, p. 125/22.

[68]Ibid., 5: p. 153/137.

[69]Ibid., 7: p. 204/3055.

[70]Ibid., 9: p. 245/46.

[71]Ibid., 1: p. 286/113.

[72]Ibid., 33: p. 373/140.

[73]Ibid., 15: p. 420/111.

[74]Ibid., p. 55.

[75]Ibid., 13: p. 376/157.

[76]Ibid., 3: p. 110/55.

The use of *tere vari* is also more frequent than *qurban jaun*. The marsiyas of Anis and Dabir provide numerous examples of such idiom that suggests that women of Muslim families used a language which was not very distinct from their Hindu counterparts and that they shared the beliefs, customs, and superstitions of Hindu women. Such examples pepper the marsiyas of Anis:

> *Zainub ne kaha kyon mujhe visvas na aaye*[77]
> *bin -byaahe mere laal ne kyon laash uthaai*[78]
> *main maa hun, na sahib, mujhe yeh baat na bhaai …. Akbar meri atthara baras ki kamaai.*[79]

All the ladies say at the time of the death of Zainub's sons:

> *sab ne kaha lo sheh ki bahin ho gayi be-aas*[80]

Kubra, the newly-wed wife of Qasim, mourns his death:

> *vo kahti thi ke jaag ke taqdir so gayi*
> *bibi na pakron haath ke main raand ho gayi.*[81]

Zanub says:

> *daulat koi maa jaye se pyari nahin hoti'*[82]
> *dekha jo lahu bacchon ka, chhati umand aayi nazdik tha mar jaaye Yadullah ki jaai*
> *par Fatima ke sabr ki shaan usne dikhaai sab se ye kaha neg lagi meri kamaai*[83]
> *hai hai ye tumhe kis ki nazar kha gayi bacchon'*[84]
> *mujh ko bahut khayal hai Zehra ki jai ka.*[85]

Women, especially in the Braj and Purabi region, use *jai* and *jaya* for daughter and son in north India. At many places Imam Husain is referred as *Fatima ka lal* and *Asadullah ka lal* (son).[86] Husain addresses his sister as *bhaina*,[87] *bali* is used for a young girl;[88] and *raand* is a frequently used expression for a widow.[89]

These colloquial words and phrases are quite common in the marsiyas of Dabir too: *Kunba, hujiye (huyeye), chah, charcha, sidhare hai (gaye hain), suhagan, dhyan,*

---

[77]Ibid., 9: p. 262/145.
[78]Ibid., 9: p. 262/46.
[79]Ibid., 9: p. 262/146.
[80]Ibid., 10: p. 294/157.
[81]Ibid., 12: p. 347/148.
[82]Ibid., 10: p. 294/159.
[83]Ibid., 10: p. 296/173.
[84]Ibid., 10: p. 97/1771.
[85]Ibid., 5: p. 147/93.
[86]Ibid., 5: p. 150/119; 6: p. 173/7; 8: p. 243/35.
[87]Ibid., 7: p. 204/55; 12: p. 325/13.
[88]Ibid., 5: p. 148/104.I
[89]Ibid., 8: p. 244/37.

Rabba, churcha hua, tap (fever),[90] *Yadullah ki jai, Asadullah ki jai, 'Ali ka lal bhaina, munh dhaapna.* Dabir uses *aswar* for *sawar* in the Charan tradition.[91]

Many Braj and Awadhi words are woven into the fabric of Anis's marsiyas, such as *lahu, nirala, dhyan, dhun, kunba, charcha, ran, nar, tan, tap, pahar, byaah, bhaina,* and *visvas.*[92] Apart from this, there is a typical blend of Indian and Persian phrases. Some of these show the impact of the *zaban-i charani*, the language of bards:

> *jo khet mein sar sabz ho sawant vahi hai.*[93]
> *jo baat pe sar de wo sakhawat ka dhani hain*[94]
> *shashdar nahin hote jo shuj'at ke dhani hain*[95]
> *hathon ko jorti hai ye bhaina asir -i gham.*[96]

The word *sidharna* is used variously and frequently, indicating the death of a revered person or his departure:[97]

> *yeh kahate hi bas gulshan-i duniya se sidhare* [98]
> *puchha na jannat ki taraf kaun sidhara.*[99]

Anis's idiomatic diction provides the nuances of the conversational style of the gentry that included Hindus and Muslims both. There are some archaic expressions borrowed from the charan tradition which are generally used in the description of battle: *bag lena,*[100] *bag firana,*[101] *ghore ko garmana,*[102] *ghore ko pherna,*[103] *kamar bandhana, khet parna,*[104] *kariyal jawan,*[105] and so on:

> *phirta hua lashkar mein chholava nazar aaya*[106]
> *Hazrat ne kaha lut gayi baba ki kamai.*[107]

---

[90]Hyderi, *Intikhab-i Marasi-i Mirza Dabir*, p. 56/95; p. 57/99; p. 78/204; 2: p. 101/73; p. 122/176; 3: p. 144/93; p. 151/125; 93; p. 151/125; 17: p. 550/23; 8: p. 327/132.

[91]Ibid., 19: p. 597/25; 13: p. 449/38; 11: p. 396/47

[92]Husain, *Anis ke Marsiye*, 1: p. 84/138; 1: p. 85/147; 2: p. 97/33, p. 99/45; 5: p. 151/123; 5: p. 408/39; 6: p. 187/91; 7: p. 204/55; 10: p. 273/35; p. 288/23; 12: p. 325/13; 10: p. 301/13; 2: p. 339/96; 14: p. 392/94; 16: p. 4267/2; 17: p. 453/31.

[93]Ibid., 9: p. 246/52; *Sawant* (brave).

[94]Ibid., 9: p. 246/51.

[95]Ibid., 9: p. 258/120; '*chhor kar bag, fars ko zara garmaya*' (10: p. 30/12).

[96]Ibid., 7: p. 204/55.

[97]Ibid., 10: p. 279/71; p. 280/73.

[98]Ibid., 8: p. 237/114.

[99]Ibid., 10: p. 297/3.

[100]Ibid., '*sun ke ye bag jo li ...*': p. 182/ 82.

[101]Ibid., 6: p. 192/121, '*bag ghore ki firana tha ke barchhi khai.*'

[102]Ibid., 6: p. 188/100.

[103]Ibid., 7: p. 216/127.

[104]Ibid., 10: p. 280/75 '*tori hai safen jang mein jab khet pare hain.*'

[105]Ibid., 14: p. 393/99 '*ran par jo charha ho, vahi jaane ke ye kya tha.*'

[106]Ibid., 15: p. 414/74 *chhalava* is a spirit, which quickly changes form.

[107]Ibid., 15: p. 419/104.

Dabir literally uses the idiom peculiar to women in women-centric situations:

le le ke balayen kaha chhati se laga kar lo aag lagi maang mein barbad hua ghar[108]
ye aatma ki aanch hai, vari, khafa na ho.[109]

Anis has also provided illustrations of *rekhti*, the idiom of the harem, which was used for the first time by his grandfather Mir Hasan in his masnavi, *Sahar ul Bayan* and popularized as a form of poetry by Insha and Rangin.[110]

main sadqe jaun mujh ko tumhari bala lage[111]
Dharka hai ke ghabara ke chale aayen na ran se[112]
sadqe gayi kuchh kaam hai yan aake sidharo[113]
sadqe gayi pani mujhe darkaar nahin hai.[114]

Sometimes the language of Anis and Darib resembles that of the *sabha* and *jalsa,* the urban theatrical representations of Lucknow. Banu, the wife of the Imam speaks to Zainub in the following manner:

ki arz haath jor ke, aye khwahar-i Imam main hun kaniz aapki aur ye pisar ghulam.[115]

Anis makes graphic use of similes from Indian mythology. This suggests that in spite of the efforts of Sauda, Mir, and Nasikh, who tried hard to eliminate the *bhakapan* from Urdu, some of the characteristics of riti poetry remained ingrained

---

[108]Hyderi, *Intikhab-i Marasi-i Mirza Dabir,* 9: p. 355/126.
[109]Ibid., 14: p. 473/14; there are many more examples of the typical idioms and phrases of women of the Awadh region in the marsiyas of Dabir:

> *hai hai mujhe to aur ye visvas ab hua* (1: p. 57/97).
> *taqdir mujhe unki maut aisi raas laaye* (1: p. 66/141).
> *bisvas mujh ko aata hai tashvish hoti hai* (3: p. 131/33).
> *kis ki nazar lagi meri ma ki kamai ko* (7: p. 278'45).
> *aakhir kahan sidharte ho kuchh batawo to* (10: p. 362/19).
> *aye nur-i nazar kis ki nazar kha gayi tum ko* (9: p. 354/124).
> *ye lal teri chand si surat ke main sadqe* (9: p. 337/38).
> *ye byah meri ladli ko ras na aaya* (9: p. 337/35)
> *nausha zamane se sidhara* (9: p. 352/112).
> *ghar lutne ka, sar khulne ka, visvas nahin hai* (13: p. 446/22).
> *pani se nihalon ko hara sab ne kiya hai* (13: p. 447/27).
> *maine abhi beton ka lahu munh pe mala hai* (13: p. 449/38).
> *beta kisi ko dagh na bete ka de khuda* (14: p. 471/10).
> *mar jaaye ma, pe lakht-i jigar se juda na ho*
> *marsiya, aye bagh –i taba 'rang-i bahar –i sukhun dikha,*
> *wo boli, han kaleje pe paththar dharungi main* (14: p. 473/20) .
> *bibi ki kokh ujar gayi, hye hye ghazab hua* (17: p. 555/47).

[110]Azad, *Ab–i Hayat:* p. 333.
[111]Husain, *Anis ke Marsiye,* 7: p. 200/30, 32.
[112]Ibid., 8: p. 245/44.
[113]Ibid., 8: p. 245/45.
[114]Ibid., 15: p. 409/48.
[115]Ibid., 18: p. 490/69.

in the poetry of those Urdu poets who hailed from Delhi. To quote an example, where Anis is praising the sword of Imam Husain:

> mojud thee har ghaul mei aur sab se juda thi dam kham bhi, lagavat bhi, safai bhi, ada bhi,
> Ik ghat pe thi aag bhi, pani bhi hawa bhi amrit bhi, halahal bhi, Masiha bhi, qaza bhi.[116]

There are several examples in Anis of the style of poetry that developed in Lucknow and thrived on figures of speech like riyayat-i lafzi:

> pyare hamre bhai ko bhai hai kya jagah.[117]

Riyayat-i lafzi, popularized in Lucknow by Miyan Amanat during the mid-nineteenth century, also found expression in Dabir's poetry:

> pyare ki badi aah mere sar pe na aayi haye haye, teri aayi hui sab ghar pe na aayi[118]

Anis deals with rukhsat in a manner that foregrounds the dramatic aspect of the marsiya and evokes emotion, intonation, and histrionics at the time of recitation. An excellent example is the way Anis describes the rukhsat sought by Akbar from Zainub and Banu, who, after great persuasion, allow him to go for battle. But they want him to go in the attire of a bridegroom, which is an Indian custom amongst the Rajputs. Akbar refuses and says:

> ham kis tereh se pahne, yah shadi ka paharavan Abbas namdar ne paya nahin kafan
>   bhai ke gham mein chaak ghareban hai Shah ka
>   mar kar kafan mile yahi jora hai byah ka.[119]

This entire episode is stretched over thirty-five verses.[120]

At the time of rukhsat for the battlefield, Zainub tells her sons to take care of each other:

> bhai kisi hangam mein bhai ko na chhore … dono mein koi 'aqada kashai ko na chore.[121]

Amad has all the glamour of contemporary urban theatrical representations, jalsa and sabha, and one is reminded of the arrival of the actors on stage.[122]

> hai shor-i amad amad-i shah-falak sarir[123]
> tha shor ke amad hai ye mahbub-i khuda ki[124]

---

[116]Ibid., 1: p. 81/141.
[117]Ibid., 5: p. 146/93.
[118]Hyderi, Intikhab-i Marasi Mirza Dabir, 15: p. 515/101.
[119]Husain, Anis ke Marsiye, 16: p. 431/49.
[120]Ibid., 16: pp. 426–432/20–50, 52–5.
[121]Ibid., 9: pp. 248/60–5.
[122]Ibid., one is reminded of the amad in Indarsabha:
    'sabha mein doston Indar ki amad amad hai'
[123]Ibid., 4: p. 122/2; p. 123/11.
[124]Ibid., 8: p. 229/67.

amad hai karbala ke naitan mein sher ki deorhi se chal chuki hai sawari diler ki
ab jaati hai ran ko 'Ali Akbar kisawari.[125]

The amad of Imam Husain in the battlefield is described by Dabir as if he is
proceeding to the court and not to the battlefield:

mujre ke liye 'arsh ke sukkan nazar aaye Qur'an ke sayyare liye haft salam aaye
sitare ye kahte huye manind-i ghulam aaye hoshiyar, janab aaye, huzur aaye, Imam aaye.[126]
tashrif janib-i dar-i daulat Husain laye
khudam panj-i naubati i- hashmat bajate aaye[127]
ghul par gaya mahal mein hai amad huzur ki.[128]

Here he is virtually describing the processions of the Awadh rulers. The
Imam is projected like a king. He is *Sultan-i din, Sultan-i mashriqain.*[129]

Anis's sarapa is generally short and in the contemporary tradition. He
describes the beauty of his hero and not his valour. While describing the sarapa
of Abbas and Qasim he says:

ankhen wo ghazalan-i khatan jin pe tasadduq rukhsar wo nazuk ke chaman jin pe tasadduq.[130]
rukhsaron pe gesu hain ke ke hai chaand gahan mein.[131]

The sarapa of the warriors of Husain is presented by Anis in this way:

rukh chaand se raushan, to badan phulon se khushbu rukhsaaron pe sumbul se latakte huye gesu[132]

Not all marsiyas of Dabir have sarapa, but whenever he does include it, he
delineates it in full.[133] He was the first to write the sarapa of Hur.[134]

He provides minute details of every limb of his hero. Even the pupils, eyelashes, and eyebrows do not escape his attention, as one finds in the sarapa of
Ali Akbar.[135]

Bain, a Persian word meaning separation, is borrowed in its present
connotation in marsiya from Punjabi folk poetry and tappa songs, which were
woven around the theme of love and vexation caused by the memory of the

---

[125]Ibid., 17: p. 454/37 .

[126]Hyderi, *Intikhab-i Marasi-i Mirza Dabir,* 2: p. 110/117 D.

[127]Ibid., 3: p. 133/34.

[128]Ibid., 10: p. 359/7.

[129]Ibid., 12: p. 420/26.

[130]Husain, *Anis ke Marsiye,* 11: p. 307/53.

[131]Ibid., p. 307/49.

[132]Ibid., 15: p. 404/15.

[133]Hyderi, *Intikhab-i Marasi-i Mirza Dabir,* 15: p. 499/503; see sarapa of Abbas (8: pp. 305–312/22–55).

[134]*ab tak kisi ne Hur ka sarapa kaha na tha* (ibid., 3: p. 149/115).

[135]'*putli hai koh —i tur -i tajalli*' (ibid., 6: p. 244/41); '*ye tir-i kahkashan hai kaman-i hilal hai*'
(6: p. 244/42; p. 247/57; p. 248/62, etc.).

departed beloved. Sikandar and Sauda, who hailed from Punjab, introduced it in their marsiyas and gradually it became a fixed feature of marsiyas in Lucknow. The bain in Anis is quite detailed, generally stretching from fifteen to twenty verses and sometimes to thirty. At the death of Akbar, he ends with:

Likhu haram ke bain to, hoti hai ik kitab[136]

Significantly in most of his marsiyas, the bain is performed by Zainub.

Dabir is at his poetic best while dealing with bain and the description is most nature.[137] Dabir does not always conclude his marsiyas on bain. At some places, the bain is devised at the time of rukhsat.

There were certain rituals associated with bain, which are described by Anis in his poetry.[138] These were typical expressions of grief:

pyaase suye firdaus sidhare mere ghar se.[139]

Bain employs the spoken idiom and the customs associated with mourning, especially widowhood (randapa), the most important symbol of which was a

---

[136]Husain, *Anis ke Marsiye*, 16: p. 447/149.

[137]*aye mere randape ke sahare* (Abbas's wife to her sons). See Hyderi, *Intikhab-i Marasi-i Mirza Dabir*, 8: p. 326/125.

   han bain karo lash pe sehre ko barhao; ibid. (9: p. 355/128).
   ro ro ke bain Fatima Kubra ne ye kahe; ibid. (12: p. 441/134).
   Iran ke ujale Arabistan ke ujale. Ibid. (15: p. 515/103). The relationship with Iran is strengthened because of the Iranian origin of the Awadh dynasty.

[138]See, Husain, *Anis ke Marsiye.*

raanden saf-i matam se uthin khole huye sar (9: p. 266/172).
Zainub ne sar par duhaththar kai maare (9: p. 266/168).
Bikhra ke sar ke bal haram sath sath the (12: p. 324/11).
deorhi se chalo matami saf ghar mein bichhao (15: p. 418/98).
gardan mein la ke shaal-i 'aza dal dejiye (Akbar to Zainub, 16: p. 431/48).
matam ki saf pe baith gayi koi nohagar (14: p. 398/128).
randsala lavo zuja- i'Abbas ke liye (14: p. 398/129).
bikhra diye Husain ki bahinon ne sar ke baal (14: p. 398/130).
jis tareh peet ta hai koi sogvar sar (14: p. 397/124).
chillaya chaak karke gareban ko sogvar (14: p. 398/126).
maare gaye jihad mein 'Abbas bawafa (14: p. 398/127).
kal thee suhagan aaj to main sogvaar hun (14: p. 399/135.
aye gul –badanon, kis ki nazar kha gayi tum ko (9: p. 265/165).
Fizza, the wife of Abbas performs bain:
bhaati thee jis ke baalon ki bu aapko kamal ussne tumhaare sog mein bikhara diye hain bal (13: p. 375/151).

[139]Ibid., 9: p. 265/166; Husain mourns the death of Abbas and performs bain in the following manner:

   Ghurbat mein lut gaya mera ghar hai hai hai sidhi na hogi ab ye kamar hai hai hai
   Taza hai aaj dagh-i pider hai hai hai kata gaya chhuri se jigar hai hai hai
   Abbas kya jahan se gaye ham guzar gaye
   Muhsin hua shahid Hasan aaj mar gaye (14: p. 394/103).

randsala, probably a shawl. This ritual is peculiar to Awadh of the nineteenth century. The wife of Hazrat Abbas tells Zainub:

> *bibi ye sab hamare randape ke taur hain.*[140]

There is a new connotation of *jihad* and *ghazi* in the marsiyas of Anis and Dabir. The battlefield of Karbala is the platform of the struggle between right and wrong. It is projected as a jihad in that sense and the warriors on the Imam's side are *ghazis.*[141] One marsiya of Anis opens with these lines:

> *kya ghazian-i fauj-i khuda nam kar gaye*[142]

Dabir uses the term *lashkar-i kuffar* for the army of the enemy of the Imam.

> *yak baar pari lashkar-i kuffar mein halchal*[143]

Dabir also uses the term jihad as a variant of war[144]

Manzarnigari is Anis's forte. His poetry depicts nature in all its colours and he uses graphic similes to portray it. Some of his marsiyas provide excellent descriptions of scenic beauty. The description of the burning heat of the desert of Iraq, where the tragedy took place, or the fatal thrust of the warriors, or the hardship of their travel is, however, dealt with just as a ritual. In fact, the flora and fauna and scenes he describes are wholly Indian. He talks about a blue dawn, morning breezes, dewdrops, the chirping of birds, the sounds made by peacocks, and even deep forests infested with lions and other animals.[145] While describing the *subeh-i Ashur,* Anis speaks of the *sabza zar sehra* instead of the hot sand.[146] He is virtually delineating the north Indian plains with their lush green meadows (sabza zar sehra):

> *vo nur- i subh aur vo sehra wo sabzvar vo tairon ke ghaul darakhton pe beshumar*
> *chalna nasim subh ka, rah rah ke bar bar ku ku vo qamriyon ki vo taus ki pukar.*[147]

One of the finest examples of Anis's poetry is in the lines:

> *chalna wo bad- i subh ke jhokon ka dam ba dam murghan- i bagh ki wo khush ilhaniyan ba ham*
> *wo aab u tab-i nahar wo mauzon ka pech u kham sardi hawa mein, par na zyada bahut na kam*
> *kha kha ke ous aur bhi sabza hara hua*
> *kha motiyon se daman-i sehra bhara hua*[148]

[140]Ibid., 5: p. 166/211.
[141]Ibid., 'tazi ko tez karke ye ghazi ne di sada', 16: p. 440/103; 18: p. 502/140.
[142]Ibid., 18: p. 482–506.
[143]Hyderi, *Intikhab-i Marasi-i Mirza Dabir,* 16: p. 537/87.
[144]Ibid., 11: p. 409/110; also p. 399/63.
[145]Husain, *Anis ke Marsiye,* 'jab bolte the sher to dar jate the bachhe', 10: p. 269/6.
[146]Ibid., 7: p. 195/6; p. 195–6/1–8.
[147]Ibid., 12: p. 323/3.
[148]Ibid.

Sometimes Anis opens his marsiyas with a description of nature.[149] His marsiya *'jab qat' ki masafit- i shab aftab ne'* is one of the finest example of the depiction of the scenic beauty in Urdu literature.

Manzarnigari in Dabir, by contrast, is more of a ritual. He indicates the end of spring season as:

kul ek hafta bagh mein gul mehman hai sabza gul-i bahar ki rukhsat ka pan hai[150]

While describing dawn, he says:

laila-i shab ke husn ka gulshan khizan hua[151]
tha sham se birhaman —i shab jo qamar- parast
khurshid ne lagai ise zarb pusht-i dast[152]

Generally speaking, the manzarnigari of Dabir is for the display of *san 'atgari*.

Dialogues form an important ingredient of marsiya literature and often bear a resemblance to the *samvad* (conversation) of Ramlila. For instance, when the Imam reaches the battlefield, a dialogue commences with the enemy:

maidan mein aa ke kahane laga Shamar be-adab taqat 'Ali ki kya hui larte nahin ho ab

Husain replies:

tu janta hai ibn-i Ali ko haras hai
mujh ko faqat Rasul ki ummat ka pas hai[153]

Dialogues are woven into the fabric of Anis's marsiya, opening with the line, *'farzand-i payamber ka Madina se safar hai'*, to the extent that it appears as if it has been written for stage presentation. Everyone is seen leave-taking and meeting friends and relatives, exchanging compliments and conversing with each other. What Anis presents here is a perfect picture of a family gathering.[154] This situation has great dramatic possibilities that Anis exploits through dialogues.

Like Anis, Dabir has also devised dialogues that remind us of theatrical representations. In the battlefield, the Imam observes all those courtsies (*tehzib-i akhlaq*) for which Lucknow is famous. When enemy asks for an introduction, the Imam introduces himself like the shurfa of Lucknow:

tum kaun ho, farmaya ke gharib azli hun batji ka nabizada Husain ibn 'Ali hun.[155]

---

[149]For instance, see his marsiyas, *'tai kar chuka jo manzil-i shab karvan-i subh'*; *jab zulf ko khole huye laila-i shab aayi'*; *'phula shafaq se, charkh par jab lalazar subh.'* See Ibid., pp. 195–217, 268–98, 323–49.

[150]Hyderi, *Intikhab-i Marasi-i Mirza Dabir*, 1: p. 53/77.

[151]Ibid., 3: p. 127/7.

[152]Ibid., 3: p. 129/14.

[153]Ibid., 2: p. 100/48.

[154]Hussain, *Anis ke Marsiye*, 3: p. 102–21; also see, 9: pp. 253–5/94–103; 10: p. 274/36–8; 12: pp. 324–6/11–19; 13: pp. 362–3 /75–9.

[155]Hyderi, *Intikhab-i Marasi-i Mirza Dabir*, 2: p. 116/145.

In the marsiya, 'kis ka 'alam Husain ke mimbar ki Zeb hai', there are many situations which appear to be part of a stage show and have dialogues and action both.[156] Dabir sometimes opens his marsiyas with a dialogue. One such example is the marsiya 'asghar pe jab ki pyas ki shiddat sawa huyi', where the entire episode of the martyrdom of Asghar is related through dialogues.[157]

In the battlefield Husain tries to convince the qaris and Hafiz-i Qur'an, that they have memorized the Quran without properly understanding its meaning.:

> har lafz ke Imam ne ma'ni dikha diye darya- i 'ilm khushq zuban se baha diye[158]

A dialogue in the samvad style begins with the qaris and the leader of the enemy, Umar.[159]

Another good example, which highlights marsiya's affinity with theatre, the dialogue between him and Umar, when Akbar comes to the battlefield:

> kya kahna tere husn ka afvah sab mein hai
> Akbar tera hi nam mubarak Arab mein hai [160]

Also,

> Banu ka char gesuon vala, tu hi hai aah Naushervan ke ghar ka ujala, tu hi hai aah binnat-i Ali ki goud mein pala, tu hi hai aah chashm u chiragh Syed vala, tu hi hai aah.[161]

All these verses were rendered with the same intonation as in the recitational form of drama. The conversation between Husain and Zainub is a good example of it. Some verses appear to be written for stage representation:

> Hur to udhar se aaya, idhar se Imam aaye aaqa ne donon haath mulaqat ko barhaye [162]
> maqtal hai chasn fasl-i bahari ki hai amad,

which deal with the martyrdom of Akbar.[163] In the marsiya, 'Asghar pe jab pyas ki shiddat siwa hui', Husain makes a small grave for Asghar and puts his blood-stained tauq on it and says to Banu:

> Bibi ye tere hasliyon wale ki qabr hai Banu ye tere goud mein pale ki qabr hai[164]

This ritual is observed as jhule ka matam.

---

[156]Ibid., 12: pp. 440–1/128–33.

[157]Ibid., 17: pp. 545–68; 'Shah bole tum logon ne chhora hai kisi ko shishmahe ke bhi gham mein karvaya mere ji ko' (2: p. 116/145). The dialogues commence for long in this way (2: pp. 116–21/149–70).

[158]Ibid., 3: p. 141/76.

[159]Ibid., 3: p. 138–41/62–78.

[160]Ibid., 6: p. 251–4/78–906; p. 252/83.

[161]Ibid., 6: p. 253/84.

[162]Ibid., 7: pp. 278–9/47–55; 7: p. 287/90.

[163]Ibid., 15: p. 495–519.

[164]Ibid., 17: p. 555/48.

Some of the marsiyas of Dabir have the traits of *qissa*. For instance, see the beginning of the marsiya, '*dast-i Khuda ka quwwat-i bazu Husain hai*':

kahte hain sahiban-i tawarikh beshtar jis saal naam-i shah par para qarrua, safar.[165]

In the marsiya, '*aye shams u qamar nur ki mehfil hai ye mahfil*', Dabir relates events/episodes in the same manner as is done by a *sutradhar* (anchor person), who prepares ground for the entry of actors on stage:

es vaqt haram kheme main ghabraye huye hai ham shaql-i nabi bahar-i vida aaye huye hai.[166]

In a marsiya by Dabir, Akbar, knowing that his aunt Zainub will not easily allow him to go for battle, asks her mother to bring his dress from her. However, Sakina, the younger sister of Akbar, has already reported to Zainub that *bhaiyya* (brother) is going somewhere and mother is crying. Suddenly Zainub appears with the dress in her hand. Dabir writes:

nagah namudar huin Zainub-i ghamnak chehre pe male khak, gareban kiye chak
hamrah liye Akbar-i gulfam ki poshak ghusse se badan r'asha mein aur surkh rukh-i pak.[167]

This is reminiscent of some scenes from a contemporary play, *Indarsabha*. Anis appears to be well versed in Indian mythology. In a marsiya, which deals with the martyrdom of Abbas, one can find a parallel with a *Krishna lila* episode where the river Jamuna was trying to touch the feet of Krishna through its waves. It is typical Indian imagery.

dala miyan-i nahar mein jo asp-i saba shitab
maujen barhin barai qadam bosi-i janab uchhli 'alam ko chumne ko mahiyan-i ab[168]

One may refer in passing here to the *rivayats* composed in the Deccan. One of these projects Asghar as *bal* Krishna. The mourning songs, *deha*, current in the rural areas of Awadh and its vicinity, present Imam Husain as Krishna.[169] Another interesting phenomenon in these marsiyas is that Husain and his family hear the voices from the beyond from departed souls, especially Hazrat 'Ali and Fatima, the parents of Husain. Like Indian gods and divinities, they remain invisible and make announcements, comparable to *Dev bani*, by way of warning or appreciation. This feature, which assigns divinity to the Imam's family, is certainly borrowed from Indian mythology and indigenous theatre.

awaz phir Ali ki ye aayi ke aye pisar[170]

---

[165]Ibid., 18: pp. 569–91.
[166]Ibid., 13: p. 445/16.
[167]Ibid., 13: p. 449/34.
[168]Husain, *Anis ke Marsiye*, 14: p. 391/86.
[169]*Hasan thhare jamuna kinare,*
  bajaven bansi jamuna ki ret mein
[170]Husain, *Anis ke Marsiye*, 14: p. 397/121.

This idea of *akash bani* is more pronounced in the marsiyas of Dabir. God in the manner of Indian gods grants a boon to Husain:

awaz ye aayi ke wafa karte hain ham bhi
kya mangte ho, maango, 'ata karte hain ham bhi[171]
Hazrat ne kaha khun bhare haathon ko utha kar Rabba, mere Shiyon ko jahannum se riha kar
Rabba, mere zavvron ki tu 'umr sawa kar Rabba, jo mujhe royen bahisht un ko 'ata kar[172]
aayi ye nida dekho meri vada u wafai[173]
ek qaza ko aayi, nida asman se
tham tham, ke tir chhut ta hai Hur ki kaman se[174]

In Dabir's marsiyas Fatima is always there to share the grief of the family and even to provide instructions regarding rituals, etc.[175]

Dabir has delineated in detail the rituals and cultural practices followed on the occasion of death. By this time, the rituals related to mourning (*dastur-i 'aza*) were formalized in Awadh. Dabir's marsiyas provide a fuller view/glimpse of these. After the death of Hazrat Abbas, Husain asks Zainub to make arrangements for mourning (*sog ka saranjam*) thus:

han sog ka Hyder ke syah farsh bichhawo han rakht-i 'aza jis mein wo sanduq mangawo
wo sab ko ye jore 'azadar banawo shappar ki 'aza ka hamen tabus pinhawo
tum pahno kali kafni aal 'aba mein
jo Fatima ne pahani thi nana ki 'aza mein
nauhe mein na 'Abbas kahe, na kahe saqqa jo bain kare, ro ke hai Husaina
baqi koi dastur-i 'aza rahne na paye sab ek ek karke pursey ko aayen[176]

Dabir's marsiyas depict the superstitions of Indian women at the time of death.
When the widow of Abbas noticed that the dresses of Sakina and Akbar were to her children given as dresses for mourning (*poshak-i aza*), she was very annoyed and said to Banu:

dono haath jor ke Banu se ye kaha thahro Khuda ke vaste, hai hai, yeh kya, yeh kya?
kyo layi farsh-i sog yeh bin byahe ka libas Zainub bhi be hawas hai laundi bhi be hawas

---

[171]Hyderi, *Intikhab-i Marasi-i Mirza Dabir*, 2: p. 122/175.
[172]Ibid., 2: p. 122/176.
[173]Ibid., 2: p. 122/177: The dialogue with the invisible God continues up to band 179, p. 122.
[174]Ibid., Akash-bani 3: p. 157/157. Also see: *'us vaqt aayi alam –i lahut se nida* (11: p. 398/58; this was at the time of rukhsat of Husain to the battlefield).
aayi sada ye arsh se aye hamil-i bala (11: p. 399/60; at the time of rukhsat to Husain by Zainub).
[175]Ibid., Fatima says to Zainub:
aye meri jayi saman-i syom bhi kuchh kar lo (see 8: p. 329/141)
aayi ye nida, pas hun main, dur kahan hun (8: p. 329/140).
randsala bahu ke main pinhane ko hun aayi ik hulla, pur nur hun, firdaus se lai (8: p. 329/141).
aayi nida 'Ali ki tu kyon behawaas hai (7: p. 285/78, at the time of Hur's death).
[176]Ibid., 8: p. 326/128; 8: p. 326/129; p. 327/132 .

sab kunba ab to jita hai Akbar ki aas par
sadqa utarun bachchon ko main is libas par
bas ab sidhariye ke mera saaya par na jaaye [177]

Some practices related to Indian marriages are also incorporated in the marsiyas:

alqissa 'aza khane mein ye byah rachaya filfaur dulhan, Fatima Kubra ko, banaya
Qasim ko udhar khil'at-i shahana pinhaya phulon se ghul -i bagh-i Muhammad ko basaya
bahane sar-i nausha pe aanchal ko urha kar
qurban huin masnad-i zarin pe bitha kar
sigha shah bekus ne parha ba dil -i maghmum randon mein mubarak ki, salamat ki hui dhum. [178]

To sum up, it may be said that marsiya is representative of the compositeness and resilience of Awadh society, wherein the idioms and conventions of the other were freely adopted; a society that had faith in the strength of coexistence of diverse cultural groups. Marsiya took on indigenous poetic, musical, and linguistic elements and had the vibrance of Indo-Persian traditions nurtured in northern India over the centuries. It became instrumental in inspiring modern Urdu and Hindi poetry of the early twentieth century, and we find Hali, Shibli, Iqbal, Josh, Prasad, Pant, Nirala, Mahadevi Verma, echoing the clarion call of marsiya in musaddas form.

[177]Ibid., 12: p. 441/130; 12: p. 441/131; 2: p. 441/132.
[178]Ibid., 9: p. 332/14–15.

OF GRAVEYARDS AND GHETTOS: MUSLIMS IN PARTITIONED WEST BENGAL 1947–67

Joya Chatterji

T
hroughout the last century, there has been a Muslim graveyard in Selimpore. This suburb, just south of Calcutta in the 24 Parganas,[1] was home to many many Muslims before Partition. Some were considerable landowners, part of the vanquished Muslim aristocracy settled by the British in south Calcutta in the late eighteenth century.[2] In times past, the burial ground belonged to one such wealthy Musalman. Originally intended for the owner's family, the cemetery in time came to be used more generally by local Muslims. Spanning an acre, the unfenced plot straddled Selimpore Road and was bounded on the south by a large pond. Houses occupied by Muslims stood at its northern edge. Beside them was a small shrine or dargah, probably the tomb of a minor *pir*.[3]

Acknowledgements: I am very grateful to Ananya Kabir, Barbara Daly Metcalf, and Samita Sen for providing information and helpful insights; and to Anil Seal for his comments on the chapter as a whole.

[1]Selimpore has since been included in the city and now falls within Ward 92 of the Calcutta Municipal Corporation.

[2]Bose writes that 'after the fall of Oudh, the Nawab was given a place of residence in Ward 75; and so were the descendants of Tippu Sultan of Mysore in Ward 78'. Nirmal Kumar Bose, *Calcutta, 1964: A Social Survey* (Bombay, New Delhi, Calcutta and Madras: Anthropological Survey of India, 1968), p. 64. Their retainers and staff followed in large numbers, as did the traders, scholars, and divines they patronized, and settled in the Tollygunge area, not far from Selimpore. M.K.A. Siddiqui, *The Muslims of Calcutta: A Study in Aspects of Their Social Organisation* (Calcutta: Anthropological Survey of India, 1974), p. 21.

[3]Selimpore's dargah does not find a place on Siddiqui's list of important *astanas* and dargahs in Calcutta. Siddiqui, *The Muslims of Calcutta*, appendix II, pp. 132–3.

During the upheavals of Partition, Muslims left the area in large numbers. Many more fled Selimpore after the fearful Howrah riots of 1950, and squatter colonies of Hindu refugees from East Bengal sprang up in the suburb.[4] One of these colonies, Shahidnagar, was located on the south-eastern edge of the burial ground. Others, including Bapujinagar and Adarsha Palli, formed what the police report described as 'a sort of ring around the burial ground'. Soon refugees from these colonies began to encroach upon the graveyard, gradually nibbling away at its edges. Once they got their foot in, they began to challenge the right of the few remaining Muslim families to use the graveyard to bury and honour their dead.

In the early 1950s, the refugees repeatedly tried to get the graveyard closed down on 'health and sanitation' grounds, arguing that it was 'located in a built up area ... in the heart of refugee concentrations'. When the Muslims refused to shut it down, Saralananda Sen, a journalist working for *Jugantar*, demanded action from the Calcutta Corporation. In March 1955, when the Muslims brought a body there for burial, Sen orchestrated a protest by the neighbouring refugees and bullied the family into burying the body instead at the graveyard at Anwar Shah Road, a couple of miles away in Tollygunje. Since burial grounds in Calcutta were intended for the exclusive use of specific Muslims sects, ethnic, or occupational groups,[5] this is likely to have caused considerable embarrassment in Selimpore.

Two months later, a burial did take place at Selimpore. But this was only able to go ahead when a charity for burying Muslim paupers—the Anjuman Mafidul Islam—intervened. The Anjuman's head, S.M. Salahuddin, successfully petitioned the Standing Health Committee of the Calcutta Corporation for permission to conduct the burial. After this, the Muslims claimed that the refugees began to harass them in other ways as well: refugee children desecrated their graveyard by playing 'Holi' on it, or by using some part of it as a football ground.

Matters came to a head a year later in 1956, when the Muslims tried to observe Shab-e-barat ceremonies at Selimpore. On '*Shobrat*', as it is known colloquially in Bengal and Bihar, Muslim communities gather in burial grounds to remember their dead. The ceremony starts in the evening, when descendants of the dead bearing trays of *halwa* and *parathas* walk to the cemeteries, distributing food to the poor. All night they pray by the graves, which have been adorned

---

[4]'Formerly the area was largely inhabited by Muslims but during the riots of 1950, a good number of Muslims left the area and only a few of them have stayed there. At the moment, the area is full of refugees'. Chief Administrative Officer, Anjuman Mufidul Islam to Dr B.C. Roy, 3 Apr. 1956. Government of Bengal, Intelligence Branch, File Number 2856/55 (henceforth GB IB, F. No. 2856/55, and so on).

[5]Siddiqui, *The Muslims of Calcutta*, p. 11. We do not know anything about this particular family's sect or ethnicity. However, the fact that the burial ground had a dargah on it, and was the site of Shab-e-barat ceremonies (see later in the chapter), suggests that it catered chiefly to Sunnis of the Barelvi persuasion. The Anwar Shah Road cemetery, in contrast, would have been intended mainly for the use of Shias.

with flowers, incense, and candles. The festival is a vital part of the ritual calendar for Sunnis in Bengal, and these little graveyards hence are central to their spirit of continuity and community.

On this occasion, however, things went badly wrong. As the *maulvi* began his prayers at the Selimpore cemetery's south-eastern corner, refugees from the adjacent Shahidnagar colony gathered threateningly. Intimidated, the maulvi abandoned the ceremony. Later that night, the Shab-e-barat was allowed to proceed but only because the police provided protective cover. When the Muslims lodged an official complaint, the refugees countered it with the claim that they had purchased the corner of the ground on which the maulvi had conducted his prayers. The local policeman who was instructed to settle the dispute upheld the refugees' dubious claim. He also dismissed as 'baseless' Muslim complaints about refugee boys using the graveyard as a football field, concluding that these allegations of harassment had been 'maliciously manufactured'.[6]

This little tale aroused my curiosity, not least because of its striking parallels with the notorious 'pir burial' case of 1924 in Calcutta's New Market.[7] In 1997 I went to Selimpore. There was no proper road to the site, and going down the narrow muddy track by rickshaw was like a journey to a place that time had passed by. All that now remained of the burial ground was a small corner, perhaps a sixth of the cemetery's original size, to the north of the road and adjacent to the shrine. Some elaborately carved tombstones still stood on what remained of the graveyard, decaying relics of once imposing graves of the big men who had owned the land. A few Muslim families still lived there, also to the north of the track, but in extremely reduced circumstances. When I asked the elderly *mujawir* or custodian of the darga, who has tended the dilapidated shrine and graves for more than half a century, he told me that for many years there had been no burials. The last, he reminisced, had taken place 'under police protection' 'when Suhrawardy and Fazlul Huq were our leaders'. Since then, he said, the main plot to the south of the road—which had neither a boundary wall nor masonry graves— had been encroached upon and vandalized, and was used as a football pitch by the neighbourhood boys.[8] This part of his story was undoubtedly correct since a makeshift goalpost stood provocatively at one end of the ground.

This vignette is a microcosm of what Partition has entailed for many Muslims of West Bengal. Recent historical work on Partition's human cost has concentrated

---

[6]This description of events at Selimpore is based on the lengthy report by the Additional Superintendent of Police, DIB 24 Parganas, dated 20 Apr. 1956, GB IB, F No. 1010/56 (24 Paraganas).

[7]For details about the heated campaign for the exhumation of the body of a *fakir* buried in 1924 in Calcutta's New Market, see Kenneth McPherson, *The Muslim Microcosm: Calcutta 1918–1935* (Wiesbaden, 1974); and Pradip Kumar Datta, *Carving Blocs: Communal Ideology in Early Twentieth-century Bengal* (Delhi, 1999), pp. 109–47.

[8]Author's interview with Khaleel on 26 May 1997, Selimpore.

on refugees who were driven across borders by the violence it unleashed. Partition's effect on the minorities it created on both sides of the border—minorities who for a variety of reasons chose not to emigrate to the 'right' new nation—has not often been examined. This chapter, which will attempt to set the Selimpore story within this wider context, is intended as a modest beginning in that direction.

I

It is now a commonplace to assert that the Muslims of the Indian subcontinent are not a homogenous community; yet it needs forcefully to be reiterated in any discussion of West Bengal. Muslims in West Bengal were divided in many ways, by their varied ethnic origins, occupations, sects and status, and were far more heterogeneous than their fellows in the agrarian tracts of eastern Bengal. Islam's expansion into the western tracts of Bengal has a longer and more complex history than its more recent inroads into the east. Islam first came to the west as the religion of the garrison towns and of its cosmopolitan new ruling elite: noblemen, merchants, soldiers, and saints from as far afield as Turkey, Arabia, Persia, and Abyssinia. Even after its social base grew more plebeian, Islam in these parts continued to have urban and cosmopolitan characteristics. Well into the twentieth century, the Bengali Muslim aristocracy continued famously to insist upon its foreign ancestry and to speak Persian or Urdu rather than Bengali. The earliest indigenous converts to Islam in western Bengal were drawn, it seems, from urban artisan castes—whether the weavers (jola), tailors (darji), circumcisers (hajam), or bow-makers (tirakar)[9]—whose function was to supply the needs of these city-based Muslim noblemen.

Long after the Mughal conquest, which pushed Islam deep into the Padma delta and into reclaimed forests and marshes in the north and south-west of Bengal, in its West Bengal setting Islam remained predominantly a religion of city folk. As Calcutta developed into the East India Company's base for its transactions in Bengal and its incursions into upper India, and as a centre of industry and trade, West Bengal's Muslim population came to be even more varied. In the 1770s, for instance, Calcutta attracted Cutchi Memons from Kathiawad, and not long afterwards, Muslim traders from Delhi and Lucknow. 'Rankis' claiming to hail from Iraq came to monopolize the hide trade and Pathan leather merchants from the North-West Frontier set up shops around the Nakhoda mosque. In the late nineteenth century, skilled craftsmen from distant parts of India were drawn in growing numbers to this city of opportunity; and many Muslim butchers, bakers, tailors, carpenters, cigarette makers, bookbinders, and leather workers settled in its suburbs.[10]

[9]Richard Eaton, *The Rise of Islam and the Bengal Frontier, 1204–1760* (Oxford, 1993), p. 101.
[10]McPherson, *The Muslim Microcosm*, pp. 9–15.

In the early twentieth century, weavers from up-country sought work in the jute mills along the Hooghly. They were followed by a much larger influx of unskilled Muslims, drawn by the lure of jobs on the shop floors of Calcutta's burgeoning industries. Another development in the twentieth century was the emergence of a small but significant Muslim middle class which came to play an increasingly visible role in the city's life. Mainly of Bengali origin, these 'English-educated' matriculates and graduates moved to Calcutta and other large towns of the west when white-collar Muslims began to benefit from government patronage and its positive discrimination on their behalf. With *bhadralok* ambitions, these Muslims preferred not to live cheek by jowl with their ruder co-religionists in Calcutta's sprawling and insalubrious suburbs, and settled in the respectable central area around Park Circus.[11] Each successive wave of migration and settlement thus tended to graft another layer onto the palimpsest of Muslim Calcutta. By 1947, it had become a tessellated mosaic of 'distinct sub-communal groups', each with its own unique and shifting history.[12]

By this time Muslims were to be found not only in the towns and cities but also in large numbers among the peasant communities in the countryside, particularly in the northern districts. But even here there was much variety. Not all of West Bengal's Muslim peasants were of local origin. Many, such as the Shershabadiyas, had moved to north Bengal to bring new land under the plough when the notoriously fickle Ganges changed its course, laying bare rich alluvial tracts in Malda.[13] Others were local people, converted after a fashion by the soldier-saints who proselytized in Bengal in the seventeenth and eighteenth centuries, and whose version of Islam still contained many elements of older folk religions and cults.[14] Most of these rural Muslims were Sunnis, as indeed was the vast majority of Bengal's Muslim population—the Shia Communities of Murshidabad, Hooghly, and Dacca were tiny islets in a Sunni sea. The Census of 1931, perhaps the most reliable enumeration of Bengal's population in the first half of the century, discovered that there were more Muslims in villages than in towns in the province as a whole. But in many parts of the west, particularly in Burdwan division, it remained the case that more Muslims lived in the cities than in the countryside.[15]

---

[11]Ibid., p. 5.

[12]Ibid., p. 11.

[13]Legend has it that the Shershabadiyas belonged to Sher Shah's personal army and had been rewarded with land grants in Shershabad paragana. Asok Mitra, *The New India*, p. 4.

[14]By the mid-nineteenth century, when Buchanan conducted his survey, about 70 per cent of Dinajpur's population was Muslim, but they forgot 'the rules of their law on many points'. Montgomery Martin, *The History, Antiquities, Topography and Statistics of Eastern India: Comprising the Districts of Behar, Shabad, Bhagalpoor, Goruckpoor, Dinajepoor, Puraniya, Rungporr and Assam* (London, 1838), pp. 723–6. For more details on the folk Islam of the Bengal countryside, see Eaton, *Rise of Islam*, and Asim Roy, *The Islamic Syncretist Tradition in Bengal* (Princeton, 1983).

[15]*Census of India, 1931*, vol. v, part I (Calcutta, 1933), p. 387.

Even the most cursory description of the Muslims of West Bengal at the time of Partition reveals that they were a very mixed bag indeed, containing a bewildering variety of social, ethnic, linguistic, regional, and sectarian groupings. They included the learned and the rude, *ashraf* conquerers as well as numerous lowly converts, city men and peasants, and all manner of outsiders drawn from every corner of Hindustan and beyond. Nor were they evenly distributed throughout the land. In some districts of the west, for example in Murshidabad and undivided Nadia, Muslims outnumbered Hindus; in rural Malda, Dinajpur, Cooch Behar, the 24 Parganas, and Birbhum, they formed large and visible communities. In parts of the industrial belt, among them Calcutta, Bhatpara, Dumdum, Kumarhati, and Asansol, one in four and occasionally as many as one in three of all the locals were Muslims. In Garden Reach, Muslims were as numerous as Hindus.[16] By 1947, certain parts of Calcutta had already become dominantly 'Muslim' areas, notably Park Circus, Bowbazar, Ekbalpur, and Karaya. In contrast, Muslims were few and far between in other parts of western Bengal, particularly in Bankura and Darjeeling.

Partition affected this extraordinarily diverse community in ways which are complex, resistant to analysis, and, because the evidence is so elusive, incapable of precise documentation. Neither government records nor scholarly studies provide a systematic investigation of this subject. Assessing the fate of Muslims was no part of the remit of the many voluminous surveys of displaced people commissioned by the Government of West Bengal. The official record contains a single passing reference to Muslim refugees, and that was in the early days.[17] In the half century after Partition, the decennial censuses abandoned the British practice of listing by religion the statistics of occupation, literacy, marriage, and migration. In consequence, the important changes which Partition wrought upon the Muslims of West Bengal have to be teased out from scanty, sometimes anecdotal, evidence, and their inwardness has often to be discovered in most unlikely and rebarbative sources.

In obvious ways, Partition dramatically reversed the position of the Muslims of West Bengal. For a decade before 1947, Muslims had enjoyed political dominance over united Bengal, and had asserted themselves socially and culturally even in areas where they were outnumbered by Hindus.[18] Partition reduced them to an exposed and vulnerable minority. After 1947, Muslims all over West Bengal lived in fear—hardly surprising, given the Calcutta Killings of 1946, the pogroms

[16]See Statement VIII. 3, ibid., p. 278.

[17]At the time of the 1951 Census, the State Statistical Bureau conducted a survey of displaced Muslims, which is referred to in *The Survey of Unemployment in West Bengal, 1953, First Interim Report*, vol. I, part I (Government of West Bengal, 1953), p. 5. However, despite every effort, it has not been possible to locate this survey.

[18]See Joya Chatterji, *Bengal Divided: Hindu Communalism and Partition, 1932–1947* (Cambridge, 1994), pp. 213–19.

in Bihar, and the deadly succession of murder and intimidation in Calcutta in the months and years after Partition.[19]

Muslim reactions to their predicament, of course, were not of a piece. They could not have been. Different Muslims responded differently when they realized their lives and property were at risk. Among the many factors which determined their actions were how easily they could take their assets away with them, how effectively they could deploy their skills to earn a living in the east, what contacts they had there, and how their prospects elsewhere compared with what they might still hang on to in the west if they stayed put and tried to weather the storm. It mattered whether they lived in clusters or were scattered thinly in isolated pockets; it also mattered whether they were near the border or far from it.

Packing one's bags and fleeing to East Bengal was an obvious response. Yet there is no accurate record of how many Muslims crossed the border into east Pakistan. In 1951, the Pakistan census counted 700,000 Muslim '*muhajirs*' in East Bengal,[20] of whom two-thirds, or 486,000, were known to be refugees from the west.[21] But the number of Muslims who fled eastwards was probably much higher. The 1961 census of Pakistan mentions 850,000 people in East Bengal, who in 1951, were recorded as having been born in other parts of the subcontinent and now possessed citizenship of Pakistan, and a further 125,000 who were 'non-Pakistanis from India'.[22] If all of these were refugees, by 1951, Muslim refugees in East Bengal numbered about a million, of whom perhaps seven out of ten came from West Bengal. In 1964, Indian Muslims once again fled in large numbers to East Pakistan in a second wave, perhaps of roughly the same order of magnitude as the first. Most came from West Bengal and the north-east of India.[23] So rough and ready estimates suggest that perhaps a million and a half Muslims left West Bengal for eastern Pakistan in the two decades after Partition.

The largest Muslim exoduses from west to east were sparked off by communal violence. The biggest of them was probably from Nadia in 1950–1, which Asok Mitra—civil servant and the first census commissioner of West Bengal—describes as a movement of refugees travelling in both directions, amounting almost to an exchange of population. Namasudras driven out of East Bengal during the Jessore riots retaliated by pitchforking the entire populations of Muslim villages out of

---

[19]There was a clear correlation between the patterns of Muslim exoduses from Bengal and the communal rioting which provoked them.

[20]'Muhajir' was the term used to describe persons who had moved to Pakistan 'as a result of Partition and of the fear of disturbances connected therewith. Persons who came for that reason are muhajirs for census purposes, no matter from where, when or for how long a stay they have come'. *Census of Pakistan, 1951, vol. 3, East Bengal, Report and Tables* (Karachi, n.d.), p. 39.

[21]Ibid., p. 80.

[22]*Census of Pakistan Population, 1961, vol. 2, East Pakistan* (Karachi, 1964), pp. 11–31.

[23]A.F.M. Kamaluddin, 'Refugee problems in Bangladesh', in L.A. Kosinski and K.M. Elahi (eds), *Population Redistribution and Development in South Asia* (Dordrecht, 1985), pp. 221–2.

Table 1: Hindus and Muslims in Calcutta 1901–51

Year	Hindu population	Muslim population	Muslim population as a percentage of the Hindu population
1901	603,310	270,797	44.9
1911	672,206	275,280	41.0
1921	725,561	248,912	34.3
1931	796,628	281,520	35.3
1941	1,531,512	497,535	32.5
1951	2,125,907	305,932	14.4

Source: *Census of India, 1951, vol. VI, part III, Calcutta City*, p. xv.

India into Pakistan. Between 100,000 and 200,000 Muslims from Nadia were tossed across the border by savage Hindu mobs baying for revenge.[24] Smaller numbers continued to escape from the latent hostility and sporadic outbursts of violence towards Muslims in Calcutta. According to the West Bengal government, by 1951, 15,000 Muslims had emigrated to East Bengal from Calcutta city alone 'through fear of disturbances'. The actual numbers were probably much higher. The 1951 Census discovered 130,000 fewer Muslims in Calcutta than it expected to find.[25] It is not unreasonable to deduce that part of the explanation for this demographic anomaly was that very large numbers of Muslims from the city disappeared by stealth into Pakistan (see Table 1). We know that large numbers of Muslims left Howrah after the riots of 1950. Thousands more migrated in the early 1960s, when a rash of anti-Muslim pogroms broke out not only in West Bengal and Assam, but also in Madhya Pradesh and Uttar Pradesh. Every time Hindus and Muslims fell upon each other, whether in India or in Pakistan, Muslims left their homes in droves. The riots in East Bengal, the troubles over the accession

[24]To the best of my knowledge, no official figures have been published on the number of Muslims who fled from Nadia in 1950. An article published in *Paigam* in 1956 stated that 60,000 Muslim families had been forced out, which would put the number of persons at roughly 240,000, given an average family of four. *Paigam* (15 Sept. 1956). Of course, not all of them went to East Bengal, but that many did is suggested by the Pakistan census which counted 137,000 refugees in Pakistani Nadia (renamed Kushtia) in 1951. *Census of Pakistan, 1951, vol. 3, East Bengal, Report and Tables*, p. 39. This is corroborated by Nakatani's study of exchanges of property between Muslims leaving for East Bengal and incoming Hindu refugees in a Nadia village. Tetsuya Nakatani, 'Away from home: The movement and settlement of refugees from East Pakistan in West Bengal, India', *Journal of the Japanese Association for South Asian Studies*, no. 12 (2000).

[25]*Census of India, 1951, vol. VI, part III, Calcutta City*, p. xvi. This figure was based on projections for 'normal' growth derived from the 1931 Census figures, which Asok Mitra, the author of the 1951 Census, believed with good reason to be much more reliable than the count taken in Wartime in 1941. If Mitra's projections for Calcutta's Muslim population had been based instead on the 1941 Census, the number of 'missing' Muslims would have been considerably larger.

of princely Hyderabad and Kashmir, and the bloodletting in Jubbulpore all pushed many Muslim families over the edge into emigrating to Pakistan. In 1964, in the wake of the serious communal rioting sparked off by the Hazratbal incident,[26] another 800,000 Indian Muslims left for East Bengal. Most of these migrants were from West Bengal or the north-east.[27]

Other Muslims left in a more considered way, in circumstances which were less dramatic. Government servants with the option of serving either in India or in Pakistan had six months in which to make up their minds. Many top Muslim officers understandably decided to serve in Pakistan. All but one of the nineteen Muslim Indian Civil Service officers in Bengal opted to join the Government of Pakistan.[28] In their train followed large numbers of humbler public servants— orderlies, peons, clerks, tellers, watchmen, and police constables—who left on a scale sufficiently large to cause a temporary crisis after Partition at the administrative base in West Bengal. Of course, it was not always easy to distinguish between government employees who went of their own volition and those who were persuaded to go, in other words between those who jumped and those who were pushed. There were ugly hints of a systematic campaign of intimidation launched to 'persuade' Muslims in government service to quit West Bengal and go to Pakistan.[29] Nor was it uncommon for Muslims of pelf and purse to send

[26]Hyderabad, the Kashmir war, and Jubbulpore led to relatively modest migrations, but the 1964 violence following the Hazratbal incident was on a much larger scale, and led to very significant exoduses from both sides of the Bengal frontier. The incident which sparked off the troubles was the mysterious disappearance of the *muy-i-muqaddas* (the sacred hair of the Prophet Mohammad) from the Hazratbal shrine in Srinagar in Kashmir. (For details, see Muhammad Ishaq Khan, 'The significance of the dargah of Hazratbal in the socio-religious and political life of Kashmiri Muslims', in Christian W. Troll (ed.), *Muslim Shrines in India: Their Character, History and Significance* [Delhi, 1992].) Each of these incidents of violence was usually was followed by the surrender by Muslims of a 'sacred space'. A police report, describing the repercussions of the violence in Karachi and Jubbulpore in Calcutta speaks of 'a sense of panic among some sections of Muslims at Dilkhusa Street (Park Circus) and Kalabagab areas. These Muslims apprehend that Hindus may retaliate on them on the occasion of Holi …. S.M. Salahuddin contacted several Mohalla sardars of Phulbagan and Tantibagan in Beniapukur … and instructed them to ask Muslims of these areas to remain quiet during the Holi festival'. 'Repercussions in Calcutta of the incidents in Pakistan', SB note, dated 1 Mar. 1961, GB IB, F.No. 1278/59 (part I). 'Remaining quiet' in the context of Holi would have meant allowing noisy Hindu processions to pass mosques without let or hindrance.

[27]Kamaluddin, 'Refugee problems in Bangladesh', pp. 221–2.

[28]Chakrabarty, *With Dr B.C. Roy*, p. 45.

[29]In June and July 1947, persons never identified by the police launched a campaign of murdering Muslim policemen in Calcutta and Howrah in broad daylight, no doubt '*pour encourger les autres*'. On 26 June 1947, an up-country Muslim constable on duty in Calcutta was shot dead at close range. No one was brought to book. GB IB, F. No. 614/47. On 23 June, another constable was shot at and injured while on patrol at Madhusudan Biswas Lane in Howrah. 'No culprits were traced'. Howrah District Report, dated 11 Oct. 1947, in GB IB, F. No. 614/47. On 7 July 1947,

family members to hedge their bets in Pakistan, while the heads of the households stayed on to maintain their stakes in land and business in West Bengal.[30] In some instances, Muslims who had property in West Bengal were able to make deals with propertied Hindus from the east by which they exchanged, whether legally or in less formal ways, their plots and holdings with each other.[31]

But for every Muslim who reacted to Partition by quitting India, many more stayed on. Most of those who remained were the weak and poor who had no assets, no connections and little by way of skills to deploy in a new life across the border.[32] But it is significant that many of those who could most easily have migrated to Pakistan elected to remain in India. These included rank-and-file Muslim government employees, like those whom Asok Mitra found holding on to their jobs when he was posted to Malda in 1947 and later to Murshidabad in 1949.[33]

Those who stayed on in the bitterly anti-Muslim climate of post-Partition West Bengal adopted strategies of survival which varied according to circum-

---

in a high-profile example of these trends, S.S. Huq, who was in charge of Muchipara police station, was murdered. Ibid. On this occasion, the army had to be called out to put down the violence which took place after his funeral in which forty people died and about 200 were injured. Chakrabarty, *With Dr B.C. Roy*, pp. 50–1. On 2 July 1947, two constables, one Hindu and one Muslim, were on duty at Satcowrie Chatterjee Lane, Howrah, when the Muslim was shot in the back and later died of his injuries. Again 'no culprit was found'. GB IB, F. No. 1123/47.

[30]A study of a Muslim family from Barasat, some of whose members migrated to Pakistan in 1964, is a case in point. The immediate nuclear family consisted of the parents and their nine children, of whom only three subsequently migrated to Pakistan, following their paternal uncle. One brother left Barasat for another village in West Bengal. The rest remained where they were. 'There seemed too much at stake: their property for example. By this time everyone in the family was comfortably off, each with his own side business, mostly shopkeeping. That they had their own high school in the village was mentioned as a plus point. Besides no one wanted to go to a "backward place" leaving behind their property. So the general feeling was to keep an open mind about it.' This study shows how the resource base, social mobility, kinship connections, and the stage in the life cycle of individuals all played a part in determining who migrated to Pakistan and who stayed behind. Meghna Guhathakurta, 'Families uprooted and divided: The case of the Bengal partition', unpublished paper presented at a workshop on Alternative Histories and Non-written Sources: New Perspectives from the South, La Paz (May 1999).

[31]In a typical case in September 1950, a Muslim of Fulnapur 'migrated to Pakistan after exchanging some properties with a Hindu'. In another instance, in April 1950, a Muslim of Baramaricha in Sitalkuchi in Cooch Behar left for Paksitan in 1950, giving over his *adhiar* right to planted jute to a Hindu refugee. These, and many other similar instances, are reported in the 'Fortnightly Reports of Border Incidents in West Bengal' (henceforth FRBI) for 1950, GB IB, F. No. 1238A—47. Also see Nakatani, 'Away from home'.

[32]As Van Hear has argued, 'Migration abroad is rarely an option for the poorest households, even though they may be among the most vulnerable in terms of economic or physical security.' Nicholas Van Hear, 'Refugee diasporas: Trans-national links among displaced people in South Asia and beyond', unpublished paper presented at a seminar on Displaced People in South Asia, Chennai (Mar. 2001).

[33]Mitra, *The New India*, pp. 1, 49.

stance.[34] But almost everyone who stayed on recognized that they had no choice but to eat humble pie, proclaim allegiance to India, and subscribe to the doctrine of a communal harmony which had ceased to exist in practice, however much people paid lip-service to the principle. The literate among them would certainly have read between the lines of the Congress Working Committee's resolution which, even as it assured 'the minorities in India' that the Congress government would continue to protect 'to the best of its ability their citizen rights against aggression', warned them that 'it would not tolerate the existence within its borders of disloyal elements' and expressed its readiness to provide 'full facilities ... to those who wish to migrate from the Indian Union'.[35] In effect, Congress had thrown down the gauntlet to all Muslims who remained in India, challenging them to prove their loyalty to the new Republic.

In response to this crude call for Muslims to 'assimilate', even the most influential Muslims felt they had publicly to renounce their old allegiances. Once India gained Independence, former leaders of the powerful Muslim League began to dissociate themselves from it. In November 1947, Huseyn Shaheed Suhrawardy, recently Premier of Bengal, convened a conference of Muslim leaders in Calcutta to discuss their future policy. Most of them took the view that the League 'had ceased to exist' and that 'Muslims must now independently steer their course in independent India'. Their resolutions proclaimed the need for harmony and cooperation between the two governments of India and Pakistan. Reporting on the conference, the *Star of India* urged 'a fusion ... be effected between the League and the nationalist Muslim leadership', claiming that Partition had eroded every real distinction between them.[36] If political Muslims were to survive and prosper in West Bengal, they could see that the Muslim League had to be allowed to die a quiet death.

It soon became obvious, and not only to those Muslims who had truck with the Muslim League, that it was not enough simply to repudiate the League. 'Allegiance and loyalty to the state' had to be displayed in more positive ways.[37]

[34]Describing his experiences as District Magistrate in 1947 and 1948, Asok Mitra refers to the 'recurrent tendency' amongst Malda's Hindus 'for a witch-hunt of Muslims'; and describes the list prepared by the outgoing magistrate of Murshidabad of 30,000 'undesirable Muslim families'. Ibid., pp. 24, 29. The police files too are redolent of anti-Muslim attitudes, and not just in the period immediately after Partition.

[35]Congress Working Committee Resolution, dated 24 Sept. 1947, All India Congress Committee Papers, First Instalment, File Number G-30 of 1946 (henceforth AICC-I, F. No. G-30/ 1946, and so on).

[36]*Star of India* (14 Nov. 1947), GB IB, F. No. 1045–7.

[37]Vallabbhai Patel in his characteristically blunt style demanded 'practical proof' of Muslim loyalty, insisting that mere protestations of loyalty were not enough. His comment: 'You don't know what it is costing the government to protect you' was hardly calculated to reassure Muslims. Cited in Mushirul Hasan, *Legacy of a Divided Nation: India's Muslims since Independence* (Delhi, 1997), p. 148.

Table 2: Party-political profile of Muslim candidates in general elections in West Bengal 1952–67*

Year	Congress	Opposition parties	Independents	Total Muslim MLAs
1952	21 [17]	14[0]	45 [2]	19
1957	28 [20]	13[3]	55[2](one CPI-supported)	25
1962	31[17]	38[4]	50[3]	24
1967	31[18]	30[14]	48[5]	37

*Square brackets show number of victorious candidates.

Source: Dilip Banerjee, *Election Recorder* (Calcutta, 1990).

The Muslim Conference of November 1947 in Lucknow called upon 'the Mussalmans of India to be members only of non-communal political parties and advise[d] them to join the Indian National Congress'.[38] Many Bengali Muslim notables saw merit in this advice and those who could, contested the 1952 elections on Congress tickets (see Table 2). For the bigwigs amongst them, this Damascene 'conversion' to Congress was made easier by the factional wars within the Bengal Congress and by Dr B.C. Roy's uncertain grip over the Assembly. Partition had created the anomaly of a West Bengal Congress dominated by East Bengalis, and after Partition the party witnessed a spectular burst of fratricide as different factions struggled to capture the organization and ministry. Consequently Premier Roy and party boss Atulya Ghosh were eager to welcome these Muslim grandees into their assembly party in support of their faction in the House.[39]

But bringing Leaguers into the Congress was not always a smooth process, especially at the grass roots, where many Hindu members of the Old Guard in

[38]This resolution was moved by the communist S.A. Brelvi and supported by Dr Z.A. Ahmed and Humayun Kabir. AICC-I, F. No. G-23/1946–8.

[39]The factions opposed to Roy and Ghosh saw what was happening but could do little about it, as any protest could easily be denounced by the ruling group as being motivated by communal and anti-Muslim sentiments. Writing in protest against Dr B.C. Roy's admission of a Muslim to the Congress Assembly Party, Amarkrishna Ghosh declared that 'the inclusion of Muslims and Anglo-Indians should be decided on a principle to be approved by the Central Parliamentary Board. ... Even in this province, if one Muslim is now admitted into the Congress Assembly Party, many others would apply for such admission and it would be difficult to resist their admission on logical grounds. And the inclusion of many Muslim members into the Party may not be advisable at this juncture of Indian politics'. Amarkrishna Ghosh and eight others to Sitaramayya, 4 Mar. 1949, All India Congress Committee Papers, Second Instalment (henceforth AICC-II), F. No. PB-3(i)/1949. In reply, B.C. Roy was quick to occupy the moral and 'secular' high ground, defending the inclusion of Shamsul Huq, elected as an independent candidate 'who has always been working with Congress since 1924 .... I am perfectly sure that the Congress will not in any case countenance such a proposition that we oust an applicant simply because he happens to be a Muslim, or that the inclusion of Muslim members would be inadvisable'. B.C. Roy to Kala Venkatarao, 9 Apr. 1949, AICC-II, F. No. PB-3(i)/1949.

Congress refused to become bedfellows with their enemies of yore.[40] Nor were these alliances of convenience seen as a boon by all Muslim nationalists. Before 1947, in resisting the blandishments of the Muslim League, they had stood against the tide and had been exiled to the margins of Bengal Muslim politics.[41] Now that their party was in power in West Bengal, they might reasonably have expected their loyalty to be rewarded when the loaves and fishes were being doled out. Instead, Congress patronage now went to Muslims who could most convincingly promise to deliver the political goods, and the Muslim nationalists were not usually amongst them. For instance, in 1950, Jehangir Kabir, a nationalist of long standing, asked to be given the Congress ticket to a Muslim seat in the Central Legislative Assembly which the Congress Parliamentary Board had allocated to another, and more recently, recruited Muslim would-be politician. Kabir's claim rested on his own record of commitment to the party and the fact that 'the other recommended gentleman never belonged to Congress and has no political past. As far as we know he is not even today an ordinary Congress member'.[42] But his request was ignored. The Congress ticket went to Kabir's rival.

It was not only the ruling coterie of Congress which put realpolitik above all else: every political faction joined in the race to sign up influential Muslims regardless of their political antecedents. When by-elections were held in the 24 Parganas central Muslim constituency in 1951, Atulya Ghosh was disconcerted to find that Prafulla Ghosh's Krishak Majdoor Praja Party (KMPP) had put up against its man 'Jenab Khairul Islam, a noted Muslim Leaguer, son of Maulana Akram Khan, ex-president of the Bengal Muslim League and present president of the Muslim League of east Pakistan'. Given the ruling faction's own fallible record, its complaint against other parties 'associating with noted Muslim Leaguers who are still doing all sorts of mischief against communal harmony' was a case of Atulya's sooty kettle calling Prafulla's pot black.[43]

---

[40]One pamphlet lamented the fate of the Congress, demanding to know 'how is it that the newly elected Deputy President [of the Malda District Congress Committee] Janab Latif Hussain (Arapur) who was a member of the district Muslim National Guard and who was never even a delegate of the Congress, how has he suddenly become Deputy President? ... How has Janab Mohammad Sayyad, who was the secretary of the Malda Jila Muslim League and who never represented the Congress been appointed to the Working Committee of the Malda District Congress?'. The pamphlet claimed that the lack of scruples with which Muslims of doubtful credentials were being drafted into the Congress had driven true Congressmen, including the author himself, out of the organization. Bibhuti Bhushan Chakravarti, 'Ihai ki Congressi adarsh?' (Are these really Congress ideals?), in AICC-II, F. No. PB-3/1951.

[41]Their marginality is reflected in the fact that Congress had put up only two Muslim candidates in the 1946 elections, both of whom were trounced at the polls by Muslim League rivals. See Chatterji, Bengal Divided, p. 130.

[42]Jehangir Kabir to Sardar Vallabbhai Patel, 9 Sept. 1950, AICC-II, F. No. PB-3/1950.

[43]Wright has argued that Congress factionalism has not tended to work to the advantage of genuine representatives of Muslim opinion, and therefore has not been good for Muslims. There

The cynicism with which Congress welcomed prominent Muslims into its fold was often mirrored by equally hard-headed calculation on the part of those Muslims who decided to join up. A typical case was that of Mahbub Huq.[44] whose visit to Jalpaiguri in 1957, 'ostensibly' to canvass support for Congress in the election, was the subject of a long and panic-stricken intelligence report. According to the police, Huq had joined Congress soon after Partition, although later he was to become a citizen of Pakistan. While still in India, he kept close connections with the Mohammedan Sporting Club and gave a lot of money to the Azad Kashmir Fund. In the Inspector's opinion, this was ample proof that his support for Congress was less than sincere. He had sold most of his assets in India in 1951, but continued to derive 'secret earnings' from Muslim-owned tea estates, which were the source of the monies which paid for the 'palatial' house he built for himself in Dacca. According to the police, 'one of his satellites', a Hindu Sanitary Inspector, had helped him get his loot out of India and into Pakistan. So he was shocked to find that Huq's visit to Jalpaiguri in 1957 was 'warmly backed by the President of the Jalpaiguri District Congress Committee, by a former Vice-President of the Bengal Provincial Congress Committee, by two [Hindu] MLAs and by a [Hindu] member of the Council of States'.[45] This assessment was probably jaundiced by the anti-Muslim and anti-Pakistani paranoia of the officer who penned the report. But the saga does give some hint of the stratagems deployed by resourceful Muslims who were able successfully to hedge their bets, maintaining alliances, property, and connection on both sides of the border and playing both ends against the middle. Often with the connivance of the Congress establishment, well-connected Muslims were able to survive Partition by these devices, and sometimes even to do well out of it.

This selective induction of some influential Muslim notables into the political establishment eased their return to prominence in West Bengal's post-Partition order, but was hardly evidence of a genuine change of heart amongst West Bengal's Hindu political elites in their underlying attitudes towards Muslims. In 1951, Dr Roy's government began to 'cleanse' the border zones of Muslims, 'presumably ... because it [was] thought that they might be unreliable elements in times of trouble', a strategy which provoked a sharp reprimand from Nehru but reflected the prevailing view in Bengal that Muslims were inherently 'disloyal'.[46] Many Muslim

---

is merit in this thesis. But in the unique circumstances of divided Bengal, some Muslims were able to take advantage of Congress factionalism to gain a ticket back into the mainstream of politics. Theodore P. Wright, Jr, 'The effectiveness of Muslim representation in India', in D.E. Smith (ed.), *South Asian Politics and Religion* (Princeton, 1966), p. 130.

[44]This is not the man's real name, which has been changed to protect his anonymity and to comply with the specific request of the head of the Intelligence Branch in Calcutta.

[45]Copy of the Report of the DIO, dated 13 Feb. 1957, GB IB, F. No. 114–57.

[46]Jawaharlal Nehru to Dr B.C. Roy, 15 Sept. 1951, cited in Chakrabarty, *With Dr B.C. Roy*, pp. 192–3.

politicians continued to complain about the Congress party leadership's latent hostility towards them.[47] In 1956, one Muslim from Bengal wrote to Nehru that his people were being systematically cut out of the electoral roll, and Government orders affecting their lives and times were published only in papers which most of them did not read. So 'the feeling of the Minority Community [was] that they [were] being deprived of [the right to vote] intentionally and in an organised manner'.[48]

Nor did the grudging acceptance of a few Muslim leaders into the Congress fold do much to improve the sense of security among the rank and file. While B.C. Roy was opening the door for Muslim bosses to enter the Congress Assembly party, Congressmen on the ground waged petty and vicious wars against defenceless Muslims. The Congress Committee of Ward 25 in Calcutta in the Kidderpore area, for instance, gained a reputation for being 'a danger to local Mohammedans'. Its members once forced '22 Mahommedans to leave possession of a room and their belongings were carted away to a distant tank. Some of the men were locked up in the Congress office. Police rendered [them] no assistance ... because [their tormentors had] Congress backing'.[49] This incident was not untypical—after Partition just as before it, the hooligans who hounded Muslims wore *khadi topis* as often as khaki shorts.[50]

In significant ways, Partition helped to create new fault lines and construct new layers of stratification among West Bengal's Muslims. It created a gulf between the fortunate few who were able to find a secure place in the new order and the great majority who did not. Ordinary Muslims faced intimidation and harassment in their day-to-day lives and were particularly vulnerable whenever communal tension flared into open violence. They too tried in little ways to adopt various strategies for survival, but the options open to them were much more limited. Holding fewer court cards in their hands, staying on required them to make sacrifices, accept defeats, and absorb losses.

In much the same way as the Muslim elites who had been given lodgement by the Hindu establishment, they too tried to show they were ready and willing to assimilate, albeit lower down the social scale, and quietly to accept their

[47]Zacharia asked to be allowed to 'submit a memorandum to the Congress High Command about the state of affairs of the Muslims in West Bengal—who are about 26% of the total population which is not a negligible number, but their position is not the same as [that] of their co-religionists living in other states .... A large number of ours are still very staunch Congressmen but they are compelled to remain outside for the time being because of the present undesirable High Command of the West Bengal State Congress Committee'. A.K.M. Zakariah to Lal Bahadur Shastri, 26 Apr. 1952, AICC-II, F. No. PB-21/1952.

[48]S.M. Salahuddin, Chief Administrative Officer, Anjuman Mufidul Islam to Jawaharlal Nehru, 28 July 1956, AICC-II, F. No. PB-21/1956.

[49]R. Ghosh to Sardar Vallabbhai Patel, AICC-II, F. No. PB-3(i)/1949. Ghosh resigned his Congress membership in protest against this incident.

[50]The small caps made of homespun cotton were a badge of Congress membership, just as the khaki shorts were the insignia of the Rashtriya Swayamsevak Sangha volunteers.

minority status. One way of demonstrating this was their readiness to surrender previously entrenched rights to the public observance of their religious rituals and their claims to public space. Under British rule, rights of holding public rituals were governed by precedence—a local community was permitted to perform a ceremony or hold a procession in a public place provided it had done so in the past and had established a 'customary' right to do so.[51] Disputes over precedents in the conduct of festivals lay at the root of much of the communal violence in the last days of the Raj. Yet this was one British rule to which the government of independent India continued firmly to adhere. In 1948, the Home Department issued a memorandum, circulated to all district officers, which reiterated that Muslims had rights to sacrifice cows: 'So far as the celebration of Bakr-Id is concerned, the principle which has always been followed in cases of dispute is that previous custom should be maintained. *No innovations should be allowed*';[52] and this rule was upheld and enshrined in the statute book in the West Bengal Animal Slaughter Control Act of 1950.[53]

It was no small concession for Muslims voluntarily to abjure precedents which assured them the continued rights, precedents which were the product of hard-fought and historic victories. It was a particularly significant step for them to renounce entrenched rights to perform the perennially controversial ritual of cow sacrifice. And yet this is what many Muslims now chose to do. Perhaps because the issue was so highly charged, so public, and so bound up with issues of power and history, this was one visible gesture humble Muslims could make which broadcast the fact that they understood their predicament and accepted the new realities. In 1947 and 1948, there were numerous occasions when police anticipated trouble at Bakr-Id, only to find that Muslims had chosen, of their own accord, or after some 'persuasion', not to perform *go korbani* or cow sacrifice. In a typical instance in October 1947, police were called to the Champdany jute mill after street meetings of Hindus urged Muslims to give up go korbani. Expecting trouble, the police rushed in force to the area but discovered that the Muslims had decided of their own volition not to make a stand. They found that 'Muslims who are in a minority are afraid of wounding the religious feeling of the Hindus by sacrificing cows. Accordingly, the Muslims of Champdany Jute Mills met together in the Champdany mosque ... and decided not to ... [sacrifice] any cows'.[54]

Sadly, such gestures were not always enough to buy Muslims security. All

---

[51]For a discussion of this policy, see Chatterji, *Bengal Divided*, pp. 212–13; and K. Prior, 'Making history: The state's intervention in religious disputes', *Modern Asian Studies* (1993).

[52]The Memorandum of 1948 is quoted in a letter, dated 11 Sept. 1950 from the Secretary to the Government of West Bengal, Home (Police) Department to all district officers of West Bengal, GB IB 1802–57 (part I). Emphasis in the original.

[53]Government of West Bengal, Department of Agriculture, Animal Husbandry and Forests, circular no. 8016-Vety., dated 25 June 1957, GB IB, F. No. 1802–57.

[54]SDPO Serampore's report, dated 21 Oct. 1947, GB IB, F. No. 167/47.

too frequently, Hindus took the unbending view that Muslims no longer had any right to perform cow sacrifice *under any circumstances*. So when Muslims voluntarily, and in a considered way, gave up established rights to sacrifice cows, far from accepting this as an olive branch which required some quid pro quo, Hindus dismissed it as an inevitable sign of weakness, a gesture deserving neither recognition nor reward. Instead, they seemed intent on forcing the issue to a final solution. In 1948 and 1949, there were many occasions when Muslims were given strife for sacrificing cows even where there were well-established precedents for their doing so, and when they had taken care to perform the sacrifices well out of sight and earshot of Hindus.[55] Even after the West Bengal Animal Slaughter Control Act in 1950 laid down clear guidelines permitting go korbani at Id, provided it was done according to established precedent, with permission, and in a private place,[56] cow sacrifice remained an issue which continued to inflame Hindu–Muslim relations, and Muslims, step by step, were forced, sometimes covertly, sometimes by open threats and sometimes by their own decision, to give up their traditional rights. In one case, for instance, on hearing that a cow had been sold to a Muslim in a Purulia village before Bakr-Id, the local Hindus organized a public meeting 'with a view to discuss their future programme over the alleged cow slaughter'. The following day, the police visited the village and met the leading members of both communities. 'The Hindus proposed that the Muslims should not slaughter cows any more in the village to which [a Muslim gentleman] who commands respect of the Muslims of the area agreed on behalf of local Muslims'.[57] In another case, Muslims of Bil Barail, who traditionally distributed beef during Bakr-Id at a public mosque, were forced to give up the practice. In protest, they 'refrained from doing Korbani on Bakr-Id day in that particular mosque'.[58] The new Hindu mood of aggressive assertiveness soon spilled over to affect other Muslim public rituals. In June 1949, for instance, a dispute erupted in Kandi between Muslims taking a *tazia* in licensed procession and Hindus who refused to allow them to trim back branches of a sacred tree which prevented the tazia getting past. It was the Muslims who had to back down, persuaded by one of their leaders 'at a secret meeting' that the 'authorities would redress their grievance in due course'.[59] And once they had backed down, the new 'precedent' was there to be used against them in the future. Once a

[55]GB IB, F. No. 69A-49 (Murshidabad).

[56]Government of West Bengal, Department of Agriculture, Animal Husbandry and Forests, circular no. 8016-Vety., dated 25 June 1957.

[57]Note of the SP DIB Purulia dated 25 June 1959, GB IB, F. No. 1802/57 (part II). The name of the gentleman in question has been withheld to protect his anonymity and in accordance with the express wishes of the head of the Intelligence Branch in Calcutta.

[58]'Situation report on the Bakr-Id festival in West Bengal', 20 June 1959, GB IB, F. No. 1802–57 (part II).

[59]Weekly Confidential Report, Murshidabad district, for the week ending 6 Nov. 1949. GB IB 69A/49 (Murshidabad).

traditional right to sacred space or performing rituals had been lost, it was unlikely to be given back.

This is why the story of the graveyard at Selimpore, itself a tiny episode in the wider history of West Bengal's Muslims, warrants its place in the larger account. Calcutta's landscape is dotted with Selimpores. Most Muslim burial grounds in the city bear similar marks of retreat and defeat. Part of the burial ground for Muslim paupers at Park Circus, which had no boundary wall and no masonry graves, was being used in 1997 as a football ground, despite complaints to the Corporation on whose ground it stood.[60] The custodian of the burial ground at Gobra, founded in 1896 by Zillur Rahman on *waqf* land, told a similar story. The cemetery had originally covered some twenty bighas (about six acres) in the heart of a Muslim-dominated locality and close to a mosque on Ashgar Mistri Lane. In 1964 during the Hazratbal riots, scores of Muslims left the area and the locality was occupied by refugees from East Pakistan: 'How they regularised their plots is not known.' Gradually, they occupied more and more area of the paupers' graveyard, which had no boundary wall and no masonry graves, until three-quarters of the cemetery had been captured. Appeals to the Corporation for permission to erect a boundary wall were unsuccessful. The new occupants have since set up a tannery on that ground, and also use part of it as a football ground. In 1989, another riot broke out over the burial ground, but no decision was taken to restore it to its Muslim owners. By 1997, all that remained of the graveyard—still beautifully tended—was about an acre of land covered with masonry graves.[61]

Selimpore is thus but one instance of the processes by which Muslims were gradually coerced into surrendering their traditional claims to public spaces, retreating meekly into less visible and mendicant postures. As these vignettes indicate, anodyne narratives of 'cultural assimilation' in the creation of secular independent India gloss over the rather harsher dynamics of intimidation, surrender, and loss which were recurring themes in the same story.

II

It was not only the boundaries of sacred and ritual space that were redrawn in the aftermath of Partition. Partition set in train a process by which the physical

---

[60] Author's interview with Mushtaque Hossain, Secretary, Muslim Burial Board, 27 May 1997, Calcutta.

[61] Author's interview with Syeed Munir at Gobra III burial ground, Calcutta, on 27 May 1997. Most of the details were confirmed by Mr Nurul Hasan of the Anjuman Mufidul Islam in his interview with the author on 3 June 1997 in Calcutta. A very similar story was related with regard to the Raja Bazar private burial ground, where reportedly a third of the paupers' burial ground has been captured and turned into a football ground. If more 'objective' evidence is needed of this pattern, it is provided by Nirmal Kumar Bose's survey of Calcutta in 1964. His analysis of land usage in Calcutta's wards shows that in almost every ward of Calcutta where Muslims had once been dominant, land occupied by burial grounds shrank between 1911 and 1961. 'Table showing area occupied by each kind of land use in 65 wards in 1911 and 1961', Bose, *Calcutta 1964*, pp. 15–23.

space occupied by Muslims was progressively reduced and rearranged. It also accelerated the process, already under way long before 1947, by which the boundaries demarcating 'Muslim areas' came to be more sharply delineated. The combined effect of these twin developments was to force Muslims to huddle together in discrete pockets. If in death Muslims were deprived of their traditional graveyards, in life they were forced to live in what rapidly became Muslim ghettos.

In many ways, this 'clustering' and 'ghettoization' of Muslims reflected the limitations and constraints within which efforts by ordinary Muslims to survive the traumas of Partition had to work. During riots, flight was for many the only option. Whether fleeing Muslims escaped to Pakistan or merely to safer areas in West Bengal, each exodus resulted in Muslims losing some property to dominant communities.

When Muslims fled, many hoped to return once normalcy was restored; their exoduses were intended as temporary retreats, not permanent departures. But all too often, experience belied optimism. Notwithstanding the agreement between India and Pakistan that evacuee property in Bengal was to be held in trust until its rightful owners came back,[62] Muslim refugees were seldom able to repossess their homes and these flights invariably turned out to be one-way journeys with no points of return. When they did try to come home, Muslims usually found that their property had been grabbed by others. And it is abundantly clear, despite Prafulla Chakravarty's protestations to the contrary, that the new occupants were usually Hindu refugees from East Bengal.[63] Police files bear eloquent testimony to the hostile reception which met Muslims who returned. In August 1950, almost four months after the Howrah riots, police reported that

a tense feeling is prevailing amongst the East Bengal refugees of the district who are residing in vacant Muslim houses over the question of their ejectment as many of the Muslim house owners have since returned and started cases [under section] 448 I.P.C. The refugees are trying to gain public sympathy on their behalf. Their eviction would not be an easy task unless they are rehabilitated elsewhere.[64]

In another typical incident on the Nadia border, 'Muslims returning from Pakistan with their families and personal effects' in the aftermath of massive riots were attacked and looted by a party of thirty or forty refugees and were

---

[62]The Evacuee Properties Act of 1951 stated that 'a migrant Muslim family from West Bengal, returning within 31 March 1951, would be entitled to reoccupy the deserted property'.

[63]Prafulla K. Chakrabarti, *The Marginal Men: Refugees and the Left Political Syndrome in West Bengal* (Calcutta, 1990), pp. 105–8. His insistence that the plight of Muslim refugees was no 'great calamity in the midst of such misery' reveals an unattractive depth of prejudice on this issue. It is no doubt the same mindset which lay behind the government's failure even to record the number of displaced Muslims.

[64]Report on the political activities of the refugees and corruption in the refugee camps for the week ending 20 August 1950, GB IB, F. No. 1838–48 (KW).

driven away from the village. 'They were forced to take shelter with the Muslims of Sonadanga'.[65] Yet they were not safe there either. On 23 August 1950, five Muslims in Sonadanga were driven out by refugees and their property was looted. As the police report explained:

After the migration to Pakistan of the Muslims of this village about 5000 Hindu refugees have been living here after occupying the Muslim houses either by virtue of documents of exchange or finding them vacant. The return of Muslims almost daily in large numbers has caused great commotion among the refugees who are unwilling to accommodate them.[66]

As in this instance, often Muslims coming back home would find that in their absence whole colonies of refugees had settled on their lands and taken over their houses. In Nakashipara near the Nadia border, Muslims found that Namasudra refugees had built over a hundred huts on their land in Radhanagar and Birpur *mouza*. In this case, as in so many others, once refugees had squatted on Muslim land with the support of neighbourhood leaders and their bully-boys, it was virtually impossible to winkle them out.[67] In April 1950, a meeting was organized at Hanskhali under the 'presidentship of Bikash Roy (Congress) [at which] he urged the refugees not to vacate Muslim houses occupied by them, nor to allow any Muslim to enter there'. That same month, police reported that a volunteer group had been formed, ominously calling itself the Santan Bahini.[68] This thuggish organization provided the threatening umbrella of muscle power under which refugees grabbed vacant Muslim homes. Muslims without connections were powerless to do anything about it. They had no choice but to return to Pakistan or to take refuge in Muslim ghettoes where they hoped to find safety in numbers. Even when returning Muslims had the status and confidence to lodge complaints with the police against the Hindu refugees who had grabbed their property, they found that they could not get their property back, because the refugees were well organized, had established political connections, and were determined to stand their ground.[69]

Patterns of Muslim settlement and landownership were altered in other, openly aggressive, ways. Often Muslims who had chosen *not* to take flight were driven out of their homes, bag and baggage. Once again, Hindu refugees played

[65]Report of D/C Kotwali PS, dated 25 Aug. 1950, GB IB, F. No. 1809–48 (Nadia).

[66]Report on the political activities of the refugees and corruption in the refugee camps for the week ending 3 Sept. 1950, GB IB, F. No. 1838–48 (KW).

[67]Extract from abstract dated 6 May 1950, GB IB, F. No. 1809–48 (Nadia).

[68]The volunteers in Bankim Chandra Chatterjee's famous political novel, *Anandamath,* called themselves 'Santan'; used in the context of post-Partition Bengal, the name evoked powerful images of anti-Muslim vigilante violence.

[69]In Cossimbazar in July 1950, for instance, a police party was attacked when it 'tried to eject refugees from a house belonging to a member of the minority community'. *Hindusthan Standard* (5 July 1950).

a leading role in this deeply unattractive saga. Most cases of forcible eviction occurred in the border districts such as Nadia where refugees settled in large numbers on the property of Muslim evacuees and then tried to capture more land by intimidating the few remaining Muslim families and forcing them also to quit. In September 1950, about fifty Namasudra refugees who had settled at Paikpara near Krishnaganj in Nadia entered the Muslim part of the village and 'asked' the Muslims to leave in order to make room for Hindu evacuees from East Pakistan. Overnight they put up huts on Muslim-owned land 'with the object of compelling the landowners to settle the lands with them'.[70] In another incident on 25 December 1950, about a hundred refugee families in the middle of the night forced their way into the house of a Muslim of Nowdapur, P.S. Tehatta, beat him up, and attacked the other Muslims in the village 'and commanded them to go away to Pakistan leaving all their properties'.[71] Nadia saw the worst of these incidents, but they were in evidence all along the dry stretches of a long rural border.[72]

There was little the overstretched rural policemen could do to protect the Muslims, even when they were minded to do so.[73] In these outlying rural border

[70]Report on the political activities of the refugees and corruption in the refugee camps for the week ending 18 Sept. 1949, GB IB, F. No. 1838–48 (part III).

[71]Copy of radiogram message from O/C Tehatta P.S., dated 26 Dec. 1950, GB IB, F. No. 1809–48 (Nadia).

[72]In May 1950, police commented on 'a general tendency amongst the Namasudra evacuees, settled recently near Bongaon, to terrorise the Muslim residents of the Indian Union so that they may go away to East Pakistan by exchanging their houses and properties'. Report on the political activities of the refugees and corruption in the refugee camps for the week ending 7 May 1950, GB IB, F. No. 1838–48 (part IV).

[73]One grave incident in Ranaghat in June 1950 graphically reflects this predicament. On 25 June 1950, a party of six policemen was on its way to three Muslim villages in Ranaghat in response to a complaint that cattle belonging to Muslims had been stolen by Hindu refugees. The brave sextet was met by a crowd of 'one thousand to fifteen hundred refugees' carrying lathis, marching towards Muslim villages: 'From a distance of 150 cubits roughly, the S[ub] I[nspector] Nepal Mukherjee challenged the crowd to stop and to explain why they were proceeding in such an unusual manner and so armed. In answer to this challenge, some members of the mob reported that they would go to villages Purbanagar and Khagradanga but they did not halt to explain any further. These two villages are thick Muslim pockets. The S[ub]I[nspector] suspected that the mob was marching with [the] obvious purpose of looting the properties of the Muslims. He further shouted at the mob to halt giving them due warning. The mob did not show any sign of changing their attitude. The S[ub] I[nspector] then asked his men to load their rifles and take position. The mob became aggressive and one of them dashed against the S[ub] I[nspector]. This man was immediately arrested. At this the mob fell out in batches to round up the small police party. No alternative was then left to the police party but to open fire to protect their rifles and their lives .... The mob then retreated a few steps back and then reorganised there for fresh attack. Five shots were then fired ... [which] wounded one man. The mob then became puzzled and fled carrying the wounded man in hot haste in different directions in the heavy rains. The police party then chased them and succeeded in arresting three others .... The police party tried to trace the wounded man

areas, state authority was thinly spread and deeply compromised, and the police gave Muslims little protection. For their part Muslims sometimes put up resistance, whether by fighting back,[74] or by forging factional alliances with local Hindus who had little liking for the incursions and carryings-on of the refugees[75] or sometimes even by hiring Hindu mercenaries to protect them.[76] But as numerous abandoned Muslim villages graphically testify, these efforts had little lasting success. In Nadia, something akin to a total exchange of population between India and Pakistan took place, similar to the events in the Punjab in nature if not in scale. But elsewhere Muslims who were forced to abandon their lands remained in West Bengal and took shelter in Muslim-dominated areas on the Indian side of the border.

In time, as each incident of rioting and tension sparked off a diaspora of frightened and vulnerable Muslims to safer areas, and as each temporary flight became a permanent exile, where Muslim communities had been small and less conspicuous before Partition, now they either disappeared altogether or shrank into tiny little clusters. Huddled together, hemmed in by refugee colonies which sprang up around them, these tiny Muslim 'pockets' were like little enclaves, surrounded and squeezed by hostile neighbours. Like Selimpore, they tended to have the air of the ghetto about them.[77]

In contrast, Muslim-dominated areas in West Bengal gradually absorbed larger and larger numbers of Muslims displaced from other parts of the state. Chiefly in northern Bengal, not surprisingly such 'Muslim belts' became larger, or at least

---

but with no result. They got help from none in the village as the inhabitants there are all refugees. There is no rural police, the village en bloc being deserted by the Muslims some time back'. 'Report of enquiry into the firing opened by the police against a riotous mob on 25 June 1950'. GB IB, F. No. 1809–48 (Nadia).

[74]At Kalupur beside the Ichhamati river, a pitched battle was fought between the Muslims of Kalabhas village, 'exclusively a Muslim pocket' and the 'Kalupur people who are exclusively Namasudra refugees'. Unusually the outcome was that refugees attempting to loot the Muslim village were beaten back by Muslims 'armed with lathis, sharkis and other weapons'. Report of the SDO Ranaghat on the Kalupur incident of 2 Sept. 1950, U/S 148/355 IPC, GB IB, F. No. 1809–48 (Nadia).

[75]In one incident in Nadia in June 1950, when refugees of the Dhubulia camp attacked Muslims of Hansadanga village, 'the Muslims resisted and were assisted by the goalas of Hansadanga. The refugees were beaten back …. On returning to the camp, the refugees spread rumours that they had been attacked by Muslims without any provocations and that two of them had been killed'. This led to widespread looting and burning down of Muslim homes and property, even though the refugees 'met with organised resistance from the goalas'. Extract from abstract dated 10 June 1950, GB IB, F. No. 1809–48 (Nadia).

[76]Note dated 19 April 1950, GB IB, F. No. 1238/47 (Cooch Behar).

[77]See, for instance, Mahadev Basu's *Anthropological Profile of the Muslims of Calcutta* (Calcutta: Anthropological Survey of India, 1985). Based on fieldwork conducted in 1973 and 1974, Basu describes one (and by all accounts typical) Muslim *basti* or slum in Narikeldanga 'as quite repulsive to the eye', choked with garbage, its drains filled with faeces, and its tiny hutments dark and unventilated (p. 2).

more densely settled, and ever more exclusively Muslim in their composition. There are also indications that these belts became the favoured destination of returning Muslim evacuees from East Pakistan who came back to India but were unable to go home. We do not know much about this reverse migration. Despite the terms of the Inter-Dominion Agreement of 1948 between India and Pakistan which was intended to encourage Bengali refugees on both sides of the border to return home, in fact Muslim evacuees were strongly discouraged from returning to India, and they were explicitly denied help in so doing.[78] So, by its very nature, this immigration was clandestine and few attempts were made before the mid-1970s to assess its size or scale. And yet one surviving run of the 'Secret Fortnightly Reports' for 1957 indicates beyond doubt that a steady flow of Muslims in this period entered West Bengal by stealth and settled there.[79]

That the process began soon after Partition is suggested by reports from Malda as early as 1949, when Muslims from Rajshahi in East Bengal had reportedly begun to trickle into Malda at the rate of one or two families a week. Malda was a northern border district with a large Muslim presence. Despite the fact that

[78]There were clear directives from Delhi making it plain that the return of Muslims to India was not to be tolerated. In May 1949, a Secretary at the Ministry of Rehabilitation in Delhi wrote to the Chief Secretary of the West Bengal Government about the Government of India's 'considerable anxiety' about the working of the permit system. 'The permit system was introduced with a view to stop one-way traffic from Pakistan as the return of such Muslims was adversely affecting the rehabilitation schemes of the Government of India. Despite our request (dated 14 December 1948) that the applications for the conversion of a temporary permit into a permanent one by Muslims who came to India after 10 September 1948 should not be entertained, we are informed by our High Commissioner in Pakistan that a large number of such recommendations are being received by him .... In this connection I am to draw your attention to my letter ... of 18 April 1949 in which you were requested not to recommend cases for the grant of permits for permanent settlement to Muslim evacuees except in cases of genuine hardship. As you are presumably aware we have over 7 lacs [sic] of displaced people receiving free rations in camps in India. The Government of India attaches great importance to their early rehabilitation .... Return of Muslims from Pakistan is bound to [retard] the rehabilitation of displaced persons. In the circumstances it is hoped the Provincial Governments will not allow permits for permanent settlement to Muslims wishing to come back to India till the displaced persons have been satisfactorily rehabilitated'. C.N. Chandra, Government of India, Ministry of Rehabilitation to the Chief Secretary, Government of West Bengal, 9 May 1949. GB IB, F. No. 1210–48(4). This was followed by a stern reminder on 6 June 1948. Ibid.

[79]The 'infiltration of Muslims into Indian territory without travel documents' was reported fortnight after fortnight all through 1957 from the border districts, from 24 Parganas, Nadia, West Dinajpur, Jalpaiguri, Darjeeling, Murshidabad, and Malda. Towards the end of the year, cases were regularly reported from these districts of Pakistani Muslims being prosecuted for 'illegal entry' and for 'violation of passport rules'. In the first half of November 1957, twenty-one Pakistani Muslims were charged in West Dinajpur for 'violation of the passport rules while in Jalpaiguri eight of them were prosecuted for the same offence. In Cooch Behar certain Pakistani Muslims ... [were charged with] illegal entry'. Secret fortnightly report for the first half of Nov. 1957 for West Bengal, GB-IB, F. No. 1210–48 (4).

'suitable steps [had] been and [were] being taken to discourage such migration', the slow, surreptitious, but steady dribble of Muslims continued, in particular into the Muslim-dominated Kaliachak area along the border.[80] That these migrants were absorbed by the Muslim communities of Malda is suggested by an undercover officer's finding in 1949 that

the Muslims who are coming to this dominion are facing very little difficulties to settle, as they are being helped by their community to settle .... It is interesting to note that the Muslims who are coming to this end from Pakistan to settle are not begging for help from anyone else or from the Government.[81]

Again, we do not know for certain who these people were, although the report suggests that 'destitutes' and 'economic migrants' were mixed among returning Muslim evacuees.[82] However, it is not difficult to see that the result of this migration was a gradual increase in the size and density of the populations living in these Muslim belts, particularly those situated close to the border with Pakistan.

The cumulative impact of these displacements can be seen in the striking fact that by 1961 just under 30 per cent of West Bengal's Muslim population lived in only fifty *thana*s or police sub-districts along the border with East Pakistan. In this handful of localities, Muslims had come to make up about 40 per cent of the total population. Their numerical weight was particularly marked in three distinct zones of 'particularly strong concentration, each consisting of a chain of contiguous border police stations'.[83] In each of these zones, in the border thanas of West Dinajpur, Malda-Murshidabad, and the 24 Parganas respectively, Muslims constituted between half and four-fifths of the total population. Significantly, Kaliachak—where the first instance of this reverse migration was discovered in 1949—was one of these zones, and by 1961 Muslims constituted over 65 per cent of its total population. This pattern of clustering was also in evidence— though perhaps not quite so sharply—in other rural districts, such as Birbhum, where there had been a strong Muslim presence before Partition. By 1961, the Muslims of Birbhum had clustered together in the north of the district and had become the majority community there; by contrast, in south Birbhum they were less than 10 per cent of the population. It was as if Partition violently shook the great kaleidoscope of Bengali Muslim society, pushing it into a new pattern: Muslims all over West Bengal moved away from areas where they had lived in

[80]Weekly Confidential Report for the week ending 31 Dec. 1949, GB IB, F. No. 69A/49 (Malda).

[81]Copy of a report by the DI O (I) of Nadia district dated 12 August 1949. GB IB, F. No. 1809–48 (Nadia).

[82]Ibid.

[83]These zones were Chopra-Islampur-Goalpokhar in West Dinajpur, Kalichak-Shamshirganj-Suti-Raghunathganj-Lalgola-Bhagawangola-Raninagar-Jalangi-Karimpur in Malda and Murshidabad and Sarupnagar-Baduria-Basirhat in the 24 Parganas. *Census of India 1961*, vol. XVI, part I-A, p. 222.

small communities and moved towards areas where they were more numerous. Small Muslim localities shrank or disappeared, large Muslim belts became larger, more densely populated, and more exclusively Muslim.

Another remarkable feature of this series of displacements is that it led to a sharp fall in the number of Muslims living in the towns and cities of West Bengal. In 1931, about three out of every ten town-bred persons in Bengal as a whole had been Muslims, and that proportion had been higher still in the west, where Muslims were 'comparatively more numerous in the towns'.[84] By 1971, only one out of ten city-dwellers in West Bengal was a Muslim. The Census of that year noted that most towns and cities, particularly those around Calcutta and on the western bank of the Hooghly, 'show[ed] the effects of Partition as far as the religious composition of the population is concerned'. By 1951, West Bengal's urban Muslim population had dropped sharply; and the decline continued thereafter, 'steadily but rather slowly'.[85] In 1964, when Nirmal Kumar Bose conducted a detailed survey of Calcutta, he found that in many wards and *mohallas* previously inhabited mainly by Muslims, refugees had edged them out and established a dominant Hindu presence.[86] Muslims long settled in these areas had left the city altogether or had 'moved into greater concentration' in other wards. The net effect was a decline in the overall numbers of urban Muslims in West Bengal, and for those who hung on in the city, the usual pattern was to cluster together in pockets of increasingly dense concentration.[87] When he conducted his survey of Calcutta's Muslims in 1969, Siddiqui too was struck by the way in which 'recent historical events' had forced them 'to cling together even more closely to meet the situation. The process that had started the withdrawal of the Muslims from South Calcutta in the mid-forties ... has continued. This tends to concentrate them in compact areas'.[88]

We do not know where all these town-bred Muslim refugees went. A certain proportion must have migrated to towns in East Pakistan. But it is interesting that the Census of East Bengal taken in 1951 shows that less than one out of every ten West Bengali muhajirs settled in Dacca district, by far the most urbanized area in the east. Far greater numbers—almost two-thirds—migrated to Kushtia, Rajshahi, Rangpur, and Dinajpur: areas that were altogether more bucolic.[89] And we know that the Muslims who moved out of the cities but stayed in West Bengal

[84]*Census of India 1931*, vol. v, part i, p. 387.

[85]The census commissioner concluded that this pattern of decline 'reflects the greater mobility of urban populations' due to 'economic factors' and no doubt such considerations played a part. *Census of India, 1971, Series 22, West Bengal, part i-A*, pp. 278–9.

[86]Bose listed wards 3, 14, 16, 34, 77, 78, 79, and 80 as areas formerly occupied by Muslim labourers and artisans, whose Muslim inhabitants had been largely replaced by refugees. Nirmal Kumar Bose, *Calcutta: 1964*, p. 33.

[87]Ibid., pp. 39–40.

[88]Siddiqui, *The Muslims of Calcutta*, p. 26.

[89]*Census of Pakistan, 1951*, vol. iii, *East Bengal, Reports and Tables*, p. 81.

gravitated towards certain Muslim-dominated clusters, all of which were rural backwaters. We also know that returning Muslim evacuees did not usually go back to their houses in the towns; they too were eventually absorbed into these rural Muslim-majority corners.

It seems impossible to escape the conclusion that West Bengal Muslim refugees after Partition mainly migrated from towns to the countryside. This is in itself a remarkable fact, since every study of migration in South Asia insists that its main direction has been citywards. Historically people in South Asia have mainly moved from villages to cities; smaller numbers have moved from one town to another or, in a minority of cases, from one rural area to another. Migration from towns to villages is almost unheard of.[90] And yet this is what West Bengal Muslims appear to have done in very considerable numbers after 1947. The significance of this fact for our understanding of migration in South Asia is potentially very great, but this is not the place to tease it out. Here it is enough to note that twenty-five years after Partition, West Bengal's Muslims were no longer the city creatures they had once been. They now lived predominantly in the countryside.

Partition thus dramatically changed the profile of the Muslim population of West Bengal. It redistributed them, and not merely spatially. Like a great earthquake, it flung them out of the cities and towns of the south, pushing them northwards to the great rural Muslim settlements along the Ganges or eastwards towards the border and beyond it. In so doing, it rubbed away some of the age-old differences between Muslims of the west—historically more urban in their setting—and their agriculturist co-religionists in East Bengal.

Even the 10 per cent who stayed on in the cities experienced upheaval and change. The communities which remained were transformed by the fact that they had to absorb refugees from more dangerous parts of the city, often into areas which had been reduced in size and usually by abandoning ritual and public space. Inevitably these communities, which had once been 'distinct sub-communal groups', now became more ethnically diverse. Basu's study of Muslim bastis in Calcutta in 1974 showed that they were mainly 'multi-ethnic'.[91] Not surprisingly, few of the old communities had been able to survive these traumas without abandoning their hereditary trades. Not a single Ansari in Basu's survey was still a weaver in 1974; the majority lived by making bidis, pulling rickshaws, hawking fish, or by taking jobs as lascars. In 1974 hardly any Raiens still sold vegetables and the Sisgars had completely given up making bangles.[92] Of course, some of their members had done well, joining the urban bourgeoisie: some Ansaris and

---

[90]That migration in the Bengal area historically followed this pattern is demonstrated in Hariparasad Chattopadhyaya, *Internal Migration in India: A Case Study of Bengal* (Calcutta, 1987).

[91]Basu, *Anthropological Profile of the Muslims of Calcutta*, p. 5. Also see M.K.A. Siddiqui, 'Life in the slums of Calcutta', *Economic and Political Weekly* (13 Dec. 1969).

[92]Basu, *Anthropololgical Profile of the Muslims of Calcutta*, pp. 14–15.

Raiens, in particular, had been able to educate themselves and enter the learned professions. But for most, the loss of old localities and old ways of life—which for most urban Muslims had revolved around hereditary skilled craftsmanship—brought poverty and hardship. For some at least, there was little choice but to join the rough-and-tumble world of the manual labouring classes.[93]

In these different ways Partition, sometimes in rushes and sometimes in imperceptible ripples, displaced and transformed countless Muslim communities all over western Bengal. Some left for Pakistan in the immediate aftermath of Partition, others left in fits and starts during the following decades, which were disfigured by endemic communal troubles. The many who stayed behind also suffered their share of dislocation and distress, often being forced in times of crisis to seek shelter in 'safe' areas, their temporary flights usually ending up as permanent displacements. Many Muslim families who had previously lived in relative harmony cheek by jowl with Hindu neighbours gradually moved out of these mixed settlements, now opting instead to live in localities where their co-religionists had the advantage of numbers and were better insulated from their Hindu neighbours. When they left, their property was quickly seized by Hindu refugees. Others were forced out of their homes and land by Hindus, usually refugees. So large numbers of Muslims were themselves turned into refugees, whether in the formal sense of being evacuees who moved to Pakistan or as 'internally displaced' persons, who had crossed no international borders but had nevertheless been dispossessed, losing their homes and their traditional means of livelihood, and being compelled to throw themselves on the mercy of their co-religionists in enclaves which increasingly became exclusively Muslim ghettos.

In time, these different processes of displacement came to impose new patterns of Muslim presence in West Bengal. Muslims now occupied considerably less land in the province than they had done before Partition and they were increasingly confined into smaller and more tightly packed locations. The extent to which these areas became sharply defined as Muslim and distinct from Hindu neighbourhoods is underlined by the way the police perceived them. From 1948 at least until 1957, the police maintained surveillance over what they described as 'Mohammadan pockets', which were duly listed, with a careful record kept of any changes in their composition, right down to the number of firearms owned by their inhabitants. These clusters appear to have become relatively stable in shape and size by the mid-1950s. In 1957, only in one district, Howrah, did the

---

[93]Among the Sheikhjees, for instance, while almost 80 per cent still clung to their hereditary calling in trading in cattle and dairy produce, almost one in five had taken up 'hard manual labour' by 1974. Ibid., p. 16.

Intelligence Bureau identify significant changes in the number, size, and location of these Muslim 'pockets'.[94] It was almost as if the larger partition of Bengal had sparked off an endless series of lesser partitions in the innumerable neighbourhoods of West Bengal, the Great Divide being mirrored in many smaller divisions in the communal topography of a changing province.

Partition thus failed to solve the root problem of the growing alienation of Muslims from Hindus in undivided Bengal. If anything, it intensified that alienation. Partition increased the social gulf as well as the physical distances separating Hindus from Muslims. It rendered more impermeable the boundaries between them. It also transformed the basic characteristics of the Muslim peoples of West Bengal, who now lost much of their historic and once highly visible presence in the towns and cities of a province whose urban profiles they had in the past done so much to shape. In those clusters where Muslims now huddled fearfully together, memories of relative prosperity and better times quickly faded in tackling the grim realities of the present and facing the even grimmer prospects of the future. Once fairly prosperous Muslim settlements were rapidly metamorphosized into slum-like ghettos of the underprivileged and the poor. In these sad communities, Muslims who were too poor and disadvantaged to migrate to Pakistan were now, in some sense, the dominant force. But in these ghettoes there were other ominous trends. Increasingly inhabited, squeezed, and crowded by Muslim outsiders from other parts of West Bengal, who had been reduced from being skilled artisans to mere labourers, these Muslim neighbourhoods were a new phenomenon, ghettos which grew larger as they absorbed indigent migrants from elsewhere in Bengal and from East Pakistan itself.

Selimpore and its graveyard with which we began is a microcosm of the big picture. The visible decay of a once prosperous Muslim neighbourhood, the way it came to be a shadow of its former self, the dilapidation of its once imposing graves, the surrender by the few remaining Muslims of their rituals and rights, the suburb's lack of civic amenities, appalling even by Calcutta's inglorious standards, and the gross poverty of its denizens, all are reflections of a much broader tale of the decline of the Muslims of West Bengal. Once masters of the province, Partition pushed them both literally and figuratively—to its margins.

---

[94]Memo no. D-4270, dated 7 Feb. 1947, GB IB, F. No. 270/56. Sadly, the intelligence files which contained the original list of Muslim pockets (GB IB 126–48) appear to have been destroyed or lost, as also the updated full list prepared in 1951 (GB IB 2154–51). But the very fact that such a precise record was made and updated, and that such tight arrangements were made for their surveillance, indicates that these clusters were largely stable formations and regarded as such by the authorities.

FROM BEEHIVE CELLS TO CIVIL SPACE:
A HISTORY OF INDIAN MATRIMONY

Nupur Chaudhary and Rajat Kanta Ray

I

The idea of 'concord' is old in Indian civilization. In the Shahbazgarhi inscription, where the idea finds its first datable mention, Emperor Ashoka pronounces that concord is commendable. Verily, if a person disparages other sects because of inordinate attachment to his own, he damages his sect by acting in that way. People, said the emperor, 'should learn and respect the fundamentals of one another's Dharma'.[1] Such was the ideological foundation of India's beehive society. Mis'ar Bin Mulhalhil, an Arab geographer who visited the port of Saimur on the west coast in CE 942, witnessed a cellular social formation there. Besides Hindus, there were Musalmans, Christians, Jews, and Parsees, and below the main temple of the Hindus on the mound, he noticed 'mosques, Christian churches, synagogues, and Fire temples'.[2] Islam as it entered India, fitted into a system that segregated the population sexually, occupationally, and ritually into self-contained communities.

The idea of concord between the sects and castes implied that the communities should live together separately: every community, every locality would manage its own affairs and this would promote coexistence and mitigate conflict. Historically, the idea took shape in a cellular social formation, upheld by the ideology of

[1]D.C. Sircar, *The Inscriptions of Ashoka* (Delhi, 1957), p. 51.

[2]H.M. Elliot and John Dowson, *The History of India as Told by its Own Historians* (reprint Allahabad, 1964), vol. 1, p. 97.

syncretism. This was a world apart from the modern ideal of a civil society, and the ideology of secularism which upholds it.[3]

In old India, the cellular formation of the society, which closely resembled the beehive, implied that the communities formed separate cells in one whole, the cells being constituted into exclusive marriage circles. The idea of syncretism was predicated on avoidance of conflict arising from matters of sex and faith. These matters belonged properly to the community; and since these differed from one community to another, it implied a barrier to intermixture. That, paradoxically, was the principle of unity.

Caste, in particular, was an exclusive marriage circle. Marriage among Hindus is still caste based. Among Muslims, too, caste is present in a matrimonial form, especially among the lower orders. Even among the higher classes of Muslims, well-understood divisions are still in force. The shooting down in court of a *mohajir* boy by the gunmen of the *biradari* of a Pathan girl who had married him in defiance of her community is a case in point.[4] This happened in broad daylight in the high court of Karachi in Pakistan. In the villages of Uttar Pradesh, too, there have been instances of eloping couples—typically a Dalit boy and an upper-caste girl—being hunted down by community elders and strung up from the nearest pole. The idea behind such actions is that the honour of the community depends on the purity of the woman's body. Pairing is, therefore, a matter of community control, and arrangement of marriage by elders is still the norm, preferably while the girl is still very young.

In late antiquity, Al-Biruni, describing the gender system of the Hindus, had noted the fact that Indians married their children young;[5] Muslims in India, too, came to follow this practice, the married girl child being given over to the possession of her husband as soon as she reached puberty.[6] Child marriage strengthened community control and promoted separation of the communities. Intermixture would disturb the arrangement. There was an implicit social compact, each community agreeing to respect the right of other communities to control woman's body in the same manner as it claimed for itself. It was this which bound the beehive formation together. The syncretistic ruler Akbar, in an effort to prevent the occurrence of conflict over this sensitive issue, prohibited intermarriage between the communities.[7]

One problem which arose repeatedly in this context was the possibility that love might occur across the barriers dictated by caste and community. The

---

[3]For a discussion of this idea, see Sudipta Kaviraj and Sunil Khilnani, *Civil Society, History and Possibilities* (Cambridge, 2001).

[4]Irfan Hussain, 'All for Love', *Asian Age* (10 March 1998), originally published in *Dawn*.

[5]Edward C. Sachau (ed.), *Alberuni's India* (reprint New Delhi, 1983), p. 154.

[6]Jaffur Shureef, *Qanoon-e-Islam or the Customs of the Mussulmans of India*, trans. and ed. by G.A. Merklots (Madras, 1895), pp. 35–6.

[7]Muhammad Mujeeb, *The Indian Muslims* (London, 1967), p. 262 n.

experience of grievous separation, known by the characteristic term *viraha*, was a constant feature of life in India; it arose from communal and other prohibitions which acted as barriers between love and marriage. Sufi and Bhakti tales, such as those centring on the extramarital affairs of Yusuf and Zulaikha and Radha and Krishna, made viraha quintessential to the experience of divine passion. Folk tales, too, such as the love of Sasui and Punhoon in Sindh and of Heer and Ranjha in the Punjab, revolved around tragedies arising from barriers to love. During the same period, scores of illiterate minstrels of East Bengal, both Hindu and Muslim, sang of the sufferings of love. The theme of these ballads was dictated by social prohibitions, including the all-pervasive injunctions against communal intermixture. Viraha, which became itself an ingredient of syncretism, implied acceptance of separation, sublimation of the erotic urge, and harmony-in-pathos. The term coined by literary critics to describe this state of the mind, which was given the highest place in medieval Vaishnava poetry, is 'union in spirit' (*bhava-sammilana*). In this state of mind, the lovers voluntarily agree to part for the greater good, but remain attached to each other in spirit.[8] Not all the tragedies in these devotional and folk tales arise from prohibitions against inter-communal or inter-caste union. In practically every instance, however, the barrier in force is due to the custom of the community (for example, the prohibition against consanguine marriage among the Hindus), which is the medieval equivalent of the law.

A brave new generation of lovers belonging to the 1920s, 1930s, and 1940s broke away radically from this idea. They defied the barriers of caste and community with the aim of achieving union, not in some spiritual realm but in this world. Out of these actions emerged the contours of a different social formation: a civil society of self-governing individuals rather than a beehive society of self-contained cells. This was a society in which marriage might be contracted under the laws enacted in British India as against the customs of the community which necessarily confined marriage within the caste and the religious community. The acts which sanction marriage of widows, civil marriage outside the circle of the community, and a legally defined age of consent had been passed in the second half of the nineteenth century. All the same, it was not until the first four decades of the twentieth century that there was a notable resort to the legal opportunities provided by colonial legislation and the existence of law courts. This was due to what Rabindranath Tagore perceived as silent change in society, as opposed to the fanfare of largely ineffective social reform.[9] The marriageable age of girls among the educated classes had increased by the 1920s and 1930s. There was an ever-larger number of educated young women and men who might be tempted to go

[8]Rajat Kanta Ray, *Exploring Emotional History: Gender, Mentality and Literature in the Indian Awakening* (New Delhi, 2001), pp. 88–112.
[9]Rabindranath Tagore, 'Nari' (1936), in *Rabindra Rachanavali* (Birth Centenary Edition), vol. 13, p. 378.

against the dictates of community and to contract their marriages according to their own individual wills. This had not happened on such a scale earlier, though there are isolated instances in the nineteenth century which presaged this later social process. Statistically far more significant is the number of marriages across the traditionally defined circles that occurred in the period between 1900 and 1947. The sharp reaction of orthodox circles to these so-called 'scandals' exhibited the principle of communalism in action in the sphere of marriage. The reaction sought to transform the cells in the beehive into exclusive and mutually opposed boxes. The courting couples had to face opposition and they asserted their individual wish in what they saw as their own affair.

The ideological conflict involved in this clash of wills revolved around the question: 'Is s/he a born member of the community guided by its collective will, or an individual whose life and love were to be determined by his/her own preference? The couples were in effect asserting, sometimes intentionally but most often unintentionally, that in this matter they were members of the nascent civil society rather than the existing communities. With that, of course, the love of old, wounded by communal separation and solaced by syncretic culture, came to an end. A new, more optimistic, love was born. This happened even before the legal machinery which would allow it full play was complete. It was not before 1955 that the Hindu Marriage Act was passed, and even then a common civil code proved impossible to achieve. In Pakistan and Bangladesh, no radical pieces of legislation such as the Hindu Code Bill were introduced at all. Nevertheless social change promoted the voluntary sexual choice of the individual throughout the subcontinent, albeit haltingly and tentatively. This was a transition from Gemeinschaft to Gesellschaft, from born community to free association, from syncretism to secularism, and from community-centred life to individualistic existence.

The terms 'community' (Gemeinschaft) and 'society' (Gesellschaft), coined by German intellectual Ferdinand Toennies around 1887,[10] arose out of a process of modernization that has everywhere, even if imperfectly, turned the old communitarian societies into modern civil societies. This implies a transition from birth to merit, heredity to association, communalism to individualism, gregariousness to privacy, custom to law, and hierarchy to equality in the eyes of the law. The emergence of civil society is and was, to use the phrase which Sir Henry Maine coined from his Indian experience in the same generation as Ferdinand Toennies, an advance from status to contract. Old Indian society was founded upon hereditary relationships which were regulated according to a hierarchy. The social structure, based upon castes and communities, was not congenial for the growth of a civil society. Nevertheless the emergence of the

---

[10]For a discussion, see Otto Gerhard Oexle, 'The Middle Ages through modern eyes: A historical problem', *Transactions of the Royal Historical Society* (sixth series), 9 (1999), p. 131.

rule of law in British India, followed by the growth of an English-educated elite which came to call itself the 'educated middle class', created a public arena and fostered the bonds of voluntary association in the course of the nineteenth century. A society of self-regulating individuals whose relations are contractual and not based on hereditary communal ties implies a new intellectual outlook, expressing itself through what the educated middle class called public opinion. The outlook of the emerging civil society, rational, scientific, secular, libertarian, and humanistic, differed from the spiritual, devotional, syncretistic, hierarchical, and patriarchal outlook of old. In so communitarian a society, however, the transition was imperfect and the tensions generated by the process turned the cells of the beehive into embattled blocs in the newly consolidated public arena. The new love, and secularism, had no less formidable forces to contend with than the old love and syncretism.

II

In the old society, reputation (*man*) and lineage (*kul*) were closely interrelated: both were formidable obstacles to love. A girl contemplating elopement with her father's herdsman reflects:

> Lineage and reputation, I'd give up for thee
> For the privilege of wiping the sweat off the body.[11]

She finds out in no time that falling in love with a likable man brings no end of trouble ('*sujan chinya pirit kara bara bisham letha*'). Such is the tenor of the eastern Bengal ballads, which were sung by minstrels in Mymensingh, Chittagong, and other districts of deltaic eastern Bengal in the period between the fifteenth and eighteenth centuries.[12] The chorus in *Dhopar Pat* sings, 'The pain of separation burns me like a flame. I loved but not a day have I been happy.'[13] Here, as elsewhere, caste is the insuperable obstacle. A washerman's daughter flees with a prince. The prince washes clothes to feed her. The princess of the town falls in love with him, and makes him a prince again. The washerman's daughter commits suicide. Lineage prevails over love.

This is as true of Muslim society as of the Hindu community. A comparison

[11] '*Ichha hoy tomar lagya chhari kulman. Muchhaiya shital kori anger gham*', 'Miashal Bandhu', Dinesh Chandra Sen, *Purbabanga Gitika*, 3 vols (Calcutta, 1926, 1930, 1932).

[12] We have used here both the Bengali edition of Dines Chandra Sen and his English translation series, but the translations, unless otherwise stated, are ours. We have found the commentary of Dusen Zbavital particularly useful. Dines Chandra Sen (ed.), *Mymansingha Gitika* (Calcutta, 1923); Sen, *Purbabanga Gitika*; Dinesehandra Sen (trans.), *Eastern Bengal Ballads*, 4 vols (Calcutta, 1923, 1926, 1928, 1932). Dusan Zbavital, *Bengali Folk Ballads from Mymensingh and the Problem of Their Authenticity* (Calcutta, 1963).

[13] Sen, *Eastern Bengal Ballads*, vol. 2:1, p. 9.

of the fate of Malua (in the ballad entitled 'Malua') with that of Aina Bibi (in the ballad entitled 'Aina Bibi') would underscore the point. The Hindu girl commits suicide in order to save her husband's reputation, because she had been imprisoned in a Muslim household, a misfortune that must result in loss of caste. The Muslim wife, for her part, despite the courage she showed in rescuing her spouse, is pronounced to be unchaste (*asati*) because she had left home all by herself to search for her missing husband. To save his reputation and to enable him to marry again, she leaves home with the gypsies. She comes back for a last look at her husband and drowns herself in the river.

It is not that love invariably ends in such tragedies in the eastern Bengal ballads. There are instances of happy inter-communal union in the ballad entitled '*Dewan Isha Khan Masnad Ali*'. Isha Khan, one of the Bara Bhuyan of Bengal who fought with the Mughal invaders, was a Pathan chief who carried off the daughter of the neighbouring Hindu landlord, Kedar Roy. In the ballad, she declares her love for him despite the communal barrier which separates them: 'You saw me when I was bathing—my mind yearns for you—I care not for my religion or my society. In you I will find all that is dear to me. If you feel any compassion for me, hasten to meet me.'[14] But for one such happy union, it will not be difficult to cite several affairs which have a sad end.[15] A zamindar's son flees with a gypsy girl, and both are killed by the girl's vengeful guardian.[16] A great chief's son flees with the gardener's daughter, and then abandons her for a courtesan; she takes poison.[17] A prince elopes with a low-caste Dom's wife, and is killed by the poisoned arrows of the enemy. She takes poison too, with these last words on her lips:

I grieve not, dearest, at my last breath
Pray I have you in life and in death.[18]

The ideal of an eternal union beyond all the ruptures in the world persists in several other ballads. The grieving lover hears the words of his lost love in a whisper from below the grave: 'I have no flesh on my body, and no blood, and no veins. Yet I have not forgotten you, nor have I untied the knot which binds me to you' (*gave nai re gost amar lou ar shita / bhuli nai re tomar katha khuli nai re gira*).[19]

Commenting on the inter-communal love affairs which are commemorated

---

[14]Ibid., p. 251.

[15]See the ballad of Surat Jamal and Adhua, an inter-communal affair which ends in tragedy. Ibid., pp. 391–419.

[16]'Mahua', ibid., vol. 1:1, pp. 1–30.

[17]'Ratan Thakurer Pala', *Purbabanga Gitika*, IV. 2, pp. 321–37.

[18]'Shyam Ray', *Purbabanga Gitika*, III.2, p. 294. '*Ami je maribo bandhu re tate dukkha nai / Jiyane marane bandhu tomare jeno pai*'.

[19]'Nuranneha O Kabarer katha', *Purbabanga Gitika* IV. 2, p. 129. The objection to a happy union in this instance, however, arises, not from a communal barrier, but from the accidental discovery that she is his sister. Both hero and heroine are Muslims.

in these ballads, the modern editor of these old narratives remarks, 'The poets of Mymensingh have faithfully narrated the story of love between the youthful men and women of both communities and they found nothing objectionable in it.' What is remarkable about the modern translator's critical perception as distinct from the spontaneous verse of the minstrels is the new fear that objections might arise from the audience, which is indeed the sign of a changing age. The editor goes on to give a list of all the affairs cutting across the Hindu–Muslim divide: the love between Momina Khatun and Kalidas, the romance of their son Isha Khan and Subhadra in the next generation, and the affair of the daughters of Kedar Ray and Isha Khan's sons in the third generation, as well as the love of Adhua Sundari, the daughter of the Brahmin Raja Dubaraj, for the youthful *Dewan* of Baniachang. 'These stories', says the editor, 'are in the form of songs which were sung by professional rhapsodists before the Hindus and Muhammadans of the localities where the events actually happened. The poets wrote the narratives without being influenced by bigotry, hence no one took objection to what they wrote.' Sadly he adds, in an implicit comment on the transformation of the beehive cells into exclusive boxes in modern times, that the minds of both the communities have been embittered on these very issues. The operative principle was no longer accommodation but exclusion.

One might question the editor's assumption that the events narrated in the ballads actually happened more or less in the form in which they are recounted. The stories might indeed be true indicators of the mentality of the age, but they cannot be treated as exact accounts of what happened. For historical authenticity, one must turn to the Persian chronicles. One true story, which concerns Saiyid Musa of Garamsir and the wife of a Hindu goldsmith of Agra, is narrated by Badauni exactly as he heard it from the lover's brother. The brother, whose name was Saiyid Shahi, had assisted in the affair, and had then recorded its tragic outcome in verse. Badauni, who had access to the poem and is good enough to provide extracts from it, dwells on the pain and sufferings of the separated lovers as they pine for each other in a love that is chaste and self-denying.[20] The failure and triumph of their love declare the victory of the spirit of syncretism in a cellular society which sublimated earthly love into *taswawuf* and bhakti.

Sayyid Musa, who belonged to a distinguished *Sayyid* family of Kalpi, came to Agra to pay homage to emperor Akbar. In the Mughal capital, he came across Mohini, whose beauty was like 'gold of the purest standard'. As the imperial camp left Agra on a campaign to conquer the fort of Ranthambhor, Musa managed to stay behind, living close to the house of his beloved on the banks of the Jumna. Whenever he ventured out to meet Mohini, he was thwarted either by the watchmen of the town or the goldsmiths of her caste. Two years and four months

[20]Al-Baduoni, *Muntakhabu-t-Twarikh*, trans. by W.H. Lowe (reprint Delhi, 1986), vol. 2, pp. 113–21.

elapsed before Mohini bid him undertake a desperate rope-climbing act that took him to her bedroom. Instead of engaging in passionate embrace, the lovers remained 'united yet apart' till morning. The brother Saiyid Shahi who sings here of the glory of the 'true love which has driven out all thought of desire' is quoted verbatim by Badauni on this point. What the chronicler himself described as chaste affection had its denouement in the lovers escaping secretly to the house of a trustworthy friend. The goldsmith community, backed by the magistrate, laid siege to the brother's house, forcing the lovers to part. For fear of calumny, she concocted an improbable story of having been transported to the land of the fairies. The silly Hindus, remarks Badauni patronizingly, believed this; nevertheless they took the precaution to lock her in.

Overcome by the pangs of separation, the lover lost his sanity. The affair became the talk of the town. Fearing dishonour, Mohini sent word to Musa to leave Agra but to leave behind a friend through whom she might stay in touch with him. The hapless Musa left for the imperial camp at Ranthambhor. Mohini found she could not live without him, so she hatched a hare-brained scheme to flee to her lover. Predictably her relatives, actively assisted by the magistrate, caught up with her. Hearing this news, Musa hurried back to Agra, where his beloved was kept in close confinement by her relatives. Neither good advice, nor show of force, nor threats and reproach by the members of his community could restrain him. At this stage, a friend, Qazi Jamal, came to their help. He contrived for Mohini to escape from her home. But the venture proved abortive. The Qazi and Mohini were apprehended and her relatives put her in chains. Musa breathed his last in 'vexation and despair'. As his bier passed below the windows of the incarcerated Mohini, in a fit of insane desperation she broke her chains and jumped down. She chanted the name of Musa at his grave, recited the confession of faith in the presence of a Muslim divine, and 'surrendered her soul to her beloved' (that is, the Creator).

True to the spirit of the age, Musa's brother took solace in the thought that the lovers were united in the garden of paradise, hidden from all mankind. If unfulfilled love had been their lot in 'the transitory world', Musa and Mohini were nevertheless believed to have had their deliverance: 'from the pain and grief of separation they were freed', and for ever. But this fulfilment they reached, according to the notions of the age, only after they had made the great crossover. Conjugal bliss was not possible in the world as then constituted. The cellular social formation, strengthened by the imperial decree forbidding all intermarriages that might provoke religious strife and communal tension, thwarted the union. From its inception, the romance was fated to follow the trajectory of spiritual love which would deny itself fulfilment in physical union. Both the communities took advantages of the state dictate to prevent the couple from breaking the barriers that protected their separate existence, but society at large found consolation in the idea of a spiritualized love cutting across the communities. 'O Sayyid why dost thou weep?', wrote the disconsolate brother.

III

The nineteenth century witnessed the manifestation of an inchoate civil society among the circle of English-educated persons. This nascent social formation had certain features which marked it out from the older social structure. The new 'society' consisted of individuals who collectively constituted a public. Such a public had not existed earlier.[21] People were born into communities. Now, however, individuals associated with one another voluntarily. Side by side with the community, there sprang up the association, and as the public sphere constituted by these associations gained in importance and influence, communities could no longer afford to remain immersed in their local and communal affairs alone. Theoretically, this public was one body, and not a series of communities. It was distinguished from the government by the rule of law, which applied to all and sundry. Legally, the colonial rulers themselves were bound by the publicly promulgated regulations which they had passed for their subjects. As all the subjects of the British government in India were put under the same regulations without distinction, they were thereby constituted into one collective body called the public, members of which were equal in the eye of the law. The law was a new force in Indian society: distinct from the custom of the community, it emanated from the legislative acts of the colonial government and the judicial decisions of the law courts. The rule of law manifested itself in the judicial and land revenue regulations passed by Lord Cornwallis during 1791–3. While this in due course provided a powerful reason for every individual to associate voluntarily with other members of the public in order to influence the law to his own convenience, in the vast social space beyond this enlightened public, the castes and communities not only continued to exist, but were in fact impelled to extend their activities to the public sphere. As the cells of the beehive began to dissolve, what emerged was not necessarily an open civil space, but a public sphere often cluttered by exclusive boxes.

Nevertheless, there was now an entity which called itself the public. The young Rabindranath Tagore noted the emergence of this still adolescent entity in a public funeral oration in 1894. Indian society, as he put it, was a household-dominated society. It was constituted by the bond of every person to the elders at home. The social space outside the home was narrow because society was split up into castes, communities, and lineages. The home in turn was segmented in the inner apartments and the outer apartments. Women were not allowed outside. In the midst of all these constraints, the youthful poet noticed the recent emergence of an entity called the public. He used the English word because

---

[21]For a discussion of the idea of 'Offentlichkeit' (publicity) and the emergences of a public sphere in the world at large and in India, see J.R. Goody, 'Civil society in an extra-European perspective', and Partha Chatterjee, 'On civil and political society in postcolonial democracies', both in Kaviraj and Khilnani, *Civil Society*, esp. pp. 150–1, 166–70.

there was no Bengali equivalent. The existence of the public implied the birth of the private. Again, he used the English word in his Bengali address. There was no private space between man and wife in the joint family of old. The rise of individualistic relations between men and women ran counter to the old patriarchial caste-bound society. The coming out of women in public contradicted the old society based on hierarchical status, separation of the home from the outside, and the division of the outer space into communities.[22]

The new form of organization did not yet (and still does not) extend to the whole surface of Indian society. Old India, the India of castes and communities, persisted in amorphously changing forms, and the scope of civil society was narrow. The lower orders of the population were compartmentalized in localities, communities, and castes, and the cells were in the process of being transformed into boxes. It was the educated middle class, with its notion of enlightenment, which claimed above all to represent public opinion. This claim was based on the fact that its interpersonal relationships were reorganized in a strikingly novel manner. Its society exhibited the reformed relationships. The middle class was unquestionably a part of the emerging civil society, and arguably its only visible form. The public might theoretically mean everybody, in practice it meant at first the middle-class leaders of public opinion. Their claim to this leadership was based socially on the rise of private individualistic relationships among themselves.

The English-educated middle class had a lifestyle that marked it out from the rest of the population. The desire for English education compelled most students to move out of their village homes and into distant towns away from their families. They had to pass through formal competitive examinations: this was, psychologically speaking, a severe test, because such examinations were quite unknown in the country. Those who passed and got into service had again to face the prospect of being away from their ancestral homes. Because of the speed and safety provided by the train and steamer, they tended to travel with their wives to the town where they had got their new employment, and there, as in school earlier, they had to negotiate a rigid and novel 10 a.m. to 5 p.m. daily work schedule. The modern work schedule, together with the school and college examinations, tried and tested the young men, and success required a reorganized household. The reorganization of the household in turn required educated young women who would be able to teach their children and to run clean, efficient homes. That in turn meant social reform and all that it implies—a reorganization of interpersonal relationships within the home and outside, in other words a new gender ethic.

The change was achieved silently in the course of the nineteenth century. The challenges to the matrimonial order, as yet, were few and far between. The real upsets came later. There were, however, certain 'notorious' instances in this

[22]Rabindranath Tagore, 'Shoka-sabha' (1894), in *Rabindra Rachanavaali*, vol. 10 (Calcutta, 1989), pp. 292–4.

period which indicated the gradual creation and halting extension of civil space in the matrimonial sphere. The entire spectrum of relationships in that sphere had so far been moulded by communal and patriarchal authority. Now there were departures.

The earliest instance is the elopement of Basantakumari, the widow *Rani* of Burdwan, with lawyer Dukhinarunjan Mookerjee, a favourite student of M.L.V. Derozio of the Hindoo College. She belonged to the Punjabi Khatri caste, he was a Bengali Brahmin. His biographer does not mention the date of this marriage, which was performed according to Hindu rites by a Brahmin who had been liberally rewarded, but he adds that because of the uncertain legality of an inter-caste widow marriage (the Hindu Widow Remarriage Act inspired by Ishwar Chandra Vidyasagar in 1860 still lay in the future), Mookerjee contracted a civil marriage with the Rani before an English magistrate in the police court of Calcutta.[23] This, too, was of uncertain legal validity; it was not until Act III was passed in 1872 that the native subjects of the British empire in India got access to civil marriage. The new Act required those who wanted to take advantage of it to declare that they did not belong to any of the established religious faiths. Before this, the only choice before the parties would have been to live in sin, something conventional society despite all its orthodoxy was willing enough to overlook. What is significant about the elopement of Basantekumari with Dukhinarunjan is the attempt at marriage, which constituted an unambiguous ideological challenge to the established matrimonial order. Indeed, he prided himself on the fact that he had committed a threefold violation of this order by contracting 'a widow marriage, an inter-caste marriage and a civil marriage at the same time'.[24] It is, however, evident that he was only partially successful in this defiance. He lived with his new wife in distant Lucknow. Among his friends in the erstwhile Derozian circle, he lost Reverend Krishnamohan Banerjee, who disapproved of what he regarded as an immoral act.

The uncertainty of the position in this regard persuaded Jnanendramohun Tagore, who conceived the romantic desire to marry Reverend Krishnamohan Banerjee's daughter Kamalmani in 1851, to convert to Christianity before going through the rites. His father, the Hindu patriarch and zamindar Prasannakumar Tagore, disinherited him immediately, though he was his only son.[25] Even his uncle Debendranath Tagore, a less conservative man, wrote to his friend Rajnarayan Bose: 'It is difficult to find among men a more mercurial character than Jnanendra Babu.'[26] Jnanendramohan shifted to London where he taught Hindu law in the

[23]Manmatha Nath Ghosh, *Raja Dakshinaranjan Mukhopadhyay* (Reprint Calcutta, 1981), pp. 42–3.

[24]Ibid., p. 43.

[25]Purnendu Patri, *Gata Shataker Prem* (Calcutta, 1987), pp. 10–12.

[26]Letter from Debendranath Tagore to Rajnarayan Bose, 26 July 1851, in Debendranath Tagore, *Patravali* (Calcutta, 1988), vol. 1.

university as a full-fledged barrister. His unforgiving father refused to help him out when he fell into financial difficulty and would not even meet the two young grandsons whom his despairing son had sent home. But Jnanendramohan fought back, aided by British law, in claiming his inheritance after the death of his father.[27]

Despite the patriarchal attitude Debendranath Tagore displayed on this occasion, the matrimonial needs of the growing Brahmo community induced him soon afterwards to think aloud before his friend about the law regarding marriage and the need for abolishing caste.[28] The matter was settled by Act III of 1872, which provided for civil marriage by an individual willing to disown his or her community.

The reminiscences of Haimabati Sen show at work the process by which a reformed Brahmo marriage circle was formed out of the broader and more orthobox Hindu community. Her husband, a drunkard and whoremonger, died of abscess of liver and pneumonia in 1876.

She was no more than eleven years of age at the time. 'Shame on you, Hindu society, great is your glory,' she writes. 'I bow a thousand times at the feet of parents who would in this way turn a daughter's life into a desert.' Nowhere else, she adds, would one find such a society. 'Such oppression of women is possible only in India; in no other country are such customs in vogue.'[29] Fleeing from misfortune, she took refuge in the Brahmo community. Those were days when there was no public space for gentlewomen to wander abroad alone. The villagers caught her and handed her over to a watchman. Eventually she found shelter in a Brahmo household in east Bengal, and then travelled by railway and steamer to Calcutta to train as a doctor. This was a few years before Tagore's funeral oration in which the young poet noted how easier and safer public transport was enabling men to take their wives from the ancestral place to the place of work and how in consequence the rigid compartmentalization between home, that is the space reserved for women, and the public sphere, which had so long been limited by the absence of women, was breaking down.[30]

In her new social circle, Haimabati overheard the enunciation of a new doctrine of marriage: 'Among Brahmos, boys and girls marry according to their own choice when they are grown up. We do not go for arranged marriages.'[31]

She soon discovered to her cost that the matrimonial reform was far from complete even in the reformed circle. An old Hindu mother was thunderstruck when her son Satish (who was in the habit of moving in that circle) took it into his head to court her. Why should her son, a highly eligible Brahmin lawyer,

[27]Bipin Bihari Gupta, *Puratan Prasanga* (reprint Calcutta, 1989), pp. 294–5.

[28]Debendranath to Rajnarayan, 20 January 1854, *Patravali*, pp. 23–4.

[29]Geraldine Forbes and Tapan Raychaudhuri (eds), *The Memories of Dr Haimabati Sen: From Child Widow to Lady Doctor* (New Delhi, 2000), p. 98.

[30]Ibid., pp. 149–207; Tagore, 'Shoka-sabha'.

[31]Forbes and Raychaudhuri, *Memories of Dr Haimabati Sen*, p. 227.

marry a grown-up woman of 30 (actually Haimabati was only 23 in that year—1889), and a Kayastha and widow to boot? Satish Chakrabarti desired his mother's consent for the marriage. Hem, too, conceded, 'It is better to have the consent of a family and kinship group than to live the life of an outcaste.'[32] Angered by the mother's sexual insinuations about their 'courtsi' and 'court-fee',[33] Hem called off her engagement with Satish despite her growing affection for him. Even in the reformed circle, caste, widowhood, and the girl's age were formidable barriers which proved more powerful than the unspoken attachment. In accordance with the well-worn tradition of sublimation of interdicted erotic urges, she wrote to him, 'Our engagement has to be terminated, do forgive me .... You are the only child of your mother, the only source of her peace and happiness .... Please make sure your mother does not suffer again. If you ever think of Hem, please remember this request of hers.'[34]

Her alarmed guardians hurried her into a marriage with a Brahmo gentleman who had met her once or twice in the presence of a third party. Kunjabihari Sen, her second husband, lived on her income as a lady doctor and used to give her a beating whenever she would not do the household chores to his liking.[35] In her old age, once again a widow, she discovered that conditions had changed very much in the intervening period. The young generation of the 1920s consulted their own happiness and in her view they did not care for their parents. As an aged mother and mother-in-law, she lamented the fact that there were fewer joint families among educated people: 'I think of these developments in recent times as evil ways.'[36]

Social change was, at long last, catching up with colonial legislation. The important legislative acts passed under the Crown are the Indian Divorce Act of 1860 (to which only Christians had access initially), the Hindu Widow Remarriage Act of 1860, the Civil Marriage Act of 1872 (technically known as Act III of that year),[37] the Age of Consent Act of 1891, the Child Marriage Restraint Act of 1929 (popularly known as the Sarda Act), and the Dissolution of Muslim Marriages Act of 1939. These enactments slowly changed the sexual ground rules for those individuals—a growing number in the early twentieth century—who were willing to take recourse to the courts of law. This band of individuals used the law to make or break their marriages in ways not provided for by the customs of their communities. They would not have been able to do so but for the changed

[32]Ibid., p. 225.
[33]Ibid., p. 228.
[34]Ibid., pp. 232–3.
[35]Ibid., pp. 234, 347.
[36]Ibid., p. 267.
[37]It entitled Brahmos and others who contracted civil marriage to claim divorce under the Indian Divorce Act of 1860.

social atmosphere. Nationalist politics in its various manifestations aided the process. Revolutionary terrorism, the Non-Cooperation Movement, and the Indian National Army's war against the British changed the social atmosphere. These events and the emergence of women's organizations significantly expanded the public domain and increased the participation of women in that sphere. The 'scandals' and sensations in orthodox circles at this time are symptoms of the challenge posed by the individualistic women and men of the twentieth century: a visible assault on the existing matrimonial order and a bold attempt to realize a new sex-gender system.

The nineteenth century incidents recounted in the preceding paragraphs occurred mostly around prominent persons in society. In the 1920s, commoners entered the picture, and isolated instances of defiance coalesced into a consolidated challenge to patriarchy setting off alarmed reactions from deep within orthodox circles. Court decisions, which mostly moved in the liberal direction in the interpretation of 'Hindoo' and 'Anglo-Muhammadan' law, substantially aided colonial legislation and nationalist and early feminist politics in fostering the challenge.[38] Legislation was still very incomplete. Christians and Brahmos had access to the legal opportunity of divorce, but not Hindu women trapped in brutal marriages. Muslim women, too, found the law of divorce in Islam heavily weighted against them.[39] It is not until the Hindu Code Bill came up in independent India that we find a step being taken to offer individuals belonging to the larger community an opportunity to exercise their will in this vital aspect of life.

The large number of inter-caste, inter-communal, interprovincial, and interracial marriages that occurred in the late colonial period, and which so alarmed orthodox circles in every community, would not have been possible but for one new development. This was the fact that the young women and men, though they came from very differently constituted communities, yet somehow belonged to the same sort of society. After all, sexual intercourse, which would necessarily follow upon marriage, requires a certain physical and social acceptability. The English-educated middle class to which they belonged shared a common appearance, a common lifestyle, and common social values. Without this they could not have entered into such personal and intimate relationships. They belonged, in fact, to a community of their own, a single new community cutting across all provinces and all communities. The transition from the old love to the new love involved a

---

[38]For these broad changes, see Geraldine Forbes, *The New Cambridge History of India IV. 2: Women in Modern Indian Struggle* (New Delhi, 1990); Barbara Southward, *The Women's Movement and Colonial Politics in Bengal: The Quest for Political Rights, Education and Social Reform Legislation (1921–1936)* (New Delhi, 1995); Janaki Nair, *Women and Law in Colonial India: A Social History* (New Delhi, 1996).

[39]Rokeya Sakhawat Hossein, 'Narir adhikar', in *Rokeya Rachanavali*, ed. by Abdul Kadir (Dacca, 1873), p. 314.

transition from non-consensual marriage to consensual marriage, from communal-cellular society to civil society, from hierarchical patriarchy to individualistic and voluntary sociality, and from syncretism to secularism. The process shook up the very foundations of the existing society. No wonder there was a scandalized outcry. The objections were wide-ranging and included complaints of sect, community, caste, religion, language, province, race, consanguinity, and parental right. Above all, there was a rooted objection to love between a grown-up maiden and a young man. For this in itself constituted and still constitutes the most fundamental threat to the forms of patriarchy prevalent in the subcontinent.

The Sarda Act of 1929 provided the immediate context for these controversies. The reaction was particularly sharp in Bengal. J.C. Bhattacharya, who described himself as a Congress worker, published a book in English criticizing the liberal members of his organization who had supported the bill. Entitled *Mysteries of Married Life*, it recounted the 'misdeeds' of courting couples in Bengal and other provinces, and was in effect a book of scandals, though ostensibly a social tract written in defence of child marriage.[40] This was followed by yet another book of scandals, written in Bengali by a person who took the feminine pen name Shailasuta Devi. In size and salacious detail, it surpassed Bhattacharya's English tract.

Parinaye Pragati[41] (Progress in Marriage), written by this unreservedly conservative Bengali writer, boldly ventures to give an exhaustive list of what s/he describes as examples of 'love for free' (*bina mylye prem*). The writer sports the unusual name of Shailasuta Devi, but no one can mistake him for a woman. In his strident criticism of consensual marriages and his heaping of ignominy on females who stray out of their community to ensnare unsuspecting males of a different background, he betrays his patriarchal male identity. He records no less than forty-nine marriages, all of them consensual and all in some way or other violating existing marital codes. Though the 'love marriage system of the Anglophile Bengali society' is the special object of his attention, he casts his net wide and incorporates entanglements that occurred elsewhere. The characters in this panorama are real persons, some of them eminent men and women from society's creamy layer, others of no distinction at all save their marital and sexual 'lapses'. Daughters and wives of eminent barristers, landlords, social reformers, and occasionally an actress or a princess, vie with nurses, rustic Vaishnavis, and even a lowly Kaivarta damsel, to make or break marriages by dubious legal means. The male characters are no less colourful: eminent politicians, society leaders,

---

[40]J.C. Bhattacharya, *Mysteries of Married Life* (Mymensingh and Calcutta, n.d.), vol. 1. The internal evidence makes it clear that the book was published in 1930.

[41]Shailasuta Devi, *Parinaye Pragati* (Calcutta, n.d.), vol. 1, The Bengal Book Agency, no. 2, College Square (East), published by R. Chakravarthy, Mymensingh, prefaces by Shri Shailasuta Devi, Bhawanipur, Calcutta; vol. 2, revised 2nd edn (Calcutta, n.d.), Oriental Agency, 18, Shama Charan De Street, published by R. Chakravarthy, 90, Harrison Road, Calcutta.

journalists, zamindars, ministers-to-be rub shoulders with commoners from all walks of life—clerks, tradesmen, small-time professionals, and so on.

The writer of the book of scandals is sharply critical of the liberated females who invade other communities in search of prized catches as husbands. The reaction is part of that process which by then is transforming the cells in the beehive into warring blocs in the public arena. The book lists twenty-one women married into other castes. The list includes a low-caste Kaivarta girl who married one Professor Sushil Chandra Maitra, a Kulin Brahmin of high standing. The author also recounts how Bina Chattopadhyay, a widow, 'got hold' of the renowned painter Mukul Dey, and proceeds to narrate how Nagendranath Ganguly, the separated husband of Rabindranath Tagore's youngest daughter Mira Devi, found consolation in the divorced woman Maya Ray. A typical instance of inter-caste marriage is that of Jyotsna Mitra, who belonged to the Kayastha caste, and journalist and freedom fighter Gopal Sanyal, of Brahmin caste. Among these inter-caste marriages, there are two widow marriages, three instances of women's bigamy, and one remarriage of a lady who was a divorcee. By far the most sensational marriage is a bigamous one: Mrs Sisirkana Mukherjee simply walked out of her husband Jogesh Chandra Mukherjee's home to marry his friend Bhabatosh Sen, a much-married merchant, according to 'Arya Samaj rituals'. Mrs Mukherjee was a Brahmin, her second husband was not. In a reversal of these caste roles, Bina Ray, not a Brahmin, married Nripendra Krishna Chattopadhyay, a Brahmin, and at that time a Professor at Banaras Hindu University.

There was some overlap of caste and communal categories in the long list assiduously assembled by 'Shailasuta Devi'. Sita Chatterjee, daughter of eminent Brahmo leader and publisher Ramananda Chatterjee, and herself a novelist of no mean repute, received a proposal of marriage from Sudhir Chaudhuri, budding writer and staff member of Ramananda Chatterjee's famous monthly magazine, *Prabasi*. Despite the fact that Chaudhuri was a Hindu belonging to a lower caste, his employer, the father of the bride, consented to the match after some reflection. This was a cross-caste, cross-community marriage between a Brahmo lady of Brahmin origin and a Hindu gentleman of Kayastha caste.

In all, *Parinaye Pragati* featured eleven intercommunity marriages. The list reads like a veritable who's who, and may be broken down into the following categories: (1) two Hindu–Muslim marriages, that is, Ashalata Sen and Kazi Nazrul Islam, and Aruna Ganguly and Asaf Ali; (2) one Brahmo–Muslim marriage, namely Shanti Das and Humayun Kabir; (3) five Hindu–Brahmo marriages, the most celebrated being the widowed Rani of Paikpara Mrinalini Sinha's marriage with Brahmo leader Keshab Chandra Sen's second son Nirmal Chandra Sen, and that of the divorced Nirupama Devi, princess of Cooch Behar, with noted poet Sisir Sen; and (4) three Hindu–Christian marriages. These marriages, it need hardly be said, provoked severe opposition and drew caustic comments from the author, demurely posing as an artless progressive. What he, in fact, represents is the communalization of the public sphere, which, too, is a new development.

'Shailasuta Devi' did not stop there. Casting his dragnet further than Bengal, he went on to record a few interprovincial and interracial marriages too. Among the four interprovincial marriages, one, namely that of Hasan Ara Aziz (a Bengali Muslim girl) and the banker Lala Harkishan Lal's son Kanai Lal Gauba (Punjabi Hindu), was an inter-community marriage at the same time. Another notable interprovincial and intercommunity marriage was that of dedicated social worker Malati Sen (a Brahmo-Baidya girl studying in Rabindranath's Santiniketan) and her Hindu fellow student Nabakrushna Chowdhury (leading freedom fighter and later Chief Minister of Orissa).

The book records four interracial marriages, serving with mordant delight the following highly newsworthy items: (1) the marriages of the Cooch Behar princesses Sudhira Devi and Pratibha Devi with two English stage-actor brothers Henry and John Mander; (2) the marriage of Alexander Benoit (a French academic in Santiniketan) and his student Sudha Chattopadhyay; (3) 'Maitland' (ICS) marrying a Lalita Ray. The tongue-in-cheek presentation is interspersed with crocodile tears shed in apparent sympathy with the persecuted progressives; but occasionally the author breaks out in righteous wrath against them. It becomes clear from the tone that this author could not have been a woman.

Behind the ironical pleasure and lurking anxiety, there lay an acute awareness of rapid social change in the 1920s and 1930s. As new public spaces emerged, individuals sought the help of laws to make or break their marriages. Some of these laws emerged out of court rulings or social reforms, a few were bolstered by colonial legislation, and a few others, such as the Vishuddha Siddhanta and Arya Samaj marriage laws, were of uncertain legal validity.

The beehive was crumbling. Nowhere was this more evident than in the breakdown of marriages originally contracted within the proper cells. The law helped individuals break out of their native marital cells, enabling them to exert their will in matters of sexual choice, and to contract new conjugal liaisons that cut across caste, community, province, and race. The reaction to this was the emergence of hostility in the public sphere.

 Parinaye Pragati recounts three sensational divorce cases. In each case it is the wife who seeks divorce. Lilian Palit-Mullick and Romola Sinha-Gupta had no legal means to obtain a divorce, but each created a situation that induced the husband to initiate the divorce proceedings in order to preserve his self-esteem. Lilian, daughter of well known lawyer and philanthropist Taraknath Palit, and Romola, daughter of Lord Satyendra Prasanna Sinha, were both Brahmo ladies of high social standing. After obtaining divorce, Romola married Bhagalpur zamindar and Congressman Deep Narayan Singh, and Romola for her part married Serampore zamindar and Congressman Tulsi Gossain. The third lady, a rank commoner named

Padmasana Ghosh, was a Hindu woman who had no means of obtaining divorce from her oppressive husband, so she converted to Islam and thereby obtained dissolution of her unwanted marriage.

While commenting on Lilian Mallik's sensational divorce case, Shailasuta Devi made the caustic remark: 'Christian, Brahmo, England-returned and progressive females are not socially diminished by illicit love affairs, divorce cases, etc.' J.C. Bhattacharya, the 'Congress worker' who wrote the English tract against the Sarda Act, shared this point of view. The Sarda Act, he feared, would promote free mixing, and free mixing, to his way of thinking, was bad. Quoting extensively from the proceedings of the divorce case of

the Right Hon'ble Romola Gupta, daughter of the late Lord Sinha of Raipur, and daughter-in-law of Col. K.P. Gupta, and [wife of] Mr N.N. Gupta, Municipal Magistrate, on account of Mr T.C. Gossain, M.L.A., Bar-at-Law, Zamindar and a National Leader being one of the big fives [sic] of the Swarajist Group of Bengal,

the author dwelt on certain new social features he disapproved: freedom of women, unrestrained upbringing, and lavish lifestyle among the elite, and above all the Child Marriage Restraint Act of 1929. All these, he said, produced the love affairs that were proliferating in contemporary India.[42]

The *Mysteries of Married Life* and *Parinaye Pragati* provide salacious but not very reliable details of love marriages in Bengal and elsewhere until the beginning of the 1930s. The two tracts do not, of course, reflect the point of view of the lovers themselves. More accurate accounts of the love affairs, and occasional glimpses of the point of view of the lovers, may be obtained from court records relating to divorce. The published law reports of the high courts turn upon technical points of law relating to marriage and divorce, but they sometimes contain interesting and reliable facts. The unpublished court records, especially the plaints for divorce, contain statements by the parties involved, and are more valuable. Occasionally, letters are reproduced in the plaints, and from them an idea may be formed about the feelings and notions of the persons involved. As individuals who took recourse to law in these matters are the very persons who represented the nascent civil society of India, the sentiments that moved them are of interest to the social historian.

The court records relating to the divorce of Lilian and Sisir Mullick, with Deep Narayan Singh as co-respondent, are a case in point. Sisir Mullick's plaint contains details, including self-revelations of the parties concerned, that are not to be found in the prejudiced account given in *Parinaye Pragati*, which refers to it as 'perhaps the first case of divorce among the Bengalis'.[43] English education,

---

[42]Bhattacharya, *Mysteries of Married Life*, vol. 1, p. 7.

[43]Shailasuta Devi, *Parinaye Pragati*, vol. 1, p. 213.

wealth, altered ideas of life, and a new self-assurance produced the following letter from Lilian Mullick (nee Palit) to her husband Sisir, on the basis of which the latter presented his petition for divorce in the High Court of Calcutta in 1913.[44]

> Prince of Wales Hotel
> Harrogate
> June 20th, 1912

Dear Sisir,

I am willing to let you know that I do not intend to return to India .... I have taken the course which although not warranted by society or convention—yet seems to me the only right one to take, and I have openly joined my life with Deep's .... I bitterly regret all the unhappiness you have experienced through me—but you know I strove my best and it is only when I found it absolutely impossible to bring you happiness I feel justified in taking my own. I have dropped the name of Mullick and taken that of Singh. If you take a divorce we shall take steps to legalise our union—if you refuse to do so our union remains as it is.

Mrs D.N. Singh
C/o. either Grindlay's or Cook's
(London)

Had Lilian Mullick been born earlier and in the older legal and social context, she would not have been able to write the above letter and sign herself Mrs D.N. Singh. She would have ceased to be a gentlewoman and would have become the mistress of a rich landlord. As it is, her life took a different course. The only daughter of eminent lawyer and philanthropist Sir Taraknath Palit, she was rich and accomplished. Her brother was Rabindranath Tagore's friend Lokendranath Palit, ICS, and her husband a rising barrister in the High Court of Calcutta, and a junior to the legendary lawyer W.C. Bonnerjee. Born in England in 1879, she had received, according to her husband's petition for divorce, 'various academic honours and distinctions both in England and from Calcutta University'.[45]

Her family belonged to the progressive circles of society, and it is a legal fact of vital importance that her marriage with Sisir Kumar Mullick on 6 October 1902 was contracted under Act III of 1872, which automatically entitled the couple to take recourse to the Indian Divorce Act if the need arose. It was a consensual marriage witnessed by Sir Satyendranath Tagore, ICS, and Lokendranath Palit, Zilla and Sessions Judge, and the bride's brother. A son, named Ajit Kumar Mullick, was born to them on 7 March 1907. Apparently the marriage was going all right. But fate (this can also be read as individual will) decreed otherwise.

[44]The letter is reproduced in the Petition by Sisir Mullick asking for divorce in the Court of the Honourable Judge Jenkins, Calcutta High Court, dated 4 September 1913. See Suit No. 22, 1913, High Court of Judicature, Matrimonial, Calcutta.

[45]Plaint dated 4 September 1913, Suit no. 22 of 1913.

Lilian made her first acquaintance with Deep Narain Singh in England. He was her husband's schoolmate and a friend of her brother. A barrister-at-law and a wealthy zamindar of the district of Bhagalpur, he was, at the time when the drama unfolded, a member of the Legislative Council of the Lieutenant-Governor of Bengal. Though married to a lady from his own community, Ramanandi Devi, and the father of a daughter, Prabhavati, he pressed his suit with the gifted and vivacious Mrs Mullick in England. She for her part was attracted to the eminent public figure from Bihar, a man of higher social standing than her staid, unambitious husband who lived in the house gifted to her by her father, Sir Taraknath Palit.

The incidents leading to the institution of an adultery charge against Lilian Mullick as respondent and Deep Narain Singh as co-respondent can be pieced together from Sisir Mullick's statement in the witness stand on 31 August 1914[46] and his earlier plaint submitted to the High Court of Judicature (Matrimonial Jurisdiction).[47] Sisir Mullick charged that he had previously taken objection to 'her conduct with Deep' and he forbade her to have any communication with the latter. 'Upon hearing scandal,' he said, 'I remonstrated with her in April 1912. She promised not to have any communication with him. She did not admit any impropriety.' Mullick added, 'Deep and she were very intimate friends. They knew each other for a long time. I had no suspicion.'

After this, Lilian left for England on 14 May 1912 'on the alleged ground that she required the change on account of the state of her health'. Shortly afterwards, she wrote him the letter of 20 June quoted earlier. In his petition, Sisir charged that

on different occasions between the 12th and 16th June 1912 in the Hotel Cecil in the Strand London W.C. and in the month of September 1912 and thence forward until about the end of the same year 1912 at No. 185 Clearance Gate Gardens Baker Street London and from about the beginning of present year 1913 up to the time of the institution of this suit at No. 38 Hanover Gate Mansions Regents Park London N.W. ... including various places in Norway where the Respondent and Co-Respondent have during the summer of the present year 1913 made a tour together travelling and living and cohabiting together as man and wife the Respondent has committed adultery with the Co-Respondent.

Evidently, after 20 June when Lilian wrote that fateful letter announcing the termination of her marriage with Sisir, the latter painstakingly collected proof of her infidelity so that he could institute divorce proceedings on 4 September 1913, creating a sensation in the highest circles of Calcutta society and inflicting tragedy on the aged Taraknath Palit who was still alive. Neither Lilian nor Deep Narain contested the suit. A close friend of the Palits, the Honourable Justice

[46]Sisir Mullick's statement as a witness in the Court of Justice A. Chaudhuri, Suit No. 22 of 1913.

[47]Plaint dated 4 September 1913, Suit no. 22 of 1913.

Ashutosh Chaudhuri, presided over the matter. Manik Rustomji Mehta, a common friend of Lilian and Sisir and himself a barrister, gave evidence for the prosecution that Lilian and Deep had been living as man and wife and that she was passing as Mrs Singh in London.[48] The marriage was terminated on 31 August 1914.

Meanwhile, an out-of-court settlement had been arrived at between the petitioner and the respondent and co-respondent. Lilian had already made it clear in her letter of 20 June 1912 that she would not fight for the custody of the 7-year-old son Ajit Kumar. Sisir, for his part, gave up the claim of Rs 150,000 as damages to be paid by Deep. Lilian was made to gift her house, No. 40 Ballygunge Circular Road, to Ajit in a deed and Deep was made to assign sufficient property yielding a net annual income of £400 in Lilian's name. Sisir stated in a gesture of concern that he wanted 'to see the lady well provided for in spite of her failing so that she may not be stranded'.[49] Lilian thereafter married Deep in London, and became a British citizen. They returned to Bhagalpur in the latter half of the 1920s.[50]

Not every unhappy wife was as fortunate as Lilian Palit. The Hindu wife, however ill-treated, had no prospect of divorce. What could she do in this situation? We have referred to the sensational case of Padmasana Ghosh Majumdar above. There was no legal scope for Padmasana, a Hindu lady, unlike the Brahmo Lilian, to get herself a divorce. So in 1929 Padmasana converted to Islam and applied for a divorce of nullity of marriage. She had duly given notice to her husband Bireshwar Ghosh Majumdar to convert to Islam and his refusal as expected provided her with the grounds. Justice Panckridge satisfied himself that the conversion of Padmasana Ghosh was bona fide, and granted her a decree annulling marriage under the authority of the *Hedaya* and the procedure mentioned therein for a Muslim convert annulling a marriage with an unbeliever. *Parinaye Pragati* implied sarcastically that Ayesha Bibi (as Padmasana Ghosh renamed herself) could now go forward, single and liberated, to capture young male hearts.[51] Conservative Hindu legal opinion expressed dissatisfaction with the judgement in terms of bitter irony: 'The Mahomedan Law ... seems just at present to be in great demand for dissolution of Hindu marriages.'[52] The rule of law and the emergence of the

---

[48]Statement of Manik Rustomji Mehta as witness in favour of the Appellant Sisir Mullick in the Court of the Honourable Justice A. Chaudhuri, 31 August 1914, Suit no. 22 of 1913.

[49]Sisir Mullick's statement as witness, 31 August 1914, Calcutta High Court, Suit no. 22 of 1913.

[50]Chitragupta, 'Uttradhikar niye ekti jatil mamla', *Ajkal* (newspaper) (3 January 1988).

[51]Shailasuta Devi, *Parinaye Pragati*, vol. 1, pp. 210–12.

[52]N.L. Sengupta, reporting in *Calcutta Law Journal*, 50, Reports of cases (July–December 1929), pp. 40n–44n. Sengupta spoke a truer word than he believed. Other hapless Hindu wives from common ranks followed in the train of Padmasana Ghosh. In 1945, a 20-year-old Ayesha Bibi alias Atreyi Chakraborty (before her conversion to Islam) obtained dissolution of her unhappy marriage with Subodh Chakraborty in the same manner. Ramen Gupta, 'Panchash bachhar aage: Swamir atyachar theke mukta hoyechhila Atreyi', *Vartaman* (newspaper) (19 August 1995).

public sphere thus stimulated both the growth of a civil society and the articulation of communal blocs in modern India.

Four years later we come across a no less sensational resort to the court of law by an unhappy wife in order to remould her life in defiance of the community. Here again a Hindu wife converted to Islam to effect a release from her otherwise indissoluble tie with the husband. She then reconverted to Hinduism and married again, this time under civil law. Married to one Haripada Ray since 1918, she had three children by him. To escape from a bitter and unhappy marriage, she went to Calcutta, educated herself in Saroj Nalini High School and took up a job as a schoolmistress in Puri in 1933. On 17 May 1933 she converted to Islam and in September obtained a dissolution of the marriage in a civil court. The husband did not contest the suit. Thereupon she entered the Arya Samaj, and on 13 December 1933 she was reconverted to Hinduism by the Hindu Mission. On that very day she married her lover Krishna Benoda Ray under Act III of 1872, amended by Act 30 of 1923. In February 1934 the former husband commenced a legal suit for restitution of conjugal rights because after her reconversion to Hinduism he deemed his rights to have revived. The judicial decision that finally emerged after years of contention was that the first marriage stood dissolved for all time to come. The lady and her new husband were paid all costs and allowed to continue in their new-found conjugal happiness, but not before a massive legal wrangle that raged from 1933 to 1939.[53] In a series of bold moves, the lady turned religion into the very weapon by which to secure her personal freedom in a court of law.

The picture that emerges from these divorce proceedings in the courts of law is one of determined individual initiatives against heavy odds. The lovers twisted this way and that way to effect the union they desired. Colonial law provided but narrow loopholes for escape through the formidable barriers of custom. Sometimes, but not always, they cleared out a path through the difficulties that faced them. Divorce and consensual marriage were part of the same social process and both expressed free will. A civil society was in the offing.

IV

From the 1920s onwards, the opening up of the public sphere to women and their participation in the freedom struggle transformed the lives of many women, a process reflected in the marital histories of famous and not so famous personalities of the time. The lives of Sucheta Kripalani, Kamaladevi Chattopadhyay, and Lakshmi Sahgal are illustrative instances. All three married outside the community they were born into.

Sucheta, daughter of a Bengali medical officer of the Punjab government,

[53] AIR, Calcutta, 430.

had a paternal grandfather who belonged to the old Brahmo Samaj, and was brought up in a liberal household. She was convent educated and, in order to support her family after her father's death, she started teaching at the Banaras Hindu University. She came to know Acharya Kripalani through her cousin Dhiren Majumdar who was Kripalani's comrade-in-arms. They came close to each other during a tour with Father Elwyn in 1934.

'From that time, he and I used to correspond with each other, and whenever he came to Banaras he met us. Well, we fell in love with each other but we thought it was not possible to marry, because Kripalani's life was dedicated to the country, and Gandhiji was very much opposed to his marriage.' The ambience within Gandhi's inner circle was hardly conducive to a love relationship. She turned down Jamnalal Bajaj's invitation to her to become Principal of Wardha Mahila Ashram when she discovered that Vinoba Bhave was undergoing a fast of penance because a young man and a young woman had fallen in love with each other. 'These things rather frightened me. The atmosphere there was too puritanic, too rigid.' However, Sucheta rode down Gandhiji's objections on this issue, and after two years' intense emotional stress she married Kriplani in 1936.[54]

Kamaladevi shared the same modern upbringing as Sucheta. A syncretic, liberal atmosphere prevailed in the mixed circle of her comfortable, upper-middle-class home in Mangalore. Her grandmother presided over a literary circle of sagacious looking gentlemen. Her mother played several instruments and was versed in Hindustani, Carnatic, and Western music. She gave Kamala a good education and taught her to read and write in two languages outside her mother tongue. In the open Konkanese society of Mangalore, girls could act in plays staged by Margaret Cousins. The mother gave Kamala the space to act in plays, participate in sports and dance, and to go beyond existing social conventions. She sent her to England and did not object to her involvement in the civil disobedience movement. Kamala's passion was the theatre. It was there that she found her mate. In Berlin she met the Bengali revolutionary Virendranath Chattopadhyay, whose poet-musician brother Harindranath teamed up with her 'for sharing of dreams and ambitions to devote ourselves to create a new theatre in India'. As Harindranath, Kamaladevi, and a troupe of artists, both men and women, moved from place to place staging plays and carrying on a 'crusade' for effecting 'a renaissance of the stage', the professional team spirit was transformed into a more personal and intimate one.[55] Her marriage was part of the transition of a syncretic coastal society into a secular civil society.

We would like to conclude this series of self-made marriages with the life and times of Lakshmi Swaminadhan (later Sahgal). She symbolized a new

---

[54]'But I will not give my blessing but will pray for you,' was Gandhiji's decision on the issue. Oral History Transcript no. 206, testimony of Sucheta Kripalani, 29 January 1968, Nehru Memorial Museum and Library, New Delhi (henceforth NMML).

[55]Kamaladevi Chattopadhyay, *Inner Recesses, Outer Spaces* (New Delhi, 1986).

individualistic ideology of life and love that would overcome all obstacles. Born to a Western-educated Madras Brahmin barrister named Subharama Swaminadhan and a Keralite Nair socialite and freedom fighter named Ammakutty Menon, Lakshmi inherited her father's intelligence and her mother's boldness. Ammakutty Menon, who spoke English, played tennis, and rode horses with equal ease, is remembered by her other daughter Mrinalini Sarabhai as the queen of Madras society in her time. Ammakutty inherited her mother A.V. Ammu Amma's courage: this grandmother had dealt with marauding Mopla insurgents single-handedly. A social news column relating to her progeny gives a fascinating rundown of four generations of determined women who spoke for themselves:. Ammu Amma's daughter, Ammu—a Swadeshi and women's activist, member of the Constituent Assembly, and MP for fifteen years; her elder daughter, Lakshmi Sahgal: Netaji Subhas Chandra Bose's second-in-command and women's activist, and gynaecologist; her sister Mrinalini Sarabhai: danseuse, teacher, and human rights activist; Mrinalini's daughter Malika: dancer, publisher, and, again, activist; Sahgal's daughter, Subhashni Ali: CPI (M) leader, former MP and trade union activist; Ammu's granddaughter by her son, Srilatha Swaminadhan: CPI (ML) wholetimer.[56]

While the two sons of Ammakutty and S. Swaminadhan subserviently allowed the parents to make academic and career choices for them, the daughters inherited the resolute Menon streak and chose their individual careers and husbands. Lakshmi opted for medicine and, against her father's wishes, decided to study in Madras instead of going to England. Mrinalini Swaminadhan finished her schooling in Switzerland but, as resolutely as her elder sister and at an even earlier age made up her mind, much to the consternation of her sophisticated and elitist mother, that dance was her calling. She went off to train in Tagore's University at Santiniketan, and mastered classical dance. She met and married the physicist Vikram Sarabhai, son of Gujarati industrialist and Gandhian Ambalal Sarabhai, and with his aid set up the dancing academy on which she had set her heart.

But it was Lakhsmi Swimandhan above all who displayed the characteristic individual initiative in remoulding her personal life. She became the denizen of a brave new world that suddenly opened up against the backdrop of the World War II and the ongoing freedom struggle. The 1930s saw her enter college and then get into an unwise marriage. In 1936 she married B.K.N. Rao, a pilot with Tata Airlines. In her memoirs she writes:

It was an unfortunate choice on my part as, temperamentally, we were not suited to each other. Being self-willed and obstinate I was not prepared to subdue my personality and play the role of a good wife. We parted within six months of our marriage but got divorced only in 1946, after my return from Burma.[57]

[56]Sona Thakur and Bisakha De Sarkar, 'Family pride', *The Telegraph* (14 June 1998).

[57]Lakshmi Sahgal, *A Revolutionary Life: Memoirs of a Political Activist* (New Delhi, 1997), pp. 8–9.

Her life in Madras was at a dead end. Upon parting from her husband, she qualified for the MBBS degree of Madras Medical College. She practised in a hospital for a year, then she left for Singapore in June 1940. She explains the decision in her autobiography thus: 'My reasons for going were, first, to be free of a marriage that was causing embarrassment to my family, and also to join a college mate who had already gone to Singapore and started his practice.'[58] Her friend from college days told her that she would do very well as there was a large south Indian community in Singapore that would welcome a woman doctor. She responded favourably to the offer: 'I also felt I would have greater scope for standing on my own without constant familial pressure.' This is what she wrote in 'her autobiography in its original form' in the late 1960s.[59] The version of her departure that she gave to Peter Ward Fay in the 1980s is less reticent:

I stayed with him (her husband) in Bombay for six months but we didn't get on at all, so I came back to Madras and finished my studies. Meanwhile I fell in love with a classfellow of mine who was a year senior to me. But my husband refused to give me a divorce.[60]

This made Lakshmi restless. Her mother and sister had left on a world tour in 1939. Her classfellow (whom she calls 'K' in Peter Fay's book) had gone off to practise in Singapore. In the version of her life that she gave Fay, 'She followed him there.' In her autobiography which was written earlier, there is a more guarded version of her intention: 'My maternal uncle's son and his wife lived in Singapore, so I set out to visit them keeping my options open.' Still later she told two journalists who interviewed her in June 1998 that she had moved to Singapore to live with a man she was involved with.

From June 1940, when she arrived in Singapore, to July 1943, when she joined the Indian National Army under Subhas Chandra Bose, Lakshmi and 'K' practised together from their clinic on Geylang Road, on the east coast of Singapore. In her autobiography she hardly refers to the kind of personal association she had with 'K', whom she simply refers to as 'my colleague'. But from the story she narrates to Peter Fay about these turbulent times, we are able to reconstruct the social aspect of the relationship. Till the fall of Singapore on 15 February 1942, they did not live in the same house. Though the journalists Thakur and De Sarkar would have us believe (or maybe they got the impression) that they lived together, it is apparent from Fay's narrative that Lakshmi lived with her first cousin Kutty and his wife Padmini. In so far as their professional life is concerned, 'he did the

---

[58]Ibid., p. 9

[59]Ibid.

[60]Peter Ward Fay, *The Forgotten Army: India's Armed Struggle for Independence 1942–1945* (Delhi, 1994), p. 43. In an interview to Shri S.L. Manchanda in Kanpur on 17 November 1973, Lakshmi Sahgal carefully avoided a personal reason for going to Singapore. She said, 'When I went to Singapore in 1940, I had no idea of settling there. I had gone on a visit to see some of my relatives ... and intended to come back.' Oral History transcript no. 277, NMML.

general side, and I did the gynecology and obstetrics.'[61] Apart from the local Chinese and Malays, they treated many Indians, mostly from Madras and Kerala. The practice flourished. By the end of 1940, she and 'K' almost finished paying the instalments on their little Morris car. Ammu and Lakshmi's younger sister Mrinalini passed through Singapore in the autumn of 1940. Mrinalini Sarabhai told Fay that their clinic was doing well. 'Lakshmi and "K" had plenty of patients who could pay.'[62]

In the professional, impersonal world of Singapore in the 1940s, not many bothered about the personal relationship between the two. Though Lakshmi found Singapore totally without character, a city whose god was money,[63] its generally modern air and bustling activity gave them a certain degree of anomymity and personal space, something they would not have had in Madras. Socially they mixed mostly in the large Indian business and professional community, most of whose members were Gujaratis, Parsees, Marwaris, and an assortment of Chettiars and other south Indians. They went about freely in this society, called on mutual friends, closed the clinic on Sunday noons, picked up a friend to go swimming, and watched movies in the evening.

Around this time, someone from quite close quarters observed them circulating in society and found it worthwhile to write two pages privately on their association. Subimal Dutt, an ICS officer posted in Singapore at the time, writes in his personal diary about a particular evening when he saw Lakshmi and 'K' together.[64] He, however, gives 'K' the name of 'Dr Abraham' [Dr Ibrahim] on the day he first wrote about him:

In the evening Guha hosted a buffet party for Ram Rao. There were about fifty to sixty guests present. There was plenty of food though no lady had supervised the arrangements. A few ladies however came from Mamaji's house. All of them were good-looking. Rama Rao came with Dr Abraham and Dr Lakshmi. Singapore society has accepted the couple as husband and wife. They move together, are invited together—though they live in separate houses.[65]

He first saw them in K.P.K. Menon's house where he had been invited for a tea party. Later on he records his first impressions of Lakshmi and narrates a significant detail about her personal life:

I saw a good-looking lady at Menon's party. Thought she was Menon's daughter. Dr Ibrahim was there at the party. He is a young doctor who has arrived recently to set up a [medical]

---

[61]Fay, *The Forgotten Army*, p. 14.

[62]Ibid., p. 45.

[63]Sahgal, *A Revolutionary Life*, p. 15.

[64]Unpublished diary of Subimal Dutt, ICS, written mainly in Bengali, mixed with English on occasion. The entries on Dr Ibrahim and Dr Lakshmi are dated 27 May 1941 and 17 August 1941. Both entries are in Bengali, which we have translated into English. We are grateful to Supriya Guha, whose maternal uncle Subimal Dutt was, for use of the diary.

[65]Ibid., entry dated 27 May 1941.

practice. I later on came to know that the two are lovers. The lady is married—a doctor by profession. Met Ibrahim in the Madras Medical College and fell in love with him. She could not give up that love and therefore left her husband's home.[66] She has come all the way to Malaya to gain Ibrahim's company. But the husband will not give up so easily. So the chance of marrying Ibrahim is very remote.[67]

To a Bengali civil servant, however highly placed in the Westernized social circle, such an unconventional relationship was still uncomfortable. He records in his private diary: 'I really do feel constrained in their company.'[68] Yet if one looks through his eyes and seeks to visualize the Indian community in Singapore, one has to admit that on the whole it was a liberal non-judgmental society—a transplanted community that could not afford the luxury of imposing strict moral codes. Dr Ibrahim and Dr Lakshmi made up an efficient medical team, their own 'countrymen', whose services could be counted upon in a foreign land, with a raging World War that could be brought to their thresholds any day. One must also remember that the Indian National Army would be formed shortly out of the same society.

In December 1941, the Japanese attacked Malaya. As the War intensified and the evacuation of Singapore started, Lakshmi had to make up her mind whether she should leave or stay. The 'K' factor seems to have been decisive at this stage. 'Being able-bodied and a doctor, "K" would not be allowed out. So they all remained.'[69] As the War slowly advanced to their doors, they dug trenches, attended at an aid post, and kept their clinic open. In February 1942, they began treating the Singapore casualties. On 15 February, Singapore fell.

It is not clear whether Lakshmi continued to stay with her cousin or moved in with Dr Ibrahim at this point. But there is an indirect reference that in the spring of 1942, under Japanese occupation, they were living and working together. The Japanese were encouraging doctors to return to their work. She says at this point: 'We went back to our home in Katong. It was in a bad state, and we had to reopen our dispensary, so we were very, very busy.'[70]

And yet, unknown to herself, Lakshmi was inching towards a new phase in her professional and personal life. Prem Kumar Sahgal, a colonel in the British Army that had just surrendered to the Japanese, was at this point officer-in-charge of one of the POW camps in Singapore. In May 1942, he came to their dispensary looking for medical supplies, with a John Somasundaram in tow. Somasundaram's family had been well known to the Swaminadhan family back in Madras. As Lakshmi

[66]From Lakshmi Sahgal's autobiography, however, we learn that she left her first husband in 1936 and met her fellow student Ibrahim in Madras Medical College in 1938.

[67]Subimal Dutt's diary, entry dated 17 August 1941.

[68]Ibid.

[69]Fay, *The Forgotten Army*, p. 65.

[70]Ibid., p. 89.

recalls, 'One afternoon he and Prem came in an army lorry and John introduced Prem and said, "We've come from our camp and we have this transport here, we want medicines badly".' Ibrahim and Lakshmi let the two have some of the medical stores, and Lakshmi added a tin of jam.[71]

A new relationship would arise out of the turn of events in a world in turmoil, but not yet. The old relationship with 'K' survived till Lakshmi Swaminadhan met Subhas Chandra Bose in July 1943 and decided to honour his request that she should take his women's regiment in hand. He had an office ready. Her first task would be to recruit. She went back to the clinic and told 'K'. As she recalls, 'He took it very badly. He was convinced that after this we were finished.' She could see that he thought she would be so occupied with her new work that she would not have time for anything else. 'And that,' Lakshmi Sahgal later told Peter Fay, 'is what happened'.[72] This is the last glimpse we have of the mysterious 'K', or, to be more exact, Dr Ibrahim. A chapter in Lakshmi Swaminadhan's life came to an end as she plunged into the War in the jungles of Burma.

As she joined the War for the liberation of her distant home, the relationship with Prem Kumar Sahgal, now a major in the Indian National Army, developed from casual acquaintance to close comradeship. Even before this, as Prem debated within himself whether he should join the Indian National Army of Mohan Singh in the summer of 1942 (before Netaji's arrival), he had consulted her on the point. Lakshmi Swaminadhan knew she would join the War if she got a chance, but she had no chance then and she did not press her views upon her new friend. But Prem began to see a good deal of Lakshmi, usually with John Somasundaram, and they talked a good deal.[73] Even before she met Subhas Chandra Bose and left Dr Ibrahim for good, Prem Sahgal had gained her friendship and trust. And it is this relationship which would become her mainstay in life at the end of the War. When Dr Ibrahim and Dr Lakshmi finally parted, what kind of a wrench was it for either? The sources are silent on this.

There is no hint of how the relationship between Prem and Lakshmi developed during the years of jungle war. Between 1942 and 1945 he served as Bose's press attaché and she was the commander of the Rani of Jhansi regiment in Burma. They met off and on, but she is quite silent on the nature of the relationship in her autobiography. She got her divorce from Rao as soon as the INA trial began in Delhi. She was free to marry Prem now. The Tamil-Malayali doctor married the dismissed Punjabi soldier in March 1946. This was but the latest in a series of interprovincial marriages which had begun in the late nineteenth century with the rise of the Brahmo Samaj. Way back in 1877, a Bengali Brahmo youth named Madhusudan Sarkar had married the Punjabi Hindu girl Biswaba Devi of Lahore

[71]Ibid., p. 88.
[72]Ibid., p. 218.
[73]Ibid., p. 94.

according to Brahmo rites under Act III of 1872.[74] It would be the same Act which would come to Lakshmi's rescue and bring her the divorce she needed to marry Prem.

Her quest for romance, adventure, professional challenge, and unexplored avenues of life coalesced in the twin figures of Netaji Subhas Chandra Bose and Major Prem Kumar Sahgal. From her first husband Rao to her lover and true friend Ibrahim and onwards to her life-mate Sahgal, from the silken cocoon of Madras to Singapore and the Rani of Jhansi regiment and the jungles of Burma, Lakshmi Swaminadhan's marital, medical, and martial odyssey represents in miniature the epic of India's journey to a civil society.

V

What are the broad conclusions that emerge from this historical study of gender relations? What stands out is the profound transformation of the private sphere wrought by the transition from custom to law and from status to contract. Indian civilization is historically rooted in a cellular social formation which we have compared to the beehive. Ideologically and culturally its embodiment, as Rabindranath Tagore saw, was syncretism.[75] The close but inconclusive encounter between modernity and Indian civilization fostered an alternative to this. The alternative is known by the Western term secularism, which in its turn is rooted in a different type of social formation nowadays described as 'civil society'.

Syncretism and secularism represent alternative strategies of conflict resolution in Indian history, especially in matters relating to faith and sex. Syncretism recognizes that faith and sex belong properly to the community. Acceptance of marriage and religious practice as communal concerns coexists with love across the communities and imbibing of one another's religious practices. Secularism is an altogether different strategy for resolving conflicts: matters of faith and sex become 'private' and they belong properly to the individual and not to the community.

Behind this lies a new mental scheme: the rise of a value-laden public–private polarity, each with a recognized value of its own. Throughout the modern world, the new public sphere with the concomitant area of private concerns provided the framework of a civil society. In the Indian instance of modernity, however, the emergence of the public sphere was accompanied by the crumbling of the beehive formation and the polarization of 'communal' and 'national' blocs: anti-colonial nationalism expressed itself in the public sphere through Indian nationalism, Hindu nationalism, and Muslim nationalism. The civil space in which the individual could regulate his or her religious and sexual concerns was circumscribed by the

---

[74]Prabhatchandra Gangopadhyay, *Banglar Nari-Jagaran* (in Bengali, Calcutta, 1946), p. 84.

[75]'*Sthapan*' (establishing harmony amidst differences). '*Bharatiya Itihas*' (1902) in *Rabindra Rachnavali*, vol. 12, p. 1029.

polarization of hostile blocs and the public contentions about these very matters. In this historical process, private matters were at the same time communal, political, and national matters. The process was therefore characterized by sharp conflict. 'Communalism' of the new variety was the modern opposite of the old syncretism: that ideal way of living life amicably of which Ghalib speaks in a ghazal:[76]

> Ham muwahihad hain
> Hamara kesh hai tark e rusum
> Millaten jab mit gayin
> Ajza-e-iman ho gain
>
> Our creed is 'God is one'
> Our cry, 'Abandon rituals!'
> So that communities dissolve
> To constitute one faith.

But in India's modern transformation, communities did not dissolve: on the contrary, they mobilized as blocs in the public sphere and there was virulent opposition to inter-religious and inter-caste marriages. It is the emergence of the public sphere which in the first instance made those marriages possible, but that very process, which involved the entry of communities en bloc into this influential sphere, generated new obstacles, namely political, to such marriages. Before these things began to happen, there was nothing 'private', nor was there a 'public'; at least not in the sense of the new values with which these imported terms were loaded. Instead, there was 'seclusion' (khalwat), and there was its opposite, 'gathering' (majlis). In yet another ghazal, Ghalib says:

> Mere hone men hai kya rusvai?
> E who majlis nahin, khalvat hi sahi.[77]

'Why should my meeting you put you to shame? Alright, if not in the gathering, meet me in seclusion.'[78]

In so far as there was a public, the community itself represented it and constituted it; there was hardly any public outside the community, unless it might be the tavern, the coffee house, or the courtesan's salon. The introduction of the rule of law, which bound the colonial government and subjected all individuals to its power on terms of legal equality (thereby creating the individual qua individual), shaped the public sphere, a sphere lying beyond the communities and lineages in which men and women had so long been encapsulated. The process gave birth to civil law. At the time in question, the women of the subcontinent who belonged

---

[76]Trans. Russell.

[77]Ibid., p. 77.

[78]Russell translates the above verse thus: 'Why should my meeting you put you to shame? Alright, meet privately, not publicly.' Strictly, however, khalwat means seclusion, retirement, where there is no bar to carnal act. Majlis is gathering, assembly, concourse.

individuals who might no longer be subject to communal custom and patriarchal control, and might indeed assert their right to a private sphere.

We have seen that the old syncretic society spoke for love across the communities. This was an ideal of spiritual and not marital love. Syncretism did not advocate marriage beyond the communal circle. Though a high spiritual value was accorded to such love, there was no provision here for the earthly and sexual happiness of the individual. Accepting the communal framework of society, syncretism spiritualized extra-communal erotic love and articulated the concept of harmony-in-pathos.

The ascent of civil society in colonial India was based upon the earthly individual and not the spiritual self. The members of that society were bolder in their search for happiness here and now. The tentative manifestation of civil society brought with it new questions, reflecting a troubled sense of the dilemma posed by the good of the community and the happiness of the individual. Subimal Dutt, who was mentally troubled by the affair of Dr Ibrahim and Dr Lakshmi in Singapore, wrote secretly in his diary on 17 August 1941.[79]

But who am I to judge? How long can society survive, ignoring the calls of the human heart (*manusher hridayer anvan*)? But then who will reconcile the demands of society (*samajer dabi*) and the demands of the heart (*hridyayer dabi*)? [There is] a dichotomy between the two and we suffer because there is no resolution. The Cathay is showing the film *Lady Hamilton*. Before her departure Lady Nelson told Lord Nelson that she would never allow another woman to take the title of Lady Nelson. Nor did she allow it. Who is to judge? Who was the most guilty of the three—Lord Nelson, Lady Hamilton or Lady Nelson? [To me], it is Lady Nelson who suffered most—it was her own husband who prevented her from sharing in his glory.

These are questions all modern societies have faced at one time or another. Indian society encountered the questions in an acute form in the late colonial period as its beehive formation crumbled and civil society failed to replace it effectively.

Lakshmi Swaminadhan was fortunate enough to get her release from her husband B.K.N. Rao, because they had contracted a civil marriage. As her daughter Subhasini Ali puts it while recalling her own divorce, 'Marriage is a social contract, not a sacrosanct institution. If it doesn't work, it's better to dissolve it.'[80] For millions of Hindu women, however, there was no escape clause in the British-defined 'Hindu law' of marriage. Independent India passed the Hindu Marriage Act in 1955. Paradoxically, divorce provisions were more liberal therein than in civil law. At the time in question, the women of the subcontinent who belonged to the Muslim community had provisional access to divorce, but only on the terms

---

[79]Translated by us from the original Bengali diary in the possession of Supriya Guha.
[80]Radhika Sachdev, 'Subhashini Ali: A feminist to the core', *Hindustan Times* (5 May 2002).

of their husbands. Independent India adopted no civil code for the benefit of every woman, nor did Pakistan and Bangladesh. All too often and throughout the subcontinent, love hangs on the gallows. Yet, however incomplete the reform, the 'progress in marriage' that so alarmed its critics has unmistakably expanded the private sphere. Love, formerly condemned to secrecy (khalwat), and typically embodied in extramarital affairs, nowadays increasingly seeks the right to exist openly (majlis) in the form of marriage.

of their husbands. Independent India adopted no civil code for the benefit of every woman, nor did Pakistan and Bangladesh. All too often and throughout the subcontinent, love hangs on the gallows. Yet, however incomplete the reform, the 'progress in marriage' that so alarmed its critics has unmistakably expanded the private sphere. Love, formerly condemned to secrecy (khalwat), and typically embodied in extramarital affairs, nowadays increasingly seeks the right to exist openly (majlis) in the form of marriage.

ACTORS

JOINT NARRATIVES, SEPARATE NATIONS: QURRATULAIN HYDER'S *AAG KA DARYA*

Kumkum Sangari

In *Aag ka Darya*, for the first time a woman writer, Qurratulain Hyder, annexed over twenty-five centuries of Indian history as a subject matter. The grand nationalist visions of a pluralist civilization had till then been a male domain elaborated, among others, by Rabindranath Tagore and Jawaharlal Nehru, while women had been for almost two centuries the subjects of colonial, nationalist, or sectarian histories, often invented and usually patriarchal.

'Civilization' has of course been a heavy and fraught term, laden with the baggage of colonial superiority, imperial design, and anti-colonial assertion. In late-eighteenth-century England, the term 'civilization' signified a state of social order and refinement in conscious historical or cultural contrast to savagery and barbarism.[1] In the nineteenth century, 'civilization' became an expansive European project that progressed, in colonial ideologies and practices, by 'educating', subjugating, or eliminating inferior races. In India, a colonial indigenism, jointly crafted by Indian elites and British administrators, helped Hindu chauvinists to appropriate the term. This Hindu chauvinist discourse of culture and civilization made a double move: on one side it posed as anti-colonial and sang the glories of an ancient Vedic-Hindu India, and on the other, it ascribed all the evils of this newly minted Hindu civilization to medieval Muslim invasions to build a xenophobic 'nationalism'. The end of direct colonialism did not, however, consign civilizational contentions to the archives of history. At the end of the twentieth century, American neo-conservatives refurbished the discourse of civilization to justify a resurgent

[1]Raymond Williams, *Keywords* (Glasgow: Fontana, 1976), p. 48.

imperialist, anti-Islamic, and professedly 'Western' formation—an aspiration that is neatly encapsulated in the title of Samuel Huntington's *The Clash of Civilizations and the Remaking of the World Order*. In 2003, the remaking of the world order sanctioned the loot, plunder, and vandalization of the invaluable artefacts of a great ancient civilization in Iraq, artefacts that ironically were as pertinent to the early history of Christianity as of Islam.

At this time, when the term 'civilization' has been pressed into such sectarian use, or relegated as a politically incorrect master narrative, it may be illuminating, even elegiac, to return to a moment when the very need to invoke a 'civilization' arose from the desire to go beyond narrow religious identities. In the 1930s and 1940s, the more inclusive and non-sectarian Indian nationalists upheld the idea of a secular civilization that could encompass settlers and residents, support wider cultural formations, and contest the pernicious two nation/two culture theory that preceded the partition of India and Pakistan in 1947. In this period, the discourse of antiquity also carried the more ambivalent anti-colonial and nationalist resonances of the 'already civilized': old civilizations like India did not need to be civilized by new nations like Britain. The more significant meaning, however, stretched into carrying the anguish of partition: that of a civilization as having greater binding force than a nation. Civilizations were not divisible into nations, national boundaries came and went; civilizations endured. Civilizational unity was percieved as made up of long-term and contemporary bonds, the *textures* of lives and memories and friendships. Culture consisted of an embeddedness that gave an identity but not a separate identity. Indeed a 'separable' identity spelled grave loss, suffering, and evacuation: the 'separable' identity was thinner, less substantive, depleted, and artifical. Though published in 1959, *Aag ka Darya* belongs to this moment.

I

The innovative structure of *Aag ka Darya* had no precedent. The novel is staged in four historical periods: first, the expansion of the Mauryan empire under Chandragupta in the fourth century BC; second, the end of the Lodi dynasty and the beginning of Mughal rule in the late fifteeenth and early sixteenth centuries; third, the late-eighteenth-century beginnings of East India Company rule until its consolidation in the 1870s; and fourth, the two decades leading up to the 1950s that encompassed nationalist struggle, Partition, and Independence. These constitute four sequential yet discrete experiential moments that can neither be made amenable to a causal and teleological reading, nor slotted in as the discontinuous fragments characteristic of a high modernism. They are more readily grasped as a single constellation, as an individual attempt to apprehend a 'civilization', and as a doubled gesture repeated in a different conjuncture when the author's own English version, *River of Fire*, appeared in 1998. This was a fifth moment, rendered invisible by labels of transliteration or mistranslation, yet so powerful that I was compelled to reread *Aag ka Dariya* backwards from *River of Fire*. It is a novel recomposed by the author: the changes in some narrative sequences and narrative voices remodulate it both in intention and effect. The basic spatial and temporal structure, however, remains unchanged; the four moments remain linked to each other through sedimentation and retrieval.

In each of these moments, a set of characters reappear with partly altered names either as different persons or in recognizably similar situations. Women and men, scholars, historians, travellers, seekers, and (potential) artists, they relive individual trajectories of mutilation, desertion, uprooting, exile, wandering, and settlement, often repeating a 'cycle' of withdrawal into personal and/or spiritual resolutions in the face of gross violence. For instance, Champak in the first story, daughter of the chief minister, is deserted by her prince-fiancé who becomes a Buddhist *bhikshu* but she rejects the same option for herself; she is separated by war from Gautam Nilambar, captured and forced to join the harem of an old *mantri*; she becomes fat, middle-aged but remains attached to Gautam. Champavati in the second story is the sister of a learned Brahmin pandit in Ayodhya; she agrees to wed Syed Abdul Mansur Kamaluddin and seems ready to convert to Islam but Kamal, the travelling scholar, never returns; she searches for him, then joins a band of Vaishnav *sannyasins* and retires to Brindaban. Champa Jan in the third story is a rich and intelligent courtesan in Awadh who dallies with a British nabob and members of the Muslim elite such as Abdul Mansur Kamaluddin Ali Reza Bahadur known as Nawab Kamman. She falls in love with the *bhadro* Gautam Nilambar Dutt, a loyal East India Company servant, she waits for his return in the train from Calcutta. Her middle age is spent as a *chowdhrain* of *tawaifs* in Lucknow. Looted and destroyed in the 1857 revolt, she eventually becomes an old beggar who still lurks at the railway station, still in love with an ultimately indifferent man. Champa Ahmed in the fourth story, daughter of a genteel lawyer who supports the Muslim League, is a petit bourgeouis, self-fictionalizing social climber, an outsider in the upper class Lucknow circle, who plays out a series of relationships with various men including Gautam Nilambar and Cyril Ashley in England, ends up not marrying any of them, works in England for a while, and returns in 1954 to set up a legal practice with her father in her home town, Benares.

Another central character, Abdul Mansur Kamaluddin of Nishapur appears for the first time in the second story. The son of a Persian mother and an Arab father, he comes to 'Hindustan' in 1476 in search of fortune on the advice of a Phoenician Jew, becomes a court translator in Jaunpur, begins to write *The Marvels and Strange Tales of Hindustan*. He passes through an 'intellectual' romance with Ruqqaiya Bano Begum, a kinswoman of Sultan Husain Shah, then falls in love with Champavati. Separated by war, he makes no real effort to find her until it is too late. When Jaunpur is destroyed by Sikandar Lodi, he deserts the sultan he serves, encounters Chistiya Sufis, Buddhist bhikshus and Kabir, and finally settles down in Bengal, tills the land, and marries the Sudra Sujata Debi. His elder son goes into Mughal service, and because of this Kamal is dubbed a traitor, beaten, and left to die by Sher Shah's soldiers. In the third story, he is symbolically split between two characters who may or may not be his descendants: the impoverished Bengali boatman Abdul Mansur, and Kamal, a hereditary landowner in Awadh. This Kamal, though married, is an admirer of Champa Jan and befriends Gautam Nilambar. Later he recounts the events of 1857 to Gautam—as a sign of Hindu–Muslim unity, a tale of British atrocity, a proof of the valour of militant women. He goes to England with Mallika Kishwar's party to plead against her deposition. When he returns two years later, after the revolt, he finds his city, Lucknow, in ruins. Kamal in the fourth story is split between two cousins: the Switzerland-returned Amir Raza who does not marry Champa Ahmad and migrates to Pakistan and the ardently socialist and nationalist Kamal Reza who studies in Cambridge, comes back to a derelict Lucknow, but cannot find a job; the land reforms impoverish his parents, their ancestral property is unfairly confiscated as evacuee property; dispossessed, they are compelled to emigrate to Pakistan.

In each part, the characters become more complex as they are inflected by their previous persona—they are distant from yet related to the earlier characters. For instance, each story revolves around waiting and/or deserted women: Champak of the first story and Champavati of the second story are deserted women, Champa Jan of the third story is a woman who waits, while Champa Ahmad of the last story breaks the pattern and decides, after a series of failed relationships, to set up a legal practice. Or, in the second story, Syed Abdul Mansur Kamaluddin is a travel writer, scholar of comparative religions, translator, and composer of popular Bengali devotional poetry: as historian, exile, wanderer, seeker, and in the male privilege of deferral, he is a counterpart of Gautam of the first story; both are uprooted by war and weary of continuous bloodshed. As a multilingual cosmopolite, and potential renunciate Kamaluddin carries traces of the Buddhist prince Hari Shankar of the first story. Caught in political calamities, connected to each other through relations of love and friendship, the characters exist in the fullness of each historical moment as well as stretch across time.

II

Aag ka Darya acquires its coherence as a narrative not in its content (the four stories are not of equal length, they can be contracted or enlarged, episodes can be replaced by others, as indeed they are in *River of Fire*), but in its structure—the spatializing of four (five) moments. Even as it occupies the linear time of recorded history, it also unfolds as spatial concurrence.

The spatial concurrence of different temporal periods in *Aag ka Darya* is distinct from a simple cultural continuity; it involves both continuity and retrieval, and, more broadly, an idea of history that is itself infused with forms of concurrence. The objective historical coordinates and semantic analogues for this metaphor spread across the late nineteenth and early twentieth centuries in historiography, theatre, early cinema, and literary modernism. Again, many notions of recurrence and concurrent time, old and new, indigenous, colonial, and imperial were circulating in the century that preceded *Aag ka Darya*, and these lurk beneath the structure of the novel. They are variously acknowledged, incorporated, or displaced. For instance, the colonial period spawned many theories of 'decline' that ranged from T.S. Eliot's conservative notion of decay and fall of a monumentalized Europe and his vision of history as a debris that had to be spatially reassembled, to the imperious and Eurocentric Spenglerian world view of cyclic decline. These theories of decline are noted and startlingly inverted in the novel in which becoming modern is both old and new, heartbreaking but still promising. *Aag ka Darya* belongs to, and *River of Fire* records, a particular moment when popular culture and popular colonial-national retrievals were yet not-quite-archive, not-yet-postmodern-pastiche, but a sedimented overfull and paradoxically contemporaneous archive, which gave a sense of fullness, a fullness that was destroyed by Partition but remembered and experienced as loss and as pressure. Though concurrence had become a modernist device as with T.S. Eliot, here concurrence is still affective, a historical sediment, that was secured, temporarily, by a secular nationalism.

Aag ka Darya thus enforces a secular nationalism imaged as a civilizational strength with still retrievable potentials, that is nationalism in itself is a source of and a support for concurrence. This is borne out in the structure of the novel: a series of historical tableaux that stretch across time through repetition, affinity, and inflection, 'familial' lineages of disposition and vocation without, necessarily, blood descent, a dialogic arrangement of sections and characters in the river of fire that as metaphor flows backwards and forwards, a topographic stability in which the same space is crossed and recrossed in different times by different persons. The affinities across time, character, and religion make 'religious' divisions unsustainable: true nationalism (regardless of its origin) becomes a recession of parochial identities. Evidently this was a particular sort of nationalism, one that was closely linked to Nehru's civilizational vision.

III

Ancient and medieval 'culture' for Hyder, whether Arab, European, or Indian was a cross-national traffic, always conflict-riven, yet always familiar with, affected or influenced by, and aware of 'other' cultures, and at times almost cosmopolitan. Hyder's preface to the 1968 edition, tries on the lines of Jawaharlal Nehru's *The Discovery of India* to make a creative relation between in-migration (including that of Aryans, Arabs, and Turks) and cultural diversity, and also celebrates the civilizational capacity to synthesize and develop a varied and mixed culture. For her too India is part of a unique civilization, a unity that encompasses diversity, a complex of linkages and differences that defines the entire subcontinent, and contemporary Indians are products of this Indic civilization rather than of its nations. As in Nehru's text, in *Aag ka Darya* the syncretic is not just secular and multi-religious, it is also the dynamic of constant change, always poised on the new, that surrenders neither to an 'insider's' hegemonic assimilation nor to an 'outsider's' imperious hegemony.

For Hyder, as for Nehru, civilizational unity did not regiment cultural diversity into a single pattern, it lay in a common popular culture comprising philosophy, history, myth, epic, legend, and in the lability of traditions which were adapted, changed, and invented. Similarly, the modern adventure is not limited to national boundaries, and it is neither a repetition nor a denial of the past. The first story displays the ancient commingling of Greek, Vedic, Buddhist, Persian, the second the peak of medieval religious syncretisms, while the third and fourth explore the hybridization both of the British—from innkeeper to nabob—and the Indian—from feudal aristocracy to the colonial middle class. In each period there is an interplay of different epistemologies, languages, and literatures.

Hyder's civilizational view has been borne out by historians.[2] Ancient and medieval 'India' was part of a large Asian constellation stretching to the Middle East, parts of Europe and China, a geographical universe that persisted till the nineteenth century (evident in north-Indian *dastaans* which encompassed Central Asia, South Asia, and China). In such a continuously re-constellating view, 'India' is never an insular or ingrown entity. If for Hyder, civilization is a category that extends beyond national, religious, and state boundaries, and includes not just literature,[3] music or art but also affective structures, then these affective structures have in turn produced many of the coherences of that civilization. *Aag ka Darya* seems to bear out Irfan Habib's contention that the 'idea' of India as a cultural unity was not a modern secular invention but a much older one, that it was a product of conquest (Mauryan emperor Asoka's inscriptions in 250 BC) and travellers' visions or a view from outside (Alberuni's *Kitab-ul Hind* in the eleventh

[2]Romila Thapar points to the notable absence of Hindu and Islamic monoliths in ancient and medieval India. Arabs, Turks, Afghans, and Persians were both contiguous and familiar, linked by trade, settlement and conquest, and intermarriage. Not only did boundaries shift often but there was a marked exchange with Central and western Asia even in pre-Islamic centuries; Indian traders and Buddhist monks lived in Central Asia and China. There were varied identities even then of caste, language, sect, and occupation. Ideologies were governed by many factors other than religion such as caste, occupation, and access to resources. The dialogue between Bhakti and Sufi cults created a syncretic, composite culture, as did intermarriage into local communities which, along with conversion, generated an eclectic adoption of un-Islamic practices and produced a process of antagonism and adjustment. See 'The tyranny of labels', *Social Scientist* (September–October 1996), pp. 280–1.

[3]Zahida Hina points out that Hyder places literature beyond national, religious, and state boundaries. See Zahida Hina, 'Urdu literature and the patriarchal family', in Neelam Hussain, Samiya Mumtaz, and Rubina Saigol (eds), *Engendering the Nation State*, vol. 2, (Lahore: Simorgh, 1997), p. 38.

century), while the affect-laden idea of India as a distinctive composite culture or a common heritage emerged from immigrants and converts (such as Amir Khusrau's *Nuh Sipihr* in 1318).[4]

Indeed the basic problematic of the novel, in which much revolves around love, seems to be a classic secular one: how was the subcontinent to be defined as a historical community shaped by ancient, medieval, colonial, and ongoing interactions and intertwining of languages, settlements, and religions, and how was the line between diversity and systemic inequality, between religion and culture, to be drawn and navigated? How was historical evidence to be used to refute stereotypes, how was religious difference to be understood in ways that were at once historical and experiential, how could this complexity be narrated to reclothe the denuded stereotypes of communal propaganda and the stark evacuation of Partition?

At one level, of course, each character makes his or her 'India'—therefore civilization is a dynamic and changing concept, also an inevitably contested one. (The most poignant is Kamal's India in the fourth story.) At another level, the novel insistently grounds these individual visions in chunks of history, projects the persona of a scholar novelist, and annexes what had largely been the provenance of male writers of the historical novel (few women wrote historical novels). The persona harks back to the tutelary woman of the nineteenth-century popular writing,[5] and usurps the pedagogic authority that had been bestowed on 'good and dutiful' women in the past century, but with a new confidence that exploits the social, political, and nationalist legitimacy of the teacher in the 1940s and 1950s. The pedagogy too is in a new register. The authorial persona appears as a learned woman, a '*vidushi*', who displays her learning and ability to read Indian history and world history, the history of religions and of music, but who subverts the exclusive 'Vedic-Hindu' model of the learned woman. Indeed as a woman learned in *multiple* traditions, she puts this nineteenth-century stereotype to a secular use.

IV

The 'answers' in the novel go beyond the Nehruvian problematic and arrive at what can only be called an 'ex-centric' or centrifugal nationalism, as opposed to an insular or sectarian nationalism, a culture constituted by travel, worked out through love configured in tropes of travel and transience. In other words, a diffuse civilizational identity that is as much a matter of political modes of discovery and retrieval as of direct lines of inheritance, and an 'ex-centric' nationalism that can look backwards and outwards and be a space for commingling.

[4]See Irfan Habib, 'The envisioning of a nation: A defence of the idea of India', *Social Scientist*, 27:9–10 (September–October 1999).

[5]See Kumkum Sangari, *The Politics of the Possible* (Delhi: Tulika, 1999), ch. 6.

The novel is densely populated with travellers. They travel because of the dislocation of war, famine, poverty, economic need; for conquest, profit, pleasure, education, (Buddhist) proselytism, curiosity, spiritual quest. The exigencies of wandering, settlement, and uprooting structure families and relationships, bonding and desertion. Love, cohabitation, and marriage across boundaries are not only a part of this episteme of travel but also subject to the exigencies of travel—desertion and separation recur in almost every story. Travel within India is as important as in-migration and out-migration. The proper history of the subcontinent seems to be a history of travellers from time immemorial: the overlap of 'separate' historical periods, the way they shade into one another, the way narratives, artefacts, and ideas of one-time travel across time and space, and how these come to be linked through life histories, through the continuations of poverty, domestic service, the caste order, social hierarchy, and instrumental modes of legitimation. This entire complex is gained through 'repeating' a set of protagonists over twenty-five centuries.

V

Every traveller is literally or metaphorically entangled in a multi-religious web, a web that has a certain resilience, and persists despite Partition, for instance in East Pakistan. Hyder obviously prefers anti-institutional and anti-caste religions, and is drawn to webbed multi-religious terrains, to devotional traditions that explicitly deny religious division, and to universalistic monotheisms or Vedantic abstraction that could be read in generously non-sectarian ways. The question of belief, around which most lives circle, is not fixed into Orientalist versions of a 'spiritual East' or read through traditionalist frames, rather it is an intellectual and philosophical journey primarily concerned with *time* and *death*. All religions deal with these existential questions and that is why religions have always been so attractive and so persuasive. There are many travelling students of the meaning of mortality in *Aag ka Darya*. And yet in the novel all religions 'fail' either to bring solace or to effect a permanent closure—the references to materialism, scepticism, atheism, agnosticism, and so on are designed to display the other currents which flow along with religious belief, eddy around it, even submerge it. If religions unfailingly raise questions of time and death, they equally unfailingly cannot supply definitive answers.

Indeed, the diagnosis of transience which lies at the heart of the impulse to believe in something permanent and unchangeable has more continuity than religious sects. This diagnosis of transience, that coils inside a number of ancient and medieval religious options, and was attached to a variety of religious and renunciatory systems—Buddhist, Vedantic, Bhakti, Sufi—is the overarching trope in *Aag ka Darya*. The understanding that all things pass holds together all transient phenomena including travel.

This may well have been a way of winning a certain poise and distance from 1947. It was certainly a way of *reclaiming* the subcontinent from the violence that had torn it apart, pulling it into a consoling civilizational *longue duree* in which the repeated destructions of the composite culture of Awadh (in 1846, 1857, 1947) could be accommodated to the recurrent rise and fall of kingdoms (reminiscent of Ibn Khaldun's fourteenth-century philosophy of history). It was also a position that could at once mourn a loss and demand a future. *Aag ka Darya* held together, concurrently, a vast temporal and spatial 'civilizational' spread that asked now for a loyalty that was different from older loyalties of region, religion, or language: a loyalty to the idea of a civilization that was wider, deeper, and more compelling than its division into separate nations.

FROM PRINCELY COURT TO HOUSE OF COMMONS: D.O. DYCE SOMBRE (1808–51) FROM SARDHANA TO LONDON

Michael H. Fisher

I. COMPOSITE CULTURES AND IDENTITIES

Despite the efforts of governments, politicians, and commentators (including some 'post-colonial' theorists) to establish clear legal and cultural categories based on abstract and fixed criteria, historians can contribute to current debates by demonstrating how contingent and inadequate are such absolute definitions. Such putatively dichotomous classifications include: Black versus White, Indian versus European, subaltern versus elite, the colonized versus the colonizer, sane versus insane. This chapter argues for a more nuanced approach in which identity is highly context sensitive and the same person could hold strongly varying identities in different locales or in relations with different people. Nor were all identities ascribed; people negotiated them in ways that cross-cut categories. Finally, each person in a relationship might perceive and record it in strikingly discordant ways.

The worldwide arena of the British empire created and reflected symmetrical power relationships in a series of contact zones. Pratt defines these as 'social spaces where disparate cultures meet, clash, and grapple with each other, often in highly asymmetrical relations of domination and subordination.'[1] Even this definition, however, may presuppose separate and distinct cultures, rather than recognizing the composite nature of each. In many situations (through history and today), individuals in many relationships sound out the terms by which to present themselves and search for signs by which to assay the relative identity of the other.

---

[1]Mary L. Pratt, *Imperial Eyes: Travel Writing and Tranculturation* (London: Routledge, 1992), p. 4.

On occasion, the respective signals and perceptions of the parties might differ fundamentally, leading to exploitation, contempt, and/or misunderstanding. In most situations, however, people work out reciprocal understandings that enable them to function and exchange. When relationships are personal or intimate, as domestic or sexual ones, the issues of identity can be particularly complex and fraught with misunderstanding.

This chapter analyses salient ways that David Octerlony Dyce Sombre (1808–51) participated in and represented his interactions in three contact zones: Sardhana and surrounding north India, Calcutta, and Europe. Based on evidence drawn from his personal diary, official colonial records, and first-hand observations by his contemporaries, we can highlight the particular instability and context specificity of his identity as he entered a series of relations in each locale. At different times and in a range of relationships of unequal power, he appeared variously Black and White, Indian and European, subaltern and elite, colonized and colonizer, sane and insane; nor did his male gender or social class mean the same thing everywhere and to all people.

II. SARDHANA AND SURROUNDING NORTH INDIA

Like many princely Indian states, diverse peoples came together to produce Sardhana's composite court culture. The founder of this small (240 sq. mile) princely state near Meerut, Walter Reinhardt alias Sombre or Somru (c. 1720–78), was one of several Catholic European mercenaries who established themselves as rulers in north India during the conflict-ridden late eighteenth century.[2] His de facto successor, Farzana Zeb al-Nissa Begum Sombre (1741/53–1836), rose from obscure origins through the Persianate world of *tawaifs* to become his consort.[3]

---

[2]He has variously been identified as an Alsatian from Strasbourg, a German from Trier/ Trèves in Rhineland Palatinate, an Austrian from Saltzburg, a German Swiss, and a gypsy. He epitomized for his British enemies the inverse of European virtues. They regarded him as: the infamous mass murderer of 150 helpless British men, women, and children prisoners at Patna; a turncoat mercenary who sold his European military skills to enemies of the British (including the French East India Company, Shuja al-Daula, Mir Qasim, the Bharatpur Jats, the Raja of Jaipur, Hafiz Rahmat Khan, Najaf Khan, the Marathas, and the Mughal emperor, among others); a coward who fled at crucial moments in defeat but claimed credit for victory. For historical and fictional accounts of Reinhardt, see: H.G. Keene, *Hindustan Under Free Lances, 1770–1820* (London: Brown, Langham, 1907), pp. 16–17; National Archives, *Fort William-India House Correspondence*, vol. 4, pp. 132–4, 258, 263, 313–14; Antoine Louis Henri Polier, *Shah Alam II and His Court* (Calcutta: Asiatic Society, 1989), pp. 93–6; K. Reinhardt, *Wegweiser zu den Quellen der Geschichte des deutschen Nabobs von Sardhana in Indien Walter Reinhardt genannt Sombre* (Völkingen: Selbstverlag, 1993); Peter Weber, *Maharadscha Reinhardt, Feldherr des Grossmoguls* (Berlin: Propyläen, 1943).

[3]For historical and fictional accounts of her life, see: Thomas Bacon, *First Impressions and Studies from Nature in Hindostan*, 2 vols (London: W.H. Allen, 1837), vol. 2, p. 76; Vera Chatterjee, *All This is Ended: The Life and Times of H.H. the Begum Sumroo of Sardhana* (New Delhi: Vikas, 1979); Amarendra Dasa, *Jebunnisa* (Kalikata, Surabhi Prakasani, 1962); Makkhanalal Gharg, *Sahi Drsya, Arthata, Samaru*

After his death, she took control over his estate, his first wife (another Muslim woman), and his son. She herself led the 3–4000 strong Sardhana army mostly composed of Jat and Muslim soldiers with predominantly European officers.[4] She ruled Sardhana's mainly Jat and Taga populace through Hindu, Catholic, and Muslim officials, using primarily Persian for her records and personal seal. Indeed, in 1781, three years after Reinhardt's death, she herself converted to Catholicism, taking the name Joanna Nobilis.[5] In 1794, she married a much younger French officer in her service (who soon thereafter died when her army briefly mutinied).

During Begum Sombre's fifty-eight years of rule, Persian, Urdu and English, and their associated cultures were all current at the Sardhana court. The Begum lavishly patronized Muslim, Hindu, Catholic, and Protestant festivals, rituals, and institutions. Many notable visitors from across Asia and Europe enjoyed Sardhana's hospitality, receiving receptions the Begum considered appropriate to their status and background. Begum Sombre also adjusted her practice of purdah according to the audience and times (that is, secluding herself from Muslim and Hindu dignitaries but not from Britons). While most of these diverse visitors found something about the Sardhana court that they could relate to, they also found it difficult to classify in conventional communal or political terms.

Begum Sombre also shaped her family according to her own design.[6] She arranged the marriage of Reinhardt's biological son to the daughter of a French officer in her service. She then recruited a half-Scots and half-Indian officer, George Alexander David Dyce (d. 1838), to marry their daughter, Julia Anne Reinhardt (aka Juliana Anna Domenica Theresa Reinhardt, 1787–1820). Thus she transcended customary gender categories in selecting a variety of relations for her late consort's biological descendants.

Her political alliances were as diverse as her cultural and familial choices.

Arua Begama Samaru ke Jivana-caritra (Kasi: Nagaripracarini Sabha, 1926); Durba Ghosh, 'Naming', *Gender and History* (forthcoming); Friedrich Halm, *Begum Somru: Trauerspiel in fünf Aufzügen* (Leipzig: Philipp Reclam jun., 1900?); Reginald Heber, *Narrative of a Journey*, 3 vols, 2nd edn (London: John Murray, 1827), vol. 2, pp. 277–80; Victor Jacquemont, *Letters from India*, 2 vols (Karachi: Oxford University Press, 1979), vol. 2, pp. 246–8; J.S. Lall, *Begam Samru: Fading Portrait in a Gilded Frame* (New Delhi: Roli Books, 1997); Patrick Nair, *Sardhana: Its Begum, its shrine, its Basilica* (Meerut: Prabhat Press, 1963); Mahendra Narain Sharma, *Life and Times of Begam Samru of Sardhana, A.D. 1750–1836* (Sahibabad: Vibhu Prakashan, 1985); Amita Sher, *Begum Samru: The Most Beloved* (Lahore: Sang-e-Meel Publications, 1993); Nicholas Shreve, *Dark Legacy* (Arundel: Bookwright, 1996).

[4]Sharma, *Life and Times*, pp. 147–9, appendix F.

[5]Yet, one of her Catholic chaplains wrote in 1824 to the Catholic College of Propaganda in Rome: 'It is true that this princess is a Christian because she has been baptized, but to all intents and purposes she is still a true Mohammedan.' Fr. Adeoldatus of Fanto to Congregation of Propaganda, 28 Nov. 1824, quoted in Fulgentius Vannini, *Hindustan–Tibet Mission* (New Delhi: Capuchin, 1981), p. 245.

[6]See Michael H. Fisher, 'Becoming and making "family" in Hindustan', in Indrani Chatterjee (ed.), *Family in Past Time* (Rutgers: Rutgers University Press, 2003 and Delhi: Permanent Black, 2003).

She continued her affective and military support of the imperial Mughals throughout her rule, long after they wielded much effective power. Indeed, the Mughal empress entrusted her with carrying marriage invitations and other personal communications to the outside world.[7] In 1803, the Begum also strategically shifted her military and political backing from the Marathas to the British, which secured her continued rule over Sardhana until her death.[8] But she continually tested the limits of British strictures over herself, her family, her policies, and her state.

The Begum eventually chose David Octerlony Dyce Sombre (1808–51) as her heir.[9] The genetic great-grandson of Reinhardt, he himself embodied elements drawn from many traditions, and his protean identities varied widely according to the context and relationship. In Western popular 'biological' calculation based on 'blood', he was three-eighths 'Indian' or 'Black' and five-eighths 'European' or 'White' (which included German and French Catholic and Scots Protestant ancestors). Begum Sombre took him from his mother as soon as the forty days of post-partum impurity had ended. She named him David Octerlony Dyce; as an explicit statement of his identification with the Begum and his great-grandfather, in 1834 he himself added Sombre to his name.[10] Thus Dyce Sombre grew up as the Begum's potential heir through highly complex relationships, none of which were genetic.

Dyce Sombre's inheritance proved insecure, dependent principally on the uncertain desires of the Begum, the policies of the British, and the adversarial actions of his biological father. The Begum clearly taught him how to comport himself and act as an Indian 'prince', by having him look over her shoulder as she ruled. One British woman noted him as a ruler-in-training: 'Behind [the Begum] on the cushions was perched David Dyce … a child of five or six years of age, in a full court suit, coat, waist-coat and shirt of crimson satin with a sword dazzling at his side and cocked hat.'[11]

Yet the Begum, despite her efforts to convince the British otherwise, had no power to convey to Dyce Sombre anything but her personal property. The

[7]See A.D. [Mrs Ann Deane], *Tour Through the Upper Provinces of Hindostan* (London: C. and J. Rivington, 1823), pp. 150–75.

[8]Herbert Compton, *A Particular Account of the European Military Adventures of Hindustan, from 1784 to 1803* (London: T. Fisher Unwin, 1893), p. 409.

[9]See Ram Babu Saksena, *European and Indo-European Poets* (Lucknow: Nevil Kishore, 1941), pp. 86–94; Nicholas Shreeve, *Indian Heir* (Crossbush: Bookwright, 2001); and a transcription of the Dyce Sombre diary, *From Nawab to Nabob: The Diary of David Ochterlony Dyce Sombre, 1833–8*, ed. by Nicholas Shreeve (Crossbush: Bookwright, 2000).

[10]Dyce Sombre Diary, Oriental and India Office Collection (hereinafter OIOC), L/L/63 (434), entry dated 17 Apr. 1834 (hereinafter cited as Diary with date). He had earlier considered adding Reinhardt. Diary 25 July 1835.

[11]Mrs [Mary Martha Butt] Sherwood, *Life of Mrs Sherwood*, ed. by Sophia Kelly (London: Darton, 1867), p. 483.

British political Residents in Delhi who exercised indirect rule over Sardhana disapproved of the Begum's wish to adopt Dyce Sombre as her political heir. Indeed, the British generally had difficulties categorizing the Begum, ascribing a range of incompatible ancestries and ambiguous gendered descriptions onto her.[12] Thus neither the Begum nor Dyce Sombre fit legally or culturally into any clear colonial classification.

During Dyce Sombre's youth, the Begum and his father contested for control over Dyce Sombre and Sardhana as well. The Begum raised Dyce Sombre as a Catholic, making him critical of the religious beliefs and practices of his father and later Muslim, Hindu, and Protestant sexual partners. Yet he also scoffed at the Catholic priests attending her court. His father apparently convinced the Begum to have him educated privately (1813–14) with a Baptist evangelist missionary, Reverend John Chamberlain (1771–1821)—whom the British finally expelled from north India for stirring up religious sectarian tensions with his public preaching.[13] The Begum and Dyce then sent him for schooling to the Reverend Henry Fisher, of the Anglican Church Missionary Society and St. Johns Church, Meerut, for four years (sometime during the period 1817–24), taking instruction in English language and manners with other sons of mixed ancestry including the Skinners.[14] Dyce Sombre dwelt for years afterward on the emotional and cultural conflicts he went through due to the rising conflicts between the Begum and his father, dependent on both even as they struggled with each other for power.

When Dyce Sombre's biological mother died in 1820, the Begum's quarrel with his father, Dyce, erupted. Beyond control over Dyce Sombre, a related issue was the education and status of his sisters (Ann May born 1812; Georgiana born 1815): should they be raised as Catholic, in purdah, and in Sardhana, as the Begum

[12]British writers identified her variously as Kashmiri, Hindu, Georgian, Mughal, and Arab Sayid, as well as 'masculine' in her regnant role. One British visitor in 1794, seeking an appropriate metaphor, proclaimed her an 'eastern Clorinda' (after that legendary female warrior from Persia or Egypt with Christian associations who fought bravely, but futilely, against the Crusaders). India Political Consultations 4, 23 May 1836, no. 66, OIOC; Bacon, *First Impressions*, vol. 1, p. 35; J. J. Higginbotham, *Men Whom India has Known*, 2nd edn (Madras: Higginbotham, 1874), pp. 406–8; Herbert Compton, *Particular Account of the European Military Adventures* (London: T. Fisher Unwin, 1893), p. 403; William Henry Sleeman, *Rambles and Recollections* (Karachi: Oxford University Press, 1973 reprint), p. 594; Keene, *Hindustan*, p. 76; Major William Thorn, *Memoir of the War in India* (London: T. Egerton, 1818), p. 386; W. Francklin, *The History of the Reign of Shah-Aulum: The Present Emperor of Hindostaun* (Lucknow: Pustak Kendra, 1973, reprint of 1798 original), pp. 105–8; Thomas Twining, *Travels in India a Hundred Years Ago*, ed. by William H.G. Twining (London: James R. Osgood, 1893), pp. 262–4.

[13]John Chamberlain, *Memoirs*, ed. by William Yates (Calcutta: Baptist Mission Press, 1825); Diary 28 May 1835.

[14]Heber, *Narrative*, vol. 2, pp. 274, 277–80.

wished, or by their father in Delhi with him as anglicized. The Begum won custody over them and married these sisters respectively to an Italian Catholic and a British Anglican officer in her service. Both couples eventually settled in Europe.

In 1825–6, Dyce attempted a coup to take Sardhana for himself as the heir to his late wife's grandfather's estate, supplanting the Begum. He failed to raise popular or military support in Sardhana. He also futilely sought British political, military, and legal backing for his claims, including through a series of legal court cases against her and her estate that lasted until his death in 1838.[15] Dyce Sombre himself had to choose between loyalty to his father—which meant the security of a modest pension for himself and employment in an agency house in Calcutta—or the insecurity of attachment to the Begum with the potential pay-off of her entire estate. He chose the latter and, as a reward for his close personal attendance on her, she eventually entrusted management of Sardhana to him, appointed him Colonel over her army, obtained from Pope Gregory XVI his appointment as Chevalier of the Order of Christ, declared him her personal heir, ceded Badshahpur (an *altumgha jagir* or personal estate) to him, and gave him Rs 3,600,000 (£360,000) cash (which he immediately invested in East India Company bonds).

As an unusually intimate account of life in Sardhana during the 1830s, and his own travels thereafter, we have Dyce Sombre's personal diary. Apparently introduced to the diary genre by his British teachers, Dyce Sombre consistently followed particular protocols, thus shaping its form, and its value as evidence. Although he grew up multilingual (Persian, Urdu, and English), he wrote his diary predominantly in English, and followed a format which he associated with that culture. His diary's occasional Persian phrases are of two sorts: literary citations and sexually-related remarks which he apparently designed to be unintelligible to a chance or notional anglophone reader. His intended audience was explicitly himself, with self-exhortations, admonitions, and reflections scattered through the pages. He used his diary as a record of his expenditures, income, personal accomplishments and failures, as well as auguries, and moral lessons to himself for the future. He believed in the larger significance of all that occurred to him, with the esoteric relationship between events revealed only in glimpses, which retrospective analysis of his diary could provide him. For example, when he eventually learned about the death of his mistress Dominga (which had occurred months earlier), he reconstructed his own prescience of the event: 'On referring to my diary, I find that on the 27th [the day before she died], in the afternoon, I was very low spirited and cried at table.'[16] He kept a rough original record, updated daily or every few days, and then went back to annotate and amend his

[15]Bacon, *First Impressions*, vol. 2, pp. 47–8.
[16]Diary 21 Nov. 1837.

entries, as well as periodically recopy the initial entries into a more polished version. While he did not seem to have intended this diary to be read by others, he did indicate that he considered it of potential interest to the public. For example, he recorded reading *Passages from the Diary of a Late Physician* by Samuel Warren (Edinburgh: W. Blackwood & Sons, 1832), which led him to reflect: '[I] Forget lots; if I could write, or rather print my words, like the author of the Diary of the late Physician, oh! what I could dictate.'[17] Of Dyce Sombre's entire diary, which he apparently wrote for most of his adult life, only two sections have survived. His estranged widow apparently destroyed most of the parts of it that he had retained. The surviving two parts of the diary cover his last years in India (1833–8) and a year travelling in Europe (1847–8); they were entered as judicial evidence and thus preserved. Throughout, his strong egocentric voice enables us to reconstruct his own candid perceptions, which often contrast markedly from the accounts of him by others. Overall, therefore, careful use of this diary can provide remarkable evidence about his shifting and contested roles as he moved among localities, cultures, and relationships, in north India, Calcutta, and Europe.

The Mughal court culture and imperial dynasty, long associated with the Begum, interrelated with Dyce Sombre in complex ways. Due to their status as nominal sovereigns, the Mughals took symbolic precedence over the Begum. Yet her relative wealth and their impoverished status, combined with her Catholicism and their Islam, meant that Dyce Sombre felt disdainful of them, even as he showed nominal submission. For example, when the Mughal imperial prince, Mirza Muhammed Shah, visited Sardhana, he received honours from the deferential Begum including a handsome *ziyafat* (welcoming feast), eleven-gun salute, *nazr* (presentation), and *rukhsat* (leave-taking ceremony). But Dyce Sombre rebuffed the prince's polite hints for more gifts, referred to such a visit as a 'begging expedition'.[18] Dyce Sombre denigrated this imperial prince's lack of an education beyond the Quran and Sadi's *Gulistan*, and called his *khilat* (robe of honour given in return) pitiful. Dyce Sombre also met personally with the wives of Mughal imperial princes, apparently considered close enough to that family to be admitted to their presence.[19] His public face showed respect for them and vice versa, but his private remarks revealed his resentment and sense of superiority toward them.

In addition, Dyce Sombre consorted frequently with the poets, dancers, and musicians who centred culturally on the Mughal imperial court but also looked to Sardhana for income. He frequently had liaisons with some of these women. Again, his lavish gifts and words of devotion to them conflict with his personal lust to possess them, and then pay them off when he tired of them or they became

[17]Diary 12 Aug. 1835.

[18]Diary 24–7 Dec. 1833. Dyce Sombre took a similar attitude toward other Mughal princes visiting Sardhana: Diary 27 Feb. 1834, 25–8 Nov. 1834, 23–7 Dec. 1834, 17 Mar. 1835.

[19]Diary 16 Dec. 1834.

pregnant. In this world of Persian and Urdu literature, music, and dance, he was an extravagant but a demanding and often exploitative patron.

Emulating his biological father, Dyce Sombre also associated with British officials and officers in the Company's service. As the Sardhana court physician Drever stated:

The society in which the said D.O. Dyce Sombre moved was chiefly composed of the European civil and military servants of the said East India Company, at Meerut and Delhi, and others, and the language usually spoken amongst those admitted on terms of equality, except with her Highness [the Begum] herself, was principally English, and the manners much the same as those of English people in India.[20]

With them, Dyce Sombre wore European-style dress, although at some functions he wore what he called his 'Hindustani clothes'.[21] In the secret brotherhood of Freemasons, as a 'Royal Architect', he stood higher in status than many Britons when they all donned that ritual apron and other accoutrements and was, in theory, a brother to all other Masons. Yet his relations with Britons remained fraught with tensions.

Dyce Sombre's lavish hospitality, frequent but incompetent wagering, and expertise in recruiting dancers and prostitutes, gained him tolerated access to young British men, although not as a warm friend or companion.[22] He resented their financial demands on him, but also feared their rejection if he did not continue to give. Once they owed him money, he held that over them while they kept him on the margins of their society. Typically, one young officer, Bacon, asked Dyce Sombre for the use of the Begum's palace in Delhi in October 1834 but did not express much gratitude for this favour when given:

At Delhi, the Begum Sumroo had a very handsome mansion, which for several years she had not frequented: this I coveted as a residence during my stay at Delhi, and a note to my good-natured friend, Dyce Sombre, at once secured it to me. With his usual kindness and good-nature, moreover, Dyce sent extra servants over to Delhi, with orders to the moohkteya to get every thing in readiness for my arrival.[23]

Bacon then belittled the accommodation and Dyce Sombre as well.

For some male Britons, the price to Dyce Sombre of their companionship meant his introducing them to, and often paying for, Indian courtesans. To some

[20]Affidavit of Thomas Drever, 24 June 1844, in D.O. Dyce Sombre, *In Lunacy: In the Matter of David Ochterlony Dyce Sombre, a Person Found to Be of Unsound Mind* (London: Hansard, 1851), pp. 31–40.

[21]Diary 1 Aug. 1834. See also Diary 10 Aug. 1834.

[22]Sir Charles Trevelyan, letter, 19 Aug. 1843 in D.O. Dyce Sombre, *Mr Dyce Sombre's Refutation of the Charges of Lunacy Brought Against Him in the Court of Chancery* (Paris: Dyce Sombre, 1849), p. 8.

[23]Bacon, *First Impressions*, vol. 2, pp. 203, 217ff; Sleeman, *Rambles*, p. 504. The Begum's palace in Delhi in Chandni Chawk became the office of Delhi Bank, later of Lloyd's Bank, it is currently a centre for wholesale electrical equipment shops. Percival Spear, *Twilight of the Mughals* (Cambridge: Cambridge University Press, 1951), pp. 149–50.

small measure, therefore, Dyce Sombre shared status with these courtesans: he obtained the companionship of Europeans which he valued partly by providing access to the sexuality of Indian women. He was most comfortable in riotous carousals where class, race, rank, and gender proprieties were submerged by drink.

While in north India, Dyce Sombre had more formal but still ambiguous relations with elite British women. He apparently conceived of his possible sexual relationship with them only through marriage. He believed that his position as heir to the Begum's fortune made him coveted by many European parents as their son-in-law, and some Britons may have agreed. After one dinner with General John Ramsay, Commander of the Meerut division, Dyce Sombre ran into 'Mrs Something, the late Miss Bishop, now a widow, to whom I was to be married once'.[24] Dyce Sombre regularly regarded himself as on trial as a groom:

I cannot express my very great acknowledgments to the Genl [Ramsay] & his family; he is always behaved in the most handsomest manner ever since I have known him. As a further mark of his kindness, he asked me to hand one of the ladies to the dinner-table in the eveng altho' there were 2 field officers, besides those that handed Mrs Ramsay & Mrs Brulton. I have very good chance of getting married, if I like, but I must not be in a hurry. Miss Fraser, who is not a bad-looking girl, I could get also; in fact, it was reported all over Meerut that I was going to get married to her; apropos the General read an advertisement in the *Meerut Observer* of a gentleman seeking for a wife! Many fellows called after breakfast; amongst them a Miss Woodcock, a guest of Hamilton's; very dark girl for an European, but not bad looking, by all means.[25]

A few months later, he overheard the Begum discussing with a Sardhana courtier 'my marrying Miss Ramsay'.[26] Perhaps to impress his prospective mother-in-law, Dyce Sombre arranged an Indian dance for her: 'Had nautching, which Mrs Ramsay said was the first time they ever saw.'[27] Such a marriage alliance between Dyce Sombre and the Ramsays may have been considered appropriate only by one side; while it is clear that the Begum and Dyce Sombre contemplated such a European marriage, there is no confirming evidence that the Ramsays entertained such an idea. Indeed, General Ramsay supported the disinheritance of Dyce Sombre through the British annexation of Sardhana, yet he subsequently asked Dyce Sombre for a personal loan, which the latter refused (although the husband of one of his sisters provided it).[28] Thus Dyce Sombre moved among several classes of elite Britons but his relations with these women and men were filled with cross-purposes, conflicting expectations, and adversarial agendas.

Dyce Sombre's most consistently egalitarian relations were with elite north Indian families of mixed Indian and European ancestry, like his own—particularly

[24]Diary 31 July 1834.
[25]Diary 2 Apr. 1835.
[26]Diary 7 July 1835.
[27]Diary 23 Oct. 1835.
[28]Diary 1–2 Dec. 1837.

the Skinners with whom he grew up. The roles and identities of people variously called 'Anglo-Indians', 'Indo-Britons', or 'Eurasians' in Indian, British, and colonial history remained highly problematic for all sides.[29] Although Dyce Sombre remained on very friendly terms with the Skinners, he never (in the extant evidence) mentioned a marriage alliance with that family, who were Anglicans. He did, however, consider an alliance with a French Catholic mercenary comparable in class to himself: General Jean Francois Allard (1785–1839), a Napoleonic cavalry officer who, after Waterloo, went via Persia to Punjab, where he served Ranjit Singh as a mercenary for many years. In 1834, on his way to France, Allard stayed both at the Begum's court and with British officers at Meerut, receiving honour from both. Dyce Sombre felt an affinity for him: 'Monsr Allard came was introduced to H.H.; he talks Persian pretty well for a foreigner.'[30] Allard's two daughters reflected his 'marriage' with a woman in the Punjab: 'They both looked as if they had hill blood in them.'[31] Allard also impressed Dyce Sombre by respecting the latter's appointment as honorary Colonel from the French government: 'Genl Allard saw the French brevets I have got, & much approved of them, & said would take a copy to France with him.'[32] They kept up a warm correspondence and exchange of gifts for years, which included Allard reportedly proposing a marriage alliance of his niece with Dyce Sombre.[33]

At degrees in society below Dyce Sombre were various people living at the Sardhana court. His English and Italian brothers-in-law vied against him for the Begum's approval and clearly resented his inheritance of the vast bulk of the Begum's wealth. Among the Catholic priests at the Sardhana court, he was a child of the Church, a plentiful patron, a wayward sinner, a drinking companion, and a scoffing cynic.

The numerous courtier families at Sardhana also depended on the Begum's fickle patronage and Dyce Sombre's influence with her. Dyce Sombre claimed flirting, or sexual, relationships with the daughters of these families, especially Catholic ones. He occasionally pressured these courtiers to allow him access to their women's quarters, generally barred to non-family members. Since they had daughters for whom marriage with Dyce Sombre might bring wealth and increased status, they were placed in a difficult position to refuse his intrusion. For example,

I & [a British companion] Marshall went to call on old Derridons .... I gave a hint to see Madame & he immediately consented to my going in with him .... [Marshall had to stay

[29]See Christopher Hawes, *Poor Relations: The Making of a Eurasian Community in British India 1773–1833* (London: Curzon, 1996) and Durba Ghosh, 'Colonial companions', Ph.D., University of California, Berkeley, 2000.

[30]Diary 30 Sept. 1834.

[31]Diary 1 Oct. 1834.

[32]Diary 3 Oct. 1834.

[33]Diary 14 Nov. 1834, 15 Dec. 1834, 15 Jan. 1836, 31 Dec. 1836, 24 Jan. 1837, 4 Mar. 1837, 21 Apr. 1838.

out] for which I was not sorry .... The Madame recd me very graciously, & kissed my cheek, & introduced me to her sister, & then afterwards to her daughters; Isabella, with whom I was rather in love with, was bashful; she has a boy about 2 years old; the rest of the daughters did not take my fancy. M[arshall] got impatient, & wrote me a note, saying that either to come out soon, or call him in.[34]

The next month, Dyce Sombre tried less successfully to repeat the entry: 'Altho' I hinted [Derridon] to take us into his zenana, but he would not, & parried off my hint by saying that they are not ready to receive us, & the rain had completely upset them.'[35] A few months later: 'After church, I & Marshall went up to have a peep at the zenana, where [Derridon's] girls had gone too.'[36] The worried parents' hoped-for reward for letting Dyce Sombre have access to their domestic sphere was a wedding with him: 'The girls were again paraded before me.'[37] Dyce Sombre was determined to enjoy this access but not to pay the price, since he considered their aspirations to his hand 'impudence'.[38] Such intrusions thus became a contest between Dyce Sombre and the men of such courtier families over his status: potential family member or exploitative outsider, patron who could not be denied or immature libertine who must be excluded.

Some women in the court had more continuing relations with Dyce Sombre which gave them some mixed prestige but no real security. He retained two long-time mistresses in the Begum's palace whom the Begum never officially acknowledged, although she accepted this arrangement and recognized their children by Dyce Sombre. One of these women, Dominga (d. 1838), was Catholic. Sardhana's Catholic families expected Dyce Sombre to favour her over his other women, but he rather asserted his possession over her than seems to have been respectful of her. Dyce Sombre's other long-time mistress, Hoosna (fl. 1835–52), a Muslim, apparently came from the courtesan class from which the Begum herself originally emerged. While Dyce Sombre personally favoured Hoosna over Dominga, he recognized the relatively higher status of the latter. They submitted to his occasional abusive behaviour in order to retain their tenuous positions in the palace. Hoosna had a daughter, Josephine Urbana (1834–5), with Dyce Sombre. The daughter had formal Catholic and Muslim rituals performed for her, by a Padre and a *Qazi* respectively, as well as Hindu folk rituals performed by the women of the family.[39] Dominga had at least three children with Dyce Sombre, all of

[34]Diary 29 June 1834.
[35]Diary 4 July 1834.
[36]Diary 8 Nov. 1834.
[37]Diary 14 Dec. 1834.
[38]Diary 2 Dec. 1834.
[39]e.g., Diary 13 Apr. 1835: 'Laura was burnt in the forehead with a coral, but it had no immediate effect on her.' After her Catholic burial, her mother had a young pig burned near her mother's house. Diary 10 May 1835.

whom died in infancy: Walter George (1832–3), Laura Celestina Roselia (1834–5), and Penelope (1836–8). Indeed, none of Dyce Sombre's acknowledged children survived. Thus his relations with each of these women was partly informed by her culture and family status and partly by her personally.

Although Dyce Sombre exercised his power over his mistresses and the Begum's dependent courtiers, he necessarily attended deferentially on the Begum, in whose hands his future lay. Although he was clearly emotionally attached to her, he also manoeuvred to continue as her favourite. At her death (27 January 1836), she left Dyce Sombre (in addition to the £360,000 she had already transferred to him) most of her extensive personal property including her palaces and other buildings in Sardhana, Meerut, Delhi, and Agra (worth about £150,000). He would enjoy the interest from this estate until age 30, when he would acquire full possession of it.[40] The East India Company, however, annexed Sardhana and commandeered her army, confiscating their accoutrements; he began lawsuits (which lasted thirty-seven years) against these seizures. After her death, he left Sardhana, touring north India with Hoosna and Dominga but, unwilling to accept his comparatively reduced status as dispossessed heir to a now defunct state, he settled nowhere. He then entered the quite different contact zone of Calcutta and tried for a time to work out his identity there.

III. CALCUTTA, THE COLONIAL CAPITAL

The complex cultural environment of early nineteenth-century Calcutta, proved difficult for Dyce Sombre to navigate successfully. Some Europeans there attributed to him an inferior biological racial identity more strongly than ever before in his experience. Others recognized Dyce Sombre's wealth, status as heir to a former 'native princess', and descendant of Europeans in his patrilineage, although each of these meant different things in Calcutta than in Sardhana. Further, he had to fight against his own father to hold on to this wealth. At one point, a lawsuit by his father froze the disputed money and landed Dyce Sombre briefly in jail. Only his father's death in 1838 finally settled this dispute and made Dyce Sombre a fabulously wealthy man.

Yet his mixed ancestry meant that some Europeans disrespected him as 'Black' and told him so to his face. He records one such incident in which a European woman told him: 'O you blk bgr, if it was not for your money, no European would speak to you.'[41] Unfortunately, little more can be known about this woman or the circumstances of the remark. Nevertheless, other Europeans shared her contempt for him.

[40]Bacon, *First Impressions*, vol. 2, p. 59; Keene, *Hindustan*, p. 103; Sleeman, *Rambles*, p. 610.
[41]Diary 4 July 1837.

In contrast, Dyce Sombre recorded with pride how on several occasions the Governor General's sisters invited him into their drawing room. There, they sat next to him and paid him attentions:

Recd. an invitation ... in the name of Miss Edens for their party this evening, & it ran thus in the postscript ... 'and on every alternate Tuesday eveng during your stay in Calcutta;' it was very flattering, & of course I determined to go ... tho' I did not wish it at first, or else could have easily left my card at Govt House, & was sure to get an invite, this being the etiquette .... The eldest Miss Eden did me the honour to sit near me, & had a few moments' chat; saw many natives well dressed, but without kumurbunds, some of them, who looked very disrespectful. There was a Baboo, who pretends to be, I am told, a very clever man. I introduced myself to him, and talked to him in Persian, wh he talks pretty fair.[42]

Dyce Sombre described his gratification at the personal honour bestowed upon him by these British ladies, his own mastery over both European etiquette and Persian culture, and his distancing of himself from other Indian guests who, he believed, did not show enough sartorial respect for their hosts. Dyce Sombre repeated such visits over the course of his stay in Calcutta.

At the same time, Dyce Sombre also explored Calcutta's seamier neighbour-hoods and rowdier people. He revelled with British junior officers, one of whom arranged for him to hire a European prostitute: 'I believe she is the first European I have touched.'[43] He also noted other women whose sexual availability he found he could buy, whom he identified by their ethnicity as Jewish or Armenian.[44] It is clear that Dyce Sombre had difficulty distinguishing among those women who were sexually available to him and those who were not, perhaps on personal grounds, perhaps on those of ethnicity. He noted: 'Saw a beautiful English girl at Mrs Maxwell's, in Bow Bazar, but she would not agree; saw her again at the theatre in the eveng.'[45] Yet he later picked up various women at Mrs Maxwell's and Mother Brook's, houses of ill-repute.[46]

He also found the rules about the distinction between dance performances and sexual offerings different from north India. After the rules were explained to him, he apparently respected them. Once at an Indian dance in Calcutta:

All 8 or 9 sets [of dancers] are not worth looking at even, with the exception of one Armenian girl, who I had known before (but not as a dancing girl) in Imambary-lane .... I sent for her, but she refused; saying, it was not Calcutta custom to do this when they came to dance; probably it was better, in the [venereal diseased] state I am in.[47]

[42]Diary 7 Feb. 1837.
[43]Diary 25 Mar. 1837.
[44]Diary 10 June 1837, 21 Jan. 1838.
[45]Diary 16 May 1837.
[46]Diary 17 May 1837, 19–21 June 1837.
[47]Diary 1 Jan. 1838.

In another instance, he seized the jewels of a madam of an Indian brothel with whom he was disputing and brawled in the streets with the door-guard, barely escaping arrest.

In these unsavoury incidents, his name and identity became highly contested. He tried to disguise who he was so as to escape public censure from respectable citizens and arrest. The sex-workers and their pimps tried to discover his identity so as to blackmail him with threat of disclosure.[48]

After his father's death, once his inheritance was secured, Dyce Sombre determined to move to Europe. Before he could do so, he felt he had to dispose of his mistresses, Dominga and Hoosna, and surviving child, Penelope. As vestiges of his Sardhana past, he had tried to hide them in Calcutta. He further felt they would not be appropriate companions for him during his new life in Europe and had to be decisively dealt with, yet he could not easily abandon them either.

He initially proposed sending Dominga back to Meerut with a pension. Since there was a smallpox epidemic there, however, she preferred remaining in Hooghly, across the river from Calcutta, under the care of a Catholic priest, Father Gondoli, with a monthly pension of Rs 60.[49] Dyce Sombre insisted that he retain custody of their child, Penelope, but that he not be publicly seen with her. Then, they concurred that she should marry, as was appropriate to her status, a European. The priest located Mr Leyding 'a gentleman earning 400 per month, but [he] wants cash in advance', some Rs 10,000.[50] After extensive negotiations, Leyding received his money, while Dominga received a pension of Rs 150 per month, custody of Penelope until Dyce Sombre returned from Europe, and various other gifts; she married Leyding on 28 April 1837.[51]

Dominga's marriage, however, proved unhappy. She was often unwell. Further, Dyce Sombre continued to visit, demand attention from her, and give gifts to them which must have added to their domestic tensions.[52] Dominga died less than five months later.[53] Dyce Sombre then tried to reclaim her property, which caused further tensions with her husband.[54] Eventually Dyce Sombre and Leyding divided her estate but Dyce Sombre paid for her burial and tombstone at a Portuguese Church in Moorghatta.[55]

Further, while Dyce Sombre desired to take his daughter, Penelope, with him to England, he also wished not to be publicly associated with her. Therefore he arranged for her to travel by a separate ship, entrusted to a European couple,

[48]Diary 18–30 Jan. 1838, 7 Feb. 1838.
[49]Diary 11–13 Feb. 1837.
[50]Diary 23 Feb.–2 Mar. 1837.
[51]Diary 3–19 Mar. 1837, 28 Apr. 1837.
[52]Diary 7 May 1837, 24 May 1837, 9 June 1837, 18 June 1837, 3 July 1837.
[53]Diary 21 Nov. 1837.
[54]Diary 3–5 Dec. 1837, 21 Dec. 1837, 1–12 Jan. 1838.
[55]Diary 24 Dec. 1837, 5–11 Jan. 1838.

Major Edmund Herring and his wife, whose passage Dyce Sombre paid in exchange for their custody of his daughter. Sadly she died soon after the ship set sail.[56] Thus Dyce Sombre made only half-hearted efforts to rid himself of Dominga and also retain but also deny their daughter.

Similarly Dyce Sombre only incompletely divested himself of his other long-time mistress, Hoosna. Hoosna, they felt, should marry a Muslim. One of Dyce Sombre's long-time retainers, a 25-year-old bearer named Sayid al-Din alias Sheikh Edoo whom he had originally intended to bring in his suite to Europe, proved willing to marry her, in exchange for appropriate compensation and a pension of Rs 200 per month.[57] They married on 25 March 1837, but Dyce Sombre could not bring himself to relinquish her. Five days later and periodically over the next month, he apparently had sex with her again, paying Edoo Rs 2000 in gold as compensation.[58] Hoosna insisted that Dyce Sombre escort her in public, displaying herself with him from his open carriage, which he reluctantly did. Only with Dyce Sombre's final departure for England did he leave her.[59] Not surprisingly, Hoosna and Edoo did not have a congenial marriage; they separated, with Edoo and Hoosna eventually receiving separate pensions from Dyce Sombre.[60] With all his Indian sexual relations ended, Dyce Sombre set out for Europe to begin his new life there.[61]

IV. THE PASSAGE TO BRITAIN

Aboard ship to Britain, the confined society of the British made Dyce Sombre feel uncertain and isolated. His identity was not clear to him, neither as a European nor an Indian, one of the paying passengers but not a full participant in their society. He thus shrank from social contact, remaining much in his own cabin: 'Generally speaking, [the other passengers] are all cold, because I am an outcaste, alias an 1/2 caste.'[62] Apparently to compensate for his sense of insecurity, he flaunted his wealth through excessively generous tips to the captain and crew and pledges on publicly visible subscription lists.

After he reached Britain in June 1838, he sued the East India Company in British courts and also established himself in high society. The first did him no good, however. He filed lawsuits in order to reverse the Sardhana annexation

[56]Penelope died on board the *Duke of Buccleigh* about 23 Feb. 1838.

[57]Diary 25 Feb. 1837.

[58]Diary 30 Mar.–18 May 1837.

[59]Diary 3–5 Dec. 1837.

[60]Dyce Sombre to Reghelini, St Petersburg, 6 Nov. 1844, and to Syed Oodeen alias Sheik Edoo undated letter, L/L/64 (441), pp. 291–2, 438, OIOC.

[61]Due to constrains of space, this chapter omits discussion of Dyce Sombre's complex roles during his brief visit to South East Asia and China.

[62]Diary 26–31 Mar. 1838.

and also to recover the Begum's seized personal property. These cases dragged on until 1865, fourteen years after his own death. The courts finally found the annexation illegal (yet not reversible) and awarded compensation to Dyce Sombre's estate for the confiscation of the Begum's personal property.

In contrast to these official frustrations, Dyce Sombre immediately entered the British social and political elite on the most intimate terms. Since he was somewhat swarthy in complexion, obese, and frequently unhygienic in his person, his physique does not seem to have been particularly attractive, but his wealth and Oriental associations were. He had transferred most of his liquid assets to England, yielding a princely cash income of about £20,000 annually.[63] To establish his credentials in London, he applied for and received a coat of arms and assumed the title of Colonel (as former commander of the Begum's troops and holder of brevets from the French).[64] One of the most influential of the Britons whom he had known in India was Sir Stapleton Cotton, Viscount Combermere, a hero of wars in Europe and India; he had met Dyce Sombre while Commander-in-Chief there. Dyce Sombre informed Combermere 'that he was anxious to get into society in London'.[65] Soon his wealth and connections established him as one of the most eligible bachelors of the social season.

Only a few months after his arrival in England, Dyce Sombre met the Honourable Miss Mary Anne Jervis (1812–93), daughter of Viscount St. Vincent. She was widely known in select society as a lively and vivacious woman. She had a much applauded voice when she sang in aristocratic gatherings. She and Dyce Sombre soon developed a strong interest in each other. Dyce Sombre consulted Combermere among others about whether to formally propose marriage. Despite their advice to the contrary, he did so and she accepted.

Her father, Viscount St. Vincent, also consulted their friends about this engagement. Given Dyce Sombre's wealth and social standing, the issue of his race was evident but did not seem to bother neither Miss Jervis nor the society around them. St. Vincent, a former slave owner in Jamaica, had defended slavery in Parliament as necessary before 'Negroes' could be useful and productive.[66] Yet he said he regarded Dyce Sombre as 'a very honourable and good young man ... and that there could be nothing against him but his colour, and that, [St. Vincent] immediately added, was his Daughter's concern'.[67]

Nonetheless, conflicts arose between Dyce Sombre and Miss Jervis over their disparate expectations of her behaviour. Dyce Sombre expected her to never go

[63]Dyce Sombre, *Mr Dyce Sombre's Refutation*, p. 246.

[64]*Illustrated London News* (12 July 1851), p. 42c.

[65]Affidavit of Combermere, 2 Mar. 1844, L/L/63 (434), Documents Appendix 1, pp. 7–10, OIOC.

[66]Lord St. Vincent Speech, 4 June 1833 in Hansard, *Parliamentary Debates*, 3rd series, vol. 18.

[67]Affidavit of Combermere, 2 Mar. 1844, L/L/63 (434), Documents Appendix 1, pp. 7–10, OIOC.

out alone and to submit to his authority. She expected to continue her fashionable life, elevated by his status and supported by his fortune.[68] This led to further clashes. Dyce Sombre tried to enlist the support of St. Vincent in curtailing his daughter's freedom of movement; when he supported his daughter instead, Dyce Sombre accused him of alienating her affections and threatened to challenge him to a duel.[69]

The engaged couple also quarrelled over another fundamental issue of identity. They had agreed that all their sons would be raised Catholic and all their daughters Anglican. Dyce Sombre now insisted that, if no sons were born to them, any daughters would also be raised Catholic. He finally conceded to her position on this hypothetical issue. After obtaining a dispensation from the Archbishop of Canterbury and the Pope for their marriage, and contracting a pre-nuptial settlement which gave her £200,000 in case of his death, they were married on 26 September 1840 in the fashionable Anglican St. Georges Church, Hanover Square, and then privately by Catholic rites.

Their honeymoon to Italy got no further than Brussels before she became quite ill for eight weeks. It is not clear when he informed her about his frequent history of venereal diseases. After their return to England in December 1840, however, their differences escalated. During their visits to the country estates of the Duke of Wellington (April 1841), the Marquis of Hastings (May 1841), and the St. Vincents themselves (June 1841), Dyce Sombre began to make allegations to his hosts about his wife's immorality, including her being an opera singer (hence being a *tawaif*), her criminal sexual intercourse with men of all classes, and her committing incest with her father. Under pressure from his shocked hosts, he grudgingly backed down in his public accusations but clearly did not relinquish them.

In the summer of 1841, Dyce Sombre and a companion, Mr Frederick Villiers, purchased sufficient votes for them both to be elected to Parliament (29 June 1841) in the Whig Radical (Liberal) interest from Sudbury. Catholics had been allowed to enter Parliament since 1829 but it was unclear if people from India qualified, particularly people born outside British territory, in princely states. Indeed, a decade earlier, Jeremy Bentham had reportedly proposed Rajah Rammohun Roy as a candidate for Parliament, but this was never tested since Roy did not stand.[70]

While his successful entry into Parliament added a social cachet to Dyce Sombre, his career there proved limited to nine months (August 1841–April

---

[68]Affidavits of Hon. Mary Anne Dyce Sombre, 25 June 1844, in Dyce Sombre, *In Lunacy*, pp. 1–25.

[69]Dyce Sombre, *Mr Dyce Sombre's Refutation*, pp. 113–15.

[70]Jeremy Bentham, *Works*, ed. by John Bowring (New York: Russell and Russell, 1962), p. 66.

1842) and six votes. Losing candidates filed petitions against seventy-three newly elected Members of Parliament. One of these accused Dyce Sombre of being disqualified for election on two grounds: first he 'was not born a subject of this realm, and had never been naturalized, and was therefore incapable of sitting in Parliament' and second, his and Villiers' elections should be voided 'on the ground of extensive bribery'.[71] In the hearing of the Election Committee, the first charge was held in reserve in case it would be needed. It was not. The Committee declared both Dyce Sombre and Villiers guilty of 'gross systematic and extensive bribery' and ordered their elections 'controverted'. Proceedings to disenfranchise the borough of Sudbury began at the same time, which occurred a few years later. Thus Dyce Sombre, Villiers, and the Sudbury voters all misjudged the changing values and regulations of British society and the extent to which elections could be purchased in the post-1832 Reform Bill era.

While living in London, Dyce Sombre had mixed relations with many of the other elite Indians there. He hosted dinners for various Indian diplomats and royalty and involved them in his pleasures. While they appreciated his generosity, some commented unfavourably on his eccentricities.[72]

Similarly, many British elite also accepted Dyce Sombre's largesse but his unconventional behaviour made them increasingly uncomfortable. When his personal conflicts with his wife worsened, she collected her relatives and their leading friends. They all pleaded with Dyce Sombre to relinquish his accusations against her, which he refused.

Yet British property laws favoured husbands over their wives. From March 1842, he took control over the allowance given her by her father. While Dyce Sombre promised to buy her anything she asked him for, and constantly showered her with costly presents, he refused to allow her independent control over any money, claiming that she would use it to buy sex. He accused her of having lovers hidden about their apartments in the posh Clarendon Hotel, and even introducing them into their bed as he slept.

An extended trip to Scotland and frequent visits by leading British physicians failed to check Dyce Sombre's accusations and increasingly unconventional behaviour. Dyce Sombre visited a famous mesmerist, Dr Elliottson, demanding that his wife be hypnotized into finding him more attractive; when Elliottson

---

[71] 'Minutes of Evidence taken before the Select Committee on the Sudbury Election Petition', *Parliamentary Papers Sessionals 1842*, vol. 7, pp. 847–942; 'Minutes of Evidence: Second Reading of the Sudbury Disenfranchise Bill', *Parliamentary Papers Sessionals 1843*, vol. 6, pp. 503–89; 'Report of the Commissioners ... to enquire into the Existence of Bribery in the Borough of Sudbury', *Parliamentary Papers Sessionals 1844*, vol. 18, pp. 247–561; *Times* (9 Apr. 1842); Arthur Barron and Alfred Austin, *Reports of Cases of Controverted Elections in the Fourteenth Parliament of the United Kingdom* (London: Sweet, Maxwell & Son, 1844), pp. 237–62.

[72] See Fisher, *Counterflows*, ch. 8.

expressed surprise at Dyce Sombre's unethical request, Dyce Sombre challenged him to a duel. Indeed, Dyce Sombre issued a series of challenges to duels, against men he believed had insulted his wife's honour, including doctors who examined her and people they met at social occasions. He attempted to induce her to share his feelings by alleging that he, too, had been offered women by the elite in British society. He urged his wife to challenge these women to duels in defence of his honour. He began to threaten her with pistols and knives, vowing to cut off her nose as adulterous women in India were treated. He asserted that good and evil spirits were battling for his mind; on the orders of an evil spirit, he cast his wife's wedding ring into the fire and shaved off his eyebrows. He sent challenges to Directors of the East India Company, threatening them with duels. He also appealed to Queen Victoria against the Company.[73] Finally, the physicians attending him convinced his reluctant wife that Dyce Sombre must be restrained, so as not to do harm to her or himself. In the presence of several eminent physicians and her family, a doctor and two keepers took physical charge of Dyce Sombre on 30 March 1843.

At this point in the development of British psychiatry, debate raged over the very nature of madness, as well as its treatment. There was no official distinction between the two conditions of lunacy and sanity; gender and class affected the state's attitude toward the alleged lunatic as well. As a gentleman of means, Dyce Sombre was never in danger of incarceration in an asylum. Nor was he ever actually treated in order to be cured. Rather, over the remainder of his life, he was almost continually being tested by individual, or boards of, doctors in order to classify him as either sane or, if not sane, the degree to which his lunacy made him a threat to himself, his wife, or his property. At first, he remained in the Clarendon Hotel, separated from his wife, but under the observation of his keepers, until he aimed a pistol at one of them.[74] His doctors then housed him in an imposing villa called Hanover Lodge near the Regent's Park zoo.

Although Dyce Sombre could go out in the company of his keepers, he clearly felt his confinement. For a time, he refused any hot food. He drew up a new will, disinheriting his wife but giving his fortune in trust to the East India Company (with large gifts to prominent Directors) for a school and other projects in Sardhana. He signed this will 'in the Prison of Hanover Lodge'. Further, he wrote letters of appeal to the American Government, to be delivered to the American Ambassador in London.[75] As he later described this to the Russian Government:

By the intrigue of my enemies, I was, under the pretext of being insane, kept under strict watch for four months .... My things were taken from me, trunks and boxes broken open, sealed letters, packets, letters, and even my will, which is reckoned a sacred thing in

[73]Dyce Sombre, *Mr Dyce Sombre's Refutation*, pp. 519–20.
[74]*Times* (2 Aug. 1843).
[75]Unattested will dated 10 May 1843, in Dyce Sombre, *Dyce Sombre Against Troup*, p. 45.

all parts of the world, were opened and read, and then given up to persons who may make whatever use they pleased of them.[76]

He further identified the spirit tormenting him as a man whom he had fatally imprisoned while he had been managing Sardhana. The Begum herself appeared before him to witness his remarriage with his wife. He saw himself conversing with the late George III in a madhouse. In short, his doctors found much to record and report about this well-publicized case.

A Commission of Lunacy was drawn up and heard in Hanover Lodge before the Lord Chancellor and a special jury, attended by a crowded gallery of the elite of British society and numerous newspaper reporters. Dyce Sombre objected to the proceedings on several grounds. One, holding hearings at 11:00 a.m., before he ordinarily arose, was an insult to his honour. Second, this was a plot against him by his enemy, the East India Company. Third, the hearings should really be aimed at justifying his repudiation of his wife by demonstrating her immorality. Dyce Sombre refused an advocate, preferring to represent himself. While his cross-examination of witnesses made some points that the Chancellor recognized as legitimate, his actions generally failed to convince the jury of his sanity.

In his judgment, the Lord Chancellor summed up the central issues of the case. These issues would remain salient ones until Dyce Sombre's death. First, what was Dyce Sombre: 'European' or 'Asiatic'? If European by 'blood' (as Dyce Sombre insisted, claiming that most of his ancestors had at least some European blood) or by education (as several witnesses insisted, primarily based on his four years studying with Reverend Fisher), then, the Lord Chancellor opined, Dyce Sombre was clearly a lunatic.[77] No sane European would act with his irrational jealousy. However, if he were Asiatic by blood (as most witnesses asserted, based on the fact that his parents each had some Indian blood) or by upbringing under Begum Sombre, then were his actions—particularly with regard to his possessive attitudes towards women—normal or abnormal by Indian standards?

On this last point, evidence would remain divided. Many Europeans, self-proclaimed experts in 'Asiatic' culture, argued that the system of female seclusion prevalent in families of his class indicated an inherent obsessive jealousy. They argued therefore, given Dyce Sombre's Asiatic nature, he was being perfectly reasonable, no matter how inappropriate such attitudes were in Europe: 'When [his actions] are interpreted by a reference to Asiatic feelings and modes of thought, [they] are by no means indicative of unsound mind.'[78] Several witnesses questioned

---

[76]Journal or Report of the Medical Council of St. Petersburg, 17 Dec. 1844, L/L/65 (452), OIOC.

[77]Dyce Sombre, *Mr Dyce Sombre's Refutation*, p. 19; *Times* (9 Aug. 1844, 2 Mar. 1849, 7 Mar. 1849).

[78]Sir Charles Trevelyan, letter, 19 Aug. 1843, in Dyce Sombre *Mr Dyce Sombre's Refutation*, pp. 8, 13, 256.

the competence of any English jury to comprehend Indian values, so foreign to their experience.

In contrast, other European 'experts in Asiatic culture' argued that the normal attitudes of Indians towards their women were essentially similar to those of Europeans, and therefore that Dyce Sombre was abnormal in either culture. The Begum's long-time physician, Drever, testified

from his long and intimate acquaintance with the said Dyce Sombre in India and with the natives of India, he is satisfied that neither the education and habits of the said D.O. Dyce Sombre, nor his Eastern parentage, can account for the delusions entertained by the said D.O. Dyce Sombre, but that the same arose from insanity.[79]

The Lord Chancellor and jury concluded on 8 August 1843 that Dyce Sombre (even if Asiatic by blood) had enough European experience to be judged of unsound mind. They declared him lunatic retroactively from 27 October 1842.[80] This led to the order for the establishment of a 'Committee of the Person' as guardian over him.

Second, was Dyce Sombre a threat to his property? The Chancellor heard little evidence that he was, but nevertheless ordered the establishment of a Committee of the Estate to control his money. Thus, while Mrs Dyce Sombre received a handsome annual allowance of £4000, all Dyce Sombre's expenses had to be approved by the Chancellor, pending the constitution of the Committee. Later, the Chancellor put Dyce Sombre on an allowance of £60 per week but required him to submit receipts for every penny. This led to a pattern by Dyce Sombre of demanding receipts for every expenditure, and disputing bills down to the cent, even at the cost of much fuss in restaurants and public places. His defenders attributed his minute scrutiny of even tiny bills as a proof of his rationality. His attackers used it, given his vast income and the lavish society in which he moved, to allege his irrationality. Partly convinced of his careful use of his money, the Chancellor eventually raised his allowance from his estate to £5000 per year, about a quarter of its income.

Now officially declared insane, Dyce Sombre spent much of the rest of his life trying to get this judgment reversed. As he wrote in frustration: 'Dead men are never heard, otherwise they would be taken for ghosts; and such is the case with Chancery Lunatics. I am a dead man, according to the existing law.'[81]

Although Hanover Lodge proved not a particularly healthy dwelling place, Dyce Sombre remained there another month, and his further improbable

[79]Drever, Affidavit, 24 June 1844, James Ranald Martin, Affidavit, 20 Feb. 1849, in Dyce Sombre, *In Lunacy*, pp. 31–40, 176–8.

[80]This invalidated the will and other transactions which Dyce Sombre had concluded during the five months prior to his being put under restraint.

[81]Dyce Sombre, *Mr Dyce Sombre's Refutation*, p. 244.

assertions were carefully recorded by his doctors.[82] In order to remove any cause for irritation, Dyce Sombre received from the Chancellor the freedom to travel wherever in Britain he chose, accompanied by a doctor and two keepers. From 9 September 1843, Dyce Sombre toured Bath, Bristol, Gloucester, Birmingham, and Liverpool. As long as he behaved normally, as his keepers reported that he did, he was able to move about these cities freely. In Liverpool, he thought to purchase a pleasure yacht for his amusement. Instead, in the middle of the night (21 September 1843), he fled his keepers and disappeared. They, aghast at having lost their charge, had the police search the city. They apprehended a tall, dark East Indian, who turned out to be the steward of a ship in port. Next, the authorities feared that kidnappers had seized Dyce Sombre for his money, since he had a considerable amount of cash on his person. In reality, Dyce Sombre had escaped to France, where he appeared once again in high society.

In Paris, and then elsewhere on the continent, Dyce Sombre assembled evidence of his sanity. He took affidavits from his servants, landladies, tradesmen, society companions, and a series of distinguished doctors, all testifying to his perfect reason. Over the years, he submitted fifty-two such affidavits, from individuals or groups, including from thirty-two medical doctors. Included among these was the Board of Russian Medical Experts, Dyce Sombre having gone to St. Petersburg for four months in 1845, his explicit goal being 'to receive a certificate from the medical men of the country, and with that document to return to England and reclaim the remnant of my once brilliant fortune'.[83]

Impressed with this extensive evidence in support of the repeated petitions from Dyce Sombre for a reversal of the judgment of lunacy, successive Lord Chancellors held five exhaustive hearings. In opposition, agents of the Committees of the Person and the Estate gathered affidavits from his acquaintances and servants attesting to Dyce Sombre's irrationally, belligerent behaviour, and immoral conduct. One of his landladies gave two affidavits, one on each side of his sanity question. Most important for the court, each of the nine medical experts whom the Chancellor appointed, in repeated examinations over the years, came unanimously to the same conclusion: Dyce Sombre remained lunatic.

British newspapers laid out all these investigations, hearings, and opinions in graphic detail for the public's edification and amusement. The unbridgeably divided opinion among the most distinguished members of the medical profession who specialized in lunacy in Britain and the continent illustrates today, as it did then, the inadequacies of such cultural categories as 'sanity' and 'insanity'. Further, some newspapers proved largely unsympathetic to Mrs Dyce Sombre, portraying her as a manipulative gold-digger who won out over her simple-minded Indian victim.[84]

[82]Lord Chancellor's Judgment, *Times* (7 Mar. 1849).
[83]Dyce Sombre, petition, 6 July 1847, L/L/65 (452), OIOC.
[84]*Age* (newspaper) (13 Feb. 1852).

In this view, her gender and aristocratic class counted against her, while his gender and ethnicity gained him some popular support.

Also entered into the record were other acts which demonstrated Dyce Sombre's efforts to shape his fate, efforts which British society, and the Lord Chancellor, found indicative of his unsound mind. Dyce Sombre sought to have the Jockey Club of Paris, where he was a welcome and frequent member, hold a formal trial about his wife's immorality. Dyce Sombre offered bribes (ranging from £1500 cash to an annuity of £250 per year) to the wives of the Lord Chancellor and several of the Chancery-appointed medical doctors, as well as Prime Minister Lord John Russell, in exchange for their support for him. He openly visited prostitutes in each European city he visited, and frequently got into trouble with the police for his promiscuous solicitation of virtually any nubile unaccompanied woman he saw on the street. In each case, his wealth and social class got him released from confinement. When his obesity, general bad health, and frequent cases of venereal disease made him impotent, he hired and trained prostitutes to give him full body massages, 'shampoos'.[85] His inquisitive landlords and landladies observed and reported his unconventional behaviour, further enhancing his unsavoury public reputation as unrestrained by morality.

Dyce Sombre also wrote works that he thought would set the record straight. Because his youngest sister and her husband did not support him, he anonymously published a pamphlet, in English, Italian, and French, alleging her illegitimacy and his immorality (alleging him a parricide of low birth). This publication led to the conviction for libel of the printer.[86] Undaunted, Dyce Sombre compiled and published a 591-page book: *Mr Dyce Sombre's Refutation of the Charge of Lunacy Brought Against Him in the Court of Chancery* (Paris: the Author, 1849). This book laid out his case in extensive detail, with vast amounts of documentary evidence supporting his contentions. Yet none of this restored his status as sane in British law.

Throughout the trials, hearings, and rehearings, Mrs Dyce Sombre maintained that she was lovingly loyal to her husband, but that he needed to change his attitudes and behaviour for the protection of himself, herself, and their property. She arranged surprise visits with him that came off badly.[87] Even on the eve of his death, she wrote affectionately to him.[88] She thus maintained her role as loving wife.

[85] Affidavits of Johan Frederic Chretien Furhberg, 8 Oct. 1853, and Amede, 8 Oct. 1853, Depositions of Witnesses, L/L/64 (441), vol. 2, pp. 405–8. See Michael H. Fisher, *First Indian Author in English: Dean Mahomed (1759–1851) in India, Ireland, and England* (New Delhi: Oxford University Press, 1996).

[86] Dyce Sombre, *Mr Dyce Sombre's Refutation*, pp. 257, 265ff; Troup Affidavit, 11 Dec. 1846, in Dyce Sombre, *In Lunacy*, pp. 103–4.

[87] Affidavit of Mary Anne Jarvis, 20 Feb. 1849, in Dyce Sombre, *In Lunacy*, pp. 179–80.

[88] Mrs Dyce Sombre to Dyce Sombre, 14 June 1851, in Dyce Sombre, *Dyce Sombre Against Troup*, p. 990.

Dyce Sombre never cleared his name. Disease severely debilitated his body and mind and he finally succumbed to an infection in his foot which spread through his body. He died in London (1 July 1851). His body was buried there, but he directed that his heart be returned to Sardhana and entombed next to the Begum. His wife and the East India Company conducted long and expensive legal battles over his estate. If his last will was proven valid, the Company would inherit as trustees for a school in Sardhana. But it was finally set aside, his wife inheriting virtually his entire wealth. She then was herself widely celebrated in high British society as 'the Begum', occasionally wearing the Indian clothes Dyce Sombre had given her, assuming her late husband's attractive Oriental aura.

V. CONCLUSION

The case of Dyce Sombre suggests particularly strongly the multiple and often conflicting ways that identities were defined and functioned in contact zones in India and, somewhat differently, in Britain. While as a whole, his case is unusual, none of the elements were unique to him. The identities of many people conflicted with abstract and fixed definitions. Constructions of gender roles created inequities that cut across other categories and were often strikingly inconsistent in India and Britain. In each location, people negotiated their respective relationships and standing on the basis of unequal power.

Like Sardhana, many Indian princely courts had composite cultures, drawing together people of different backgrounds. Various people of mixed ancestry like Dyce Sombre held particularly problematic roles under colonialism, as visible products of intimate intercourse between Europeans and Indians that some racial theories and colonial dichotomies tried to deny.[89] Typically among courtiers, the currently chosen heir apparent gained power but also resentment. Prostitutes and mistresses might loathe their treatment, but also sought to gain monetarily from it.

The relationship between people living in such princely states and the British also varied. Courtiers and rulers opposed, tolerated, or collaborated with British colonialism. The legal status of inhabitants of 'Indian India' as opposed to 'British India' remained frequently contested and unsettled in this period. Indeed, the Begum was a ruler but not sovereign; she could freely dispose of her personal property but not state property. Yet it took thirty-seven years of court cases before the legal distinction between these was settled.

In British India, the standing of Indian noblemen and women was often ambivalent. They were elevated by their class and wealth but were marginalized by many Britons as one of the colonized. Britons developed theories about 'Black' versus 'White' races, about 'martial races' and 'effeminate races', and tried to

---

[89]See Hawes, *Poor Relations*.

impose policies based on those theories.[90] Yet those theories and policies were cultural constructs not based on the lives of real people. At least some high-ranking British officers seem to have considered wealthy men of mixed ancestry like Dyce Sombre as potential sons-in-law. Then the issue would be the subordination of their daughters on gendered grounds and the identities of their descendants. Lower-ranking British officers also permitted men like Dyce Sombre into their society, but under distant and non-reciprocal terms. As with many Anglicized Indians, some of the lodges of the Freemasons provided a different hierarchy, not based on race but rather their own esoteric order.

The social world of Calcutta also contained many different inconsistencies about identities. Indian-displaced Indian noblemen like Dyce Sombre were invited by the Governor-General's sisters to their 'at homes'. But lesser-ranked Britons objected to their presence among them, resenting their wealth even more due to their status as colonized and 'Black'. Nonetheless, some European prostitutes, whatever their personal feelings might have been, sold their bodies into intimate relations with Indians who would pay.

The tens of thousands of Indians who, like Dyce Sombre, also travelled to Britain by this time all negotiated identities often quite different from those they were familiar with in India. Many Indian men used their power as male by gender to subordinate British women, including those they married. Some used their wealth to rise into the highest circles both socially and politically. Even a slave-owning aristocrat accepted Dyce Sombre as son-in-law, based on his property and putative class status, and despite his Catholic religion and physique.

Although Dyce Sombre rose higher than most, he proved unable to remain there. Only when Dyce Sombre made himself vulnerable by excessive transgression of British social conventions, particularly concerning gendered behaviour, however, did he become subject to confinement. His English wife eventually gained his entire fortune (which later went to her second husband, Baron George Cecil Weld Forester) and also some of his Oriental mystique. Significantly, British public opinion at that time tended to favour him and other Indian husbands as innocent victims of their British wives' greedy ambitions.

In addition, the status of Indians as British subjects in Britain was also controversial. Dyce Sombre's legal right to enter Parliament was never resolved. For the electors of Sudbury, Dyce Sombre's money outweighed his virtually total lack of connection to their borough. Other Indians were elected starting a half century later, including Dadabhai Naoroji (1825–1917, who ran for Parliament in 1886 and won in 1892) and Mancherjee Merwanjee Bhownaggree (1851–1933, who won in 1895 and 1900). Sitting in the Parliament of imperial Britain,

---

[90]See Mrinalini Sinha, *Colonial Masculinity: The 'Manly Englishman' and the 'Effeminate Bengali' in the Late Nineteenth Century* (Manchester: Manchester University Press, 1995).

these men might participate in public discourse and influence colonial (and British domestic) policies, although Dyce Sombre did not speak or vote through any legislation.

British society also remained generally unresolved about the nature of sanity. During this period, in addition to learned medical discussion, many controversial cases received widespread popular attention. In his case, British definitions of his 'race' as 'European' or 'Asiatic' based on biological criteria confronted definitions based on his education and deportment. For him to have accepted being 'Indian' might have freed him from confinement as a lunatic. Yet he would not concur and instead liberated himself. On the continent, his legal status was that of a sane man, although his behaviour often offended local morals.

Dyce Sombre's private record of his life, contextualized with other historical evidence about him, provides an index of his complex, asymmetrical, yet intimate social and cultural interactions in three contact zones. Further, his own writings often reveal gaps between his perceptions and self-representation and those of others. All this demonstrates the dangers of simple characterizations concerning identities, especially under colonialism. His identities as Black and White, Indian and European, colonized and colonizer, subaltern and elite, sane and insane, remained highly contested, each cross-cutting his gender and class identities, with diverse implications for his agency and relationships in each locale.

SHARIF CULTURE AND COLONIAL RULE: A MAULVI—MISSIONARY ENCOUNTER*

Mushirul Hasan

A branch of Islamic literature in which didactic morality is a frequent subject of treatment is that concerned with *adab*, manners, and 'professional' etiquette.[1] Used in its most general sense as a greeting, adab is also defined as correct behaviour in the process of a person being educated, guided, and formed into a good Muslim.[2] Thus the eighteenth century French adventurer, Antoine-Lois Henri Polier (*c.* 1741–95), used phrases like 'gentlemanly' behaviour, 'candour', and 'loyalty' to express proper conduct. Polier's image of local people is based on their relationship to success and power, not their status within the varna hierarchy. He therefore deploys a vocabulary to identify them in terms of the professions they pursue, relates to them on professional grounds, and judges their conduct by using the urbane and upper class notions of proper conduct popularized by the Mughals.[3] In the post-Mughal capital of Lucknow and the erstwhile Mughal *subah* of Awadh, the social identifiers continued to be the caste- and community-neutral categorizations.[4]

---

*An earlier version of this chapter appeared in C.F. Andrews, *Zakaullah of Delhi* (Delhi, 2003), introduced by Margrit Pernau and me.

[1] Rueben Levy, *The Social Structure of Islam* (Cambridge, 1957 edn), p. 235.

[2] Ira M. Lapidus, 'Knowledge, virtue, and action: The classical Muslim conception of adab and the nature of religious fulfilment in Islam', in Barbara Daly Metcalf (ed.), *Moral Conduct and Authority: The Place of Adab in South Asian Islam* (Berkeley, 1984), p. 39.

[3] Muzaffar Alam and Seema Alavi (eds), *A European Experience of the Mughal Orient* (New Delhi, 2001), pp. 60, 61.

[4] Ibid., p. 57.

Both in Delhi and Lucknow, the old culture did not vanish despite colonial rule's intrusive role.[5] While clinging to established traditions, acquisition of knowledge and the strict observance of professional codes being part thereof, individuals and families became part of and not distanced from an ever-changing social and cultural landscape. They earned respect and fame not because they were wealthy or powerful, but because of their moral stature and professional standing. Thus the death of Hakim Mahmud Khan of Delhi, also mentioned by Abdul Halim Sharar (c. 1860–1926) in his book *Lucknow: The Last Phase of an Oriental Culture*, moved Khwaja Altaf Husain Hali (c. 1837–1914) to write an elegy of great pathos and power.

The wealth that is so scarce in the market of the world today,
Thy graveyard is endowed with it in abundance.[6]

The death of Mirza Asadullah 'Ghalib' (c. 1797–1869) and Saiyyid Ahmad Khan (c. 1817–98) evoked similar responses from Hali.[7] Years later, *Comrade* (Calcutta, Delhi) mourned the demise of Hakim Abdul Aziz, the renowned Lucknow physician, and the scholar Aga Kamaluddin Sanjar. Founder of the Madrasa-i takmil-ut tib and a physician of exceptional attainments and experience, the *Hakim* enjoyed repute as a leading exponent of *yunani* medicine. 'We still await,' the paper concluded its obituary with the comment,

the birth of … eminent physicians like the late Hakim Abdul Aziz, or poets of the power and versatility of the late Aga Sangar. Hitherto, the products of the 'New Spirit' have had to depend for light and inspiration on men who had formed their minds and characters on the faith and culture of the past.[8]

What made Mahmud Khan, Abdul Aziz, and Aga Kamaluddin Sanjar so endearing to their contemporaries? This is, in part, answered by a document produced by the All India Muhammadan Educational Conference. Published in Lahore with essays from Aligarh's leading lights, this treatise reiterates the codes of behaviour that the Prophet—'the noble paradigm'—followed.[9] It is, in all probability, inspired by *Akhlaqul Ashraf*, or 'Ethics of the Aristocracy', authored by Ubayad-i Zakani, the fourteenth-century Persian parodist and satirical

---

[5]This is evident from the essays of Rashidul Khairi (c. 1870–1936) in *Dilli ki akhri bahar* (Delhi, 1937).

[6]Some of the Urdu lines and their translations are in *Hali's Musaddas: The Flow and Ebb of Islam*. Translated, and with a critical introduction by Christopher Shackle and Javed Majeed (New Delhi, 1997), p. 46.

[7]Some of the obituaries or *marsiyas* (elegies) in poetry are in Khaliq Ahmad Nizami (ed.), *Armughan-i Aligarh* (Aligarh, 1974). The emotionalism expressed therein illuminates several aspects of social and cultural history.

[8]*Comrade*, 21 October 1911.

[9]*Risala-i Conference mutaaliq tamaddun-o-ma'asharat* (Aligarh, n.d.).

writer.[10] Other works on ethics were also in circulation, notably the *Akhlaq-i Nasiri* written by celebrated astronomer Nasiruddin Tusi, the *Akhlaq-i Jalali* by philosopher Jalaluddin Dawani, and the *Akhlaq-i Muhsini* compiled by Husain-i Kashifi. While translations of these books were printed at Hertford for Anglo-Indian officials,[11] their original Persian version guided Delhi's Urdu writers who compiled such works with similar titles. Broadly speaking, the hallmark of high culture, according to them, was not worldly power and material possessions but knowledge, intelligence, refinement, and personal and professional integrity in private and public persona. Those possessing these attributes were the standard-bearers of the much celebrated *sharif* milieu.

Maulvi Muhammad Zakaullah (*c.* 1832–1910), the grand old man of Delhi, fulfilled nearly all the qualifications laid down in late-nineteenth-century religious and ethical texts. In his obituary published in August 1911, one of his best friends described him as *Karimun nafs* (noble-minded, of a generous soul), *Karimul akhlaq* (most generous and noble), *Wasihul nazar* (broad-minded, with breadth of vision), humble or *Munkasirul mizag*, *Raushan dimagh* or enlightened, and *Fayyaz tabah* or generous and beneficent.[12] The paradigm of sharif culture is essentially ideal and many of its protagonists fell considerably short of this ideal. But Zakaullah, who was influenced by Islam's ethical norms and moral precepts and by Persian moralist Shaikh Sadi's (1184–1292) *Bustan* (The Fruit Garden) and *Gulistan* (The Rose Garden; the Urdu translation printed in Nastaliq type was priced at Rs 32 in 1809), paid special attention to the acquisition of knowledge and to gentlemanly conduct. At the same time, his conception of adab and public and private morality was different from that of some of his contemporaries in so far as he affirmed that virtues such as honesty, truthfulness, loyalty to friend, and concern for the poor and needy, had a place in any great civilization. In other words, the Islamic ethical ideal was not very different from the ethical ideals of other religions. 'Such is the potent combination of earnest, truthful and utilitarian ideas,' Zakaullah writes, 'that remove darkness and ignorance from this world .... Their protagonists underline unity and harmony rather than discord and disunity. Their ideas, though derived from different sources, ultimately merge into a stream and impact on nations and communities in much the same way.'[13]

This example serves to situate Zakaullah, his novelist friend Maulvi Nazir Ahmad (*c.* 1836–1912), and his biographer Charles Freer Andrews (*c.* 1871–1940), son of a minister of the Catholic Apostolic Church. In the triangular narrative that follows, I have not re-traversed the ground covered by Andrews, except to add to

---

[10]Edward G. Browne, *Literary History of Persia* (Cambridge, 1992), vol. 3, pp. 244–9.

[11]Ibid., pp. 442–3.

[12]Maulana Muhammad Yahya, *Sairul Musannifin* (Delhi, 1928), vol. 2, p. 211.

[13]Maulvi Nazir Ahmad, quoted in Maulvi Muhammad Zakaullah, *Tahzibul Akhlaq-e Arya Hind, Yaani Hinood* (Delhi, 1891), p. 1.

the information here and there, and to give it perhaps a new actuality and perspective. Let me add another caveat. Sharif culture in Delhi's context was inclusive with a strong imprint of religious plurality and cultural synthesis. Yet I deal exclusively with the cultural and intellectual trends amongst the Muslim literati largely because they figure time and time again in Andrews' master text. I draw upon this text to illuminate certain neglected features of Delhi's cultural and intellectual ambience.

I

While all the problems of definition and treatment of terms like 'colonialism', 'nationalism', revivalism', 'reformism', and 'modernism' have still to be worked out, there is virtual unanimity among historians that the colonial impact on Delhi's Muslim elites was by no means the same as on their counterparts in Bengal. While British rule led to the service communities' displacement or impoverishment in Bengal, similar groups in Delhi, having long been connected in one way or the other with the Mughal court and administration, were weakened but not uprooted lock, stock, and barrel. Quite a few individuals did well, and made the colonial bureaucracy work. Of all persons, Zakaullah stated that 'it is the Royal House of Victoria that has thus raised my family to its former dignity and affluence'.

The opening lines of Nazir Ahmad's novel, *Ibn-ul-Vaqt* (A Son of the Age), are: 'What made Ibn-ul-Vaqt so prominent was the fact that he adopted the English lifestyle at a time when even to learn English was considered blasphemy and to use English goods an act of apostasy.'[14] Even if the Muslim communities did not necessarily adopt the English lifestyle, they recognized foreign rule as an unchanging fact of life. Thus Mufti Sadruddin Azurda rose to become the highest official in the Delhi judiciary, while Maulana Fazl-i Haq Khairabadi (c. 1797–1861) obtained a post in the Company's service as *serishtadar* in Delhi's civil court. Mirza Asadullah Khan Ghalib wrote to the nawab of Rampur on 13 January 1858 that it was not, after all, such a bad thing to be a *namak-khwar-i sarkar-i angrez*—an eater of the salt of the English government.[15]

The reason why Delhi's Muslim elites retained their position, if not predominance, is that Urdu remained the official language and a necessary qualification for government employment. Saiyyid Ahmad learnt no English, but he could still be employed in the Sadr Amin's office at Delhi (18 January 1837). This meant that representation of such individuals in the administrative apparatus— judicial and executive—was not adversely affected. What is more, a specifically Indo-Muslim culture survived the deleterious effects of colonial rule, and the

[14]Nazir Ahmad, *Son of the Moment*. Translated by Muhammad Zakir (New Delhi, 2002).
[15]Peter Hardy, 'Ghalib and the British', in Ralph Russell (ed.), *Ghalib: The Poet and His Age* (Delhi, 1997 rpt), p. 163.

inner cultural, intellectual, and moral resilience of the Urdu-speaking elites, though enfeebled, was by no means beyond repair.

What created this resilience was the commanding position occupied by certain families in Mughal India, and the loss of it moved some to raise the banner of revolt and others to dispute whether or not India under the British was transformed into a *dar al-harb* (land of war). All this provided a foundation for the popular Muslim belief in the British threat. The fear was authentic, and the aggrieved sections exploited it. The *mujahidin*, for example, played with a smouldering fire that suddenly flared into a conflagration in the north-western part of India.[16] But such outbursts, caused by the almost sudden loss of power and patronage, petered out before long. Once the wings of the hard-core mujahidin and their sympathisers were clipped, what sustained the service elites' diverse communitarian perspectives was the will to reorder their lives differently. In so doing, they found it easy to adhere to the Islamic value system represented in the persona of the Prophet and the four Khalifas (Abu Bakr, Umar, Usman, and Ali), rather than the Islamic way of life supposedly threatened by the unbridled intrusion of the West. This they did to almost near perfection, negotiating the Islamic ethical domain with relative ease, and, in the process, proving its relevance and establishing its legitimacy.

What fortified the resilience after 1857, despite the retribution faced by scores of families at the hands of the British, is the high moral ground they occupied even at a time of growing uncertainties and mounting cultural and intellectual anxieties. Of all the examples assembled by historians, but hardly ever interpreted to convey its true import, is that of Ghalib.

In January 1842, the Secretary of the Government of India came to interview candidates for a Professorship in Persian at Delhi College (originally the Madrasa of Ghaziuddin Khan).[17] Ghalib was called for interview. When he arrived in his palanquin, the Secretary was informed, and at once sent for him. But Ghalib stood waiting for the Secretary to come out of his office and extend him the customary welcome. When the Secretary did finally come out and explained that he could

---

[16]Qeyamuddin Ahmad, *The Wahhabi Movement in India* (Delhi, 1994); Peter Hardy, *The Muslims of British India* (Cambridge, 1972).

[17]For the histories of Delhi College, Avril A. Powell, *Muslims and Missionaries in Pre-Mutiny India* (London, 1993), pp. 195–202; Gail Minault, 'Saiyyid Ahmad Dehlavi and the "Delhi renaissance"', in R.E. Frykenberg (ed.), *Delhi Through the Ages: Essays in Urban History, Culture and Society* (Delhi, 1986); her 'Qiran Al-Saadain: The dialogue between Eastern and Western learning at Delhi College', in Jamal Malik (ed.), *Perspectives of Mutual Encounters in South Asian History* (Leiden, 2000); and her *Secluded Scholars: Women's Education and Muslim Social Reform in Colonial India* (Delhi, 1998), especially on gender issues; Narayani Gupta, *Delhi Between Two Empires 1803–1931: Society, Government and Urban Growth* (Delhi, 1981); Nina Dey Gupta, 'The Halycon yesteryears of Delhi College: A chequered history', in Mushirul Hasan (ed.), *Knowledge, Power and Politics: Educational Institutions in India* (Delhi, 1998); Aziz Ahmad, *An Intellectual History of Islam* (Edinburgh, 1962).

not extend a formal welcome to a person seeking employment, the poet replied, 'I contemplated taking a government appointment in the expectation that this would bring me greater honours than I now receive, not a reduction in those already accorded me.' The Secretary replied, 'I am bound by regulations.' 'Then I hope that you will excuse me,' Ghalib said, and went away.

Zakaullah's career also illustrates a form of resilience that is, in some ways, unique to him. His life work was his attempt to persuade his co-believers not to abandon the use of their mother tongue: 'To forget it, despise it, is to lose one of the strongest factors in the building up of national character.' Though he knew English, he did not speak it unless it was absolutely necessary. He doggedly set himself the task of translating modern scientific textbooks into the Urdu spoken in north India. Although the verdict has gone against him with Muslim institutions, notably the Aligarh Muslim University, adopting English as the vehicle of higher education, Zakaullah's intervention illustrates the self-pride in a linguistic-cultural tradition and his creative attempt to safeguard it with the aid of translations of scientific work into Urdu. Translation of English prose into Urdu had already started at the Fort William College in 1800, but gradually spread to Patna, Faizabad, Hyderabad, Lucknow, Delhi, and Ghazipur. This trend gained impetus with the setting up of the Royal Translation Bureau in Lucknow and Hyderabad (founded in 1834), the Vernacular Translation Society of Delhi College (1842), the Scientific Society (1863), and the Christian missionary organizations with their presses at Serampore, Sardhana (Meerut), Mirzapur, Ludhiana, and other places.

What I have earlier called resilience (not to be construed as 'arrogance', 'self-conceit', or 'vanity') was sustained in various ways and through different institutions, mosques and traditional schools being just two of them, and found tangible expression in—and that indeed is my next point—Delhi's cultural and intellectual milieu. True, the world was fractured after Lord Lake's entry into Delhi in 1803, but that did not prevent the flowering of music, yunani medicine, Urdu prose and poetry, and historical scholarship. 'High traditions of the past,' commented Andrews, who had access to traditional Muslim families in the old city, 'were kept alive in every home by the stories of religion which mothers taught their children.'[18] Again, what this did was to keep intact the cultural and intellectual fabric, though quite often within the bounds of tradition. It also provided sustenance to the liberal humanism of the nineteenth-century north Indian Urdu-speaking elites, which forged a place for itself in Urdu literature produced mostly at the Delhi College, founded in 1825 with an English Principal, J.H. Taylor.

In the first edition of *Asar-us Sanadid* ('The Vestiges of the Great'), a study of Delhi's ruins and extant monuments published in 1847, Saiyyid Ahmad included

---

[18] Andrews, *Zakaullah of Delhi*, p. 12.

a chapter on the most successful and well known of the traditional intellectual elites. He extravagantly complimented them by saying,

People of [this city] do not have their counterparts in any other lands; here every individual combines in him thousands of virtues and is a nosegay of innumerable arts; and one and all they are dedicated to scholarship and writing. Morality is instinctively ingrained in their character that if one were to comment on only one aspect of it, thousands of books on ethics could be produced. Yet [these scholars] are modest and considerate; their regard for friendship is beyond description, and they are utterly without envy and they never nurse a grudge.[19]

Doubtless, the changes ushered in by the British were real and they did, indeed, heighten cultural and religious fears. But they did not disturb, at least before the 'Mutiny' days, the normal flow and rhythm of life. No wonder, Andrews mentions the 'great abundance' within the city between 1830 and 1850, the 'easy-going existence',[20] and 'an urbanity' existing from close daily contact and kindly feeling.[21] A glimpse of such daily contact is offered by a graphic description of the Delhi elites, their daily lives, and their old boy networks:

Shamsul Ulama Munshi Zakaullah left his home from Kucha-i Chalan every evening at 6.00 P.M. to reach the Town Hall in Company Bagh. Maulvi Nazir Ahmad from Batashon ki Gali, Master Piyare Lal from Dariba, and Maulvi Ziauddin from Aksarrehat Kuan would also gather at the same place .... That evening, Munshi Zakaullah came to Maulvi Nazir Ahmad's house. I found them exchanging notes. Just then arrived Maulana Azad [1888– 1958]. Maulvi Nazir Ahmad owned a Victoria that he used for his outings. All three of us set out on our short journey. In Khari Baoli we met Hali. At Maulana Azad's insistence, he too joined us .... A discussion on poetry ensued. That included a comparison of Zauq and Ghalib. We stopped at Lahori Gate ... [followed by a description of the place].[22]

Each individual mentioned herein sought out the society of learned and clever men, and delighted in their converse. Their lives were avowedly based on the assumption that friendship and personal relationships were, by far, the most important thing in life.

Reaching Delhi in 1810, Ghalib found the conflict between the 'traditionalists' in religion and the 'radical' reformers 'raging vigorously'.[23] Indeed, Delhi was the centre of those active and distinguished discussions and investigation that afterwards fructified in the establishment of Delhi College. It was here that knowledge flowed in every direction, commented Maulvi Karimuddin Panipati (c. 1821–79), a student at the Oriental Department of Delhi College in 1840,

---

[19]Quoted in Hafeez Malik, *Sir Sayyid Ahmad Khan and Muslim Modernization in India and Pakistan* (New York, 1980), pp. 328–40.

[20]Andrews, *Zakaullah of Delhi*, pp. 4, 5.

[21]Ibid., p. 12.

[22]Rashidul Khairi, *Ismat* (1935); his *Dilli ki Akhri Bahar*, pp. 124–5.

[23]Ralph Russell and Khurshidul Islam, *Ghalib: Life and Letters* (Delhi, 1969), p. 31.

brother of Maulvi Imamuddin (*c.* 1831–1900), and a convert to Christianity. 'As the mulla makes for the masjid, so scholars flocked to Delhi,' he wrote.[24] Leaving aside such exaggerated claims, there is no denying that even though Delhi lost out to Lucknow as the focus of intellectual life, it was still the favourite haunt of innumerable scholars, writers, poets, and musicians. 'This was a golden age for poetry,' declared Karimuddin. 'Everybody from the king down to the beggar was smitten with the poetic craze.'[25]

The intellectual vitality animating Delhi's society led to a slow but steady proliferation of newspapers and magazines. Karimuddin himself rented a place in Hauz Qazi to start a printing press and publish translations of the most well-known Arabic classics. By the 1840s, Delhi had seven printing presses. Facilitated by the establishment of the first litho press around 1835, *Dihli Urdu Akhbar* came out in 1836. It was Delhi's first Urdu newspaper. Five papers with the common name of *Sadiqul-Akhbar* were in circulation. *Saidul Akhbar*, started by Saiyyid Ahmad Khan's brother in 1837, *Fawaidul Nazirin*, *Qiranul-Saadain*, and *Mufid Hind* were the other Delhi papers.[26] They were precursors to the spurt of publications later, especially after *Comrade*, the influential English daily, moved from Calcutta to Delhi. Following the Turko-Italian war in 1911–12, *Comrade* turned Delhi into a storm centre of the pan-Islamic campaign.

All said and done, the pan-Islamic euphoria was a tame affair compared with the fury of 1857–8. Yet, despite the anti-British rhetoric reverberating here and there and the raising of the banner of revolt by Saiyyid Ahmad Barelwi (*c.* 1786–1831), the wounds of 1857 were more or less healed within a decade. This provided British officials some breathing space, but, more importantly, it led the Muslim literati—traditional and modern—to take stock of existing attitudes towards a government that had come to occupy the physical spaces, stay and not to return to the cool climes of Great Britain. The self-introspection that took place produced varying reactions. Some chose to decline contentedly in the lap of a feudal but decaying culture, but those exposed to the winds of doctrine blowing from the West announced the tidings of the dawn and pointed the way to the light of the sun. Contrary to the suppositions of several British writers, they engaged with the living present. Ghalib described Saiyyid Ahmad's editing of *Ain-i Akbari*, a major sixteenth-century text by Abul Fazl (*c.* 1551–1602), as a futile endeavour to extol the past, which ignored the scientific accomplishments of the British.[27]

---

[24] Akhtar Qamber, *The Last Mushairah of Delhi* (Delhi, 1979), p. 39.

[25] Ibid., p. 40.

[26] Abdul Salam Khurshid, *Sahafat: Pakistan-o-Hind Mein* (Lahore, 1963), pp. 103–11.

[27] Put aside the *Ain*, and parley with me;
   Open thine the eyes in this world,
   And examine the [life] of Englishmen,
   Their style, their manner, their trade, and their art.
Malik, *Saiyyid Ahmad Khan*, p. 58.

He was generally put off to find people stuck in the past, oblivious to the present. When people spoke of the 'good old times', Zakaullah told them that 'those times, as a whole, were not good, when they are compared with the days in which we are now living. They were full of corruption and decay'.[28] Such was his enthusiasm for the 'new age' that he defined history as *Tariful waqt* (appreciation of time).[29] Above all, he privileged the advance in science over past accomplishments: 'Such a development we have not witnessed or even dreamt of in any other century.'[30]

The change of dynasty was fixed and ordained by God: 'Only by contact with a fresh and younger civilisation could life and vigour flow back into ... the community and into India as a whole.'[31] Cynics construed this as subservience to John Company or the Crown, a charge levelled against Saiyyid Ahmad as well. But this was no more than a crude attempt to tarnish the reputation of visionary men. When, as an officer in the Education Department, Zakaullah attended a Durbar at Delhi, he avowed to his biographer that he felt degraded by bowing before a foreign ruler. And yet he held that the House of Timur was destined to collapse; it pleased him to fancy that Allah had raised the Royal House of Queen Victoria to succeed the Royal House of Jalaluddin Muhammad Akbar.

Being 'Muslim' and observing Islamic practices was not a problem under Pax Brittanica, a point made by Muhammad Ismail (c. 1781–1831), the nephew of the influential *alim* Shah Abdul Aziz (c. 1746–1824). Saiyyid Ahmad pursued the same argument,[32] recommending, though from a different perspective, a modus vivendi with the British. The real and daunting challenge, to which Zakaullah and his contemporaries alluded, was to preserve the essential ingredients of sharif culture, and to defend the corporate Muslim identity not vis-à-vis the Hindu population which posed no serious threat, but against the culturally hegemonic West.

Broadly speaking, this too produced two kinds of responses. Deoband's Dar al-ulum, an educational haven for Muslims in distress, was typically traditional with all the ingredients of orthodoxy.[33] After an initial flurry of anti-British activity, its founders focused on eliminating 'false accretions' derived from the Sufis and the Shias and Islamicizing every aspect of religious and everyday life. Their visions

---

[28]Andrews, *Zakaullah of Delhi*, p. 19.

[29]Zakaullah, *Muqaddimah-i Tarikh-i Hindustan* (Aligarh, 1915), p. 1.

[30]Quoted in Irfan Habib, 'Munshi Zakaullah and the vernacularisation of science in nineteenth century India', in N.K. Sehgal, S. Sangwan, and S. Mohanti (eds), *Uncharted Terrains: Essays on Science Popularisation in Pre-Independence India* (Delhi, 2000), p. 134.

[31]Hugh Tinker, 'Between Old Delhi and New Delhi: C.F. Andrews and St Stephen's in an era of transition', in Frykenberg, *Delhi Through the Ages*, p. 358.

[32]He stated that the British government did not interfere with the Muslims in the practice of their religion. Saiyyid Ahmad Khan, *Review of Dr Hunter's Indian Mussalmans: Are They Bound in Conscience to Rebel Against the Queen?* (Banaras, 1872).

[33]Barbara Daly Metcalf, *Islamic Revival in British India Deoband, 1860–1900*. With a new preface to the paperback edition (Delhi, 2002).

were meant to be a challenge to the world in general, and the West in particular, and as such had become powerful beacons for large numbers of backward and impoverished Muslims living in a cruel and uncertain world. On the contrary, Delhi College and Aligarh's MAO College, with all their ambiguities and ideological fissures, spearheaded a heterodox movement, with a strong emphasis on Western learning and reconciliation with the West. Nonetheless, regardless of the depth of theological dissensions and the incompatibility of their goals, all three institutions shared a common project—to evolve and pursue communitarian strategies in order to negotiate with the reality of British rule.

Ideological rivals within both camps competed to demonstrate their Muslimness, each side accusing its opponents of being overly submissive on the Muslim/Islamic issue. On occasion, the level of rancour between them suggested an imminent break, but that did not occur so long as they were united in furthering the yearnings, real or imaginary, of the community. So that when the going was tough, especially during the early phase of the Khilafat movement (1919–20), the Muslim divines (*deendaar*) from Deoband and the worldly men (*duniyadar*) from Aligarh joined hands to save the Khilafat.[34] Though contemporaries attached much significance to this distinction, it was in effect a spurious one. Whether located in Deoband or Aligarh, individuals and groups freely moved from one domain to the other and traversed each other's terrain uninhibitedly. The sharp divide between the deendaar and the duniyadar was an imaginary construction based on a textual analysis, and without reflecting the unities between the conflicting world views and ideologies. The unity forged during the Khilafat days resulted in more conferences being held, more protests being issued, and more articles in newspapers being published.

What is more, the fraternization of the 'traditionalists' or the 'modernists' in any phase of the nineteenth or twentieth century did not mean the dilution of faith or the abrogation of the fundamental tenets of Islam. Zakaullah, for example, left off during the greater part of his life many of the outward religious observances. Still, he upheld the Islamic values of moral piety, humility, courtesy, hospitality, generosity, fearlessness, and loyalty to friends.[35] He knew that this heritage was the base of his people and the backbone of their historical existence. Caring towards friends and family, he saved enough for his parents to perform the pilgrimage to Mecca, and paid for the education of his younger brother, and the marriage expenses of his three sisters and two brothers. Cutting across class, caste, or territorial boundaries, this constituted the essence of sharif culture. No wonder, Zakaullah reminded Andrews of 'the old saints or patriarchs who

[34]Mushirul Hasan, *Nationalism and Communal Politics in India, 1885–1931* (New Delhi, 1991), ch. 6; and Muhammad Ali, *My Life A Fragment: An Autobiographical Sketch of Maulana Muhammad Ali*. Translated and annotated by Mushirul Hasan (Delhi, 1999), p. 80.

[35]Zakaullah, *Tahzibul Akhlaq-i Arya Hind*, pp. 3, 128.

lived in the presence of God'.[36] 'The purity of his nature,' he stated, 'shone out in his face.'[37]

Government employment or the growing passion for Western learning made no difference to Zakaullah's outward manners and customs that were so much a part of Delhi's sharif environment. His dress, his habits, his domestic life, and his religious life—all that he valued most dearly—remained unchanged.[38] Abdul Qadir, the Urdu writer who knew him well during the years 1907 to 1908, recalled: 'In his dress and manner of living he was old fashioned and he stuck to that style, but he was quite progressive in his ideas.'[39] Progressive or not, he remained true to the same social and cultural ideals that shaped the personality of Delhi's Urdu-speaking elites and informed their world view.

II

Charles Freer Andrews, who came to India to promote the Cambridge University Brotherhood in Delhi, was drawn to Islam, its history and culture soon after reaching Delhi in April 1904.[40] But unlike T.W. Arnold (c. 1864–1934) and Theodore Morison (c. 1863–1936), who taught at Aligarh and researched on Islam at Aligarh's MAO College,[41] he could not sustain his interest owing to his involvement in the Gandhian movements and his bonding with Rabindranath Tagore (c. 1861–1941). Yet the lasting treasure in his recollections of his Delhi years was his close bonding with Zakaullah and Nazir Ahmad. 'Delhi will always remain Old Delhi to me,' he wrote, 'on account of the vivid recollection of these two noble old men.' For this reason Delhi became his 'first love'. Nothing could take its place in the romance of Indian life. Teaching at St. Stephen's College—an 'Alexandria on the Banks of the Jamuna'—he recalled: 'We had no such brilliant array of students in modern times such as existed in Zakaullah's days.'[42]

An ideal biographer must be endowed with a spice of vanity, or in any case, must be thoroughly interested in himself.[43] Now, Andrews was not greatly interested in himself. Instead, he revelled in meeting Zakaullah and his friends and describing details of their lives. No wonder, his autobiography abounds in generous tributes, not only to Zakaullah, the vibrant symbol of the 'Delhi renaissance', but to his other comrades like Nazir Ahmad and Hakim Ajmal Khan (c. 1863–1927). He

---

[36]Andrews, *Zakaullah of Delhi*, p. 138.

[37]Ibid., p. 153.

[38]Ibid., p. 118. This is also borne out by Nazir Ahmad's account (pp. xii-xiii).

[39]Abdul Qadir, *Gleanings* (Patna, 1947), pp. 166–7.

[40]Tinker, 'Between Old Delhi and New Delhi', p. 359.

[41]For Arnold, see Katherine Watt, 'Thomas Walker Arnold and the re-evaluation of Islam, 1864–1930', *Modern Asian Studies*, 36:1 (2002).

[42]Tinker, *The Ordeal of Love*, p. 33.

[43]H.A.L. Fisher, *Pages from the Past* (Oxford, 1939), p. 176.

recalled meeting them each evening at the reading room on the library roof, and discussing subjects of common interest. Such cultural encounters between a 'Muslim sage' and an Anglican priest were the first of their kind in Delhi, and were, in many ways, comparable with T.W. Arnold's interactions in Aligarh and later in Lahore where he moved to teach. But, while their exchanges enabled them to uncover the inner fundamental truth of all religions, they did not produce the result Andrews may have desired, that is, reconciliation between Islam and Christianity. They did, however, enable Andrews to understand what it meant to be a Muslim under a colonial dispensation. Others tried, but their efforts fell short of expectations. The colonial mindset did not allow an appreciation of the true nature of Indian Islam. Though policy decisions were, after 1857, finely tuned to draw the estranged Muslim communities into the bureaucratic fold, the intellectual discourses ran parallel to the high politics of the Raj. With some notable exceptions, late-nineteenth-century writings on Islam reinforced colonial stereotypes, imaging Indian Islam as inimical to the West and representing its followers as the Other.

It is hard to establish, moreover, whether or not the quiet and unobtrusive dialogue conducted in the lanes of Shahjahanabad led some of Andrews' proselytizing Christian colleagues—who had burst on the Delhi scene with the establishment of various missions—to soften their hostility towards Islam and its adherents. The chances are that it did not. Andrews is silent on the matter. What he is explicit about is that Zakaullah and Nazir Ahmad were the best exponents of inter-faith harmony and understanding. Nazir Ahmad, in turn, paid back the compliment and held Zakaullah and Andrews as the models for fostering love and understanding between the followers of Islam and Christianity. He talked of Andrews as 'a living example of the same kind of cordiality (during the early years of Islam) existing between Islam and Christianity.'

The rationale behind the constant reference to Andrews' biography is this: although focused on Zakaullah, it provides an entrée into the lives of not two charismatic figures but the trio—Zakaullah, Nazir Ahmad, and Andrews—and the intellectual influences which helped to shape their mind. *Zakaullah of Delhi* needs to be revisited also as an evocative introduction to Delhi's cultural, religious, and intellectual life. To the author's credit, he revisits a city bruised by the 'Mutiny', resurrects its painful past, recovers its cultural heritage, and, in the process, discovers the joy of living in it. Sections dealing with the transition from the Mughals to the coming of the British contain a great deal that springs directly from Andrews' own research; but it applies also to the rest of the narrative. He writes from first-hand knowledge.

Hence the book's scope is considerably wider than the title suggests, for it provides an account of the whole complex of divergent ideas and interpretations to which the revolt of 1857 gave rise, and the hugely complex problems encountered by the Muslim elites in coping with the alien West. Thus the book's coverage extends to an era that was already receding into the background during Andrews' lifetime. Andrews began collecting materials for his book in 1912, the year he met Tagore. This momentous meeting inspired him to complete the project of writing Zakaullah's biography. What Zakaullah stood for in Old Delhi, both in education and religion, had its counterpart in Tagore's work at Santiniketan. 'Without any direct link of connection,' he observed, 'Munshi Zakaullah's own spirit may be felt there in the poet's ideals as they are being put into practice.' Then, at the beginning of 1914, in answer to an appeal, he went to South Africa, where Gandhi was putting his method of satyagraha into practice against the government's treatment of Indians.

Andrews wrote on Zakaullah in Calcutta's *The Modern Review* in April 1911, but his pressing engagements interrupted the book's completion. During his voyage from Colombo to Marseilles he put together his notes and drafts, and probably completed the final draft in 1928 at his Cambridge home. It was serialized in *The Modern Review*. When the book finally appeared a year later priced at 7s. 6d., it received a mixed response in the West. Some introduced a discordant note,[44] but most complimented the author.[45] *The Moslem World* welcomed the biography of a Muslim of the old school, and one who had broad sympathies and a loving heart. 'The background of Delhi before the mutiny,' commented the reviewer, 'and that of the foundation of the Aligarh movement are of interest, and the portrait of Zakaullah with his religious devotion, Old World courtesy, and gracious hospitality stands out clearly and vividly.'[46] T.W. Arnold commended it in the *Bulletin of the School of Oriental Studies*: Zakaullah belonged, so he wrote, to a 'distinctive type in Muslim society' that seeks knowledge in the best Islamic tradition without any thought of reward and without regard for remuneration. He bemoaned that the life of the majority of such persons was, from the very nature of the case, uneventful and the historian does no more than to give a few dates and list their writings. 'The student looks in vain,' concludes Arnold in the same vein as I have done in an earlier section of this essay, 'for a representation of personality and a revelation of the inner character of such men.'[47] *Zakaullah of Delhi* does just that.

III

The wind has blown away the dust of men
Unnumbered from your lane:
Yet your true lovers are not daunted: men
Come to your threshold still.[48]

[Mir Taqi Mir]

[44]*Journal of the Central Asian Society*, 116, part 4 (1929), p. 551.
[45]The royalties, as with the profits on the Gandhi biography, were allocated to Santiniketan.
[46]*The Moslem World*, 20 (1930), p. 214.
[47]*Bulletin of the School of Oriental Studies* (London), 5, part 3, pp. 623–4.
[48]Ralph Russell, *In Pursuit of Urdu Literature: A Select History* (London: 1992), p. 48.

Zakaullah of Delhi offers many useful insights. One of them relates to 'the rapid efflorescence of men's mind'. The men he had in mind constituted a small but influential group of Muslims in the old city. What made them different from the others was this: They 'did things on their own initiative and thought things out for themselves'. They represented what is commonly described and accepted as 'the Renaissance in the north of India'. Though it came later in time than the Bengal movement and was less enduring in character, their efforts matched the achievements of Ram Mohun Roy [*c.* 1772–1832] in Bengal.[49]

The theory of a Delhi renaissance is a grand myth invented by no other than Andrews. On his first visit to India and during his first exposure to Delhi, this graduate of Cambridge's Pembroke College discovered a general enlivenment of the city. He noticed the development of Urdu prose, the translation of scientific works in that language, the flowering of scientific curiosity, and the growth of the printing press. The Delhi College, though now a shadow of its glorious past, still offered hope to those who valued Western education. Andrews therefore describes these features with much feeling and eloquence.

Though Delhi College's development remained a subject of contention, it was a major educational enterprise. In 1854, it had 333 students, of whom 112 were Muslims. It had an English branch where English language and literature and modern European sciences were taught and an Oriental branch in which Arabic, Persian, and Sanskrit were taught, along with geography, mathematics, and sciences. Above everything else, it had been a nursery of science teaching and a catalyst of major works on scientific subjects.[50] The doctrines of ancient philosophy taught through the medium of Arabic verse were 'cast in the shade before the more reasonable and experimental theories of modern science. The old dogma ... that the earth is the fixed centre of the universe was generally laughed at by the higher students of the Oriental as well as by those of the English Department of the College'.[51]

Zakaullah defined science as 'a knowledge which has truth, an absolute truth, and nothing but the truth'.[52] He used to tell Andrews 'with kindling eyes how eagerly these scientific lectures were followed, and how, after each lecture, the notes used to be studied, over and over again, and copied out by many hands. It was like entering into a wholly undiscovered hemisphere of the human mind'. Enthusiastic teachers also taught the young students. They were allowed to experiment with unknown chemical gases. They were invited to dip into the mysteries of Magnetism, which was just then coming to the fore as a freshly discovered science. 'There was much yet to come; but these things formed actually for them a new world.'[53]

---

[49]Andrews, *Zakaullah of Delhi*, pp. 38, 46.

[50]For example, *Mazharul Mazamin* by Mazharul Haq. He was tutor of the Nawab of Pataudi.

[51]Ram Chandra, quoted in Andrews, *Zakaullah of Delhi*, p. 39.

[52]Habib, 'Munshi Zakaullah and the vernacularisation of science', p. 134.

[53]Andrews, *Zakaullah of Delhi*, pp. 42–3.

Quickened by the breath of the new curiosity, Delhi College achieved much more than encouraging scientific studies. It contributed to the development of Urdu prose as a vehicle for the transmission of knowledge. It mediated between Eastern and Western cultures and mentalities, and did so in the vernacular, contributing to an Urdu-speaking and reading public that belonged to different religious persuasions.[54] Even though hot-headed *mullahs*, theologians, and publicists sustained their campaign against Western education and its supposed negative impact on Muslim beliefs and practices, Delhi College embarked upon changes in the traditional academic curriculum and created a climate for fostering liberal thought and the rational spirit. Its leading lights lived with the sense that they were making history, and creating a new society. For its alumni, the college remained 'a home of pleasant memories in the far distant past', and retained its liberal, scientific, and humanistic spirit. 'If I had not studied in Delhi College,' stated Nazir Ahmad, 'I would have been a maulvi, narrow and bigoted.'[55]

These were, admittedly, major gains. But they were not good enough to support the theory of a 'Delhi renaissance'. Even the impact of the 'New Learning' engendered by Delhi College was short-lived and much less far-reaching in its ultimate effect. Although the college blazed the trail in initiating a dual system of education, its merger with Lahore's Government College in April 1877 brought to an end the dream of its founders. The flowering of science came to a standstill, while the liberal and rational spirit was overtaken by strident communitarian aspirations.

The sound and fury of 1857 overshadowed the college's impressive beginning. While the clouds of uncertainties loomed large on the horizon before its actual closure, the college was attacked; its rich collection of manuscripts and books was burnt down, and Taylor, the English Principal, was killed by the mutineers. By the time a temporary revival occurred from 1864 to 1877, Delhi College had lost its distinct personality. One of the principal reasons was that Urdu, a major catalyst for Delhi's cultural and intellectual regeneration, ceased to be the medium of instruction. This was, in retrospect, the beginning of an inglorious era in the history of the Urdu language. Though Urdu prospered in certain ways until Independence and Partition, it could not regain its pre-eminence in the administration and bureaucracy. The language being squeezed out of the school and college curriculum hastened its demise. As in Bengal where English substituted Persian in 1835, English eventually replaced Urdu in Delhi.

Even at the best of times, the so-called Delhi renaissance found no resonance in the lives of common Muslims. A movement associated with such famous names and full of so momentous a future passed through a region without effecting a major transformation in outlook. In this respect, the influence of ideas was

[54]Gail Minault, 'Qiran Al-Saadain', in Malik, *Perspectives of Mutual Encounters*, p. 277.
[55]Quoted in Gupta, *Delhi Between Two Empires*, p. 131.

disappointingly small in relation to the possibilities. Here in Delhi, as indeed elsewhere, a great extension of the scientific domain did not take place. It remained confined to the pages of Saiyyid Ahmad's *Tahzibul Akhlaq* or the *Aligarh Institute Gazette*. Nor did the reach of the Delhi renaissance or the many-sided outbursts of intellectual energy extend beyond Delhi. One indication of this is that people like Zakaullah and Nazir Ahmad, though respected during their lifetime for their creativity and scholarship, vanished into the mists of history. There can, indeed, be no more significant illustration of the way in which they were forgotten even during their lifetime than the Muslim League session at Delhi in December 1910 making no mention of Zakaullah's death a month earlier in the same city. *The Tribune*, published from Lahore, a city where Zakaullah's writings were read and appreciated, carried an obituary of Major Goold-Adams (8 November 1910), but not Zakaullah.

I V

Faith stops me, if impiety pulls me towards itself;
Ka'ba is behind me, the church is in front of me.

[Ghalib]

Zakaullah of Delhi is important in yet another respect. Andrews, the author, does not hesitate to develop his own ideas of a pluralist historical trend far beyond the purely political sphere, and his study illustrates very well the strength and the weakness of the composite traditions that he celebrates with such abandon. Thus he talks of 'the amalgamation of customs and usages' among the Hindus and Muslims alike, and refers to fairs, melas, and other forms of festivities as expressions of plurality and composite living.[56] In all of this, Zakaullah appears as a presiding deity over Delhi's multicultural and multi-religious society, and Andrews writes with feeling, if sometimes repetitively, on his catholic outlook, tolerance, and forbearance.

Andrews points out that Zakaullah tried bridging the gulf separating the two religious communities, though he exaggerates in describing him as 'one of God's peace-makers who brought unity among the children of men by his goodness and love'.[57] What he is right about is that Delhi's grand old man was, as Nazir Ahmad put it, 'untainted by that spirit of religious bigotry, prejudice, or superstition', and that he did not draw religious boundaries in his personal and professional conduct.[58] Every evening when Pandit Tulsi Ram's family lighted the lamps to worship, they included the name of Zakaullah, in the prayer repeated at that time, along with the names of other close family members.[59]

---

[56]Andrews, *Zakaullah of Delhi*, p. 15.
[57]Ibid., p. 129.
[58]Nazir Ahmad, in ibid., pp. xiii–xiv.
[59]Andrews, *Zakaullah of Delhi*, p. 145.

In the last eight chapters, Andrews demonstrates how Zakaullah's reactions to the post-1857 developments conformed to the highest standards expected of a wise and intelligent man. He fills out the story by material derived from friends and family that bears on his personal and professional life. He, thus, endeavours to establish the greatness of his hero, his secularity, and the nobility of his mission. There is, in all this, a clear, honest, and unaffected affinity between the biographer and his subject.

Biographers idealize their subjects, and why should they not if they do genuinely inspire them. Andrews' strenuous efforts to establish Zakaullah's 'secular' credentials carried a special meaning and signification. Essentially, he used Zakaullah to fortify the era's secular ideologies that were being assailed by Hindu and Muslim revitalization movements. He regarded his legend as a symbol—and often a very apt symbol—of the Gandhian initiatives to promote Hindu-Muslim fraternity and understanding. In this sense, *Zakaullah of Delhi* has a single theme.

Yet such scholarly interventions, though timely, praiseworthy, and important in themselves, could not foster Hindu–Muslim togetherness either in Delhi or elsewhere. The politics of representation had created a wedge and undermined the inter-community front created by his mentor, Gandhi, during the Khilafat and Non-Cooperation campaigns. The conflict was more than a struggle for power and patronage; it was also a battle for myths, religious faith, and history. Groups amongst Hindus and Muslims fought it out with a primal fervour that led inevitably to violence. This collision of passions and politics lit a dreadful fire—few knew this as well as Andrews did. Yet Andrews, a man imbued with a missionary zeal and fervour, could not abandon the hope of Hindu–Muslim reconciliation. By writing Zakaullah's biography he hoped to provide the healing touch and offer a role model worthy of emulation. Hence Nazir Ahmad's optimism:

Far-sighted, tolerant, and wise men, like Munshi Zakaullah, have already in their own lives found out the art of avoiding these things [religious disputes of various kinds]. They have learnt how to prevent beforehand these painful religious disputes. Their lives are living examples of harmony and concord .... After a time, it is hoped that those newspapers that are notorious for exciting bitter contention and hatred between the two communities,—the Hindu and the Musalman,—will vanish and come to nothing. Every good man must wish for this to happen.[60]

The prophecy did not come true; Hindu–Muslim squabbles intensified after the death of Zakaullah and Nazir Ahmad. Their differences were never-ending, surfacing in almost every arena. Both 'Muslim' and 'Hindu' politics made demagogic use of religious symbols; both were easily drawn into extreme positions and lost control of events. But the sentiment expressed by Nazir Ahmad mirrored yet

---

[60]Nazir Ahmad, in ibid., p. xv.

another contemporary reality, that is, the presence of individuals who were unmoved by the communal claptrap and cherished, what in modern parlance is described as, multiculturalism.

V

Only the survivors come forth in the rose, the tulip.
What faces have gone under the dust!

[Ghalib]

Nazir Ahmad, who wrote an introduction to *Zakaullah of Delhi*, conformed to the standard of a virtuous citizen. He had his share of reverses, but affection and admiration attended him throughout his life. He was mild, courteous, and gracious in his manner, but formidable in debate. No wonder, he wrote *Chand Pand*, a series of plainspoken articles on good manners, common sense, anger, avarice, pride—whether of wealth or beauty—timidity, immodesty, and envy. He devotes the last few pages to the inculcation of religious and moral maxims. He was interested in language and literature, in religion and politics, in the prosperity and permanence of the British empire, and in the happiness and well-being of his wide circle of friends. 'What makes him typically Indian Muslim,' writes Muhammad Mujeeb (1902–85), the historian of Indian Islam, 'was his informality, his humour, his being under the spell, as it were, of the living idiom of Delhi, his wordy speech and writings.'[61]

Nazir Ahmad was a nineteenth-century liberal humanist within the Islamic frame. Going against the contemporary theological trend, he advocated *ijtehad* (interpretation) in matters of faith in the book *Al-ijtehad* (1908). His interest in women's education, reflected in his extensive writings,[62] went considerably further than that of Saiyyid Ahmad.[63] He showed the evils of polygamy, and argued for widow remarriage. Some of his ideas were expounded in *Mirat ul-urus* (The Bride's Mirror), a forerunner to Hali's *Majalis un-nisa*, and its sequel, *Banatun nash* (literally 'Daughters of the Bier').

Mirat ul-urus gives an account of two characters, Asghari and Akbari, the former a girl of sound ideas and habits and the latter a wayward and undisciplined girl of the same family. Asghari's good manners endeared her in the parents-in-law's house, while Akbari suffered for her shortcomings in her husband's house. The whole of the tale is told in the words of everyday life in sharif society, the true Urdu of Delhi, and not the high-flown dialect of pedants and poets. The incidents are natural, such as are well known in every father-in-law's household,

---

[61]Muhammad Mujeeb, *The Indian Muslims* (London, 1967), p. 532.
[62]Zakaullah, *Talimul Khisal* (Delhi, 1892), pp. 35–6.
[63]Minault, *Secluded Scholars*, p. 35.

and the ways of the *zenana* (women's wing) are introduced in such a way as to allow some insights into the domestic realities of everyday life in a Muslim family. Their language, their likes and dislikes, their fondness for their children, their importance in the family circle, their gross ignorance, their spitefulness and petty intriguing, all received illustration. This picture bears no exaggeration. Nazir Ahmad paints from life and leaves the tale to teach its own moral.[64]

The novel had 'the singular virtue of being admirably adapted for the perusal of the females of India. It cannot fail to interest their imagination as well as instruct their minds'. UP's lieutenant governor added: 'It also brings to light the vast influence exercised by the women of India, and the manner in which that influence may be crowned with the highest results when education is added to intelligence and virtue.'[65] *Mirat ul-urus* mirrors, moreover, Nazir Ahmad's commitment to secular education and reveals, at least to a historian if not to a linguist, several facets of family and social history in late-nineteenth-century Delhi. Notice the following:

In accordance with the family custom, my daughters also were taught by the eldest ladies of the house to read such small vernacular tracts as 'the Holy Quran and its Teaching', 'A Letter on the Last Day', 'The Way of Salvation', etc. It was a house in which reading and writing formed a constant topic of conversation at all times. I noticed that even my little daughters, taking their cues from us men, had quite a longing of their own for the acquisition of knowledge. At the same time, however, I became convinced that purely religious subjects of study are not suited to the capacities of children, and that the literature to which my children's attention was restricted had the effect of depressing their spirits, of checking their natural instincts, and of blunting their intelligence.[66]

Born in 1830 in an *ashraf* family of Bijnor, Nazir Ahmad had his early schooling at Delhi's Aurangabadi mosque, and the rest at Delhi College (1846–53). He taught at Kunjah in Gujrat district, Punjab (1854–7), served as deputy inspector of schools in Kanpur (1856) and Allahabad (1857), and as deputy collector (1863 and 1872) in Kanpur, Gorakhpur, and Orai (district Jalaun). A prolific writer, he wrote an elementary treatise on the art of writing the Persian character (*Rasmul-khat*: 5th edition, Delhi, 1919); a Persian primer, originally written by Amir Khusrau (c. 1253–1325) of Delhi (*Nisab-i Khusrau*, or Khusrau syllabus); an introduction to Persian grammar for beginners, advocating its study solely on the ground of its being necessary for an Urdu scholar (*Sarf-i saghir*); a series of selected stories for children intended to attract their attention and improve their understanding

---

[64]This is based on M. Kempson, Director of Public Instruction to R. Simon, Secretary to Government, N.-W.P., 22 July 1869, *Statistical Abstract of British India*, 1869, vol. 23, p. 38, Oriental and India Office Collections, British Library, London.

[65]R. Simon to Kempson, 20 August 1869, *Statistical Abstract of British India*, p. 41.

[66]Nazir Ahmad, *The Bride's Mirror Mirat ul-Urus: A Tale of Life in Delhi: A Hundred Years Ago.* Translated from the Urdu by G.E. Ward (New Delhi, rpt 2001), pp. 1–2.

(*Muntakhib-ul-hikayat*, or Selection from Parables). The *Al Huquq wa al faraiz* (On Rights and Duties), in three volumes, aimed at ensuring peace and spiritual satisfaction by fitting the *sharia* into contemporary life or contemporary life into the sharia.[67] *Mirat ul-urus*, a hugely successful novel, *Ibn-ul waqt* (Son of the Moment), and *Banatun nash*, as also his Urdu translation of the Koran (1896), added to his fame. He earned contemporary esteem by translating, at the behest of William Muir, the lieutenant-governor of the North-Western Provinces, the Indian Penal Code (*Taazirat-i hind*) and the Law of Evidence (*Qanoon-i shahadat*). In 1863, two years after completing this project, he was rewarded with the post of deputy collector in the Revenue Service (hence, his conventional title of 'Deputy' or 'Dipty' Nazir Ahmad).[68] His translation of *The Heavens* attracted the notice of Hyderabad's Prime Minister. He was invited to the Deccan to join the Revenue department.

'Dipty Sahib' grew up to see the extinction of the Mughal power, the coming of the British, and the sudden shifting of horizons in art, literature, and politics. Though living in Allahabad at the time of the 1857 upsurge, he knew what had rocked Shahjahanabad. But without being overwhelmed by the swiftness of the changes around him, he also endeavoured to promote an Anglo–Muslim rapprochement in the cultural and intellectual realms. This, according to him, did not involve acquiescence in all of Western values or transgressing the boundaries of traditional codes of social behaviour and cultural patterns, but creating new channels of aspirations and creativity. Saiyyid Ahmad, whom Nazir Ahmad greatly admired, held the same view while pressing his own agenda against heavy odds. Inevitably, the two drew sustenance from each other. Wrote Nazir Ahmad:

Except in the sacred formula of Islam, 'there is no God but One: and Muhammad is the Prophet of God,' I have never, during the whole of my long life in this world, seen Musalmans in India so united as on this present very urgent question of their higher education at Aligarh.[69]

Typical of his devotion to the *Saiyyid* was his response to the students' strike against the British-dominated staff and administration at the MAO College in 1907. Distressed by what he perceived as a threat to the Saiyyid's mission, he retorted to the strikers: 'You are slaves. What can slaves do? Get back to your books and work.'[70]

---

[67]Mujeeb, *Indian Muslims*, p. 410. Strangely, Mujeeb discusses Nazir Ahmad's views in some detail but makes no reference to Zakaullah. The omission is, to say the least, intriguing. There is at least a passing reference to Zakaullah and Nazir Ahmad in Jawaharlal Nehru, *The Discovery of India* (Bombay, 1947 edn), p. 348.

[68]For an excellent summary of his life and works, Russell, *In Pursuit of Urdu Literature*, pp. 112–20, and his 'The Development of the Modern Urdu Novel', in T.W. Clark (ed.), *The Novel in India: Its Birth and Development* (London, 1970), pp. 118–22.

[69]Nazir Ahmad, in Andrews, *Zakaullah of Delhi*, p. vii.

[70]Tinker, *The Ordeal of Love*, p. 39.

With his astounding range of vocabulary and his colloquial style, Nazir Ahmad led his readers out of the traditional mode of thinking into new vistas of hope and endeavour. All his life he desired 'to attain simplicity of diction, as well as purity of sentiment' to reach out to his ever-growing readership. Though he offended a section of the ulama by his frank and candid views,[71] many of his contemporaries admired his erudition, wit, and his felicity of thought. They also valued the Shamsul Ulama's association with the MAO College in Aligarh, the Muhammadan Educational Conference, the Tibbia College in Delhi, and the Anjuman-i Himayat-i Islam of Lahore. The University of Edinburgh conferred upon him the LLD degree. The Punjab University did likewise. The government rewarded him with prizes and honours befitting a man of his wisdom and creativity. An edition of 2000 copies of the *Mirat ul-urus* (The Bride's Mirror), lithographed in the best style, was ordered for government use, and recommended to the Board of Examiners as a textbook of examination.

VI

The walls and doorways of my house are mourning
Are as meadows overgrown with grass;
Where is this spring, why ask how autumn looks?

[Ghalib]

Nazir Ahmad's fellow traveller 'on life's difficult journey' was no other than Khan Bahadur Shamsul Ulama Maulvi Muhammad Zakaullah. Both were prized products of Delhi College. Nazir Ahmad studied Urdu and Arabic, whereas 'Master' Ram Chandra (*c.* 1821–80), a recent convert to Christianity, 'sowed in his [Zakaullah's] mind and heart a seed of another kind, namely a love for mathematics'.[72] At a time when scepticism towards Western learning prevailed, Ram Chandra's growing influence on Zakaullah raised some eyebrows, though fears of his conversion to Christianity were ill-founded. Nazir Ahmad, who was himself criticized by the Muslim orthodoxy for being drawn to Christianity under the magic spell of Andrews, asserted that his friend was 'a strict Unitarian Musalman, trusting in one God with His full attributes as understood in Islam'.[73] He had himself invited the wrath of religious conservatives by writing on the wives of the Prophet of Islam (*Ummaahat ul Umma*) and introducing, in his translation of the Koran in Urdu, parenthetical clauses here and there to elucidate the meaning of the text. Andrews, too, clarified that 'never by any word that passed from his

---

[71]He is reported to have said: 'If you look into their position you will find that you can learn two lessons from the maulvis—first hypocrisy, and second idleness. How can a community prosper when people like these are its leaders and counsellors?' Russell, *In Pursuit of Literature*, p. 119.

[72]Andrews, *Zakaullah of Delhi*, p. ix.

[73]Nazir Ahmad, in ibid., p. x.

lips in my presence did I gather that he regarded himself as anything else than a true Muslim'.[74]

Zakaullah may have been attracted to some aspects of Christianity under Ram Chandra's influence, but Andrews endeavoured to dispel this impression. Anxious to enhance rather than damage his friend's reputation, he wanted Zakaullah's mission to be understood and not misconstrued. The need was all the more great in the late-1920s, the years Andrews spent writing his book, because at that time Hindu–Muslim relations in Delhi and elsewhere had reached their lowest ebb. The Nehru Committee Report, published just a few months after he sailed for London in May 1928, fuelled tensions and deepened political and cultural anxieties.[75] In this climate, Andrews invoked the ideals cherished by Zakaullah throughout his long public career.

Born in a house in Kucha Balaqi Begum, situated between the Jama Masjid and the Delhi Palace on 20 April 1832, Zakaullah had an aristocratic Turkish ancestry. His grandfather Hafiz Muhammad Sanaullah was a man of considerable stature and learning, and it was his overbearing influence that shaped the young Zakaullah's mind. Equally, his father Hafiz Sanaullah's piety and saintly character earned him much esteem. Like his ancestors who had gained respect in society as teachers in the Mughal court, Sanaullah tutored the youngest son of Bahadur Shah 'Zafar' (r. 1837–58), the fallen hero of the short-lived 'Mutiny'. He even offered him refuge when parts of Delhi were ablaze, and the British bayonets were out in the open hunting the recalcitrant descendants of Akbar (c. 1556–1605) and Shah Jahan (c. 1628–58). But the prince would have known that his fate was sealed. He escaped to Jaipur, from where he was taken a prisoner to Rangoon.

Beginning in Meerut, the revolt in Delhi burst like a bubble. British troops, having suffered some initial reverses, seized Qudsia Bagh and Ludlow Castle on 8 September; three days later they bombarded and destroyed the Kashmiri Gate bastion. Ghalib's Delhi was stormed on 14 September, the day he noted,

As for the writer of these words, his heart did not quake, nor did his steps falter. I stayed where I was, saying, 'I have committed no crime and need pay no penalty. The English do not slay the innocent, nor is the air of this uncongenial to me. Why should I fall a prey to groundless fancies and wander stumbling from one place to place? Let me sit in the same deserted corner blending my voice with my lamenting pen, while the tears fall from my eyelashes to mingle with the words of blood I write.'[76]

While Ghalib busied himself writing the *Dastambu* (A Popsy of Flowers) and vacillating in his attitudes towards the British, the starry-eyed representatives of John Company captured Bahadur Shah at Humayun's tomb. His crown was removed; his expensive robe discarded from his person. He would have felt

[74] Andrews, *Zakaullah of Delhi*, p. 149.
[75] Hasan, *Nationalism and Communal Politics*.
[76] Russell and Islam, *Ghalib*, p. 141.

indignant and humiliated, but his protest, if any, was of no avail. Tried between 27 January and 9 March 1858, Bahadur Shah was found guilty, transported to Rangoon in October, and imprisoned there. The Mughal emperors—from Babur (c. 1483–1530) to Jahangir (r. c. 1605–27)—wrote their memoirs. None would be written hereafter. The royal family had been, finally, edged off the stage. British and Sikh soldiers had already ransacked the palace in Lal Qila, once the home of Shah Jahan, and carried away the valuables. On 20 September 1857, Jama Masjid was taken over. Officers and soldiers clambered up the minaret and 'saw the whole city and country like a map below our feet; all Delhi was ours'. They danced about, drank beer and brandy, and lit fires in the mosque. More celebration took place at the home of Colonel Baird Smith. Midnight came, corks popped, fireworks exploded.[77] The city's 160,000 inhabitants were driven out into the open. Every citizen wanting to return after expulsion had to pay a fine: Muslims paid 25 per cent of the value of their real estate, Hindus only 10 per cent. Thousands were killed after perfunctory trials or none at all. The mutineers and other rebels were executed. They were strung up on a platform in front of the Kotwali in batches of a dozen at a time.

Hali, who fled back to Panipat on the outbreak of the revolt and was robbed of all his possessions save a Koran tied in a scarf around his neck, told his audience in 1874 'Do not go into the ruins of Delhi. At every step priceless pearls lie buried beneath the dust.'[78] Mian Muhammad Amin Panjakush, an excellent writer, and Maulvi Imam Bakhsh, whose nom de plume was Sahbai, and his two sons were shot dead, and their bodies thrown into the Yamuna. Maulvi Muhammad Baqar (c. 1810–57), educated at Delhi College and proprietor of *Dilhi Urdu Akhbar*, was arrested and executed. His son Muhammad Husain 'Azad' (c. 1830–1910), a Delhi College graduate (1854), was expelled from his house at bayonet point.

The world turned black before my eyes .... Abandoning a well-furnished house, with twenty-two half-dead souls I left the house—or rather, the city. And the words fell from my lips, 'Hazrat Adam left Paradise; Delhi is a paradise too. I'm his descendant—why shouldn't I leave Delhi?' In short, I became a wanderer, and God knows how and where I found myself.[79]

Ghalib told his friend:

I write a letter to Munshi Nabi Bakhsh Sahib and receive his reply, and today I get a letter from you, and your name is still Munshi Hargopal and your takhallus Tufta, and the city I live in is still called Delhi and this muhalla is still named Ballimaron muhalla—

---

[77]David Blomfield (ed.), *Lahore to Lucknow: The Indian Mutiny Journal of Arthur Moffat Lang* (London, 1992), pp. 57, 97.

[78]Gupta, *Delhi Between Two Empires*, pp. xviii-xix.

[79]Muhammad Husain Azad, *Ab-e Hayat: Shaping the Canons of Urdu Poetry*. Translated and edited by Frances Pritchet in association with Shamsur Rahman Faruqi (Delhi, 2001), p. 367.

yet not one of the friends of that former birth is to be found. By God, you may search for a Muslim in this city and not find one—rich, poor, and artisans alike are gone. Such as here are not Delhi people.[80]

Ghalib stayed in Delhi for the entire period between the coming of the mutineers from Meerut on 11 May and the successful British assault upon the city on 14 September. 'The tumult of arrests and killings' reached his lane, renting 'the heart of every man with fear'. He wrote bitterly of the execution of the three nawabs of three small estates in Delhi's neighbourhood. His brother's house, close to his, was plundered. His family went away. This was another sorrow, another calamity that descended on him like an avalanche. 'We live,' the poet wrote, 'in anxious thought for bread and water, and die in anxious thought for shroud and grave.'[81] Delhi had become a city without a ruler, a slave without a master, a garden without a gardener.[82] The *Fughan-i Dilli* (The Lament of Delhi), a collection of forty poems on Delhi's ruin and plunder, says it all.

This was Zakaullah's Delhi, a city where everybody could have echoed Ghalib's sentiment—*Main Andalib Gulshan-i na-afrida hun* (I am the *bulbul* of the garden uncreated). The varying fortunes of the city in war and peace become part of the general sweep of Delhi's social history. But for an individual whose family had been closely connected with the Delhi court, the eclipse of the Mughals and Bahadur Shah's unceremonious removal caused a great psychological blow.[83] For a family brought up with notions of stability and political acquiescence, it was deeply embarrassing to discover, in the words of Zakaullah, that 'Hindustan had become the arena of the mighty whirlwind and the blazing fire'.[84] For a family steeped in learning and scholarship, the loss of the city's great libraries was most painful. One of them belonged to Nawab Ziauddin Ahmad Khan of Loharu: it had supplied the manuscripts from which Henry Elliot compiled his eight volumes of translated excerpts on the history of India.[85]

Zakaullah did not write anything resembling *An Account of the Loyal Mohamedans of Indians of India* (1860–1) or *Asbab-i baghawat-i Hind* (1858), but 'the shock of those last Mutiny days was beyond all bearing'.[86] Imam Bakhsh, shortlisted in 1842 along with Ghalib and Momin Khan 'Momin' (1800–52) for an appointment

---

[80]Russell and Islam, *Ghalib*, p. 151.

[81]Ibid., p. 143.

[82]Quoted in Hardy, 'Ghalib and the British', p. 68.

[83]Rajat Kanta Ray, 'Race, Religion and Realm: The Political Theory of "The Reigning India Crusade", 1857', in Mushirul Hasan and Narayani Gupta (eds), *India's Colonial Encounter: Essays in Memory of Eric Stokes* (New Delhi, 1993).

[84]Andrews, *Zakaullah of Delhi*, p. 145.

[85]Francis Robinson, 'The Muslims of upper India and the shock of the Mutiny', in Hasan and Gupta, *India's Colonial Encounter*, p. 193.

[86]Andrews, *Zakaullah of Delhi*, p. 75.

in Delhi College, taught him Persian and Arabic. When Saiyyid Ahmad lived in Delhi from 1846 to 1854 as *Sadr Amin*, it was he who assisted him in writing *Asar-us sanadid* that won him the honour of a Fellowship of the Royal Asiatic Society in 1864. Zakaullah revered Imam Bakhsh, and deeply mourned his loss. To his students at the Muir Central College in Allahabad (established in 1872),[87] he would say that he felt as if Imam Bakhsh was present even while lecturing to them.[88]

The *Maulvi* was dead, but his other icon, the mathematician Ram Chandra escaped the mob fury. A prominent Delhi citizen told Andrews how when Delhi was taken over by the mutineers from Meerut at about 10 o'clock, he met Zakaullah hurrying towards Delhi College in order to save Ram Chandra. But the professor had already escaped in disguise to the open country.

Family hardships compounded personal losses and tragedies. Zakaullah's house near the Red Fort was demolished, and the family sought refuge among the tombs of Nizamuddin Auliya (*c.* 1238–1325), some three miles away from the city wall.[89] Their property was confiscated without any compensation, and on one occasion the father and son, though eventually let off, were summoned by Captain Wilson to explain their antecedents. In such trying times, his mother sold her ornaments to buy books for her children. This must have caused great pain to a sharif family, but then her children's education was her first and foremost priority. Education was a family asset, as it had always been from the time Zakaullah's ancestors moved from Ghazni into Hindustan. It was the passport to success, the key to Zakaullah's own fame and eminence.

Muslims proudly quote two *hadis* (Prophet's Traditions), of which one makes it the bounden duty of every Muslim to seek knowledge, while the other is the widely quoted counsel of perfection, which bids man 'seek knowledge, even if it be in China'. Zakaullah did so throughout his life. He taught in Delhi College, Agra College (1855–69),[90] and at Allahabad's Muir Central College (1872–86) as 'Professor of Vernacular Science and Literature'. He headed the Delhi Normal School, and served as deputy-inspector of schools in Bulandshahar and Moradabad (1869–72). The contacts he would have made on these occasions and his visits to conferences and meetings qualified him to interpret to his fellow-countrymen historical and contemporary issues.

Though he led a busy and hectic life, teaching, reading, and writing were his preoccupations. This extraordinary tenacity had brought him so close to Imam Bakhsh and Ram Chandra. His clear and sharp intellect enlarged his friendship circle that included Nazir Ahmad, Maulvi Karim Bakhsh, Rai Piyare Lal 'Ashob',

[87]For details, see H.R. Nevill, *Allahabad: A Gazetteer* (Allahabad, 1911), vol. 23, p. 147.

[88] Andrews, *Zakaullah of Delhi*, p. 60.

[89]This is where Ghalib was buried on 15 February 1869.

[90]The Agra College was founded in 1823. For details, see H.R. Nevill, *Agra: A Gazetteer* (Allahabad, 1921), vol. 8. pp. 130–1.

Kanhya Lal, Mir Babar Ali, Master Nand Kishore, and the Arabic scholar Maulvi Ziauddin, who testified against Ghalib in a libel suit against Miyan Aminuddin of Patiala.[91] His affinity with creative writers and scholars created a powerful bonding with his Delhi College colleagues, Muhammad Husain 'Azad', Hali, a lifelong friend, and Maulvi Samiullah Khan (*c.* 1834–1908) whose biography he completed just a year before his death in 1910.[92] During his last fatal illness, he sent messages through Andrews to Nazir Ahmad, then flickering like a flame.

Zakaullah received honours, recognition, and appointments for his loyalty to the Crown. The charm and simplicity of his personality and the weight of his scholarship gained from the first the admiration of those who knew him. He was a key figure in the Scientific Society started at Ghazipur on 9 January 1864, and a regular contributor to Saiyyid Ahmad's *Tahzibul akhlaq*, *Maarif*, *Makhzan*, and Kanpur's *Zemana*. He served as vice-president of the Anjuman Taraqqi Urdu, founded in 1903 to foster the learning and instruction of Urdu, and it was probably at his insistence that Delhi hosted the 1894 session of the All-India Muslim Educational Conference.[93]

A close friend of Saiyyid Ahmad, he played a large part in the Aligarh College affairs, serving as Trustee from 1892 onwards, and as member of the Board of Management. It was he who supported the idea of founding the college at Aligarh and not elsewhere.[94] But, then, serious difference of opinion occurred over the diffusion of knowledge in Urdu. At first the Saiyyid strongly advocated the teaching of sciences through the medium of the vernacular, but later he endorsed the official line that 'the great object of the Government ought to be the promotion of European literature and science among the nations of India'.[95] Zakaullah differed with Saiyyid Ahmad, agreeing with many later theorists in thinking that the medium of instruction should have been Urdu not English. He also did not share Saiyyid Ahmad's outright rejection of traditional school;[96] instead, he believed in achieving some degree of synthesis between the traditional and modern syllabi.

[91]Russell and Islam, *Ghalib*, pp. 361–2.

[92]Zakaullah, *Sawanih Umri: Haji Muhammad Samiullah Bahadur, C.M.G.* (Delhi, 1327 A.H./ 1907). According to Zakaullah, Maulvi Muhammad Hamidullah, son of Maulvi Samiullah and an employee in India Office, London, first mooted the idea of a Muhammadan Educational Conference. This view is hotly contested. Abdul Rashid Khan, *The All India Muslim Educational Conference: Its Contribution to the Cultural Development of Indian Muslims 1886–1947* (Karachi, 2001), pp. 20–1.

[93]Saiyyid Ahmad to Members, Managing Committee, Muhammadan Educational Conference, 21 July 1894, in Atiq Ahmad Siddiqi (ed.), *Sir Syed's Correspondence* (Aligarh, 1990), p. 202.

[94]Zakaullah to Saiyyid Ahmad, n.d., in Siddiqi, *Sir Syed's Correspondence*.

[95]Graham, *Life and Work of Syed Ahmed Khan*, pp. 313, 314.

[96]*Report of the members of the Select Committee for the Better Diffusion and Advancement of the Learning Among the Muhammadans of India* (translated), 1872, quoted in C.H. Philips (ed.), *The Evolution of India and Pakistan 1858 to 1947: Select Documents* (London, 1962), p. 179.

While contesting some aspects of the Saiyyid's educational blueprint, Zakaullah shared the overall perspectives of his lifelong friend, and backed his initiatives.[97] Both believed, as Zakaullah stated, that 'without a full acceptance of the results of modern science and a full knowledge of them also, the East must inevitably fall behind the West'.[98] Both held out the ideal of Muslim regeneration in unison with rather than in opposition to the British,[99] and for this reason they developed a strong aversion to the Indian National Congress founded in December 1885. The Saiyyid stridently criticized its activities, whereas Zakaullah, despairing of public affairs and preferring instead the peaceful pastures of knowledge, couched his protest in mild terms.

Both rejected pan-Islamism. During their lifetime, the pan-Islamic surge threatened to wreck their effort to prop up the Anglo–Muslim alliance in India; so they wanted to cut the silver cord that tied Muslims to the international community of 'all believers', personified in the Khilafat. Both spoke against the Turco-philia among some of their co-religionists, arguing that they were legally bound to obey the writ not of an external Khalifa but of the British Indian government.

Zakaullah maintained a low profile in public life, allowing his icon, Saiyyid Ahmad, to steal the limelight. The Saiyyid was an indefatigable letter-writer; Zakaullah was not. A very private person, he was also too shy and nervous to speak in public. Like 'a nightingale of a thousand songs' before his friends, he was 'tongue-tied, like a mute, in the presence of an audience'.[100] He was a man born to follow, not to lead. He needed a hero; and he found one in the great Aligarh reformer.[101] He was too sage, too tolerant, to force his way to worldly distinction.

VII

We kept writing the blood-drenched narratives of that madness
Although our hands were amputated in the process.

[Ghalib]

[97]In his evidence before the Education Commission (1883), Saiyyid Ahmad opined, 'Vernacular education is no more regarded as sufficient for our daily affairs of life. It is only of use to us in our private and domestic affairs .... It is English education which is urgently needed by the country, and by the people in their daily life.'

[98]Habib, 'Munshi Zakaullah and the vernacularisation of science', p. 134.

[99]There are eight letters from Saiyyid Ahmad to Zakaullah in Shaikh Muhammad Ismail Panipati (ed.), *Maktubat Sir Saiyyid* (Lahore, 1972), vol. 1, pp. 207–12.

[100]Andrews, *Zakaullah of Delhi*, p. 141.

[101]'His eyes used to light up with eager enthusiasm at the mention of the name of Sir Saiyyid Ahmad Khan', wrote Andrews. 'There could be no question who was Munshi Zakaullah's greatest living hero; it was Sir Saiyyid Ahmad.' Andrews, *Zakaullah of Delhi*, p. 95.

It was characteristic of his energy that Zakaullah had time to concentrate on his personal research and the motivation to write books. He started writing at the age of 19, and, by 1910, he had published 147 books with infinite skill and patience. Though their quality is uneven, they illustrate the span and scholarly nature of his activities. His first work was on playing cards and chess, an entertaining guide to forms of leisure and recreation in early-nineteenth-century Delhi. *Tuhfatul hisab*, the book published next, dealt with modern mathematics based on questions and answers. At that time, Zakaullah was only 19 years old. He also wrote two books on mensuration, one of which—*Risala ilm-i masahat*—was commissioned by Aligarh's Scientific Society and Roorkee's Thomson Civil Engineering College. Some of his later works are solid enough to be useful for reference, and to deserve a long life. But Urdu's virtual disappearance from India has made that impossible. Most of Zakaullah's books have either vanished from our libraries, or gather dust in bookshelves.

Abdul Qadir claims that Zakaullah wrote about 70,000 pages of printed matter, which appeared in about hundred volumes. Besides, he contributed 10,000 pages to numerous newspapers, magazines, and periodicals. Several thousand pages of manuscript were found in boxes at the time of his death.[102] How could he produce so much? Zakaullah himself credited his mother for imposing a strict regimen that enabled him to write four pages every day of his life. Like other women in her generation, she accepted her role as mother, wife, and housekeeper who saw to her husband's needs, and to the cleaning, cooking, mending and child rearing. According to Abdul Qadir:

She used to get up at about 3.30 a.m., to offer her *tahajjud* [optional prayers], which were followed by the morning prayers, after which her daily routine of household started. She used to have a nap for half an hour between 8.30 and 9 a.m., after finishing the important part of her morning's work .... She made a point of doing some spinning every day and kept a strict discipline in the house .... Maulvi Zakaullah used to say that he owed to his mother's regular habits his regularity and the methodical nature of his work.[103]

Zakaullah was in full swing in the 1890s. He published *Tahzibul akhlaq Arya Hind ya'ani hunood* (Morals and Culture of the Hindus: 1890), *Muhasinul akhlaq* [(Laudable Morals), a work that takes an explicit position against early marriage],[104] *Mukarramul akhlaq* (Venerable Morals: 1891), *Taalimul akhlaq* (Moral Education: 1892), and *Taalimul khisa'al* (Guide to Character-building: 1892). *Talimul intizamam*

[102]Qadir, *Gleanings*, p. 162. For summary of Zakaullah's publications, Rafat Jamal, *Zakaullah: Hayat aur Unke Ilmi aur Adabi Karname* (Delhi, 1990) pp. 179–244, and Habib, 'Munshi Zakaullah and the vernacularisation of science', pp. 141–3.

[103]Qadir, *Gleanings*, pp. 165–6, and the account of his contemporary Asghar Abdur Razzaq Kanpuri in Asghar Abbas (ed.), *Intikhab Zakaullah* (Lucknow, 1983), pp. 8–9.

[104]Zakaullah, *Muhasinul Akhlaq* (Delhi, 1891), p. 110.

(Guide to Education: 1892), a comparatively small book of 110 pages, deals with savings (*kifayat sha'ari*), investment, the judicious use of material resources, and charity. These have a strong moralistic tone; their style is often technical rather than simple. The specialized vocabulary used in *Muhasinul akhlaq*, a book of 515 pages, makes it inaccessible. Some of his other writings, too, are in part rather specialized for the general reader, in part rather elementary for the professional historian.

In the 1870s, Zakaullah published *Silsilatul ulum*, a series of twenty-three volumes of mathematical works in Urdu. Published under the aegis of Aligarh's Scientific Society and the Scientific Society of Bihar, the publication and sale of the first seventeen volumes were organized by Saiyyid Ahmad. Copies were bought by, among others, the *Nizam* of Hyderabad and the *Maharaja* of Patiala.[105] Zakaullah, in turn, generously allowed the MAO College to publish and prescribe any of his publications.[106] Four of the volumes are translations of Euclid (about 300 BC), the Greek geometer who founded a school in Alexandria and whose chief work, *Elements* (thirteen books) is the basis of many later works in geometry. In addition, Zakaullah produced four treatises on plane and one on spherical trigonometry, the latter a translation of the best work on the subject by the English mathematician, Issac Todhunter (*c.* 1820–84), author of standard textbooks on mathematics, and treatises on the history of mathematical theories of probability, attraction, elasticity. He translated Todhunter's work on differential and integral calculus, as also school manuals by Galbraith and Haughton of the Queen's College in Ireland. All these translations are remarkable for careful and exact rendering. They are free from inelegance of speech, and the technical terms employed are those commonly received. The figures are drawn correctly, indeed remarkably so, considering that they are lithographed.

The translation of such and so many mathematical works was a monumental feat. The government thought so:

The appearance of a series of mathematical works in Urdu just at this time is a welcome support to the argument for teaching science in the vernacular, and *I can only say that I want no better books for a thorough course of pure mathematics than those now under review*. The course contained in the *Silisital ulum* is sufficient to carry the student up to the B.A. standard. (Emphasis added)[107]

---

[105]Saiyyid Ahmad to Raja Jai Kishen Das, 19 April 1871, in Yusuf Husain (ed.), *Selected Documents from the Aligarh Archives* (Aligarh, 1967), pp. 104–5.

[106]Zakaullah to Saiyyid Ahmad, 26 February 1873, in Husain, *Selected Documents from the Aligarh Archives*, p. 239.

[107]The above summary and quotations are based on Memo No. 10 of 3 May 1872 issued by the Secretary, North-West Provinces under Article XIII entitled 'Meritorious Books by Native Authors'. *Statistical Abstract*, pp. 280–1.

Not surprisingly, Zakaullah was rewarded for 'the industry displayed in the preparation of this excellent series of scientific works, and for his public spirit in publishing them'. The Director of Public Instruction added:

I think the highest degree of credit attaches to the honest and careful completion of the task he has undertaken. The labour has been very great, and no small amount of mathematical talent appears in the style and quality of the work. It bears the character of a scientific work rather than a literary performance, but as an important aid to education.[108]

Zakaullah's well-known biographies are on his friend Maulvi Samiullah (in two parts) and on the first half of Curzon's viceroyalty (*Curzon namah*: 1907). He transferred his personal loyalty to Queen Victoria, whom he idealized in *Victoria namah*. Her place in history was side by side with that of Asoka and Akbar, an analogy that became an axiom of his historical thinking.[109] These books, with excerpts from contemporary sources, contain much useful information and lively comments. But judged from the standpoint of biographical literature, they are much less interesting than the works of Shibli Numani (c. 1837–1914).

Tarikh-i Hindustan, published by Muhammad Ataullah in the old city, is Zakaullah's magnum opus. In all, he scripted 7169 pages, a truly laborious feat. Tempting the reader's curiosity and reminding him of the surprising range of his interest in history writing, the first volume appeared in 1897. The *Aligarh Institute Gazette* reissued it in 1915. Providing a full and painstaking account starting from Arabia with the rise and expansion of Islam and concluding with the Arab conquest of Sind and the Delhi Sultanate (c. 1206–65), his preface is erudite. The sections dealing with his didactic and utilitarian purposes of history, though unoriginal, foster among students an appreciation of history and historical processes. Studying the past, he wrote, is a guide to avoid fatal errors and to deal with adversity. And knowledge of history and historical processes sensitizes people to the currents of change and develops in them the spirit of perseverance and patience.[110] He sets out certain historical laws, drawing on the insights of British and Muslim historians, including Ibn Khaldun (733–808/1332–1406), the great Arab historian.[111] But he fails to live up to the standards that he set for his readers. He criticizes the tendency in the West to demonize Muslim dynasties,[112]

---

[108]Secretary to Director of Public Instruction, North-Western Provinces, 15 June 1872, *Statistical Abstract*, p. 282.

[109]Muhammad Aslam Syed, *Muslim Response to the West: Muslim Historiography in India 1857–1914* (Islamabad, 1988), p. 60.

[110]Zakaullah, *Muqaddimah*, p. 64, and his *Makaramul akhlaq*, pp. 532–5.

[111]It is the introduction to his *Kitab al-Ibar* (Book of Examples and the Collection of Origins of the History of the Arabs and Berbers).

[112]Zakaullah, *Tarikh-i Hindustan Uruj-i Saltanat Inglish: Lord Auckland ke Ahad Saltanat se Lord Dalhousie ke Ahad Tak* (Delhi, 1879), vol. 1, p. 14.

but he is himself too enamoured with the West to be objective, detached, and reflective.[113] 'Even dark aspects of their [Western] civilization appear pleasant', he wrote in an article.[114] For this bizarre expression of unrestrained loyalty, Andrews, the biographer, had this to say:

Zakaullah was, to the very depth of his being, a hero-worshipper, whose spiritual nature always depended on having some personality to serve with devotion. He could hardly exist without an atmosphere of loyalty to some higher person about him than a fish can exist without water, or a man can breathe without air.

The next two volumes, illustrated by extracts from Persian and British sources, are chronologically arranged, covering the Khaljis (c. 1290–1320), the Tughlaqs (c. 1320–1412), the Saiyyids (c. 1414–51), the Lodis (c. 1414–1526), and the reigns of Babur and Humayun. Subsequent volumes turn to regional kingdoms, whereas Iqbal nama-i Akbari covers Akbar's reign (c. 1556–1605). This book of 1056 pages does not add much to earlier conclusions about Akbar.

Volume six is devoted to Jahangir. It is followed by yet another tome on Shah Jahan. The last three volumes deal with Aurangzeb and his successors. Herein Zakaullah does not trace or examine the loss of Mughal power, or analyse its course; instead, his enthusiasm for Aurangzeb (c. 1658–1707), whom he admired for his piety and religious devotion—a mirror image of himself—is unabashedly uncritical. He attributes the Mughal decline not to Aurangzeb's religious intolerance or his prolonged and protracted Deccan campaigns, but on his weak and inept successors.

In the first edition of volume one, he made certain sharp remarks about his dealing with Bahadur Shah, but he afterwards expressed regret. He used to say that he could not meet any member of the erstwhile Mughal household without feeling a pang of remorse for what he had written. His justification, though, was that his views were those of a historian; and history writing did not allow any favour to be shown even to the high and mighty.[115]

What Zakaullah is best at is retelling in detail and in quasi-fictional style, with heightened emotion and effective use of the novelist's art, the story of the futile revolt in 1857. The saga of 1857, as indeed aspects of British rule, are brought alive in a set of publications brought out from 1879 onward. He is critical of Aurangzeb's successors, but fulsome in praising the East India Company. Extolling its achievements, he concludes with an uncritical note: 'In short, the East India Company established the glory and majesty (shaukat) of Europe in the east, replacing a barbaric (wahshiana) government with a sophisticated (shaista) and civilized (muhazzab) one.'[116]

---

[113]For a brief but critical appreciation of his history writing, see Saiyyid Abdullah, Sir Saiyyid aur unke Namwar Rufaqa ki Nasar ka Fikri aur Fanni Jaeza (Delhi, 1960), pp. 224–5.

[114]Quoted in M.A. Syed, Muslim Historiography in India, p. 63.

[115]Andrews, Zakaullah of Delhi, p. 19.

[116]Zakaullah, Tarikh-i Hindustan, vol. 2, part 3, p. 215.

The *Tarikh-i Hindustan* and his multi-volume *History of the Rise of the British Empire* make, in part, fascinating and instructive reading, even though in his preoccupation with details Zakaullah has little time for reflection and analysis. This is especially so when he copiously quotes from Henry Elliot and J. Dowson's *History of India as Told by its Own Historians*, and the other British historians of India. Judicious selection of facts and compression would have enhanced the narrative's quality, but the very scale of the effort makes for somewhat heavy going. And the account itself makes a less exciting story than might have been expected.

Finally, contrary to Andrews' contention that studying India's ancient past was 'one of the delights of his life, both as a scholar and a patriot', Zakaullah reveals a singular lack of sympathy, as does Shibli, for the pre-medieval period.[117] Despite the compliment paid to his skills as a historian by the French Orientalist Garcin de Tassy (*c*. 1794–1878), the *Tarikh* is vastly inferior to the Indo-Persian chroniclers.[118] The voluminous material is

a paraphrase of the chronicles and history is seemingly used to mean a collection of the different witnesses and facts, and not as a correlation, interpretation, or judgement of those facts. As in the Persian chroniclers, it is full of minute, vivid description of battles and festivities, with a preponderant interest in war and the court, and the significance is mixed up with the unimportant. Criticism or analysis of causes is hardly attempted.[119]

Urdu historiography developed in the nineteenth century, but only slightly. Saiyyid Ahmad showed the path with *Jam-i Jam*, a brief tabulated account of the kings of Timur and his edition of Ziauddin Barani's *Tarikh-i Firuz Shahi* (1862) and the first lithographed text of Abul Fazl's *Ain-i Akbari*. But Muslim historians writing in Urdu remained virtually tied to medieval Indian chroniclers, and uncritically adopted their methods and styles of representation. Though aware of Western methodology, they failed to break the mould. More often than not, they turned apologetic in response to the denunciation of Islam in certain circles, and, in the process, invented their 'glorious' phase of Islamic history with its heroes. As Shibli did while chronicling the life of Umar ibn al-Khattab (*c*. 634–44), the second orthodox *Khalifa*, al-Mamun (*c*. 786–833), Khalifa of Baghdad (*c*. 813–33), Abu Hanifa (*c*. 699–767), a Muslim jurist and founder of the Hanafi school of jurisprudence, al-Ghazali (*c*. 1058–1111), the Arab philosopher called by some the 'Father of the Church of Islam', and Jalaluddin Rumi (*c*. 1207–73), the Persian

[117]See, for example, Shibli Numani, *Maqalat-i Shibli* (Azamgarh, 1937), p. 194; Z.H. Faruqi, 'Sir Saiyyid and Maulana Shibli', in Mohibbul Hasan (ed.), *Historians of Medieval India* (Meerut, 1968), p. 240; and for an analysis of Shibli's historical works, Aziz Ahmad, *Islamic Modernism in India and Pakistan 1857–1964* (London, 1967), pp. 77–85.

[118]Zakaullah translated his collection of five lectures as *Risala-i Tazkirat*. Ed. Tanvir Ahmad Alvi (Delhi, n.d.).

[119]A.B.M. Habibullah, 'Historical writing in Urdu: A survey of tendencies', in C.H. Philips (ed.), *Historians of India, Pakistan and Ceylon* (London, 1961), p. 489.

poet and the author of many exquisite *masnavi*s, or *mathnavi*s, a collection of double-rhymed verses containing ethical and moral precepts.

Backed by the proliferation of the Urdu press, such efforts developed in the Muslim readership a false sense of cultural and religious superiority, a point Saiyyid Ahmad alluded to in his evidence before the Education Commission in 1883. Often, they failed to distinguish between reality and words and symbols; more than once they preferred to believe in fictions and fantasies. But the non-Muslims, who were proficient in Urdu and used it as their language of communication, had little patience with religious and cultural orthodoxies and their assertion through religious decrees (*fatawa*) or public debates (*munazira*). In effect, the pro-Muslim and pro-Islamic bias of the Muslim historians triggered off the trend to write parallel 'Hindu' and 'Muslim' histories that were rooted in invented and imaginary traditions of the past. History writing in Urdu was, consequently, reduced to polemics. Respectable 'historians', often swayed by the rhetoric of the publicists and political propagandists, turned publicists. They were much less read by the audience they targeted, that is, Muslims, who accessed a wide variety of religious texts, that is, commentaries on Koran and *Hadis* literature (compilation of the traditions of the Prophet). Non-Muslim readers, too, shunned such writings. Besides their content that often hurt their cultural sensibilities, they were increasingly swayed by the polemics of the Arya Samaj, especially in the Punjab and in parts of the North-Western Provinces. Increasingly, the appeal of Muslim historians diminished.

Zakaullah was no exception. He was conscious of his Indian Muslim identity, as well his professional obligation as a historian. But, like Shibli and Ameer Ali (*c.* 1849–1928), he too failed to intellectualize this duality creatively. Often his Muslim identity stood in the way of an objective historical enquiry. As a result, his writings did not set a secular trend in Urdu historiography or make the succeeding generation of historians rethink their methodology and approach.

VIII

The Coronation Durbar was held on 12 December 1911, in Delhi, the newly chosen imperial capital. The State entry into Delhi led by King George V and Queen Mary went through the Red Fort and onto the big maidan between the Fort and the Jama Masjid. An eyewitness described the pomp and pageantry:

At the time I had an easy feeling that the realities that lie behind politics are pretty thin, & looking back that must, I think, explain why as a whole the people, the real India, surged past the old Fort walls upon which the King & Queen sat alone panoplied in all the cumbrous additaments of their calling. I could not see them, but I did see perhaps 100,000 people washing up to the walls in great waves of many-coloured humanity and emotion breaking from them like foam in the music of uplifted hands and voices. That was a superb and a most moving spectacle.[120]

Andrews witnessed the Durbar. Nazir Ahmad would have heard the shout of 'God Save the King-Emperor', echoed in the lanes and by-lanes of the Old City.[121] But there was no Zakaullah to witness the curtain being drawn on another phase in Delhi's history. He had died on 7 November 1910, and was buried at the shrine of Shah Abdul Salam Faridi, a Sufi of the Chishti order. In Kucha Balaqi Begum all was quiet that evening, but for the mourners reciting '*We belong to Allah, and to Him we shall return*', and ending with the Koranic prayer 'We come into the world with clenched fists but leave it with open, empty hands and nothing lasts. May the souls of the dead rest in peace.' Just then, the *muezzin*'s call of *Allah-o-Akbar, Allah-o-Akbar* came from the nearby Jama Masjid, described by the visiting English writer, E.M. Forster (*c.* 1879–1970), as 'a most glorious building—the courtyard raised on huge basement, colonnaded with sandstone galleries, and paved with marble'.[122]

'The divine stream of eternal life,' Zakaullah would have quoted from his friend's book *Ab-e hayat* (Ghulam Husain 'Azad' died the same year) 'is flowing yet, on the banks of which, from age to age, all five gatherings are assembled. The "Water of Life" is making the rounds. The water of the stream captures a picture of the passing of time. And the waves go on bidding farewell to this external life.'[123]

[120]Malcolm Darling to E.M. Forster, 4 February 1912, *Selected Letters of E.M. Forster*. Edited by Mary Logo and P.N. Furbank (London, 1983), vol. 1, p. 129.

[121]He died on 3 May 1912.

[122]Forster to Maura Mary Forster, 31 October 1912, *Selected Letters of E.M. Forster*, p. 146. Forster reached Delhi in mid-October 1912 and stayed with Dr M.A. Ansari [*c.* 1880–1936] at Mori Gate.

[123]Azad, *Ab-e hayat*, p. 429.

LIVING TOGETHER SEPARATELY: THE 'ULAMA OF FARANGI MAHALL C. 1700–C. 1950

Francis Robinson

One day in May 1980, the diners in the ground floor section of the Kwality restaurant in Lucknow's Hazratganj looked up from their meals to see a most unusual sight. A group of traditionally dressed Muslims was moving somewhat self-consciously through the tables towards the stairs which would take them to the private dining room on the upper floor. They were a striking sartorial vision, wearing a range of styles, some from the nineteenth century, and particularly in the form of head wear, some of which would draw attention in the Chawk let alone Hazratganj. These were 'ulama of Farangi Mahall—Matin Miyan, 'Abd al-Rahman Sahib, Mufti Rada Ansari, Fakhir Miyan Bahr al-'Ulum, and descendants of the saint of Bansa, Mushir Miyan and Hashim Miyan Razzaqi, who with myself were all guests of the famous Lucknow bookseller, Ram Advani. Ram had been aware of the great hospitality I had been receiving from the Farangi Mahallis and Razzaqis over the past four months and wished to show his gratitude on my behalf.

Once we had sat down and begun to eat I realized that no one seemed willing to talk. I put on my best British good manners and strove to draw everyone into conversation. It quickly became clear that my sallies were unwelcome. The Farangi Mahallis and Razzaqis wished to eat in silence out of respect for their host. It was a companionable silence. When the guests had eaten their fill, conversation did develop. But it was not long before the guests said their thanks and their farewells, and descended the stairs to leave to the startled gaze of the diners below. All concluded, as far as I knew, that it had been a most successful event. We all knew, too, how unusual it had been for the Farangi Mahallis and Razzaqis to make the mile and a half journey from the Chawk to dine in the Kwality restaurant, Hazratganj.

This anecdote serves to introduce the Farangi Mahall family of learned and holy men as one which has lived separately from other religious communities, but equally for the most part has been happy to coexist with them. Indeed, for much of its history, family members have seen their past and to some extent their future through a family and a Muslim lens. From time to time they have been concerned to draw clear distinctions between their world and those of others. Of course, it could be argued, and probably rightly, that a family of Muslim learned and holy men was more likely than most to live 'separately' within India. This said, we will note that, when in the twentieth century some shareable public spaces opened up, Farangi Mahallis were able to join other communities, though in small numbers and generally for a restricted time.

Like many of *sharif* descent, or those who liked to pretend to sharif descent, the Farangi Mahallis traced their line back to the time of the Prophet. It was their ancestor, Ayyub Ansari, who had been the Prophet's host at Medina, and it was he who had been the Prophet's standard bearer, and subsequently the leader of a naval expedition against Constantinople, c. 638, in which he died.[1] The Farangi Mahallis then traced their descent through the eleventh-century mystic, 'Abd Allah Ansari of Herat, whose descendants migrated to India in the early years of the Delhi Sultanate, establishing themselves in the region of Panipat. In the fourteenth century, one Ala al-Din migrated eastwards, settling in the village of Sihali in Awadh. From the mid-sixteenth century, they were able to trace their ancestors in large numbers of documents relating to their rights in land down to the point when their ancestor, the great scholar, Qutb al-din Sihalwi, was murdered by neighbouring zamindars in a squabble over land, and the emperor Aurangzeb made the famous donation in recompense to his four sons of the sequestered *haweli* of a European indigo merchant in Lucknow—Farangi Mahall.[2]

The learned and holy men of Farangi Mahall were also conscious of their various contributions to Muslim rule. They knew that Qutb al-din Sihalwi and his pupils had brought *ma'qulat* scholarship to its peak in the late-seventeenth- and early-eighteenth-century northern India, a peak which was recognized in West Asia. They knew, too, that Qutb al-Din's son, Nizam al-din, had reformed the madrasa curriculum, which came to be called the Dars-i Nizami, so that it was a much more effective training for administrators. Indeed, not only was it adopted

---

[1]The seventeenth-century Ottoman chronicler, Evliya Chelebi, has a marvelously sardonic description of how Mehmet Fatih with the help of a dream of his Shaykh al-Islam discovered Ayyub Ansari's tomb at Eyup.

[2]This profoundly sharif vision of the Farangi Mahalli past is set out in Mawlana Mawlwi Muhammad 'Inayat Allah, *Tadhkira-yi 'ulama-I farangi mahall* (Lucknow, 1928).

throughout India but it had also been endorsed by the East India Company, when it established the Calcutta madrasa. But Farangi Mahalli contributions did not end with improved forms of education, they also knew that their ancestors had served Indian Muslim rulers: the Mughals themselves, and Mughal successor states, the Nawabs of Farrukhabad, Rampur, Awadh and Arcot, the Begums of Bhopal, and most especially the Nizams of Hyderabad.

Their vision of their past, a classically sharif vision, meant that many Farangi Mahallis would have sympathized with the rhetoric of Mohsin al-Mulk and Imad al-Mulk who drafted the Muslim address to Viceroy Minto in 1906. They had come to India from Arabia and while in India had long been associated with the exercise of Muslim power. Equally, from the mid-nineteenth century onwards, there was a dimension of their consciousness which embraced the Islamic world, but particularly West Asia, and which was especially sensitive to the advance of Western power there. Thus, in 1878, when Russia went to war against the dying Ottoman empire, 'Abd al-Razzaq of Farangi Mahall founded the Majlis Mu'id al-Islam and campaigned throughout north India to raise funds for the Ottoman cause. His grandson, 'Abd al-Bari, performed the Hajj three times, studied and taught in Mecca and Medina, and visited Baghdad, Damascus, Beirut, Alexandria, and Cairo. He kept a house in Medina so that, as he declared in his will, he might be regarded as being a resident there when he went to heaven, and maintained a correspondence with Muslims of the region, amongst them Young Turks and Sharif Husayn of Mecca. It is hardly surprising that, from the moment that the Ottoman empire entered its death throes in 1913 to 'Abd al-'Aziz's announcement of his kingship of Saudi Arabia in January 1926, most of his energy and imagination should have been focused in this direction, and that in the process he should have drawn many members of his family, as well as many Muslims, with him.[3]

Another perspective on the sense of themselves that the Farangi Mahallis had in India is provided by the religious guidance they followed and offered. The Farangi Mahallis paid enormous respect to the Qadri saint Sayyid Shah 'Abd al-Razzaq of Bansa, who died in 1724. In his 1917 essay on the 'urs at Bansa, 'Abd al-Bari declared that for the 'ulama of Farangi Mahall, however learned they were, 'attendance at this 'urs, has been a means of reinforcing faith'.[4] Indeed, traditionally at the ceremonies of the 'urs, the Farangi Mahallis were given the place of greatest prominence. On the other side, representatives of the holy family of Bansa were present at all the key moments of the family's life whether the official occasions of the madrasa or the death of family members. To bring the saint's blessings, the

---

[3]For 'Abd al-Bari's life and his focus on West Asia, see 'Abd al-Bari and the events of January 1926' in Robinson, 'Ulama of Farangi Mahall, pp. 145–76.

[4]'Abd al-Bari, 'Urs-I Hadrat-i Bansa (Lucknow n.d., but internal evidence suggests 1926), p. 10.

family always tried to have at least one member of the saint's family staying with them, as they did on the occasion of the dinner in the Kwality restaurant.

In following the traditions of Bansa, as far as it has been possible to discover, the Farangi Mahallis followed only those recorded by their ancestor, Mulla Nizam al-Din (d. 1748). The *mulla* had been a friend and *khalifa* of the saint. His narration of the Banswi tradition in his *Manaqib-i Razzaqiyya*[5] places the saint in a world which is clearly populated by Hindus, indeed, on one occasion the saint is attracted to a Hindu boy.[6] The anecdotes, however, that are told are concerned to show Muslim superiority, as a Hindu mystic is revealed to be materialistic,[7] or the distinction between a Muslim and a Hindu position on the transmigration of souls.[8] Equally, the saint is demonstrated to be a strong supporter of those who uphold the law and dignity of Islam, as when he congratulates a disciple who had fasted during a hot monsoon Ramadan when travelling to Bansa,[9] and as when he praises a host at a *qawwali* concert for upbraiding his guests for going into ecstasy at songs in Hindi but not doing so when they hear verses from the Quran.[10]

There is no hint in the Farangi Mahalli tradition, as represented by the written record, or my personal involvement with the family over thirty years, of support for the religious practices expressed in Nawab Muhammad Khan Shahjahanpuri's two *malfuzat* collections *Malfuz-i Razzaqi* and *Karamat-i Razzaqi*, which belong to the latter half of the eighteenth century. These express concerns not just for the *sharia* but for religious harmony in Awadh. The saint shows respect for taziyas and the Muharram processions of Shias. He shows marked respect for the Hindu religious world, and receives it in return. Thus he is present at Diwali celebrations, watches *bakhtiyas* performing the life of Krishna, and has visions of Ram and Lakshman; in turn, Krishna would send his *salam* to the saint. Such acts, as one might expect, were a step too far for 'ulama. There were important distinctions which had to be maintained.[11] Disciples, however, who belong to this tradition were honoured nonetheless; Hasrat Mohani, *murid* of 'Abd al-Wahhab and author of poems in praise of Krishna and Mathura, is one of the few non-family members to lie in the family graveyard—in a separate section. Shias and Hindus were always welcome at the family's madrasa.

As far as formal religious guidance is concerned, although the evidence is

---

[5]Mulla Nizam al-din's *Manaqib-I Razzaqiyya* was originally in Persian. The edition used here is the Urdu translation made by Sibghat Allah Shahid Farangi Mahall (Lucknow, n.d., but probably in the 1930s or 1940s). The translation was made at the request of the *sajjadanashin* at Bansa, Sayyid Shah Mumtaz Ahmad Razzaqi.

[6]Nizam al-Din, *Manaqib*, p. 64.

[7]Ibid., p. 19.

[8]Ibid., p. 38.

[9]Ibid., p. 24.

[10]Ibid., p. 19.

[11]For a discussion of this point, see Robinson, *'Ulama of Farangi Mahall*, pp. 64–6.

not considerable, in the late nineteenth century, the Farangi Mahallis seemed rather more accepting of the requirements of living harmoniously in a largely Hindu society than the reformers. Whereas Rashid Ahmad Gangohi of Deoband issued a *fatawa* 'that discouraged social and business intercourse with Hindus, forbade attendance at Arya Samaj lectures (unless one were skilled in debate) and deemed illegitimate the appearance of being Hindu, whether in dress, hairstyle or the use of brass instead of copper vessels',[12] the fatawa of 'Abd al-Hayy of Farangi Mahall declared that, although a Muslim most certainly could not accept a Hindu donation for a mosque, he could eat food prepared by a Hindu, wear clothes washed by a Hindu, and abstain from cow sacrifice, provided it was to avoid a riot and not because he thought the beast was holy.[13]

At this juncture, it is important to reiterate that the Hindu world only seems to have a small purchase on the Farangi Mahalli mind during the eighteenth and nineteenth centuries. Let us look briefly at three works by Farangi Mahallis covering the period from c. 1800 to the early twentieth century. They are: the malfuzat of Anwar al-Haqq (c. 1822) with some additional elements of family history, *al-Aghsan al-Arbaa*, by Wali Allah Farangi Mahalli (c. 1855),[14] the life and malfuzat of 'Abd al-Razzaq, the *Anwar-i Razzaqiyya*, by Altaf al-Rahman Qidwai,[15] and *Salah Falah* by 'Abd al-Khaliq Farangi Mahalli, which was a commentary on the times.[16] The first describes an entirely Muslim world; Hindus do not appear in any way, shape, or form. Apart from the usual mystical and biographical concerns, the main focus is on the problems that this family of Sunni 'ulama had in dealing with the Nawabs of Awadh and their courtiers, and the growing presence of the British both as a source of employment and as a great power in relation to the Nawabi state. The second work covers the life of 'Abd al-Razzaq, including his journey to Madras when young, his involvement in the Mutiny uprising, and after that event his increasingly strong awareness of the British, whom he detested. It also contains substantial coverage of his sayings and miracles. There are only four points in this extensive work where one might gather that 'Abd al-Razzaq lived in a land which was also peopled by Hindus. Two come as throwaway comments: he recalls that on his journey to Madras in his youth he found blessing in the lands ruled by Hindus which were not present in those ruled by Christians,[17] and he speculates that Muslims came to use fireworks at the festival of Shab-i Barat as a

[12]Barbara Daly Metcalf, *Islamic Revival in British India: Deoband, 1860–1900* (Princeton, 1982), p. 153.

[13]'Abd al-Hayy Farangi Mahalli, *Majmua-yi Fatawa Hadrat Mawlana 'Abd al-Hayy Marhoom, Farangi Mahalli*, 10th ed. (Lucknow, 1985), vol. 1, pp. 57, 115, 149, 170.

[14]Wali Allah Farangi Mahalli, *al-Aghsan al-arba'a*, Nadwa ms., Lucknow, n.d.

[15]Altaf al-Rahman Qidwai. *Anwar-I Razzaqiyya* (Lucknow, n.d.).It is family tradition that 'Abd al-Bari dictated this text to Qidwai, who acted as his amanuensis.

[16]Muhammad 'Abd al-Khaliq, *Salah Falah* (Lucknow, 1909).

[17]Qidwai, *Anwar*, p. 61.

result of the influence of Diwali celebrations.[18] Two come in demonstrations of the spiritual power of the *Mawlana*. In the first he succeeds in preventing the relations of a Hindu Raja, who had secretly converted to Islam from cremating his remains,[19] and in the second he demonstrates to a Muslim, drawn to mysticism by Hindu *jogis*, the greater satisfaction of an Islamic spiritual path.[20] Indeed, 'Abd al-Razzaq saw the future in terms of an almost apocalyptic struggle between Muslims and Christians. The time will come, went one of his sayings, that

the world will be divided into two camps, one under the Muslim flag and the other under the Christian flag. The people under the Christian flag will get food cheaply and those under the Muslim flag will pay dearly for it. At that time it will be difficult to protect the faith.[21]

Indeed, it is striking, although we should not really be surprised, how Islamically focused the Farangi Mahallis were as they considered the future in India. The years after the Muslim address to Viceroy Minto in 1906 saw the beginnings of increasingly intense reflection on the future of Muslims in India and purposeful action. In 1909 'Abd al-Khaliq of Farangi Mahall published *Salah Falah* or his suggestions for the betterment of Muslims. The world view he expresses is substantially changed from that of 'Abd al-Razzaq. It is one which reflects both the press discourse of several decades as well as a view of India expressed in British writings. He regards the British Raj as a good thing; a suppressor of disorder and a source of justice and progress.[22] His world, moreover, is distinctly formed in terms of 'Hindus' and 'Muslims'. He writes of the rise and decline of India in the pre-British period in a language of Hindu–Muslim conflict,[23] of the Mutiny uprising being Hindus versus Hindus and Muslims versus Muslims,[24] of how well the *mahajans* have done under British rule,[25] of how Hindu lawyers had all been in favour of Sir Sayyid when he came to Lucknow in 1886 to make his Qaisarbagh speech, and of how the *Sayyid* had succeeded in offending many through his attitudes to Hindus [in fact Bengalis].[26] The 'Hindus' have emerged in 'Abd al-Khaliq's consciousness as they have not appeared in family discourse before. His prime concerns, however, remain as purely Muslim as 'Abd al-Razzaq's had been, though his emphases were diametrically opposed; Muslims had slipped behind, he argued, because they had failed to follow the Islamic exhortation that they

[18]Ibid., p. 45.
[19]Ibid. pp. 88–90.
[20]Ibid., p. 93.
[21]Ibid., p. 128.
[22]Khaliq, *Salah,* pp. 16–40.
[23]Ibid., pp. 12–15.
[24]Ibid., pp. 26–8.
[25]Ibid., pp. 33–4.
[26]Ibid., pp. 41–2.

advance in knowledge. Sayyid Ahmad Khan's Aligarh initiative was just what Muslims should be following.[27] He talks proudly of the presence of Islam in Britain and in the USA, of its rapid advance in Africa, and of a British report which tells of half the population of China being Muslim![28] Islam, he declares, is progressing in India through conversion.[29] The upshot is that, problems of Shia–Sunni rivalry apart, which absorb a quarter of the book, Islam has a bright future in India and in the world.

Given this view of a Muslim future in India, in which Hindus appear primarily as the subject of conversion, though to be fair not aggressively so, it was to be expected that the first Muslim organization to be founded in this period by the Farangi Mahallis (apart from their madrasa in 1907) was focused completely on a Muslim future. In 1910, responding in part perhaps to the great agitation which surrounded the campaign for separate electorates in the Morley-Minto reforms,[30] and in part perhaps to the establishment of the Muslim League's headquarters in Lucknow in that year, 'Abd al-Bari presided over the refounding of the Majlis Mu'id al-Islam. It aimed, amongst other things 'to try to help the Muslims attain progress in worldly matters, while keeping in mind the injunctions of the shariat'.[31] Its members found themselves subsequently involved in, amongst other things, 'Abd al-Bari's Anjuman-i Khuddam-i Ka'ba organization, the struggle to protect the holy places, and the Cawnpur Mosque campaign.

The period of the World War I saw no broadening of their perspective. At this time we are privileged to be able to listen to Farangi Mahallis, and their associates, discussing matters amongst themselves in the pages of *Al-Nizamiyya*, a house journal to which mainly younger members of the family contributed from 1915 to 1919. The purpose of the journal had a specific Muslim focus, and its contributors were Muslims, although it did publish *nath* poetry in praise of the Prophet by a Hindu, Raja Kishen Pershad 'Shad', chief minister of Hyderabad. Amongst its aims were 'the progress of Islam and the encouragement of Muslims to follow its tenets, in all possible ways' and 'the strengthening of unity amongst Muslims'.[32] In subsequent issues we find 'ulama probing into the nature of nationality and how it may be preserved. Ibn Khaldun's idea that it was group solidarity or party spirit (*'asabiyya*) which enabled groups to survive, and in favourable circumstances to dominate others, seems to have been their starting point. 'It was group solidarity,' argued Muhammad Yunus of Farangi Mahall, 'that had enabled both the Aryans to maintain their national existence amongst

[27]Ibid., pp. 43–4.

[28]Ibid., pp. 71–5.

[29]Ibid., pp. 76.

[30]'Abd al-Bari had been a strong supporter of separate electorates in the great campaign for them in 1909.

[31]Francis Robinson, *Separatism Among Indian Muslims: The Politics of the United Provinces' Muslims 1860–1923* (Cambridge, 1974), p. 276.

non-Aryans and the English to maintain their dominion over India.'[33] Later he added that it was high moral principles which enabled a nation to progress. Islam had brought the Arabs to an advanced state, and, when they neglected it, they declined.[34] In the same vein, Sibghat Allah of Farangi Mahall argued that nations survived by protecting their national characteristics (*qawmisi'ar*), and the secret of doing so lay in *ta'assub*, that is prejudice in favour of one's group, which was precisely what Islam endorsed.[35] In the same issue Sayyid Amin al-Hasan Mohani brought the discussion to the point of action needed in the present. Missionary work (*tabligh*) had enabled a handful of men in the Prophet's time to form and rule a universal community. This was what was needed today to achieve the higher end of nationality (*qawmiyyat*) and democracy (*jumhuriyyat*).[36] There was no sense in this Wartime period, in which Indian nationalist feeling was growing and in which a Lucknow Pact was to be signed, of any nationalist vision that was not purely Muslim. The Shahabad riots of autumn 1917, in which many Muslims were killed by Hindu mobs protesting against cow sacrifice, led Sibghat Allah of Farangi Mahall to reflect on the importance of maintaining the symbols of difference. Muslims must maintain their identity by protecting their chief characteristics of which sacrifice (*qurbani*) was one. Hindus had a sense of solidarity which underpinned their nationalism. They avoided Muslims who they regarded as untouchables or barbarians (*mlecchas*), and despite Muslim rule they had not allowed themselves to be absorbed into Islam.[37]

The Farangi Mahallis' focus remained no less distinctively held within a narrow Islamic frame when they had to confront a real issue of devolution of power in India. In 1917, in the aftermath of the Lucknow Pact, but also in that of the Shahabad riots, their Majlis Mu'id al-Islam had an opportunity to present an address to Secretary of State Montagu and Viceroy Chelmsford, who were touring India to gather opinion on constitutional reform. 'Abd al-Bari's telegram calling 'ulama to meet to consider their address made his position on collaboration with Hindus clear: 'Mussalmans nominal leaders and outward co-religionists are in delusion of union with infidels. If ulama keep silent Mussalmans will suffer great loss. The matter must be consulted over and a deputation of ulemas presented before Sec of State.'[38] The draft address which emerged from this meeting only confirmed their separate vision, their anger at Hindus, and their need for protection

---

[32] *Al-Nizamiyya*, 1:1 (March 1915).

[33] Muhammad Yunus, 'Tarikhi qawmen kyonkar banti hayn', ibid., pp. 19–24.

[34] Muhammad Yunus, 'Hamari taraqqi ke raz', *Al-Nizamiyya*, 1:3 (May 1915), pp. 23–7.

[35] Sibghat Allah Shahid, 'Qawmi si'ar ka tahaffuz', *Al-Nizamiyya*, 1:3 (May 1915), pp. 29–30.

[36] Sayyid Amin al-Hasan Mohani 'Tabligh', *Al-Nizamiyya*, 1:3 (May 1915), pp. 15–22.

[37] Sibghat Allah Shahid, 'Islam ka sab se aham usul: "qurbani"', *Al-Nizamiyya*, 3:8–9 (Oct./Nov. 1917), pp. 49–57.

[38] 'Abd al-Bari to Tajuddin, 13 Oct. 1917, copy of the text of a telegram, 'Abd al-Bari Papers, File 10, (English) Farangi Mahall.

against them. It required some very nimble work on the part of Hakim Ajmal Khan and Dr Ansari to remove most of the elements which could be seen as undermining Hindu–Muslim unity and the Lucknow Pact, and to replace them with a formulation that the government was to describe as 'a nakedly impracticable demand for the predomination of priestly influence'.[39]

In the Khilafat period it could be argued that the Farangi Mahallis softened their views towards Hindus, which to some extent they did. It was Gandhi who was the key figure in building a relationship. He had heard of 'Abd al-Bari from Mushir Husayn Qidwa'i when he was in England, and it is believed that they first made contact when Gandhi attended the 1916 Congress in Lucknow. They came into regular contact as Gandhi campaigned for the release of the 'Ali Brothers and against the Rowlatt legislation. When he came to Lucknow he would stay in Farangi Mahall; to this day Farangi Mahallis point to the room in the *Mahalsera* in which Gandhi stayed and the papaya tree (though by now surely a replacement) to which the Mahatma would tie his goat. When during 1919 the Khilafat issue became pressing, it was 'Abd al-Bari who courted Gandhi to the extent that in the following year he was able to boast: 'I have made Mahatma Gandhi to follow us in the Khilafat question.'[40] By June 1920 Gandhi was heading a small committee of Khilafatists to put non-cooperation into practice and by September, with Muslim help, the Congress had been won for Gandhi and for non-cooperation.

The remarkable period of political action which followed has been trumpeted as a period of Hindu–Muslim unity, which it was, and Hindu–Muslim friendships which were to endure the nationalist struggle were made in it. But for the vast majority of Farangi Mahallis it was not seen thus. Just as 'Abd al-Bari thought of Gandhi being won for the Khilafat so they saw the Congress in general being won for the cause. Everything, moreover, was fine so long as the tensions between the nationalist movement's search for power in India and the 'ulama's pan-Islamic dreams did not clash. But, of course, they were bound to do so.

As in 1922 and 1923, the prospect of elections to the Montagu–Chelmsford councils became closer, many politicians began to focus on the prospect of real power; the direct action favoured by 'ulama in pursuing their pan-Islamic causes became less attractive. At the same time, the new assertiveness of Muslims in the towns and cities of India, and their prominence in Congress affairs, had galvanized Hindus into acting as Hindus. In the autumn of 1922, the Hindu Sabha was refounded as the Hindu Mahasabha. In spring 1923 Swami Shraddhanand launched the Shuddhi movement amongst the Meos, and in the summer of 1923 northern India was wracked by Hindu–Muslim riots. 'Abd al-Bari, along with several Muslim organizations, leapt to the defence of their co-religionists. The erstwhile protagonist

[39]For how Ajmal Khan and Ansari worked the changes, see Robinson, *Separatism Among Indian Muslims*, pp. 284–6.
[40]Ibid., p. 293.

of Hindu–Muslim unity now told his followers to forget about trying to accommodate Hindu feelings. He urged them to sacrifice cows declaring that

if the commandments of Shariat are to be trampled underfoot then it will be the same to us whether the decision is arrived at on the plains of Delhi or on the hilltops of Simla. We are determined to non-co-operate with every enemy of Islam whether he be in Anatolia or Arabia or in Agra or Benares.[41]

By the end of the Khilafat period, arguably the first really intense north Indian Muslim engagement in the public sphere at the national level, Hindus were firmly in the Farangi Mahalli consciousness.

In dealing with the Farangi Mahallis we have tended to treat them as an undifferentiated group. But it should be clear that we have been dealing in large part, though not wholly, with those in the dominant (in numbers at least) line of descent from Qutb al-Din Sihalwi, that of Mulla Sa'id, and in particular those attracted by the leadership of 'Abd al-Razzaq and his grandson 'Abd al-Bari. Until the 1937 elections, the politically minded of these, like the influential Mawlana Inayat Allah, head teacher of the Madrasa Nizamiyya, tended to be supporters of the Congress. But, at this point, they began to turn to the Muslim League of which in 1942 'Abd al-Bari's son, Mawlana Jamal Miyan, became Honorary Assistant Secretary.

Others, however, for instance the younger brothers of the author of *Salah Falah*, Mawlanas 'Abd al-Hamid and 'Abd al-Majid, from the side of the family descended from Qutb al-Din's third son, Mulla Nizam al-Din, through the great eighteenth-century scholar 'Abd al-'Ali Bahr al-'Ulum, took a pro-British and anti-nationalist line. There was a history of ill-feeling between the descendants of Mulla Sa'id and Mulla Nizam al-Din going back to the time in the early nineteenth century when 'Abd al-Bari's great-grandfather, Mulla Ala al-Din, had been preferred as successor to Bahr al-'Ulum as sajjadanashin over the great man's son 'Abd al-Rab. In 1912 ill-feeling broke out again when both 'Abd al-Hamid and 'Abd al-Majid resigned as teachers from the Madrasa Nizamiyya in protest over 'Abd al-Bari's anti-government stance on pan-Islamic issues. In 1918 they were rewarded with a government grant to set up their own madrasa in opposition to Madrasa Nizamiyya. Throughout World War I and the Khilafat Movement they issued fatawas in support of the government and against the pronouncements of 'Abd al-Bari. Both were awarded medals of Shams al-'Ulama.

From the 1930s, one or two others, inspired in large part by the Progressive Writers Movement, broke with their family's sharif Muslim view of the world. Hayat Allah Ansari, for instance, founded a communist study circle, published a pro-Congress Urdu socialist weekly, *Hindustan*, from 1937 until it was closed by

[41]For this statement and the strength of 'Abd al-Bari's feelings at this time, see ibid., p. 339.

censorship in 1942. He edited the Congress *Qawmi Awaz* newspaper from 1945 to 1972, won the Sahitya Akademi Award for the best Urdu novel for his *Lahu ke Phul* (Flowers of Blood), and was President of the Anjuman-i Taraqqi-i Urdu. A staunch Nehruite, he was nominated to the Rajya Sabha. There was also Mufti Rada Ansari, who taught at the Madrasa Nizamiyya from 1936 to 1943 until his radical nationalist activities forced him to resign. He was secretary of the Lucknow branch of the Progressive Writers Association, holding meetings at Farangi Mahall. A communist, he strongly opposed the Muslim League. From 1948 to 1969 he was on the staff of *Qawmi Awaz*, leaving it to become a lecturer in Sunni theology at Aligarh Muslim University. In later life he used to refer to his communist days as 'the time when I was misguided'. There was also Nasim Ansari, son of the active Khilafatist and dedicated teacher, Mawlana Shafi, who joined the Progressive Writers Association and supported communism, though not actively, before becoming Professor of Surgery at Aligarh Muslim University. Two of his sisters took the unprecedented step for Farangi Mahallis of marrying Hindus: Wasima married Keshwant Singh and was active in communist circles in Lucknow in the 1950s and 1960s, Khadija married Professor Anrud Gupta, and at least up to the 1980s both were known to be communist sympathizers.

From their arrival in Lucknow in the late seventeenth century down to the early twentieth century, the Farangi Mahallis had been able largely to ignore the Hindu world about them. Part of the sharif world of Muslim governing traditions, they taught in madrasas and served at the courts of Muslim princes. Only two Hindus appear in their record in positions of honour, both in the early twentieth century. One was Raja Kishen Pershad who, like many of his fellow Kayasths, Khatris, and Kashmiri Brahmins, influenced by the world of Muslim courts, was able to contribute to sharif literary culture. The second was, of course, Gandhi, 'Abd al-Bari's key ally in the Congress. It is important to note, however, that throughout 'Abd al-Bari's intense engagement with the nationalist movement, in which thousands of letters and telegrams were received and sent, he had only one Hindu correspondent—Gandhi.[42] When Hindus appear in the record the Farangi Mahallis keep themselves, it is as benchmarks, for instance as better rulers than the British, or as presenting examples of behaviour Muslims should avoid as in the *Manaqib-i Razzaqiyya*, or as the mirrors in which Muslim superiority might be revealed as in the *Anwar-i Razzaqiyya*. The Hindu presence seems detached from their consciousness, as detached as that of the Farangi Mahalli 'ulama from the world of Hazratganj when they came to dine in the Kwality restaurant.

[42]From c. 1912 to 1926 'Abd al-Bari's correspondence and telegrams were carefully kept in letter books from which the range and intensity of his correspondence may readily be ascertained. Farangi Mahall papers, Lucknow and Karachi.

From the beginning of the twentieth century, it was increasingly clear that the structures of power which sustained the sharif world view were crumbling. In British India the remnants of Muslim court culture were steadily being stripped out of the state machinery; Persian had been replaced by the vernaculars and now Urdu itself, in the Persian script, was under threat from Hindi in the Nagri script. At the same time, a madrasa education was no longer a route to government service; qualifications were needed from the state system of education and for the levels of government to which the sharif aspired these had to be in English. Only by taking service at the courts of Muslim princes was it possible, for the most part, to remain insulated from the new non-sharif world.

Those who remained in British India were confronted not just by a state machine, in which Muslims would have to engage with other peoples and cultures on terms not of their own making, but also by a growing public sphere, in which they failed to engage with others at their peril. This sphere was there in the press, in the local, provincial and national arenas of politics, in the political organizations that formed to compete in these arenas, and in the new associations which formed to pursue activities ranging from film and literature to tennis and cricket. Here were opportunities to work together in public, even if they did not do so in private. A few took these opportunities, and it helped to have an income to enable them to do so. Most, however, either continued to live together separately in the new India, sustaining fragments of the once all-powerful sharif culture, or largely for financial reasons left India for Pakistan, West Asia, Britain, and North America.

MILLAT AND MAZHAB: RETHINKING IQBAL'S POLITICAL VISION

Farzana Shaikh

T he canonization of Muhammad Iqbal (1877[1]–1938) as the patron saint of Pakistan meant that much of his thinking, at least in that country, has been selectively employed to expose the intellectual bankruptcy of the idea of composite culture.

The aim, more often than not, has been to concentrate on those parts of Iqbal's thinking that best vindicate the Partition of India and justify the creation of an exclusive Indo-Muslim state. One damaging consequence of this endeavour has been to treat the early phases of Iqbal's intellectual trajectory with their broad universalist overtones as something of an embarrassment. Works of serious scholarship, often painstakingly mounted by Pakistani scholars, suggest that Iqbal's early fascination with pantheistic Sufism and with the possibilities of India's

Acknowledgements: I am deeply indebted to Professor T.N. Madan, whose sustained comments on the original version of this chapter have been invaluable in helping me develop what I hope is a more rounded and complex picture of Iqbal, the man, and his thought. I am also grateful to Mushirul Hasan and Barbara Metcalf for their searching questions, which were both fair and pertinent, despite our differences over some aspects of Iqbal's thinking. Thanks too to Seema Alavi, who gave freely of her time to help unveil the beauty of Iqbal's Urdu poetry.

[1]There remains some confusion about Iqbal's date of birth, which is variously cited as sometime between the 1873 and 1877. Iqbal himself gave his date of birth as 'the third of Dhi-Qa'd, 1297 AH (AD 1876)'; see his 'Lebenslauf', in S.A. Vahid (ed.), *Thoughts and Reflections of Iqbal* (Lahore: Shaikh Muhammad Ashraf, 1964), p. 28. However, Vahid notes that the third of Dhi-Qa'd, 1294 AH actually corresponds to 1877. See also S.A. Vahid, *Iqbal: His Art and Thought* (London: John Murray, 1959), p.3. Curiously none of these dates matches that given by Iqbal's son, Javid Iqbal, who cites 1873. See Javid Iqbal, *A Note-book of Allama Iqbal* (Lahore: Shaikh Ghulam Ali, 1961), p. vi.

cultural pluralism were essentially unrepresentative of his thinking as a whole, if not aberrations unworthy of the high Islamic idealism for which he came to be better known.[2] Much is made of Iqbal's own repudiation of both pantheistic Sufism and cultural pluralism while little attention is paid to the violence Iqbal inflicted upon his mental universe to effect this transition from his 'youthful' to his more 'mature' self.[3] Paradoxically, the need to divide up Iqbal's thinking has proved to be just as compelling among Iqbal's many admirers in India today. They look to his early poems for confirmation that Iqbal was once passionately committed to the Indian nationalist ideal, hoping thereby perhaps to offset Iqbal's later preoccupation with Muslim separatism that laid the basis for Pakistan.

The argument developed in the next few pages will seek to distance itself from both these approaches by teasing out the continuities in Iqbal's thinking over time. This it will seek to do by showing how Iqbal drew throughout on recognizably Islamic themes of universalism and exclusivism to sustain contradictory positions, and by doing so exposed some of the unresolved tensions within a broadly Islamic tradition. It will also suggest that the much-vaunted political 'break' between Iqbal's early 'nationalist' self and his later sharply defined Muslim 'separatist' stance is better understood as a transition within a single religious tradition. What this signified in the case of Iqbal was a shift away from an early preoccupation with Islam's broad humanitarian ethos, which with its emphasis on the universal truth of all religions allowed him initially to respond to the appeal of a 'composite' nationalism that transcended social and political diversities. Later, however, Iqbal's quest for Quranic truth meant that he was led increasingly in the direction of a more exclusivist vision sustained by the quintessentially Islamic notion of *tawhid* or monotheism. What this demanded was the urgent delineation of 'a fiercely restrictive identity (as) the *sine qua non* of any wider human relation or relevance'.[4]

It should be clear from this that there is no question here of endorsing the commonly held view that Iqbal 'graduated' in any sense from a 'narrow' love of country (India) to the lofty realms of Islamic universalism, or of conflating Iqbal's

---

[2]Typical of this genre are some of the contributions in Hafeez Malik (ed.), *Iqbal: Poet-Philospher of Pakistan* (New York: Columbia University Press, 1971).

[3]This is not to suggest that there are no references in the literature to Iqbal's 'mental conflict'. The scholar, S.A. Vahid, well known for his critical commentaries on Iqbal alludes to it in his *Iqbal*, pp. 9–14, as do several contributors in Malik, *Iqbal*. However, the focus has tended either to be on Iqbal's anguish over the outrage he caused among Muslims disturbed by the audacity of his poetic voice, notably in his *Shikwa* and *mathnavi*, *Asrar-i-Khudi* upon his return from Europe in 1908, or the loneliness he suffered in a life devoid of any real emotional attachment. What is missing is any sustained discussion of the intellectual travails endured by Iqbal as he sought to loosen the grip of his Indian heritage by renouncing the universalist ethics of the Quran which had made possible its appreciation in favour of a more exclusivist concern with the laws of Islam.

[4]Kenneth Cragg, *The Pen and the Faith: Eight Modern Muslim Writers and the Qur'an* (London: George Allen and Unwin, 1985), p. 28.

Muslim identity in a general sense with his espousal of 'Islamist' doctrines.[5] What is being emphasized rather is a *continuum*, defined by Iqbal's ceaseless preoccupation with Islam, first as a universal faith and then as a specific political ideology. This is what lent coherence to his thinking and what helps explain its multiple contradictions. Ultimately what was distinctive about Iqbal's approach to the idea of 'living together separately' was precisely the manner in which he drew on his religious tradition to shape and reshape his own troubled passage from being 'Muslim' to becoming 'Islamic'. His early preoccupation with questions of religious tolerance, freedom, and justice, which translated easily into the language of composite Indian nationalism, clearly echoed moral values in the Quran that encourage participation in the wider human condition. Later, his concern with what he called 'the specific inwardness' of the Muslim community,[6] was no less inspired by Quranic injunctions that urge a bold recourse to the Law and an acknowledgement of the 'power equation within (the Prophet) Muhammad's own mission'.[7] As a recent and highly perceptive critic reminds us: 'Although his interests range widely, Iqbal essentially *belongs to, and speaks from within, the Islamic tradition* employing for his purposes its historical, religious, philosophical and literary resources.'[8]

I

It may be instructive at this point to begin by dwelling briefly upon how Iqbal might have framed his response to Humayun Kabir's grand exposition on composite culture, which sets the tone for this volume. Kabir's own vivid description is worth quoting:

From immemorial times (India) has tried to achieve a unity for the heterogeneous elements that make up the totality of her life.... She has not only survived but also maintained and developed a continuous culture. Different races have met and fought and fraternised on her soil. She has absorbed all of them into her blood .... She has lived through recurrent centuries of war and pestilence. She has triumphed over natural calamities and human misrule.... It is a story of unity and synthesis.[9]

[5] The pitfalls involved in engaging in the latter have recently been highlighted again by Mushirul Hasan, in Mushirul Hasan (ed.), *Islam, Communities and the Nation: Muslim Identities in South Asia and Beyond* (Delhi: Manohar, 1998), pp. 7–24. See also Akeel Bilgrami, 'What is a Muslim? Fundamental commitment and cultural identity', *Economic and Political Weekly* (May 1992), pp. 16–33.

[6] Muhammad Iqbal, *The Reconstruction of Religious Thought in Islam* (Lahore: Sang-i-Meel Publications, 1996), p. 146.

[7] Cragg, *The Pen and the Faith*, p. 27.

[8] Mustansir Mir (ed. and trans.), *Tulip in the Desert: A Selection of the Poetry of Muhammad Iqbal* (London: Hurst, 2000), pp. 4–5. The emphasis is mine.

[9] Humayun Kabir, *The Indian Heritage* (Bombay, Asia Publishing House, 1955), p. 33.

Two elements in this otherwise elegant presentation would have disturbed Iqbal: Kabir's emphasis on assimilation and the importance he attached to the material basis of national unity. Both ran directly counter to Iqbal's main operating assumptions. The first emphasized that the Muslim religious community (*millat*) was not open to assimilation—it assimilates; the second, that the basis of national unity lay not in the material foundations of society but in a common religious creed (*mazhab*).

Those familiar with the corpus especially of Iqbal's early poetical works are likely to challenge the view that these assumptions were representative of Iqbal's thinking on composite culture over time. They will emphasize that as a young man, at least until his early 30s, Iqbal showed every sign of being a passionate Indian nationalist dedicated to cultural pluralism. They will point to the exultant refrains of the *Tarana-i-hind*:

> *sare jahan se achchha hindustan hamara*
> *hum bulbulein hain is ki, ye gulistan hamara*
>
> The best land in the world is our India
> we are its nightingales; this is our garden.[10]

and claim as some have that it is the nearest 'to a truly non-communal national anthem of India'[11] with no hint in defence of either millat or mazhab as narrowly understood categories. Others will suggest that Iqbal's poem, '*Naya shivala*' (A new Shiva Temple) should be read as further incontrovertible proof of his early commitment to the desirability of composite culture. They could even cite Iqbal's blanket condemnation of priests and preachers—both Hindu and Muslim—and construe this, and unreasonably, as evidence of his distaste for religious division and, by implication, support for composite nationalism.

> *Sach keh doon aye Brahmin. Agar tu bura na mane*
> *Tere sanam kadon ke buth ho gaye purane....*
> *Tang akey meine akhir dair-o-haram chorra....*
> *Aa ghairiyet ke parde ek bar phi utha dein,*
> *Bichhron ko phir mila dein, naqsh-i-dui mita dein*
>
> Let me tell you truth, Brahmin, if you will not be offended,
> The idols of your temple have become old....
> Finally I became tired: I abandoned temple and mosque....
> Come, let us once again raise the curtain of estrangement;
> Let us once more unite the estranged: let us erase every trace of duality.[12]

---

[10]Muhammad Iqbal, '*Milli tarana*', in D.J., Matthews (trans.), *Iqbal, A Selection of the Urdu Verse* (London: School of Oriental and African Studies, 1993), pp. 16–17.

[11]Iqbal Singh, *The Ardent Pilgrim: An Introduction to the Life and Work of Mohammad Iqbal* (London: Longmans, Green, 1951), p. 24.

[12]Muhammad Iqbal, '*Naya shivala*', in Matthews, *Iqbal*, pp. 18–19.

Yet, although the broad thrust of these observations is generally well grounded (and well taken), it is debatable whether the differences between Iqbal, the young poet and Iqbal the man who emerged as the acknowledged ideologue of Indo-Muslim separatism can usefully be cast and understood in terms of the categories of nationalist discourse. Rather it would seem that a closer reading of Iqbal suggests that even in his so-called nationalist phase Iqbal's thinking did not so much *converge* with mainstream Indian nationalism as *run parallel* to it. In this he was quite unlike Jinnah, for example, who, it is commonly maintained, began as an Indian nationalist and ended up a Muslim nationalist. Iqbal, it seems to me, began as a 'Muslim' and ended up an 'Islamist', engaged primarily in the restoration of Quranic law as the basis of a socio-political order in human society.

Nevertheless, there is no doubt that much of Iqbal's early work appears to blend easily with the emerging discourse of composite Indian nationalism. However, what needs also to be more clearly recognized is that much of this work was inspired and nourished by a broad universalist tradition well rooted in traditional Islamic discourse. It was this that allowed Iqbal to portray early on as in his poem, 'Nala-i-yatim' (Cry of the Orphan),[13] the plight of his own religious community—its condition of political bondage and its spiritual and economic poverty—as universally symptomatic (in this case) of the fate of India as a whole. Another poem 'Taswir-i-dard' (Portrait of Anguish), written in 1904, also invokes the great universal themes of human freedom and equality. Here Iqbal clearly frames his reflections on the state of Hindustan under colonial rule within the larger question of the relationship between Love and Liberty:

> *Chaman main aa kya rehna jo ho be aabru rahna*
> *Jo samjhe tu to azadi hai posheeda muhabbat mein*
> *Ghulami hai aseer i imtiaz ma o tu rahna*

> What is the good of living in the garden if it is a life of disgrace?
> In Love is hidden Liberty, if only you could see
> Bondage is discrimination between you and me.[14]

'Naya shivala' (New Temple), written soon afterwards and frequently held up as proof of Iqbal's 'nationalist' credentials is equally anchored in these universalist preoccupations. Iqbal's aim here is to salvage the universal truth of all religions— a characteristically Islamic precept—and to do so by ridding them of the debilitating forces of doctrine, here represented by the Brahmin and the *mullah*. Indeed it is tempting to argue that Iqbal's 'Naya shivala', despite its Hinduized vocabulary,[15]

---

[13]On the public reaction to the poem, which was first read at the annual session of the Anjuman Himayat-i-Islam in 1900, see Hafeez Malik and Lynda P. Malik, 'Life of the Poet-Philosopher', in Malik, *Iqbal*, p. 16.

[14]Mohammad Iqbal's 'Taswir i Dard', in *Bang-i-Dara* in *Kulliyat-i-Iqbal* (Rampur, Parveen Book Depot, 1970), p. 67.

[15]Iqbal's use of Hindi vocabulary (in bold) in the composition of 'Naya shivala' is believed by some critics to demonstrate his lack of prejudice:

was intended not so much to combine the elements of Hinduism and Islam in a new faith but to *preserve* the essential truths distinctive to each religious tradition. It would seem then that, arguably, Iqbal's new temple was categorically not *of* India but merely *in* India.[16]

However, the point worth reiterating in this regard is that Iqbal was working with idioms derived essentially from within his own Islamic tradition—idioms that were geared to retrieving the universalist essence of his faith rather than with laying the foundations of an 'Indian nation'. His poem 'Zuhd o Rindi' (Piety and Profligacy) published in 1903 is a good example. It aims directly to recast the meaning of Muslim piety by freeing it of the web of doctrine and the weight of 'the ordinances of Islam'.[17] Here the ideal Muslim is one who refuses to 'regard the Hindus as infidels' and is prepared to reach out to dissenters by even countenancing 'a little Shi'ism'.[18] The fact such notions of Muslim piety and religious tolerance sat comfortably with the prevailing discourse of composite Indian nationalism ought not to blind us to Iqbal's central preoccupation at the time—the development of a humane society implicitly grounded in the universalist tenets of the Quran.

It was precisely the universalist thrust of Iqbal's early preoccupation with the meaning of his faith that also rendered him sensitive to the symbolism of other religious and philosophical traditions including, not surprisingly, Hinduism. Two of his poems from this period, 'Ram' and 'Aftaab (tarjumah i gayatri)', stand out in this respect. The first is an extraordinary homage to the Hindu god, Ram, which helps Iqbal articulate his belief in the single Truth of all religious traditions when stripped of their distorting accretions.

Labrez hai sharab e haqiqat sey jam i Hind
Sab falsafeh hain khatthe maghrib key Ram i Hind...
Hai Ram key wujud pey Hindustan ko naz
Ahl i nazar samajhtey hain us ko Imam e Hind

Aa ek nya shivala is **des** main bana dein...
Har subah uth kai gayen **mantar** wo meethe meethe
Saray **pujarion** ko mai **preet** ki mila dein
Shakti bhi **shanti** bhi bhagatoon ke geet me hai
Dharti ke **basiyon** ki **mukti preet** mai hai

Come let us build a new altar to Shiva in the land...
Every morning, let us get up and sing those sweet, sweet chants;
Let us give all those worshippers the wine of love to drink.
In the song of the devotees there is both power and peace
Salvation for the inhabitants of the earth is in love.
Muhammad Iqbal, 'Naya shivala', in Matthews, *Iqbal*, p. 19.

[16]Riffat Hasan, 'The development of political philosophy', in Malik, *Iqbal*, p. 141.
[17]Muhammad Iqbal, 'Zuhd o Rindi' (Piety and Profligacy), in Matthews, *Iqbal*, p. 11.
[18]Ibid.

Brimmed is India's flask with the wine of Truth,
For Western philosophers, the charm of Ram, is a sure sign....
For India, the existence of Ram is of great pride
India's leader he is reckoned, manly and divine.[19]

The second is inspired by the Hindu prayer, the gayatri mantra (the prayer of Gayatri, the goddess and consort of Brahma and mother of the Vedas). Here Iqbal invokes the power of the Sun (Aftaab), the presiding deity to whom the ancient prayer is dedicated, to illuminate the Self and reveal the path to wisdom. Rarely cited in Pakistani commentaries on Iqbal, both poems are clearly a testimony of Iqbal's pride in acknowledging the influence of his Vedic roots to proclaim his belief in the unity of the Divine spirit and, by extension, the unity of mankind.[20]

Iqbal's indebtedness to his Vedic heritage, which he would later recast as the 'Aryan stamp' on the Semitic essence of his faith,[21] has not received anything like the attention it deserves. Iqbal's family background could provide a clue to his appreciation of Vedic culture; but by the same token it could also account for Iqbal's own ambivalence towards that culture in his later, more pronounced, 'Islamist' phase. What is less often acknowledged, especially in Pakistani studies, is Iqbal's possibly quite recent Hindu ancestry, which is generally glossed over in favour of portraying a household suffused with Muslim piety.[22] S.A. Vahid is an exception, though even he while noting that Iqbal's family were descended from Kashmiri Brahmins takes care to stress that it 'accepted Islam about three hundred years before (Iqbal's birth)' in Sialkot, now part of Pakistani Punjab).[23] This account has been disputed by fresh claims that Iqbal's grandfather Shaikh Rafiq changed his name from Sahaj Ram Sapru after converting to Islam just before settling in Sialkot around 1857.[24] As for Iqbal himself, it is worth noting that he explicitly referred to his Brahmin extraction on at least one occasion, in a Persian verse:

Look at me, for in Hind thou wilt not see again,
A man of Brahmin extraction versed in the mystic knowledge of Rum and Tabriz.[25]

[19]Cited in S.G. Abbas, Dr Muhammad Iqbal: The Humanist (Lahore: Iqbal Academy, 1997), p. 31.

[20]Muhammad Iqbal, Aftaab (tarjumah i gayatri), Bang-i-Dara (Lahore: Shaikh Mubarak Ali, 1930), pp. 30–1.

[21]Muhammad Iqbal, The Development of Metaphysics in Persia: A Contribution to the History of Muslim Philosophy (London: Luzac, 1908), p. 99.

[22]Malik, Iqbal, pp. 4–5

[23]Vahid, Iqbal, p. 3.

[24]Ram Nath Kak, Autumn Leaves: Kashmiri Reminiscences (Delhi: Vitasta, 1995). See also the electronic version in http://www.koausa.org/Books/AutumnLeaves/part4html [30 October 2003].

[25]Cited in Vahid, Iqbal, p. 3. Iqbal's preference for expressing himself in Persian, which became a pronounced feature of his later work, is often explained as a consequence of his growing interest in more recognizably 'Islamic' themes. But Iqbal's Kashmiri Brahmin roots may also have endeared him to Persian. According to Francis Robinson, Kashmiri Brahmins were among a

Whatever the claims for and against Iqbal's Brahmin ancestry, there can be no question that Iqbal was deeply familiar with, if not fascinated by, the philosophical doctrines of the Hindu Vedanta. This surfaced clearly in his doctoral dissertation, *The Development of Metaphysics in Persia*, submitted to the University of Munich in 1907 and published in 1908.[26] While the work has generally been singled out as evidence of Iqbal's intellectual engagement with Persian Sufism and especially its governing doctrine of *wahdat al wujud* (unity of being), what is just as revealing is Iqbal's readiness to acknowledge the superiority of Vedantic thought as vital both to the experience of fundamental religious truth as well as to its systematic exposition. Indeed, for all his admiration of Persian Sufism at this stage, it was the Vedanta that offered Iqbal a glimpse of what he was to seek for the rest of his life—a spiritually driven rationality that was at odds with both pantheistic Sufism and Western intellectualism.

Astonishingly, Iqbal was drawn to Brahminical thought precisely for its rejection of the dualism of spirit and matter, which he was later to single out also as the hallmark of an Islamic world view. 'The subtle Brahmin', he wrote,

sees the inner unity of things; so does the Persian. But while the former endeavours to discover it in all aspects of human experience, and illustrates its hidden presence in the concrete in various ways, the latter appears to be satisfied with a bare universality, and does not attempt to verify the richness of his inner content.[27]

But Iqbal also envied and understood the Brahminical talent for systematic thinking in the service of a higher end. 'The Hindu,' he claimed,

while admitting like the Persian, the necessity of a higher source of knowledge, yet calmly moves from experience to experience, mercilessly dissecting them, and forcing them to yield their underlying universality. In fact the Persian is only half conscious of Metaphysics as a *system* of thought; his Brahmin brother on the other hand, is fully alive to the need of presenting his theory in the form of a thoroughly reasoned out system.... In the one case we have only partially worked out systems of thought; in the other case the awful sublimity of the searching Vedanta.[28]

Ultimately, however, the extreme intellectualism of the Indian Vedantist was ill-suited to the poet in Iqbal. He found the Indian Vedanta a 'cold system of thought'[29] that could not respond to the human need for Love. This is what he believed Persian Sufism with its synthetic blend of 'Semitic and Aryan formulas'

---

handful of small communities who still cherished the use of Persian long after its decline elsewhere in the subcontinent by end of the nineteenth century. See Francis Robinson, *The 'Ulama of Farangi Mahal and Islamic Culture in South Asia* (London: Hurst, 2001), p. 32.

[26]Iqbal, *The Development of Metaphysics in Persia*.

[27]Ibid., p. viii.

[28]Ibid.

[29]Ibid. pp. 105–6

was better able to deliver, predicated as it was upon a more 'complete view of human nature'.[30] Nevertheless Iqbal recognized that the links between Persian Sufism and Hindu thought would remain close, bound as they were by their common regard for pantheism.[31] Indeed he believed that the 'wildly pantheistic' bias of some Sufi schools, best represented by the Muslim mystic Hussain Ibn Mansur (better known as Hallaj), stemmed as much from the influence of Neo-Platonic ideas of the immanent nature of Divine Reality as from 'the true spirit of the Indian Vedantist (who) cried out "I am God"—Aham Brahma asmi'.[32]

II

Iqbal's eclecticism and the universalist bent of his poetry and philosophy were subjected to intense pressure during his residence as a young student in Europe from 1905–8. Two aspects of European life are now generally recognized to have exercised a profound influence on him. The first was the force of national rivalries, or what Iqbal deplored as the 'race idea', on the human mind; the second was the ruthless energy of the West, which aroused in him feelings (in roughly equal measure) of admiration and revulsion.

That Iqbal raised urgent questions about the merits of nationalism during his European sojourn there is no doubt. That he did so because of his belief in the inherent incompatibility of nationalism with Islamic values is also beyond question. But what is also significant about Iqbal's encounter with European nationalism is that it helped crystallize for him the difference between patriotic love (*vataniyat*)

[30]Ibid. p. 106. For Iqbal, Sufism's greatest exponent was the twelfth-century mystic, Shaikh Shahabal Din Suhrawardi, also known as Shaikh al Ishraq Maqtul, whose work Iqbal summarized as 'uniting speculation and emotion in perfect harmony'. Ibid., p. 150.

[31]Iqbal spells this out explicitly by drawing on his detailed knowledge of Vedantic metaphysiics and suggesting that it had a vital bearing on the thinking of the eighth-century Sufi mystic, Al-Jili, whose notion of Divinity came close to 'the idea of the phenomenal Brahma of the Vedanta'. Ibid., p. 163.

[32]Ibid., p. 115. The noted Iqbal scholar, Anne-Marie Schimmel, has maintained that Iqbal's generally dismissive attitude to Hallaj continued until at least 1927. She cites in evidence verses from Iqbal's *Zabur-i-Ajam* (Persian Psalms), published in June of that year, in which Iqbal warns against the monist philosophies of Hallaj and Shankara, the celebrated exponent of the Vedanta.

> Do not speak of Shankara and Mansur!
> Search for God always in the way of the Ego!
> Be lost in thyself in order to realize the Ego!
> Say 'Ana'l Haqq', and become the Siddiq of Ego!

By 1928, however, Schimmel argues, Iqbal's thinking on Hallaj had undergone a profound change owing partly to his familiarity with the work of the eminent French scholar, Louis Massignon, whose studies on Hallaj prompted Iqbal to revise his opinions and conclude that 'the martyr saint could not have meant to deny the transcendence of God'. See Iqbal, *The Reconstruction of Religious Thought*, p. 88. See also Anne-Marie Schimmel, 'Mystic impact of Hallaj', in Malik, *Iqbal*, pp. 310–24

and the kind of total allegiance demanded by nationalism (*qaumiyat*). Like many Indians of his generation, Iqbal could be forgiven for mistaking the one for the other. This confusion was not, however, to last long; Iqbal's stay in Europe brought home to him more starkly than ever before the realization that nationalism ultimately entailed translating the love of country into undivided political allegiance. Iqbal's understanding of its full implications for Muslims in India and elsewhere have been well rehearsed in the scholarly literature. It points unanimously to his rejection of territorial Western nationalism as diametrically opposed to Islam's supra-territorial impulse, and to his unease with the idea of the 'nation' superseding the global fraternity of the Islamic millat as the main focus of a Muslim's allegiance.

It was while he was in Europe that Iqbal was forced to express more explicitly what had been latent in his thinking. This, it is generally assumed, involved a clear demonstration of his belief in the inherent superiority of Islamic universalism over and above the kind of territorial nationalism then sweeping Europe and increasingly favoured by the purveyors of 'composite nationalism' in India. However, this assumption has proved to be deeply problematic. For, even while Iqbal gave eloquent voice to Islam's concern for mankind as a whole as a far more desirable alternative to the consolidation of communities 'determined by birth, locality or naturalisation',[33] he stimulated what has rightly been described as 'the growth of a very virulent species of nationalism among his community'— a nationalism which demanded, paradoxically, 'a territorial focus as the condition for its appeasement'.[34] Unless this glaring contradiction is to be dismissed merely as 'an aberration of vision'[35] on Iqbal's part or a case simply of Iqbal not always being true to the spirit of his message[36] (which he is said to have intimated on at least one occasion),[37] we need to search harder for an explanation.

The way forward may lie in setting aside some standard assumptions about Iqbal's intellectual trajectory. Two arguments are worth pursuing in this regard. First, that by the time Iqbal was engaged in employing the idea of the universal Islamic community as a weapon against nationalism, his understanding of Islamic universalism had already undergone a subtle but profound transformation. Where once his celebration of humanity bore a resonance for both Muslims and for 'people of any religion or no religion at all',[38] it was now cast in terms primarily of his own quest for Quranic truth. Second, that the demands of this search for

---

[33]Muhammad Iqbal, 'Islam as an ethical and political ideal', in Vahid, *Thoughts and Reflections*, p. 50.

[34] Singh, *The Ardent Pilgrim*, p. 234

[35] Ibid.

[36] Ralph Russell, 'Iqbal and his message', in Ralph Russell, *The Pursuit of Urdu Literature: A Select History* (London: Zed Books, 1992) p. 185.

[37]'Iqbal himself does not know what Iqbal is, I swear to you by God, I am not joking', 'Zuhd-i-Rindi', *Bang-i-Dara* in *Kulliyat-i-Iqbal* (Rampur, Parveen Book Depot, 1970), p. 56.

[38]Russell, 'Iqbal and his message', p. 181.

Quranic truth drove Iqbal to subject his universalist vision to an increasingly restricted view of 'a society (millat) exclusive in the sense of having a well-defined creed (mazhab) and a well-defined outline'.[39] By 1910 the outlines of this society were already taking shape. 'In order to maintain the health and vigour of such a (Muslim) community,' he wrote,

the development of all dissenting forces in it must be carefully watched, and a rapid influx of foreign elements must be checked or permitted to enter the social fibre very slowly, so that it may not bring on a collapse, by making too great a demand on the assimilative power of the social organism.[40]

Iqbal now stood on the brink of a major undertaking that involved a bold recourse to the law, the object of which he would signify in 1930, was the *recreation* of a community where

even the immutability of socially harmless rules relating to eating and drinking, purity and impurity, has a life-value of its own inasmuch as it tends to give such a society a specific inwardness, and further secures that external and internal uniformity which counteracts the forces of heterogeneity always latent in a society of a composite character.[41]

The challenge here was to restore the Quranic purity of the Muslim community even at the expense, temporarily, of narrowing the Islamic vision of a spiritual fraternity.

It is only by appreciating the urgency of Iqbal's need to reclaim Quranic truth as he understood it, rather than by any reference to Iqbal's self-conscious discourses on Islamic universalism after 1908, that it becomes possible to understand why the idea of cultural 'compositeness' that lay at the heart of the Kabir's vision should have held such little appeal for him. There is of course no question that Iqbal was profoundly sensitive to the *land* of India, especially in the period before 1908. His depictions of India's lakes and mountains, its tulips and its roses, its nightingales and its cuckoos are often exquisite. Indeed some critics have not hesitated to draw comparisons between Iqbal and the great English Romantic poet, William Wordsworth, whose work nurtured Iqbal's pantheism and helped deepen his mystic appreciation of nature.[42] Since then, generations of Indian nationalists have also been inspired by the majesty of Iqbal's natural descriptions of India and drawn sustenance from his poems such as 'Himala', 'On the banks of the Ravi', and 'Glow-worm'. Nevertheless it is the case that what these poems ultimately suggest is an idea of vataniyat or patriotism rather than

[39]Letter to Dr Nicholson, 24 January 1921, in Vahid, *Thoughts and Reflections*, p. 98.

[40]Muhammad Iqbal, 'The Muslim community', in Vahid, *Thoughts and Reflections*, p. 381.

[41]Iqbal, *The Reconstruction of Religious Thought*, p. 146

[42]S.A. Vahid, 'Nature in Iqbal's poetry', in S.A. Vahid, *Studies in Iqbal* (Lahore: Shaikh Muhammad Ashraf, 1967), pp. 172–97.

any real understanding of the *historicity* of the Indian nation. I would argue that it was precisely the ahistoricity of Iqbal's thinking that significantly weakened his appreciation of India's composite culture.[43]

This is not to say that Iqbal had *no* sense of history; indeed it can be argued that the glories of the Muslim past are a constant theme in Iqbal's poetical and philosophical works, especially in the period after 1909. However, there is little in the corpus of Iqbal's work to convey a sense of history, whether Islamic or Indian, as in any way an interactive or cumulative, let alone a 'syncretic', process. Even Iqbal's early work in his so-called 'nationalist' phase appears to be quite devoid of the kind of historicity associated with the Nehruvian vision in which 'India appeared as a space of ceaseless cultural mixing, its history a celebration of the soiling effects of miscegenation and accretion'.[44] Instead what we find in the young 'nationalist' Iqbal are passionate references to the physical attributes of his country, Hind, which, he declared, its Muslims loved as dearly as any of its other communities. But what they cherished, Iqbal's poetry makes clear, were Hind's Himalayas, its rivers, and its 'gardens of delights'. There is no reference here to any sense of attachment to a common history or culture—no celebration of common myths, nor of shared melodies, nor even of common heroes. What Iqbal evokes for us rather is a sense of place and of locality—the necessary ingredients one might say, precisely, of vataniyat or patriotism—but not the attachment, let alone the political allegiance, to a bounded territory with an 'imagined' historical past that is presupposed by modern nationalism.

Iqbal, as we have observed earlier, was inclined like most of his generation to confuse patriotism with nationalism. This confusion was expressed most famously in his poem, 'Vataniyat', written shortly after his return from Europe, and

---

[43]T.N. Madan suggests that this rejection of historicity stems from the difficulty of reconciling Islamic thought with 'secular time'. He cites as evidence the leading contemporary Muslim scholar, Seyyed Hossein Nasr (*Islamic Life and Thought*, [New York: State University of Albany Press, 1981], p. 7) for whom history as the domain of ideas and institutions that are humanly derived negates the 'unitary perspective of Islam' according to which 'all aspects of life, all degrees of cosmic manifestation are governed by a single principle and are unified by a common centre .... In essence, everything, is sacred and nothing profane'. See also T.N. Madan, *Modern Myths, Locked Minds: Secularism and Fundamentalism in India* (New Delhi: Oxford University Press, 2003), pp. 152–3. There is also here fascinating comparison to be made with Iqbal's understanding of 'secular time'. 'In Islam', he wrote, 'the spiritual and the temporal are not two distinct domains, and the nature of an act, however secular in its import, is determined by the attitude of mind with which the agent does it. It is the invisible mental background of the act which ultimately determines its character. An act is temporal or profane if it is done in the spirit of detachment from the infinite complexity of life behind it; it is spiritual if it is inspired by that complexity.... The Ultimate Reality, according to the Quran is spiritual .... All that is secular is, therefore, sacred in the roots of its being .... There is no such thing as a profane world'. Muhammad Iqbal, 'The principle of movement in the structure of Islam', in Iqbal, *The Reconstruction of Religious Thought*, pp. 134–5.

[44]Sunil Khilnani, *The Idea of India* (New Delhi: Penguin Books, 1998), p. 169.

published in the final section of his first collection of poetry, *Bang-i-Dara*.[45] Here what he has in mind is clearly the phenomenon of nationalism with its divisive consequences and, more disturbingly, its claim to rival religion as the focus of men's allegiance.[46] Indeed, Iqbal had no hesitation in concluding that the 'garment' of nationalism would be the 'shroud' of religion.[47] Nevertheless Iqbal was gradually to become more aware of the vital distinction between qaumiyat (nationalism) and vataniyat (patriotism or love of country). In his address to the All India Muslim Conference in Lahore in 1932, he declared:

I am opposed to (it) nationalism because I see in it the germs of atheistic materialism which I look upon as the greatest danger to modern humanity. Patriotism is a perfectly natural virtue and has a place in the moral life of man. Yet that which really matters is a man's faith, his culture, his historical tradition. These are the things which in my eyes are worth living for and dying for, and not the piece of earth with which the spirit of man happens to be temporarily associated.[48]

In a rejoinder to Jawaharlal Nehru on the Ahmedi question in 1936, he made this clear. His observation is worth quoting in full:

Nationalism in the sense of love of one's country and even readiness to die for its honour is a part of the Muslim's faith: it comes into conflict with Islam only when it begins to play the role of a political concept and claims to be the principle of human solidarity demanding that Islam should recede to the background of a mere private opinion and cease to be a living factor in the national life.[49]

I would like also to suggest here that the absence of any real feeling of attachment to a bounded territory in Iqbal's early work is perfectly consistent with his ambivalence towards what he was later to refer to as 'earth-rootedness'— that is the engagement with a particular territory or piece of earth. If so, Iqbal would not have been unusual among Muslims, for whom the freedom from primordial and native ties has always been deeply symbolic of the Prophet Muhammad's renunciation of his links with his birthplace in Mecca and of his migration to Medina, there to mark the moment of Islam's emergence as a socio-political ideal. At its heart, Iqbal reminded his audience in 1930, lay a conception

---

[45]Muhammad Iqbal, 'Vataniyat' (Bang-i-Dara), in *Kulliyat-i-Iqbal*, in Urdu (Aligarh: Educational Book House, 1999), p. 160.

[46]'*In taaza khudaon mein baraa sab sey vatan hai*' (The biggest of these new gods is the nation). Ibid.

[47]'*Jo perhan us ka hai wo mazhab ka kufan hai*' (That which is its [the nation's] garment is religion's shroud). Ibid.

[48]Iqbal's presidential address delivered at the annual session of the All India Muslim Conference at Lahore on 21 March 1932, in Vahid, *Thoughts and Reflections*, p. 197.

[49]'Reply to Questions raised by Pandit Jawahar Lal Nehru', in Vahid, *Thoughts and Reflections*, p. 289.

of 'not as an earth-rooted creature, defined by this or that portion of the earth, but as a spiritual being understood in terms of social mechanism, and possessing rights and duties as a living factor in that mechanism'.[50] This also explains why the Nehruvian, and possibly the Kabirian, idea of a common history grounded in the 'soil of India', as it were, would exercise so negligible an effect on Iqbal.

The attractions of this kind of freedom from local attachment would remain a characteristic feature of Iqbal's thinking. It was, not surprisingly, in his poetry that Iqbal was most fully to develop this theme. Several critics have remarked upon the symbolic importance of the eagle or hawk motif in Iqbal's poetry as a means of gaining access to some of Iqbal's ideas on life and society, and especially his idea of freedom.[51] They suggest that Iqbal was drawn to the eagle and the hawk precisely because of their capacity to soar above any earthly station.[52] A typical example is his poem 'The hawk' (sometimes translated as 'The eagle') in *Bal-i-Jibril* (Gabriel's Wing), published in 1936 in which Iqbal sings in praise of the hawk's freedom-loving nature.

> Farewell to this land of the earthbound, whose craving
> It needs only water and food to appease!
> Joy to my soul is the stillness of deserts—
> My nature since time first began has scorned ease
> No languishing love notes, no zephyr of springtime
> For me, no fair flower-reaper: I must depart
> From the nightingale's haunts, from these dwellers in gardens
> Whose charms come too near to seducing my heart....
> Through the kingdom of birds and Ascetic I roam:
> The hawk builds no nest, for the hawk needs no home.[53]

There were of course other aspects of the life of the eagle and the hawk that were increasingly to fascinate Iqbal and explain the shift away from his earlier passion for the sublime existence of those 'songsters of the glade' (*Payam-i-mashriq*)[54]—the nightingale and lark. The eagle and hawk were both deeply suggestive of Iqbal's emerging philosophy of vitalism, the purpose of which was unquestionably to fortify the Muslim. Here there was no place for images of

---

[50]Iqbal's presidential address delivered at the Annual Session of the All India Muslim League at Allahabad on 29 December 1930, in Vahid, *Thoughts and Reflections*, p. 173.

[51]Mir, *Tulip in the Desert*, pp. 92–9; Vahid, *Studies*, p. 18. It is important to bear in mind, as Mir reminds us, that Iqbal's eagle was essentially a construct, which cared little for the kind of 'ornithological accuracy' that might distinguish an eagle from a hawk or a falcon. Mir, *Tulip in the Desert*, p. 92.

[52]Mir, *Tulip in the Desert*, p. 92.

[53]'The Hawk', in V.G. Kiernan (trans), *Poems from Iqbal* (London: John Murray, 1955), p. 59.

[54]Translations of 'Payam' from A.J. Arberry, *Tulip of Sinai* (London: The Royal India Society, 1947), p. 45.

gentle nightingales whose lives were framed by 'red roses (and) summer air', [55] for, though pleasurable, theirs was an enervating existence. A new ideal would replace it. This was to be embodied in the life of the eagle, which shuns the garden in favour of the austere but health-giving environment of the desert.

> We do not make nests in a garden or a field—
> We have our own paradise in mountains and deserts.
> We regard picking up grain from the ground as an error,
> For God has given us the vastness of the skies.
> If a bird of noble stock scrapes his feet on the ground,
> He becomes more despicable than a house bird. [56]

For some seasoned critics of Iqbal's poetry, the subtext is clear: 'Muslims must stop living indolent lives and develop the power to fly like the mountain eagle.' [57] For others, too, Iqbal's lyric poetry from this point on shows all the signs of a 'robust vitality and manliness which is singularly lacking in Oriental lyric poetry. He now sees in the eagle and the hawk a beauty which is more inspiring than the beauty of the nightingale and the lark'. [58] Iqbal himself expressed this radical shift in a powerful prayer in his *Zabur-i 'Ajam* (Persian psalms):

> No desire my spirit moves
> Save the prayer: An eagle spirit,
> Lord, bestow upon thy doves! [59]

Francis Robinson, who correctly observes the gradual hold of 'Arabian Islam' as a desirable ideal in Iqbal's thinking, has spelt out the political implications of this message. [60] It entailed waging war on what Iqbal vividly described as 'all the solvents of Ajam (which) had finally divested (Arabian Islam) of its original character'. [61] In doing so, Robinson suggests, Iqbal 'spoke for those ashraf who had already turned for their religious inspiration towards Arabia' and who, in grappling with the fearful prospect of the modern national state, recalled their past with its memories of 'power and its management'. [62]

---

[55]Ibid., p. 44.

[56]Muhammad Iqbal, 'The falcon's advice to its youngster', in Mir, *Tulip in the Desert*, p. 97.

[57]Mir, *Tulip in the Desert*, p. 92.

[58]Vahid, *Studies*, p. 18.

[59]A.J. Arberry, *Persian Psalms*, pts I and II (English verse translation) (Lahore: Shaikh Muhammad Ashraf, 1948), p. 57.

[60]Robinson, *The Ulama of Farangi Mahal*, p. 40.

[61]Muhammad Iqbal, 'Stray thoughts (II): Islam and Mysticism', in Vahid, *Thoughts and Reflections*, p. 82. In Iqbal's poetry Ajam signified Persia but also referred more widely to the non-Arab world.

[62]Robinson, *The Ulama of Farangi Mahal*, p. 40.

III

It is perhaps not so surprising then that when Iqbal finally did engage with 'history', soon after his return to India from Europe in 1908, it was not India's 'national' history that held his attention but the 'universal' history of Islam, which like the Muslim millat transcended the narrative of contingent, man-made boundaries. Iqbal's 'Milli tarana' (Hymn to the millat) written around this time with its exalted rhythms:

> *Cheen-o-Arab hamara, Hindustan hamara*
> *Muslim hain hum, watan hai sara jahan hamara*

> China and Arabia are ours, Hindustan is ours
> We are Muslims, the whole world is our homeland

has been read as much as a paean to the 'universal' Muslim community as an appeal to Muslims to reclaim their pivotal position in world history.[63] This sentiment is captured repeatedly in poems such as 'Sicily' and Iqbal's even more moving tribute to the mosque at 'Cardoba'. But Iqbal was now also driven to invoke the power that once lay with Muslims to regain the world. In grand, metaphorical language, in an originally untitled *ghazal*, later cast as 'Beyond the stars', the poet consoles an eagle, who has lost his nest, to rise above the terrestrial world and seek out other realms.

> Do not be content with the world of colour and smell,
> Other gardens there are other nests, too.
> What is the worry if one nest is lost?
> There are other places to sigh and cry for!
> You are an eagle, flight is your vocation:[64]

One could of course argue that Iqbal's fascination with the universalist claims of the Muslim millat, especially after his return from Europe in 1908, naturally predisposed him to adopt an ahistorical stance more concerned with the broad sweeps of Islamic civilization than with territorially constricted history of India and its Muslims. I would suggest though that there was another process at work here, which was to render Iqbal's thinking increasingly resistant to the historical bent of the emerging discourse of composite Indian nationalism. This was his growing hostility to Persian Sufism, which brought him, albeit indirectly, into conflict with the votaries of 'cultural India'. Iqbal's disillusionment with Persian Sufism appears to have taken hold sometime during his European sojourn, when buffeted by the intellectual currents of late German romanticism then sweeping the continent he suffered something of an intellectual and personal crisis. Its

---

[63]Russell, *The Pursuit of Urdu Literature*, p. 180.
[64]Muhammad Iqbal, 'Beyond the stars', in Mir, *Tulip in the Desert*, p. 96.

most lasting effect was to persuade him to embark on a quest for authenticity not unlike that associated with the great seventeenth century Indian Muslim champion of orthodoxy, Shaikh Ahmed Sirhindi (known also as Shaikh Ahmed Mujaddid Alf Thani). His influence on Iqbal has been acknowledged by scholars,[65] while Iqbal himself made no secret of his admiration for the Shaikh's endeavour to purge Indian Islam of foreign influences. In a poem, 'To the Punjab pirs', Iqbal singled out Sirhindi, described here as the 'Reformer', as the one

> Whom Allah sent in season to keep watch
> In India on the treasure house of Islam[66]

Iqbal's intellectual and emotional journey away from Persian Sufism and its governing doctrine of *wahdat al wujud* entailed a twofold process of negation and purification.[67] The first led Iqbal steadily to reject all borrowed thought as a distraction from the search for Quranic truth. The second drove him to sharpen the contours of the millat and restore the purity of its original mazhab. Greek, especially Platonic philosophy, represented for Iqbal one of two main foreign influences which by way of Persian Sufism had diluted and contaminated the original Islamic message. The other, he came to believe, was Vedantic monism which had corroded the substance of the Quranic message. Both had destroyed the inherent vitality and dynamism of Islam and hastened the political decline of the millat. To regain its power, the millat had to reject Platonism. This idea Iqbal endeavoured to convey not only in the controversial first edition of his mathnavi, '*Asrar-i-khudi*' (Secrets of the self), published in 1914, which criticized the apparently life-negating philosophy of neo-Platonism espoused by revered Persian Sufi poet, Khwaja Hafiz, but also in correspondence most famously with the eminent Cambridge scholar, R.A. Nicholson. 'My criticism of Plato,' he wrote, 'is directed against those philosophical systems which hold up death rather than life as their idea, systems which ignore the greatest obstruction to life, namely, matter and teach us to run away from it instead of absorbing it'.[68]

But the quest for purity could not stop at the expurgation of Greek philosophy: it required the repudiation of the whole corpus of Sufi thinking as it had evolved in India, with its blend of neo-Platonism and Vedantism and the syncretic Indian 'national' ideal that flowed from it.

That Iqbal was driven to do so must be explained by situating him in part within the broad currents of Indo-Muslim orthodoxy which had first emerged most clearly in the sixteenth century as a reaction against Mughal emperor Akbar's

[65]A.H. Kamali, 'The heritage of Islamic thought', in Malik, *Iqbal*, pp. 240–2.
[66]Muhammad Iqbal, 'To the Punjab pirs', in Kiernan, *Poems from Iqbal*, p. 58.
[67]Singh, *The Ardent Pilgrim*, p. 82.
[68]'Introduction' by R.A. Nicholson, in Muhammad Iqbal, *Secrets of the Self*, trans. by R.A. Nicholson (London: Macmillan, 1920), p. xvi.

experiment in religious syncretism (Din-i-ilahi), and then developed steadily through the eighteenth century under the reforming zeal of the great Muslim intellectual, Shah Waliullah of Delhi. T.N. Madan, who has recently explored the development of this tradition of orthodoxy, has highlighted some of its defining features. In the case of Sirhindi he observes a threefold argument involving, first, a concern with revival with a view to restoring the original purity of Islam; second, the imperative of strengthening the community against outsiders (Hindus) but also against the injurious activities of insiders (Shias); and third, bringing into focus the state or political power as an instrument of revival and reform.[69] For Shah Waliullah, the scheme of reform was more clear-cut: 'First, "purification" of the prevailing Muslim way of life, corrupted by survivals from pre-Islamic Arabic religions, borrowings from Hinduism... and, second, the revival of Muslim political power.'[70]

The parallels between these traditions and the trajectory of Iqbal's own intellectual and political development can scarcely be missed. Like Sirhindi, Iqbal was concerned not just with the question of orthodoxy but most characteristically with 'the reconstruction of religious thought' that would decisively unveil the Quranic truth. And while there is little of Sirhindi's antipathy to Shias in Iqbal's thinking, Iqbal's controversial position on the Ahmadis suggests a similar willingness to narrow the definition of the community, and even to put into question Islam's universalist vision of 'ever enlarging its limits by example and persuasion' in the interests of securing the 'eternal solidarity' of the community.[71] But it is likely that the contradictions of this stance would have escaped Iqbal for whom by this time the philosophical idea of khudi, which he defined as 'self-hood rather than selfishness', constituted the very basis of his humanitarian ideal. So too with the question of political power; like Sirhindi and Waliullah after him, Iqbal was to become increasingly conscious of the possibilities of effecting and securing reform through the exercise of political power, albeit within the parameters of a purposeful social order. Indeed, the similarities between Shah Waliullah and Iqbal were to become ever sharper with Iqbal's growing awareness of the importance of restoring political power to Muslims if only to salvage Islam's spiritual force. For Waliullah,

---

[69]Madan, *Modern Myths*, pp. 125–6.

[70]Ibid., pp. 128–9. Some Muslim scholars, notably Fazlur Rahman, have cast doubt on the centrality of purification in Shah Waliullah's programme of Islamic reconstruction and reform in India, arguing that it was because of Waliullah's pupils and sons that the 'definite Sufic interpretation of the universe' in his thinking came to be obscured. It was through their activities, Rahman argues, that 'the "purification" element in [Shah Waliullah's] teaching received greater emphasis from the totality of his catholic approach'. Fazlur Rahman, *Islam* (Chicago: University of Chicago Press, 1979), p. 203.

[71]See Iqbal's 'Reply to questions raised by Pandit Jawaharlal Nehru' and his 'Letter to the "Statesman"', in Vahid, *Thoughts and Reflections*, pp. 257–94

'the fundamental cause of both the moral and the political decline of Indian Muslims was their ignorance of the Quran and the Prophetic tradition'.[72] For Iqbal it lay, quite simply, in the neglect of the Law.

In 1917 he spelt out the essence of his thinking that was henceforth to govern both his philosophical and his political deliberations. 'Our birth as a society,' he declared,

was due only to our subjecting ourselves to a system of Law believed to be divine in origin; ... no student of Muslim thought and literature can deny that the tendency to ignore the Law—the only force holding together Muslim Society was the direct consequence of a false Mysticism born of the heart and brain of Persia.[73]

Earlier the young Iqbal, in a remarkably prescient passage in his doctoral dissertation, had vividly captured the process by which the Law had come to be diluted. He wrote:

The Persian, though he lets the surface of his life become largely Semitised, quietly converts Islam to his own Aryan habits of thought. In the West the sober Hellenic intellect interpreted another Semitic religion—Christianity; and the results of interpretation in both cases are strikingly similar. In each case, the aim of the interpreting intellect is to soften the extreme rigidity of an absolute law imposed on the individual from without.[74]

There were of course external factors that also prompted Iqbal to subject Sufism to critical scrutiny. The crisis in the Balkans in 1912–13, which he, along with many other Muslims of his generation, experienced as the humiliation of Islam, led him to pose urgent questions about the forces that had diluted the activist essence of the Quranic message. But what is interesting about Iqbal's thinking at this stage is not just his ambivalence towards Sufism but his growing unease in relation to Western modernity, and its by-products—materialism and nationalism. Their corrupting influence was a theme that Iqbal was to develop at great length in his later work, though the seeds of that conviction were almost certainly sown during his European sojourn.

One is tempted here to sympathize with the feelings that may have engulfed the young, academically gifted Iqbal, who was raised as the son of a tailor in the rural backwater that was Sialkot in the 1870s and 1880s, and who, on his first visit to Europe, was forced to wrestle with the contradictions arising from a spiritually impoverished West that had decisively supplanted the pre-eminence of his own millat. Iqbal's rage and incomprehension were captured in his classic poem, 'Shikwa'. In many ways its spirit is eerily reminiscent of the discourse of modern-day Islamists

[72] Muslim, Modern Myths, p. 129.
[73] 'Stray thoughts (II): Islam and Mysticism' in Vahid, ed., Thoughts and Reflections, p. 81.
[74] Iqbal, The Reconstruction of Religious Thought, pp. 22–3.

still confounded by the question of why devotion to the faith has not secured for Muslims the political power that they deem to be their birthright.

> There are people of other faiths, some of them transgressors...
> Your blessings are showered on the homes of unbelievers, strangers all.
> Only on the poor Muslim, Your wrath like lightning falls.[75]

A comparison between Iqbal and his near contemporary, Maulana Abul Kalam Azad, in this regard is both instructive and revealing. Born into a learned family in Mecca around 1888 and conversant in both Arabic and Urdu, Azad's experiences abroad left him with impressions that were very different from those of Iqbal. Even if Azad's accounts of these sojourns in West Asia and France in the early 1900s are sometimes contested,[76] what is not in doubt is that they fuelled Azad's abiding belief in the resilience of his religious community and its ability to forge a confident partnership with others. In a vein that was to become characteristic of his political creed in later life, Azad wrote in 1912:

Now, members of a brotherhood of four hundred million believers in the unity of God are afraid of two hundred and twenty million idol worshippers of India .... You must realize your position among the people's [sic] of the world. Like God himself, look at everyone from a lofty position.[77]

This self-confidence and sense of elation exuded by Azad stands in marked contrast to the deeply pessimistic spirit that haunted Iqbal upon his return to India. The social and political transformation Iqbal had witnessed in Europe and which now threatened to engulf India, made him deeply wary of change. While intellectually he continued to explore the possibilities of innovation, he grew ever mindful of the need for security and safety. W.C. Smith explains this curious position by suggesting that when confronted with the prospect of far-reaching change, Iqbal was inclined to favour *taqlid* (conformity) over *ijtihad* (independence of thinking), which meant that in the context of India on the threshold of national liberation, Iqbal was happier about talking of innovation than about seeing innovations practised.[78]

Iqbal's personal odyssey away from Sufism, which coincided with this mood of pessimism upon his return from Europe, was to have profound effect on his attitude to the emerging discourse of composite nationalism in India. Its vision

[75]Muhammad Iqbal, *Shikwa* and *Jawab-i-Shikwa*, Complaint and Answer: Iqbal's Dialogue with Allah, translated from the Urdu by Khushwant Singh (Delhi, Oxford University Press, 1981), p. 41.

[76]Aijaz Ahmad, 'Azad's careers: Roads taken and not taken', in Mushirul Hasan (ed.), *Islam and Indian Nationalism: Reflections on Abul Kalam Azad* (Delhi: Manohar, 1992), pp. 152–5.

[77]Quoted in Ian Henderson Douglas, *Abul Kalam Azad: An Intellectual and Religious Biography*, edited by Gail Minault and Christian Troll (New Delhi: Oxford University Press, 1988), p. 144.

[78]Wilfrid Cantwell Smith, *Modern Islam in India* (Lahore: Shaikh Muhammad Ashraf, 1969), p. 161.

of a common Indic culture, based on a process of assimilation and synthesis, was too deeply reminiscent of what he associated with the corrupting tendency of Sufism to make 'the many into One'. In an often-cited comment on *tasawwuf* (Islamic mystic Sufism) Iqbal emphasized that the idea of *wahdat* (unity) was neither desirable nor intrinsic to Islam. Wahdat, he maintained, was a philosophical theme that was deeply tainted with pantheistic Sufism. 'Islam,' he wrote, 'has nothing to do with *wahdat* and *kathrat* [plurality]. The essence of Islam is *Tawhid* and the opposite of the latter is not *kathrat* but *shirk* [the fundamental transgression of attributing partnership with God]'.[79]

But Iqbal was not only at odds with the philosophical basis of syncretic, composite Indic culture, he was also unable to engage with its historical premise. For while the votaries of 'cultural India' were seeking urgently to 'construct' a historical past to sustain a composite Indian nationalism, Iqbal was being driven to negate the past in order to reclaim the purity of the Muslim millat. That process of negation had begun with his violent renunciation of pantheistic Sufism and what he believed were its attendant evils of quietism and the corroding influences of neo-Platonic and Vedantic thought. Iqbal now embarked on a process of historical 'purification'—his 'principle of movement'—whose objective was to rid Islamic thinking of its excrescences and its impurities. This involved the urgent recasting of the Muslim millat to restore its essential character as.a spiritual community unfettered by local history; it also involved purging its mazhab to strip it of the layers of alien influences that had vitiated the community's capacity for political autonomy.

'The expression "Indian Muslims",' Iqbal wrote soon after return to India in 1910,

however convenient it may be, is a contradiction in terms, since Islam in its essence is above all conditions of time and space. Nationality with us is a pure idea, it has no geographical basis. But in as much as the average man demands a material centre of nationality, the Muslim looks for it in the holy town of Mecca.[80]

What is immediately significant about this passage is Iqbal's attempt to reclaim the purity of the millat by denying it any historical mooring. I would argue that this denial of history was essential to Iqbal's new, Islamist agenda, which required a cultural break with the past and the influence of its delusive metaphysics in order once more to unveil the hard and crystal core of the prophetic revelation. This vision clashed directly with the Nehruvian ideal, which allowed for no possibility of a return to past purity or historical cleansing. Indeed the more the Nehruvian

---

[79]Muhammad Daud Rahbar, 'Glimpses of the man', in Malik, *Iqbal*.

[80]Muhammad Iqbal, 'Islam as a moral and political ideal' in Vahid, ed., *Thoughts and Reflections of Iqbal*, p. 51.

ideal turned away from religion to a shared *historical* past as the basis of a composite Indian nationalism, the more imperative it became for Iqbal to draw attention to the trans-historical essence of the Islamic millat to underline its freedom from any material limitation.

Here it is worth stressing that Iqbal was not always clear or consistent about the precise relationship between the religious community and the nation. In his presidential address to the Indian Muslim League in 1930, he told his audience that 'the Muslims of India are the only people who can fully be described as a nation in the modern sense of the word'. But, he emphasized, this did not mean that any religious community is qualified to be a nation. The Hindus, he claimed, 'are not a nation [although] this is what they are striving for'. Iqbal returned to the theme in 1938 during his now famous debate with Maulana Husain Ahmed Madani.[81] In a series of tart exchanges, Iqbal rounded on the Maulana for having the temerity to suggest that Indian Muslims should embrace the *qaum* in exchange for the freedom to continue as a millat, unfettered in the practice of its religion and the application of its personal law. What is worth noting is that Madani like Iqbal held the millat to be superior to the qaum, comparable in some sense to the relationship between heaven and earth (though Iqbal regarded this as mere pretence on Madani's part).[82] What distinguished them was Iqbal's difficulty in reconciling his conception of the millat with the attributes of the qaum. This was evident as far back as 1924, long before his clash with Madani, in his poem, 'Mazhab'. In it Iqbal declares that what really distinguishes the millat is its character as a community guided above all by prophetic Law. A qaum, on the other hand, has no such divine stricture attached to it; indeed it may or may not be a religious community.[83]

This distinction was fundamental for Iqbal, and it was to resurface in his debate with Madani. Here, even more explicitly, Iqbal drew attention to the qaum as an essentially material configuration defined sometimes by its geographical contours, sometimes by shared historical experiences. By contrast, the millat was an essentially spiritual community that transcended all temporal and spatial

[81]Muhammad Iqbal, 'Statement on Islam and nationalism in reply to a statement of Maulana Husain Ahmad, published in "*Ehsan*" on the 9th March 1938', in A.R. Tariq (ed. and comp.), *Speeches and Statements of Iqbal* (Lahore: Shaikh Ghulam Ali, 1973), pp. 229–46.

[82]According to Iqbal, 'By saying that he [Madani] has not used the word "millat" in his speech, the Maulana seems to pretend that he regards *millat* as something higher than nation.... In actual practice, however, he has left no place for *millat* by preaching to the eight crore Muslims to lose their identity in the country, and therefore in the majority and to make nation a heaven and to ignore the fact that Islam will thereby be reduced to the status of the earth'. Ibid., p. 235.

[83]Do not compare your *millat* with other nations of the West,

   Your distinction lies in being the nation of the Prophet of Islam

   Their unity rests on territorial nationality

   Yours in the strength of your *mazhab*

'Mazhab' (Bang-i Dara), in *Kulliyat-i-Iqbal*, p. 248.

boundaries. Iqbal spelt out more clearly what this implied for the participation by Muslims in the emerging Indian 'nation'. He argued that while the millat could absorb the qaum, it was inconceivable for the millat to be absorbed into the qaum without also forgoing its mazhab. It was this that prompted Iqbal to make his final ringing declaration to Madani, affirming that 'the *millat* or *ummat* embraces nations but cannot be merged in them'.[84]

There was one final aspect of Iqbal's thinking on the millat which by underlining its ahistoricity accentuated its antipathy to the Nehruvian discourse on a common Indian national culture. This was Iqbal's treatment of the Muslim millat as a 'given'. Indeed the roots of Iqbal's problematic relationship with the governing assumptions of composite nationalism are, I believe, deeply grounded in his understanding of the Muslim religious community (millat) and the nature of its creed (mazhab). The community of Islam, he wrote (for a lecture delivered in 1910 at Aligarh University), 'abhors all material limitations' whether of race, tribe, or territory. It is not, he claimed, 'dependent for its life principle on the character or genius of a particular people' but is quintessentially 'non-temporal' and 'non-spatial'.[85] The vitality of such a community could not be sustained without also sustaining its religious creed (mazhab), the distinction of which was that it was 'something more than a creed...above all conditions of time and space'.[86]

Two consequences flowed directly from Iqbal's emphasis on the Muslim millat as a 'purely abstract idea' and on his notion of mazhab as organically linked to temporal power. The first imparted to his thinking a degree of ahistoricity, which accounted for his general disregard for a 'shared historical past' that was deemed to be constitutive of Indian nationalism in the Nehruvian sense. The second led him to posit a relationship between a Muslim's religious creed and the focus of his political allegiance, which became increasingly difficult to reconcile with the homogenizing agenda of the Indian nation state. In a brief correspondence with Nehru in 1937, Iqbal acknowledged that it was primarily the idea of nationalism as a 'political concept' that had brought it in conflict with Islam. This it would seem was the nub of Iqbal's problem with the Nehruvian vision. For it was predicated precisely on the idea of the 'nation as a political concept, and by definition a political project'. It was this that Iqbal could not concede. For to do so, as Gyan Pandey has so eloquently put it, would be to 'acknowledge [the nation's] historicity...to open up the question of who should wield power and to what end'[87]—questions that for Muslims like Iqbal, accustomed to regarding power as their birthright, were clearly non-negotiable.

---

[84]In Tariq, *Speeches and Statements*, p. 240.

[85]Iqbal, 'The Muslim community', p. 377.

[86]Iqbal, 'Islam as a moral and political ideal', pp. 50, 51.

[87]Gyanendra Pandey, *Remembering Partition: Violence, Nationalism and History in India* (Cambridge: Cambridge University Press, 2001), p. 160

REINVENTING ISLAMIC POLITICS IN INTERWAR INDIA: THE CLERGY COMMITMENT TO 'COMPOSITE NATIONALISM'

Barbara Metcalf

In 1947 two separate states were created in South Asia, India and Pakistan, the latter as a homeland for Muslims. As in the case of Israel, created as a religious homeland at the same time, a substantial part of the Muslim traditionally educated religious leadership opposed a religiously defined state. The fact that both movements, Zionist and Pakistan, were led by secularly educated people committed to a secular state would seem sufficient to explain this stance.[1] But the Indian leadership, the *'ulama*, in fact, took their position for the simple reason that for a quarter of a century before the Partition they had worked actively with non-Muslim Indians precisely to secure the whole of India as a religiously plural state independent from Britain.[2] With increasing confidence, members of the *'ulama*—unlike secular Muslims associated with Jinnah and the Muslim League—articulated a rationale for embracing a secular, plural democracy and a commitment to what they called 'composite nationalism'.[3]

---

[1] Yohanan Friedmann, 'The attitude of the *Jamiyyat-I Ulama-i Hind* to the Indian National Movement and the establishment of Pakistan', in Gabriel Baer (ed.), *The Ulama in Modern History*, Asian and African Studies VII (Jerusalem: Israeli Oriental Society, 1971), pp. 157–83.

[2] A small group of dissident 'ulama organized the Jami'at Ulama-i Islam in Calcutta in 1945. Their leading figures included disciples of Ashraf 'Ali Thanawi (1863–1943): Shabbir Ahmad Usmani, Zafar Ahmad Usmani, and Muhammad Shafi'. See Rizwan Malik, 'Muslim nationalism in India: Ashraf Ali Thanawi, Shabbir Ahmad Uthmani and the Pakistan Movement', *Pakistan Journal of History and Culture*, 17:2 (1997), pp. 73–82; Parveen Rozina, 'Jamiat al-Ulema-I-Hind: Its formation and organization', *Pakistan Journal of History and Culture*, 16:1 (1995), pp. 27–36; A.S. Sayyid Pirzada, *The Politics of the Jamiat Ulema-i-Islam Pakistan, 1971–77* (Karachi: Oxford University Press, 2000).

[3] I exclude from consideration here the region of Kashmir, whose Muslim population has

In the end, when India and Pakistan gained Independence, the Muslim population of British India was divided into roughly three parts: one-third in East Pakistan, where civil war in 1971 led to the independence of Bangladesh; one-third in West Pakistan; and one-third in India. Together these Muslim populations have formed almost half of the world's Muslims. The political fortunes of these countries have varied widely, and the course of political life in Pakistan, in particular, has fluctuated dramatically with democracy yielding regularly to military rule and global political interests transforming internal political life. In India, Muslims constitute some 12 per cent of the population, and, at numbers somewhere between 130 and 160 million at the turn of the twenty-first century, constitute either the second or third largest Muslim population in the world.[4]

The Muslim population of India has received relatively little international attention since most outsiders assume that the significant Muslim population is in the Middle East. Indeed, *The New York Times* columnist Thomas Friedman framed an article on Muslim Indians as 'Today's News Quiz', since he expected readers, like himself, to have no previous idea at all of the size of the Muslim Indian population, let alone familiarity with its participation in electoral democratic politics. India, he correctly pointed out, had no jihad-oriented, let alone Islamist, political parties; and it had, apparently, not produced a single participant in the international jihad stretching from Chechnya through Kashmir and Afghanistan to Bosnia. There was not even a national Muslim party.[5] The situation of Muslims in India had often not been easy, in particular given the ascendance of Hindu 'fundamentalists' in the past decade. But Friedman's point was sound—Muslims in India after Independence embraced secular democracy.

This chapter focuses on the decades before Independence, granted in 1947, when the foundation for that political stance was laid. In particular, it discusses the Islamic reasoning of one of its foremost exponents, Maulana Husain Ahmad Madani (1879–1958), a distinguished scholar and political spokesman who flourished in the mid-century decades.

I. POLITICS BETWEEN THE WARS

When the British established their rule over India in the mid-nineteenth century, the state functioned with the participation of limited numbers of 'loyal' elites.

---

organized independently of Muslims elsewhere in India. Kashmir has not been a cause for Muslim Indian organizations or spokesmen.

[4]Population estimates are available from http://www.cia.gov/cia/publications/factbook/index.html by country. India's population is given as 1,045,845,226 with 12 per cent Muslim population. Pakistan's population, 97 per cent Muslim, is given as 147,663,429; Bangladesh, 133,376,684, is said to be 83 per cent Muslim. Indonesia is the largest Muslim population, some 88 per cent of 231,328,092 people.

[5]Thomas L. Friedman, 'Today's News Quiz', *The New York Times Quiz*, 20 November 2001.

They created what one historian has called 'a simulacrum'[6] of the old pre-colonial Mughal polity. Only at the end of the first decade of the twentieth century, following the first of three major 'Council Acts' providing for limited franchise, did a new public life begin to appear. But World War I marked the real divide. India itself suffered in the War both from internal economic disruptions and loss of life from heavy military deployments in Europe; and politically conscious Indians were horrified at the devastation that Europe had wrought. During the War, Indians had been promised, moreover, progress towards the self-determination that was a central diplomatic theme of the times. In 1919, a second Councils Act increased Indian participation in elections and councils. Members of the 'ulama were central actors in the varied and lively political experimentation of the following years.

They were, for a start, active in the Khilafat Movement that followed World War I. It was short-lived and fundamentally ill-conceived in its goals since it latched on to the preservation of the Ottoman caliphate—of no importance whatsoever to the Indians of the subcontinent through most of their history—as a symbol of Muslim glory. The dismemberment of the Ottoman empire was seen by Indians as a symbol of British colonial perfidy. In that sense, the movement to preserve the caliphate was less about the Ottomans than about India, with the fate of the Ottomans conflated with India's own. For this reason, Gandhi embraced the movement. Khilafat leaders failed to see the strength of Arab and Turkish nationalism, forces with which in principle they should have been sympathetic. The Turks themselves in 1924 abolished the caliphate. Nonetheless, the movement gave secular, Westernized leaders a kind of 'Islamic' rather than only a 'Muslim community', or interest-based, identity. It also drew popular Muslim participation into political movements for the first time. And it marked a new role for the traditionally educated 'ulama, including Maulana Madani.

In 1919, leading 'ulama founded an association, the Jami'at Ulama-i-Hind (the Association of Indian 'Ulama), not as a separate political party but as a forum to speak for Muslims and support the movement for independence.[7] Maulana Madani would play a significant part in the organization over most of its first four decades.

Maulana Madani responded to the changing circumstances of the day with hard-headed pragmatism. There were two dimensions to his political strategy. One, he recognized that nationalism, democracy, and the importance of public opinion were the political currency of the day. And, second, in the context of

---

[6]Peter Hardy, *Partners in Freedom and True Muslims: The Political Thought of Some Muslim Scholars in British India, 1912–47* (Lund, 1971).

[7]The Jamiat has been relatively little studied. Friedmann, 'The attitude of the Jamiyyat-I Ulema-i-Hind'; Yohanan Friedmann, 'The *Jamiyyat-I Ulema-i-Hind* in the wake of Partition', *Asian and African Studies*, 2:2, pp. 181–211; Peter Hardy, *Partners in Freedom and True Muslims: The Political Thought of Some Muslim Scholars in British India, 1912–47* (Lund, 1971); Rizwan 2006?

British India, he, like everyone else, not just the clergy, imagined the society as consisting of the distinctive 'official' categories of colonial India. Of these, putative religious identity was centrally important. His 'composite nationalism' was thus 'composed' of religious 'communities'—Hindu, Muslim, Sikh, Christian— who would participate in a fundamentally secular political life to deal with law and order, economic life, and so forth, with communities themselves sustaining distinctive customs and personal law as they long had done. There is an ongoing debate among historians of the extent to which colonial categories like 'caste' and 'religion' were created or simply acknowledged by the British. What no one disputes is that these categories, in the case of religion most dramatically after 1920, took on a new, corporate, politicized meaning that shaped individual identities as well.

II. MAULANA HUSAIN AHMAD MADANI

Who was Madani? Husain Ahmad did not come from a family of 'ulama. His was a family of landholders in the eastern United Provinces who fell on hard times during the anti-British uprising of 1857. His orphaned father learned no Arabic and, instead of a religious education, followed an English track to become a schoolteacher, and then headmaster, of a small school. Given his family history, he, not surprisingly, loathed the English. He cultivated the inner life of Sufism and was a serious poet in the local regional languages in which he wrote songs of the sort so central to the devotional religious style common to both Hindu and Muslim traditions in this region.[8] At the end of the nineteenth century, he migrated to Medina, the site of the Prophet Muhammad's grave and the focus of Sufi longing through devotion to him.[9]

Husain Ahmad and his elder brother grew up with the dual experience of residence in Medina, a cosmopolitan setting, crossed by Muslims from all areas, and sojourns in the small country town of Deoband in India where both were educated in the new style, formally organized madrasa that had been founded in 1867. Deoband trained young men in the traditional Islamic disciplines with an emphasis on hadith scholarship as a guide to deliberate reform of customary practice; Deobandis particularly targeted what they saw as false Sufi and Shi'i practices as well as the 'heresy' of the Ahmadis or 'Qadianis' that emerged at the end of the

[8]Husain Ahmad Madani

[9]His paternal grandfather and his grandfather's two brothers were killed and most of the family property was lost. When, at the urging of friends concerned with his progress in the educational system, Husain Ahmad's father set out to learn some English, he dreamed that his hands were soiled from the privy. The dream confirmed in him, one biographer asserts, his hatred of the English (Hifzu'r-Rahman in Hussain Ahmad Madani, Naqsh-i hayat (Impression of a Life), 2 vols (Deobandh: Maktaba diniya, 1953).

century.[10] Madani also received Sufi initiation from one of the great saints and scholars associated with the school. His relationship with Maulana Rashid Ahmad Gangohi (1829–1905), whom he only knew shortly before the latter's death, continued through dreams to shape his entire life. At Deoband he also became attached to the principal at the time, Maulana Mahmudul Hasan (1851–1920) whom his followers later honoured with the title, the Shaikh of India, the Shaikh ul Hind. Madani spent many years in Medina, himself acting as a teacher to students from many countries once his own education was complete.

The story might have ended there except that, during the World War I, Madani got caught up with the activities of Mahmudul Hasan, now in Medina, who had ties to people who saw the War years as an opportunity to challenge colonial rule militarily. (Muslims were not alone in this. There were similar efforts in Bengal as well as one that linked Punjab and San Francisco.) This stance, it is worth noting, was a dramatic break with the loyalism of the day, as characteristic of those at his religious school as it was, for example, of the Indian National Congress. This particular 'conspiracy' seems to have imagined links with Ottomans and Afghans who would join with freedom lovers in India to oust the colonial rulers. Madani, Mahmud Hasan, and several others were arrested and interned in Malta for four years.

From this brief biography, there would seem to be clear elements that influenced Husain Ahmad's path of anti-British activism and cooperation with non-Muslims, not least his early life in India and his experiences of interacting with Hindus, as well as his family's experience of colonial reprisals and alienation. Also significant was his residence abroad, which for him, as for so many others including Gandhi, helped him see India as a whole and not as the mosaic of irreconcilable social groups the British held it to be.

Finally, like colonial subjects throughout the world, prison or internment proved to be not only an experience taken as a metaphor for the larger condition of society, but also a school for radicalism and an occasion for forming new kinds of social ties. Madani himself wrote of his first prison experiences in the guise of a biography of the Shaikh ul Hind with the rather romantic title, *Prisoner of Malta (Asiir-i malta)*.[11] As Madani describes life in Malta from 1916 to 1920, he mixed with Germans, Austrians, Turks, and other Indians, including one Bengali Brahmin accused of manufacturing bombs. Madani, like so many others in such circumstances, saw internment as an occasion to study and talk with the other prisoners, free, moreover, of colonial surveillance. There was no CID. This prison experience marked a watershed in his life. Instead of growing old in Medina, as he might have, Madani subsequently moved permanently to Deoband where he

---

[10]Madani advocated the Sunni position in contestation over rights with Shi'as in Lucknow in the late 1930s.

[11]Husain Ahmad Madani.

would become principal of the school; help organize Muslims to firmly support the Congress party; and return periodically to jail.

III. IND.A AS AN ISLAMIC LAND

I turn now to consider three issues in the intellectual interpretations Maulana Madani brought to bear to shape his political stance in the years leading up to Independence, starting with 'India as an Islamic Land'. Shortly before Independence, Madani wrote an essay, 'Hamara Hindustan aur uske faza'il' (India: Our land and its virtues).[12] He used an old genre of Arabic literature 'fazai'l', in which writers celebrated the merits or virtues of different lands.[13] But he used it to jump into what might be seen as a competition over the historical 'biography' being created for the Indian nation. The Hindu terrorist, Vinayak Damodar Savarkar (1883–1966) and other Hindu nationalists, the intellectual fathers of today's virulent Hindu nationalism, insisted that India was a Hindu land, sacred only to Hindus and not to so-called 'foreign' Muslims and Christians. Muslims had no ties to India, he insisted: their holy places were all in Arabia just as Christian holy places were all in Palestine.[14] Madani did not challenge this argument directly; he simply made an Islamic claim to trump it.[15]

Madani, quoting earlier writers in this genre, made the perhaps surprising following points:

• India is in fact for Muslims the second holiest place on earth next to Mecca because Adam descended on Adam's Peak, in Ceylon, after his expulsion from paradise.

• Thus, since Adam is understood as the founder of the Islamic prophetic tradition, India was the site of the first revelation, the first mosque, and the first place from which pilgrimage to Mecca was performed.

• In India, 'the eternal light of Muhammad' was first manifested in Adam.

• Since Adam was in India, all humans, being descended from him, are also

[12]Husain Ahmad Madani, 'Hamara Hindustan aur uske Fazail' (India: Our land and its virtues), trans. by Mohammad Anwar Hussain (New Delhi: Jamait Ulama-I-Hind, n.d. [1941]).

[13]The most exhaustive presentation of the merits of India along these lines was in fact written by Ghulam 'Ali Bilgrami, an eighteenth-century Indian who based celebration of India on Qur'anic verses and prophetic hadith; the recorded sayings of holy men; scholarly commentaries; and love poetry in both Sufi and (Hindu) bhakti traditions. Bilgrami also sought out reports from contemporary travellers, and he himself voyaged to Ceylon. See Ghulam 'Ali Azad al-Bilgrami, 'Subhat al-mirjan fi athar Hindustan', ed. by Muhammad Fade al-Rahman al Nadwi al-Siwani. 2 vols (Aligarh: Jamiat Aligarh ali Islamiyya, 1976–80 [1764]. Trans. by Carl Ernst in Donald S. Lopez, Jr (ed.), Religions of India in Practice (Princeton: Princeton University Press, 1994), pp. 556–63.

[14]Vinayak Damodar Savarkar, Hindutva: Who is a Hindu, excerpted in Stephen Hay (ed.), Sources of Indian Tradition (New York: Columbia University Press, 1988 [1923]), pp. 293–5.

[15]Ibid.

Indian—although, to be sure, 'among various communities residing in India, Muslims alone, because of Adam, can legitimately claim they are the original inhabitants of the land'.[16]

The colonial narrative of Indian history, first formulated in the late eighteenth century, had been to position Muslims as foreigners, thus making British rule seem less intrusive and, by vilifying Muslim rule, more benign. Key elements of that narrative were appropriated by Indians generally to account for their subjection. Today, Hindu extremists justify ethnic cleansing on the basis of this same narrative of Muslims as foreigners. Madani made his case on the defensive.

Madani made a further, perhaps startling, comparative point, namely that Muslims, 'unlike Hindus and Zoroastrians', did not burn or expose, but rather buried, their dead, so that 'even after death, a Muslim remains attached to the soil' and at the time of Judgment will rise from the very spot where buried. According to their own beliefs, moreover, Madani continues, Hindus and some other groups of Indians believe that souls after death take on new forms so that 'there is no guarantee that a Hindu soul ... will again take birth in India' at all. The grave of a Muslim by contrast is a place of resort for living Muslims, and a sanctuary till the Day of Judgment. For the dead person, Madani explains, the 'grave is like Radio Station ... where messages are received and transmitted', particularly as others pray and do good works on behalf of the deceased.[17]

Madani's final, and for him irrefutable, argument, was that the Prophet Muhammad loved his homeland so that his followers in India could hardly do otherwise.

Madani's scalpel, in short, excised the colonial/Hindu nationalist story, at the same time as it excavated the Islamic tradition in order both to socialize Muslims to the loyalties of modern nationalism—and to encourage other Indians to accept them. Madani's celebration of India as an Islamic land resonated with old arguments made by earlier writers, but he was very much a product of his times in tying that celebration to a commitment to the territorial loyalty of a modern nation state.

IV. MUSLIM HISTORY IN INDIA: AGE-OLD PRESENCE AND RESISTANCE TO INDIA'S 'SLAVERY'

Madani created, moreover, as earlier writers in this genre did not, a modern, linear narrative in which Muslims had a major place in the history that defined the emerging nation. The argument had two parts. One, articulated in particular in the Faza'il tract, was one more susceptible to the historian's eye than the

---

[16]Madani, 'Hamara Hindustan aur uske faza'il'.
[17]Ibid.

association with Adam. This was simply that Muslims had made India their home for over 1000 years, and that in fact most of those now Muslim were descended from earlier inhabitants. Companions of the Prophet, moreover, had visited Indian soil; thousands of scholars, Sufis, and martyrs lie buried here; India boasts millions of mosques, tombs, and other Islamic institutions. This was the Muslims' ancestral home and, he insisted, they had no greater ties to Muslims beyond the subcontinent than did Hindus to their fellow religionists abroad. This was a response both to Hindu nationalist claims to the contrary, as well as to interpretations made of the Khilafat agitation.

A second theme in Madani's historical writing focused on recent history and positioned Muslims at the forefront of what he called 'resistance to India's "slavery".' In this regard, Madani contributed to the creation of a genealogy of anti-British Muslim nationalism, which made further exuberant claims for Muslim nationalist legitimacy. Madani argued not merely that Muslims were anti-British, but they were the *most* anti-British. Madani constructed an anachronistic story that positioned Muslims as the first nationalists. Its landmarks were an 1803 fatwa on the status of India after the British occupation of Delhi in 1803; what he described as the anti-colonial jihad of Sayyid Ahmad Shaheed and others who attempted to carve out a state on the frontier in the early nineteenth century; 'ulama participation in the 1857 Mutiny; and, of course, the conspiracies of World War I that brought him and others to Malta.[18] The Indian National Congress, by contrast, was, from his perspective, a laggard, long niggling over minor constitutional adjustments and proclaiming its loyalty. It was Muslims who earliest and most courageously opposed exploitative, tyrannical imperialism.

The 'ulama of the Jamiat Ulama relentlessly opposed the British. It is too easy to attribute this opposition to 'religion' or 'religious fanaticism', assuming that Muslim leaders opposed the British because of a conflict with their Christianity. Madani's opposition was based concretely on an analysis of what the British did. Madani's second major prison writing, *Naqsh-i hayat*, written in Naini prison in 1944, included a fierce, hard-headed attack on colonialism with a focus on exploitation, capitalism, the particularly anti-Muslim policies of the British, and the ruin of India's economy. Not for Madani, Nehru's contemporaneous romantic quest in *The Discovery of India* (1944)—written while he was in prison during the War—for an organic Indian civilization as the focus of a historical exploration. The English-educated, socialist lawyer wrote poetry; the Islamic mystic wrote an economic critique of colonialism.

---

[18]Historians can challenge each of these presumed landmarks. The status of *dar ul harb*, for example, can be seen as a ruling made on technical grounds only to impact such issues as taking interest; the jihad, fundamentally, was no more than a variation of the regional state-building activities that were the currency of the day; the rule of the 'ulama in the 1857 uprising is exaggerated and misinterpreted.

Madani often addressed his concerns to the welfare of Muslims, but on the matter of the colonial presence he addressed Indians as a whole: Muslims were part of the nation, and all Indians faced common problems. In May 1945, as World War II came to an end, Maulana Madani presided over the annual meeting of the Jami'at Ulama, held in Saharanpur. His eloquent presidential address or *khutba*, was tightly focused on what he spoke of as 'the stain of India's slavery and [the current period as] the worst of times'. In sixteen precise points he reviewed the Wartime offenses of the 'humanity-crushing policy' of the 'utterly selfish and merciless' British who, he argued, had left India 'half dead'. He denounced the declaration of War on India's behalf and he spoke in the nation's voice: 'What do I have to do with enmity or friendship, war or peace, with anyone? I am neither Germany's enemy nor friend, nor am I America's .... I long for one thing, and one thing only, and that is freedom.'[19]

He continued point by point on what he saw as British contempt for the interests of Indians: police firings; imprisonment without trial; abuses under the Defence of India Act, the Army bill, and the establishment of special courts; censorship; the seizure of mills and factories and control of production; the confiscation of grain; the export of trains and engines from India to the detriment of internal travel, shortages of petrol and petroleum; and the tragedy of export of India's goods through the United Kingdom Commercial Corporation to the Allies 'with no concern for the poverty and hunger of India'. Alluding to the horrific suffering of the 1943 Bengal famine, he argued that India had deteriorated into a veritable hell.[20]

In this entire address, delivered by one of the great religious scholars of the age speaking to an audience comprising mostly other clerics, there was no discussion whatsoever of what one would construe as doctrinal or scriptural issues—not a quote from a sacred text, not an argument about divine law, nothing. Instead we have someone addressing economic and political issues alone. Madani, who himself did not know English, quoted English newspapers, Shakespeare, the ardent Bengali nationalist, Surendranath Bannerjee; he knew the details of repressive legislation; he was outraged by the differential treatment of dissidents in England and those in India. His remarks were informed by the new political theory of the age, not Islamically derived, that takes the interests and the voice of

[19]Husain Ahmad Madani, *Intikhab khutbat jamiat ulama-yi hind* (Selection of sermons/addresses to the Jamait Ulama Hind), ed. by Shuja'ta 'ali Sandilvi (Lucknow: Uttar Pradesh Urdu Akademi, 1988).

[20]Ibid., pp. 154–9. Indivar Kamtekar provides a nuanced study of the differential economic impact of World War II in Britain and India, confirming many of the points Madani made. Kamtekar also identifies industrialists and others in India who profited, but Madani sees rather the suffering of the poor and modestly paid who saw the value of their income decline. Indivar Kamtekar, 'A different war dance: State and class in India 1939–1945', *Past and Present*, no. 176 (2002), pp. 187–221.

the 'public' as the ultimate arbiter of political life and that defends 'civil liberties'—using the neologism, *huquq shahariyat*—as a human entitlement.[21] He called the British to account, for example, by the differential treatment of Indian and British anti-War sentiment. The British were allowed freedom of speech; Indians were not. An '*alim* like Madani was in no sense limited in his purview to sectarian issues of worship, doctrine, and spiritual guidance.

V. 'COMPOSITE NATIONALISM' AND 'TRADITIONALIST' PRAGMATISM

Finally, my third theme, how did Madani justify his alliance with the non-Muslim dominated Congress leadership? In 1940 the Muslim League, led by Jinnah, had taken the negotiations over various constitutional schemes to their logical end by proposing a separate state for Muslims, a state, as alluded to in the preceding pages, intended to be organized on secular grounds and not on religiously specific principles. The debate revolved around the definition of the nation. Madani insisted on a territorial definition of the nation, from which perspective he simply accepted the fact that people of multiple religious groups lived within the boundaries of India. He denied the League's 'two nation theory' that insisted that Muslims needed a territory of their own. Madani also, like Nehru, regarded the League as a party of the aristocratic nawabs in the pocket of the British whose interests were served by 'divide and rule'.

Although of much less significance at the time, a second challenge to Madani's stance also emerged at the end of colonial rule, namely an 'Islamist' position led by Maulana Maududi and his party, Jama'at-i Islami, founded in 1941.[22] Maududi opposed both the scheme of Partition, which basically provided two secular states, and the Congress goal of a united India. He held out a vision of what can be called 'Islamist rule'. Islamist orientations worldwide have also included the Muslim Brotherhood, which originated in Egypt, the ideologists of the Iranian Islamic revolution, and, of interest most recently, several of the Afghan jihad movements in opposition first to the Soviets and then to the Taliban. The Islamist movements are ones typically led by secularly educated professionals and technical people committed to an 'Islamic system', as they call it, parallel to other systems of the twentieth century like Marxism and capitalism, that shapes all aspects of life: thus Islamic economics, Islamic society, Islamic governance, Islamic sciences, and so forth. The Islamist movements in principle, moreover, if not in practice, are not nationalist.[23]

[21]Madani, *Intikhab khutbat jamiat ulama-yi hind*, p. 156.

[22]Charles J. Adams, 'The politics of Maulana Maududi', in Donald Eugene Smith (ed.), *South Asian Politics and Religion* (Princeton: Princeton University Press, 1966), pp. 371–97.

[23]Maududi, it is worth noting, in his own career represented the variety and probing and continuous rethinking characteristic of so many individuals and movements in the inter-War years.

In 1939 one of Maulana Madani's followers sought his guidance after reading a persuasive essay by Maududi. Madani replied with a ringing refutation.[24] The heart of Madani's argument—appealing to a historian—is that theory gets you nowhere. '*Siyaasiyyaat* (politics) is not resolved', he says, 'through *falsafiyyaat* (philosophy)'.[25] If people fail to pay attention to history and to contemporary constraints, if they hide their eyes from the conditions around them, they are self-destructive, or, as he says, they might as well commit suicide. For Madani, the reality of the day was the constitutional movement; the need to gain the support of the population as a whole; and a united front against the British. In relation to this last, Maududi's effort to add the creation of 'an Islamic order' to the conflicting movements already in place could not be more inappropriate.

Maududi's essay had specifically denounced the Muslims who supported the Congress on the grounds that a Muslim could not accept the leadership of a non-Muslim. This for Madani was proof that Maududi lived in a dream world, abstracted from the reality in which the Muslim population of India actually lived. Just think, he wrote, what this would mean. By this argument every Muslim participating in a Municipal board, or a District board, or an Assembly, or a Council, or a trade or industrial administrative board—all of them—would have to resign, since, given the relative size of the Hindu and Muslim populations, they were probably following orders of non-Muslims! Then, of course, with no income, they would fall into poverty and famine, and descend—and along with them their whole families, their children, ultimately the whole Muslim people—down the *ghats* of *fana*. Madani inverted the meaning of fana, or obliteration, the final stage of the Sufi, from ascent to descent, from a positive to a negative value. Muslims with Maududi's vision would also have to live without treatment by non-Muslim doctors, the work of non-Muslim engineers, the buildings of non-Muslim architects, the administrative work of non-Muslim bureaucrats, and so on.

His father had a Western style education and a law degree, but he was ambivalent about that education, devoted to Sufism, and educated his son at home. In the years after the World War I, Maududi was an enthusiastic supporter of Congress, turned to journalism, and embraced fully the Khilafat movement. In 1921 he was invited to edit the official newspaper of the Jamiat Ulama-i-Hind. By this time he had learned English and was increasingly interested in Western learning, but he also studied traditional Islamic texts in Delhi at the same time. The collapse of the Khilafat movement, and the communal violence of the 1920s, left him, like so many others, adrift, and in his case led him to question the morality of nationalism, making him, one might note, part of a larger transnational discussion in the period after the Great War. Maududi's focus turned to revival among Muslims and a vision of a model Islamic community. Still, although in later years his Jamat Islami would be held up as a complete antithesis to the quietism of the internal missionary movement, Tablighi Jamaat, linked to the Deobandi ulama, he initially was a great admirer of the Tabligh movement, and his published description of its work in the late 1930s first introduced it to many.

[24]Husain Ahmad Madani, *Makhtubat-i shaikhu'l-islam* (letters of Shaikhu'l Islam), 4 vols, ed. and Introduction by Maulana Najmu'd-din Islahi with a Foreword by Maulana Qari Muhammad Tayyib Qasimi et al. (Deoband: Maktaba diniyya, 1950/51), vol. 1, pp. 395–401.

[25]Ibid., p. 396.

Second, Madani writes, given that among Muslims themselves there is hardly consensus on religious grounds, just *what* would Islamic rule mean? He has a list here too to call attention to those differences: Easternism, Westernism, Shiism, Qadianiyat, Khaaksaariat, Adam taqlid. 'Each person', Madani points out, 'considers *his* reasoning beyond that of Plato or Socrates',[26] and—showing again how he had imbibed the new political world of his day—adds the reminder that in a free country, the only sources of authority are persuasion, guidance, and advice. All this suggests that Madani's opposition to Islamist politics did not only derive from India not being a majority Muslim country. Even among Muslims there could be no agreement on the nature of proper Islamic rule.

The official Congress position and the official Jamiat position were, in this period, congruent. But behind the Jamiat positions were arguments, disseminated not only by individual letters but also by publications, periodicals, and by public meetings, that insisted on an Islamic justification for their stance. In this letter, for example, Madani made an analogy between the required canonical prayer, whose rules are subject to individual characteristics and contexts (for example whether a person is sick or well, travelling or staying in one place). Imagine right now, was his argument, how the context of India must impact the choice of political strategy. What dream world was Maududi living in, he implied, to think that in the mixed population of India, with the varieties of Islamic interpretations current, he could enforce the rules he drew from theoretical premises like stoning, prohibition, or monetary compensation for murder?[27] Rules like these, Madani concluded, could not possibly be morally obligatory: they were simply not *farz* in India as it was.[28]

VI. BEYOND ARGUMENTS: THE CHARISMA OF AN ISLAMIC LEADER

It is not enough to know the ideological positions of the clergy leadership to understand their influence. Even a formal institutional history, important as it is, is not enough. A leader like Madani also commanded intense personal loyalty. He lived at the core of a world of profound male sociality, dependent variously on shared political ideas, shared sectarian orientation, and shared networks of scholarship and spiritual guidance. His activities, as reflected in his letters, included a centrally important commitment to religious education and to spiritual guidance. His life was organized around cycles of worship and feasts and fasts. Visions and

[26]Ibid., p. 399.

[27]On other occasions, he and his colleagues further pointed to what was taken as an analogous episode in the life of the Prophet Muhammad, the Treaty of Hudaibiyah, when he allied with various non-Muslims, including Jews. Maulana Anwar Shah Kashmiri, Madani's Deobandi colleague, wrote an influential tract on this issue. Ibid., pp. 402–3.

[28]Ibid., p. 400.

dreams played a constitutive part of his everyday life. Loyalty to him reached beyond his immediate circle to those who encountered him in public events as well as those who knew him through the printed word, a process that was central to formation of larger public identities that increasingly became part of the personal identity of individual Indians in the twentieth century.

In this regard, it is interesting to return to the formative experiences of Madani's life. The then director of the Deoband academy, Qari Muhammad Tayyib Qasimi, writing about Madani in the mid-1950s, offered an interpretation of what shaped his life different from mine as given here. First, he ignored Madani's early childhood in India, and divided his life into three stages marked by place of residence: Medina, Malta, and Deoband. Residence in Medina because it is a central focus of Islam, he wrote, allowed Husain Ahmad to breathe in spiritual fullness, *jami'at*. Residence in Malta, because he was in the company of the Shaikh ul Hind, whom Tayyib calls the greatest personality of the age, caused the wave of fulfilment, *jami'at*, in moral or ethical deportment to flow over him. And finally, the years at Deoband brought him to a place of flowing together with others *ijtimaa'iyat*. Taiyyib's interpretation of significant life experience is thus centred on relationships—in this case to the Prophet through his city; to the Shaikh ul Hind during internment; and to the community of like-minded Muslims brought together in India. It was this profound male sociality, as I called it in the preceding discussion, that according to Tayyib made Madani the influential figure, *markazi shakhsiyat*, he would become.[29]

A frequently retold story suggests what were seen as Madani's personal and moral qualities. This story, the first of three stories chosen by the editor of the multi-volume edition of Madani's letter to illustrate his character, hints at the larger world in which he lived.

When Hazrat Maulana Madani returned from his final hajj we people were present at the station in Lahore for the honour of seeing him (*sharf-i ziyaarat*). Among those in relationship with him was Saahibzaada Muhammad 'Aarif, from district Jhang who then accompanied [Maulana Madani] as far as Deoband. He reports the following story. On the train, there was also a 'Hindu gentleman' who experienced a call of nature and went to attend to it. Clearly unhappy, he came right back. Hazrat Maulana Madani understood [what had happened], and immediately … went to the toilet and cleaned it completely. Then he said to the Hindu friend, 'Please go, the toilet is completely clean. Perhaps because it is night you couldn't see it properly.' To make a long story short, [the Hindu gentleman] got up and went, and [found] the toilet completely clean. He was very moved and with great conviction [*aqiida*] said, 'Your honour's [*huzuur*] kindness [*bandanawaazii*, cherishing of servants] is beyond comprehension'.

One must place next to this the tradition of the Jewish guest of the Prophet Muhammad [s.a.s.] that comes to hand. The guest dirtied the bedding of the Prophet Muhammad during the night (55) and with his own blessed hand he cleaned it. So excrement

[29]Muhammad Tayyib, in ibid., pp. 3–4.

can be taken as a sign [*siraagh*] of selflessness and self-discipline [*be nafsi* and *nafs kushi*] of the people of the Prophet, and the demonstration of the Prophet's own beauty.[30]

Here are four brief comments about what, I believe, this story implicitly conveyed to those who heard it and told it.

1. Madani was a charismatic figure. He was endowed with spiritual power that comes from power over the self (nafs kushi). He was a living model of the Prophet in his humility. Indeed, his followers believed him to be a descendant of the Prophet Muhammad and affixed '*sayyid*', to his name, a claim he himself seems to have neither accepted nor denied. The locative 'Madani' further underscored his tie to the Prophet. The people on the train station were there to do *ziyaarat*, the pilgrimage owed to a holy person or a holy grave. He simultaneously carried the prestige of mastery of Islamic scholarship (although to be sure political life took precedence over actual scholarly writing). The structure of the story is that of a Sufi tale [*hikaayat*], in which an outsider is awed by the holy person's power or charisma, in this case a person with multiple connections to the living and the dead. Increased numbers had ties to someone like Madani because of the media, like the inexpensive publications in which stories like this are found.

2. Madani was like Gandhi. He wore *khadi*. He cleaned the latrine.[31] He knew that 'public opinion', not the will of viceroy or sultan, had to be the foundation of political life. Related to this:

3. Madani was often on a train. He inhabited the geographical space of India. If one were telling his life, one strategy would be simply to map his travels because he represented a new pattern among the 'ulama generally of frequent travel.

4. And, finally, Madani inhabited this vast space of India with dignity and pride in a way that served as a metonym for the Muslim community as a whole. Muslims, like Madani, believed themselves to be the best of communities; and in the glowing moment of recognition in this story, the humbled and wiser Hindu gentleman accepted the bandanawaazii of their representative whose worthy and superior status was thus acknowledged. Madani may appear to be engaged in a humble task but his was the humility of the truly great.

This story is a reminder that Madani believed himself to be fully committed to the welfare of all the people of India, but that he saw India, as did most political actors of his day, as comprising not individuals, as liberal political theory would have it, but a 'composite nation' with communities defined, above all, by religion. This was in large part a legacy of colonial rule. Madani sought to secure, and was seen as securing, the well-being and dignity of Muslims above all. The view of India as community-based was built into the constitution of the new republic by the recognition of separate, religiously defined, codes of personal law. This was

---

[30]Najmu'd-din Islahi in ibid., pp. 53–5.

[31]As the Richard Attenborough film, *Gandhi* (1982), makes clear, the great symbol of Gandhi's allegiance with the poor in a pollution-obsessed society was cleaning latrines.

accepted with varying degrees of commitment, by Muslim and Hindu leaders alike, even while, for a leader like Nehru, they were expected to be short term and for others they were regarded as a long-term guarantee of communal control. This fundamental contradiction in Indian constitutional arrangements persists, and the Muslim leadership, including Madani's heirs in the 'ulama, are fully committed to sustaining it in the form of separate religiously defined personal law.

The subject of India's lack of what is called 'a uniform civil code' is a large one, but to an outsider is likely to be seen as detrimental to individual liberties, as does any vision that posits religious community generally as standing formally between the individual and the state. Similarly, Madani's participation in the competition of who got to India first, discussed in the preceding pages in relation to India's 'virtues', would seem irrelevant to a polity founded as a liberal democratic state. Such anachronistic judgments can be dismissed as unfair: Madani was a man of his times.

Nonetheless, one central fact remains. Madani challenges what are common stereotypes of the political thought of Muslim clerics. He was a participant in modern political life, he was cognizant of social and political issues, he was concerned with the real problems of poverty and civil liberties, he was committed to democracy. His son, who succeeded him as president of the 'ulama association has been elected to parliament several times. Madani's solutions were driven not by abstract principles but by what worked. He was, moreover, someone whose religious life was rich and complex, steeped in the high tradition of Arabic learning and simultaneously embedded in the world of spiritual relationships with the holy and pious, both living and dead, so characteristic of Indian religious life.

Discussion of Muslim politics these days often assumes that all can be explained by fanaticism or irrational unrest—with phrases like 'the Arab street'—or by a priori assumptions of the sort that 'Islam' is incompatible with democracy. Analysts often turn to sacred texts, for example on such subjects as jihad, assuming that they can extrapolate from scriptural quotations to current behaviour, as if the meaning of isolated texts was transparent and Muslims lived detached from the world they lived in.[32] Such approaches could never explain Madani's sermon on British exploitation and abuse of civil liberties, nor could they have imagined his burning devotion to those radio transmitters of saintly graves that fuelled his Indian nationalism. A thinker like Madani in his time participated fully in modern life, and he took into account common human concerns with freedom, justice, and economic well-being. His actual behaviour, as well as his own teaching of looking at the world clearly, deserve attention from those trying to understand Muslim politics today.

[32]Ranjit Hoskote, 'Modernities of the Islamic world', *The Hindu Magazine* (16 Feb. 2003). http.//www.thehindu.com/thehindu/mag/mag/2003/02/16/stories.

THE COLONIAL CONTEXT OF MUSLIM SEPARATISM: FROM SAYYID AHMAD BARELVI TO SAYYID AHMAD KHAN

David Lelyveld

I. INTRODUCTION: THE HISTORIOGRAPHY OF THE COMPOSITE CULTURE

'Ganga–Jamna' as defined in Fallon's nineteenth-century Urdu, or rather, Hindustani–English Dictionary means 'a mixture of any kind' and 'a mode of adjusting interest of a loan (the debtor being credited with the interest of the instalments paid by him, while he is debited, per contra, with the full amount on the original loan)'; 'ganga–jamni', feminine, on the other hand, was defined as 'a mixture of gold and silver, or of brass and copper' or 'an earring made of such mixed metal'.[1] Only later, towards the mid-twentieth century, did the phrase refer to the 'mixture' of cultural forms associated with Muslims and Hindus, particularly in north India, and more or less as an allusion to a Mughal heritage. It was another way of talking about the so-called 'composite culture', with affectionate condescension, as a matter of mere decoration, the sort of thing one was likely to see in the Parsi theatre or its cinematic successor, the costume dramas of Sohrab Modi. The trivialization of supposed mixtures of diverse cultural traces, 'Hindu' and 'Muslim', in language, art, or, as a matter of fact, religious practice, had been the stock-in-trade of official British colonial ethnography, as in the comment in

---

[1]S.W. Fallon, *A New Hindustani–English Dictionary* (Banaras: E.J. Lazarus and Co. and London: Trübner and Co., 1879; facsimile edn Lucknow: Uttar Pradesh Academy, 1986), p. 1009; word for word the same in John T. Platts, *A Dictionary of Urdu, Classical Hindi and English* (Oxford: Clarendon Press, 1884), p. 919.

the Gurgaon District Gazetteer that Meos, or rather *the* Meos 'keep the feasts of both religions and the fasts of neither'.[2] Grounded in Orientalist notions of what could count as genuine religious authority, British official observers construed deviations as evidence of Indian ignorance and their own greater knowledge.

It was toward the final decades of the nationalist movement and the early years of Independence that the task of developing a serious historiography and positive evaluation of the mutual cultural influences of Muslims and Hindus became a matter of earnest concern. Aside from Nehru's *The Discovery of India*, Tara Chand, Sayyid Abid Hussain, Humayun Kabir, and Muhammad Mujeeb exemplify in their different ways the enterprise of developing a literature on the composite culture.[3] What Abid Hussain called 'the national culture of India', was characterized by harmonious Muslim and Hindu interaction but had little to do with other sorts of cultural identity, linguistic or regional for example, that might have been part of such a project. In response to the politics of Partition and the mobilization of political constituencies around symbols of separate religious identity, these writers constructed a common history and the possibility of a shared future. They offered, most of all, grounds for saying that people do not have to be murderously antagonistic just because they are, among other things, in various senses of the terms, Hindu or Muslim.

The Ganga–Jamna image, however, could also raise issues of who would owe how much to whom in a cultural economy of old debts and bitter competition. Now, more than a half-century later, one can see that the celebration of composites or syncretism for all its good intentions was not all sweetness and light. The two rivers, after all, suggest a *sangam*, an ultimate confluence into a single, onflowing body of water, the Jamna merging into the Ganga: *darya men fanah ho jana*. From Nehru's perspective, the idea of India's unity was paramount. The claims of cultural diversity loomed as problems to be overcome or at least reduced to the private sphere; they should not stand in the way of India's progress as a strong, prosperous, democratic nation, sharing, out of a common history, a sense of common purpose. The slogan of unity in diversity was meant to give the lie not only to colonial denigration of the possibility of India's Independence, but also to those who denied the possibility of common citizenship across religious boundaries once Independence had been won. The celebration of syncretism, on the other hand, could also serve as a strategy for establishing dominance over

[2] *Punjab District Gazetteer*, vol. IV, A: *Gurgaon District* (Lahore: Civil and Military Gazette Press for the Punjab Government, 1911), p. 70.

[3] Jawaharlal Nehru, *The Discovery of India*, reprint edn (New Delhi: Oxford University Press and the Jawaharlal Nehru Memorial Fund, 1981); Tara Chand, *Influence of Islam on Indian Culture*, 2nd edn (Allahabad: The Indian Press, 1963); S. Abid Hussain, *The National Culture of India* (Bombay: Jaico Publishing House, 1956); Humayun Kabir, *The Indian Heritage*, 3rd edn (New York: Harper, 1955); M. Mujeeb, *The Indian Muslims* (London: George Allen & Unwin, 1967).

those who otherwise might not owe their primary allegiance to a monolithic national community.

As so much else in modern Indian history, a central question about this idea of a national, composite culture is the extent to which it was formulated out of the encounter with the colonial state. The authors associated with the idea of the composite culture, as well as other authors with more parochial brands of nationalism, all looked to history to document and legitimate their definitions of national community. But at some level or other, they all realized that India or whatever alternative they had in mind remained to be 'discovered'. Writing history was part of the anti-colonial struggle, part of the project of nation making.

Over the past ten or fifteen years, however, there has been renewed debate about the extent to which one can attribute the formulation of modern Indian society, including institutions and ideologies of India as a nation, to colonialism. Peter van der Veer, for example, has made a good case for the pre-colonial roots of much of the various nationalisms that inhabit India today. What he shows is that one cannot really make an either/or choice about how much to emphasize the colonial experience as opposed to what came before British rule: the task of history is to take up not only the deep continuities, but also the interruptions and the overlapping contingencies in all their complexity. Still, as van der Veer felicitously puts the case, 'Nationalism is a discourse that transforms preexistent forms of culture'.[4]

One might well say the same about colonialism. At least that is what I want to examine here in considering the ways in which one sort of opposition to the idea of a composite culture was formulated in the nineteenth century, namely what came to be known as Muslim separatism. Muslim separatism, for all its pre-colonial bits and pieces, arose as a consolidated movement in the context of the colonial encounter. But that need not be the end of the story. What started as separatism in the colonial situation could later be adapted to a pluralist, democratic nation state as an alternative to either amalgamation or marginalization. On the other hand, this very act of consolidation could also stand accountable, like nationalism itself, for its effort to create monolithic aggregations of people and subject them to oppressive forms of dominance. There are, I will suggest, other alternatives.

II. COLONIAL KNOWLEDGE ABOUT 'THE MUSLIMS OF INDIA'

The formulation during the colonial period of the Muslims of India as a social category, as opposed to the worldwide *ummah,* or far-flung Sufi networks, or

---

[4]Peter van der Veer, *Religious Nationalism: Hindus and Muslims in India* (Berkeley: University of California Press, 1994), p. 193.

very local communities of Muslims does not mean that pre-colonial Muslims failed any more than anyone else to identify with India. As one Barha Sayyid said to a Lodi comrade in arms on the battlefield in 1597, 'We and you are Hindustanis; there is no resource but to die.'[5] There was no other land to return to. But from the outset of British rule in India in the late eighteenth century, it was an axiom of colonial knowledge and the exercise of ruling power, most immediately in the formation of legal codes, that Muslims constituted a separate, aggregate social entity. It was in the context of the colonial state that the ideologies and organizations claiming to represent all the Muslims of India emerged and received both official and public recognition.

First published in 1871, *The Indian Musalmans* by W.W. Hunter (1840–1900), provides a useful example of the place of colonial knowledge in the construction of social categories.[6] I will start with the syntax: how there came to be a 'the' in front of 'Indian Musalmans', that is how could all Muslims in British India be fit into a single noun phrase? As for the predicate, that comes in its subtitle: *Are They Bound in Conscience to Rebel Against the Queen?* The concept is even more powerfully set in motion by the full narrative sweep of the book itself. Often reprinted, Hunter's book lends itself with extraordinary transparency to deconstructive analysis. In fact you do not really have to be an ordained deconstructionist; the book detonates itself.

Hunter's point of departure, after the introduction of what is presented as a problem of contemporary urgency, is to go back to the early decades of the nineteenth century and the career of Sayyid Ahmad of Rae Bareilly (1786–1831), who starts off, Hunter claims, as a bandit among the so-called Pindaris, but then makes an opportune career change to become what Hunter sarcastically calls a 'Prophet' or 'Apostle' among the Pathan tribes of the north-west, who respond to his message 'with frantic enthusiasm'. The message is a call to war, jihad, against the Sikh kingdom of Ranjit Singh, and such a war takes place leading to the death of Sayyid Ahmad and his learned disciple, Shah Isma'il (1779–1831) at Balakote in 1831. But the jihad continues over the following decades, with central headquarters in Patna and widespread support all the way from eastern Bengal, now not only against the Sikhs but, after the annexation of Punjab in 1849, directly against the British themselves. Hunter goes on to a series of brief, thrilling vignettes of frontier battles between British troops and the 'Fanatic host', culminating in 1863 with an extended account of troop movements, dangerous encounters, heroic British victories at the Afghan frontier, the historic source, Hunter points out, of India's conquerors.

---

[5]Nawwab Samsam ud-Daula Shah Nawaz Khan and 'Abdul Hayy, *The Maathir-ul-umar*, trans. by H. Beveridge, 2nd edn revised by Baini Prashad (Patna: Janaki Prakashan, 1979), vol. 1, p. 55.

[6]W.W. Hunter, *The Indian Musalmans: Are They Bound in Conscience to Rebel Against the Queen?* (London: Trubner & Co., 1871; reprint edn Lahore: Premier Book House, 1968).

It turns out that Hunter has more or less accurately reproduced the overall gist of the archival record.[7] Official documents bear many of the same rhetorical markings that Hunter transferred into his text, words like 'fanatical', used as factual descriptions, and many of the same anxieties, such as the danger of the fact that there were Muslims in the British Indian army. 'Where there is a Muhammadan', says one official dispatch, 'he is a man to be watched'. 'Where a population is at once ignorant and fanatical, as are the Mahomedans of India, seditious preaching ought to be a substantive offense'.[8] What the documents of several decades and far-flung regions of India reveal is a deeply entrenched anxiety that there exists a massive, well-connected, and potentially violent popular movement that they can know little about.

From at least the 1830s, British officials gathered and translated the writings associated with Sayyid Ahmad Barelvi's movement, sometimes confining them to records, frequently publishing them in learned journals such as that of the Royal Asiatic Society.[9] In addition, intelligence reports and trial testimony provide extensive documentation of sermons, private utterances, and intercepted letters that British authorities treated, justifiably, as evidence of resistance. The archival record, based on trial depositions and intelligence reports, also reveals divergent interpretations and policies among British officials, as well as circumstances that might mitigate the more alarmist concerns of people like Hunter. They report that one promise held out by religious preachers against British rule among poor cultivators in eastern Bengal, for example, is the abolition of rent. Some evidence suggests that people who gave financial aid to the jihad did not really know what it was or who the enemy was supposed to be. But in general these records indicate the concept, at least the possibility in the minds and actions of some South Asian Muslims, of drawing out of various local concerns a combined sense of Muslim community that ought to have, if it does not already, a unified set of beliefs and practices and ultimately a destiny of political autonomy. In all of this, Hindus are peripheral. The great antagonists are, first of all, British rulers, and secondly, Muslims who do not make religion their chief concern.

The historical question that causes Hunter, his predecessors, and colleagues the greatest concern is how British power interacts with the ongoing process of

---

[7]Selections from the Records of the Bengal Government, no. XLII: Papers connected with the trial of Moulvi Ahmadoolah of Patna and Others, for Conspiracy and Treason (Calcutta, 1866); see also Muin-ud-Din Ahmad Khan (ed.), Selections from Bengal Records on Wahabi Trials (1863-1870) (Dacca: Asiatic Society of Pakistan, 1961); Peter Robb, 'The impact of British rule on religious community: Reflections on the trial of Maulvi Ahmadullah of Patna in 1865', in Peter Robb (ed.), Society and Ideology: Essays in South Asian History (New Delhi: Oxford University Press, 1993).

[8]Muin-ud-Din Ahmad Khan, Selections from Bengal Records, pp. 45–6, 112.

[9]Maulavi Isma'il. Shahamat Ali, Mir, 'Translation of the Takwiyat-ul-Imam, preceded by a notice of the author', Journal of the Royal Asiatic Society of Bengal (London) 13 (1852), pp. 310-72; 'The Wahhabis in India', Calcutta Review, 50:110, pp. 73–104; 51:101 (1870), pp. 177–92.

far-flung religious amalgamation, to what extent the drive toward a unified Muslim community within the boundaries of British rule is a response to the challenge of foreign domination, and the displacement of institutions brought about by colonial rule. What Hunter adds to the archival record is a narrative frame that holds together, however imperfectly, a single set of social identities, turning on India's status, according to Muslim religious authorities, as *dar al-harb*, the abode of the enemy. In Hunter's account, it is the British Government of India that unites South Asian Muslims and separates them from Muslims in other parts of the world.

III. CAN THE WAHHABI SPEAK?

Unlike many objects of British colonial observation and encapsulation, the Tariqah-i Muhammadiyya, as the movement associated with Sayyid Ahmad Shahid often called itself, developed a considerable body of accessible self-expression. In addition, there are many other Muslim sources, created both before and after W.W. Hunter's book, that are relevant, often by way of opposition. As I have said, some of these texts, in Persian, Urdu, Bengali, and occasionally Arabic, entered into the processes of colonial construction by way of official investigation. Wahhabi literature, written and oral, was addressed to a wide Muslim public and dealt with a considerable range of religious issues. Although these texts were not created solely to address the sorts of questions and anxieties that British officials brought to them, they arose under conditions created by the colonial situation. At the same time, this particular movement bears some similarity and may well have had substantive historical links with a number of other movements of the late eighteenth and early nineteenth centuries located elsewhere in the Islamic world.[10] All of these so-called Wahhabi movements made similarly universal claims about the nature of God's revelation to humanity and the errors in belief and practice among contemporary Muslims. Among their differences, however, were the fields of their operations, the audiences they addressed, and the techniques they used to communicate their ideas. Sayyid Ahmad Shahid and his disciples constituted their movement, which claimed to be nothing less than sole legitimate authority for an all-encompassing formation of Islam in India, by taking advantage of techniques and resources that had come to India under British auspices. These included travel, postal services, and, later, telegraphy, but perhaps more interesting are new forms of oratory as well as widespread use of printing, particularly in what came to be known as Urdu, which, increasingly in preference to Persian, they used throughout India, even among audiences that might not initially have access

---

[10]William R. Roff, 'Islamic movements: One or many?', in William R. Roff (ed.), *Islam and the Political Economy of Meaning* (Berkeley: University of California Press, 1987), pp. 31–52; Nehemia Levtzion and John O. Voll (eds), *Eighteenth-century Renewal and Reform in Islam* (Syracuse, NY: Syracuse University Press, 1987).

to the language, as in the case of the Bengalis gathered in Patna on the way to the North-West Frontier or, once they got there, among the Pathans they sought to mobilize into the struggle.[11]

It has been suggested that the introduction of evangelical Christian preaching after 1813 set the example and stimulated the response of Sayyid Ahmad and Shah Isma'il.[12] There is also a substantial relationship with John Gilchrist's enterprise at Fort William College, the formulation of a 'simple' Urdu prose in printed books to teach British officials and military officers 'the command of language and the language of command'.[13] This is not the place to go into the complex history of the origins of Urdu prose and the role of Gilchrist and Fort William College, except to mention that a number of the '*munshis*' who created these texts were connected to the religious milieu of Delhi from which the so-called Wahhabis also came. Gilchrist bought a private press and presided over the development of a movable type for Persian and Urdu that became the model, in the 1820s, for the publication of books based on the utterances of Sayyid Ahmad and the writings of Shah Isma'il, as well as the first printed Urdu translation of the Qur'an, printed as interlinear gloss between the Arabic lines, in 1829. The printer had been directly inspired and authorized by Sayyid Ahmad, who explicitly assured him that such a text was a commendable task for the benefit of Muslims, not a violation of Islam. The printer was the son of a Fort William munshi.[14]

Starting with Sayyid Ahmad Barelvi's great tours of northern India and developing into a system of travelling preachers, the movement used the whole matrix of communications—roads and steamships, printing and postal services, common currency for transferring funds—to spread an all-India message.[15] They also engaged Muslim opponents throughout India. Opposition to British rule was only part of their concerns, and attention to Hindus was relatively rare and intermittent. More important was to establish ideas about religious authority, ritual practice, mystical experience that would unite Muslims. There is a strong suggestion in the literature that Sayyid Ahmad claimed political as well as religious

---

[11]Ghulam Rasul Mahr, *Sarguzisht-i mujahidin: y'ani Hazrat Sayyid Ahmad Shahid ki jamayat mujahidin nl ek sau sal men Islam ka ahyar Islami hukumat ki bi-hali aur mulk ki azadi liye jo jihad kiya un ka mufasil sarguzisht* (Lahore: Kitab Manzil, 1956), vol. 4: 1831 to the present.

[12]Marc Gaborieau, 'Late Persian, early Urdu: The case of "Wahhabi" literature (1818–1857)', in Francoise 'Nalini' Delvoye (ed.), *Confluence of Cultures: French Contributions to Indo-Persian Studies* (New Delhi: Manohar, 1994), pp. 170–96.

[13]Bernard S. Cohn, *Colonialism and Its forms of Knowledge: The British in India* (Princeton, N.J.: Princeton University Press, 1996).

[14]'Abd al-Qadir, *khatimah, Muzih al-Qur'an* (Calcutta, 1829; Paris: École des langues orientales); Mahr, *Sarguzish-i mujahidin*, pp. 305–9; see also Khwaja Ahmad Faruqi, *Urdu men vahabi adab.* (Delhi: Sh'oba-i Urdu, Delhi University, 1969).

[15]Francis Robinson, 'Technology and religious change: Islam and the impact of print', *Modern Asian Studies*, 27:1 (1993), pp. 229–51.

authority, and, at least for some, this claim carried over beyond his death, which some of his followers refused to accept. The Muslims to be united were within the orbit of British power, though sometimes across the borders and sometimes within the princely states.

IV. FROM RESISTANCE TO DIALOGUE

Though bound together in the same field of forces, Muslims of Tariqah-i Muhammadiya and British rulers of India did not speak to each other. When they did not take pains to conceal what they had to say through coded messages or official secrets, they simply assumed that the audiences they addressed were self-contained. But as British officials carefully gathered intelligence in order to formulate a unified Muslim policy, another Sayyid Ahmad, Sayyid Ahmad Khan, pointed out that Indian Muslims, at least some of them, followed closely what British rulers had to say about them: 'Natives anxiously con all articles bearing upon the feelings with which their rulers regard them. Articles sneering at them or misrepresenting their thoughts and feelings, sink deep into their soul, and work much harm.'[16]

Hunter's volume and Sayyid Ahmad Khan's response to it were part of a more explicit engagement between British officials and at least some Indian Muslims with the concept of 'the' Indian Muslims as an object of official policy to be negotiated, a public to be mobilized, and knowledge to be disputed.[17] In his critique of Hunter, Sayyid Ahmad openly identifies himself as a Wahhabi, and throughout his life and work, he cited Shah Isma'il Shahid as a major influence on his thought.

Sayyid Ahmad Khan's critique of Hunter is not only a defence of Indian Muslims in general; more specifically, it purports to speak on behalf of the Tariqa-i Muhammadiyah. Throughout Sayyid Ahmad's life, Shah Isma'il Shahid, who preached in the nearby Jama Masjid when Sayyid Ahmad was a boy growing up in Delhi, remained a major influence both in his ideas about religion and, to some extent, his rhetorical style in a language that Shah Isma'il called *salis* Hindi and that Sayyid Ahmad Khan helped develop into modern Urdu prose. The core ideas of this restatement of Islam was *tauhid*, an uncompromising belief in the oneness of God, and the authority of God's revelation to the Prophet Muhammad—that is unencumbered by the mediation of saints or the historical accumulation, as they saw it, of rules, practices, and interpretations that separated Muslims from the source of religious truth.

[16]Sayyid Ahmad Khan, *Review on Dr Hunter's Indian Musalmans: Are They Bound in Conscience to Rebel Against the Queen?*, reprint edn (Lahore: Premier Book House, n.d. [1871]), pp. 5–6.
[17]Altaf Hussain Hala, *Hayat-i javid*, reprint edn (Lahore: A'inah-i Adab, 1966 [1901]), pp. 196–203; P. Hardy, *The Muslims of British India* (Cambridge: Cambridge University Press, 1972), pp. 70–91.

Like Sayyid Ahmad Barelvi, Sayyid Ahmad Khan was no 'alim, but unlike his predecessor, the second Sayyid Ahmad did not stand forth as a charismatic leader. Instead, his religious writings and orations were presented as matters of dialogue, collaboration and persuasion. Sayyid Ahmad started publishing in the early 1840s, about a decade after Balakote, in Delhi and Agra, where the challenges of British rule and European ideas were powerfully visible. Christian Troll has ably described the religious controversies initiated by Protestant Christian missionaries, writing and preaching in Persian and Urdu, starting with Carl Gottlieb Pfander in Agra just shortly before Sayyid Ahmad arrived in nearby Fatehpur Sikri as an East India Company *sadr amin*. Sayyid Ahmad was closely associated with Pfander's major Muslim interlocutor, Maulana Nur ul-Ḥassan, and his early writings are part of a collaborative response to these missionary challenges.[18]

At the same time, Sayyid Ahmad had a separate source of inspiration and interest: mathematics and science. Rooted in Islamic scholastic traditions, his grandfather, uncle, and other associates had been keenly interested in ideas, methods, and instruments that had been introduced to India by Europeans. One of his early works was an Urdu translation of his grandfather's Persian treatise on the compass for the Vernacular Translation Society in Delhi in 1846. Another was an Urdu work, again adapted from a Persian source, on mechanics for British government schools in the North-West Provinces.[19]

In later years, one of the chief concerns of Sayyid Ahmad Khan, like many of his British contemporaries, was to show that modern science was not inconsistent with religion, in his case rationalist interpretations of Islam that he derived from his association with the family of Shah Vali Ullah, the grandfather of Shah Isma'il Shahid. Sayyid Ahmad was also influenced by his slightly younger contemporaries who had made Delhi College in the 1840s a place of vigorous intellectual activity by translating and adapting European scientific works.

In addition to theology and science, Sayyid Ahmad's major interest was history, notable in his account of the archaeology of Delhi and his printed scholarly editions of some of the major classics of Indo-Persian historiography. As Troll points out, Sayyid Ahmad's ideas about history were probably informed by his judicial career and court procedures about the uses of documentary evidence. What Sayyid Ahmad learned from history is that the contexts and conditions of knowledge change over time. For Sayyid Ahmad, this idea of historical change, perhaps rooted in Shah Vali Ullah's theory of sacred history, could be characterized as *taraqqi*, that very nineteenth-century concept, progress. Relevant to Sayyid

---

[18]Christian Troll, *Sayyid Ahmad Khan: A Reinterpretation of Muslim Theology* (New Delhi: Vikas Publishing House, 1978), pp. 61–9; see also Avril A. Powell, *Muslims and Missionaries in Pre-Mutiny India* (Richmond, Surrey: Curzon Press, 1993).

[19]Troll, *Sayyid Ahmad Khan*, pp. 146–7.

Ahmad's ideas about religion, the progress of historical understanding made it possible to interpret passages in the Qur'an as metaphorical or historically contextual. It was also possible to supersede traditions of Hellenistic science, long associated with Islamic scholasticism, by taking up the experimental science of contemporary Europe.

The course of Sayyid Ahmad's intellectual development carried him from the most severe and exclusive purism to a bold eclecticism, although he would always argue that he was still motivated by the same religious commitments with which he had set out. In his religious writings he moved from a refutation of opponents, especially Christian missionaries, to a careful examination and appreciation of their ideas. Starting in 1861, he took up the task of preparing a Muslim commentary on the Bible, which departed from the standard Muslim insistence that Jews and Christians had so corrupted God's revelation that there was nothing to be learned from it. To carry on this task, Sayyid Ahmad had to enlist the assistance of people who knew English, which he never learned. He also studied Hebrew to deal with the Old Testament. Soon after he established the Scientific Society, first in Ghazipur, then in Aligarh, to carry on the sort of · work that the Delhi Vernacular Translation Society had initiated two decades before: the translation of European books, particularly those dealing with modern science. It was only in the 1870s that he became fully committed to English education, though he had already provided such an education to his own sons.

At the same time, Sayyid Ahmad developed much more inclusive ideas about what it meant to be a Muslim. In an era in which differing Muslim groups were continually issuing *fatawas* against each other as infidels and heretics, with Sayyid Ahmad himself a frequent target of such denunciations, the institutions that were associated with what came to be known as the Aligarh movement reached out to all Muslims—and often invited non-Muslims to take an active role as well. In a lecture in Lahore in 1884, translated in Troll's book, Sayyid Ahmad even spoke of the Muslims of Gurgaon who wore dhotis and practised Hindu customs that they thought of as Islamic.

The *Qazi* performed the marriage and the Brahmin led the bride around the fire .... There was nothing on the basis of which they could call themselves Muslims, except their faith in God and His Messenger. But I assure you, I consider their faith to be much more solid than my own faith (why should I mention somebody else's?).[20]

He had travelled a long way from Shah Isma'il.

For Sayyid Ahmad, the political context of these transformations, particularly after 1857, was the dominance of British power in India. Although Sayyid Ahmad was no believer in democracy and had no concept of nationalism, he attempted

[20]Ibid., p. 310.

to formulate, both ideologically and organizationally, ways for Muslims to participate in a society that was not ruled by Muslim kings or legitimated by Muslim religious authority. He understood that in India and, of course, the British empire as a whole, Muslims were a minority and that governing authority would continue to be held by non-Muslims. What Muslims could hope for under these conditions, he argued, in his review of Hunter. was that India would neither be *dar ul-Islam* nor *dar ul-harb*, neither the abode of Islam nor the abode of war, but rather *dar ul-amn*, the abode of peace. This would mean that Muslims would be free to practise fully their religion and also to participate, along with others, in developing India as a civil society. The oratory, printing, and organizational practices associated early in the nineteenth century with the so-called Wahhabis were transformed under the leadership of Sayyid Ahmad Khan into a public sphere, characterized by voluntary associations, open debate, and the exercise of persuasion rather than compulsion. He also realized that Muslims would benefit by working with non-Muslims, British and Indian, Hindu and Christian, in pursuing shared goals, most particularly the advancement of education.

What Sayyid Ahmad Khan and his associates offered Muslims in India was a rooted cosmopolitanism, founded on a sense of identity that was strong enough to reach out to others without losing itself. The term he used in many of his writings and organizational efforts was Musalmanan-i Hind, the Muslims of India, two nouns, no adjectives, and no subordination of one concept to another. It was open to all types of Muslims, including those with unorthodox beliefs and practices or doubtful piety. They belonged to India and had a right, as Muslims and as Indians, to participate fully in India's progress. There would be seepage, tributary streams, backwaters, canals, maybe, *khuda na khwasta*, a dam or two. Some water might even cross national boundaries. The Ganga and the Jamna constitute fluid, interlocking networks that cannot be contained by monolithic, dual, or even countable categories of identity.

BIBLIOGRAPHICAL ESSAY

Adnan Farooqui and Vasundhara Sirnate

'The singular thing about India was that you could only speak of it in the plural.... This pluralism emerged from the very nature of the country; it was inevitable by India's geography and reaffirmed by its history.'

—Shashi Tharoor in *India: From Midnight to the Millennium* (New Delhi: Viking, 1997)

WHOSE LAND IS IT ANYWAY?

The essays in this volume serve the purpose of reinvigorating academic interest in a past where cultures and communities were not viewed as monolithic entities and all cultural boundaries were porous enough to allow for a certain degree of permissible interaction. What usually resulted were syncretic traditions, which drew on the enormous reserves of varied cultures present in the Indian sub-continent. This syncretism was exciting insofar as it lent to the cultural tapestry a blend of religion, tradition, and ritual that testified to a certain brand of historical religious tolerance. Indian religious history can be categorized into the Indus valley, Indo-Brahminical, Indo-Sramanical, the Indic, the Indo-Islamic, and the Indo-Anglican types.[1] There is a residual transmission of culture from each of these periods into the following ones. The final two types in the classification are called the New Indic formations and with their essentially distinct cultural visions have produced crosscurrents of far-reaching

[1] Classification taken from Larson, Gerald J., (1997) *India's Agony Over Religion*, New Delhi: OUP.

consequence that are manifest even today. Post-Independence and a five decade long experiment with democracy, the much idealized notion of secularism has been questioned on the ground that it has failed to deliver the tolerance and accommodation for all religions and cultures that it promised. In 1996, Shahid Amin wrote, 'we all live today in a 1026–1528–1992 present and not in the 1757–1885–1947 of the past.'[2] The antagonism in India today is between groups asserting their cultural dominance over other groups in many ways, the chief being through the accession of state power, which in some cases also disadvantages minority religious cultures. Much academic work has investigated India's syncretic traditions and this bibliography attempts to classify some of the more important works that highlight instances of cultural hybridism in the eighteenth, nineteenth and twentieth century histories of the Indian sub-continent.

To begin with Mushirul Hasan's *Making Sense of History: Society, Culture and Politics* (New Delhi: Manohar, 2003) focuses on the manner in which the syncretistic tradition and perception have been challenged and undermined at times by various contesting ideologies. Chief amongst these are orientalist scholarships that helped to perpetuate exclusive and conflicting modes of culture, the advancers of Muslim separatism and, in contemporary India the Hindu nationalists that think in terms of reinvigorating the Indian nation with a strong sense of Hindutva. *The Eighteenth Century in Indian History: Evolution or Revolution* (New Delhi: OUP, 2003) edited by P. J. Marshall, is a collection of essays that explore the debate about the nature and pace of change affecting India roughly between 1700 and 1800. In *Hinduism and Modernity* (London: Blackwell, 2003) David Smith undertakes a comprehensive survey of Hinduism in relation to modernity. He traces Hinduism on its journey through encounters with the rationalist discourse in the West, colonialism and orientalism and the central problem of contemporary Hinduism which is the rise of Hindu nationalism. *India: Living With Modernity* (New Delhi: OUP, 1999) by Javeed Alam is an account of the formation of linguistic communities formed between the eighth and fourteenth centuries that provided the spatial core and the spiritual basis for the growth of tradition—literary, aesthetic, social, and cultural. Alam believes that in India the cultural and linguistic boundaries were never coterminous with the statewide territory, in contradiction to the earlier European nationalisms, which believed that the boundaries of a nationality were coterminous with that of the state. *Communalism, Ethnicity and State Politics* by Sajal Basu (Jaipur: Rawat, 2000) focuses on varied expressions and assertions of identity that have redefined ethno-regional politics. Based on empirical evidence the book shows that ethnic groups and communities' lives have been shaped by sentiments and myths rather than by historical facts.

[2]Quoted in Eaton, Richard M., (2003) *India's Islamic Traditions, 711–1750*, New York: OUP.

Gurpreet Mahajan in *Identities and Rights: Aspects of Liberal Democracy in India* (New Delhi: OUP, 2001) makes the case for constitutionally invoked cultural harmony and champions the cause of the individual in any community. K.N. Pannikkar's (ed.) *The Concerned Indian's Guide to Communalism* (New Delhi: Viking, 1999) contains essays on Hindutva and its relation to conversions, media and gender. Romila Thapar's essay in this collection 'The Tyranny of Labels' discusses historical interaction and objects to the use of blanket terms like 'Hindu' and 'Muslim' as such terms erase precision with reference to social groups and is thus methodologically invalid and historically inaccurate. Such terms, argues Thapar, belittle the fact that there have always been links between socially diverse groups. Lloyd Rudolph (ed.) *Cultural Policy in India* (New Delhi: Chanakya, 1984) focuses on cultural policies that the book contends have always been neglected. The essays in this book reopen an investigation into the institutions and processes that reproduce and construct national values and identities. *Pluralism, Equality and Identity: Comparative Studies* by T.K. Oommen (New Delhi: OUP, 2002) argues for a positive value orientation to cultural heterogeneity. Oommen recognizes that modernity has created sharp cleavages that have led to the emergence of a restless, intolerant heterogeneity. He also explores the importance of identity conferring differences and primordial allegiances that are often recalcitrant. Boris Klyuev's *Religion in Indian Society: The Dimensions of 'Unity in Diversity'* (New Delhi: Sterling, 1989) argues for a synthesis of diversity.

One of the influences on Indian culture was Europe. Muzzaffar Alam and Seema Alavi's translation *A European Experience of the Mughal Orient: The I'jaz-i-Arsalani (Persian Letters 1773–1779) of Antoine-Louise Henri Poliere* (New Delhi: OUP, 2001) is a fascinating account of the complex network of cultural interaction between Europeans and Indians in the Eighteenth century. This interaction generated a lot of literature in both European and Indian languages. This book is a collection of letters of a Franco-Swiss military officer employed by the East India Company, to a range of Indians—the Emperor, nobles and ordinary citizens. The merit of the book is its sensitivity to the complex syncretic Indo-Persian culture which had been nurtured over two hundred years of Mughal rule and which was also under threat of being torn apart on caste and religious lines by the Eighteenth century British orientalist scholarhip. Seema Alavi's edited volume *The Eighteenth Century in India* (New Delhi: OUP, 2002) shifts the focus of the debate on understanding whether the nature of the colonial political culture was alien or reinvented.

India's Agony Over Religion by Geral James Larson (New Delhi: OUP, 1997) believes that the post-1947 secular state is a forward caste Neo-Hindu state operating pervasively and purposively on the surviving variegated pre-modern layers of religious life and behavior patterns. The 'hybrid' discourse of the secular state is itself a religious discourse in modern India.

CHALLENGING THE TRADITIONAL ANTAGONISM
BETWEEN HINDUISM AND ISLAM

Believing that Indian Islamic traditions were 'hybrids' and thus inevitably 'syncretic' or that South Asian Muslims were conflicted in their religious identity, many scholars would interpret the colonial or the post-colonial era reform movements as destined to correct, or at least try to correct, the 'distortions' of Islam in pre-colonial South Asia. Is Islam best understood as a foreign intrusion in South Asia? Over the course of twelve centuries had Islamic tradition become 'indigenized' as natural elements of India's cultural landscape? In Richard M. Eaton's edited volume *India's Islamic Traditions, 711–1750*, (New York: OUP, 2003) seventeen essays discuss Islamic traditions in India and negotiate the terrain of Hindu-Muslim encounters in various fields of literature, theology and political power. The purpose of the essays is to focus on the melds between Hindu-Muslim faiths that ultimately developed a common culture. The essays challenge the notion of monolithic Hindu and Muslim religions, the fixity of bounded religious communities and stress on the importance of highlighting a common tradition to give a fillip to secularism. Susan Bayly's essay 'The South Indian State and the Creation of Muslim Community' looks at the nawabi rule of Tamil Nadu and the development of a culture informed by both Hindu and Muslim religions. Vinita Damodaran and Maya Unnithan-Kumar's edited book *Post-colonial India: History, Politics and Culture* (New Delhi: Manohar, 2000) contains essays that focus on the history of modern India, the types and processes of political and economic empowerment, and the forms of cultural representations and post-colonial identities. Mary Searle-Chatterjee's essay in the same volume 'Women, Islam and Nationhood in Hyderabad' captures the subject of the alienation of Muslim minorities. Accordingly, the rise of religiously defined movements among both Hindus and Muslims in the 1980s has sharpened communal divisions and undermined the culture of religious accommodation in Hyderabad.

Moving to more current times, Peter Gottschalk in *Beyond Hindu and Muslim* (Oxford: Oxford University Press, 2000) undertakes a study of the village of Arampur in Bihar where local narratives incorporate both Hindu and Muslim histories. He stresses the importance of such a blend of narratives in fashioning a group identity. *At the Confluence of Two Rivers: Muslims and Hindus in South India* by Jackie Assayag (New Delhi: Manohar, 2004) apprehends the vital importance of Hindu–Muslim relations in contemporary India. It is argued that an analysis of these relations is often reduced to stereotypes and the complexities of the mutual relations of attraction and repulsion which Hindus and Muslims have maintained are ignored. Assayag studies the situation of Muslims in Karnataka, where the dynamics of the cultural forms of pair alterity/identity has seldom been studied. Hindu–Muslim relations are explored in the village and urban milieu through saints, fakirs, hybrid cults and even within the individual, community, everyday life and festivals. Assayag also looks at communal conflict and demonstrates how new boundaries, even if they are secular, today highlight a communitarian exclusivism, which extends to the core of collective memories.

In *The Wahhabi Movement in India* by Qeyamuddin Ahmad (New Delhi: Manohar, 1994) the history of this movement is traced from its founder Sayyid Ahmad of Rae Bareli to the climax of the movement in the Ambeyla War of 1863 against the British. The movement was initially organized for socio-religious reforms in Indo-Islamic society in the Nineteenth century. However, the Wahhabi movement in India was significant as an instance of early resistance to British rule and therefore challenges the notion of the purported Muslim disloyalty to the Indian nation which forms a part of the Hindutva rhetoric. Another interesting read is *Impact of Hindu Culture on Muslims* by Mohsen Saeidi Madani (New Delhi: MD Publications, 1993) which, as the title suggests, discusses the impact of Hinduism on birth, marriage customs, festivals, dress and food of Muslims that have lived in India since the Eleventh century.

Gail Minault's seminal work 'Women's Magazines in Urdu as Sources for Muslim Social History' in the *Indian Journal of Gender Studies* (vol. 5:2, 1998, pp. 201–13] stresses on the contribution of Urdu women's magazines as sources of information of their educational and social reform. The magazines, she says, are also important in understanding middle class Muslim society as it emerged in the early twentieth century and what influenced its eventual character. Her other work is *Secluded Scholars* (New Delhi: OUP, 1999) is a documented account of individuals, organizations and institutions that were influential in furthering Muslim girls' education in colonial India. Papiya Ghosh's essay 'Partition's Biharis' in *Comparative Studies of South Asia, Africa and the Middle East* (vol. 17(2), 1997, pp. 21–34) focuses on the bonds of religion and biradari that pushed through the homogenizing political trajectories of the 1940s and seeks to explain some of the complexities within the Bihari Muslims in the Partition diaspora as well as in contemporary Bihar.

Frederique Apffel-Marglin's interesting piece titled 'Of Pirs and Pandits: Tradition of Hindu-Muslim Cultural Commonalities in Orissa' in *Manushi* (No. 91, Nov–Dec 1995, pp. 17–26) talks about the intercultural involvement of both Hindus and Muslims in the other communities traditions and festivals. The author is struck by the ritual similarities between the two communities in a small district in Orissa and the presence of a Muslim Pandit and a Muslim pir that Hindus worship. *Devotional Islam and Politics in British India: Ahmad Raza Khan and his Movement, 1870–1920* by Usha Sanyal (New Delhi: OUP, 1999) is an emphatic understanding of the diverse, contending forms of discourse in the politico-cultural arena of modern Islam in India. Through the study of the fatawas and tracts of Ahmad Riza Khan, Sanyal analyses the religious discourse of the Ahl-e

Sunn which was at the core of a process of identity formation and which had wider ramifications for relations with competing Muslim, non-Muslim groups as well as the colonial state.

Atis Dasgupta in 'Islam in Bengal: Formative Period' published in *Social Scientist* (No. 370–71, Mar-Apr 2004, pp. 30–41) looks at the religious discourse which was taking place in Bengal between the Sahajiya syncretic tradition and Sufism of Islam from the thirteenth to the seventeenth centuries. 'The Indian 'Ulama and Freedom Struggle' by Yoginder Sikand in *Muslim India* (No. 253, vol. 22(1), January 2004) talks about how large sections of the Indian 'ulama were in the forefront of the Indian freedom struggle. They were pragmatic and wanted a united and free India.

Islamic Society on the South Asian Frontier: The Mappings of Malabar, 1448–1922 by Stephen Frederic Dale (New York: OUP, 1980) is a study that shows how two frontiers shaped the modern history of the Muslims of Kerala, the oldest Islamic community in South Asia and how the European encounter combined with the Hindu dominated land evolved an Islamic community whose most prominent cultural characteristic was religious militancy. *Muslim Civilization in India* by S.M. Ikram and Ainslie T. Embree (New York: Columbia University Press, 1964) is an edited volume that in addition to the political narrative, also gives an account of the cultural developments, the changes in political philosophy and institutions, the rise of Indo-Muslim law and above all those religions and intellectual movements which proved more powerful than rulers.

Hamza Alavi's 'Misreading Partition Road Signs' in *Economic and Political Weekly* (November 2–9, 2002) says that it is no longer useful to ask if the Partition could have been avoided. The different perceptions of the shared history of India and Pakistan have, perhaps, contributed in some measure to create barriers of prejudice between the two nations. However, there are issues of history that need to be looked at again. This article attempts to highlight some of those contentious and often ill-understood issues. Offered here is an attempt by a sociologist-cum-social anthropologist to highlight some issues. Against the intensified communalization of civil society and the emergence of new modes of racism in contemporary India, Rustom Bharucha's essay 'Muslims and Others: Anecdotes, Fragments and Uncertainties of Evidence' in *Economic and Political Weekly* (October 4, 2003) juxtaposes different histories of the 'other' through critical insights into the construction and demonization of the Indian Muslim, along with subaltern performers and indigenous people, among other minorities. Working through anecdotes and fragments, bits and pieces of history, and the backstage life of theatre, this disjunctive discourse on the 'other' agitates liberal assumptions of cultural identity by calling attention to the uncertainties of evidence by which ethnic identities are politicized in diverse ways. Bharucha's other essay worthy of mention is 'Enigmas of Time-Reflections on Culture, History and Politics' in *Economic and Political Weekly* (March 25, 2000) which focuses on the manner in which improvisations in traditional theatre, where times are at once fluid and interchangeable, and the ecology embedded in ritual cultural practices that ensures their continuity, the anti-historical prejudice in colonialist readings of 'Indian time' in juxtaposition with fundamentalist readings of the 'Indian past'.

OTHER CULTURAL BLENDS

'Rethinking Meo Identity: Cultural Faultline, Syncretism, Hybridity or Liminality?' by Shail Mayaram published in *Comparative Studies of South Asia, Africa and the Middle East* (vol. 17(2), 1997, pp. 35–45) focuses on the Meos of Mewat and their extraordinary blend of cultures. Mayaram's thrust are communities like the Meos of Mewat that fall between religious traditions like the Muslim Merat, Bhatti, Mussalman and Kayamkham Rajputs and Khanzadas of Rajasthan, Malhana Rajputs of central India, all of which occupy an indeterminate space between Hinduism and Islam. Homi Bhabha's notion of hybridity is one of the most recent concepts of cultural theory that expresses the intercultural encounter. Hybridity suggests how two entities combine to produce a third. The liminal helps constitute a third space that does not presuppose binarism but seeks to transcend the binary mode of thought and understanding. *Kinship And Rituals Among the Meo of Northern India: Locating Sibling Relationship* by Raymond Jamous (New Delhi: OUP, 2003) presents the kinship system of the Meo, a Muslim community of Rajput caste of north India, where the brother–sister relationship transcends the distinctions between consanguines and affines to pervade relations both before and after marriage. In terms of family and kinship, and associated ceremonies, myths and legends, the Meo have long been regarded as unusual among Indian Muslims. They forbid what is regarded as a diacritical Muslim kinship practice patrilineal parallel-cousin marriage as well as cross-cousin marriage, and follow north Indian, Hindu kinship rules.

Shahjahanabad: The Sovereign City in Mughal India, 1639–1739 by Stephen Blake (Cambridge: Cambridge University Press, 1992) is the first study of a pre-modern Indian city as a sovereign city. Blake demonstrates how all aspects of life centered on the emperor and the nobles in Shahjahanabad (Old Delhi). He talks about the domination of the landscape by their palaces and other architecture and also the people's cultural life by the nobles and how the economy was also controlled by those who controlled a large portion of the state revenue. *Historic Delhi: An Anthropology* edited by H.K. Kaul (New Delhi: OUP, 1998) is a traveller's account providing a comprehensive picture of Delhi through the ages. *Delhi Between Two Empires, 1803–1931: Society, Government and Urban Growth* by Narayani Gupta (New Delhi: OUP, 1998) is a sociopolitical history of the city of Delhi from the British conquest over the Mughals to when Delhi became a city in the modern sense.

The Making of Colonial Lucknow, 1856–1877 by Veena Talwar Oldenberg

(Princeton: Princeton University Press, 1984) examines the history of Lucknow and demonstrates how the results of its transformation after the 1857 Mutiny continues to provide the city even today challenging conventional views of the extent of British intervention in India. Later Indian administrations accepted the socio-political, economic and physical changes. *Rulers, Townsmen and Bazaars: North Indian Society in the Age of British Expansionism, 1770–1870* by C.A. Bayly (Oxford: OUP, 2002) is a path-breaking work on the social and economic history of colonial India. It traces the evolution of North Indian towns and merchant communities from the decline of Mughal rule to the consolidation of Britain's empire in India following the 1857 mutiny.

P.K. Datta in *Carving Blocs* (New Delhi: OUP, 1999) looks at communalism as it developed in Bengal in the early twentieth century. He sees communalism as an organized ideology saturated in violence. Peter Robb in *A History of India* (London: Palgrave, 2002) analyses India's civilizations and its empire through the ages as they tangled with regional rule and heterodox cultures. The volume edited by Stephen Hay *Sources of Indian Tradition* (New York: Columbia University Press, 1988) remains one of the most important and widely used texts on civilization and cultural links in South Asia. *Islamic Revival in British India, Deoband, 1860–1900* by Barbara Daly Metcalf (New Delhi: OUP, 2002) focuses on the most important Islamic seminary of the period, Deoband. This book studies the vitality of Islam in late nineteenth-century north India. Mushirul Hasan (ed.) *Islam and Indian Nationalism: Reflections on Abul Kalam Azad* (New Delhi: Manohar, 2001) offers a thorough reappraisal of Abul Kalam Azad. *Lucknow: Memoirs of a City* by Violette Graff (ed.) (New Delhi: OUP, 1997) focuses on 250 years of Lucknow's history.

The Ulama of Farangi Mahall and Islamic Culture in South Asia by Francis Robinson (New Delhi: Permanent Black, 2001) is the first full-length treatment of Islamic scholars, teachers, and leaders. It addresses the issues of the establishment of specific traditions of scholarship and mysticism in the eighteenth-century Awadh, the place of these traditions in Perso-Islamic culture. *Between Tradition and Modernity* by Fred Dallmayr and G.N. Devy (New Delhi: Sage, 1998) talks about the need to come to terms with India's complex historical tapestry. *My Life: A Fragment— An Autobiographical Sketch of Maulana Mohammad Ali* by Mushirul Hasan (ed.) (New Delhi: Manohar, 1999) illumines how figures like Maulana Ali reflected on the changes ushered in by the colonial government and their impact on his community and the nation.

Shrines and Neighbourhood in Early Nineteenth Century Pune, India by Lawrence W. Preston (*Journal of Historical Geography*, vol. 28(2), April 2002, pp. 203–15) looks at shrines in the ritual, ceremonial and political spheres of Pune and makes distinctions between the major temples of the high Sanskritic Hindu tradition and their subsidiary shrines of regional and folk deities and the relation of Muslim shrines to Hindu places of devotion. C.G. Hussain Khan's study 'Muslim Kinship in Dravidian Milieu' in the *Economic and Political Weekly* (November 15, 2003) explores the institutions of kinship and marriage in a Karnataka Muslim community. In this region though Muslims retain their separate identity by following their own customs and practices, using their own language and maintaining strict endogamy and communal restrictions, there is clear tendency on their part to fall in line with the local dominant non-Muslim socio-cultural practices. In 'Hindu and Islamic Transnational Religious Movements' published in *Economic and Political Weekly* (January 3, 2003) Shail Mayaram makes the argument that there has been a phenomenal intensification of transnational religious networks and of new international players and styles oriented to missionisation, religiosity, spiritual rejuvenation, creating and recreating community. This article makes some observations regarding the transformation of religion under globalization and new modes of transnationalism in the context of a discussion of the Tablighi Jama'at and the Vishwa Hindu Parishad. Yoginder Sikand's 'Islamic Perspectives on Liberation and Dialogue in Contemporary India: Muslim Writings in Dalit Voice' in *Economic and Political Weekly* (Sep. 14, 2002) is an analysis of a survey that suggests that increasing numbers of Muslims, particularly from long-marginalized 'low' caste groups, are now demanding that their voices be heard, thereby seeking to challenge the established Muslim leadership as spokesmen of Islam and representatives of the community. These voices of dissent are significant in that they offer an interesting case of 'lay' perspectives on Islam that emerges from a situation of struggle against oppression.

'Lucknow Nawabs: Architecture and Identity' in *Economic and Political Weekly* [Sep. 7, 2002] by Simonetta Casci talks about how the distinctive culture of Lucknow represents an important phase of transition in the definition of modern identities that coincided with the decline of the Mughal empire and the increasing role of the East India Company in Indian affairs. Lucknow's architecture, its town planning and monuments, mirrors the refashioning of identities through the fusion of different cultures and styles.

Penumbral Visions: The Making of Polities in Early Modern South India by Sanjay Subrahmanyam, [New Delhi: Oxford University Press, 2000] analyses how political structures in south India underwent the transition from Vijayanagara to early colonial rule. Its focus is on south-eastern India, but the discussion is wide-ranging and comparative. *Kingship and Political Practice in Colonial India* by Pamela G. Price (Cambridge: Cambridge University Press, 1996) focuses on the two former 'little kingdoms' of Ramnad and Sivaganga which came under colonial governance as revenue estates. She demonstrates how rivalries among the royal families and major zamindari temples, and the disintegration of indigenous institutions of rule, contributed to the development of nationalism and identity amongst the people of southern Tamil country. The author also shows how religious symbols and practices going back to the seventeenth century were reformulated and acquired a new significance in the colonial context. Arguing for a reappraisal of the relationship of Hinduism to politics, Price finds that these symbols and practices continue to inform popular expectation of political leadership today.

Islam and Muslim History in South Asia by Francis Robinson (New Delhi: OUP, 2003) is a collection that draws our attention to the subtle, dynamic and complex relationship between Islamic law and practice, the close interaction between religious ideas and piety on the one hand and changes in material life on the other, and the capacity of elites and individuals alike to make choices that may well owe more to religious faith than to 'rational' self-interest. From Contact To Conquest: Transition to British Rule in Malabar, 1790–1805 by Margaret Frenz (New Delhi: OUP, 2003) focuses on the construction and legitimation of rule by élite local groups in Malabar and the implications of British conquest. At the centre of the study is an exploration of the clash of sovereignty that occurred when two very different concepts of rule collided that of the British, built on the Euro-centric notion of the state with an all-pervasive administration, and that of the Malabar élite, a complex indigenous idea of the state based on redistributive processes. A major contribution to academic literature on the region, this book combines detailed case study with broader ideas about the phenomenon of conflicting cultures and the resulting negotiation of new values within the spheres of politics, society, and economy. Aligarh's First Generation: Muslim Solidarity In British India by David Lelyveld (New Delhi: OUP, 2003) explores the nature of Muslim cultural identity in India in the nineteenth century, and the changes it underwent, in the context of colonial rule. The author examines the history of the Muhammadan Anglo-Oriental College (Aligarh Muslim University) during the first twenty-five years of its existence, the period when the first generation of Muslims educated in English graduated from the college. The author argues that as Muslim social identity was closely tied to the political traditions of the late Mughal period, there was an urgent need to find methods of adapting received concepts of family and religion to the ideological and institutional challenges of colonialism and nationalism.

David Lelyveld's study of the Muslim effort to maintain social and cultural continuity shows how Aligarh gradually prepared a new generation for the political and cultural leadership of a newly formulated Indian Muslim community. The unconventional narrative interweaves scholarly analysis with literary genres (biographies and anecdotes) and devices such as symbolic motifs. Imperial Simla: The Political Culture of the Raj (second edition) by Pamela Kanwar (New Delhi: OUP, 2003) talks about the mystique that has enveloped Simla for over a century in British and Indian eyes stems as much from its being a cultural enclave for the British elite in India, as from the fact that it was a seat of government, magnificently located and splendidly isolated. The author draws on contemporary reports, official documents and personal interviews with old residents of Simla, to present an immensely lively and well-documented picture of the social, historical and political development of this hill-station-cum-capital. Social And Religious Reform: The Hindus

Of British India by Amiya P. Sen (New Delhi: OUP, 2003) is a volume that is perhaps the first work to focus on 'reform' as a disputed concept. It retraces some of the critical contestations around the phenomenon of reform as it affected the largest community of British India—the Hindus. The essays in this volume identify major issues within the history of socio-religious reform among Hindus that grew into passionate public debates. *Communal Identity in India: Its Construction and Articulation in the Twentieth Century* by Bidyut Chaktabarty (ed.) (New Delhi: OUP, 2003) is a collection of essays that address the contested issue of community identities as they evolved historically the course of the twentieth century in India. They explore both the circumstances and the forms in which identity, communal identity in particular, is recast in a transitional post-colonial society like India. *Literary Cultures in History: Reconstructions from South Asia* by Sheldon Pollock (New Delhi: OUP, 2003) is united by a twofold theoretical aim: to understand South Asia by looking at it through the lens of its literary cultures and to rethink the practice of literary history by incorporating non-Western categories and processes. The questions these seventeen essays ask are accordingly broad, ranging from the character of cosmopolitan and vernacular traditions to the impact of colonialism and independence, indigenous literary and aesthetic theory, and modes of performance.

On Becoming an Indian Muslim: French Essays on Aspects of Syncretism translated by M. Waseem (New Delhi: OUP, 2003) is a selection of fifteen essays by modern French intellectuals that focus on the significant contributions of the Indian mystics Kabir, Dara Shikoh, Jayasi, Pir Shams, Waris Shah, Ghazi Miyan and Ramdeo Pir, the Bhartrhari Jogis of Gorakhpur and Mahatma Gandhi. The concluding essay is by the translator himself and focuses on the followers of the Agha Khan, otherwise known as the Ismaili Khojas. M. Waseem's translation of all the essays is clear and precise, and his substantive Introduction outlines the gradual amalgamation of different religious elements during the spread of Islam as described by well known scholars such as Charlotte Vaudeville, Louis Massignon, Jules Bloch, and Francoise Mallison among others.

CONTRIBUTORS

Joya Chatterji is Lecturer at the Department of International History, London School of Economics, UK.

Nupur Chaudhary is part time Lecturer at the Department of History, Presidency College, Kolkata.

Adnan Farooqui is a research scholar at the Centre for Political Studies, School of Social Sciences, Jawaharlal Nehru University, New Delhi.

Michael H. Fisher is Danforth Professor of History at Oberlin College, USA.

Najaf Haider is Associate Professor of Medieval History at the Centre for Historical Studies, Jawaharlal Nehru University, New Delhi.

Mushirul Hasan is Professor of Modern Indian History, Jamia Millia Islamia, New Delhi.

David Lelyveld is Professor of History and Associate Dean of Humanities and Social Sciences, William Paterson University, USA.

Gurpreet Mahajan is Professor at the Centre for Political Studies, Jawaharlal Nehru University, New Delhi.

Shail Mayaram is Senior Fellow at the Centre for the Study of Developing Societies, Delhi.

Barbara Metcalf is Alice Freeman Palmer Professor of History at University of Michigan, Ann Arbor, USA.

Annie Montaut is Professor of Hindi, INALCO, Paris.

Rajat Kanta Ray is Professor and Head of the Department of History, Presidency College, Kolkata.

Francis Robinson is Professor of the History of South Asia, Royal Holloway, University of London, UK.

Asim Roy is Research Fellow at the School of History & Classics, University of Tasmania, Australia. Formerly he was also the Director of The Asia Centre in the Tasmania University.

Kumkum Sangari is Professorial Fellow at the Centre for Contemporary Studies, Nehru Memorial Museum and Library.

Kerrin Gräfin Schwerin is Privatdozentin at Free University, Berlin.

Farzana Shaikh is Research Associate at the Centre of South Asian Studies, University of Cambridge, UK.

Vasundhara Sirnate is a graduate student at the Department of Political Science, University of California, Berkeley.

Madhu Trivedi is Reader at the Department of History, School of Open Learning, University of Delhi.

Peter van der Veer is Professor at Utretcht University, Netherlands.